CONSTITUTIONAL LAW OF TI UNION

PEARSON
Education

We work with leading authors to develop the strongest
educational materials in law, bringing cutting-edge thinking
and best learning practice to a global market.

Under a range of well-known imprints, including Longman,
we craft high quality print and electronic publications which
help readers to understand and apply their content,
whether studying or at work.

To find out more about the complete range of our
publishing, please visit us on the World Wide Web at:
www.pearsoned.co.uk

CONSTITUTIONAL LAW OF THE EUROPEAN UNION

Sionaidh Douglas-Scott
SCHOOL OF LAW, KING'S COLLEGE LONDON

Harlow, England • London • New York • Boston • San Francisco • Toronto
Sydney • Tokyo • Singapore • Hong Kong • Seoul • Taipei • New Delhi
Cape Town • Madrid • Mexico City • Amsterdam • Munich • Paris • Milan

Pearson Education Limited
Edinburgh Gate
Harlow
Essex CM20 2JE
England

and Associated Companies throughout the world

Visit us on the World Wide Web at:
www.pearsoned.co.uk

First edition 2002

© Pearson Education Limited 2002

The right of Sionaidh Douglas-Scott to be identified as author of this work has been asserted by her in accordance
with the Copyright, Designs and Patents Act, 1988.

ISBN 0582 317177

British Library Cataloguing-in-Publication Data
A catalogue record for this book is available from the British Library

10 9 8 7 6 5 4 3
07 06 05 04

Typeset in 10/13 Sabon by 68
Printed in Great Britain by Henry Ling Ltd., at the Dorset Press, Dorchester, Dorset, DT1 1HD

The publisher's policy is to use paper manufactured from sustainable forests.

BRIEF CONTENTS LIST

CONTENTS

PREFACE

Writing books about the EU is a hard task. EU law has, perhaps more than any other area of law, been prone to change and upheaval. As the last century drew to a close, a swift succession of intergovernmental conferences resulted in a seemingly neverending process of treaty amendments (Maastricht 1992, Amsterdam 1996, Nice 2000). And the process continues, with more changes foreseen at a further IGC in 2004. The accession of new member states has also changed the face of the EU – with the most dramatic, those of the 'new' democracies of Eastern and Central Europe, planned to take place over the next couple of years. None of these events has made the polity that is the EU any less complex or perplexing. As a constitutional entity, it is a very messy creature, whose law and legislative processes often seem incomprehensible. The EU is also distant from its citizens. As has often been said, it lacks an 'affective' dimension. How will it its institutions function in an enlarged EU, of perhaps 27 states? What sort of role will the EU play in the post-September 11 world? How will it meet the challenges of global terrorism?

The aim of this book is to set out, as clearly as possible, a crucial core of information and reflection on the current EU. European citizens may not be over-excited by the EU, but they need to be better-informed, so they may see what is at stake (and so, arguably, do non-EU citizens!) Regardless of what the IGC of 2004 decides, the EU already has a Constitution – it just does not have a transparent, intelligible, or ultimately meaningful one. In writing this book, I have attempted to make this Constitution more apparent. In so doing, have made use of comparative law, political theory and philosophy, and international relations – but only in order to set the EU in context and render it more intelligible, not to obscure or further complicate its processes.

No doubt only too aware of the pressing challenges facing the EU, the European Council, meeting in Laeken in December 2001, declared the convening of a constitutional convention on the future of Europe, with the former French President, Valéry Giscard d'Estaing, as its Chairman. This commenced work in March 2002. In addition to a Chairman and 2 Vice Chairmen, the Convention has 102 other members, composed of representatives of the Heads of States and Government, and of the national parliaments, as well as the European Parliament and European Commission. Significantly, the accession candidate countries are also represented on the Convention on equal terms to the current members, although they may not overturn any consensus of the existing member states – a stipulation which has already caused some resentment. The Convention is charged with scrutinising certain 'key issues arising from the Union's future development' namely: the question of the division of competences between member states and EU; the simplification of the myriad of EU legal instruments; the issue of how to increase democracy, transparency and efficiency in the EU; and the possible drafting of a Constitution for the EU. The

Convention works as openly as possible, placing all its official documents in the public domain and by March 2003 is to draw up a final document.

The Laeken Declaration was drafted with grand phrases, starting with the proclamation, 'Europe at a Crossroads' (not the first time this phrase has been used in the past 10 years). The grand rhetoric has since continued, with comparisons made between the EU Convention and the Philadelphia Convention, which met in 1787 to frame the Constitution of the newly independent United States. Noble speeches have been given by Romano Prodi, President of the European Commission, and Giscard D'Estaing (who speaks of a 'dream of Europe') and many others.

Will the Convention, and the IGC which is tabled to follow it in 2004, live up to these noble aspirations? 'Convention' is an evocative word, redolent of the revolutions in France and America in the 18th century. The 21st century European Convention no doubt proceeds in the spirit of good will, hard work, and a hope to succeed. But it is not the Philadelphia Convention. Its Chairman, Giscard d'Estaing, and its Vice-Chairmen, Giuliano Amato and Jean-Luc Dehaene, may be experienced European politicians, but do they possess the radical vision of a James Madison? The Convention's task is not an easy one. The challenges facing the EU are so large, and opinions as to what steps should be taken to deal with them are so many and so diverse – as a quick glance at the Convention's official documents already reveals. There is the danger that the Convention will disintegrate into a talking shop, or that it will produce a report that will be shelved, as have been so many grand and solemn reports in the EU's history. Whether Europe faces a 'constitutional moment' in the early years of this new century remains to be seen.

I have debts of gratitude in particular to the following people for advice and discussions about EU law – Andrea Biondi, Piet Eeckhout, John Gardner, Miguel Poiares Maduro, Peter Oliver, Wulf-Henning Roth and Alexander Turk. Keith Ewing has been a supportive and encouraging editor throughout. I am also very grateful to Pat Bond and David Cox at Longman, as well as David Richards, for their co-operation and very hard work on the editing of this book. Arash Amel was a helpful research assistant. In carrying out research, I benefited from grants from the British Academy and the Centre of European Law at King's College.

I have aimed as far as possible to state the law as it stood in April 2002, and have written the book on the assumption that the Treaty of Nice, not yet ratified, will come into force.

On a personal note, I would like to say thank you to my family, for suffering me while I was writing this book. This book is dedicated to Peter, whose love and support have been invaluable.

TABLE OF CASES

Court of First Instance (Chronological)

Court of First Instance (Alphabetical)

National Courts

European Court of Human Rights

TABLE OF LEGISLATION

COMMISSION NOTICES AND OTHER SOFT LAW MEASURES

COMPLAINTS

RESOLUTIONS

RULES OF PROCEDURE

NATIONAL LEGISLATION

EIRE

TABLE OF TREATIES

ACKNOWLEDGEMENTS

We are grateful to the following for permission to use copyright material

Chapter 14 reprinted from 'In Search of Union Citizenship' in *Yearbook of European Law*, 18, edited by Eeckhout, P. and T. Tridmas, by permission of Oxford University Press © Oxford University Press (2000); Chapter 15 reprinted from 'A Constitution for Europe' © Hart Publishing (2000).

In some instances we have been unable to trace the owners of copyright material, and we would appreciate any information that enable us to do so.

PART ONE

STRUCTURES

1

THE EUROPEAN UNION IN SEARCH OF AN IDENTITY

THE IDEA OF EUROPE

In this millennial time, both Europe's law, and Europe itself, lack a straightforward identity. For example, 'European law' is a very unsatisfactory term – an expression used as shorthand for a variety of (sometimes) interlocking legal systems – namely, EC law (i.e. the law of the European Community); EU law (being wider and more intergovernmental than EC law, but often confused with the former); the law of the European Convention on Human Rights (a creature of the Council of Europe); or, most generally, a group term for the family of legal systems in Europe, widely diverse as they are. Some of these expressions, created within the past 50 years, have evolved, going through changes and differently structured relationships. The EC, EU and ECHR are often confused by both journalists and the public, for whom they present an incoherent institutional image. And yet this confusing panoply of legal regulation, this 'European legal space',[1] relates to one of the most important legal communities in the world, with its court, the European Court of Justice, arguably the most powerful court. So we have to take these shifting, confusing, legal, cultural and geographical identities seriously.

This, however, is difficult because the very idea of Europe itself is uncertain. There have existed not one idea, but many, constantly changing over time and perspective. Europe has always been diverse. Its origins are shrouded in uncertainty. Reference is often made to the Greek myth of origin, whereby the Greek goddess, Europa, was abducted by Zeus, disguised as a bull. However, not all accepted her Greek (and hence European), nor her divine, origins. On other accounts of the myth, Europa's origins are less clear. She was an Asian girl, who had settled at some point in Egypt,

---

[1] An expression recently used by C Harding in 'The Identity of European Law; Mapping out the European Legal Space' (2000) 6 ELJ 128.

and hence also had an African connection.[2] As Fitzpatrick has asserted, 'if she [Europa] were comprehensively European, she could hardly provide the origin for a Europe that would have to exist already to make her European'.[3]

As with its origins, so, too, the notion of a European identity is a highly contested and complex concept. 'Europe' is a geographical expression, with political significance and immense symbolic weight, but what do we understand by it? It has no clearly defined or agreed boundaries and is subject to many metaphors and images – for example, the 'common European home' of Gorbachev's rhetoric, or the reference to Central Europe as 'a kingdom of the spirit'.[4]

Attempts to articulate a European identity have sometimes been given by means of an antithesis, or common European enemy. And so Europe has often been defined in relation to the 'Other': to what it is not.[5] Historically, Europe began with its differentiation from Asia, and, for a long period in its existence, its defining ethos was Christendom (although, of course, Christianity has often been a divisive force in Europe). Edward Said has described how Europeans created the Orient to perform the task of the Other.[6] This negative form of identification proceeds with a vocabulary of difference and vilification – for example, 'the Barbarians', 'the heathen' or 'despotism'[7] – although it must be admitted that such expressions were frequently used of other Europeans too. The non-European world was still conditioning a European sense of identity in the second half of the twentieth century when the politicians who set out to rebuild Europe immediately after the Second World War had to work within a framework set by Russian hostility and American sponsorship, rather than strongly 'European' guidelines.

Contemporary Europe continues to be shaky in its identity. Increasingly porous boundaries pose a threat to the identity of Europeans. Physical borders, along with their legal and political significance, can assume psychological meanings which are eroded when such radical events as the fall of the Iron Curtain and the projects of the EU for 'an ever closer union' take place, and, of course, the cataclysmic events of 11 September 2001 and beyond. A result of such shaken identities may be the triggering of primitive psychological defence mechanisms and the transfer of aggressive emotions onto vulnerable groups.[8] Outbursts of racial violence and xenophobia may be symptoms of this, as well as an attempt to single out what is non-European. Turkey has continued to have a difficult and ambiguous relationship with Europe – unacceptable as yet for EU membership (as evidenced by

---

[2] For a detailed exploration of the myth of Europa's origin, see P Fitzpatrick, who refers to the account given by R Calasso in *The Marriage of Cadmus and Harmony* (London: Cape, 1993) (P Fitzpatrick, 'New Europe and Old Stories' in Fitzpatrick and Bergeron (eds) *Europe's Other* (Ashgate, 1998)). The myth is also cited in many other sources, e.g. in Denis de Rougement's *The Idea of Europe* (New York: Macmillan, 1965).

[3] Fitzpatrick, op. cit. at 31.

[4] T Garton Ash, *The Uses of Adversity* (Cambridge University Press, 1989).

[5] J Derrida, *The Other Heading: Reflections on Today's Europe* (Bloomington: Indiana University Press, 1992).

[6] E Said, *Orientalism* (Harmondsworth: Penguin, 1995).

[7] P Burke, 'Did Europe exist before 1700?' (1980) 1 History of European Ideas 22.

[8] A Falk, 'Border symbolism' (1974) 43 Psycho-Analytic Quarterly 650.

Turkey's unsuccessful application to join the EC) and even within parts of western Europe still identifiable as the Other, blamed by nationalists for unemployment and crime and forced to suffer the consequences of otherness by violent attacks. The problems European governments experience over asylum seekers, immigration and the general control over the entry of non-EU nationals into Europe, underline the impression that there is still an Other who must be kept at bay.

At the same time, however, differentiation of Europe from non-Europe can prove problematic. The ending of the Cold War and application of former Communist countries for membership of both the EU and Council of Europe has also accentuated confusion over European **geographical** identity, for where do the boundaries of Europe stop? For Adenauer, in 1946, 'Asia stands on the Elbe'.[9] But, in more recent years, Europe's boundaries have shifted several hundred miles eastwards, a move characterised by the re-emergence of Berlin as capital of Germany, a resurfacing of the idea of 'Mitteleuropa', and the renaming of Leningrad as St Petersburg in an attempt 'to regain its lost European identity'.[10]

However, in the post-war years the expression 'Europe' has been, to a certain extent, appropriated by the EEC and now the EU, by those whose governments had declared a commitment to build a 'European Union' resting on a common aspiration to a European identity and a shared European idea. Ward, for example, writes 'Europe, it seems, was invented in 1957' (turning it into a post-war phenomenon, in rather the same way that a famous English poet found sexual intercourse to have been discovered in 1963) going on to comment that 'It was also invented as an historical idea.'[11] Thus, politicians opposed to certain aspects of the EU are labelled 'anti-European' or 'Euro-sceptic' and the judges of the European Court are said to have 'une certaine idée de l'Europe'.[12] Article 49 of the TEU states that 'Any European state may apply to become a member of the Union.' It is therefore of consequence to the applicant governments whether their countries are included in the accepted definition of Europe.

It was, however, the intention of the founders of the EEC to foster a distinctive 'European identity' to replace warring national identities, and, as the British, French, Germans and Italians had done in their deliberate nation-building myths of the nineteenth century, the founders of the EEC set out to create new myths and symbols to replace the old. Some sharp disputes within the early EEC concerned just this. For example, discord between de Gaulle and Hallstein, an early President of the European Commission, regarding how ambassadors should be received by the EEC reflected de Gaulle's determination to prevent the EEC developing symbols of statehood. There have also been repeated arguments about the role and powers of the European Parliament and its growing status as an alternative focus of legitimacy to

---

[9] T Garton Ash, *In Europe's Name: Germany and the Divided Continent* (New York: Random House, 1993) at 50.

[10] G Delanty, *Inventing Europe: Idea, Identity, Reality* (Macmillan, 1995) at 135.

[11] I Ward, *The Margins of European Law* (Macmillan, 1996) at 23.

[12] The expression used by Judge Pescatore in 'The Doctrine of Direct Effect: an infant disease of Community law', (1983) 8 EL Rev, where at p 157 he observes that 'the reasoning of the Court shows that the judges had "une certaine idée de l'Europe" of their own'.

national parliaments. Similarly, there has been resistance to the Commission's attempts to establish its legal competence over certain matters, such as education, and, in particular, opposition to 'a more European history'.[13]

Given present difficulties in delineating a tangible European identity, it may be questioned whether the European Community or Union is in fact only, in Anderson's much used phrase, an 'imagined community'.[14] Concepts such as citizenship of the Union or a foreign policy to 'reinforce' the European identity (as expressed in Article 3 TEU) suggest a certain lack of confidence as to the present strength of the European identity and a perceived need to foster and promote one. However, perhaps it is unrealistic to consider any community as occurring naturally rather than being constructed. For example, in the context of the nation state, Ernest Gellner[15] has written: 'Nationalism is not the awakening of nations to self-consciousness; it invents nations where they do not exist.' Indeed, for Gellner, who sees the formation of nation states in Europe as a necessary accessory to the process of industrialisation and the needs of nineteenth century capitalism, the European Union, with its internal market and projected monetary union, must surely be a suitable entity for a supra-national state.

If the 'European' identity is not a natural phenomenon, it is instructive to consider the reasons underlying its attempted creation. Why go to the trouble of constructing a strong European self-image rather than maintaining intergovernmental cooperation in certain key areas? To prevent further conflict in the region, to encourage economic prosperity and liberal democracy and to promote these values in the newly emerging democracies? In this, the EU has enjoyed a certain measure of success.

However, a focus on the unifying aspects of Europe's history and culture has been seen by some as Euro-nationalistic,[16] involving a one-sided emphasis on harmony, unity, continuity progress etc., whereas the divisive, violent and repressive sides of the European tradition (war, imperialism, genocide) are either ignored or treated as not essentially European. Derrida[17] has suggested that the designers of the European Union have failed to take account of, or even denied, Europe's own history. In this, Derrida's vision is surely too bleak. The idea of Europe may be one of pluralism and difference, tainted by exclusion, its history drenched in blood, but notwithstanding all of this there are positive unifying factors. In fact, one of the problems is that the EU appears to have too little confidence in asserting what is positive, what is good, where there is agreement, in the European arena. Pluralism, variety and heterogeneity exist, and should be respected, but, if anything, *pace* Derrida, the EU needs a stronger identity at its constitutional level. It is submitted that this is possible – indeed, not only possible, but desirable, and this submission is one of the over-arching themes of this book.

---

[13] Attempted by the French historian Baptiste Duroselle in *Europe: A History of its Peoples* (London: Viking, 1990).

[14] B Anderson, *Imagined Communities: Reflections on the Origin and Spread of Nationality* (2nd edn, London: Verso, 1991).

[15] E Gellner, *Nations and Nationalism* (Oxford: Blackwell, 1983).

[16] N Wilterdink, 'The European Ideal: an examination of European and national identity' (1993) 34 Archives Européennes de Sociologie 119.

[17] Derrida, *The Other Heading*.

However, it is all too clear that the EU has so far failed to achieve a solid positive identity for itself. Tortuously drafted legal instruments, institutions apparently run by greedy bureaucrats and an overwhelming focus until recently on economic efficiency have not proved very inspirational to the peoples of Europe. Current initiatives, such as the Commission's *White Paper on Governance*, or the *Future of Europe Debate*,[18] may strive to achieve a more harmonious, intelligible constitutional structure, to create more order out of the highly complex, almost incoherent state of EU affairs. This order does not exist at present and will not be easy to achieve. Such is the present state of the legal orders of Europe – complicated, overlapping, uncertain, incompatible, that for many, harmony is impossible to achieve, and not in any case desirable.[19] This author does not take that view. Nevertheless, it is necessary to argue the case for a European Union that can serve as a focus for identity, unity, and even pride, among the peoples of Europe. And in any case, the reasons why such harmony does not exist at present, and Europeans suffer from messy and fragmented constitutional structures, relate to the history of the European integration, which will be explored in a large part of this chapter.

HISTORY

Ian Ward, writing in 1996, regretted the paucity of space allotted to European history in the opening pages of many legal textbooks.[20] Perhaps he was being unfair. For in many textbooks, a historical account is not impossible to find. But if Europe was not invented in 1957, or at a pinch, 1950, where do we start? How far back do we go in Europe's often savage and brutal history to seek out the events that Derrida charges us (or at least the European bureaucrats) with having forgotten in the present quest for *capital*, for economic dominion?[21] While most accounts start with the post-war reconstruction, or may go a little beyond, to the inter-war period, some do go further back. Some make references to Charlemagne, others to a fourteenth century treatise 'on the way to shorten wars' by Pierre Dubois (Dubois' way being a permanent, continent-wide military alliance).[22] We may cite William Penn's 'An Essay Towards the Present and Future Peace of Europe', which suggested the introduction of a European Parliament to prevent war between the states. We may also look to pre- or proto-federalist writings by the likes of Kant, Rousseau, Bentham and Saint Simon. But, as Ernst Haas remarked, these remained the 'sentiments of relatively isolated persons'[23] and the sad fact remains, that, in its past, Europe was more likely to be unified by force, ruled unwillingly by a conqueror, even if that

---

[18] Commission, *European Governance: A White Paper* COM(2001) 428 final; for more information on the *Future of Europe Debate*, see the website at http://europa.eu.int/futurum. For information on the European Convention see the website at http://www.european-convention.en.int. These initiatives are discussed in Chapter 2.

[19] Such views are discussed at the end of this chapter.

[20] I Ward, *The Margins of European Law* at 23.

[21] Derrida *op. cit.*

[22] D Chalmers, *EU Law* (Ashgate, 1998) at 3.

[23] E Haas, 'The United States of Europe' (1948) 63 Pol Sci Quart 528 at 532.

conqueror did for some brief time enjoy some sort of approbation caused by their appearance of being a liberating force – as did Napoleon. Past attempts at unification were that – attempts – and most usually inchoate in the extreme.

If the more distant past provides us with an often depressing catalogue of European history, the twentieth century provides us with both the brutal history, and also a chronicle of a growing momentum toward European integration, if one of fits and starts. The tendency, and perhaps the danger, is to start at some point earlier in the twentieth century, either before or after the Second World War, and to present subsequent events in chronological fashion, as a progress, or pilgrimage, toward the apotheosis of a united European polity. The institutional architects of the EEC, Spaak, Monnet and, a little later, Walter Hallstein, designed it to be evolutionary – an entity in the process of continuous creation.[24] Even if Europe seemed (and often still does seem) to be on a journey to an unknown destination, with the benefit of hindsight it is all too easy to present European integration in eschatological terms, as an onward process. Just as the Italian art critic, Vasari,[25] writing at the end of the High Renaissance, could look back at Italian art over the previous 300 years as a march toward the grand 'terza maniera' of Michelangelo, with Giotto and Masaccio as staging posts along the way, so one might imagine some fictional (but all too probable) 'European' some time later this century, looking back at 100 years of European integration, and identifying the ECSC, EEC, SEA, Maastricht Treaty and so on, as important staging posts (or as what Bruce Ackerman has deemed 'constitutional moments'[26]) in the path to European unity.

And so, the majority of textbooks proceed. The opening chapter tends to be chronological, evolutionary in nature. I cannot pretend that this chapter will depart wildly from what has become the traditional way of proceeding. The aim of this book is to set EU constitutional law in context, and part of that context is recent legal history. To understand the wranglings of Maastricht, of Nice, as well as the EU's current lamentable lack of democracy, one has to understand its origins, the purposes of its founders. If Jean Monnet had not been trained in the French *énarque* functionalist background, if Walter Hallstein had not battled with de Gaulle, if the Court of Justice had not picked up the momentum of integration at a certain point, the EU might look different today. If we live in a world of historical contingency, rather than some Hegelian progress of the *Weltgeist,* and European integration is not set in stone, then any attempt to do justice to European law must reflect that fact. It is the methodology of this book, however, to try to provide a history of European legal integration which is not mere chronology, but one coupled with critical comment and a contextual approach, taking in legal and political theory and philosophy, as well as political science approaches to that integration.

---

[24] See e.g. Walter Hallstein, 'The European Economic Community' (1963) 78 Pol Sci Quart 161.
[25] Giorgio Vasari, *Lives of the artists. a selection*: translated by George Bull (London: Folio Society, 1993).
[26] B Ackerman, *The Future of Liberal Revolution* (Yale University Press, 1992).

The twentieth century impetus towards integration

By the early twentieth century, the momentum for European integration was growing. The pan-European movement was conceived by Count Richard Coudenhove-Kalergi,[27] a federalist, who saw this movement as a means of preserving political power in Europe, writing, presciently in 1921: 'It would still be possible for Europe to participate in the partition of the earth through timely federation. While Europe is breaking up, it must sink to complete loss of political influence, until one day, after losing its colonies, in debt, bankrupt and impoverished, it will succumb to invasion.'[28] Members of this group were intellectuals and politicians, some of whom would make a name for themselves in the post-war years, such as Pompidou, later to be President of France, or Adenauer, a post-war Chancellor of West Germany. The pan-European movement also went so far as to set up Economic Councils in Paris and Berlin.

In addition, there was also governmental input given to the idea of European integration, such as by the Briand memorandum of 1929–30, proposed by the French foreign minister and discussed by the League of Nations, which set up a Committee of Enquiry on the European Union. This committee proposed a European Federal Union, which would link states without compromising their sovereignty. An early commentator[29] accurately and presciently summed up what was wrong with the Briand plan (and also other inter-war attempts at European integration). He wrote, 'unless the statesmen and peoples of Europe . . . face the facts frankly and fearlessly . . . unless they realise that our completely changed civilisation requires a completely different method of dealing with the relations between nations . . . there can be little doubt that this European Union will bring just as much disappointment as did the League of Nations'. The Briand plan failed and, by 1934, agitation for a united Europe had lapsed into insignificance in the face of the more immediate problems posed by Hitler and Mussolini.

Post-war

If anything could discredit the notion of the sovereign state it was the horrors of nationalism, and the apotheosis of national pride exemplified by the Nazi era's glorification of the nation state. After the Second World War there were concerted efforts to find realistic ways to limit sovereignty, and the vicious circle of violence which had followed it, through some European initiative. There were two immediate and parallel tasks: to recover from the economic bankruptcy in which the Second World War had left most European countries, and to find a way out of the calamitous political bankruptcy of the old order in Europe, which had been based on the balance of power: its coalitions, reprisals and blackmails.[30] The notion of a

---

[27] R Coudenhove-Kalergi, *Pan Europe* (New York: Knopf, 1926). See also C Pegg, *Evolution of the European Idea 1914–1932* (Chapel Hill: University of North Carolina Press, 1983).

[28] R Coudenhove-Kalergi, *Pan Europe* at 24.

[29] So wrote Francis Deak of Columbia University, in 'Can Europe Unite?' (1931) 46 Pol Sci Quart 424.

[30] Hallstein, 'The European Economic Community' (1963) 78 Pol Sci Quart 175.

federal constitution for Europe had already been explored and worked out by some, such as the early federalists Spinelli and Rossi, who had drafted their Ventotene manifesto while imprisoned by the fascists during the Second World War. This stated that 'The question which must be resolved first, failing which progress is no more than mere appearance, is the definitive abolition of the division of Europe into national sovereign states.'[31] This was most definitely a federal document in nature, proposing an end to national sovereignty. Such radical ideas would have to wait, not even having reached fruition by the early twenty-first century, although Spinelli did manage to persuade the European Parliament to draw up and approve a draft European Union Treaty in 1984.[32]

Italian federalists apart, Sir Winston Churchill also, of course, made his famous speech in Zurich in 1946, suggesting a 'united states of Europe' – but it was to be a united states without apparently the participation of the United Kingdom, which seemed more than happy to stand on the sidelines, not wishing its laws to be subject to any other institution. But Britain was not the only nation for which sovereignty remained important. When the horrors and privations of the Second World War had receded sufficiently into the background once again, the former great European nation states began gaining in strength and to resist the idea of reform.

When the first step towards the future European Union was taken, its immediate impetus was a French desire to contain Germany's now resurgent coal and steel industries in the Ruhr and Saar. Putting French and German coal and steel (and those of the Benelux countries and Italy) under a common structure could contain Germany but also serve a longer term interest: the development of European political institutions, and hopefully economic prosperity. And so the Schuman[33] Declaration of 1950 stated 'the pooling of coal and steel production should immediately provide for the setting up of common foundations for economic development as a first step in the federation of Europe . . .'[34] Walter Hallstein later described the Schuman Declaration as 'a kind of founding charter for the EU'.[35]

In fact, the notion of pooling the steel and coal industries was not new.[36] As far back as 1926, the pre-war steel cartels, although a threat to competition, had been welcomed as a healer of Franco-German hatreds. What was new was the way in which it was proposed to be done under the Schuman plan. Previous plans had

---

[31] See D Weigall and P Stirk (eds) *The Origins and Development of the European Community* (Leicester University Press, 1992) at 29–32.

[32] This was not the first such attempt at a federal constitution for Europe: see, for example, the British Federal Union's Draft Constitution of 1939, drafted by lawyers, including Sir Ivor Jennings.

[33] Robert Schuman was the French foreign minister, who actualised the ideas of the civil servant, Jean Monnet, on the pooling of coal and steel. Interestingly, having been born in Lorraine, Schuman only became a Frenchman at the age of 32, and had previously fought in German uniform. F Duchêne, *Jean Monnet* (New York and London: W Norton, 1994) comments at 187 that Schuman was even more 'European than one might think'.

[34] European Parliament, *Selection of Texts Concerning Institutional Matters of the Community for 1950–1982* (OOPEC Lux 1982) at 42.

[35] Hallstein, 'The European Economic Community' at 166.

[36] Jean Monnet had proposed something very similar to the Schuman plan as early as 1941, on his first meeting with Paul Henri Spaak: see Duchêne op. cit. at 182.

envisaged some sort of intergovernmental organisation run by governmental ministers by consensus. Jean Monnet, however, wished for more power for the institutions of this new coal and steel community, which would make them more **supranational** in nature. The art of the Schuman plan was, as the then editor of *Le Monde*, Jacques Fauret, pointed out, 'to extract a policy from a need', but it was also 'a leap in the dark', as Schuman himself said.[37] The proposed new community would have an executive – a High Authority – which would be independent from the member state governments and thus take more political responsibility. It would, however, still be accountable, because it would be responsible to a new parliamentary assembly which would have the power to dismiss it. There would also be some intergovernmental input by way of a Council of Ministers, as well as a new European Court of Justice.

Thus the new European Coal and Steel Community was set up by the Treaty of Paris in 1951. It regulated a common market in coal and steel, abolishing internal customs duties, and restrictions on imports and exports in these commodities, as well as measures which discriminated against imports. Prices could be regulated, but only if there was a crisis caused by shortages or over-production. It was based on free market principles and not as interventionist in method as Monnet, the High Authority's first President, would have liked. But the new Coal and Steel Community most definitely had some federal characteristics, resulting in the removal of sovereignty from its member states.

It was Monnet's plan to move gradually – his idea being that a European federation would be built over the years on this 'first concrete foundation', as new sectors of activity would be brought within the scope of what might be described as pre-federal institutions – an idea which was carried over into the foundation of the EEC and Euratom later that decade. What Monnet could not foresee at that point was how the Council of Ministers, and intergovernmentalism, would come to dominate the politics of the EC in the next decades, as the member states asserted themselves against a perceived realisation of the federalist ideal.

The next attempted step towards European integration was, however, more federal in nature. The 1950s were a time of insecurity caused by world events. Communist threats were posed in the 1950s and early 1960s by the Korean war, the coup in Czechoslovakia and the Berlin blockade. It seemed as if western Europe might need its own security community to deal with these threats from the east. And so the French foreign minister, Pleven, proposed a plan similar to that taken with coal and steel – the pooling of common resources into a European Defence Community, which would also include a European army. And in the minds of some it was not just a Defence Community that was necessary. With something as serious as defence and a common army, surely strong common institutions would be needed to control them? Therefore, Spinelli proposed that the newly created ECSC assembly should come up with a draft for a European Political Community treaty which would see to this. According to Jean Monnet, writing in his *Memoirs*, 'Now the federation of Europe would have to become an immediate objective.'[38]

---

[37] Duchêne op. cit., at 223.
[38] Monnet, *Memoirs* (trans R Mayne, London, 1978).

But the federalising of Europe was not to be such an immediate prospect after all: the desire for a greater union of this kind came up against the rocks of national sovereignty when the French Assemblée Nationale (under the government of Mendes-France, with de Gaulle newly President) failed to ratify these draft treaties, seeing them as a threat to the domain of the nation state. Britain had never in any case wished to join, preferring to deal with security through NATO. The European Defence Community was Europe's first great crisis and defeat and many thought it had put paid to European integration forever. Although the Western European Union had already been created as a European security alliance, including Germany (an alliance that would spring into life in the last decade of the twentieth century at the time of the Maastricht treaty), defence and a common European army would remain a touchy subject for some time to come: witness the outrage in some quarters in Britain in late 2000 when the common army initiative was renewed.[39]

The relance

If the European defence and political communities had floundered, this was not an end to the integration initiative. It did, however, mean that it took a different, more oblique, turn. An earlier plan of 1953, proposed by the Dutch foreign minister, Beyen,[40] suggested integration of a different sort, in the economic field only, by abolishing barriers to trade. As Benjamin Franklin said in another context, 'No nation was ever ruined by trade.' Just a year after the EDC had floundered, a meeting of foreign ministers was held in Messina ('probably the most hazardous straits in the whole European journey'[41]) in 1955. Integration in the economic field did not appear such a great threat to national sovereignty. The Belgian prime minister Spaak drafted a report in 1956 which was to lead to the treaties of Rome (a separate treaty on atomic energy being added to appease the French) of 1957, approved by the same six countries as had signed the ECSC treaty. These came into force on 1 January 1958.

The EEC

The EEC institutions were modelled on those of the ECSC, sharing the same Court of Justice and Parliamentary Assembly. However, there was a significant difference in the relationship between the EEC's executive and its ministerial council, which would affect the operation of the EEC for some decades. Instead of a High Authority, the EEC had an executive called the Commission, with less power, representing a weakening of federalism and greater control by the member state governments.

Nevertheless, the scope and content of the EEC were of great consequence – the creation of a common market for all goods and services was 'a project of great polit-

---

[39] See I Black, 'Britain and France clash over Defence' (The Guardian 5 December 2000).
[40] According to Spaak, in his memoirs, 'the daring of Beyen's vision scared me': Duchêne op. cit. at 274.
[41] Duchêne op. cit. at 283.

ical and economic significance'.[42] The economies of the member states had once been separated by tariffs (the great historical instrument of protection), quotas and non-tariff barriers, and most of these were still rife in the post-war period. Their removal was 'truly a radical project' (although the Benelux countries had already achieved this some time earlier) and here the Treaty of Rome was most decisive, setting out a detailed programme to remove these within twelve to fifteen years, by the end of a 'transitional period' specified in the treaty. A common market was also aligned to a common external tariff: the customs union. It was more than a free trade area: in addition to providing for free movement of goods, the Treaty of Rome provided for the free movement of workers, enterprises and capital. It also contained the provisions for common agricultural, competition and transport policies. Additionally it made some provision for social policy in the field of employment (whether, as some perceived it,[43] as an attempt to 'humanise' the EEC, or simply as others would have it, to ensure a 'level playing field'[44]) and established a Social Fund and an Investment Bank. The achievement of the Common Market was to be financed by a Community Budget, which would eventually be financed by 'own resources'. However, it most certainly did not have the one economic power essential to a federal system: the control of monetary policy, especially the issuing of money by a central bank. This was seen as the preserve of member state economic sovereignty and its introduction would have to wait for another 40 years.

The neo-functionalist vision of integration

Throughout the post-war history of European integration, different theories, or models, have been proposed, with a greater or lesser degree of success, in an attempt to explain the process, or to predict its development. Although there were some federalist visions in the early years of the EEC,[45] it was the functionalist and neo-functionalist models which were seen as the most convincing alternatives to a federalist concept of integration. The ECSC treaty is a good example of an attempt to integrate along functionalist lines. By this interpretation, what Monnet would refer to as 'engrenage', supranationalism is established in one sector, and then inevitably this involves a 'spillover' into other policy areas as a result. These other sectors then, of necessity, become included in the integration process. The EEC treaty fits less clearly into this model as it is less sectoral in nature, operating over a wide spectrum of

---

[42] J Pinder, *The Building of the European Union* (3rd edn, Oxford University Press, 1998) at 11.

[43] Per AG Trabucchi in Case 7/75 *F v Belgian State* [1975] ECR 679.

[44] Article 141 EC, for example, which provides for equal pay for men and women, was originally inserted at the demand of the French, who, having more advanced non-discrimination laws on equal pay than the rest of Europe at that time, were anxious to secure that they would not be at a competitive disadvantage by the relocation of work in member states more profitable to employers. See Chapter 14 of this book for a further discussion of these matters.

[45] Some of them emanating from significant individuals, such as Walter Hallstein, the first President of the Commission, whose language, writing in 1963, was striking: 'what is really being achieved is political union in the economic field'. Hallstein, 'The European Economic Community' at 165.

economic affairs. None the less it still involved the process of 'spillover' leading theorists to develop a new model, that of 'neo-functionalism'.[46] This modification of functionalism stresses the importance of groups of political forces, or elites, within the integration process, emphasising that development takes place as a result of transfer of loyalties and activities among certain groups: 'the original form of neo-functionalism emphasises the importance of activities and loyalties of the major societal groups, and in particular the political and economic elites. Neo-functionalist theory argues that a new European "polity" is emerging because actors in several distinct national settings are persuaded to shift their loyalties, expectations and political activities towards a new centre . . .'[47]

This theory accords well in at least one way with the EEC: its domination by elites, or rather by certain groups, not generally well known by the public at large, and often caricatured as the 'bureaucrats in Brussels'. The domination of Community institutions by bureaucratic elites is partly an effect of the influence of Jean Monnet, whose background in the bureaucratic training ground of the French Civil Service is seen as accounting for the technocratic character of the original High Authority of the ECSC,[48] in contrast to, for example, the federalism of Spinelli. Undoubtedly, the EEC, in its early days, was influenced by the French political class, which was dominated by administrators, described by one commentator as 'the most formidable, well-educated political class in Europe'.[49]

In such a situation, legitimacy is to be achieved through economic prosperity, through maintenance of peace and progress, not through a particular and deliberate democratic structuring of the organisation. And, in the process, it was supposed that loyalties and affinities would gradually shift, in this case to the European enterprise, albeit an elitist one. As Lindberg and Scheingold wrote: 'The idea is that increasing affluence stoked by new technology and more aggressive business practices nurture a more benign environment, sublimating social cleavage in an increasingly successful quest for material goods and dissolving political conflict in a consensus of apathy.'[50]

---

[46] See e.g. the following works for an exploration of this theory: E Haas, *The Uniting of Europe* (London, 1958); L Lindbergh, *The Political Dynamics of European Integration* (California: Stanford, 1963); L Lindberg and S Scheingold, *Europe's Would be Polity: Patterns of Change in the European Community* (Eaglewood Cliffs NJ, 1970); see also S George, *Politics and Policy in the European Community* (3rd edn, Oxford University Press, 1996) 38.

[47] S Hix, 'The Study of the EC' (1993) 17 West European Politics 45.

[48] Which Paul Craig has described as a 'technocratic, elite led gradualism and corporate style of engagement of affected interests'. See Craig and de Burca (eds) *The Evolution of EU Law* (Oxford University Press, 1999) ch. 1. See also H Wallace and J Smith, 'Democracy or Technocracy? European Integration and the Problem of Popular Consent' in Hayward (ed) *The Crisis of Representation in Europe* (Frank Cass, 1995) 140. However, one should not take the French ENA (École Nationale d'Administration) thesis too far; another extremely influential French President of the Commission, Jacques Delors, did not even attend university, but worked for the Banque de France and trade unions.

[49] L Siedentop, *Democracy in Europe* (Penguin 2000) at 113, who goes on to criticise this (perceived) domination of the EEC by the French, which while it tried to defend the European identity against a 'facile Americanism' also led to 'the happy consequence for France of the development of the CAP' and Siedentop also asks 'is it an accident that France pays so little into the coffers of the Community budget (less in fact than Sweden)?' He also goes on to link it with Commission mismanagement and irregularity, leading to the 'private and unaccountable elite' of Jacques Santer.

[50] Lindberg and Scheingold, *Europe's Would-be Polity* at 269.

Three things are worth noting about this view. First, this is rather a impoverished view of legitimacy. It requires only a permissive 'consensus of apathy', which allows the technocrats to proceed with the important business of integration, which was thought suitable for Europe in the 1960s and has resulted in the level of apathy now felt by its citizens for the European idea. This is a sad feature of the Union's existence in the early twenty-first century. A contemporary pressing issue is that of a more suitable democratic structure for the European Union in the new millennium. This notion of a government of elites did not, however, originate in the passageways of *Sciences Po*, or the *École Nationale d'Administration* (which are specialist French higher education institutions where students train for the highest echelons of the administration), but is also redolent of what the French positivist, Henri de Saint-Simon, wrote in the nineteenth century.[51] Saint-Simon predicted that European government would in future be taken over by administration of society by bankers, industrialists and scientists: 'The government of people will be replaced by the administration of things.'[52] Saint-Simon approved of such a displacement, seeing it (in an age of optimism and faith in science) as the substitution of positive knowledge, skill and rationality for the emotive, prejudiced rhetoric of politics. Such a positivist certainty might have seemed attractive in the nineteenth century, but has now taken on an unpleasant ring, when horrific events have shown us just how far rationality may take us, a notion explored at a theoretical level by Horkheimer and Adorno in the *Dialectic of Enlightenment*.[53]

Secondly, a focus on economic integration, performed by elites, is also perhaps responsible for the subordination of political language and questions of accountability, participation and representation, to the language of economics. If one reads the Federalist Papers, detailing the background to the drafting of the American Federal Constitution, one reads impassioned debates on vital issues of the nature of government, democracy, the constraining of power. There may have been passion in the urge for European integration, but a 'common market' is a less inspiring and powerful image than the radical, revolutionary statements of well reasoned political thought that became the American Constitution, the debates over which throw up again and again words such as 'robust', 'energetic', and 'vigorous government'.[54] Such a subordination has been called 'economism', described as having deep roots in the European project able to be 'traced back to the idiom of Jean Monnet',[55] whereby the question of political institutions and democratic accountability were left largely to one side. Siedentop has suggested that we are now paying a high price for that subordination, complaining that 'has the west seen off the Communist

---

[51] Interestingly, Pascal Lamy, Delors' Chef de Cabinet and a true 'énarque' confessed to being a Saint-Simonian. Although he was later to claim in 1992 that 'Saint Simonism is at an end after the Danish no-vote', suggesting that it (i.e. Saint-Simonism) failed to brook democratic opposition. See G Ross, *Jacques Delors and European Integration* (Blackwell, Polity Press, 1995) at 69 and 194.

[52] Saint-Simon, *The political thought of Saint-Simon* [translated from the French by Valence Ionescu], (Oxford University Press, 1976).

[53] M Horkheimer and T Adorno, *Dialectic of Enlightenment* (New York: Herder, 1972).

[54] *Federalist Papers Reader* (ed F. Quinn, Washington: Seven Locks Press, 1993).

[55] Siedentop at 33.

challenge only to fall victim to an unelected elite, in its own way as arrogant and exploitative as the Community elite?'[56]

A third notable effect of neo-functionalism is that the theory seems also to involve a rather basic form of economic determinism, of the sort that old-style Marxists used to pursue (albeit with different ends in mind), i.e. it assumes that certain other improvements will follow naturally when economic progress is achieved. But surely the great moments in European integration (and even some of the less great ones!) cannot just be explained as the product of some reaction produced by underlying issue linkages? Surely political action has something to do with them, rather than just being effects or epiphenomena?

In any case, neo-functionalism as a theory was not borne out by fact, whether in its crude determinist form, or in a more sophisticated version.[57] The EEC did not progress as swiftly towards the implicitly political intentions of its Preamble, to 'lay the foundations of an ever closer union among the peoples of Europe', as might have been hoped; instead the intransigence of the de Gaulle regime in France and subsequent Luxembourg Accords led to a crisis in the Commission, which consequently became more cautious in its activities.[58] The process had not accomplished its hoped for degree of 'spillover'.

Community crisis and retrenchment

In some respects, however, the EEC made good progress in its first ten years – and its economic and commercial achievement was substantial. According to the figures given by the British Government White Paper[59] of 1971, just before the debate in the Westminster Parliament prior to Britain's entry, the abolition of tariffs had encouraged mutual trade and by 1969, intra-Community trade was 50 per cent higher. Stronger competition had forced industries to seek more efficient, lower cost production methods. Prospect for exports had increased rapidly with investment growth. In all, EC countries had a rate of GNP twice that of Britain just before UK entry. Such impressive economic progress would have been unlikely to be achieved independently of membership by the six original member states. On the other hand, in spite of its impressive economic growth, the EEC came under threat, and most particularly its institutional growth and institutional balance, from resurgent nationalism, in the form of the Gaullist challenge from France. As early as 1962 de Gaulle had stated, 'at present there is and can be no Europe other than a Europe of the States – except

---

[56] Ibid.

[57] See the later work of Lindberg and Scheingold, e.g. *Regional Integration* (Harvard University Press, 1970) which becomes increasingly complex. Neo-functionalism later resurfaced in the 1990s, see e.g. Jeppe Tranholm Mikkelson, 'Neo-functionalism: obstinate or obsolete? A Reappraisal of the new dynamism of the EC' (1991) 20 J'l Int. Studies 1; D Mortimer, '1992 and the Political Integration of Europe: neo functionalism reconsidered' (1989) 13 J'l Eur. Int. 1.

[58] See on this K H Neunreither, 'Transformation of a Political Role: the case of the Commission of the European Communities' (1971–72) JCMS 233.

[59] Commission White Paper 'Completing the Internal Market' COM (85) 310 final.

of course for myths, fictions and pageants'.[60] And so, having dispensed with the Algerian war, de Gaulle freed himself 'to give his attention to his quarrels with the federalists in the Community and the "Anglo-Saxons" outside it'.[61] This latter he managed to do quite effectively – vetoing Britain's first application to join the EEC in 1963, using his veto unilaterally at a Press Conference without consultation with France's other European partners, and offending the British by giving his infamous reasons against UK membership, 'England is in effect, insular, maritime, linked through its trade, markets and food supply to often very distant countries.'[62]

However it was the major wrangle in 1965 that brought about the so-called Community crisis. A new Commission, led by Walter Hallstein, with definite federal goals, began to assert itself. It is interesting to observe Hallstein's optimism. Speaking at Dean's Day at Columbia University in 1963, he described the treaties as 'an attempt to build on a federal pattern a democratic constitution for Europe'.[63] The statist French President, de Gaulle, sought to put an end to this. These were, after all, the sort of words that, uttered nearly 40 years later by the German Foreign Minister, Joschka Fischer, still continued to inflame Europeans.[64]

The crisis came about in this way. The Commission had put forward three related proposals as a package. First, the completion of the Common Agricultural Policy (CAP) financing regulations. Second, the introduction of the Community's own sources of revenue to replace contributions from national governments, and, third, the increase of the powers of the European Parliament by giving it some control over the Community budget. Therefore, this package combined the strengthening of EEC institutions with progress toward further economic integration. But despite the French interests in settling CAP finance, de Gaulle was not amenable to any neo-functionalist spillover, nor any federalist logic which contributed to the weakening of the position of the nation state.[65] Therefore France boycotted the EEC from 1 July 1965 – the 'empty chair policy' – and although the other five Community members continued to meet, the EEC was paralysed. In January 1966, an agreement was drawn up in Luxembourg to settle the crisis in a way which worked against greater supranationalism, by settling on an agreement to disagree on the use of majority voting in the Council of Ministers: the so-called 'Luxembourg Accords'. Where 'issues of vital national importance' were at stake, France insisted on retaining a veto, and inevitably a shift of influence took place from the Commission to the intergovernmental Council of Ministers and its committees, which became the centre of the decision-making process.[66] The need for unanimity,

---

[60] Said at a Press Conference 15 May 1962. Quoted in M Holland, *European Integration: From Community to Union* (London: Pinter, 1993) at 9.

[61] J Pinder, *The Building of the European Union* (OUP, 1998) at 14.

[62] Although there was a grain of truth in de Gaulle's view, given Britain's colonial past and continuing strong ties with the Commonwealth.

[63] Hallstein, 'The European Economic Community' at 168.

[64] An English translation of Fischer's speech may be found at http://www.jeanmonnetprogram.org./papers/00/symp.html.

[65] Such a stance did not necessarily impress the French electorate, as in the ensuing election de Gaulle failed to secure an overall majority.

[66] See W Nicholl, 'The Luxembourg Compromise' (1984) 23 JCMS 35.

brought about by the existence of the veto, ended the hope that the EEC could swiftly move toward supranationalism. Although the Luxembourg Accords were only informal, their status was never challenged, and thus it would not be until the Single European Act of 1986 that majority voting would be accepted on a more general scale. It was now clear that political unification would not be an automatic consequence of taking certain economic decisions jointly. The Community proceeded on an intergovernmental basis with its true source of political authority the governments of the member states.

Clearly, neo-functionalism was unable to explain the progress, or lack of it, of the Community from the late 1960s. It seemed to be dominated by the member states, or at least some of them, and their interests, and a theory more orientated towards intergovernmentalism might seem to provide a better explanation of these developments. We can find such theories in the liberal intergovernmentalism of Andrew Moravscik[67] and also in Alan Milward's controversial analysis of the European Community as a mechanism for strengthening state sovereignty rather than pursuing a federalist agenda.[68] These are both variants of an interstatist approach to the EC. They have their roots in the realist school of international relations, according to which states, perceived as the essential and most important actors in international politics, behave rationally (i.e. in a self-interested manner) and are motivated by a desire to enhance and maintain their power relative to that of other states.[69]

Liberal intergovernmentalism seeks to explain European integration on the basis that it suited, and strengthened, the member states' purposes to pursue that path. Such theories draw on public choice theory[70] and assume that the state will act rationally on the basis of aggregated preferences of groups in society. States will engage in economic integration on the basis of a cost-benefit analysis. As Moravscik writes: 'Following public choice analyses of domestic constituents, intergovernmental theory views the decision to adopt qualified majority voting or delegation to common institutions as the result of a cost-benefit analysis of the stream of future substantive decisions expected to follow from alternative institutional design.'[71] To give up some national sovereignty is rational if it thereby increases efficiency. The role of the ECJ has a related justification. Although international legal tribunals may again reduce state sovereignty, and this has certainly been the case with the ECJ, their role can be rationalised on the basis that they prevent other states refusing to

---

[67] A Moravscik, 'Preferences and Powers in the European Community: A Liberal Intergovernmentalist Approach' (1993) 31 JCMS 473. For a fuller statement of Moravscik's views see Moravscik, *The Choice for Europe* (Cornell University Press, 1998).

[68] A Milward, *The European Rescue of the Nation State* (Routledge, 1992). See also S Hoffmann, *The European Sisyphus: Essays on Europe 1964–1994* (Boulder: Westview, 1995) who writes of the EC regeneration of the nation state. See also G Garrett 'International Co-operation and Institutional Choice: the European Community's Internal Market' Internal Organisation, Spring 1992.

[69] See Hans Morgenthau, *Politics Among Nations* (Knopf, 1948); Kenneth N Waltz *Theory of International Relations* (Addison Wesley, 1979).

[70] See e.g. J Buchanan and G Tullock, *The Calculus of Consent* (University of Michigan Press, 1962); I Mclean, *Public Choice: An Introduction* (OUP, 1987).

[71] Moravscik, 'Preferences and Powers in the European Community' at 509.

comply with their part of the bargain and thus spoiling the situation overall – it prevents prisoners' dilemma and free rider problems.[72]

However, even more than neo-functionalism, intergovernmentalism leaves us with an impoverished role, or view, of democracy, and most particularly fails to explain the role of the European Parliament in the EU. According to intergovernmentalism, the European Union may only be a democratic polity if it derives its legitimacy from the consent of its member states.[73] The European Parliament may however block legislation in the Council of Ministers. It can thwart their wishes. Why include it?[74] But, as far as legitimacy is concerned, this seems to be an unpleasant and counter-intuitive conclusion, as the Parliament, with its direct election by the peoples of Europe, is generally thought to be the most democratic of EU Institutions. So, a theory which proposes that democracy and legitimacy may derive only from the member states seems unsatisfactory – especially as we may think that there are very good reasons for scrutiny by the European Parliament (and also judicial control by the ECJ) when they constrain what those in power wish to do.[75] Even if intergovernmentalism attempts to describe, rather than assert, a desirable account of the EU, it seems unsatisfactory.

Alan Milward proposes a similar explanation but also claims that we must be suspicious of what we take to be the 'facts' of integration.[76] He perceives the ideological rhetoric of integration as a 'deliberate smokescreen', warning that we should be particularly wary of the pronouncements of 'the great men' of Europe. Milward asserts that we should not be confused by the fact that nations no longer act in isolation into believing that this is against their national interests. Some features of the EC have been greatly to the benefit of some of its member states – witness the advantages reaped by France by the CAP. Milward suggests that the economic growth of western Europe up to 1968 (as, for example, cited by the British Government White Paper urging British membership of the EEC) was not just the result of EEC integration, but also of the fact that states were more effective in managing their economic affairs as a result. According to Milward, the 'great men', so often presented as the *jalons* of European integration, such as Monnet and Schuman, were very assiduous in preserving the nation state.[77] Milward states that, for Schuman, the nation remained the basis of his legal thought. Monnet is described as 'more nation state orientated than any other'.[78]

---

[72] For an explanation of the Prisoner's Dilemma see L Green, *The Authority of the State* (OUP, 1990) at 127 *et seq*.

[73] A view shadowed in the German Constitutional Court's Maastricht judgment, which is discussed later in this chapter and also in Chapter 3.

[74] For Moravscik's further views on this matter see Moravscik, 'Liberal Intergovernmentalism: A rejoinder' (1995) 33 JCMS 611.

[75] See the discussion in Chapter 3 of this book.

[76] Milward, *op. cit.* at 8–19.

[77] However, as Armstrong and Bulmer point out (K Armstrong and S Bulmer, *The Governance of the Single European Market* (Manchester University Press, 1998) at 44), Milward draws heavily on national archives for his research – hence a bias in favour of national government interests might be expected.

[78] Milward op. cit., at 325. Milward's thesis is discussed at some length in I Ward, *The Margins of European Law* at 54.

But we should not be misled by this enduring nationalism of the intergovernmental schools of thought into believing that there is no other way of proceeding. As Horsmann and Marshall comment, this particular vision is simply a way of 'imaging' the world – there is nothing God-given about it.[79] If states have benefited from Community membership, there have been burdens as well, such as large budget contributions in some cases, with incommensurate returns. Certainly, latterly, intergovernmentalism fails to explain the drive to integration in areas not fuelled by economic prosperity, nor giving up the veto in ever more areas. It does not explain the Commission's drive to integration, often beyond that desired by the member states.

On a normative level, the account intergovernmentalism gives of legitimacy and democracy in the EU is unattractive. According to intergovernmentalism, the EU will act legitimately if its measures have been consented to by the member states, the masters of the treaty (which may not however satisfy the channels of legitimacy through their own parliaments). But surely democracy at the European level is not just a matter of subsidiarity? It must flourish at every level – including the supranational, as well as the intergovernmental.

Stagnation

In 1969, the leaders of the six member states (with de Gaulle now dead) had met at the Hague Summit conference, determined to end the period of political stagnation into which the EEC had fallen after the Luxembourg crisis. They managed to secure agreement on four major issues. First, they agreed on the financing of the CAP, and the direct financing of the EEC from its own resources – and to that extent, issues of the 1965–6 Luxembourg crisis were resolved. (The CAP, however, would continue to eat up regrettably large chunks of the Community budget for some time to come.) In addition, they settled on two projects which have been highly contentious and which only really started to come to fruition in the late 1990s; thus, their inclusion as early as 1969 is initially surprising. They made plans for full economic and monetary union by 1980, with Werner, the Prime Minster of Luxembourg, to head a committee on this. As it turned out, these plans were wildly unrealistic. They also agreed to study the steps needed to achieve a European common foreign policy: this was to be done in a report by Davignon, of the Belgian Foreign Office. This led to the setting up of an extra-Communitarian body, European political cooperation, an intergovernmental group – the member state foreign ministers – which aimed at coordinating the foreign policies of the EEC members. Fourthly, (de Gaulle now safely out of the way) they decided to take steps to extend membership to the UK and some other countries.

Britain had continued to take refuge in EFTA, the much less ambitious European Free Trade Association, after its two unsuccessful applications for membership of the EEC. But it did eventually join, along with Ireland and Denmark, under the

---

[79] M Horsmann and A Marshall, *After the Nation-State: Citizens, Tribalism and the New World Disorder* (London: Harper Collins, 1994) at 269.

enthusiastically committed Heath Government in 1973, on, it has to be said, some-what unfavourable terms,[80] with a large budget contribution. These new member-ships brought greater diversity to the Community and new interests and attitudes, if somewhat indigestible ones, such as, in the UK's case, an attachment to national sovereignty which was to prove similar to that of de Gaulle. The new Labour gov-ernment of Harold Wilson immediately tried to renegotiate on coming into office in 1974, and this aggressive approach certainly did not diminish under Margaret Thatcher's Conservative government after 1979.

Other initiatives were taken. The European Regional Development Fund was set up when the UK joined, and the Social Fund expanded. At the Paris summit of December 1974, the heads of state and government agreed to hold regular summit meetings in future and that they would be known as the European Council from then on. This would be another extra-Community institution, the only body to have some jurisdiction in all fields, what seemed to be a triumph of intergovern-mentalism.

In spite of the bold plans of the 1969 Hague summit, the 1970s were not an impressive period in Community history. There was a severe recession caused by the rise in oil prices, and parliamentary government came under criticism in some states: in France after the events of the May '68 student riots, in Britain after the crisis of the miners' strike and the three-day week of 1973–4. Economic recession and infla-tion led to stagflation, and countries responded by protectionism. Tariffs could not be raised within the EEC, but there was a rapid spread of non-tariff barriers, e.g. state aids to industry to protect jobs. The effectiveness of Community measures weakened and growth levels fell to half of what they had been in the 1960s. Intra-EEC trade expansion stopped. But if national governments came under criticism, so did the EEC. Commission officials were often represented as faceless bureaucrats, spending far too much time in technocratic activity: devising unnecessary regula-tions for standardisation of things such as the size of apples, cricket bats and kippers. The shift of the popular permissive consensus heralded by the neo-function-alists had not come about. There was widespread disillusion with the Community objective and the EEC suffered from having concentrated too closely on economic and commercial affairs in the 1960s; it had lost what Leo Tindemans was later to call its 'parfum d'aventure'.

Further initiatives were taken to try to remedy this. At the Paris summit meeting of 1972 it was agreed that the EEC should aim at the creation of a new 'European Union' by 1980, to coincide with full monetary and economic union. This was clear-ly an unrealistic agenda. Later, in 1976, the Belgian Prime Minster, Leo Tindemans, drew up a report on European Union, investigating how the EEC's institutions might be strengthened to make for more efficient decision making and more demo-cratic control. In his view it was essential to present a Community 'with a human face'. He considered European integration to be a 'self-evident good', not a view

---

[80] Its contribution to the Community budget was to be £300 million by 1978, most of which would go into the seemingly bottomless pool of the CAP, which was rapidly rationalising European faring to the point where butter mountains and wine lakes started to appear.

which everyone shared. The kind of union that Tindemans had in mind would have required very strong political commitments from the member states – he had recommended more democratic accountability and majority voting in the Council of Ministers. In 1976 there was no commitment to such a political community and little inclination for any institutional changes. Proposals to complete any such union by 1980 were abandoned and the report shelved. In the light of this it might have been thought unnecessary to require another report so shortly after that of the very grandly named 'Three Wise Men' in 1979.[81] Many of Tindemans' proposals appeared in this report, which proposed that Community institutions be reformed so as to speed up decision-making and that European political cooperation be brought within the framework of the Treaty. But again, nothing was done. Even as late as March 1982, the cover of *The Economist* showed a tombstone with the words, 'EEC born March 25 1957, moribund March 25 1982, "capax imperii nisi imperasset"'.[82]

However, one institution not affected by stagnation was the European Court of Justice. From early days in the Community's history – its 'heroic years' – it had given judgments of great significance, introducing the doctrines of direct effect and supremacy of Community law, actions sometimes perceived as the first steps towards the creation of a European constitution out of the treaties.[83] In addition to the innovation of such foundational principles, it had also been furthering the pace of integration in a substantive sense. While the Commission was bogged down in a tedious and dilatory harmonisation process, the ECJ, in such landmark judgments as *Cassis de Dijon*, carried forward free movement by requiring member states to engage in mutual recognition of each others' products and product laws, denying them access to the domestic market only if the product failed to satisfy certain mandatory requirements recognised under Community law. It also required member states to recognise core principles of free movement such as freedom of establishment,[84] even in the absence of Community legislation which should have been, but had not been, introduced to complete the common market.

Thus, the continuance of European integration during this period was as much, if not more, a legal than a political phenomenon.[85] However, integration of this kind,

---

[81] *Report on European Institutions presented by the Committee of Three to the European Council* (EC Bull Supplt. 1–3/78).

[82] 'It seemed capable of power until it tried to wield it', cited in R Keohane and S Hoffman, *The New European Community: Decision Making and Institutional Change* (Westview, 1991) at 3.

[83] These concepts are discussed in Part II (Chapters 5–9) of this book.

[84] As in Case 2/74 *Reyners v Belgium* [1974] ECR 631.

[85] See e.g. J Weiler, 'Community, Member States and European Integration: Is the Law Relevant?' (1982) 20 JCMS; A Easson, 'Legal Approaches to European Integration: The Role of the Court and the Legislator in the Completion of the European Internal Market' (1989) 12 J'l Of European Integration 101; K Lenaerts, 'Some Thoughts about the Interaction between Judges and Politicians in the European Community' (1992) 12 YEL 1; D Wincott, 'Political Theory Law and European Integration' in J Shaw and G More (eds) *New Legal Dynamics of European Union* (Oxford: Clarendon Press, 1995).

apart from any charges of judicial activism which may have attended the Court,[86] is not unproblematic. It is deregulatory in nature and thus is known as 'negative' rather than 'positive' integration. A free flow of products, services and so on, takes place on the basis of the absence of legislation, rather than on the basis of EC regulation. There is a danger of a regulatory 'race to the bottom' and the ignoring, and setting aside, of some national laws which may exist for good reason on grounds of safety, culture, environment etc., but which nonetheless are not perceived to fall within the scope of a mandatory requirement.[87] Perhaps this was the only possible way forward at that stage in Community history. Mutual recognition was later taken up by the Commission as the appropriate methodology for completing the Single Market in its 1985 White Paper. Be this as it may, this 'integration by law' increased the role of the ECJ, even if not necessarily increasing its public profile, making it indispensable for study in a survey of European integration, although its existence did not seem to be discovered by political scientists until the late 1980s in spite of this. Indeed, there is a certain irony in the fact that, while lawyers perceived the EC as becoming 'constitutionalised' or even federalised, political scientists continue to construe it in terms of traditional intergovernmentalism.

Transformation by stealth?

The 1970s are traditionally seen as a period of stagnation, as indeed they have been described here. However, in one respect, important transformations were taking place in the Community legal order, a point that is considered fully in Weiler's famous article 'The Transformation of Europe'.[88] This concerned the expansion of the Community's competence to act. The Treaty of Rome, unlike certain federal texts, contained no enumeration of powers of the member states and the EEC. In *Van Gend en Loos*,[89] the ECJ had referred to the fact that member states had limited their sovereign rights within limited fields. However, the period from 1972 on (after a European Council meeting, at which a decision was taken to make fuller use of the 'implied powers' clause Article 308 (then 235)) saw a great expansion of Community competence, as the EEC proceeded to enact legislation on a variety of matters, such as environment, for which provision had not been made in the EEC treaty, but of which a power to act could be implied through Article 308. This period Weiler described as 'a second and fundamental phase in the transformation of Europe' in which 'the Community order mutated almost as significantly as it did in the foundational period'.[90] This mutation, although of tremendous significance,

---

[86] See the discussion in Chapter 5.

[87] See on this F Scharpf, 'Negative and Positive Integration in the Political Economy of the European Welfare State' in G Marks et al (eds), *Governance in the European Union* (London: Sage, 1996); J Weiler, 'The Community System: the Dual Character of Supranationalism' (1981) 1 YBEL 267.

[88] J Weiler, 'The Transformation of Europe' (1991) 100 Yale LJ 2407, now reprinted in Weiler, *The Constitution of Europe* (Cambridge University Press, 1999).

[89] Case 26/62 [1963] ECR 1.

[90] Weiler, *The Constitution of Europe* at 42. See also Chapter 3 for a more detailed discussion of these issues.

was not, however, subject to the objections and unpopularity which would be the case with the Maastricht treaty sometime later. Indeed, it seemed to be almost ignored by the member states, perhaps because it did not occur at their expense, but rather with their consent, as Community voting under Article 308 proceeded by unanimity. There was no apparent erosion of member state sovereignty. Therefore, 'whereas the principal political actors may have shared a common interest in the jurisdictional mutation, it was, like still water, slowly but deeply boring a creek in the most important foundation of the constitutional order'.[91] Only in this new millennium has the issue of Community competence appeared to take a new turn.[92]

Regeneration

If earlier initiatives such as the Hague summit of 1969, the 1972 Paris summit (which had set out the first EC action plans in environment and social policy) and the Tindemans and Three Wise Men reports did not seem to have resulted in the hoped for regeneration, by the 1980s things were beginning to change, although without much effect initially. In 1981 there was the Genscher–Colombo initiative (named after the foreign ministers of France and Germany) which led to a 'draft' European act, increasing Community competences.[93] This act, although never implemented, did bring about the 1983 Heads of State and Government Solemn Declaration on European Union, which, having the grand title of a Solemn Declaration, did not have a great deal of content but did state that there should be a 'renewed impetus towards the development of Community policies on a broad front' including the completion of the internal market. A year later, in 1984, the European Parliament, led by Spinelli, itself drew up a draft treaty on European Union, perceived alternately as a very radical document, or a treaty drafted 'over dinner at the *Crocodile* restaurant in Strasbourg'[94] depending on your point of view. However, it did provoke member state governments to react, and in June 1984 the European Council met at Fontainebleau and decided to set up a committee (the 'Doodge Committee') along the lines of the earlier Spaak committee to investigate institutional reform. This committee recommended the convening of an intergovernmental conference to negotiate a new treaty. The result of this conference was the Single European Act (SEA), signed in February 1986, which was not a treaty to replace the treaty of Rome, as advocated by Spinelli and the European Parliament, but rather a series of amendments to the Treaty of Rome.

The EEC treaty had survived for nearly 30 years without any major amendments.[95] However, under the SEA some significant adjustments were made. Most

---

[91] Weiler *op. cit.* at 61.
[92] See the discussion on competences in Chapter 4.
[93] See J Weiler, 'The Genscher–Colombo draft European Act: the politics of indecision' (1983) 6 J'l of European Integration.
[94] per I Ward, *The Margins of European Law* at 30.
[95] Although the institutions of the EEC and Euratom were merged with those of the ECSC under the 1965 Merger treaty.

importantly, the member states pledged to complete the internal market by 1992. Article 14 EC (8A as then was) required the EEC 'to adopt measures with the aim of progressively establishing the internal market over the period expiring 31 December 1992'. The realisation of this would demand significant legislative activity, and so the SEA altered voting procedures to introduce majority voting for most decisions necessary for the completion of the internal market, thus denying member states the power to block measures. This was done by way of a new Article 95 (then 100A), somewhat craftily expressed as a 'residual' power, a derogation from the already existent Article 94 (then 100) which required unanimity. A new legislation procedure, the cooperation procedure, was introduced to give the European Parliament, now officially called Parliament, rather than merely the Assembly, a greater role in legislation, going beyond consultation. New EEC competences were introduced in environment, technology, social policy, research and technical development, although for the most part this simply confirmed initiatives upon which the EC had already embarked.[96] It also made the first formal reference to the European Monetary System, in operation since 1979, and brought European Political Cooperation within the framework of the treaty for the first time.

The idea of completing the internal market had in fact been floating around the Commission for some time, having been initially introduced in 1981 by Karl Heinz Narjes, an EC Commissioner and the former *Chef de Cabinet* of Walter Hallstein, as a modest project, although work continued steadily on it for four years. Such a notion enthused the world of business and commerce, and Community elites, but, unlike the project of the Parliament's draft Union treaty, the idea of a single (or internal[97]) market was also popular with the member states, as it seemed not to involve threatening new supranational agencies.[98] Also, its scope for increasing prosperity had appeared to be self-evident, especially if one took the Cecchini report figures seriously.[99] Jacques Delors had become President of the Commission in 1984, making his appointment conditional on some major initiative to invigorate the EC, but of all the suggestions (most of them based on previously unimplemented initiatives generated by the Community in its recent past) which he made to the heads of state, the only one to be acceptable was that of the single market. Monetary union and institutional reform, which he also proposed, were still thought to be unacceptable, and would have to wait until the Maastricht treaty of 1992.[100] Lord Cockfield, Narjes' successor (and previously minister at the UK Department of Trade and Industry, where he had acquired first-hand experience of Europe's non-tariff barriers to trade) presented a White Paper[101] – written at great

---

[96] Under Article 308 EC.

[97] For the purposes of the discussion in this section these terms are used interchangeably, although purists would assert that there are considerable differences in meaning.

[98] See N Fligstein, and I Mara Drita, 'How to Make a Market: Reflections on the Attempt to Create a Single Market in Europe' (1996) Am J Soc. 1 at 11–13.

[99] P Cecchini with M Catinat and A Jacquemin, *1992: the European challenge. The benefits of a single market* (English edition by John Robinson, Aldershot: Gower, 1988).

[100] Although a committee on EMU was set up under Jacques Delors.

[101] White Paper 'Completing the Internal Market' Com (85) 320.

speed, within only three months – with a plan for 279 directives to be concluded by 1992 in order to complete the internal market.

However, the status of this concept of the internal market was, and still is, less than clear. Although an impressive objective, it was in fact less ambitious than the original concept of the 'common market' in the treaty of Rome, as it probably only covered fundamental freedoms of movement, rather than the common policies such as competition, transport and agriculture, encompassed within the notion of the common market.[102] Qualified majority voting did not extend to such areas as free movement of persons, nor tax, and the UK, Greece and Denmark had insisted on a Declaration being appended to the SEA that nothing would affect the Luxembourg Accords.[103] So elements of intergovernmentalism were still maintained.

Successive ambitious or even pretentiously named initiatives – the Solemn Declaration, the Three Wise Men report – had been taken, but to no avail. Why was change possible with the Single European Act? Why, if the EEC had for so long been dominated by intergovernmentalism, did the member states agree to qualified majority voting and greater powers for the Parliament? The single market initiative was possible because its impetus was clearly economic, and even those institutional changes which it introduced, such as qualified majority voting, were clearly linked to market liberalism. It contained no supranationalist rhetoric, no prophetic visions, no hints at spillover. Thus, in some ways, it could perhaps be described as falling within the rational choice assumptions which inform intergovernmentalism. It simply made sense for the member states to work hard with the Commission to complete the single market, as Margaret Thatcher, for example, with all her Euro-scepticism, well saw. It had also been a shrewd move to connect the single market with funda-mental change in the EC decision-making process, recommended by the Doodge committee. The member states were simply probably not aware of its far-reaching consequences. Further, the SEA was achieved by means of the calling of an intergovernmental conference (IGC) under Article 236 EEC (now Article 48 TEU), a formula rarely used until then which allowed for the opening of inter-state treaty negotiations by simple majority vote.[104] Such a procedure forced reluctant states to come to the bargaining table, displaying their intransigence in public, and also forced them to conclude the affair, (even if meant staying up all night, or several nights)[105] which simple Council deliberations did not. The Council had been known to let fall many a piece of ordinary legislation into purgatory by not acting at all.

But of course, other explanations have been given for the renewed impetus toward integration in the mid 1980s. George Ross[106] points to the 'political opportunity

---

[102] Article 14 EC, formerly Article 8A.

[103] Also, a Council Decision (Amendment to Council rules of procedure of 20 July 1987 [1987] OJ L291/27) was passed in 1987 which lessened the impact of the Luxembourg Accords. This set out a mechanism for going to a majority vote, and was a very important step. As Joseph Weiler has written, 'Reaching consensus under the shadow of the vote is altogether *different from reaching it under the shadow of the veto*' ('The Transformation of Europe' in *The Constitution of Europe* 71).

[104] There had only been one intergovernmental conference, that leading to the Merger Treaty of 1965.

[105] A practice which, by the time of the Nice IGC in December 2000, some heads of state were finding exhausting and intolerable.

[106] G Ross, *Jacques Delors and European Integration* (Blackwell: Polity Press, 1995).

structure' whereby a multiplicity of changing contextual circumstances combine with transformational effect. Also, the new key political figures in the EEC, the Commission leader among them, capitalised on this to reassert the Commission's role as motor of integration. In other words, individuals and institutions played their part. True, there was a great deal of the 'Monnet method' in this, but Delors was a genuine democrat, whose origins lay in the French parliamentarian, civil libertarian, traditions of the Catholic left.[107] Even the pervasive scepticism about the Commission worked in its favour: if it was not thought to be capable of generating grand ideas, then the member states would more willingly go along with it.

Neither functionalism, nor intergovernmentalism, could adequately explain what happened in the 1980s, and political scientists and international relations theorists began to look elsewhere for another model to account for the Community's progress. They drew on the work of 'new institutionalist' political scientists in the USA, which stressed the important role played by institutions.[108] As the authors of one recent work state: 'As utilised here, this approach is based on the simple presumption that, in the process of formulating EC/EU rules and policy, institutional arrangements matter.'[109] This new institutionalism rejected a choice-based view of politics that sees policy outcome as the rational product of competing interests. Unlike neo-functionalism and neo-realism, new institutionalism is not teleological in nature. It looks to the less formal as well as the formal arenas of politics, and is also concerned with institutional values (i.e. beliefs, codes, cultures, knowledge).[110] This account seems better suited to cover the years of the Delors Commission. Personalities such as Delors played a key role, exploiting the full potential of his presidency with the assistance of his Cabinet. New institutionalism does not, however, assume some heterogeneous Community institution, rather it acknowledges that there will be a high degree of sectoral difference regarding integration.

Another institution which played a key role was, as already mentioned, the ECJ. In *Cassis de Dijon*, the ECJ had made it possible for the Commission to avoid the time-consuming and frustrating task of harmonisation by simply requiring states to recognise other states' laws as legitimate, as long as they satisfied health and safety concerns. This simply left the Commission with the task of codifying some basic measures on health and safety and so on, and even contracting out technical regulation to private agencies.[111]

---

[107] See Ross, *Jacques Delors and European Integration*, for an interesting account of Delors' origins.

[108] See, for example, the work of J March and P Olsen, *Rediscovering Institutions: the Organic Basis of Politics* (Free Press, 1989).

[109] K Armstrong and S Bulmer, *The Governance of the Single European Market* (Manchester University Press, 1998) at 7.

[110] See also N MacCormick, and O Weinberger, *An Institutional Theory of Law: New Approaches to Legal Theory* (Reidel, 1986) and MacCormick (ed) *Constructing Legal Systems: 'European Union' in Legal Theory* (Kluwer, 1997) – for theoretical work which see institutions as the basics of legal systems rather than the rules or norms traditionally preferred by legal positivism.

[111] See D Cameron, 'The 1992 Initiative: Causes and Consequences' in A Sbragia, (ed) *Euro-Politics* (Washington DC: Brookings Institute, 1992) 23; K Alter, and S Meunier-Aitsahalia, 'Judicial Politics in the European Community: European Integration and the Pathbreaking Cassis de Dijon Decision' (1996) 26 Comp. Pol. Studies 535.

But, even so, reactions to the SEA were not uniformly favourable. Judge Pescatore of the ECJ described it as a 'severe setback' for the cause of European integration.[112] The presentation of the internal market as a new goal was seen as dishonest, when what in actuality was happening was the attempt to complete original targets set out in the Treaty of Rome. Completing the internal market led to an initial loss of jobs, as the Commission's own data had demonstrated. Breaking down the barriers between national markets had opened up the prospects for 'social dumping', and multinational corporations could indulge in regime shopping. Delors and the Commission had therefore committed themselves to the opening of a 'social dialogue' at European level, intimating that completing the internal market would necessitate 'flanking programmes' – one of these being the notorious Social Charter for Workers.

The SEA also involved derogations, a feature that has occurred in EC treaty making ever since, a flexibility which becomes a necessary evil in the attempt to secure agreement between sovereign states where there is no meeting of minds. It seemed at best to be a compromise between supranationalism and intergovernmentalism.[113] However, if Ehlermann's (himself a Director-General of the Commission Legal Service at that time, and perhaps not unbiased) description of the SEA as an 'outstanding success'[114] was hyperbolic and if the Cecchini report's suggestions of the gains to be made in prosperity as a result of completing the internal market were unrealistic,[115] it was nevertheless the case that, by 1992, 95 per cent of the internal market legislation had been enacted and 77 per cent of it was in force in the member states.[116]

The road to Maastricht

The Delors Commission engaged in what has been described[117] as a 'Russian Doll Strategy': when the first doll is taken apart, another is to be found inside. In the context of European integration, this connotes distinct episodes of strategic action which carry with them the impetus for further action of a different sort. Delors believed that the regeneration of European economic activity through the single market was a matter of survival or decline of Europe. But further, unlike those who took an Anglo-Saxon, *laissez-faire* approach, he believed that markets existed with-

---

[112] P Pescatore, 'Some Critical Remarks on the SEA' (1987) 24 CMLRev 9.

[113] See G Bermann, 'The SEA: A New Constitution for the European Community?' (1989) 27 Columbia J'l Transnat Law 529; see also A Moravscik, 'Negotiating the Single European Act' (1991) 45 International Organisation 19.

[114] C-D Ehlermann, 'The 1992 Project: Stages, Structures, Results and Prospects' (1990) 11 Michigan J'l Intl Law 1097.

[115] Ward goes as far as to say that 'The Cecchini report notoriously made up all sorts of unlikely figures, which a worryingly large number of people seemed to believe': I Ward, *The Margins of European Law* at 31. Although, to be fair, by the early 1990s, when the reckoning was made, Europe had started to fall into a recession, and Germany had to pay the great cost of unification – factors which Cecchini had not bargained for.

[116] 26th Report on the Activities of the European Communities in 1992 (OOPEC EC Lux 1993) at 35.

[117] Ross *op. cit.* at 64.

in a broader 'model of society', which moralised individuals and structured preferences. According to Delors, the internal market should be a humane social order
with a commitment to basic social justice, with its roots in the Social and Christian
democracy of the mainstream of continental European politics. In such a society the
citizen was to play a greater role than a consumer and the government more than
an economic tariff squad. It was the government's duty to create a wide range of
public goods, not only because of the danger of market failure and externalities but
also in response to demands of solidarity. Much of this was hateful to some
Europeans, e.g. the Thatcherite UK. And it would certainly not be easy for Delors
to achieve. The collapse of communism introduced complexities at a time when the
EU was putting all of its efforts into deepening, and intensifying, integration.
International uncertainties were at least one of the factors to mar the unity of purpose of the member states.

Nevertheless, in December 1990, two intergovernmental conferences were
opened with a view to considering further amending the Treaty of Rome to lead to
political and monetary union,[118] which seemed to be the next step in integration,
and in creating a truly single market. A committee had already been set up under
the chairmanship of Jacques Delors, and both it, and the Cecchini Report, had
argued that the costs of variable currencies were unnecessary and excessive in
Europe. If there were to be monetary union, then it would also be the case that
were states to pursue diverse political interests, then these might result in
economic divergences in currency harmonisation. Therefore, an IGC on political
union was thought to be necessary, although added as somewhat of an after-
thought. The IGC on Political Union lacked the strong starting point of the Delors'
report on EMU, and its agenda was less clear: ranging over a prospective common
and foreign security policy, changes to enhance the treaty's democratic legitimacy,
additional competences, and a range of matters such as drugs, terrorism, illegal
immigration and organised crime.

The result of these two IGCs was not two treaties but one, the Treaty of
Maastricht, grandly named the Treaty on European Union, which proved to be very
controversial in nature, if not as radical as the popular press reported, but rather, a
mixture of forward movement and retreat.

The Treaty of Maastricht consolidated the Union, by introducing the now famous
three pillar structure, composed of the EC (a title which replaced that of 'EEC' to
take account of the broader range of Community affairs), Common Foreign and
Security Policy (CFSP) and Justice and Home Affairs (JHA), which was nonetheless
to be served by a single institutional framework. However, it was not really a very
unified construct, as there was a different institutional balance within each of these
pillars, some being more intergovernmental in nature, thus allowing a smaller role
for the Commission and ECJ. This, along with all the protocols, opt-outs and declarations, made it unwieldy in nature. It was also to be a European **Union**, and not

---

[118] See F Lawson and S Vanhoonacte, *The IGC on Political Union* (Dordrecht Martinus Nijhoff, 1992);
R Corbett, 'The IGC on Political Union' (1992) 30 JCMS 271; K Middlemas, *Orchestrating Europe*
(London: Fontana, 1995) 184–204.

a federation. At first sight, the word 'Union' might appear more provocative than 'federation', implying a fusion and oneness which a federation might lack. Nonetheless, the infamous 'f word' of an earlier draft under the Dutch presidency had appeared just too politically charged and was therefore dropped. But some of the new provisions of the TEU seemed to be no more than statements of intent. Article 1 is a good example. Article 1 states: 'This Treaty marks a new stage in the process of creating an ever closer union among the peoples of Europe, in which decisions are taken as closely as possible to the citizen.'

There were important new substantive provisions, some with a most definite 'constitutional' look to them. The most dramatic of these were the provisions on economic and monetary union – inserted into the EC treaty in Articles 98–124 – which enacted the Delors proposals on monetary union and a complex timetable for its progress. These introduced an exchange rate mechanism (which almost immediately proceeded to fall apart), a common currency, and a European Central Bank. There were numerous convergence criteria to be satisfied by the member states in the steps leading to monetary union and the UK and Denmark secured opt-outs from this last stage. Also introduced into the treaty was the principle of subsidiarity, introduced in Article 5 of the EC treaty, and Article 1 TEU, as well as being mentioned in the Preamble (and the relationship between these different provisions is questionable and a good example of the ambiguity and tensions inherent in the Maastricht Treaty overall). Subsidiarity was seen by some as a very federal measure, and by others, namely the British under John Major's government, as a way of preserving national sovereignty. It was a principle taken from Catholic doctrine:[119] a somewhat curious choice, as it had not operated against centralisation in that context, whereas presumably it was supposed to ensure that decision-making took place at its proper level within the EU. Citizenship of the Union was also introduced (Article 8 EC, now 17–22) as little more than a codification of existing measures, but, nonetheless, an attempt to get to grips with the proposals of the earlier Adonnino committee of 1984, and to make Europe closer to the citizen.[120] Article 6(2) TEU inserted into the treaty a requirement to respect fundamental rights, as they were to be found in national constitutions and in the ECHR, very directly mirroring the case law of the ECJ for some time, but in the context of a non-justiciable provision.[121] All of these provisions were quite possibly in tension with the injunction in Article 6 (1) TEU on the Union to respect the identities of the member states.

There were some institutional reforms. There was an increase in qualified majority voting; and an increase in the powers of the European Parliament through the introduction of the new codecision procedure, but, as a result of this, the legislation procedure became ever more complex. New bodies were set up: the Committee of the Regions (which had consultative powers only) and a European Ombudsman.

---

[119] See the lengthy discussion on subsidiarity in Chapter 4.
[120] See Chapter 14 on Union citizenship.
[121] See Chapter 13 on fundamental rights. Although Article 6(2) has since been made justiciable by the treaty of Amsterdam.

The two other pillars, those of the CFSP and JHA, were largely intergovernmental in nature, with the ECJ and Parliament virtually excluded from their scope. The TEU was also supplemented by a large number of declarations and protocols, one of the most striking being the Protocol on the Agreement on Social Policy, necessarily in this form due to the UK's determined (and ideological) non-participation. This enacted the Social Charter of Rights of Workers of 1989, resulting in the ability of the eleven member states to make use of Community institutions, but not within the Community framework, as the UK did not participate. This has been described as transforming Community policy from 'Cinderella to ugly sister',[122] and was, at the very least, a convoluted mechanism. In what seems to have been a move against the European Court, other protocols were inserted to deal with the effects of ECJ judgments, such as those of *Grogan* and *Barber*.[123]

The Maastricht Treaty came under criticism from all angles. It seemed to be too much of a last minute compromise, patched together at the eleventh hour, with resulting Protocols and Declarations which had to be added to deal with specific member states' reservations. It also appeared to be a creature of chaos and fragmentation: what Curtin described as employing a 'bricoleur's amateurism, in its renumbering, and non-unitary structure'.[124] In so doing, there might have been attempts to 'constitutionalise' the treaties, but for those with a tidy frame of mind, this was unsatisfactory. In aiming to innovate, consolidate and redefine, it seemed only to confuse and disappoint.

Ratifying Maastricht was a tortuous process, as the member states discovered, although they managed to create some of the problems themselves. The referenda processes proved extremely troublesome. Although 69 per cent of the Irish voted in favour of Maastricht in their national referendum, the Danish initially voted narrowly against,[125] and the French then gave only a very narrow majority in favour (although in fact the French referendum was constitutionally unnecessary and the embarrassment could have been spared). A monetary crisis followed shortly after, caused partly by tight monetary policy pursued by the Bundesbank, in the wake of unification,[126] prompting the UK to leave the European exchange mechanism altogether. The European Council met in Edinburgh in December 1992, trying to figure out how best to deal with these crises. It was necessary to get the Danes back into the fold without reopening the text of the treaty which was seen as non-negotiable. Certain Declarations therefore were appended to appease the Danes,[127] and a new Danish coalition government managed to gain a 56.8 per cent vote in favour the second time round.

---

[122] E Szyszczak, 'Social Policy: A Happy Ending or Reworking of a Fairy Tale?' in O'Keefe and Twomey (eds) *Legal Issues of the Maastricht Treaty* (Law Chancery, 1992).

[123] Case C-262/88 *Barber* [1990] ECR I-1889; Case C-159/90 *Grogan* [1991] ECR I-4685.

[124] D Curtin, 'The Constitutional Structure of the Union: A Europe of Bits and Pieces' (1993) 33 CMLRev 17 at 24.

[125] K Siune and P Svensson, 'The Danes and the Maastricht treaty: the Danish EC referendum of June 1992' (1993) 12 Electoral Studies 99.

[126] D Cobham, 'Causes and Effects of the European Monetary Crisis of 1992 (1996) 34 JCMS 585; W Sandholtz, 'Money Troubles: Europe's Rough Road to European Union' (1996) JEPP 84.

[127] D Howarth, 'The Compromise of Denmark and the Treaty on European Union: A legal and political analysis' (1994) 31 CMLRev 465.

No referendum was needed as part of the UK ratification process, as treaties there are ratified by the executive, although legislation has to be passed if they are to be incorporated into national law, and it was this process which provided opportunities for opponents of the Maastricht Treaty. Opposition from both Eurosceptic Tories and from the Labour and Liberal Democrats, who opposed the UK's failure to accede to the Social Protocol, resulted in many amendments to the Bill, which only got through Parliament after the Major government called a vote of no confidence: if Tory MPs had voted against this the government would have fallen, and so the Bill was passed.[128] An action brought against ratification of the treaty in the UK also failed.[129] Further challenges were also brought in France, Spain and Denmark.[130]

Most important of the challenges, however, was that brought in the German Constitutional Court by a former German MEP,[131] on the basis that ratification violated the German Basic Law (principally Article 38, which provides for the right to vote in elections for the German Parliament and the principle of democracy). It was alleged that the TEU infringed these provisions by transferring too many powers to the EU and thus depriving the German Parliament of essential decision-making powers. Article 23 of the Basic Law (now amended) allows transfer of sovereignty by the legislature but only in so far as this does not alter the identity of the constitutional order of the Federal Republic (set out in Article 79(3) of the Basic Law, which may not be repealed). The German Constitutional Court held that the TEU did not violate the Basic Law, but it did, however, place future constraints on the progress of European integration. In doing so the German Court worked on the basis of a traditional definition of national sovereignty, describing the member states as 'masters of the treaty' and the EU as a federation, a '*Staatenverbund*'.[132] The Court decided that democracy was thriving in the member states, but that an excess transfer by the member states would weaken this. Guarantees of democracy, it stated, were held by the national parliaments, as there was no European 'demos', or people, as yet.[133] It also suggested that the Constitutional Court would not apply EU acts if the EU were to exceed its powers. Therefore this implied that it felt that the ECJ lacked a '*Kompetenz-Kompetenz*', namely, the ability to decide on questions of jurisdictional boundaries.[134]

---

[128] See R Rawlings, 'Legal Politics: The UK and the Ratification of the Treaty on European Union' (1994) PL 254.

[129] *R v Secretary of State for Commonwealth Affairs ex parte Rees-Mogg* [1994] QB 552.

[130] For France, *Decision of the Constitutional Council, Re Treaty on European Union* (December 1992–3008) J.O. de La République Française 1992, No. 5354; for Spain, *Decision of the Constitutional Court, Re Treaty on European Union* [1994] 3 CMLR 101; for Denmark, *Carlsen v Rasmussen* [1999] 3 C.M.L.R. 24.

[131] *Brunner et al v The European Union* (1994) 1 CMLR 57.

[132] Ibid. at para. 39

[133] Ibid. at 87.

[134] For commentary on the Constitutional Court's judgment, see M Herdegen, 'Maastricht and the German Constitutional Court: Constitutional Restraints on an ever Closer Union' (1994) 31 CMLRev 2235; U Everling, 'The Maastricht judgement of the German Federal Constitutional Court and its Significance for the Development of the European Union' (1994) YBEL 1; J Weiler, 'Does Europe Need a Constitution? Demos, Telos and the Maastricht Urteil' (1995) 1 ELJ 219.

Enlargement and external affairs

As well as deepening the integration process, the EU was also widening it. The increased prosperity of the SEA had made countries aware of the benefits of EU membership. Foremost among these were the EFTA countries. The EFTA community had been constituted by a series of bilateral free trade agreements, but by 1984, there was a desire to increase cooperation leading to the creation of a 'European economic space'. This led to the European Economic Area created by the Treaty of Oporto of 1991.[135] Under this agreement the EFTA states adopted all EC legislation regarding the internal market, research and development, social policy, education, consumer protection and the environment, but were unable to participate further in the EU policy process, a somewhat unsatisfactory situation, from their point of view. Austria, Finland, Sweden and Norway therefore applied to join the EU. Although the Norwegian people voted against membership in a referendum, these other three countries became members of the EU, as from 2 January 1995.

At the same time, the collapse of the former Soviet Union had made it (theoretically) possible for those former Soviet dominated countries of Eastern Europe to contemplate EU membership, most particularly the 'Visegrad' countries: Poland, Hungary, and the Czech and Slovak Republics. The EC set up its PHARE programme of 1989 to provide financial support for Central and East European reform, to help these countries rebuild their economies. They entered into 'Europe agreements': bilateral free trade agreements with the EU. In June 1993, the EU set out its so-called 'Copenhagen' criteria[136] for membership. Then, in July 1997, the Commission presented its Agenda 2000 programme, the single framework within which the broad perspective for the development of the EU and its policies beyond the turn of the century were outlined. This included opinions on candidate countries' applications for membership and in March 1998 accession negotiations with the Visegrad countries, Cyprus, Estonia and Slovenia, began. This progress was much slower than would have been wished for, internal squabbling about institutional matters blocking the progress up to, and at, the 2000 IGC.

Other events in external affairs

On completion of the internal market, the EU had become an increasingly global trading force. The conclusion of the GATT (WTO) 'Uruguay' round extended

---

[135] T Blanchet, R Piiponen and M Westman-Clément, *The Agreement on the EEA* (Oxford: Clarendon Press, 1994); F Weiss, 'The Oporto Agreement on the EEA: A Legal Still Life' (1992) 12 YBEL; M Cremona, 'The "Dynamic and Homogenous" EEA: Byzantine Structures and Variable Geometry' (1994) 19 ELRev 508.

[136] These were set out in the Presidency Conclusions of the Copenhagen Council 1993, namely:
– stability of institutions guaranteeing democracy, the rule of law, human rights and respect for the protection of minorities
– the existence of a functioning market economy as well as the capacity to cope with competitive pressure and market forces within the Union
– the ability to take on the obligations of membership including adherence to the aims of political, economic and monetary union.

global trading to new areas, such as services. However, a ruling of the ECJ prevented the Commission from asserting the power of the EU to participate without the member states in the field of services,[137] on the basis that the EC's Common Commercial Policy did not include trade in services, where competence had been traditionally shared leading to mixed agreements.

The Common Foreign and Security Policy (CFSP) had proved disappointing and fragmented in its operation so far, most particularly in the context of the ethnic Balkan wars. It proved very difficult to secure consensus on joint actions and Greece imposed unilateral economic sanctions on the former Republic of Macedonia. One of the CFSP's key functions, as originally specified in Article 2 TEU, was to assert a European identity. It contributed little to this objective by both failing to reach a clear, unified foreign policy and by presenting institutional incoherence – different EU institutions might represent the EU in international contexts – sometimes the Commission, sometimes the Council, thus presenting a particularly inarticulate identity. The CFSP seemed to be achieving little more than the EPC of pre-Maastricht days.

The Treaty of Amsterdam

Article 48 of the TEU had already provided for another IGC to take place. In 1996 a new IGC opened in Turin and a Reflection Group was set up composed of representatives of the member states, the Commission and Parliament. The issues for consideration were to be: reform of the second and third pillars, institutional structures, the hierarchy of laws and the possibility of a multi-speed Europe. The overall aim was to make Europe more relevant to its citizens, to enable the Union to work better and to prepare it for enlargement (a task that was postponed). As usual there was wrangling over an increase in qualified majority voting and relations were not improved by the lack of cooperation from the UK government on account of the BSE crisis. In the event its result, the Treaty of Amsterdam, was a less ambitious document than the Treaty of Maastricht.

First, it amended the three pillar structure: a necessary act, because a new area of freedom, security and justice had been created, common to both the EC and what had formerly been the JHA pillar. Many of the provisions previously dealt with under JHA were transferred to the EC pillar, creating a new Title IV on the free movement of persons in asylum, immigration and visas, as well as judicial cooperation in civil matters. The UK, Ireland and Denmark secured certain opt-outs from this new Title. The Schengen acquis on the free movement of persons was integrated by Protocol into the EU treaty framework, again dealing with matters within both the first and third pillar. And, again, the UK and Ireland were not parties to this. Differences between the first and third pillar (renamed Provisions on Police and Judicial Cooperation in Criminal Matters, or PJCC) now seemed less clear, and the Parliament and ECJ were given a bigger say in the third pillar. There were fewer changes to the second pillar, that of the CFSP, from which the ECJ and

---

[137] *Opinion 1/94 (GATT/WTO)* [1994] ECR I-5267.

Parliament were still largely excluded and the Commission was still subordinate to the European Council. The CFSP still suffered from a lack of clarity, particularly regarding its institutional identity, although the concept of a joint action was given greater definition, and provision was made for the possibility of some qualified majority voting (QMV) to take place in the future. Other institutional reforms were carried out. QMV was further extended. Social policy was moved into the EC pillar and the Social Policy Protocol abolished, now that the UK, with a new Labour government, no longer wished to opt out of it. There was a new Protocol on subsidiarity and a new principle of transparency added into the treaty in Article 255 EC.

But some issues could not be agreed and had to be left: the weighting of member states' votes for the QMV process, the number of MEPs, the number of Commissioners. A Protocol on the Institutions with the Prospect of Enlargement of the EU was inserted, requiring another IGC a year before EU membership reached twenty. Additionally, treaty articles were renumbered (which hardly increased transparency) and obsolete articles deleted. Fewer new competences were added than by Maastricht, although there were important provisions on fundamental rights inserted in Article 13 and Article 7 TEU. Somewhat intriguing provisions were added on the notion of flexibility, allowing some member states to integrate at a faster rate. A new Article 11 EC referred to provisions for differentiated integration, as did Title VII TEU, although these would not be allowed to affect the rights and obligations of non-participating member states.

Beyond Amsterdam and Nice

Amsterdam was not the high profile affair which Maastricht had been. Moreover it was always acknowledged that there would have to be yet another IGC in the near future in order to prepare the EU institutions for the accession of new member states, these matters having been left over at Amsterdam. In the event, it was decided that the necessary institutional reforms would have to be introduced after a single IGC, before accession negotiations with the most advanced applicant countries had reached their conclusions. Given that the EU's institutions were created with just six states in mind, and that they were experiencing difficulties even with fifteen, let alone twenty plus, the need for reform was pressing.

It was decided at the Helsinki European Council in 1999 that the IGC would consider the following issues: the size and composition of the Commission; the weighting of votes in the Council; the possible extension of QMV in the Council; and other necessary amendments to the treaties arising as regards European institutions in connection with the above issues and in implementing the Treaty of Amsterdam.

Reaching agreement on these key issues proved difficult, although eventually was achieved in Nice in December 2000, and the Treaty of Nice was signed by all member states in February 2001 but is still not ratified at time of writing. Although there was agreement on the future streamlining of the size of the Commission, this was postponed until Community membership reached 27.[138] However, greater

---

[138] See *Protocol on the Enlargement of the European Union attached to the Treaty of Nice* (SN 533/00 ANNEX 1).

powers were granted to the Commission President to allocate portfolios and to sack individual Commissioners. The reweighting of Council votes and the issue of QMV proved more contentious. The voting system prior to Nice involved the smaller member states having a disproportionately large voice in the Council. Various approaches were under discussion and agreement very hard to reach, requiring three drafts. In the event, parity was retained among the largest four countries, whose votes were increased to 29.[139] As far as QMV was concerned, there was an arduous case by case examination of the 73 articles where unanimity still applied, with cases such as taxation and social security proving especially contentious. Finally, the IGC agreed to extend QMV in some areas, but specifically not in the fields of tax and social security, and also on trade negotiations involving cultural and audio-visual issues after French pressure to keep its 'cultural' exceptions.

Nice ended almost two days late at 5 am on 11 December 2000, with a great deal of discontent at the rushed marathon sessions. Both the European Commission and Parliament were disappointed with the results, as were some of the smaller member states. The French President Chirac stated: 'The working methods will have to be changed. It is not normal to end at five o'clock in the morning, and what is even less normal is to impose on the staff of the heads of state and government a working rhythm absolutely incompatible with peace of mind – that is to say, to impose nearly no sleep during three or four days is absurd.'[140]

Unsatisfactorily, the results of some of the most controversial discussions at Nice are actually to be found in Protocols and Declarations appended to the treaty, hardly making it a very transparent document. Yet again, member states agreed that new intergovernmental talks would start in 2004 to define the precise power of national governments and Community institutions, an issue very much left unresolved at Nice. A Declaration on the Future of the Union, annexed to the Nice treaty, sets out issues for future consideration (please see p 47).[141]

One crucial reason for success at Nice was the importance of enlargement as a very necessary next step in the EU's development, a process which the existing member states were in danger of jeopardising. There has been a great contrast between the determination of the Central and Eastern European states (what Commission President Romano Prodi has described in a speech to the European Parliament as 'enormous, profound and unprecedented efforts')[142] in their preparation for EU membership and the lacklustre response of the EU member states themselves. The original aim had been for a fast track of six countries to join by the end of 2002: it now looks unlikely that there will be new EU members before 2005, especially as the EU is currently spending much of its time

---

[139] See Chapter 2 for a breakdown of each country's votes and for the voting system.

[140] 'Nice: Reaction in Quotes' (BBC News Online 11 December 2000). Similar sentiments were voiced by Prime Minster Blair.

[141] Namely, a more precise delineation of the competences between the EU and member states in accordance with subsidiarity; the status of the Charter of Fundamental Rights 'proclaimed' at Nice; a simplification of the treaties to make them clearer and more accessible without affecting their meaning; the role of national parliaments in the European architecture.

[142] Commission 100/352 October 2000.

introducing measures to combat terrorism, rather than looking outward to increase its membership.

THE CONTINUING QUEST FOR IDENTITY

So much for the history of European integration. What conclusions may be drawn from this brief summary? At the dawn of the new millennium, the problematic nature of the European polity persists. Questions of identity, both of Europe and of European law, persist in an age when both the borders of Europe and of the European legal space are ill-defined. Surely we can no longer prevaricate about making hard decisions[143] about the type of European Union that we want? The history of European integration is one in which such integration almost seems to have taken place by stealth, within a group of states for the most part unwilling to unite further, although desirous of the greater economic benefits and prosperity that such integration may bring. As a result, the Community has often seemed to be a talking shop, but one in which the hard political questions for too long have been put off: questions of constitutionalism and democracy, of the meaning of community, or union, in a Europe of such diversity. When they have been approached, such as at the time of Maastricht, they have been provocative, loathed, and outrightly rejected, and, as a result, subject to last-minute compromises leading to an unwieldy entity that barely deserves the name of polity. As a result, the language of economics still dominates politics in the European Union, 40 years after the observations of the neo-functionalists, a feature that pleases some, but perhaps should not. The sort of 'spillover' of the type alluded to by the functionalists inevitably occurs, but it is hardly a satisfactory way of proceeding with ever closer union. Economic and monetary union – a long step down the road to integration – exists among the twelve, but the inevitable decisions that accompany it – over dealings with interest rates, inflation, and their consequences for unemployment – will, in the European context, continue to be taken by bankers and bureaucrats, with a lack of democratic accountability, which makes nobody happy.[144] The European Central Bank is independent, but not accompanied by a stable economic policy body representing an overall view of the economic state of the union. However, if the Commission were to take on such a task, as its President recently suggested,[145] this would hardly be a democratic solution, as the Commission is unrepresentative and unelected.

If democracy at European level is still weak and European citizens disaffected, or ignorant of what it means to be a European citizen, we should hardly be surprised. Too little attention has been paid to what exactly is this European Union which we

---

[143] European Commission White Paper *European Governance: A White Paper* COM(2001) 428 final.

[144] For a discussion of the democratic deficit regarding the European Central Bank see P Leino, 'The European Central Bank and Legitimacy: Is the ECB a Modification of or an Exception to the Principle of Democracy?' Harvard Jean Monnet papers 1/2001, at http://www.law.harvard.edu/programs/Jean Monnet/papers/papers96.html. See also the discussion in Chapter 2 on the ECB.

[145] Prodi in speech mentioned above: Commission 100/352 October 2000.

are creating, or what it should be, and, as a result, to date, economics has out-stripped constitutionalism, but cannot replace it. The political theorist, Joseph Schumpeter, writing in the mid twentieth century, referred to political parties as the equivalents of companies offering products, in competition for consumer prefer-ences.[146] The electorate, under this description, is transformed into the consumer, in a polity in which it has little to do with decision-making, which has become a domain for experts. Such a vision may have some relevance for the EU, in the context of a government by elites, of an electorate too ignorant of its civic role (minimal in any case). Of course, in another way, Schumpeter's vision of democracy cannot apply to an EU which lacks even the democratic hallmarks of the Schumpeterian vision, in a Community in which the law-makers are hardly competing for the popular vote.

However, a related theory, sometimes suggested as applicable in the EU context, is that of *consociationalism*.[147] This involves dominance of a polity by a cartel of elites.[148] As these elites operate outside of the normal political channels they are not excluded from decision-making in the event of electoral defeat, as is the case with majoritarianism. Such government is by consensus and is thought attractive as it may render the system functional and stable. It has been suggested that this is a type of modified intergovernmentalism appropriate for the EU in its current state of development, also in the way that it characterises the symbiotic relationship between the collectivity and member states. However, consociationalism, while it gets close to providing an adequate characterisation of the EU, is hardly attractive in normative terms, as such elite distant government can hardly be a blueprint for an EU which is seeking to render itself more accountable, more democratic, more participatory, more transparent: more attractive.

This imbalance also has another result, one discussed in subsequent chapters.[149] When economic language outstrips political language then this also affects the role of individuals in the polity. The danger is that the role of consumer, the market citizen, is substituted for that of the citizen. If European citizenship has been defined largely in terms of the economic benefits of the single market until now, we should not be surprised if we are in the process of developing a European citizen who has rights, wants, preferences, joy in the 'hedonistic delights' of the supermarket, of the grave reassurances of the law courts[150] (and most particularly the ECJ, which so contributed to the development of the single market) but little conception of his or her political rights and duties in the European context (hardly well developed in any case).

---

[146] J Schumpeter, *Capitalism, Socialism, and Democracy* (Allen and Unwin, 1942); see also A Downs, *An Economic Theory of Democracy* (Harper Row, 1957); Bachrach, *The Theory of Democratic Elitism: A Critique* (Little Brown, 1967).

[147] For writings on consociationalism see A Lijphart, 'Consociationalism and Federalism: Conceptual and Empirical Links' (1979) 22/3 Can J'l Pol Sc 499.

[148] R Dahrendorf, *Society and Democracy in Germany* (Garden City: New Jersey Doubleday, 1967) at 276.

[149] See the discussion in Chapters 13 and 14.

[150] See Siedentop, *Democracy in Europe* chapter 2, also M Glendon, *Rights Talk* (Macmillan Free Press, 1991) who criticises the consumerist, atomistic nature of rights and citizenship.

However, it is not that the EU totally lacks theorists, thinkers and policy developers willing to explore a vision of the evolving European polity. Such work has been done, both in the legal and political domain.[151] Rather, its institutions seem at present to lack any pragmatic aptitude for this – an ability to work hard in the practical sphere to put such visions into action – although the Commission is maybe trying to do so with its *White Paper on Governance*. As one commentator recently complained: 'Where are our Madisons?'[152] There seems to be little confidence in law, or politics, in the European regime, in a body of rules that can embody the popular will, and be changed if it does not. There has been little faith in the concept of a European polity as a matter of civic identity and pride, little confidence that such a polity might provide even a sort of constitutional religion, a focus for loyalty and shared values amid the diversity and ethnic and national backgrounds which still characterise Europe.

Integrationists in the twentieth century hoped that federalism might provide both a uniting factor in Europe, and an attractive form of government. So far, it has provided neither, the 'f word' causing especial tension and bickering in the run-up to the Maastricht Treaty.

However, the early European federalists, such as Spinelli, were acute in appreciating what the benefits of a federalist structure for Europe might be. The requirement of different spheres of public authority, what Madison described as a 'compound republic,' can build a political system sensitive to a wide diversity of cultural, social, geographical differences, as well as promoting democracy by the separation of powers, but also by a system of 'checks and balances'.[153] The subtlety and passion of the framers of the American Constitution, and the fervour of the federalist papers, are rarely to be found in the cooler, more measured language of the reflection group, or the national representatives at the IGC, standing for their national interests. This necessarily impoverishes the language of integration.

On the one hand, Europeans should rightly be suspicious of the dangers of a premature federalism, of unifying structures which might endanger the rich pluralities of Europe, stultifying diversity and stunting difference. One sometimes sees a tendency toward the unificatory and the homogenous in EU law, with all that the unifying normative aspect brings with it. Thus, the EU is presented as a transcendent legal order, with its claims of unity and progress, and its ability to take priority over national law. In this we see EU law incorporating some of the discourse of modernity, most particularly the ECJ with its teleological evolutionary methodology, and its 'heroic' jurisprudence.

---

[151] The works of Juergen Habermas and Joseph Weiler are among the notable exceptions. The Commission's Forward Studies, working hard on aspects of Governance for the white paper, is another (somewhat anonymous) example.

[152] Siedentop, op. cit. chapter 2. James Madison was one of the key figures in the shaping of the American Constitution in the late eighteenth century. But this comment is not entirely fair. Even if Europe lacks its Madisons today there have been candidates in the past. Jean Monnet is surely one: see Duchêne, op. cit. for a penetrating discussion of Monnet's role in European integration. Ross, in *Jacques Delors and European Integration*, refers to Delors' 'deep spiritual motivations' and 'grand mission' at 55 and 70.

[153] The equivalent of which in the EU might be the still underdeveloped concept of institutional balance: this is discussed in Chapter 2.

But recent challenges have been made, or simply allowed to occur, to the unifying tendency in European law.[154] The TEU introduced the feature of opt-outs,[155] protocols and differentiated integration. Amsterdam continued this, and the concepts of closer cooperation and increased flexibility look set to stay. The Union might be built on a three pillar structure, but the architectural dynamics of that structure, with its interlocking relationships, sometime *passerelles*, defy both the 'consistency' alluded to in Article 3 TEU of its institutional framework, and also the unity and harmony of European law. There has certainly been no consensus of opinion among scholars as to the legal status of the European Union.[156]

There is the further vexed question of the relationship of the EU with non-EU bodies and laws, which may, nonetheless, be incorporated into the EU *acquis*, such as the ECHR, or Schengen (until Amsterdam outside of the treaty) or the Brussels Convention on Jurisdiction and Judgements (now the Brussels regulation). In this way, it has been suggested that we have to re-write or remap the legal map of Europe,[157] to incorporate all of these diverse legal orders or 'spaces' with a new theory, political science and language. A legal map of Europe will not be the same as a political map of Europe at the millennium. And the legal orders of Europe within this European legal space interlock and interact in complex and interesting ways. This raises a need for new approaches, particularly theoretical approaches which depart from the traditional one based on the sovereignty and unity of national law which has persisted since the seventeenth century, when the Peace of Westphalia gave rise to the 'Westphalian' notion of sovereignty.[158]

To illustrate these transformations (or mutations, even)[159] we may look at the way in which legal norms have been exported, principally those of the EC, to other orders such as the EEA and CEEC, in the way that the Roman law and the common law systems were exported to other territories in the past. But the exportation has not always been of a straightforward kind, so, for example, EFTA states may participate in 'decision shaping' but not decision making in the EC (Articles 97–104 EEA Agreement). Under the Europe agreements approximation of those countries'

---

[154] See e.g. C-D Ehlermann, 'How Flexible is Community Law? An Unusual Approach to the Concept of "Two Speeds"' (1984) 82 Michigan LR 1274; Tuytschaever, *Differentiation in European Law* (Hart, 1999); and N Walker, 'Sovereignty and Differentiated Integration of the European Union' in Z Bankowski and A Scott (eds), *The European Union and Its Legal Order* (Oxford: Blackwell, 2000).

[155] Although such opt-outs actually pre-date Maastricht Article 95 (4), introduced by the SEA, gave the member states a chance to opt out of harmonisation on certain grounds.

[156] Among those who consider that the EU has no legal personality are H Schermers., and N Blokker, *International Institutional Law* (3rd edn) (Martinus Nijhoff, 1995), while others consider that it is a legal entity – e.g. RA Wessel, 'The International Legal Status of the European Union' (1997) 2 European Union Foreign Affairs Review 109 and B de Witte, 'The Pillar Structure and the Nature of the European Union – Greek Temple or French Gothic? in T Heukels' and N Blokker, *The European Union after Amsterdam: a Legal Analysis* (Kluwer, 1998). See also D Curtin and I Dekker, 'The EU as a "Layered" International Organisation' in Craig and de Burca (eds) *The Evolution of EU Law* (OUP, 1999).

[157] C Harding, 'The Identity of European Law; Mapping out the European Legal Space' (2000) 6 ELJ 128.

[158] But as Harding notes, reality was less straightforward – see S.D. Goldstein and Keophane (eds), *Ideas and Foreign Policy: Belief, Institutions and Political Change* (Cornell University Press, 1993).

[159] Harding op. cit. at 136.

laws to EC law is to take place within certain areas although, as Harding writes, 'what might generally be referred to as a regime of norm exportation is both varied and problematic once attention moves beyond the point of basic principle'.[160] Whereas the EEA is conceived of as a permanent partnership of separate actors, the Europe agreements are seen as a temporary and transitional arrangement, a step towards integration. And a new vocabulary is built in the meantime: 'decision shaping', 'shadow enforcement' and adjudication bodies, such as the EFTA court, which engage in parallel rule development and so on. Another example might be what has been termed 'cross-referring conditionality', for instance the protection of human rights under both the ECJ and ECHR court in Strasbourg.

Such overlapping systems cannot easily be accommodated within existing frameworks, such as the federalism, functionalism, neo-functionalism, supranationalism, intergovernmentalism, consociationalism, which have already been discussed within this chapter. Such theories have been applied in the context of a bilateral relationship between two fixed units: member states,[161] and international organisations such as the EU. But in this context of fragmentation, such a two-dimensional analysis no longer seems sustainable. Instead, Europe has become a 'multi-dimensional configuration of authority'.[162] Hedley Bull has written of 'a new medievalism, an ordering of overlapping jurisdictions, segmented authority and multiple loyalties'.[163]

This is scarcely a new or radical perception,[164] but has recently become more of a preoccupation. New approaches to this complex European legal space are being developed, whether in the context of MacCormick's 'overlapping legal orders', or the belief that the European Union is an essentially contested project,[165] in an attempt to come to grips with this complexity of overlapping sometimes mutually disputed legal orders within Europe. One particular problematic is that of disputed boundaries between these orders; a poignant expression in the context of Europe's history, where disputed border territory has so often led to hostility, enmity and war. A later chapter discusses the jurisdictional battles which have been waged between national legal orders and the ECJ over the issues of the supremacy of EC law.[166] These have not proved fatal to the Community legal order, and have been the exception, rather than the rule, in integration, even if one commentator has described the potential battle between the ECJ and the German Constitutional Court as giving rise to assumptions of MAD (mutually assured destruction).[167] But so often, in the context of territorial battles between national and Community law (i.e. who is to have

---

160 Harding op. cit. 137–8.
161 Although admittedly, states may be less than homogenous, themselves subject to a multi-dimensionality.
162 Walker, 'Sovereignty and Differentiated Integration of the European Union' in Z Bankowski and A Scott (eds) *The European Union and Its Legal Order* (Oxford: Blackwell, 2000) at 32.
163 Hedley Bull, *The Anarchical Society: A Study of Order in World Politics* (Macmillan, 1997) at 254. Although this was not Hedley Bull's own preferred manner of organising international relations.
164 In fact the first President of the Euratom Commission, Armand, would often refer to 'Europe à la Carte' (cited in Duchêne op. cit. at 397).
165 Z Bankowski and E Christodoulidis, 'The European Union as an essentially Contested Project' in Bankowski and Scott (eds) *The European Union and Its Legal Order* (Oxford: Blackwell, 2000).
166 See Chapter 7.
167 J Weiler, *The Reformulation of European Constitutionalism* (1997) 35 JCMS 97.

the *Kompetenz-Kompetenz* to determine the legality of a Community act?) both parties are operating within outdated legal paradigms, whereby national constitutional law, or EC law, is placed at the apex of some legal hierarchy, some Kelsenian type machine. Perhaps, as has been suggested,[168] constitutional law has lost its traditional mooring at the peak of the sovereign state and in fact there is no longer a hierarchy, but rather a heterarchy of laws with constitutional law at its periphery, charged with the important task of regulating the interconnected worlds of law and politics. In this context, we look to other pluralistic theories to enrich our understanding: that of the mixed commonwealth[169] or systems theory analysis.[170]

How might all these different systems or legal spaces interact? One might take an optimistic view, seeing such a multiplicity as a positive and stimulating force, breaking the stranglehold which the notion of a unitary legal system has had for centuries. In this way, Arnaud invites us to rejoice, rather than to despair.[171]

However, one might take the view that these different systems are autopoetic in nature, i.e. self-referential, operating on the basis of their own system of communications, unable to penetrate each other directly, even if they do seem to overlap, and thus actually closed worlds unto themselves, a sort of purist view which has something in common with Kelsenian positivism. On such an analysis, it is difficult to see how such systems could interact with each other or influence, or export, or replicate norms, except at the most superficial of levels. Sousa Santos has described the plurality of legal orders as consisting of 'partial legal fields constituted by relatively unrelated and highly discrepant logics of regulation'.[172]

However, this seemingly unbridgeable gulf between different systems of law may be overcome, as autopoesis looks to the linkage and structural coupling of systems, even if this is done in a blind way. Under the (admittedly rather obscure) doctrine of 'structural coupling', systems use concepts which are specific to that system, where there is no shared understanding and yet pressure to interrelate. Such a vision of interlocking legal orders might be seen as either invigorating, or perhaps depressing, 'as a never-ending dance of solipsistic systems entranced in their own world'.[173] Thus, there are structural couplings, but they can result in a series of misreadings. Such a theory explains some of the problems encountered by Community law, e.g.

---

[168] See e.g. N Walker, 'Sovereignty and Differentiated Integration of the European Union'; G Teubner, *Law as an Autopoetic System* (Blackwell, 1993).

[169] See the work of Neil MacCormick for this sort of analysis in N MacCormick, *Beyond the Sovereign State* 56 MLR 1993 1; see also MacCormick N., *Questioning Sovereignty* (Oxford: Oxford University Press, 1999).

[170] See e.g. G Teubner, 'Breaking Frames: The Global Interplay of Legal and Social Systems' (1997) 45 AJICL 150; 'Global Bukowina: Legal Pluralism in the World Society' in G Teubner (ed) *Global Law without a State* (Gower, 1996).

[171] Arnaud, *Pour une Pénsée Juridique Européenne* (Paris: PUF, 1991).

[172] B de Sousa Santos, *Toward a new common sense – law, science and politics in the paradigmatic tradition* (Routledge, 1995) at 281.

[173] Z Bankowski, 'How Does it Feel to be on Your Own? The Person in Sight of Autopoesis' (1994) Ratio Juris.

the difficulties in implementing it and in transmuting concepts employed by a different legal system: witness the difficulties experienced by the English courts with the concept of proportionality during the Sunday trading saga,[174] or the difficulties the English legal system had in providing remedies for state liability in damages as required under the ECJ's *Francovich* holding.[175]

However, there are also border posts and bridging mechanisms, interactions which allow new impulses to be felt in law.[176] But these are just as likely to destabilise the national system. Systems theories propose that, as a matter of analysis, domestic law, naturally self-referential in nature, will not be able adequately to accommodate change or transformation.[177] However, other writers have suggested that, at a **normative** level, the changes wrought by EU law are not necessarily desirable. Such suggestions are prompted not by some sort of chauvinistic attachment to national sovereignty, but rather by the realisation that cultural and legal diversity is valuable,[178] an assertion which takes us back to Derrida's point, cited at the beginning of this introduction, that 'in trying to redefine itself, Europe is forgetting and ignoring its cultural history'.[179] Legrand's strong assertion that European legal systems are not converging is also based on a descriptive claim that harmonisation is not possible due to the fundamental differences between European legal cultures. For Legrand, legal systems, which may seem to be superficially similar, 'are but the surface manifestation of legal cultures . . .'[180] Legal cultures, being based on distinct and very different mentalities, are often incapable of absorbing external material. The attempt to do so, may, if Legrand is right, turn out to be something like a bad literary translation.

If we agree with Legrand, or the systems theorists, the prospects for a greater integration of European law seem distant and depressing. Indeed, it conjures up a nightmarish world of incoherence and separatism. But are legal systems as atomistic as these writers suggest? Convergence may be problematic, but surely it does take place. For some commentators, the clash, or incompatibility of legal cultures, is not a problem at all. The prospect of a common European civil code has excited some

---

[174] For a systems theory analysis of EC law see I Maher, 'Community Law in the National Legal Order: A Systems Theory Analysis' 36 JCMS (1998) 241.

[175] See Joined Cases 6, 9/90 *Francovich and Bonifaci v Italy* [1991] ECR I-5357. A. Barav, 'State Liability in Damages for Breach of Community Law in the National Courts', in T. Heukels and A. McDonnell (eds) *The Action for Damages in a Community Law Perspective* (Kluwer, 1997).

[176] See G Teubner, *Law as an Autopoetic System* (Blackwell, 1993) who sees the trial as a mechanism by which more general norms are fed into the legal system.

[177] See, for example, Teubner, who describes 'legal transplants' as 'legal irritants' (G Teubner, 'Legal Irritants: Good Faith in British Law or How Unifying Law Ends Up in New Divergences' (1998) 61 MLR 11 at 12). See also Joerges, who makes a similar point about the difficulty of absorbing 'foreign transplants': C. Joerges, 'The Europeanisation of Private Law as a Rationalization Process and as a Contest of Disciplines – an Analysis of the Directive on Unfair Terms in Consumer Contracts' (1995) 3 European Review of Private Law 175, 183.

[178] See C Harlow, 'Voices of Difference in a Polyphonic Community: The Case for Legal Diversity Within the European Union' Harvard Jean Monnet paper 3/2000, at http://www.law.harvard.edu/programs/Jean Monnet/papers/papers00.html.

[179] Derrida, *The Other Heading* (Bloomington Indiana).

[180] P Legrand, 'European Legal Systems Are Not Converging' (1996) 45 ICLQ 52, 56.

scholars such as Kötz and van Gerven,[181] for whom the prospect of the convergence of European laws is not only possible but desirable. Where Legrand is too pessimistic, these writers may be over optimistic or even simplistic. As Harlow writes: 'Integrationism was once seen as something of a loyalty test; today pluralism is squarely on the political agenda.'[182] But surely 50 years of experience has borne out the 'Europeanisation' of national law, and the normalising of its vocabulary into national legal culture. Surely the reality of the EU in a new century is that of a highly complex phenomenon, composed of interlocking, overlapping, systems, some of which relate successfully, and others which have not (yet). Perhaps it is a sign of the coming of age of the European Union, of a growing confidence in the existence of EU law as an authentic legal system, that the issue of the diversity of European legal culture is, in this new millennium, a matter of concern.

---

[181] H Kötz, 'Towards a European Civil Code', in P Cane and J Stapleton (eds), *The Law of Obligations, Essays in Celebration of John Fleming* (Oxford: Clarendon, 1998) at 243–4. W van Gerven, 'Bridging the Gap Between Community and National Laws: Towards a Principle of Homogeneity in the Field of Legal Remedies?' (1995) 32 CMLRev 679 and 'Bridging the Unbridgeable: Community and National Tort laws after Francovich and Brasserie' (1996) 45 ICLQ 507; R Caranta, 'Judicial Protection Against Member States: A New Jus Commune Takes Shape' (1995) 32 CML Rev 703. See also Chapter 9 for a more detailed discussion of these issues.

[182] Harlow op. cit. at 32.

2

INSTITUTIONAL STRUCTURES: LEGISLATIVE AND EXECUTIVE

In recent times, there has been a focus on rethinking the role of institutions, and governance generally, in the EU. In a speech to the European Parliament,[1] Romano Prodi, the Commission President, referred to 'the paradox of European integration', whereby European integration has achieved a half century of peace and prosperity, but has left its citizens disenchanted and anxious. Europe, he stated, needs a sense of meaning and purpose, which at present it lacks. If the EU is lacking in this way, then part of the responsibility must lie with its institutions. Even if one sets aside such debacles as the Commission resignation of March 1999, EU institutions are uninspirational, and sometimes worse: seemingly undemocratic, untransparent and elitist in their motivations. If the peoples of Europe have little sense of what it means to be a 'European citizen', this is surely partly on account of the lack of suitable political structures provided by the treaties or the institutions set up thereunder. In sum, the EU lacks an affective dimension.

However, this charge might appear somewhat unfair. It might be protested that the institutions, as set up under the original Treaty of Rome, were not intended to be democratic. They were set up to manage an economic community, and in order to do this they needed to be efficient, bureaucratic, technocratic. This was the essence of the Monnet method in the 1950s. But such a defence is also inadequate. The EU long ago progressed beyond a mere free trade community – the Treaty of Nice is the fourth European Treaty in seventeen years, with another scheduled for 2004[2] – but institutional developments have failed to keep pace with this. Furthermore, even simple efficiency is often sadly lacking in the Community institutional architecture: witness the mismanagement of the budget by the Commission, or the complex Byzantine legislative procedures which can take so long to pass through the Community structures. It seems quite plain that, in this new century, the institutional (and constitutional) structure of the EU is inadequate and in need of urgent rethinking.

---

[1] Romano Prodi, 'Shaping the New Europe 2000–2005': speech to the European Parliament, 15 February 2000, DN. Speech/00/41.
[2] As stated in the 'Declaration on the Future of the Union' in the Final Act of the Conference, OJ C 80/1 10 March 2001.

Yet the problem of the EU's institutional framework is not being ignored. One may point to at least five initiatives which are capable of having an impact, perhaps even a serious impact, on the way Europe is governed in the twenty-first century. These are: the institutional reforms mandated by the Treaty of Nice, in order to prepare the EU for the effects of enlargement; the current work on reforming the Commission; the project of the Commission's 2001 White Paper on Governance; the debate on the future of the EU, opened on 7 March 2001 by the Council Presidency[3] and the report of the European Convention. Clearly then, the EU does not lack an impetus for rethinking its governance. But how these initiatives might work together, with whatever synergy or lack of it, is as yet unclear.

  The Treaty of Nice picked up issues left over[4] by the Amsterdam Treaty which were held necessary to adapt the EU for larger membership.[5] These same issues are also perennial issues of EU treaty reform. These were, in essence: the issue of the size of the European Commission; the weighting of votes in the Council of Ministers; and the issue of more qualified majority voting. These are not issues which sound exciting: one recent commentator suggested that, 'when seen out of context they look like procedural problems requiring a compromise based on almost mathematical formulae'.[6] Like Amsterdam, Nice was fairly modest in scope, and these reforms do not appear to be at the essence of constitutional creation, not indicative of what Bruce Ackerman has termed a 'constitutional moment'.[7] They are nonetheless important for the efficient functioning of the Union, and its institutional balance, the first and the third, in particular, by taking the Union further away from member state domination of the EU agenda. In contrast to these institutional items on the Nice agenda, one might also mention the EU Charter of Fundamental Rights, adopted at Nice, although not legally binding, a more emotive and perhaps immensely symbolic document, but at this stage at least, of less practical significance for the business of Community decision-making than the size and composition of its organisations.

---

[3] As a result of a decision take by the European Council in Nice 2000, see Article 3 Declaration on the Future of the Union attached to Treaty of Nice.

[4] Relegated by the Amsterdam treaty to the Protocol on the Institutions with the prospect of enlargement of the European Union.

[5] The need to adapt the institutions for enlargement was the theme of two important pre-IGC documents – first, another 'three wise persons' report, *The Institutional Implications of Enlargement* – a report to the European Commission, October 1999, in this case the wise three being Jean-Luc Dehaene, former Belgian Prime minister, Richard von Weizsacker, former German President, and Lord Simon of Highbury, former chairman of BP; and a second report – *Adapting the Institutions to make a success of Enlargement* – the Presidency report for the European Council, which set a narrow agenda which was basically followed by the 2000 IGC. Also worth mentioning in this context is the document on the reorganisation of the treaties commissioned from the EUI in Florence and presented to Prodi in May 2000. This was an ambitious project entitled *A Basic Treaty for the EU: A study of the reorganisation of the Treaties*. However, the Commission concluded that it was not realistic for the IGC 2000 to carry out this exercise, and so the grander constitutional questions were left for a future date.

[6] X Yataganas, 'The Treaty of Nice: The Sharing of Power and the Institutional Balance in the European Union – A Continental Perspective', Harvard Jean Monnet Working Paper 01/01 at 7, available at: http://www.jeanmonnetprogram.org/papers/papers01.html.

[7] B Ackerman, *The Future of Liberal Revolution* (Yale University Press, 1992).

L The second significant institutional initiative of recent years is the reform of the Commission, led by Commissioner Neil Kinnock, with the aim of ensuring greater efficiency, transparency, accountability and responsibility within the Commission. This received less publicity than the wranglings of Nice, but grapples with crucial issues: how to ensure both efficiency and legitimacy within the Commission, now perceived as a somewhat discredited organisation after its mass resignation in March 1999.[8]

﬏ The third and fourth such initiatives are the most indeterminate. In the first place, the Commission has set itself the task of investigating the hugely broad issue of governance, and new forms of governance, in the EU, producing an ambitious White Paper in 2001. This project is quite plainly focused on political integration, traditionally the poor sister of economic integration in the EU, but also a concept to make the Eurosceptic's blood curdle. However, so far this project has not attracted much public or media attention, although it is at least conceivable that these might take on the sort of impetus of the 1985 White Paper on the internal market.[9]

﬏ Furthermore, in addition to the Commission's project, the European Council has taken the decision to open a debate about the future of the European Union: this stretches beyond institutional matters to include issues of widening and deepening and reform of policy and it is hoped, rather optimistically, to stimulate debate in all sections of society.[10]

The fifth such initiative mentioned above is that of the European Convention, very much related to the Future of Europe debate and the Commision's White Paper on Governance. Indeed, one wonders quite how they will all fit together. To prepare for the IGC of 2004, the Laeken European Council, meeting in December 2001, established a Convention to debate the future of the Union with a brief to consider the following matters: accountability and legitimacy of the Union; the division of competences; rationalising the Union's legislative instruments; enhancing democracy, transparency and efficiency; simplifying and reorganising the treaties; and possibly the adoption of a formal constitutional document for the EU. The Convention is to draw up a final document by 2003 which can be used as a basis for discussion at the 2004 IGC. The Convention, headed by former French president Valéry Giscard d'Estaing (a somewhat backward-looking choice, providing the Convention with a leader whose style reflects the elitism, *dirigisme* and *technocratie* of the EU's earlier days, rather than being an inspirational role for the new millennium) has 113 representatives from current member states and candidate countries as well as the European Parliament and Commission. The problem is that the Convention has an extremely broad agenda and it will have its work cut out if it is to provide a document inspiring to European citizens.

In addition to these practical steps, another concern, theoretical in nature, merits consideration. This has been the turn away from realism or intergovernmentalism

---

[8] This is discussed later in the chapter.

[9] N Lebessis and J Patterson, 'Developing New Modes of Governance 2000' working paper (Commission Forward Studies Unit, 2000).

[10] A declaration on the appropriate initiatives was taken at the European Council meeting in December 2001. For more information see the website at http://europa.eu.int/futurum.

in comparative political science, towards instead a 'new institutionalism' as a model for analysing integration in Europe.[11] This institutionalism suggests that institutions are not just the epiphenoma of self-interested individual or nation state behaviour, but rather that '*institutional* analysis is the central element of the EU conceptual toolkit'.[12] In this way institutions are seen as playing a key role in the shaping of political life, but it is not just the legal remit and formal organisational chart of institutions which is under scrutiny, but also the complex structures and processes by which they work, and they are at their most complex in the context of the EU. Just as the historian, Fernand Braudel, called for a shift in focus from kings, generals and dramatic events to the 'longue durée' – events that operated over longer time spans, and the structures that conditioned those events –[13] so this new institutionalism has stressed the power of background structures – the institutions of the EU – to shape interests and values. A new institutionalism has also pervaded the terrain of legal theory, in the institutional theory of law proposed by Neil McCormick and Uta Weinberger, in which institutions supplant rules or norms as the fundamental and foundational building blocks of a legal system.[14] Thus, at all levels, it would seem that the time is ripe for an institutional review, or accounting, of the EU.

INSTITUTIONAL BALANCE IN THE EU

Even the most superficial such review reveals that the EU's structures are not transparent, nor really amenable to analysis by the time-honoured concepts of political theory, as they have been applied to the nation state. Traditional political theory looks to the institutional organisation of the state in terms of the separation of powers, which, stated very briefly, holds that if government is to be for common good, those who formulate the laws should be distinct from those who are entrusted with their interpretation, application and enforcement. This theory can be traced back to classical times in Aristotle's work, as well as to Locke's *Two Treatises on Government*[15] but it finds its *locus classicus* in Montesquieu's discussion in *The Spirit of the Laws*.[16] Taken by itself, the traditional theory of separation of powers suffers from the problem that it is both conceptually, and practically, very difficult to separate the functions of government – and government is not strictly separated in this way in most modern legal systems – certainly not in the UK or the US. In the

---

[11] See for example, J March and J Olsen, *Rediscovering Institutions, the Organisational Basis of Politics* (Free Press, 1989); S Bulmer, 'The Governance of the European Union: A New Institutionalist Approach' (1993) 13 J'l of Public Policy 351; K Armstrong, 'New Institutionalism in EU Legal Studies' in P Craig and C Harlow (eds), *Lawmaking in the European Union* (Kluwer, 1998).

[12] S Bulmer, ' The Governance of the European Union: A New Institutionalist Approach' (1993) 13 Jnl of Public Policy 351 at 378.

[13] F Braudel, *On History* (University of Chicago Press, 1980); see also R Smith, 'Political Jurisprudence and the New Institutionalism' (1988) Political Science Review.

[14] e.g. N MacCormick and O Weinberger, *An Institutional Theory of Law: New Approaches to Legal Positivism* (Reidel, 1986).

[15] Locke, *Two Treatises on Government* (London: Everyman, 1994) Book II 143–4.

[16] Montesquieu, *L'Esprit des Lois* (Oxford: Voltaire Foundation, 1998) Book XI chapter VI. In fact, Montesquieu synthesised three doctrines from earlier thinking – those of mixed government, the balance of power, and checks and balances – all of which were seen as essential to good government.

unwritten British Constitution, the separation of powers refers mainly to the independence of the judiciary, as executive and legislative power is closely related.[17] And in the context of the US, already in the eighteenth century, the American federalists were trying to adapt separation of powers theory. So, for example, in the debates on the ratification of the American constitution, in which the theory of separation of powers was pivotal, we find James Madison and Alexander Hamilton reworking Montesquieu to stress the part played by the theory of checks and balances, whereby the three branches of government place controls on each other. Moderated in this form for a democratic society, the separation of powers takes on an almost mechanical form, suitable for the age of Enlightenment but perhaps too clockwork-like for a more flexible, unpredictable age.[18]

Such a doctrine is not easily translatable into the EU context, which, rather than smooth clockwork, has 'instead resembled Alice in Wonderland trying to play croquet with flamingos'.[19] There is no separation of powers as such in EU institutions. Indeed, the ECJ expressly rejected the doctrine in *France, Italy and UK v Commission*.[20] Although the European courts in Luxembourg are reasonably self-contained, the EU's legislature and the executive in the form of the Parliament, Council and Commission, operate in a *sui generis* way. The Parliament, although it now plays a sizeable role in the EU legislation process, has no free-standing right to initiate legislation, unlike traditional legislatures. The Council of Ministers is still perceived as the EU's main legislating body, but, being composed of national government ministers, combines both legislature and executive. The Commission is traditionally spoken of as the EU's executive, but although unelected, has the sole right of legislative initiative and issues a huge amount of (delegated) legislation.

Nonetheless, it has become common to speak of an 'institutional balance' within Community institutions, and the way in which this is evoked draws on a system of checks and balances not dissimilar to these we find in more traditional governmental systems. The EU institutions have come to operate a system of checks on each other, sometimes referred to in the context of an 'institutional balance'. The Commission must appear in the Parliament and answer its questions, as well as providing it with an annual report. The Council and Parliament check the Commission's budget accounts. Safeguards operate within various legislative procedures and the ECJ and Ombudsman are able to control institutional malpractice in various ways. Thus, it might be argued, various checks and balances operate within a series of institutions, whose functions and powers are divided along distinct (albeit *sui generis*) lines. Indeed, the notion of an institutional balance does not originate with the EC, but has a long historical pedigree and was a

---

[17] Finer et al., *Comparing Constitutions* (Oxford: Clarendon Press, 1995) at 21.

[18] See R Bellamy, 'The Political Form of the Constitution: The Separation of Powers, Rights and Representative Democracy' in R Bellamy and D Castiglione, *Constitutionalism in Transformation: European and Theoretical Perspectives* (Blackwell, 1996).

[19] K Middlemas, *Orchestrating Europe* (London: Fontana, 1995) at 214.

[20] Cases 188–190/80 *France, Italy and UK v Commission* [1982] ECR 2545, in which the UK argued that Commission Directive 80/723 was void as it argued that all law-making power was vested in the Council, whilst the Commission only had powers of implementation and surveillance. The ECJ held that there was no basis for that argument in the treaty provisions governing the institutions (at 2573).

fundamental element of the republican concept of democracy, as it helped prevent tyranny and sectional self-interests, and thus played an important part in republican discourse of the fifteenth and sixteenth centuries.[21]

However, reference to an 'institutional balance' implies something rather like a formal constitution, in which counterpoised structural features can be presented in a balanced and systematic way. The EU often seeks to present itself as a coherent and unitary polity, unified across its three pillars, and founded on the rule of law, democracy and human rights.[22] This coherent self-image is supported by the European Court of Justice, and its 'constitutional' case law, which established the doctrines of supremacy and direct effect of EC law, as well as the EU's respect for fundamental rights despite their original express absence from the treaties.[23] However, such a self-image is undermined by a closer, more persistent look at the EU's institutional structures. Indeed, trying to provide a single, effective, theory of EU institutions is well nigh impossible. For rather than unity it might seem that the EU is a fragmented, polycentric, multi-level creature – a 'post-modern' structure, as much made up of informal networks as of formal institutions. What is needed is to take account of these other features of the institutional structure of the EU which render its consideration in the formalistic terms of political theory inadequate. What is required is an understanding of how the EU institutions operate in practice, of the 'real' or substantive constitution.[24]

AN EPISTEMIC COMMUNITY?

We can be more specific about the features of this 'real' constitution. For example, the pillar structure of the EU, the mixture of the two intergovernmental pillars – the Common Foreign and Security Policy (CFSP) and Provisions on Police and Judicial Cooperation in Criminal Matters (PJCC) – and the communitarian EC, undermines the TEU's own claim to a 'consistency' of activities and the mention of a 'single institutional framework' in Article 3 TEU. In fact, the institutions play varying, and different, roles across the pillars. The Commission, Parliament and Courts are virtually excluded from the second and third pillars, where it is the Council of Ministers, and intergovernmental European Council, which dominate, leading to a lack of openness and parliamentary oversight. There is also the variable geometry, closer cooperation and subsidiarity of EU decision-making, whereby not all EU member states take part in every EU action,[25] which renders it uncertain, deviations from an already less than coherent 'constitutional' structure.

---

[21] For a further discussion of this, see P Craig, 'Democracy and Rule-making within the European Community' (1997) 3 ELJ 105; JGA Pocock, *The Machiavellian Movement: Florentine Political Thought and the Atlantic Republican Tradition* (Princeton University Press, 1975).
[22] Article 6 TEU.
[23] See Chapters 7, 8 and 13.
[24] G de Búrca, 'The Institutional Development of the EU: A Constitutional Analysis' in Craig and de Burca (eds) *The Evolution of EU Law* (Oxford: OUP, 1999).
[25] This is further discussed at the end of Chapter 4.

Another key element of this 'real' constitution is the fragmented and sectional nature of much EU decision-making, as well as the substantial part played by committees and agencies at every level of the decision-making process, undermining the formal institutions. 'Working groups' – unelected national technical experts – advise the Commission on policy, influencing the nature of draft legislation it proposes. More working groups play an important part within the Council, scrutinising Commission measures before the proposal reaches the formal Council meeting. The same is true of COREPER – the permanent representatives attached to the Council who are civil servants, who also scrutinise and agree on legislation before it reaches the Council proper – and so 80 per cent of measures have been agreed at these two levels before they reach the ministerial meetings of the Council: i.e. they are agreed by unelected technocrats or bureaucrats. Much legislation is delegated to the Commission, but it does not have a free hand to act here, as its measures are scrutinised by committees of member states' appointees, more unelected worthies who can sometimes even veto the proposals. Thus at all levels the procedure is liable to be untransparent and dominated by technocrats. But, in addition, this means that the way in which the institutions function does not correspond to a formal reading of the EC treaties, in which there is no mention of committees, nor of working groups, nor of their role in the decision-making process. Additionally, there has been a growth in the creation of autonomous agencies, such as the Office for Internal Market Harmonisation, or the Agency for the Evaluation of Medicinal products,[26] which again do not make an appearance in the formal treaties. Most of these agencies lack formal coercive powers but nonetheless play an important role in supplying information and establishing networks.

The existence of these informal, bureaucratic structures within the EU has led one commentator to refer to 'Europe-wide epistemic communities' of technical experts, 'whose technical truths transcend politics'.[27] Thus, EC bureaucracy might be seen as a complex international policy network, in which technical experts play as important a role as politicians and parliamentarians.[28] In the light of this, it has been asserted that 'Community regulation by committees of experts is difficult to fit into existing constitutional categories; and even more difficult to square with democratic legitimacy: a tough challenge of European constitutional theory.'[29] In such a loose, flowing system of technical networks, it has been suggested that, at its worst, the policy process may exhibit some aspects of the 'garbage-can' model of decision making, namely, something more akin to a loose collection of ideas than to a coherent structure, characterised by fluid participation in processes which are not

[26] See R Dehousse, 'Regulation by Networks in the European Community: the Role of Agencies' (1997) 4 JEPP 246; M Everson, 'The Independent Agencies in the European Union: Hierarchy Beaters?' (1995) 1 ELJ 180.

[27] M Shapiro, 'The Problems of Independent Agencies in the United States and European Union' (1997) 4 JEPP 276; see also P Haas, 'Introduction: Epistemic Communities and International Policy Co-ordination' (1992) IO 1, for a detailed discussion of 'epistemic communities'.

[28] K-H Ladeur, 'Toward a Legal Concept of the Network in Standard Setting' in Joerges and Vos (eds) *EU Committees* (Hart Publishing, 1999). See also S Picciotto, 'Networks in international economic integration: fragmented states and the dilemmas of neo-liberalism' (1997) 17 NW J. Int'l L Bus 1014.

[29] W Sauter, 'The Economic Constitution of the European Union' (1998) 4 Colum. J. Eur. L. 27 at 68.

even understood by the participants.[30] In an EC whose (already complex) legislation procedures have been rapidly changed by frequent treaty amendments, and where umpteen committees exist, often with no clear terms of reference, such an appellation does not seem unreasonable.

However, it has become more common, in the context of an examination of the minutiae of EU institutions and decision making, to look to a 'regulatory model' as a paradigm rather than the perhaps overly pessimistic 'garbage can'. The assertion that the EU is a regulatory structure has been made by Majone, and similar claims have been made by others.[31] It is argued that the primary task of the EU has been to deal with issues over which it can achieve greater efficiency than the member states, a throwback to its functionalist origins. Majone supports this claim by reference to the EC budget, which does not give the EC a remit over redistributive policies, but rather over regulation. The thesis of a regulatory community is supported by the nature of judicial review in the EC,[32] whereby the provisions for control of the Institutions by the Community courts are more administrative than constitutional in nature: indeed, these procedures are drawn directly from French Administrative law. The EU also lacks the range of powers traditionally associated with the nation state and is not redistributive in nature. Its institutions often seem to ignore a clear distinction between legislative and implementing rules. In this way, it is suggested that the Community is best explained in terms a supranational administrative agency, or as Majone puts it, as an 'independent fourth branch of government'.[33] EC decision-making is thus to be justified and even legitimated in terms of the expertise of its bureaucrats and the efficacy of its outcomes.

The EU has often been charged with having a democratic deficit, but legitimacy becomes less of a problem if the EC is characterised as being administrative, rather than constitutional, in nature. Perhaps administrative structures need not be all that democratic in nature: national parliaments delegate quite a lot of administrative rulemaking to bureaucracies because they wish not to be bothered with the minutiae of rule making. The rules produced by these technical bureaucracies are not subject to parliamentary scrutiny. Instead, it has been suggested that it is enough if in this context we look to transparency of the decision-making processes, the duty of the regulators to disclose the scientific basis of the rules, as well as to an increased range of participation rights for those with an interest in the regulation at issue. Majone has called for something akin to the US Administrative Procedures Act in the EU,[34] for what has been termed a 'deliberative polyarchy'.[35]

---

[30] M Cohen, J March, J Olsen, 'A Garbage Can Model of Organisational Choice' (1972) 17 Administrative Science Quarterly 1, discussed in J Richardson, 'Policy Making in the EU' in Richardson (ed.) *European Union: Power and Policy Making* (Routledge, 1996).

[31] e.g. by Lindseth, who refers to the 'administrative reality of EU institutions' in P Lindseth, 'Democratic Legitimacy and the Administrative Character of Supranationalism: the Example of the European Community' (1999) 99 Colum. L. R. at 732; see also R Dehousse, op. cit. at fn 26 and M Everson, op. cit. at fn 26.

[32] Under Article 230 EC: see Chapter 10.

[33] G Majone, *Regulating Europe* (Routledge, 1996).

[34] Majone op.cit.at 95.

[35] J Cohen and C Sabel, 'Directly Deliberative Polyarchy' (1997) 3 ELJ 313, and see also the discussion in Chapter 3.

However, this regulatory paradigm is not completely satisfactory, neither as a description of the structures of the EU, nor as a recipe for the legitimacy of its regulation. For a start, EU decision-making cannot be simply characterised as a regulatory, administrative model. How would this account for EMU, for the 'high politics' of the CFSP, or the constitutional character of much of the ECJ's case-law? EC policies extend, for example, to social policy (and indeed have always done so) as well as to education, and the EC has a growing role in tax. To characterise the EU as an administrative community is to misrepresent its nature. Too much that is constitutional persists and its institutions are of a significant nature,[36] in a way which is not merely regulatory. The history of the European Parliament, for example, illustrates this, with its real growth in legislative power, and its growing power over the executive (the Commission), taking us closer to a federal system in type. Furthermore, efficiency is clearly not, nor should it be, the EU's only or most important goal. Effective, legitimate and democratic institutions are just as important, as some of the new initiatives mentioned at the outset of this chapter would suggest. So at some stage the EU must look closely at the whole question of the constitutional structure of the Union, and the 'lamentable'[37] state of the treaties? Indeed, the time-tabling of another IGC, in 2004, to deal with these major structural issues, suggests that it already has decided to do so. The remainder of this chapter will pursue a more detailed examination of the major institutions of the EU[38] while attempting to pursue some of the issues raised in this introduction.

THE COMMISSION

The Commission has been traditionally described as the most supranational of the EU institutions: it is also what many people have in mind when they refer to the Brussels bureaucracy. And yet this is unfair, for most Community regulation is actually passed not by the Commission but by the Parliament and Council, and the Commission, although at around 21,000 employees the biggest of the EU institutions, is actually smaller than most national government departments. However, its image was certainly not improved by the infamy of the revelations of mismanagement and fraud brought to light in March 1999:[39] a state of affairs which contributed to a popular perception of the Commission as inefficient, bungling and undemocratic, as well as undermining its characterisation by Middlemas as 'at heart, an Enlightenment artefact, based on the triumph of rationality over the molten magma of human chaos'.[40]

The Commission, in its own website explaining its role and function,[41] describes itself as operating 'at the very heart of the European Union'. Since its early days as

---

[36] See the references to New Institutionalism above at fn 11.

[37] per U Everling, 'Comments on B. de Witte's "International Agreement or European Constitution?"' in J Winter, D Curtin and B de Witte, *Reforming the Treaty on European Union: The Legal Debate* (Kluwer, 1996) at 21.

[38] With the exception of the Community courts, which are dealt with in Chapter 5.

[39] See, for example, Committee of Independent Experts: *First Report on Allegations of Fraud, Mismanagement and Nepotism in the European Commission* and the discussion below.

[40] K Middlemas, *Orchestrating Europe* (London: Fontana, 1995) at 214.

[41] to be found at http://europa.eu.int/comm/role_en.htm.

the High Authority of the ECSC, when, infused with the idealism of Jean Monnet, it operated with some sort of pioneer spirit, to the heady days of the Delors I Commission, with the launching of the White Paper on the Completion of the Internal Market in 1985, it has sometimes operated with flair and ambition. What makes it so central as a Community institution is that it possesses the sole right of policy initiative (which involves both large-scale general measures, such as White Papers, as well as specific legislative proposals) giving rise to its description as the 'motor of integration', a title which it has, however, only sometimes lived up to. The Commission has been at its best when the climate for integration has been favourable. However, the Commission does not perform its role of legislative/policy initiative completely alone, it works closely with the other institutions and governments of the member states, as well as working groups of experts appointed by the member states, in order to bring these policies to fruition. It has had a sometimes tortuous relationship with these other bodies, the nature of this relationship reflecting the history of European integration.

Policy initiative has not been its only role. It has conventionally been described as 'guardian of the treaties', in that it has had the important function of ensuring that EU legislation has been implemented and applied correctly by the member states, as well as by those companies and individuals who do not have Community obligations. This has been an important function, given that some of the member states have felt it against their interests to comply with Community law. However, it has also been a time-consuming and resource-consuming role, and, in the course of Community history, alternative means, such as the direct effect of EC law, or state liability in damages, have been found to ensure that Community law is complied with.[42]

The third significant function of the Commission has been to act as the Community executive, responsible for implementing and managing policy. In this respect, it has played a significant role in the execution of areas such as agriculture, competition and trade. It has also overseen the part played in implementing these areas by national authorities. The Commission also has the considerable task of managing (or mismanaging, as it has sometimes seemed) the Community budget (97 billion Euros in 1999 according to the Commission itself)[43] as well as running the Structural Fund, which is supposed to even out disparities between richer and poorer countries of the EU. Further, the Commission plays its part in external relations: it negotiates trade and cooperation agreements with non-EC countries, on behalf of the EU. Since the 1990s, it has been managing the PHARE and TACIS programmes of financial aid to the countries of Central and Eastern Europe and the republics of the former Soviet Union. So it has a complex and multifarious role.

COMPOSITION

Who, or what, are the Commission? According to Article 213 EC, they consist, for the present, of a college of twenty Commissioners, with at least one being drawn

---

[42] These are discussed in Chapters 8 and 9.
[43] To be found on the Commission's web site: http://europa.eu.int/comm/role_en.htm.

from each of the present states of the EU, and two from the five larger ones: France, Germany, Italy, Spain and the UK. In addition to the actual commissioners, the Commission is divided up into Directorates General (of whom about 1,500 individuals constitute a mandarin elite of policy makers) which are rather like national ministries and each Commissioner also has personal advisors, or **cabinets**.

Much of the work of the IGC leading to the Treaty of Nice, as well as the negotiations at the summit itself, was spent on the vexed question of how many Commissioners there should be. In having such a focus, the Treaty of Nice was not unique: at most debates on the EU institutions over the past 30 years, the nature and size of the Commission has tended to be on the agenda. Although, in the past, it had been thought fundamental that the Commission should contain at least one national per member state,[44] the Commission's functioning as a collegiate body is endangered by the ever-greater aspiring membership of the EU which threatens to turn the Commission into an assembly. Thus, measures have been taken to keep its size down. With new applications in mind, the Treaty of Nice limits Commission membership to one per member state as from 2005, the larger states thus giving up their second commissioner. The treaty also imposes a ceiling on membership once the EU has 27 members,[45] raising the future possibility of some countries being without a Commissioner at some time.[46]

APPOINTMENT

The appointment of the Commission has been described as 'one of the messiest, often nastiest, episodes of EU decision making'.[47] Commissioners are appointed for a (renewable) term of office of five years,[48] and Article 213 EC stipulates that the Commissioners are to be 'chosen on the grounds of their general competence' and that they must be persons 'whose independence is beyond doubt'. Until recently,

---

[44] The fact that the five largest have had two members derives from the EEC's earliest history, when six members seemed too few for the Commission in 1957 so nine were chosen instead.

[45] The Council of Ministers is to lay down the basis for this, acting unanimously at some future date: Article 1(2) Protocol on Enlargement of the EU, amending Article 213 (1) EC. These arrangements can hardly be said to be transparent (if one has to look at a treaty Protocol to determine the size of the Commission), raising the possibility that the governments could not agree numbers at the actual Nice summit, thus concluding by way of Protocol. However, it is possible that some states will join before 2005, so Commission membership is likely to rise above twenty before then.

[46] In which case member states will divide up Commission membership on the basis of a rotation system based on the principle of equality. The Council of Ministers must ensure that each college reflects 'the demographic and geographic range of all the member States of the Union' (Article 4 Protocol on the Enlargement of the EU). This would seem to preclude a Commission which failed to include a national from any of the largest member states or from a geographic region, such as the Mediterranean or Scandinavia. But neither size of reduction nor detailed arrangements are laid down; they must therefore be settled by a future IGC or unanimously by the Council. Such a rotating system would not be new in Community institutions: the choice of Advocate General from the members outside the big five has proceeded on such a basis.

[47] J Petersen and E Bomberg, *Decision making in the European Union* (Macmillan, 1999) at 40.

[48] Article 214(1). Unless there are special circumstances, such as the resignation in 1999 of the Santer College, which resulted in the Prodi College taking office in September 1999 for five years and three and a half months.

Commissioners were nominated by the member state governments and it was pretty much up to those governments whom they nominated.[49] Since the Treaty of Nice, Article 214 has been amended to provide that 'The Council, acting by a qualified majority and by common accord with the nominee for President, shall adopt the list of the persons whom it intends to appoint as Members of the Commission, drawn up in accordance with the proposals made by each member state.'[50] This amendment removes the national veto so that, in future, it will be impossible for one country to block an appointment, as the UK did in 1994 in the case of the nominee for President, Jean-Luc Dehaene. It also renders the decision subject to judicial review (perhaps not an insignificant point, given the role played by the US Supreme Court in *Bush* v *Gore*[51]). It is also intended to give the President a bigger role[52] in nomination, and, if the President of the Commission is to become more prime ministerial in character (perhaps an unlikely analogue, given the eurosceptic tendencies of some member states) then maybe the Commission President should be able to select with whom they will work. The Doodge committee[53] of 1985 on 'The Functioning of European Institutions' suggested such a procedure but it was (unsurprisingly) rejected by the national governments. Now, however, practice seems to be moving more in this direction.

All those nominated, including the President, are subject, under Article 214(2), to a vote of approval by the European Parliament, a role that the Parliament takes seriously. In 1994, it required the Commission nominees to appear before its committees, in the style of US Senate hearings for federal appointees.[54] The Prodi Commission appointees also had to answer long questionnaires (available on the internet at the time, such scrutiny perhaps being hardly surprising in the light of the debacle over mismanagement earlier in 1999). This process, while increasing the role and importance of the Parliament, also introduced a greater democratic input into the Commission's appointment. This, at least, seems to be progress. Things have changed since Peters,[55] writing in 1992, made the following comments: 'If the EC is to become a genuine political entity, better mechanisms of popular political accountability need to be articulated for the Commission. As it is the Parliament has

---

[49] Where two Commissioners are nominated by the larger member states it has often been usual to appoint one each from major political parties – but this is not always the case. In the 1999 Prodi Commission, the second German Commissioner was not appointed from the opposition Christian Democrat party as expected, which caused a row.

[50] According to Article 214(2) – as amended by Nice – it is the European Council which is to nominate the President, but again by qualified majority.

[51] *George W Bush et al.* v *Albert Gore Jr. et al.* S Ct No 00-949 December 12 2000.

[52] This was designed to reflect the practice which had arisen of the President having some involvement. In the 1999 nominations, Romano Prodi, for example, discussed with the governments the sort of Commission appointments he would like to see, e.g. hoping that more women be appointed (in this he was not particularly successful with only five women members).

[53] Ad Hoc Committee for Institutional Affairs, *Report to the European Council* (Brussels 29–30 March 1985) (Luxembourg, 1985).

[54] The Parliament also asked for the remit of some Commission portfolios to be changed, for example that of the Irish Commissioner, Padraig Flynn, who at that stage had been given a remit covering equal opportunities, but was criticised by the Parliament women's rights committee.

[55] B Guy Peters, 'Bureaucratic Politics and the Institutions of the European Community' in A Sbragia (ed.) *Euro-Politics* (Washington DC. The Brookings Institution, 1992) at 93.

almost no control over the appointment of the Commission and must depend on the goodwill and competence of national governments to send the correct people to Brussels.' The growing influence of the Parliament in the Commission nomination process might be an indication of the growing 'constitutionalisation' of the treaties. The extensive questioning is surely also of value to Commission nominees, requiring them to be well-informed about their responsibilities.

Are the commissioners representative of the European people (if we can even meaningfully refer to the European people as an entity)? Given their power in shaping major European initiatives, along with their unelected status, it might be hoped that they are chosen with some sort of representation in mind. But this does not seem to have been the case. In a study of the composition of the fifteen colleges from August 1952 to January 1995, Andrew Macmullen[56] concluded that commissioners were predominately male and late middle-aged (no different from national politicians then), mostly qualified in law or economics, previously occupied as state officials, lawyers or politicians with centrist political affiliations. The Prodi Commission seems to have continued in much the same way: its average age is 52, and is male dominated, with only five of its twenty members women, in spite of Prodi's apparent efforts to achieve a better balance. None is from an ethnic background. In one way, however, it is unusual: with only four members of the outgoing college returning (Fischler, Liikanen, Kinnock and Monti, although Pascal Lamy, a veteran of the Delors Commissions, being Delors' chief of staff, returned as commissioner for trade). These four were the only ones to retain sufficient credibility from the disgraced Santer Commission.

ORGANISATION

The Commission has always been divided up into Directorates-General (DGs). There are currently 36 Directorates-General and specialised service divisions in the Commission. These are predominantly sectoral in nature, i.e. organised according to policy, although there are some which cut across the whole organisation, such as budget, legal or financial departments. These used to be numbered, some more familiarly (such as the well-known DG IV for Competition) than others. However, under the Prodi Commission, in an effort for greater transparency they are simply named for the policies they deal with, e.g. DG for Agriculture, Competition, etc.

Commissioners are not allotted DGs as such, but portfolios, which may correspond to more than one DG. Since the Treaty of Nice, Article 217 EC has been amended and considerably increased in scope to make it clear that it is the President of the Commission who allocates portfolios (a practice which occurred anyway) 'in order to ensure that it [the Commission] acts consistently, efficiently and on the basis of collective responsibility'. This has always been a sensitive function, as the character, scope and importance of portfolios have varied considerably.

---

[56] A Macmullen, 'Evaluating Integration through the Approach of the European Commission' (1997) 7 Diplomacy and Statecraft 221; 'European Commissioners 1952–95: National Routes to a European Elite' in Nugent (ed.) *At the Heart of the European Union: Studies of the European Commission* (Macmillan, 1997).

Competition, agriculture, internal market and trade have always been seen as important, but economic and monetary union, as well as external political relations, are also now perceived as increasingly significant for obvious reasons. There may be energetic lobbying by the member states to ensure that 'their' commissioner receives a certain portfolio. The composition of portfolios has varied over the years, sometimes resulting in rather bizarre combinations, such as that of Marcellino Oreja who, during the Santer Commission, was charged with relations with the European Parliament, relations with the member states over transparency, information, culture, audiovisuals, as well as institutional matters and the 1996 IGC. Such a mixture of responsibilities can mean that several Directorates-General can end up reporting to one Commissioner, which results in inefficiency.[57] Prodi, however, appeared determined to rationalise the arrangement and content of portfolios, telling the Cologne European Council in 1999, 'There will be a rational, well balanced coherent spread of portfolios...There will be no horse trading.'[58]

The President of the Commission

The role of the President has become more important, increasing in power with the Treaty of Nice. The choice of Commission President has sometimes been contentious, given that, until the Treaty of Nice was amended,[59] the President had to be appointed by a consensus of the member states. For example, the renomination of Walter Hallstein during the crisis that led to the Luxembourg Accords was contested violently by the French (mainly on the grounds of Hallstein's federalism) and had to be withdrawn. Likewise, the nomination of a favoured Franco-German candidate, the Belgian prime minister, Jean Luc Dehaene, was vetoed by the eurosceptic UK conservative government, the presidency eventually going to Jacques Santer, nobody's first choice, who later resigned in disgrace, along with the rest of the Commission. What the President makes of their position will depend somewhat on their personality. Some have been dynamic and forceful such as Delors,[60] Monnet or Hallstein, others more cautious. Since Hallstein's demise, however, 'All Presidents have to accept the Hallstein lesson that like Popes, they have no legions to confront the member states head on, and must therefore persuade or catch them with silken words.'[61] The President also, of course, has to be able to work with the other Commissioners, as well as the key DGs, to be able to attain a working majority.

As already mentioned, the President now has a role in the selection of Commissioners and decides on its internal organisation.[62] Since Nice, the President may also

---

[57] P. Ludlow, 'The European Commission' in Keohane and Hoffmann (eds.), *The New European Community: Decision Making and Institutional Change* (Boulder: Westview Press, 1991).

[58] Intervention of Mr. Prodi, Cologne European Council (3 June 1999): http://europa.eu.int/comm/commissioners/prodi/speeches.

[59] Article 214(2) now requires a qualified majority of the European Council to nominate the President.

[60] See for example G Ross, *Jacques Delors and European Integration* (Oxford: Polity Press, 1995) for an interesting account of the Delors Presidency.

[61] K Middlemas, *Orchestrating Europe* at 218.

[62] Although Article 219 really does nothing more than put into the Treaty the Commission's own rules of procedure adopted in 1999 and amended in November 2000 (OJ 2000 L308/26) in effect from 1 January 2001.

request the resignation of individual Commissioners (Article 217 (4)) thus dealing with the problem where it is the conduct of an individual Commissioner which is impugned, rather than that of the whole Commission.[63] Again, this puts into the Treaty a practice which Prodi had already instigated, the so-called 'lex Prodi' under which members of his Commission had undertaken to resign individually if called upon to do so. The President also has considerable dealings with other institutions: attending meetings with COREPER (which works with the Council) as well as meeting from time to time with the Council Presidency, the European Council, and the European Parliament.

The services

The bulk of Commission employees work full time, and are supposedly appointed (by open competition) to ensure a balanced national representation.[64] However, higher levels are often appointed on the basis of national or political affiliation rather than merit, a practice which Neil Kinnock tried to address in the Commission reforms. About two-thirds of Commission staff are involved in drafting new laws and overseeing implementation, and about 20 per cent are in research. The rest are occupied in translation and interpretation, as although the Commission works in English and French, documents must be translated into the eleven EC languages. Administration in the Commission is overseen by a Secretariat-General (headed for 30 years by Emile Noel) supported by a smallish staff of about 350. The Secretary-General chairs weekly meetings of the *chefs de cabinet*, sits in on meetings of Commissioners, helps structure the Commission's relationship with the Parliament, and generally provides support. Additionally, particularly sensitive subjects may be assigned to the Secretariat-General, rather than to individual commissioners. This was the case with the final stages of EFTA admission in 1993, which was handled by the then Secretary-General, David Williamson. The Commission is also advised by a legal service of about 80 lawyers and twenty lawyer-linguists, headed by a Director General, who is required to be consulted on all drafts or proposals and on all documents which have legal implications.[65]

Also relevant is the type of person tending to work at the Commission.[66] Originally, Jean Monnet wanted the High Authority to be an elitist body of policy-making experts rather than being bogged down in sectoral integration or parliamentary politics.[67] In reality, Commission employees are probably a little of both, as the following quotations illustrate. On the one hand, it has been said that 'staff maintain allegiance to national identities'.[68] On the other, 'The Commission recruits

---

[63] Which can be required to resign *en bloc* if a sufficient vote is garnered by the European Parliament.

[64] In fact one in four are Belgian, being secretarial and support staff and locally recruited: J McCormick, *Understanding the European Union* (Macmillan, 1999) at 92.

[65] Article 20 Commission Rules of Procedure.

[66] See Ross, *Jacques Delors and European Integration*.

[67] S Mazey, 'Conception and evolution of the high authority's administrative services (1952–1956)' in E Heyen et al. (eds), *Jahrbuch der Europäischen Verwaltungsgeschichte* (Baden-Baden Nomos, 1992) at 31.

[68] Christiansen, 'Tensions of European Governance: political bureaucracy and multiple accountability in the European Commission' (1997)4 JEPP 73 at 82.

from people who are highly motivated, risk-orientated, polyglot, cosmopolitan, open-minded and innovative',[69] and 'The majority of officials...appear to see themselves not simply as bureaucrats, but as an elite charged with implementing an historically unique project...Yet they lack the time, consideration and resources which civil servants enjoy within the majority of member states...Their careers often end prematurely and in frustration.'[70]

THE COMMISSION AT WORK

The Commission is difficult to characterise, being neither like national political office, as the Commission has no final political responsibility for the legislation it sets in motion, nor like the national civil service, as commissioners operate in a more politicised and public way. Commissioners continue to have some sort of relationship with the state that nominated them, although according to Article 213, they are prohibited from seeking or taking 'instructions from any government or from any other body'. Be this as it may, complete supranationality is in practice impossible to attain. Commissioners have very often held national political office, and can be steeped in the culture that nominated them. Governments and national ministries will frequently communicate with them. According to Lord Cockfield, the British Internal Market Commissioner at the time of the Single Market Initiative (who was accused by Margaret Thatcher of having betrayed British interests, by 'going native' and was not reappointed as a result), 'as with all lobbying activities, the dividing line between "information" and "influence" can be a very narrow one'.[71]

Member states may be represented in the Commission in a variety of ways, e.g. in senior posts in the administration and in the Cabinet of the DG concerned. When Jacques Delors was President of the Commission, his Cabinet was well-staffed by French 'énarques'. The strength of these Cabinets may undermine the Commission's independence from national politics.[72] As McDonald has observed, the Cabinets may be described as a 'structural contradiction', as they 'have regular contacts with national administrations, national lobbyists and the permanent representations. They also notoriously "parachute" their chosen national recruits directly into key service jobs, over the heads of the well-qualified and experienced officials in the services.'[73] Perhaps this is why the cabinets have been targeted for reform in the White Paper of 2000 on Reforming the Commission. However, as Nugent remarks, 'for the most part the Commissioners do go about their work impartially, otherwise the College would start to resemble the Council of Ministers'.[74]

---

[69] V Eichener, 'Social Dumping or Innovative Regulation?' (1992) EUI Working Paper 92/98 Florence, at 53.

[70] K Middlemas, *Orchestrating Europe* at 260.

[71] Cockfield, *The European Union: Creating the Single Market* (Chichester: Wiley, 1994).

[72] M Donnelly and E Ritchie, 'The College of Commissioners and their Cabinets' in G Edwards and D Spence (eds), *The European Commission* (Longman 1993).

[73] M McDonald, 'Identities in the European Commission' in N Nugent (ed.), *At the Heart of the European Commission* (London: Macmillan, 1997) at 51.

[74] N Nugent, *The European Commission* (London: Palgrave, 2001) at 93.

COLLEGIALITY AND WORKING METHOD

The concept of collegiality has always been important to the functioning of the Commission. It may also be a way of countering nationalistic influence. It has meant that in theory, important decisions should be taken at meetings of the college, and that no commissioner should show too much independence. According to Article 217 EC (as amended by Nice) the Commission 'shall work...on the basis of collegiality'. In the words of the ECJ in the *BASF* decision,[75] 'the principle of collegiate responsibility...is based on the equal participation of Commissioners in the adoption of decisions, from which it follows in particular that decisions should be the subject of collegiate deliberation and that all the members of the college of Commissioners should bear collective responsibility at the political level for all decisions adopted'.[76]

However, as Nugent notes,[77] collegiality is best thought of as an ideal, one which came closest to being achieved during Hallstein's strong presidency. In fact, as Nugent continues, 'the Commission is far from being a wholly cohesive and united institution'.[78] Inevitably perhaps, given the way in which Commissioners are appointed, in that the member states focus not on the needs of the Commission as a supranational body, but rather on who can best serve their interests, membership of the college does not result in a shared outlook: disputes and conflicts between individual Commissioners invariably arise, as for example, between Leon Brittain and Franz Fischler over the handling of the BSE crisis.

According to Article 219 EC, the Commission acts by a majority of its members. However, given the Commission's huge body of work, Commissioners act through various types of delegation in order to improve efficiency. They may use the delegation (or '*habilitation*') procedure whereby individual Commissioners themselves act through delegated powers.[79] This is usually only possible for administrative and technical matters. But the entire Commission must adopt the act as a whole.[80]

The Commission also uses the 'written procedure' to deal with much of its work. This is for cases in which relevant matters have already been agreed by the relevant DGs and the Legal Service. All cabinets are sent copies and decisions are deemed to be adopted if no commissioner has raised an objection requesting that the matter be dealt with at a college meeting.[81] Again, this procedure is not used for matters of the greatest importance, but rather for more routine and minor issues such as agricultural regulations, customs or non-controversial but urgent matters such as emergency food aid in disasters.

---

[75] Case C-137/92P *Commission v BASF* [1994] ECR I-2555.

[76] Ibid. at para. 63.

[77] Nugent, *The European Commission*.

[78] Ibid.

[79] Commission Rules of Procedure Article 11(1). See also Case 5/85 *AKZO v Commission* [1986] ECR 2585 in which the ECJ upheld this procedure as necessary for the sound functioning of the Commission's decision-making power.

[80] In *BASF* the ECJ held that the Commission could not delegate the power to adopt a decision (in this case in the field of competition law) in its definitive written form.

[81] Commission Rules of Procedure Article 10.

The remainder of matters will be dealt with in full college meetings, usually taking place in Brussels on a weekly basis, except when the European Parliament is in session, when they are held in Strasbourg. These meetings are small, held in private and discussions are confidential.[82] Unlike Council meetings, which are large-scale affairs, Commission meetings are much smaller, although the Secretary-General of the Commission will attend meetings and some other persons, such as the *Chef de Cabinet* of the President may be present. By the stage of college meetings, discussions will be at a very advanced stage, preliminary work having been done by the cabinets. The sort of matters under discussion, for example, will be proposals for Council and Parliament legislation, policy proposals in the form of White or Green Papers, such as the White Paper on Governance, or the Commission's Annual Work Programme.

FUNCTIONS OF THE COMMISSION

The Commission carries out a number of functions according to Article 211 which states:

> In order to ensure the proper functioning and development of the common market, the Commission shall:
>
> —ensure that the provisions of this Treaty and the measures taken by the institutions pursuant thereto are applied;
>
> —formulate recommendations or deliver opinions on matters dealt with in this Treaty if it expressly so provides or if the Commission considers it necessary;
>
> —have its own power of decision and participate in the shaping of measures taken by the Council and by the European Parliament in the manner provided for in this Treaty;
>
> —exercise the powers conferred on it by the Council for the implementation of the rules laid down by the latter.

This provision does not give a particularly clear view of the functions of the Commission, which are, in summary: policy initiator (including the making of legislative proposals); executive functions; and guardian of the treaties. The widespread nature of these activities ensures that the Commission has some involvement in most aspects of Community governance. However, what is notable is that these tasks and functions are not clear-cut, the Commission does not operate as a *Rechtsstaat*.

(a) Policy initiator

Article 211 does, however, provide the Commission with considerable scope for developing new initiatives or pushing forward ongoing debates. This can take a great variety of forms: the policy concerned might be general, spanning the whole framework of EC activity or quite detailed and sectoral in nature. Some important

---

[82] Commission Rules of Procedure Article 7.

policy initiatives are taken as a result of decisions in the European Council and the high profile nature of Council summits can be an important feature in supplying authority to Commission initiatives.

The Commission has described itself as 'the driving force behind European integration',[83] but it might be thought that this is an inappropriate role for an unelected body. However, the Commission has the advantage of relatively long terms of office and the benefit of no direct political influence or constraints (unlike national government ministries) so, in fact, it can be quite well-placed to shape and manage policy. It also has better access to information than the Council or the Parliament, being, as it has been described, 'at the hub of numerous highly specialised policy networks of technical experts designing detailed regulations'.[84]

Thus, it has been suggested that: 'the function of *animateur* permeates the whole structure and ethos of the Institution'.[85] This perception of the appropriateness of the role of *animateur* dates back to the early days of the Commission, and the experience of early Commission officials such as Jean Monnet, whose background in the Planning Commission of the French civil service had persuaded him of the importance of strategic planning by enlightened civil servants. On the other hand, this function of *animateur* may place a strain on the college when there is no uniting political belief or ideology within it. The Commission is not a cohesive body but rather, like the EU itself, diverse and pluralistic, reflecting a great variety of styles and cultures. As Petersen and Bomberg comment, 'One of the most enduring myths surrounding EU decision-making is that the Commission is a purposive, single-minded institution.'[86] Part of the problem is that it is fragmented, on account of the highly sectoral nature of much of its business, creating lots of small sub-communities, made up of Commission members but also advisers and experts from elsewhere. The notion of 'epistemic communities', already discussed at the outset of this chapter, has been used to refer to the development of fellow feeling among such groups.[87] The existence of such communities contributes to the fragmentation, or 'multi-organisational'[88] nature of the Commission.[89] In fact, the Commission has been described as 'a purposeful opportunist',[90] namely, an organisation which has a notion of its overall objectives and aims but which is quite flexible as to how these are carried out.

---

[83] Commission, *Adapting the Institutions to make a success of enlargement*, COM 2000, 34, Brussels.

[84] G Marks, 'Structural policy and multi-level governance in the EC' in A Cafruny and G Rosentahl (eds) *The State of the European Community II* (Boulder: Colorado, 1993).

[85] P Ludlow, 'The European Commission' in R. Keohane and S. Hoffmann, *The New European Community: Decisionmaking and Institutional Change* (Boulder: Westview Press, 1991) at 97.

[86] J Petersen and E Bomberg, *Decision Making in the European Union* (Macmillan, 1999) at 39.

[87] P Haas, 'Introduction: Epistemic Communities and International Policy Co-ordination' (1992) 46 IO 1; J Richardson, 'Actor based models of national and EC policy-making: policy communities: issue networks and advocacy coalitions' in H Kassim and A Menon (eds), *The EU and National Industrial Policy* (Routledge, 1996).

[88] L Cram, 'The European Commission as a Multi-Organisation' (1994) JEPP 199.

[89] J Petersen and E Bomberg, *Decision Making in the European Union* at 39; see also G Ross, *Jacques Delors and European Integration* (Polity, 1995) at 3 for a similar view.

[90] Cram, op. cit. at 199.

Legislative functions

The Commission has the exclusive right to draft legislation for the EC pillar. Although it is the Council of Ministers or the Council and the Parliament, acting jointly, which take the final decisions on Community legislation, they can only act on the basis of a draft proposal from the Commission. The Commission draws its specific right of initiative from various provisions in the treaty, although sometimes it acts more energetically than others. Certainly, during the 1992 programme, the Commission acted energetically, as Weiler noted: 'for the first time since the early days of the Community...the Commission plays the political role clearly intended for it by the Treaty of Rome'.[91] However, making an initiative stick involves skilful presentation of the issue, control of the agenda and media as well as support of other institutions, quite a tall order.

Only a smallish proportion of ideas for legislation actually originate with the Commission; instead, they may come from the European Council, or by a request of the Council under Article 208 EC, or from the Parliament under Article 192 EC. Rulings from the ECJ may also affect policy and sometimes prompt the Commission into action (e.g. as with the *Cassis de Dijon* case, in which the Commission issued a memorandum based on its understanding of this case and its effect on the free movement of goods). The Commission is however unique in being represented at, and contributing to (if not having the final say in), all stages of Community legislation. The Community legislation process will be discussed in more detail in the next chapter.

The Commission's own power of legislation

In addition to this right of legislative initiative, the Commission also has its own power to legislate under Article 211, something which is not always appreciated. This may take two forms. In the first such case, the Commission has a free-standing power to introduce legislation in its own right, without the participation of any other Community institution. This power is quite limited, as the treaty provides the Commission with an express basis for legislation only in very limited circumstances. Nevertheless, the member states have been unhappy with this role of the Commission as independent legislator. For example, in 1980, the Commission adopted Directive 80/723 under Article 86(3) EC (formerly Article 90 [3]) on the transparency of relations between member states and public undertakings (with the aim of establishing how much in the way of public funds was being put into them). This Directive was challenged by France, Italy and the UK before the Court of Justice. The UK argued that the Commission's power of legislation violated the principle of the separation of powers, submitting that all original law-making power was vested in the Council of Ministers, and that the Commission's powers were only executive in nature. France and Italy argued that, even if Article 90(3) did confer a law-making power on the Commission, the Commission was precluded from acting

---

[91] Weiler, *The Constitution of Europe* (Cambridge University Press, 1999) at 65.

where the Council itself could have adopted the rules in question. The ECJ rejected these arguments, stating: 'The limits of the powers conferred on the Commission by a specific provision of the Treaty are to be inferred not from a general principle, but from an interpretation of the particular wording of the provisions in question...analysed in the light of its purpose and place in the treaty.'[92]

The Court went on to hold more recently[93] that whenever the EC treaty confers on the Commission a specific task, then it impliedly confers on the Commission the powers, including legislative powers, necessary to carry out that task. It might be thought that there is a danger of the Commission misusing these powers in areas where it is difficult to pass legislation through the Council. However, this does not appear to have been the case and relatively little legislation has been passed by the Commission under these provisions.[94]

Delegated legislation and comitology

The second situation in which the Commission may itself legislate stems from derived powers. This delegated legislation deals with the detailed implementation of Council (or Council/Parliament) acts, or enables such legislation to adapt to changed circumstances. The principle of delegation was upheld by the ECJ in early case law such as *Koster* and *Meroni*,[95] although both cases supposedly limited the Council to the delegation of administrative, rather than discretionary powers.[96] As such, most EC delegated legislation is administrative and highly specific and technical in nature,[97] for example the alteration of agricultural prices, or market support measures.[98] In fact, the majority of EU legislation is issued in this way – of about 1,550–2,000 legislative instruments per year, all but 500 are issued in the name of the Commission – because the great bulk of EU legislation is administrative, technical and often agricultural, as a glance at the Official Journal will show. Moreover, the Commission now issues more directives than the Council.[99]

---

[92] Cases 188–90/80 *France, Italy and UK v Commission* [1982] ECR 2545.
[93] Cases 281, 283–5 and 287/85 *Germany, France, the Netherlands, Denmark and the UK v Commission* [1987] ECR 3203.
[94] This was nonetheless an aspect of EC law-making over which the German Constitutional court expressed disquiet in its Maastricht judgment: *Brunner v European Union Treaty* [1994] 1 CMLR 57.
[95] Case 25/70 *Koster* [1970] ECR 1161; Case 9/56 *Meroni* [1957–8] ECR 133; also Case 23/75 *Rey Soda* [1975] ECR 1279.
[96] In fact quite broad powers have been delegated to the Commission: see, for example, Case 41/69 *Chemiefarma* [1970] ECR 661, for an illustration of this.
[97] Although in some cases there is an overlap of administrative and policy law, for example the Common Commercial Policy, under which the Commission can apply preventative measures such as anti-dumping duties.
[98] It should be noted, however, that not all rules which implement EC law are passed by the Commission. Some are made by other bodies, such as European Standards bodies (Comité Européen des Normes (CEN) which are staffed by technical experts from national administrations and the business environment. For example, the 1994 Packaging and Waste Directive required packaging to be 'reusable' by 1998 but left CEN to draft detailed definitions and set thresholds.
[99] see R Dehousse, 'Towards a Regulation of Transitional Governance? Citizen's Rights and the Reform of Comitology Procedures' in C Joerges and E Vos, *EU Committees: Social Regulation, Law and Politics* (Hart, 1999) 109 at 113.

However, this is not to say that the Commission has complete autonomy, as the measures are usually subject to Council scrutiny and control. Article 202 EC states:

> ...the Council shall...confer on the Commission, in the acts which the Council adopts, powers of the implementation of the rules which the Council lays down. The Council may impose certain requirements in respect of the exercise of these powers. The Council may also reserve the right in specific cases, to exercise directly implementing powers itself.

In fact, a complex web of monitoring and safeguard measures has been put in place, most usually taking the form of committees, which are known as comitology committees and the whole issue by the neologism of *comitology*,[100] a practice which was endorsed by the ECJ in the *Koster* case.

These committees are composed of representatives of national governments, usually civil servants, to whom the Commission must submit drafts of the measures it proposes to adopt. The committee members vote by qualified majority. A Council decision of 1987[101] regulated the nature of the Council's control of measures by dividing the committees into three broad types,[102] from **advisory** committees, which have the lowest degree of control over the Commission's actions, being merely able to give advice; through **management** committees, usually associated with the CAP, which may delay the Commission's ability to act; to **regulatory** committees which may block the Commission's actions in certain circumstances. However, to complicate matters, and remove transparency – a feature all too common in the EC – there are variants on these procedures (the most constraining and unpopular of these being the *contre-filet* procedure, a variant which was finally abolished in 1999), and in all, there exist around 400 individual committees, which are 'highly complex and differentiated in nature',[103] although not all of them meet regularly; rather they are driven by demand. The 1987 comitology decision was replaced by another decision taken in 1999,[104] which, while not doing away with the tripartite committee structure, took measures which may help improve the transparency of the comitology process.[105]

Comitology undoubtedly serves some very important functions. It helps implement EC legislation; it allows the Council to maintain residual control; it provides an input from national bureaucracies; it helps the structurally overburdened Commission; it establishes links between the Commission and national networks; it informs decision-making about recent developments; and it provides building blocks for new

---

[100] The word is said to have been first used in English by C. Northcote Parkinson in *Parkinson's Law* (Harmondsworth: Penguin, 1958), in the chapter on Divisions and Councils, to denote the science of committees. The term was rarely used in the EC context before the 1987 comitology decision.

[101] 87/373 OJ L197 1987.

[102] See also Case 302/87 *Parliament v Council* (comitology) [1988] ECR 5615.

[103] W Wessels, 'The Growth and Differentiation of Multi-level Networks: A Corporatist Mega-Bureaucracy or an Open City?' in H Wallace and A Young (eds) *Participation and Policymaking in the European Union* (Oxford: Clarendon Press, 1997).

[104] 1999/468/EC OJ L184 1999.

[105] See discussion which follows below.

forms of regulation.[106] Its committees cover a very wide range of subject matters and a lot of salient issues are in fact dealt with by way of comitology. All of the following areas have been dealt with by way of comitology: technical standards for tachographs; the EC banana regime; data protection; humanitarian aid; mutual recognition of qualifications; the budget allocation of the *Socrates* and *Leonardo* education programmes; giving effect to the Common Customs Code; the common organisation of particular markets. A great many comitology measures have a direct impact on the consumer, such as regulation of the safety of foodstuffs and other goods, labelling of goods and environmental protection, to name but a few.

Comitology is, however, problematic. It results in unelected bureaucrats exercising a strong hold over Community legislation through complex processes which are not even transparent to experts.[107] The way comitology works is a mystery to most people, even EU specialists. The committees are powerfully placed to promote their own positions, especially if certain groups achieve dominance. This was the case with COPA, the transnational association of farmers' unions, which in the 1970s managed to block all EC attempts to limit EC price guarantees for major farm products, although produce exceeded demand, as conspicuous butter and sugar mountains illustrated all too well. The Council of Ministers appears to take the comitology process seriously, taking much time and effort deciding which committee process to apply, but the Commission has not raised any substantial objection to the exercise of comitology,[108] perhaps because, although comitology might appear to involve control by member states, in fact the Commission is still well-placed to determine the agenda and to control by chairing the meetings. Indeed, the Commission itself was responsible for the choice of the regulatory committee in 40 per cent of the cases in which it was used.[109]

The European Parliament, however, dislikes comitology, seeing it as an unreasonable constraint on the Commission, as well as being annoyed by the fact that it, the Parliament, has been excluded from scrutiny of legislation passed in this way. The Parliament attempted to challenge the 1987 comitology decision in a case brought against the Council,[110] arguing that the decision undermined the rights of executive control, and also democratic control by the Parliament. The challenge failed, as the ECJ held that the Parliament had no standing to bring an action for annulment.[111]

---

[106] See W Sauter and E Vos, 'Harmonisation under Community Law: The Comitology Issue' in P Craig and C Harlow (eds), *Law-Making in the EU* (Kluwer, 1998).

[107] For a general account of comitology see C Demmke, E Eberharter, G Schaefer, and A Turk, 'The History of Comitology' in R Pedler and G Schaefer (eds) *Shaping European Law and Policy: The Role of Committees and Comitology in the Political Process* (European Institution of Public Administration, 1996). Also M Andenas and A Turk, *Delegated Legislation and the Role of Committees in the EU* (Kluwer Law International, 2000).

[108] G Marks, L Hooghe and K Blank, 'European Integration from the 1980s: State Centric v Multi-Level Governance' (1996) JCMS 341.

[109] Dehousse, in Joerges and Vos, op. cit. su 99 at 111.

[110] See again case *Parliament v Council* (comitology); also K Bradley, 'Comitology and the law: Through a Glass, Darkly' (1992) 29 CMLRev 631.

[111] The Parliament's right to sue was improved by Case-70/88 *Parliament v Council (Chernobyl)* [1990] ECR I-2041 and followed by successive treaty amendments until the Treaty of Nice amended Article 230 to give the Parliament a full right of standing in the European Courts.

The Parliament's situation improved in the 1990s with the '*modus vivendi*' between the Council, Commission and Parliament, whereby the Parliament was at least asked to give its views on measures intended to implement the codecision procedure. However, comitology was an issue in two-thirds of the dossiers that went to conciliation. Comitology issues (namely the choice of the management committee, rather than advisory procedure preferred by the Parliament) were at the root of the Parliament's rejection of the Council's common position in the Directive on Voice Telephony, the first such rejection.

A new 1999 Council comitology decision[112] was represented as meeting many of the Parliament's complaints. As well as setting out, in Article 2, criteria for the choice of type of comitology committee (something which the earlier legislation had failed to do) and abolishing two variants of the comitology procedures – the *contrefilet* (double safety net) management and regulatory procedures, which were thought to be particularly constraining on the Commission – the decision gave the Parliament a greater power to participate in the process. Under Article 3, it provides that, where a draft measure, based on legislation taken under the codecision procedure (whereby the Parliament jointly enacts legislation with Council), is dealt with under comitology, the Parliament may pass a resolution opposing it. The Commission is then forced to re-examine the measure, although, according to Article 8 of the Comitology decision, it has no duty to accommodate the Parliament's views. In the situation where a regulatory committee delivers an unfavourable opinion, or even no opinion at all, the Parliament must be informed of the Commission's proposal. In such a situation, if the Parliament opposes the measure, then the Council, although it may act on the Commission proposal, 'must take account' of the Parliament's views according to Article 5 (6), although it is not bound by them. This has certainly improved the Parliament's position, putting it in a better place to monitor the administration, and to determine whether the Parliament's policy choices have been executed as the original legislation intended. However, the Parliament still has no effective veto.

Aside from being shielded from control by the democratic legislature, comitology is problematic in further ways. Its committees are not subject to judicial review under Article 230 EC.[113] On the other hand, it might be suggested that comitology deals mainly with technical measures which would not be subject to full scrutiny even in the domestic context. Comitology, however, does not just involve specialists and technical matters, for it may be difficult to separate science from policy, as in the case of pricing and development of products, for example, thus putting real political power in the hands of the technocrats. It can be very difficult to set clear boundaries of delegation between essential broad policy on the one hand and technical detail on the other, a distinction which the ECJ dictated in the *Koster* case. A lot of highly important issues are dealt with in comitology. Some writers[114] have

---

[112] 1999/468/EC 28 June 1999 [1999] OJ L 184/23, repealing 1987 comitology decision.
[113] See Case 25/70 *Koster* [1970] ECR 1161; Case 23/75 *Rey Soda* [1975] ECR 1279.
[114] i.e. Joerges and Neyer, 'From Intergovernmental Bargaining to Deliberative Process: the Constitutionalising of Comitology' (1997) 3 ELJ 271.

pointed to the quality and efficiency of the solutions produced by comitology and its smooth functioning: disagreement between the Commission and comitology committees is rare. However, this still provides no justification for its overall legitimacy. This key issue, the way in which comitology contributes to the lack of democracy or legitimacy in the EU, will be considered in the next chapter. However, the purpose of this brief examination of comitology has been to highlight its function as an important, if little realised, feature of the 'real' constitution of the EU, or at least as an aspect of that new form of governance which is the EU.

(b) Executive powers

In addition to delegated legislation, the Commission also plays an important role in the implementation and administration of Community policy. Much of EC policy is actually administered by national authorities; for example, customs authorities collect the duties imposed under the CCT on goods coming into the EC from third countries, and agricultural regulations are often implemented in the member states by national agricultural Intervention Boards. Nonetheless, the Commission tries to supervise and monitor the way in which these national authorities apply EC law. This may be difficult, as the Commission only has limited resources, the rules concerned may be difficult or complex to administer and the national agencies may be reluctant to apply EC law in the first place.

Another important executive function is that of managing the Community's annual budget[115] and running its structural funds, which have the main purpose of evening out economic disparities between the richer and poorer parts of the EU. The Commission's recent record of administration of Community funds has not been good, with the European Court of Auditors refusing to certify the Commission's accounts for five years in a row.[116]

A further such executive function is that of negotiating trade and cooperation agreements with third countries on behalf of the EU (there are agreements with over 100 such countries): for example the Lomé Convention, which links the EU with some African countries, the Caribbean and the Pacific (ACP). The Commission also negotiated the Uruguay round trade liberalisation accord on the EU's behalf.

(c) Guardian of EC law

The Commission acts as guardian of the treaties to ensure that EU legislation is applied correctly by the member states. Where necessary, the Commission has the power to institute proceedings against member states which are violating the treaty. Such actions proceed against member states under Article 226, and, although most such cases are settled at an early stage, some 50–100 references are made to the

---

[115] 97 billion euros in 1999 – in fact, rather a small sum amounting to 1 per cent of the EU's GNP, because most of the truly expensive policies, such as health, education or defence, are still financed and operated by the member states.
[116] See below.

ECJ in an average year. This function is given detailed consideration in Chapter 12. The Maastricht Treaty gave the Commission the power to apply for a fine to be imposed on a member state which has not complied with an ECJ judgment finding it to be in violation. The first such application was made in June 1999 in the case of *Commission* v *Greece*,[117] brought for the failure of Greece to apply the waste directive.

The Commission also has powers to pursue individuals and companies which are violating the competition provisions of the treaty, and it is also responsible for vetting subsidies paid by national governments to their industries and practices likely to distort competition in the single market. Within the competition field, the Commission has not only a power of enforcement, but also its own decision-making powers (of a quasi judicial nature) under Article 83 EC. It may impose large fines on those undertakings found to be engaging in anti-competitive behaviour, such as in the cases of cement and Volkswagen.

CONCLUSIONS

That the Commission plays an important and central role in the functioning of the EU is undeniable. This role, however, is problematic. The problem is that the Commission has to carry out three very different kinds of function. First, policy formulation, which requires coherent, organic and insightful organisation, and secondly, implementation, which requires mechanistic organisation along the lines of what Weber termed a classical bureaucracy: specialised, fragmented and unsuited to innovation. Thus the Commission has to balance its requirement to be dynamic and innovative, as the supposed 'motor of integration' of the EC, and a capability for smooth, bureaucratic running of the European polity. Ludlow, writing well before the Commission debacle in 1991, wrote that 'senior Commission staff are, for the most part, better at drafting directives than they are at implementing them'.[118] A lack of such a bureaucracy was perhaps responsible for the creation of semi-autonomous agencies, such as the Office for Trade Marks and Designs, Plant Varieties (and may lead to others; for example, the German government has suggested transferring the implementing powers of the Competition Directorate to a separate EU cartel office).

Recently, attention has shifted from the Commission's role in policy development to that of policy application. Partly, this has been due to the high-profile criticism of the Commission management of the EU's finances.[119] But such a change of focus also reflects a wider concern about the Commission's capacity to function as an efficient executive. The Commission's complex task is not made any easier by the need

---

[117] Case C-387/97 *Commission* v *Greece* [2000] ECR I 000.
[118] P Ludlow, 'The European Commission' in R Keohane and S Hoffmann, *The New European Community: Decisionmaking and Institutional Change* (Boulder: Westview Press, 1991) at 99.
[119] e.g. Committee of Independent Experts: *First Report on Allegations of Fraud, Mismanagement and Nepotism in the European Commission*.

to reconcile additional requirements on it, namely, public accountability; attention to member states' interests; and the need to provide independent expertise.[120] The Commission requires a dynamic force at its centre if it is not to lose a sense of clear articulation.

As the EU has grown in size, so have the Commission's tasks, but with no corresponding increase in resources. As a result, the Commission has taken up the practice of outsourcing work to the private sector, sometimes even in the case of important policy and this has not been particularly satisfactory. Two of the cases investigated in 1999 by the Committee of Independent Experts[121] concerned the management and development of significant policies contracted out to the private sector. This is an example of what Majone has termed 'indirect or proxy government',[122] and, in Majone's view, requires new forms of control and accountability, which do not at present exist but surely must be introduced.

In recent times, the Commission has taken on different initiatives, concerned with improving democracy and governance in the European Union.[123] But it still has to deal with the task of how to reconcile the demands of efficiency and legitimacy within its own organisation, and this is no easy task.

THE COMMISSION CRISIS OF 1999

Current perceptions of the Commission are doubtlessly marked by the dramatic events of the Commission's collapse and resignation in March 1999, a saturnalia of incompetence, if not of corruption. How did these events come about?

There had been concern over the Commission's management of the EU budget for some time, and, for several years in a row, the European Court of Auditors (ECA) refused to certify the EU's annual accounts (for example in 1995, on the grounds that nearly £3 billion euros seemed unaccounted for). In 1998, the European Parliament refused to give the budget discharge. But the fuse was lit not so much by the ECA's misgivings, as by a dossier handed to the European Parliament by a Commission employee, Paul van Buitenen. It concerned Commission mismanagement, much of it dealing with Edith Cresson's mishandling of the Leonardo project. For his pains, van Buitenen was suspended on half pay (and still had not been reinstated at time of writing) and apparently even put in fear of his life. He was however named 'European of the Year' in January 2000, which may or may not have been a consolation. The Commission might have been removed from office in its entirety in January 1998, if a successful vote of censure had been forthcoming from the European Parliament. In the event, the Parliament's two main groups, the Socialist and the European People's Party, were unable to agree on how to handle

---

[120] T Christiansen, 'A maturing bureaucracy: the role of the Commission in the policy process' in J Richardson (ed.) *European Union: Power and Policymaking* (Routledge, 1996) at 81.

[121] Namely the aid to Mediterranean countries (MED), and Leonardo da Vinci programmes.

[122] G. Majone, 'From the Positive to the Regulatory State: Causes and Consequences of Changes in the Mode of Governance' (1997) 17 Journal of Public Policy 139, 146.

[123] Such as the Commission's White Paper on European Governance.

the crisis, and the vote of censure did not materialise. However, the Parliament did insist on the establishment of a committee of independent experts to investigate allegations of fraud, mismanagement and irregularities in the Commission, and the Commission limped on for another two months.[124] This committee delivered its (very critical) report on 15 March 1999,[125] which included the now famous sentence, 'It is becoming difficult to find anyone (in the Commission) who has even the slightest sense of responsibility.'[126] This very quickly provoked the mass resignation of the Commission, although that same Commission in fact returned almost immediately for a further six months until the new one was sworn in[127] in September 1999 with Romano Prodi as its president.[128]

The committee's report was based on six charges of alleged fraud and mismanagement,[129] as well as on charges of nepotism, the most notorious of these being that of Edith Cresson, who had appointed an old friend (and apparently her dentist), M. Berthelot, to a succession of positions for which he seemed particularly unsuited and unqualified.[130] The committee found the Commission to have acted reprehensibly and to be 'responsible for not behaving in accordance with proper standards in public life'.[131] It has been suggested that 'in this sense the work of the committee marks a peculiarly important moment in the continuing construction of the constitution of the European Union',[132] i.e. in the sense of bringing to the fore the issue and nature of responsibility and accountability in the Commission in the public life of the EU. In fact, the notion of responsibility had already been considered, ironically enough by the Santer Commission[133] itself, which had, however, sought to separate policy from administrative responsibility, the latter being, in its

---

[124] The five members of this committee were Pierre Lelong, a former president of the European Court of Auditors; André Middelhoeck, also a former president of the ECA; Inga-Britt Ahlenius, a Swedish auditor; Juan Antonio Carrillo Salcedo, a Spanish international human rights lawyer; and Walter van Gerven, a former Advocate General of the European Court of Justice.

[125] Committee of Independent Experts: *First Report on Allegations of Fraud, Mismanagement and Nepotism in the European Commission.*

[126] Ibid. para. 9.4.25.

[127] This was partly due to uncertainties in EC procedure: although under Article 201 the Parliament could dismiss the entire Commission, and under Article 215 the ECJ could compulsorily retire individual Commissioners, it was unclear what would happen in the event of a mass resignation. In the event, the European Council settled the matter at the Berlin summit, with the result that it returned the old Commission until the new one could be sworn in.

[128] Santer finding work elsewhere, ironically enough as an MEP.

[129] Four of which were particularly significant, namely tourism, aid to Mediterranean countries (MED), ECHO, and Leonardo da Vinci.

[130] As the Committee reported, 'what we have here is a clear-cut case of favouritism. A person whose qualifications did not correspond to the various posts to which he was recruited was nonetheless employed.' Paras. 81.35–6.

[131] At para. 1.6.2. As such the Commission was consciously reflecting the work of the British Nolan Committee on Standards in Public Life, which suggested that public life should be founded on the principles of selflessness, integrity, objectivity, accountability, openness, honesty and leadership. See *First Report of the Committee on Standards in Public Life* Cm 2850 1995 and commentary on it by A Tomkins, *The Constitution after Scott: Government Unwrapped* (Oxford: Clarendon Press, 1998).

[132] A Tomkins, 'Responsibility and Resignation in the European Commission' (1999) 62 MLR 744 at 758.

[133] European Commission, *Sound and Efficient Management 2000.*

view, within the remit of the DGs. Such a notion of the separation of policy and implementation of policy seems undesirable and unworkable if commissioners are to have this much-vaunted sense of responsibility. To enhance this aspect of its first report, the Committee, when it reported for the second time, in September 1999, suggested the establishment of an EU Committee of Standards in Public Life, as well as a complete overhaul of personnel policy.[134]

The Prodi reformation

Institutional reform is obviously a crucial issue for the new Commission. It is also no easy task, for, as has been written, 'The physical and human geography of the Commission...resists change.'[135] Nonetheless, Prodi identified key changes which needed to be made, namely, to the configuration of Commission portfolios and staffing of the DGs; the déménagement of commissioners from their Breydel building into the buildings housing the DGs; and an end to certain national monopolies over key positions (no easy task, in an institution which requires the balancing of the need for multinationalism as against experience and ability).

He set Neil Kinnock, one of the few commissioners to return from the Santer Commission, with the task of heading the new reform portfolio, the Task Force on Administrative reform.[136] Its reform strategy was unveiled in January 2000, in a consultative document[137] which in turn led to the March 2000 White Paper, *Reforming the Commission*. The White Paper set down a three-year timetable, stating, *inter alia*, that, the Commission needed to introduce fewer but better legislative initiatives; that commissioners and senior officers needed to develop a sense of responsibility and to be more responsible for their activities; that the cabinets needed to be reined in; that financial controls needed to be tightened and financial management strengthened; that administrative procedures needed to be reformed.

The new approach has not been without its detractors. Part of the problem lies in disagreement over the nature of the Commission and in the tensions between its different functions, both of animateur and bureaucracy. Part of the problem is caused by differing national perceptions as to its nature. There are many contending models and approaches. Some critics of the approach taken by Prodi and Kinnock see it as a rejection of French national influence which held sway over the Commission since its earliest days as the High Authority. Kinnock has faced particular opposition from the Commission's trade unions, which threatened strike action over his abolition of certain privileges, e.g. of Commission employees' bank transfer arrangements (which allowed them to send up to one–third of their salary home on a very favourable exchange rate) and travel allowances,[138] hardly a cause for which the European public will feel much sympathy. The Prodi/Kinnock reforms do seem set

---

[134] Second Report on Reform of the Commission: *Analysis of current practice and proposals for tackling mismanagement, irregularities and fraud*, 10 September 1999.
[135] K Middlemas, *Orchestrating Europe* at 223.
[136] Which can be found at the specific website: http://europa.eu.int/comm/reform/index_en.htm.
[137] Consultative document, communication from Neil Kinnock 17/18 January 2000 at p iii.
[138] See 'EU staff bow to EU reforms', (*The Guardian*, 1 March 2001).

to be implemented, even if slowly. Reform does not happen quickly in the Commission. It took fifteen years to adapt DG 3 Industry to cope with the internal market.[139]

In spite of improvements, there has been, however, concern that the Commission was still being mismanaged. In December 1999 the European Court of Auditors refused for the fifth year running to approve its accounts because of persistent weaknesses in control of farm subsidies (for which read sums going missing), something about which the Kinnock report was silent. The Kinnock report does, however, raise the right questions, which still have to be answered. These are: what will the Commission's future functions be? What sort of organization must it be to carry them out? How can the demands of efficiency and transparency be reconciled? Nevertheless, given the multinational nature of the Commission it will surely never be the case that it will correspond to a 'neat political and administrative model'.[140]

THE COUNCIL

The Council has been described as 'the most important and probably most misunderstood' of the EU institutions.[141] It is the main political and legislative institution of the European Union and the nearest to what one finds in a conventional international organisation,[142] depending as much on diplomacy and bargaining among representatives of national interest as on collegiate interactions. Nevertheless, it has been contended that, however much realists and intergovernmentalists might aim to portray the Council as standing for the ideal of the nation state, it functions in a more complex way. For example, Wessels has written, 'the Council is not an "interstate body"... but a body at supranational level'.[143]

The Council is based in Brussels (although may hold meetings elsewhere) and is made up of representatives of the member states. Article 203 specifies that: 'The Council shall consist of a representative of each Member State at ministerial level, authorised to commit the government of that member state.' As in the case of Article 211 (which specified the powers of the Commission), Article 202, which sets out those of the Council, does not give a particularly clear account of its functions, stating that the Council shall do the following:

---

[139] Middlemas, *Orchestrating Europe* at 223.

[140] D Dinan, 'The Commission and the Reform Process' in G Edwards and A Pijpers (eds) *The Politics of European treaty reform: The 1996 Intergovernmental Conference and Beyond* (London: Pinter, 1997) at 210.

[141] F Hayes-Renshaw and H Wallace, *The Council of Ministers* (Macmillan, 1997) Introduction.

[142] B Guy Peters, 'Bureaucratic Politics and the Institutions of the European Community' in A Sbragia (ed.) *Euro-Politics* (Washington DC: The Brookings Institution, 1992) at 78; also A Moravscik, 'Preferences and Power in the European Community: A Liberal Intergovernmentalist Approach' (1993) 31 JCMS, 473.

[143] W Wessels, 'The EC Council: The Community's Decision–making Center' in R Keohane and S Hoffmann (eds) *The New European Community: Decision-making and Institutional Change* (Boulder: Westview, 1991).

—ensure the coordination of the general economic policies of the Member States;

—have power to take decisions;

—confer on the Commission...powers for the implementation of the rules which the Council lays down...

However, its main function under the EC treaty, is that listed second under Article 202, to take decisions, i.e. to adopt Community legislation, these days usually acting along with the European Parliament.

The Council now meets over 90 times a year, about every other working day.[144] Unlike the Commission, the Council is not a fixed body, but what has been described as a 'legal fiction,'[145] as its members will vary in accordance with the subject matter of the meeting in question – if agriculture is on the agenda, agricultural ministers will attend, and so on – so that it functions more like a cabinet committee. This means that the Council has been highly fragmented along policy sectors, reinforcing what Petersen and Bomberg[146] have described as 'the disaggregated, sectorised nature of EU decision making'. Its most frequent meetings are those of the General Affairs Council, which is made up of foreign ministers, meeting about fifteen times per year, and deals with foreign and security policy, general institutional and policy matters and whose role is sometimes difficult to distinguish from that of the European Council (see below) as far as general policy and agenda setting is concerned. The Council of Economic and Finance Ministers (ECOFIN) has grown in importance as might be expected, with the implementation of Economic and Monetary Union. It is not always a member of the national government who attends Council meetings; practice varies, depending on the constitutional structure of the member states. The German Lander, insisting on more representation at EU level, sometimes send their minister to represent Germany in the Council, as do Belgian regional ministers.

Article 204 EC refers to the Presidency of the Council, which plays a key role, chairing Council meetings. The Presidency rotates among the member states at six-monthly intervals and has increased in power as the EU has evolved. It sets the agenda for its six-month period, a matter which can be of considerable importance for that state's image and national pride, but a large task for a small country without great resources at hand, especially as the EU expands. Increased use of the codecision procedure has led to greater contact between the Council Presidency and Parliament, as it is the Presidency which represents the Council in formal conciliation committees.

---

[144] D Rometsch and W Wessels, 'The Commission and the Council of Ministers' in G Edwards and D Spence, *The European Commission* (Longman, 1994).

[145] Wessels, 'The EC Council: The Community's Decision-Making Center' in Keohane and Hoffmann op. cit.

[146] J Petersen and E Bomberg, *Decision Making in the European Union* at 34.

OPERATION

Much, or even most, of important Council work will have been done before it reaches the Council ministers themselves, initially in Council working groups[147] made up of national technical experts,[148] of which there are up to about 250. They provide technical and scientific information which the European institutions themselves lack, and they play a significant but little-known role in the Community decision-making process. According to Hayes-Renshaw and Wallace, about 70 per cent of EU legislation is actually decided by these groups,[149] which they describe as 'the backbone of the European system of integration'.[150] Important they may be, but transparent they are not. Their composition can be very difficult to determine and their terms of reference vary, some operating without any terms of reference at all.[151] The European Parliament has no control over how they operate, nor are they open to media comment. Judicial review of any of their actions by the ECJ is not possible. Given that they play such an important role in the EC decision-making process, their lack of openness is problematic to say the least.

Legislative measures are then sent to COREPER (the Committee of Permanent Representatives) whose role is set out in Article 207 EC, as being responsible 'for preparing the work of the Council and for carrying out the tasks assigned to it by the Council...' All Council meetings are prepared by COREPER, which meets very regularly and which is divided into two parts: the deputy permanent representatives (COREPER I) which deal with technical and economic issues, and the permanent representatives (COREPER II), consisting of senior ambassadors, which deal with more political questions. Items which have been agreed by COREPER are classified as 'A points' and are usually formally approved by ministers without discussion. Where COREPER has failed to agree, the matter goes on Part B of the Council agenda and agreement has to be reached in the Council itself. This means that, before a measure reaches the more political level of decision making – the Council itself – at least two levels of officials will have considered it.

From the EEC's earlier days, COREPER was criticised as undermining the role of the Commission by acting in the interests of the member states, but also undermining the role of the Council by pursuing technocratisation.[152] But over time, it seems

---

[147] The Commission will also have members on these groups to protect its position.

[148] The majority of whom are based not in Brussels or Strasbourg but in national capitals: see Rometsch and Wessels, *The European Union and member States: Towards Institutional Fusion?* (Manchester University Press, 1996); V Wright, 'The National co-ordination of European policy-making: negotiating the quagmire' in J Richardson (ed.) *European Union: Power and Policymaking* (Routledge, 1996).

[149] F Hayes-Renshaw and H Wallace, *The Council of Ministers* (Macmillan, 1997) at 15.

[150] Ibid. at 98.

[151] See Van der Knaap, 'Government by Committee: Legal Typology, Quantitative Assessment and Institutional Repercussion of Committees in the EU' in R Pedler and G Schaefer (eds) *Shaping European Law and Policy: The Role of Committees in the Policy process* (EIPA, 1996) at 20; Van Schendelen, 'EC Committees: Influence counts more than legal powers' in Pedler and Schaefer op. cit.; also E Vos, 'The Rise of Committees' (1997) 3 ELJ 212.

[152] A Spinelli, *The Eurocrats* (Baltimore: Johns Hopkins University Press, 1966); E Noel and H Etienne, 'The Permanent Representatives and the "Deepening" of the Communities' (1971) 'Government and Opposition'.

to have become accepted as essential to the workings of the EU, and recently it has become increasingly significant in the context of the second and third pillars of the EU, those of the CFSP and PJCC, in which the Commission has a very limited role and the Council functions as chief decision maker without the Parliament.

COREPER is an interesting and slightly paradoxical institution. As representatives of the member states, COREPER might be supposed to put forward their national dimension. The delegations, however, vary from state to state, and while 'some are microcosms of national administrations' this is not so with all.[153] And yet, as most of its members serve for a long time in Brussels, they develop a communitarian dimension, and what has been described as 'a collective rationality which transcends individual, instrumental rationality'.[154] So, for example, they may set the agenda for Council meetings in such a way as to minimise national conflicts.

COREPER works along with the Council Secretariat-General, based in Brussels, which provides the Council with administrative support.[155] The Secretariat is small (comprising approximately 2,500 officials). It plays a key role in the drafting of texts, most particularly working out the content and wording of compromises, as well as preparing all official documents for IGCs and the Presidency Conclusions after European summits: it can provide crucial support for the Presidency, especially if the Presidency is held by a small country. In addition to drafting, the Secretariat also ensures the translation of meeting documents and provides legal advice for the Council and its Committees. Additionally, it administers the Council budget. Although a small body, the Secretariat-General has been described as 'an unsung heavyweight in EU decision-making'.[156] Since 1952 only five individuals have held the post of Secretary-General itself,[157] the most recent being Javier Solana (formerly Secretary-General of NATO from 1995–9[158]) in office since October 1999 for five years, a position which has been augmented by the Treaty of Amsterdam to include the role of High Representative of the Common Foreign and Security Policy (and now also Secretary-General of the Western European Union). Dr Solana's appointment was a high profile affair, drawing attention to the EU's growing role in defence and security matters – a recent indication of Solana's approach was his criticism of EU foreign policy for being too bureaucratic and lacking in consistency.[159] On account of the pressures of the CFSP role, Dr Solana is assisted by a Deputy Secretary-General, Pierre Bossieu, who is responsible for the running of the General Secretariat and whose appointment caused some concern, on the grounds that he has not shown himself to be a high priest of transparency.[160]

---

[153] G Edwards, 'National sovereignty vs integration : The Council of Ministers' in J Richardson (ed.) *European Union: Power and Policy Making* at 137.

[154] J Lewis, 'Is the "Hard Bargaining" Image of the Council Misleading? The Committee of Permanent Representatives and the Local Elections Directive' (1998) JCMS 479.

[155] Article 207 (2) EC.

[156] Petersen and Bomberg op. cit. at 36.

[157] Appointed by the Council.

[158] http://ue.eu.int/solana/home.asp.

[159] 'Solana slates foreign policy' (*The Guardian* 23 January 2001).

[160] Described recently as an 'opponent of institutional openness' by D Dinan, 'Governance and Institutions 2000: Edging Towards Enlargement' (2001) 39 JCMS 25 at 37.

Therefore a key, and interesting, feature of the Council is the fact that most of those involved in the making of legislation are not ministers but rather national officials and technocrats whose views may sometimes be influenced by political judgement. As Wessels writes, 'each Council is at the top of a pyramid...equivalent to what is known in the States as an "iron triangle"',[161] – this may well give the impression of the Council as an institution which spends much of its time negotiating within itself. Although these 'sub' bureaucracies may have recently grown in number and significance, recognition of the importance of bureaucratic processes in the EU is not new: it was recognised by Haas some while ago.[162] What is also revealed by scrutiny of Council decision-making operations is that Community law emerges as a result of 'networks': horizontal ties between actors, operating within complex relations.[163] Haas characterised the EEC as a 'semi-lattice', continuing, 'There is a clear centre of authorisation for some activities and decisions but not for all. Lines of authority duplicate and overlap, functions are performed in fragments by many subsystems; sometimes authority flows sideways and upwards, at other times the flow is downward.'[164] These processes raise questions as to the identity of the Council of Ministers. Such practices have been increased by the proliferation of legislation procedures since Haas was writing, forcing the Council, in the context of the cooperation and codecision procedures, to forge a variety of coalitions with the Parliament in the interests of extra leverage within the Council of Ministers. All of these are still processes which are too little discussed and understood.

Voting

There are a variety of voting procedures in the Council which inevitably affect the way legislation is structured and pursued. Voting procedures in the Council differ according to the treaty article on which the measure in question is based. Some require unanimity, others a majority of votes. If the treaty article does not specify a particular majority then the act may be adopted by a majority of its members (Article 205(1)). But in most cases of majority voting, the treaty requires the Council to act by a qualified majority (QMV) whereby the votes of each member state are weighted reflecting the population but in a way that favours states with smaller populations. An increase in QMV has changed the role of the Council and, so it would seem, the entire Community, having shifted the policymaking process in the EU from that of a typical intergovernmental organisation towards something more like the policy-making and coalition-forming of parliamentary democracy. Thus, much Community law-making in the Council relies on coalition-building rather than on national vetoes. QMV has become more and more essential as the EU has become larger and larger: without it there would be paralysis.

---

[161] W Wessels, 'The EC Council' in Keohane and Hoffmann op. cit. at 140.
[162] E Haas, *Functionalism and International Organisations* (Stanford University Press, 1964).
[163] See references at fn 28.
[164] E Haas, 'Is there a Hole in the Whole? Knowledge, Technology, Interdependence and the Construction of International Regimes' (1975) 29 IO 827 at 856.

With successive amendments and enlargements the size of the qualified majority has varied from 67 per cent (when there were six member states) to 58 per cent with fifteen. However, it has always represented a large majority in terms of the population of any member states supporting the decision, and has required the support of at least half of the member states. The process has been designed so that the four largest states (France, Germany, UK, Italy) could not take decisions themselves, but also to preclude action only by the smaller states, but in this latter aim it has been less successful. After the Treaty of Amsterdam a group of member states could form a 'blocking majority' if they could muster at least 26 votes out of a total of 87 votes (the allocation of votes being set out in the treaty at Article 205(2)). However, this system was thought to be unsatisfactory, as it tended to privilege the smaller states (raising questions for the future in the case of EU enlargement, with additional small members whose votes might be at the expense of those with large populations). Therefore, the Treaty of Nice states that the system of decision by qualified majority will be modified. But this will take effect in phases, depending on future waves of enlargement, and in any case from 1 January 2005.[165]

Partly to compensate those member states which gave up the future possibility of nominating a second member of the Commission, the Treaty of Nice changes the number of votes allocated to each member state, as well as the formula for achieving a qualified majority. It imposes what is in effect a threefold majority requirement. In addition to a qualified majority of votes (between approximately 71 per cent and 74 per cent of votes, depending on the actual number of member states) and the requirement that a majority of member states should be in favour of the decision, it also introduces the so-called 'demographic safety net' requirement: 62 per cent of the population of the Union.[166] However, this is hardly a very transparent system. As a European Parliament notice points out,[167] 'the very reverse of the objective of simplifying decision-making by qualified majority voting was achieved'. One is reminded of Condorcet's attempt to apply advanced mathematics to voting in legislative bodies.[168]

However, this Byzantine practice of QMV does not perhaps accurately reflect reality in any case. This is partly because voting in the Council has been quite rare in practice, as many matters will already have been agreed by COREPER, and partly because the Council tries to secure a consensus wherever possible (although this is becoming more and more difficult as the EU increases in size). Votes are often not taken explicitly, but rather in one of the following two forms: first, implicitly, by silence, whereby no one speaks against the measure and so it is passed; and secondly,

---

[165] See Article 3 Protocol to the Treaty of Nice on the Enlargement of the European Union.

[166] Which should mean that Germany, France and Britain, with the required 62 per cent of the EU's population, could then block virtually anything they wanted: see Ian Black, 'How the Big Powers won Big Benefits' (*The Guardian* 12 December 2000).

[167] European Parliament Notice 'Overview of the Results of the Intergovernmental Conference' CM/427130 EN.doc at 2

[168] Condorcet, *Sur les élections* (Paris: Fayard, 1986).

by positive confirmation, whereby the President says 'I see the conditions for a decision are fulfilled'.[169]

Furthermore, after the crisis in the Community in 1965, following France's withdrawal from EEC matters, the member states had agreed on the 'Luxembourg Compromise' or Accords, whereby, if 'very important interests' of one or more of the states were at stake, the members of the Council would try within a reasonable time to find a solution acceptable to all of them 'while respecting all of their mutual interests and those of the Community, in accordance with those of Article 2 of the treaty'.[170] The Luxembourg Accords, whose legal status has always been unclear, but which might be considered some sort of constitutional 'convention,' did not explicitly renounce the principle of majority voting, but appeared to create a veto. This was certainly considered to be the case by the British government on its accession to the EEC, although sometimes, but rarely, decisions were adopted against the wishes of a state, such as in May 1982 when farm prices were determined for the first time by a qualified majority vote.[171] However, its status since the signing of the SEA has certainly been problematic. Although its continued efficacy has been important for realists and eurosceptics, it would seem to be incompatible with QMV, by which a government may be outvoted whatever its national parliamentary position. The Luxembourg Compromise was never accepted by the Commission or the ECJ, which in 1986 stated that 'the rules regarding the manner in which Community institutions arrive at their decisions are laid down in the Treaty and are not at the disposal of the member States or the Institutions themselves'.[172] In any case, the member states have found a variety of other means by which they can impede a measure, as the UK showed at Maastricht, and the Danes shortly after with their original 'no' vote in the Maastricht referendum.

One way in which Council business functioned in the shadow of the veto was through the concluding of 'package deals,' which gave all parties some benefits, and thus promoted a consensus (usually in the context of nightlong sessions, introducing some drama – and media attention – to Council meetings). Ever since the Single European Act introduced QMV for a great number of measures, a practice which has increased with successive treaty amendments since then, the status of the Luxembourg Compromise has itself been compromised. In 1987,[173] the Council amended its rules of procedure to allow for the opening of a voting procedure, provided that the majority of the Council's members so decide. In practice, the Council does not take a formal vote on many matters as, already mentioned, COREPER and the working parties have done much of the agreement.

---

[169] Wessels, 'The EC Council' in Keohane and Hoffmann op. cit. 147
[170] The Luxembourg Compromise Part B s1 (1966) 3 Bull. CE 10. Also see W Nicol, 'The Luxembourg Compromise' (1984) 23 JCMS 35; A Teasdale, 'The Life and Death of the Luxembourg Compromise' (1993) 31 JCMS 567.
[171] Vasey, 'Decision making in the agricultural council and the Luxembourg compromise' (1988) 25 CMLRev 725.
[172] Case 68/86 *UK v Council* [1988] ECR 855.
[173] Amendment to Council rules of procedure of 20 July 1987 [1987] OJ L291/27.

OTHER FUNCTIONS

The Council is not restricted to legislating. Its other functions under Article 202 have already been mentioned, which may be summarised as follows. It coordinates the economic policies of the member states, by means of non-binding measures (although it may impose sanctions in this context). It also confers powers on the Commission to implement Community legislation, a feature discussed in the previous section. Additionally, the Council carries out important functions with regard to other EU institutions and bodies. It appoints members of the Court of Auditors and may alter the members of the Commission and ECJ (Article 213(1) and Articles 221 and 222). It also exercises some control over the Commission, in that it can ask it to carry out studies and make proposals (Article 208) and participates in the Commission implementation of the budget. The European Central Bank must also present it with an annual report (Article 113(3)).

The Council plays a more generally important role under the other two pillars of EU, overshadowing the Parliament and Commission in these contexts. It takes the decisions necessary for defining and implementing the common foreign and security policy on the basis of general guidelines established by the European Council. It also coordinates the activities of the member states and adopts measures in the field of police and judicial cooperation in criminal matters. These pillars are much more intergovernmental in nature, and the transfer of matters previously dealt with at national level to an intergovernmental body, without much scrutiny from any parliament, will be discussed in the next chapter.

REFLECTIONS ON THE COUNCIL

The Council is very complex in its operations. It is a paradoxical institution, difficult to characterise, partly because of many inherent tensions in the way it operates. So, for example, it is both supranational and intergovernmental. The ministers who sit in the Council are leading political figures in their own countries and considerations of national politics may well motivate their behaviour. On the other hand, the Council appears more supranational than a body motivated purely by national self-interests. As early as 1958, Ernst Haas mused over why the Council of the ECSC appeared different from other international organisations, such as the OEEC (later OECD) and why such an intergovernmental body as the Council should produce decisions geared towards integration at the expense of national sovereignty. He found some explanation in the concept of 'engagement' whereby:

> if parties to a conference enjoy specific and well-articulated ends of participation, if they identify themselves completely with procedures and codes within which their decisions are made, they consider themselves completely 'engaged' by the results even if they do not fully concur with them.[174]

---

[174] E Haas, *The Uniting of Europe* (Stanford University Press, 1958) at 522.

The Council has both European and national features – COREPER perfectly illustrating these dimensions, being charged with feeding the Council national views and yet also representing EU back to the member states. The Council has been described as always looking 'Janus-like'[175] to both the member states and to the Commission, the balance of its relations with both of these changing over the years. More recently its relations with the Parliament have become increasingly important and complex, as the Parliament has become more ambitious within the Community legislation process.

Furthermore, the Council is required to operate both as executive and legislature, unlike the member states where these functions are usually separated. It also operates both as a forum for negotiating and decision-making. Yet another dimension is added by the fact that it is both general and sectoral, its meetings ranging from the large policy setting agendas of the General Affairs Council, to the highly specialised sectoral councils. Its decision-making is further fragmented by the different decision-making processes which operate across the three pillars of the EU. Yet, as well as being fragmented across sectoral lines, it suffers from a patchwork of vertical processes, caused by the inputs of the working parties and COREPER to the legislative process. This has prompted van Schendelen to argue that the legal status of the Council is not in accordance with its actual status,[176] an observation which accords with the discussion in the introduction to this chapter – that the actual workings of the EU do not accord with its formal institutional (or 'constitutional') structure. What exactly is the Council? The term 'Council' is applied to meetings at ministerial level, but should it also be applied to meetings at other levels, such as the Council working groups and COREPER? The Council seems somewhat contradictory about its own status, asserting in one recent case[177] that it was a single body comprising all its compositions, working groups and committees, and yet insisting (unsuccessfully) in another[178] that the Council Presidency was a separate institution. Such complexity has been characterised as 'schizophrenic' by recent commentators.[179]

Indeed, the problem of the fragmented nature of EEC decision-making already received attention in the 1970s. It was proposed in 1977 that the Foreign Affairs ministers in the General Affairs Council should exercise overall control over Council business (the so-called 'La Marlia' procedure) but this did not happen, partly as other ministers (especially finance ministers) dislike being 'managed' by foreign ministers. This idea has however been revived recently.[180] The so-called 'Three Wise Men' report of 1978 also considered the growing problem of fragmented decision-making in the Council and made some suggestions which were not acted upon.[181] However, with the prospect of further enlargement, the streamlining of procedures in the Council has become inevitable.

---

[175] F Hayes-Renshaw and H Wallace, *The Council of Ministers* (Macmillan, 1997) Introduction.

[176] Van Schendelen, 'The Council Decides: Does the Council Decide? (1996) 34 JCMS 531.

[177] Case T 14/98 *Hautala v Council* [1999] ECR II 2489.

[178] Report of the Ombudsman for 1997 pp 176 *et seq.*: application by Tony Bunyan for access to documents (Complaint 1054/25.11.96, *Statewatch v Commission*).

[179] Curtin and Dekker, 'The EU as a Layered International Organisation: Institutional Unity in Disguise' in Craig and de Burca, *The Evolution of EU Law* (OUP, 1999).

[180] See below.

[181] Committee of Three Report 1979 at 92: see also Bull EC 11-1979 1.5.2. for summary of report.

Reform

The Commission is not the only EU institution to require reform. If the Council is to operate effectively in the future, with new member states, considerable changes will have to be made. Indeed, even if the EU were not to increase in size, the Council's working methods would probably have to change.[182] The problems it faces may be characterised as those of productivity, efficiency and legitimacy.[183]

The Council has shown that it can be reasonably productive and efficient on occasion. During the 1992 initiative it made an impressive response to the Commission's ambitious programme of legislation for completing the internal market. It also acted swiftly on the occasion of the accession of the former East German Lander to the EU. Generally, however, it takes an average of eighteen months between a Commission proposal and a final Council decision on the matter. On some occasions it proceeds painfully slowly, as in its response to the GATT Uruguay round. Nor was its record of action during the Balkan crisis impressive.

One problematic factor is the huge variety of complex legislation proceedings: by 1995 there were some 23 different combinations of procedures for the European Parliament and Council of Ministers,[184] with conciliation procedures which sometimes involve meetings with up to 140 Parliamentarians.[185] Sometimes this complexity is due to the need for arrangements for decision-making in areas in which not all member states participate, due to opt-outs and closer cooperation provisions adding to the flexibility of the integration process.

The quality of the Council's output is not always impressive. Scharpf[186] suggests this is because of a 'joint-decision trap' which occurs if two or more levels of government have to cooperate, thus resulting in decisions which are not optimal. This has certainly been the case in the EU, although it is admittedly difficult to imagine how else the multinational EU might function.

How might procedures be improved? The reform of Community institutions seems to have been a perennial theme in European integration, in the case of the Council usually involving recommendations that COREPER, the Secretariat and the Presidency make a firmer job of coordination and management, rather than any more radical proposals. The Trumpf-Piris report of March 1999 prepared the way for 'An Effective Council for an Enlarged Union' – a series of recommendations approved by the Helsinki European Council of December 1999. One of these recommendations was to strengthen the coordinating role of the General Affairs

---

[182] This has also been the view of the European Parliament, which adopted the Bourlange Report of 1999, calling for a radical overhaul of the Council.

[183] Wessels, 'The EC Council' in Keohane and Hoffmann op. cit. at 149.

[184] This was somewhat simplified after Amsterdam. There has also been the requirement to use all languages in the legislation process, despite the cost of this. Some countries, namely Germany and Spain, have insisted on using their languages in other situations, putting the emphasis on national identity and advantage, (Dinan, 'Governance and Institutions 2000' (2001) 39 JCMS 25 at 37.)

[185] Although this is not necessarily a result of the wishes of the Parliament but rather of the Council.

[186] F Scharpf, 'The Joint Decision Trap: Lessons from German Federalism and European Integration' (1988) 66 Public Administration 239; also Scharpf, *Governance in Europe: Effective and Democratic?* (OUP, 1999).

Council, as well as proposing that the number of Council 'formations' should be reduced to a maximum of fifteen, in order to improve the coherence and consistency of the Council's work,[187] a recommendation that had already been made twenty years previously to no avail. Such reorganisation might reduce the effects of what is called 'functional differentiation', namely that the different compositions of the Councils contribute to the complexity of European governance.

The Helsinki conclusions also recommended that certain steps should be taken to render the codecision procedure more effective and that the Council should propose changes to improve it. However, some of the proposals seem banal in the extreme, for example operational recommendation 25, the concluding sentence of which reads: 'The Presidency and the incoming Presidency will take all the necessary steps to ensure a smooth transition from one Presidency to the next', hardly the sort of proposal which will revolutionise the way the EU operates. But reforming the Council's working methods is crucial. As Dinan suggests, 'Although not as well publicised as the Prodi reformation, in many respects Council reform is more consequential for the successful functioning of the EU.'[188]

Legitimacy

However, as with the Commission, the concern is not only with effectiveness (i.e. productivity and efficiency) but also legitimacy. There are real concerns as to the Council's actual legitimacy, given its key role in the EU decision-making process. Unlike the Commission, most of the Council members are elected, but this is indirect, as, unlike EP members, they are elected to **national** office, on a national rather than an EU agenda, and, as such, they have been likened to 'assemblies of sovereign entities like a conclave of medieval kings, each secure in his divine right'.[189] The Council seems not to be accountable to any other body, although it increasingly reports to the European Parliament. The COREPER network also diffuses responsibility as it is controlled neither by the European Parliament nor by national parliaments. Any accountability COREPER may have is not to any EU body but to national parliaments and electorates. This may erode their sense of responsibility for EU matters and any sense of collectivity which the Council may possess. It also ensures that national interest-based bargaining will predominate.

A second problem, which can contribute to the undermining of legitimacy, lies in the Council's lack of transparency.[190] Liberal democratic theories of governance assume that the legislation process should be subject to transparency and scrutiny and this is not the case within the Council, which on the whole still tends to legislate in secret. Indeed, a critical feature of the Council is the secrecy with which its meetings take place. These are not public, with the exception of the six-monthly policy debates on the forthcoming work programme of the presidency, or the exceptional case in which the

---

[187] See for a summary http://ue.eu.int/en/info/main8.htm.
[188] Dinan, 'Governance and Institutions 2000' at 36.
[189] Middlemas, *Orchestrating Europe* at 274.
[190] Transparency is discussed generally in Chapter 3.

Council decides to hold a meeting in public by unanimous vote.[191] However, according to Article 207(3) EC, where the Council acts in a legislative capacity it must publish the results of votes. The Council has made efforts since Maastricht to improve its record of openness, by holding some open sessions, allowing more access to documents and insisting on more clearly drafted documents; all of these featured in the Helsinki Council conclusions in the sections on transparency, which provided, for example, that 'At least one public Council debate should be held on important **legislative** proposals' and also further recommendations to 'ensure more interesting public debates'. Although these are desirable recommendations, its seems unlikely that they will make a huge difference to the way the Council conducts its affairs.

A lack of transparency also pervades its dealings with other institutions, creating an impression of deals such as inter-institutional agreements and the Conciliation procedure (discussed in Chapter 3) with the Parliament being hammered out in smoke-filled rooms. This is problematic given its major law-making role within the EU, especially given that the Council cannot be rendered accountable or dismissed.

On the other hand, much of what the Council does in its meetings takes the form of negotiating rather than legislating, and the securing of difficult and tense agreements: operations which we would not necessarily expect to be open at national government level. Perhaps we should not be too quick to condemn. If the Council fails to meet ideal targets of efficiency, effectiveness and legitimacy, then so do national governments. However, the fact that an undesirable practice occurs elsewhere does not make it acceptable in the context of the Council. Indeed, the lack of effectivity on the part of European citizens makes it all the more necessary for European institutions to strive to be more open, approachable and meaningful to the population of Europe, and provides food for thought for the Commission's work on governance as well as for the debate on the future of the Union.

THE PARLIAMENT

The evolution of the European Parliament tells us quite a lot about the development of the EC. Indeed, over the past fifteen years the Parliament has changed in status from its original function of consultative assembly (and sometimes not even that, given that there was no requirement at all to consult it on some matters) to something more like a traditional legislative body. However, the Parliament has not always enjoyed great respect; one commentary proceeds as follows: 'The Parliament suffers from its hapless image as a powerless, money wasting "talking shop", as well as from its impossible domestic arrangements,' continuing 'Even the Parliament's staunchest supporters concede that Parliament attracts incompetents and party hacks deemed unsuitable for national office, as well as committed and talented parliamentarians.'[192] So, if the Parliament is supposed to be the open, democratic face of the EU, it has also suffered from an image problem.

---

[191] Council Rules of Procedure Articles 4(1) and (2).

[192] J Petersen and E Bomberg, *Decision-Making in the European Union* (Macmillan, 1999) at 43.

COMPOSITION AND ORGANISATION

Since the Treaty of Nice, according to Article 189 EC, the number of members of Parliament 'shall not exceed 732' (although this figure may be exceeded during a transitional period on the accession of new members). Article 190(2) sets out the number of representatives per member state.[193] This allocation has not been particularly satisfactory in the past (with Luxembourg being grossly over-represented for its small population). The Treaty of Nice seems to have created further problems, with some future members, for example the Czech Republic and Hungary, being allocated seats contrary to the principle of equality and democracy, as they have been allocated fewer seats than other present members of smaller populations.[194] (This unsatisfactory allocation may result from the necessary constraints of EU evolution by treaty making, i.e. it was perhaps the result of too many overnight sessions which tried to provide some acceptable last minute *ad hoc* compensation for the weighting adopted for votes in the Council.)[195]

Members of the European Parliament lead a very peripatetic existence, for (not particularly rational) historical reasons.[196] They must commute continually between their national constituencies, Strasbourg (where the plenary sessions are held for one week every month), Brussels (where the Parliamentary committees meet and also some plenaries) and Luxembourg (where much of the Parliament's secretariat is housed). This inevitably increases the Parliament's running costs, as well as creating a schizophrenic working environment. On the other hand, the location of its main building in Strasbourg perhaps somewhat marginalises it, far away from those it is supposed to supervise and off the main arteries of the European transport system.[197] In fact, these locations were not confirmed until the early 1990s,[198] but the blame for the Parliament's peripatetic existence must lie with France, Belgium and Luxembourg, each acting out of national self-interest, rather than the Parliament itself.

---

[193] But Article 2, Protocol on the Enlargement of the EU, states that as from 1 January 2004 Article 190(2) will be replaced by a new allocation set out in Article 2 of the Protocol.

[194] See Parliament: 'Overview of the results of the Intergovernmental Conference', CM/427130 EN. doc at 4. See Declaration 20 on Enlargement of the European Union, which sets out the distribution of seats in the European Parliament for a union of 27 states.

[195] Ibid.

[196] This is because the three communities, the ECSC, the EEC and the Euratom, were not set up at the same time. The ECSC was founded in Luxembourg in 1952 and the latter two established mainly in Brussels in 1958. Strasbourg became first the seat of the Council of Europe and then in 1952 of the European Parliament, as a symbol of Franco-German reconciliation. Notwithstanding, this inconvenient arrangement, the Amsterdam Treaty formalised the location of the institutions in these three places.

[197] Shirley Williams, 'Sovereignty and Accountability in the European Community' in Keohane and Hoffmann op. cit. at 155.

[198] In Cases 258/85 and 51/86 *France v European Parliament* [1988] ECR 4821, the ECJ upheld the Parliament's decision to build a debating chamber in Brussels but stated that it could hold plenary sessions out of Strasbourg only exceptionally. Then the Edinburgh European Council decision of December 1992 established Strasbourg as the Parliament's seat, in which twelve monthly sessions were to be held, with additional plenary sessions and committee meetings in Brussels; see also Case C-245/95 *France v European Parliament* [1997] ECR I-5215.

In the Chamber, MEPs sit in political groups not national delegations. Parliament currently has eight political groups, plus some 'non-attached' MEPs.[199] Thus, its basic organisation is partisan and supranational. In the 1999 elections, the PES (the European Socialist Party) was displaced as the largest party for the first time since direct elections in 1979. During those twenty years, the two largest parties (the PES along with the conservative European People's Party) had a joint management committee, which (arguably) monopolised parliamentary affairs. This was not renewed after the PES losses of 1999 but it remains to be seen whether its loss will transform the way Parliamentary business is done.

The popular perception is that MEPs do not have a very public face, and most do not, but there have been, and are, some well-known figures. Presidents of the Commission, such as Jacques Delors and Gaston Thorn, have been drawn from former European Parliamentarians, or, such as Jacques Santer, have chosen to become MEPs (perhaps a rather curious choice on his part). There are also those who are well-known nationally such as Brandt, Spinelli or Giscard d'Estaing. Thus, one way or another, the Parliament has been able to draw upon some formidable expertise.

Members of the European Parliament have been directly elected since 1979[200] and are now (under a system first used in the 1999 elections) elected under a system of proportional representation (Article 190). MEPs are elected for a term of five years (Article 190). But electoral turnout has not been particularly good, seemingly falling every year,[201] an example of what Alexander Hamilton described as 'the alarming indifference discoverable in the exercise of so valuable a privilege as voting'.[202] This is a disappointing situation for European democracy, and, although parties produce 'European' manifestos, elections are still fought largely along national lines. A Commission proposal of January 2001, intended to subsidise those European political parties dedicated to building a 'European political consciousness', seems to have, for the time being at least, failed.[203] Even the Parliament's stand against the Commission in 1999 apparently failed to impress the public, as electoral turnout continued to decrease (falling to as low as 2 per cent in some areas of the UK). Perhaps this was partly due to the fact that the public profile of MEPs themselves has not been so good, suffering from perceptions of gravy trains and fiddled expenses. Until recently MEPs received the same parliamentary salary as members

---

[199] Political groups as at September 1999 (information may be found at http://www.europarl.eu.int/presentation/default_en.htm at 7):
EPP-ED: Group of the European People's Party and European Democrats; PES: Group of the Party of European Socialists; ELDR: Group of the European Liberal Democratic and reformist party; Greens/EFA: Group of the Greens/European Free Alliance; EUL/NGL: Confederal Group of the European United left/Nordic left; UEN: Group of the Union for a Europe of Nations; EDD: Europe of Democracies and Diversities Group; TDI: Technical Group of Independent members – mixed Group.

[200] Since the 1960s the Parliament had made repeated requests for direct elections, but had to put up with delegates from national Parliaments with a dual mandate.

[201] It fell from 56.8 per cent in 1994 to 49.9 per cent in 1999.

[202] Alexander Hamilton, *The Federalist Papers* (New York: New England Library, 1961).

[203] In order to qualify for the funds the parties had to be part of a political grouping on the Parliament that has seats in at least three states. This proposal was postponed after the Commission failed to satisfy the transparency concerns of the European Court of Auditors.

of their national parliament (which varies greatly from country to country) increased by the European Parliament by a sum to cover their costs: a system open to abuse.[204] However, provision was made by the Amsterdam treaty for a common statute for all members to remove the disparities in salary between MEPs as well as ensuring greater transparency. However, in May 1999 the Parliament rejected the Council's draft statute, on the basis that they did not wish to be taxed at variable national levels – an attitude which hardly improved its public image.[205] At time of writing the statute has not been adopted, although the Treaty of Nice inserted a new paragraph into Article 191, giving the Council the power to adopt a regulation 'governing political parties at European level and in particular the rules regarding their funding'. The Parliament is, however, concerned about its public image. A group of MEPs recently launched a campaign to clean up the Parliament, realising that MEPs had fallen into disrepute over a salaries and expenses system that was out of date, untransparent and in urgent need of an overhaul.[206]

On a possibly more positive note, MEPs would seem to have greater individual independence than their national counterparts. They suffer less pressure from strict voting disciplines, given that there is no executive which has to be backed. Under the Parliament's Rules of Procedure they vote on an individual basis and do not receive a binding mandate. Due to the relative weakness of the political leadership structure it is difficult to sanction rebel members while in office. MEPs can thus perhaps provide an important counter-weight to the Council in the legislative process, prompted by more independent considerations than the sometimes short-term ones of government ministers. Although the individual priorities of MEPs have quite an impact on how they fulfil their functions – some spend much time in the plenaries, others in committee or with their group – differences in national political culture also play a part. Members from northern European countries seem more willing to spend time on the details of technical legislation and, apparently, British members put more of an emphasis on question time.[207]

According to Article 197, members of the Parliament elect (by an absolute majority of votes cast) a President, who has the formal duties of directing its activities, presiding over sittings (although this function is often delegated), representing Parliament in external relations, ceremonial occasions and administrative, legal and financial matters. Fourteen Vice Presidents are also elected,[208] and the Presidents and Vice Presidents together form the Parliamentary bureau. The President also signs (or refuses to sign) the Community budget. Like members of the Commission,

---

[204] At time of writing, the Austrian MEPs are the best paid with around £70,000 pa and the Spanish the worst with around £29,000.

[205] In 2000 an independent report was submitted to the Parliament recommending that all MEPs should be paid c £57,000 but should adhere to a system that permitted reimbursement of only those costs actually incurred. At time of writing, talks had broken down, but the aim was to introduce a new statute by 2004, the date of the next parliamentary elections.

[206] Ian Black, 'Euro group calls on MEPs to reform' (*The Guardian*, 15 March 2001).

[207] F Jacobs, R Corbett and M Shackleton, *The European Parliament* (Harper, 2000, 4th edn).

[208] European Parliament Rules of Procedure, Rule 19.

the President is assisted by a **cabinet** or personal private office. Some past Presidents have been high profile figures, even at a time when the Parliament was not a high profile institution: the first President of the Common Assembly of the ECSC was Paul-Henri Spaak of Belgium, and the first President of Parliament in 1958 Robert Schuman of France. The Parliament's current President is Patrick Cox, in office since January 2002.

Most of the European Parliament's work is done in twenty standing committees, which prepare the work of the Parliamentary plenary sessions and play an important part in both the legislative and democratic accountability roles of the Parliament (see below). The remit of these committees was altered after the Amsterdam Treaty to provide a better fit with the EU's structure. Members are usually assigned to a committee for a five-year term of office and can develop considerable expertise during this time. Committees meet in Brussels so they can more easily oversee the work of the Commission and Council – although this in turn leads to further segmentation and a symbiotic working with the DGs – proliferating the patterned nature of the EU's decision-making process.

The Parliament's work is organised by a Secretariat, headed by the Secretary-General, with a permanent staff of c 3,500. In addition to the Secretariat there are political group staff and the members' assistants. A considerable amount of the staff work in interpretation and translation and the constraints of multilinguism impose severe delays on the Parliament's operations. They also constrain comprehension and spontaneity in Parliamentary business, of whatever kind. Of course this problem is not unique to the Parliament, but it does constrain the creation of a deliberative democracy, and possibly the mutual dialogue and understanding which contribute to the creation of European citizenship and constitutionalism. One author commented, 'The indirect irony or criticisms of an Italian member may well be completely lost in interpretation whereas the directness of a Dutch or Danish member may only seem like rudeness.'[209] On the other hand, the needs of translation may have a favourable effect on working hours: if committee meetings have to proceed beyond 6.30, they must do so without translation or interpretation.

FUNCTIONS AND POWERS

All Parliaments fulfil two basic roles: passing legislation and holding the executive accountable. The European Parliament fulfils these by exercising three main powers: to legislate; those relating to the Community budget; and its supervision of the executive.[210]

---

[209] Jacobs, Corbett and Shackleton, op. cit. at 37.
[210] Cf. M Westlake, 'The European Parliament's Emerging Powers of Appointment' (1998) 36 JCMS 431.

Legislative power

The Parliament's place in the Community legislation process has grown considerably over the years. At first, under the original Treaty of Rome, the Parliament had only a right to be consulted on some areas of EEC legislation. (However, it managed to make effective use of this, establishing a right to intervene before the ECJ, when it had no formal *locus standi* rights.)[211] Successive Treaty amendments improved the Parliament's position. The Single European Act of 1986 greatly extended the range of matters over which it had to be consulted, as well as introducing the cooperation procedure, which gave it an effective role along with the Council in the Community legislation process. The Maastricht Treaty introduced the Parliament's right of co-decision under Article 251, giving the Parliament a significant right to veto legislation. It is now the most usual EC legislative procedure, putting the Parliament and Council on an equal footing, leading to the adoption of joint acts by them. The codecision procedure now applies in legislation concerning the free movement of workers, creation of the internal market, research and technological development, the environment, consumer protection, education, culture and health.[212] Thus, the proportion of policy areas in which the Parliament is not involved has declined from 72 per cent of the original EEC treaty to 37 per cent of the post-Nice EC.[213] However, as Petersen and Bomberg comment, the codecision procedure has exposed the Parliament's weakness in dealing with highly technical matters.[214] The Parliament lacks, say, the resources of the US Congress. On the other hand, a large number of lobbyists have turned their attention to the European Parliament since 1986, especially in the fields of agriculture and pharmaceuticals. Strasbourg is now as much subject to lobbying as Brussels.

However, successive treaty amendments have not prevented the Parliament from playing a subordinate role in certain areas of EU business. It continues to enjoy only consultation rights in the field of agriculture, with no formal consultation rights under the Common Commercial Policy.[215] The tripartite pillar structure continues, too, to place barriers to the Parliament's influence, with the Parliament playing a much smaller, almost negligible, role in the non-EC pillars.

The Parliament also has no independent right of legislative initiative, which is still the preserve of the Commission. During the negotiations leading to the Single European Act, the Parliament made the case, unsuccessfully, for such a right. The Commission opposed this strongly on the basis that its sole right of initiative was a fundamental element of the constitutional balance of the EU (reasons given for this have related to the possible short-termism of the Council of Ministers, and the sug-

---

[211] Cases 138/79 *Roquette* [1980] ECR 3333 and 139/79 *Maizena v Council* [1980] ECR 3933, in which Parliament got a Council Regulation annulled on the basis that, although the Council had sought the Parliament's opinion, it had gone ahead impatiently and passed the Regulation before the Parliament's Opinion was obtained.

[212] This procedure has also increased the importance of the Parliament's sectoral committees, especially those of the rapporteurs (namely the member who drafts a report on the proposal under consideration). This report will be discussed both in committee and in plenary.

[213] European Parliament, 'Co-Governing After Maastricht' Working Paper POLI 104/rev EN. at 5.

[214] Petersen and Bomberg, *Decision-Making in the European Community* at 44.

[215] Except for the Parliament's right to be consulted regarding an extension of the scope of the CCP to international agreements concerning services: Article 133(7) post-Nice.

gestion that the Parliament is not yet sufficiently developed to present its own initiatives). The Parliament no longer calls for such a power, but since Maastricht it has had the power (now Article 192), similar to that of the Council under Article 208, to request legislative initiatives on the part of the Commission, although it has so far used this right sparingly.

The Parliament's budgetary powers

'The power of the purse has historically been the central lever for the legislative acquisition of power.'[216] The Parliament has quite significant powers in this area. It adopts the EU's budget for the following year every December.[217] As a result of the two budgetary treaties of 1970 and 1975, the Parliament exercises joint control with the Council over the Community Budget, although it is the Commission which draws up the draft Budget and is responsible for implementing it. Although the Council has the last say on 'compulsory' expenditure (i.e. agriculture, approximately 55 per cent of the Budget) the Parliament has the last word on 'non-compulsory expenditure' (NCE),[218] which relates to such things as social and regional policy, research and humanitarian aid and refugee programmes. The Parliament has also managed to shift the balance of expenditure, lowering that of the compulsory (which was originally over two-thirds) in favour of NCE. If the Parliament and the Council fail to agree after two readings of the draft budget, the Parliament has the power to reject the Budget as a whole and the procedure must start all over again.[219] The Parliament also monitors the progress of expenditure by the EU, through the committee on budgetary control, assisted by the Court of Auditors. Thus it scrutinises the management of funds and monitors activities for fraud. It gives an annual assessment of the Commission's use of funds before granting it a discharge on the use of the budget. In 1999, famously, it did not grant the Commission a discharge on grounds of mismanagement and lack of transparency.

Power of democratic supervision

The Parliament now exercises democratic supervision over a great deal of Community activities. These have grown quite considerably since the 1970s, indicating, as its increasing role in the legislative process has done, the Parliament's growing role: in this case in holding the executive, but not only the executive,

---

[216] B Guy Peters, 'Bureaucratic Politics and the Institutions of the European Community' in A Sbragia, *Euro Politics* (Brookings Institution, 1992) at 90.

[217] Since 1970 the Community budget has been financed from 'own resources,' agreed by the member states after the Parliament has been consulted. These include: customs duties levied at the EU's external borders; agricultural levies imported on products imported from third countries; 1 per cent of the VAT on goods and services throughout the EU; and a contribution from each member state calculated on the basis of the relative prosperity of each member state (but limited to 1.27 per cent GNP).

[218] A distinction which the Parliament has continually challenged.

[219] This happened in 1980, 1982 and 1985, but without lasting effect, as interim financing of the Commission's work continued.

accountable. This is a constitutional role and has been developed through both treaty amendments and informal developments.

Within parliamentary systems a relationship of accountability is essential: executive authority must have some sort of accountability and responsibility to the legislature. But the Commission was not originally very accountable to the Parliament. It was required to answer questions from the Parliament either orally or in writing under Article 197 (and more than 5,000 such questions are put every year) and could be dismissed *en bloc* if the Parliament could carry a motion of censure by two-thirds majority under Article 201, but this has never happened. However, innovations, both formal and informal, have transformed other aspects of the Parliament's relationship with the Commission. One of these concerns appointments of the members of the Commission, including its President. As early as 1981, Gaston Thorn, newly appointed President of the Commission, participated (although not required to do so) in a Parliamentary debate which the Parliament described (with what Westlake has described as 'imaginative dexterity')[220] as a 'confirmation hearing' following the practice of the US Senate.[221] The Heads of State and Government confirmed this practice through the 1983 Stuttgart Solemn Declaration and in 1985 Jacques Delors continued with the practice. It was built into the EC Treaty by Maastricht and now is to be found in Article 214. Its impact can be seen by the fact that, in 1995, the Parliament nearly denied the member states their choice of President of the Commission, Jacques Santer. The implications of this power are considerable: a President designate will have to ensure a Parliamentary majority but, on the other hand, does reap some benefits, as this may grant them 'political and moral authority'.[222]

Article 214 also provides that nomination of the Commission college as a whole is to be subject to a vote of approval by the Parliament before confirmation, tantamount to a vote of confidence, which the Parliament has not always been willing to give. As already mentioned, the Parliament has always had the power under Article 201 to obtain the resignation of the Commission *en bloc* by a vote of censure. In March 1999, following a report on the Commission's management by a Committee of Independent Experts, the Commission opted to resign rather than face a motion of censure. Parliament also exercises control over the Commission on a daily basis by scrutiny of the reports which the Commission submits to it, as well as annual public reports which the Commission is required to submit under Article 200 for general debate. The Parliament has also pushed for tighter legislative planning from the Commission, requiring the Commission to signal its political and legislative initiatives through an annual report drawn up in ever closer consultation with the Parliament.

The Parliament's powers of democratic supervision extend to the Council, which, according to Article 197, 'shall be heard by the European Parliament'. But this control extends nothing like as widely as that it exercises over the Commission. The

---

[220] M Westlake, 'The European Parliament's emerging powers of appointment' (1998) 36 JCMS 434 at 438.
[221] EU Bull 1981 No 2 48–9.
[222] Westlake op. cit. 439.

Council is under no obligation to report to Parliament but its President does present the Council's programme at the beginning of the Presidency as well as reports of what has been achieved after six months. Furthermore, under Article 4 TEU, the European Council is required to report on the progress of the European Union. But the Parliament lacks sanctions against either the Council or the European Council. Supervision of the Council is also exacerbated by the continued lack of transparency of Council proceedings. Perhaps, as Shirley Williams suggests,[223] the Parliament would be able to question the Council more effectively if it had a better idea of what was going on through greater access to the Council's meetings, minutes, and so on.

However, a good example of how the Parliament has exploited its powers to the full is that of the European Central Bank, which has operational independence but is accountable to the Parliament. This is a role which the Parliament has developed for several years, since its original dissatisfaction with its EMU role allotted under the Maastricht Treaty. Thus, even in the days of the European Monetary Institute (EMI), the predecessor of the European Central Bank, it used its rights of consultation over the appointment of the President to the utmost. Once again, it seemed to model itself on the US Senate and its role in appointments, going so far as to send the chairwoman of the Parliamentary monetary affairs sub-committee to Washington on a fact-finding mission.[224] The Parliament interrogated the candidate for President of the EMI, the Belgian banker Alexandre Lamfalussy, for three hours.[225] This procedure was given recognition under Article 113 EC, and was followed in 1997, when Wim Duisenberg, the nominee for the President of the European Central Bank, was appointed. The Parliament also drew upon detailed research on the candidates for the Executive Council of the Bank. No doubt the Parliament's exploitation of its powers in this area was helped by the fact that these appointments were given a high profile in the media due to the vested interests of the financial markets. But the Parliament also stressed the importance of the need for the creation of a democratic dialogue with the Bank, setting out what it thought this involved in its report on democratic accountability of the bank.[226] The relationship between the ECB and Parliament has been somewhat formalised in Article 113 EC, under which the ECB President is required to present an annual report to the plenary sitting of Parliament, and members of the ECB may also appear before Parliament's monetary affairs committee at regular intervals.

The Parliament's earliest involvement in appointment of EC officials was with those of the European Court of Auditors (ECA), who under Article 247(3) EC are appointed by the Council after consulting Parliament. Indeed, the Parliament saw the ECA almost as its own creation, according to Westlake, giving serious attention to its nominees, again borrowing from the US tradition of parliamentary hearings in specialised committees, in this case the Parliament's Budgetary Control commit-

---

[223] Shirley Williams, 'Sovereignty and Accountability in the European Community' in Keohane and Hoffmann, op. cit. at 163.

[224] Westlake op. cit.

[225] Westlake op. cit.

[226] European Parliament, 'Report on Democratic Accountability on the third stage of EMU', 2 April 1998.

tee, although nothing in the EC treaty forced ECA candidates to appear in this way. However, in 1993, the Council ignored the Parliament's reservations over two candidates, confirming them in any case. This was a blow to the moral authority of the Parliament, although it created nothing like the media interest occasioned by appointments to the ECB.

Maastricht introduced new supervisory powers in order to make the EU more accountable to its citizens.[227] Thus, under Article 193, it gave the Parliament the right to set up Committees of Enquiry to investigate 'alleged contravention or maladministration in the implementation of Community law'. A quarter of MEPs must request the setting up of such a committee and it must report within eighteen months of setting up.[228] This procedure existed prior to formalisation under Maastricht, with committees being set up regarding, for example, racism and xenophobia in 1985 and 1990. But it was only in 1997, after it had set up another committee of enquiry, in this case into the BSE crisis, that the importance of this procedure became clear, when it attracted media attention. The Parliament was not satisfied with the Commission's conduct of the crisis and 70 members tabled a motion for censure of the Commission. This was not eventually carried, on the Commission's agreeing to comply with conditions laid down by the Parliament within six months. However, it showed that the Parliament could compel the Commission to change its policy. Since Maastricht, the right 'of any natural or legal person residing or having its registered office in a member State' to petition the Parliament has been formalised under Article 193, although this has actually existed in practice since the founding of the EEC. The President of the Parliament assigns the petition to the Committee on petitions, which, if it finds it to be admissible, may conduct hearings and issue a report. Over the last decade or so the number of such petitions has significantly increased: there are now about 1,500 per year. In fact, the Parliament cannot redress the grievance unless it relates to the workings of the Parliament itself, but it can at least give publicity to the case, or refer it to the Ombudsman. The Parliament has, since Maastricht, also had the power to appoint an Ombudsman which is empowered to receive complaints on instances involving the maladministration in the activities of the Community's political institutions (see below). All of these powers were formalised as part of the citizenship package introduced in the Maastricht treaty, in which it was hoped that the Parliament might play its part in bringing the EU closer to the citizen.

REFLECTIONS

How to assess the role of the European Parliament in the post-Nice era? In a report prepared by the Parliament itself, it noted a 'distinct lack of agreement in assessments of the role of the Parliament',[229] (indicating perhaps a normative disagreement over

---

[227] See Chapter 14 on Citizenship.
[228] EP Rules of Procedure, Rule 136.

what the Parliament's role should be.) In this same report, the Parliament stated that, contrary to judgments which suggest that it is lacking in a legislative capacity, in fact evaluation indicates that it colegislated on a very significant amount of binding EC secondary legislation (about 80 per cent) directly affecting the citizen's way of living. The report also stressed that, with its right to press the Council of Ministers into conciliation, or to reject the Council's common position, and thus the whole proposal, the Parliament has obtained real bargaining powers to change substantive issues of legislation.[230] Therefore, although it might seem that national parliaments such as the UK Parliament have significantly greater power than the European Parliament, in that all legislation is introduced there and must be passed by it, closer scrutiny reveals certain important features. In the UK Parliament, most legislation is introduced by the government, and consequently backbenchers and the opposition probably have less power to veto and influence legislation (unless the government has a very small majority, such as the Conservative government of John Major from 1992–7) than the European Parliament does in the context of codecision.

One might expect the Parliament to be upbeat about its own powers. However, independent commentators also take the same view: as long ago as 1993, Juliet Lodge called the Parliament 'arguably one of the most vital EC institutions'.[231] Dehousse[232] has argued that, notwithstanding the 'black holes' of the two extra-EC pillars, it is not excessive to argue that the EC's institutional system is developing towards a federal system, in which the legislative power is shared by two branches, representing its population and its states. However, although MEPs might desire to serve in a full second chamber, national Parliaments might not so strongly wish for this, fearing a gain in power in the EP at their expense. Jealousy between national and European Parliaments might conceivably disappear if there were a truly European public.[233] But this seems a long way off.

According to Westlake, the incremental achievements and adjustments to the Parliament's powers 'may represent the bare bones of an emerging constitution'.[234] He continues, 'Those "bones" include an autonomous central bank nevertheless engaged in political dialogue by the European Parliament, and an emerging executive drawing its legitimacy from the Parliament.' We should not ignore these developments: as Westlake notes, the Treaty amenders 'have frequently followed Parliament's logic by transforming the conventions it so imaginatively creates into formal treaty provisions'.

---

[229] European Parliament, 'Co-Governing after Maastricht: The European Parliament's Institutional Performance 1994–1999' Working paper, DG for Research POLI 104/rev.EN at 9–10.

[230] Ibid. 11.

[231] J Lodge, 'EC policymaking: institutional dynamics' in Lodge (ed.) *The European Community and the Challenge of the Future* (Pinter, 1993, 2nd edition) at 21.

[232] R Dehousse, 'European Institutional Architecture after Amsterdam: Parliamentary System or Regulatory Structure?' (1998) 35 CMLRev 595 at 625.

[233] Note also Tony Blair's proposal for a European second chamber, made up of members of national parliaments, which did not however meet with a successful response in the UK, 'Backlash against EU second chamber', Patrick Wintour, (*The Guardian*, 29 December 2000).

[234] Westlake op. cit. at 443.

THE EUROPEAN COUNCIL

The practice of holding summit conferences attended by Community leaders (i.e. heads of state and government) and the President of the Commission began in 1969 and was put on a formal basis by the Paris summit of 1974. This was how the European Council came into being. This practice was later given legal recognition by Article 2 of the Single European Act and a more formal statement in the Maastricht treaty, Article 4 of which states that: 'The European Council shall provide the Union with the necessary impetus for its development and shall define the general policy guidelines thereof.' However, the European Council still does not have the status of a Community institution.[235]

Notwithstanding its lack of institutional status,[236] the European Council plays a very important role in the political processes of the EU. It meets at least twice a year and is presided over by the member state which holds the Presidency of the Council of Ministers. It is responsible for taking general policy decisions and was involved, for example, in the decisions to establish a European Monetary System; direct elections to the European Parliament; and enlargement of the EU. It also plays an important role in Common Foreign and Security Policy (CFSP) matters, where it sets out the principles, common strategies and guidelines which are to govern EU action.

The European Council fulfils what Craig and de Burca have described as a 'perceived need for a focus of authority at the highest political level'.[237] Indeed, for some commentators it is the key EU institution – Petersen and Bomberg, for example, comment that a 'profile of EU institutions must begin with the European Council'[238] – something which this author has clearly chosen not to do, preferring to scrutinise the older institutions first! They refer to it as 'the EU's Board of Directors', a description which likens the EU to the image of the commercial enterprise from which it seems to be trying to escape in its recent years. Most certainly, the European Council has played a very important role in setting the pace of the EC integration process, being a primary source of historic decisions, the Presidency conclusions agreed by European summits becoming 'bibles'[239] for future action. However, its scope and function are political, rather than legal, and the European Council has emerged as the *de facto* highest level decision-maker in the EU without a legal foundation for this role.[240] It functions without rules of procedure or principles of decision-making. It has no published agenda nor minutes.

If the European Council may be seen as a key source of gravitas in the European integration process, why then were the heads of Government originally absent from the EEC framework? Jean Dondelinger, in an early study of the European Council,

---

[235] The community institutions are set out in Article 7 EC.

[236] And therefore not subject to the rule of law jurisdiction of the ECJ, unless it encroaches on actions taken by the Community institutions under the EC treaty. See: Case C-253/94P *Roujansky v Council* [1995] ECR I-7 and Case C-170/96 *Commission v Council* [1998] ECR I-2763.

[237] Craig and de Burca, *EU Law* (OUP, 1998) at 64.

[238] Petersen and Bomberg, *Decision Making in the European Community* (Macmillan, 1999) at 33.

[239] Petersen and Bomberg op. cit.

[240] M Troy Johnston, *The European Council* (Boulder: Westview, 1994) at 1.

suggested that this would have been seen as intimidating the fledgling EEC institutions.[241] However, the extra-treaty nature of the European Council might seem to conflict with the 'constitutionalising' impetus of the institutional development of the EU. Indeed, in contrast to those who have stressed the European Council's heavyweight nature, von Bogdandy has suggested that: 'At the focal point of the political process one finds a legal vacuum and with it a power that is difficult to control with legal instruments. In the constitution of the Union, some elements of political rule are thus less formalised and thereby less transparent than in national constitutions.'[242] What, however, the European Council may possess, is symbolic importance – as Troy Johnston notes, the European public may be more likely to identify with Europe's (usually) elected heads of government as the Community's political executive than the unelected Commission – and this symbolic status will continue to support its role in the EU process.

THE COURT OF AUDITORS

This is the fifth of the EC's official institutions under Article 7 EC, although not set up until 1977 and fairly subordinate in status until promoted to the rank of institution by the Maastricht treaty. Although the perception of audit is of something technical, and unexciting – or even, as more forcefully expressed by Adam Tomkins, 'deeply unsexy'[243] – audit has recently shed some of its dull image to become a central concern of the EC in the late 1990s, revealing arresting facts of EU mismanagement, as in the case of the Commission crisis of March 1999.

The establishment of an autonomous EEC Budget based on 'own resources' by the 1970 Budget Treaty suggested the need for an independent audit, and, in 1973, the European Parliament presented its report, 'The Case for a European Audit Office'. Under Article 248 EC, the Court of Auditors (ECA) has the main task of auditing the accounts and the implementation of the Budget of the EU. It is independent from the other Community institutions and has a free choice in the organisation and scheduling of its auditing work. It publishes its results in a series of reports, augmented by another, special series of reports on particular areas of EU expenditure.

Under Article 247 EC, the ECA consists of fifteen full-time members with expertise in auditing matters, originating from the fifteen member states. They are appointed by the Council of Ministers, after consulting the Parliament, for a term of six years (changed from three by the Treaty of Nice). They elect a President for a term of six years. Approximately 550 staff (rather a small number, limiting the capabilities of the ECA) work for the ECA in Luxembourg, about 250 of them auditors.

---

[241] Dondelinger, unpublished paper 'Le Conseil Européen' 20 November 1975, in the library of the secretariat of the Council of Ministers in Brussels, cited in Troy Johnston, op. cit. at 4.

[242] A Von Bogdandy, 'The European Union as a Supranational Federation: A Conceptual Attempt in the light of the Amsterdam Treaty' (2000) 6 Colum. J. Eur L. 27.

[243] A Tomkins, 'Transparency and the Emergence of European Administrative Law' (1999–2000) 19 YEL.

The function of audit is to examine the acts of those responsible for management, with the double aim of improving results and accounting to the taxpayer for the authorities' use of public funds.[244] External auditing of public agencies and their use of public monies is considered a norm of good government: 'sound and flexible management was seen as part of the Weberian tradition of the state'.[245] The ECA was set up to ensure that the ever-growing Community resources would be subjected to a level of control at least equivalent to that provided for expenditure at national level and was described at its inauguration by Kutscher, then President of the ECJ, as the EC's 'financial conscience'. Under Article 248(2) it examines whether EU budgetary revenue has been received and corresponding expenditure incurred in a legal and regular manner. It also places a particular emphasis on examining whether financial management has been sound: i.e. it checks whether management objectives have been met, while assessing to what extent and at what cost this has been done (Article 248 EC). This additional focus on 'sound management' reflects northern European traditions of audit, consciously taken up by the ECA, which lacked any common European tradition of audit on which to draw. It may audit any body or person managing or receiving Community funds, including national, regional and local authorities and the recipients of Community aid.

The ECA has no jurisdictional powers (and, in fact, is not a court as its name would suggest). If its auditors discover irregularities, including fraud, this is communicated to those Community bodies responsible so they may take appropriate action. However, the ECA's discoveries are not always quickly acted upon. This can reflect (or produce) tensions between the ECA and other institutions. It took some time for the Council, for example, to follow up the ECA's reports: it was not until 1985 that the Ecofin Council formally examined the ECA's annual reports, although it has recently paid more attention to them. However, as Laffan notes, 'the Council and the Court operate to different logics. The Council is animated by a political logic and promotion of national interest, whereas the Court operates within a logic of auditing and good financial housekeeping.'[246] Member states may be the cause of financial problems which they do not wish to see highlighted. Additionally, compromise and bargaining in the Council may actually lead to management and financial difficulties because of incoherent and loose drafting.

If the ECA's relations with the Council have sometimes been distant, those with the Commission have been positively stormy.[247] Prior to the establishment of the ECA, the Commission's management of the Community budget was largely unfettered. Things got off to a bad footing when the ECA became embroiled in a dispute over Commissioners' personal expenses, after providing evidence to a European Parliament budgetary control committee, at which the President of the Commission had been forced to appear to give assurances that new controls were in place.

---

[244] This account is given by the ECA itself on its web site as http://www.eca.eu.int/EN/BROCHURE.

[245] B Laffan, 'Becoming a "Living Institution": The Evolution of the European Court of Auditors' (1999) 37 JCMS at 252.

[246] Laffan op. cit. at 260.

[247] For example, the Committee of Independent Experts' report on the Commission in 1999 noted the Commission's antagonistic reaction to the ECA's observations.

Relations did not improve under the Delors Commission, which objected to the ECA's reports (or tone of its reports) on spending in 1992, especially over the CAP. Ironically, in fact, it was President Santer who invested time and energy in improving relations with the ECA.

However, in spite of Santer's efforts to improve relations, things did not improve. It is well known that the ECA refused to certify Commission accounts five years in a row, without, however, any noticeable results until the EP stepped in and appointed a Committee of Independent Experts to investigate fraud and mismanagement in the Commission. This supports the statement made by Adam Tomkins that 'The ECA is potentially extremely powerful, yet in practice a deeply disappointing body.'[248] Why has there not been a greater response to, and uptake on, its reports? Tomkins suggests this is because although the ECA has an impressive output, it tends to engage in 'thick verbiage' and thus to talk past the Commission. Thus the Commission finds it very difficult to translate the reports into specific management reforms which can be acted upon. Whether this relationship will improve in the wake of the Commission reforms remains to be seen.

THE EUROPEAN CENTRAL BANK

Since the start of 1999, much of the EU[249] has had a new currency, the euro. The European Central Bank (ECB) was established on 1 June 1998, in Frankfurt-am-Main, and has as its main task the ensuring of price stability in the euro area.

Economic and monetary union (EMU) came about as a result of the 'Delors report'[250] of 1988–9, which proposed that EMU should be achieved in three discrete but evolutionary steps. During stage 1 of EMU, which started on 1 July 1990, in principle all restrictions on the free movement of capital were abolished. The EC treaty was amended by the TEU so as to establish the required institutional structures.[251] The second stage of EMU was marked by the establishment of the European Monetary Institute (EMI) on 1 January 1994, which had the following tasks: strengthening central bank monetary policy coordination and making preparations for the European System of Central Banks (ESCB); the conduct of single monetary policy; and the creation of a single currency. The 'euro' was chosen as the name of the single currency by the European Council of December 1995, to the

---

[248] A Tomkins, 'Transparency and the Emergence of European Administrative Law' (1999–2000) 19 YEL; see also House of Lords Select Committee on European Union 12th report, 'The European Court of Auditors: The Case for Reform' (2001).

[249] The UK, Sweden and Denmark do not participate at time of writing.

[250] This report was the product of a committee chaired by Jacques Delors, then President of the Commission; the governors of the European Central Banks; Alexandre Lamfalussy (then General Manager of the Bank of International Settlements); Niels Thygesen (Professor of Economics at the University of Copenhagen); and Miguel Boyer (President of the Banco Exterior de España). However, the origins of EMU go back much further, at least as far back as the 1969 Barre Plan and the 1970 Werner report, both of which suggested that some elements of economic decision-making should be transferred from the national to the supranational.

[251] Now Title VII EC treaty, Articles 98–124.

disdain of many, although inspirational to others, such as Wim Duisenberg, the ECB's new President, who stated whimsically: 'The euro is far more than a medium of exchange. It is part of the identity of a people. It reflects what they have in common now and in the future.'[252] In December 1996, the EMI presented the designs for the euro banknotes, artificial, constructed designs of imaginary buildings, which seemed to presage the unreal notion of monetary union. With the establishment of the ECB in June 1998, the EMI had completed its task and went into liquidation. On 1 January 1999, the third and final stage of EMU began with the irrevocable fixing of the exchange rates of the currencies of the initial eleven member states participating, which had satisfied the convergence criteria set out in the EC treaty for the adoption of the single currency. This was increased to twelve on 1 January 2001 when Greece too entered the third stage.

Article 107 EC sets out the legal basis for the ESCB. According to Article 107(1) the ESCB is composed of the ECB and the national central banks of all fifteen EU states. The Statute of the ESCB and ECB is attached to the Maastricht treaty as a Protocol.[253] The twelve central banks in the euro area and the ECB form the 'eurosystem'. The primary objective of the eurosystem is, according to Article 105 EC, to maintain price stability. Its basic tasks, also set out in Article 105 EC, are to 'define and implement the monetary policy of the Community'; 'to conduct foreign exchange operations'; 'to hold and manage the official foreign reserves of the Member states'; and 'to promote the smooth operation of payment systems'. According to Article 110 EC it may make regulations, take decisions and issue recommendations and opinions in order to carry out these tasks.

The process of decision-making in the eurosystem is centralised through the decision-making bodies of the ECB which are the Governing Council and the Executive Board. Decisions of the ECB are to be taken by a simple majority.[254] While there are member states which have not yet adopted the euro, a third decision-making body, the General Council, also exists. The Governing Council is the highest decision-making body of the ECB. According to Article 112 EC it is made up of six members of the Executive Board and the governors of the national central banks of the euro area. Its key task is to formulate the monetary policy of the euro area, which includes, where appropriate, intermediate monetary objectives, key interest rates and the supply of reserves in the eurosystem. The Executive Board of the ECB consists of the President, Vice President and four other members, chosen from persons of recognised standing and experience in monetary and banking matters by the Heads of State or government of the twelve.[255] It is responsible for implementing the monetary policy, as formulated by the Governing Council, and gives instructions to national central banks, as well as managing the day-to-day business of the ECB. The General Council comprises the President and Vice

---

[252] A Brunner, 'Welcome to Euroland', (*The Guardian*, January 1999).

[253] See also Rules of Procedure governing the European Central Bank L338 25/12/98 at 28.

[254] Article 10 Protocol on the Statute of the ESCB and ECB.

[255] A group from which the UK is currently excluded. See the comments of Romano Prodi, who stated 'To be different makes you less important in the total decision-making process', 'Join euro or lose out' (*The Guardian*, 16 February 2001).

President and governors of the national central banks in all fifteen member states. It contributes to the advisory and coordinating functions of the ECB, and prepares for possible enlargement of the euro area.

The current President of the ECB is Wim Duisenberg, the former head of the Dutch Central Bank. His appointment was controversial, as the French government had insisted on a French candidate and had only backed down on the assurance that Duisenberg's successor would be the Frenchman, Jean-Claude Trichet. Duisenberg was appointed on the understanding that he would stand down some way through his term of office. This was apparently not a very clear understanding, as he recently described it as 'slightly absurd' in the European Parliament.[256] As perhaps might be expected, appointments have been quite traditional – only one of those on the Executive Board and the Governing Council being a woman – Sirkka Hamalainene of Finland. About 770 staff work at the ECB in Frankfurt. They are recruited from all fifteen EU countries and work in close cooperation with staff of the national central banks. The ECB is divided into working units, which are grouped in directorates-general, directorates and divisions. Overall responsibility for these lies with individual members of the Executive Board.

As already stated, the ECB's primary objective, under Article 105 EC, is to maintain price stability. This has not been clearly defined in the treaty, but has been defined by the ECB itself as a year-on-year increase in consumer prices of below 2 per cent. This focus on price stability explains why the central management of the ECB did not seem unduly worried in short-term fluctuations in foreign exchange such as those of 1999 and 2000, when the euro fell from 1.17 dollars to 80 cents in less than two years. A weak euro does not damage inflationary prospects because the euroland is essentially a closed economy, with only 10 per cent of its demand supplied by imports.[257] The ECB also has the sole right to issue bank notes under Article 106 EC.

According to Article 108 EC the Eurosystem is independent and its proceedings are confidential. Indeed, research has shown a correlation between the level of central bank independence and long-term inflation rates.[258] Under Article 108 EC, neither the ECB nor the national central banks may take any instructions from any external body (which includes the Community institutions). Under Article 108, the ESCB may not grant loans to Community bodies or national government entities and the ECB has its own budget, independent of the European Community. These features supposedly shield it from policy interference and keep the administration of the ECB separate from the financial interests of the Community. The subscription of capital comes from the national central banks and not from the EU. Members of the ESCB have security of tenure, as do members of the Executive Council under Article 107, who are appointed for a non-renewable term of eight years. They may be removed from office only in the event of incapacity or serious misconduct (Article 107).

---

[256] Quoted in *The European Voice* (14–19 May 1998).
[257] See Anatole Kaletsky, 'ECB manages to keep euro weakness in perspective' (*The Times*, 30 November 1999).
[258] See e.g. A Cukierman, *Central Bank Strategy, Credibility and Independence* (MIT Press, 1992).

TRANSPARENCY AND LEGITIMACY

In its own brochure[259] the ECB states: 'To maintain its credibility, an independent central bank must be open and clear about the reasons for its actions: It must also be accountable to democratic institutions. Without encroaching on the ECB's independence, the Treaty establishing the EC imposes precise reporting obligations on the ECB.'

It is the case that the ECB fulfils certain conditions in the name of openness. It publishes a weekly consolidated financial statement of the eurosystem, reflecting transactions in the previous week. It publishes reports on the activities of the ESCB at least every quarter. It must, under Article 113(3), deliver an annual report on its activities and monetary policy to the Parliament, Council of Ministers, Commission and European Council. The Parliament may also hold a general debate on its annual report and the Parliamentary committees may question the President and the members of the Executive Board (Article 113 (4)). The Parliament has consciously modelled the operational processes of this committee on the US Senate Committee hearings of the Federal Reserve chairman. The Parliament, in its Resolution on the Amsterdam Treaty, pointed to perceived shortcomings of EMU, and set out a 'shopping list' of objectives: the provision of information; establishment of dialogue between the Parliament and the ECB; the holding of quarterly meetings between the Parliament and ECB President; the holding of an annual debate.[260] Some of this has been achieved and, in its brochure, the Bank states that 'In fact, the ECB has committed itself to go beyond the reporting requirements set out in the treaty. The President explains the reasons behind the Governing Council's decisions in an annual Press Council. Further views are published in a monthly bulletin of the ECB.'[261] However, one of the major criticisms so far made of the ECB is that it lacks openness and accountability.[262] Why is this so?

Willem Buiter, for example, has suggested that it is 'not sufficient that outcomes of monetary policy process be transparent. The whole process should be.'[263] His criticism seems to be directed at the decision taken by the Governing Council of the ECB not to publish minutes of meetings, nor to publish voting behaviour. This follows the approach taken by the Bundesbank[264] rather than the Bank of England,[265] which publishes minutes after two weeks, or the US Federal Reserve Board, after seven to eight weeks. The argument against publication would appear to be that the multinational make-up of the ECB makes publication undesirable, but Buiter complains that this leads to consensus and compromise, and that, in any case, as a result

---

[259] *The European Central Bank*, at 31, available on its website at http://www.ecb.int/about.
[260] See EP Resolution on the Amsterdam Treaty; also EP Report on democratic accountability in the third stage of EMU (2 April 1998).
[261] *The European Central Bank* at 32.
[262] W Buiter, 'Alice in Euroland' (1999) 37 JCMS 181.
[263] Buiter op. cit. at 206.
[264] See e.g. H Remsperger, 'Geheimnis und Transparenz in der Geldpolitik' (1998) lecture available at http://www.bundesbank.de
[265] Indeed, the Bank of England Act 1998 places a surprising emphasis on openness.

of rumour and hearsay, media and academic commentators can work out the voting records of individual members within a short time.

De Haan and Eijffinger[266] have been less critical of the ECB's democratic credentials. They acknowledge that Anglo-Saxon central banks like the Bank of England and the Federal Reserve are more inclined to be accountable and transparent, but with the danger of revealing their tactics. Continental banks such as the Bundesbank have been swifter to recognise the need for some ambiguity in foreign exchange market operations.

The ECB, in the section of its brochure cited above, stressed the need for credibility. However, as Hix suggests,[267] credibility is not sufficient to secure an independent and stable monetary policy. As well as being credible, a Central Bank also needs to be legitimate: it needs to have what economists call 'reputation'.[268] Reputation makes it easier for the public and the markets to accept monetary policy decisions that might appear unpopular in the short term. However, the ECB is a new institution managing a new currency and does not have a long-established reputation: it will take time for it to become a 'living institution'. Some member states may suffer more than others in the ongoing process of EMU and may be more likely to turn against a new institution such as the ECB than they would be against a more established one, such as the Bundesbank for example.[269] In such a scenario, governments in those states would be more likely to turn to political direction in the monetary policy arena. As the ECB is at least in theory independent, it cannot be forced to take up a particular monetary policy, but the member states could still influence it through the appointment process. Therefore it might be seen that, within the decision-making processes of the ECB, there is an inherent tension between independence and accountability. Although increased accountability and transparency enable the Bank to establish its legitimacy, they also provoke the politicisation of ECB decisions and internal ECB bargaining. Ultimately, these issues raise the question of how the ECB will fulfil the function of a central bank without the existence of some sort of political union. Romano Prodi has argued: 'the ECB must be independent but must not suffer from loneliness. Europe now lacks strong political structures because national states do not wish to create them.'[270] So the ECB seems set to be 'lonely' for some time to come. However, it seems that the ECB is establishing greater dialogue with the European Parliament in an attempt to avoid the pitfalls of greater accountability to the member states. As reported in *The European*:

> Mr Duisenberg understands that lack of accountability is his Achilles heel. When the good times roll, Euroland's politicians will flock to his support. But when he has to keep his hand firmly on his wallet during a downturn, he knows they will be his

---

[266] J de Haan, S Eijffinger, 'The Democratic Accountability of the European Central Bank: A Comment on Two Fairy-tales' (2000) 38 JCMS 393.
[267] S Hix, *The Political System of the European Union* (Macmillan, 1999) 298–9.
[268] B Winckler, 'Towards a Strategic View of EMU: A Critical Survey' (1996) 16 J'l of Public Policy 1.
[269] This was apparently the case in the early years of the US Federal Reserve Bank – see B Eichengreen, 'Designing a Central Bank for Europe: A Cautionary Tale from the Early Years of the Federal Reserve System', Discussion Paper no 585 (London, Centre for Economic Policy Research, 1991).
[270] *The Guardian*, 30 March 2001.

sharpest critics. That is why he has selected the Parliament as a forum in which he will explain himself and build his credibility. He rightly refuses to be answerable to national Parliaments...but his quarterly reports to the European Parliament will rapidly become as significant occasions as when the chairman of the US Federal Reserve submits himself to grilling by Congress.[271]

Whether such a relationship will render the ECB less 'lonely' remains to be seen.

THE ECONOMIC AND SOCIAL COMMITTEE

The Economic and Social Committee (ESC) is a consultative body, or 'quasi-institution', representing a wide range of economic and social activities. Thus it is supposed to provide the input of various interest groups, or, at least that of 'civil society' (as ESC chooses to define it in its own promotional literature)[272]. According to Article 258 EC, as amended by the Treaty of Nice, its membership 'shall not exceed three hundred and fifty'.[273] These members are appointed for a renewable four-year term of office. They live and work in their home countries and only come to Brussels for meetings. These members are drawn from organisations representing employers, workers, commerce, agriculture, the professions, consumers, environmental groups and so on.

The ESC describes itself has having three main functions: to advise the major institutions on legislative proposals; to promote a greater commitment from civil society to the EU; and to bolster the role of civil society organisations in non-EC countries.[274] It is probably best known for its (consultative) role in the EC legislation process. However, as consultation is only mandatory in some cases, its effect can be limited. On average, the ESC delivers about 170 advisory opinions[275] every year. These are published in the Official Journal. It is questionable how influential a role the ESC has played. According to its own website, about 60 per cent of its proposals are adopted in final texts,[276] but other commentators have perceived its influence as much more limited. According to Nugent, 'Evidence of this (lies) in the follow-up reports which the Commission produces: these tend to include relatively few unambiguous acceptances of ESC recommendations.'[277]

The ESC also suggests that it can provide valuable technical expertise through its own initiative reports: these may cover subjects neglected by other institutions and prompt the Commission to table proposals.[278] However, given that the ESC is drawn from a variety of different organisations and groups, there can be disagree-

---

[271] *The European*, 11–17 May 1998 at 5.

[272] 'The ESC: a Bridge between Europe and Civil Society' ESC 99 011-EN 1999.

[273] The current division among the member states is set out in Article 258. Post-enlargement membership is set out in the Nice Protocol on the Enlargement of the European Union.

[274] Detailed in the ESC's website at http://www.ces.eu.int/en/org/welcome-htm.

[275] About 15 per cent of these are however delivered on its own initiative, rather than as part of the legislation process.

[276] 'The ESC: a Bridge between Europe and Civil Society' available on the ESC website.

[277] N Nugent, *The Government and Politics of the European Union* (Macmillan, 1999, 4th edn) at 239.

[278] ESC own initiative work for 1999 included the following reports: Pluralism and Concentrations in the Media; Towards a Citizens' Treaty; and The impact of implementing EMU on economic and social cohesion, (source 'The ESC: a Bridge between EU and Civil Society').

ment. For example, employers and trade union representatives will clearly not always agree. The ESC itself takes the view, somewhat optimistically, that this search for agreement will be bound to improve the quality and credibility of EC decision-making, making it more comprehensible and democratic, complementing political with economic democracy,[279] as well as supplementing the popular will expressed by the European Parliament. This may make its role sound quite grand. However, in reality the ESC is in a weakish position. The Commission, Council and Parliament are not bound to act on its opinions and the range of issues for which consultation of the ESC is mandatory is smaller than that of the Parliament. The Council and Commission may also choose at what stage to refer proposals to the ESC, leaving it late enough to have already fixed their own opinions. Nor may the ESC call upon the ECJ under Article 230 to ensure that its functions are respected, as it is not an official Community institution. The ESC stresses the importance of the contribution of 'civil society' to EC legislation in indicating what impact EC action is likely to have on those most directly concerned. However, the ESC is by no means the only body to have this function. Civil, sectional interests are represented at earlier, perhaps more crucial stages of the decision-making process, such as advisory committees at the pre-proposal stage and working groups in the Council of Ministers, albeit less transparently. Thus, all in all, the importance of the ESC should probably not be over-stressed.

THE COMMITTEE OF THE REGIONS

This committee, along with ESC, is more 'quasi-institution' than institution, and was set up by the Maastricht treaty in order to involve regional and local bodies in the shaping of Community policies. Since the Treaty of Nice, according to Article 263 EC, its membership is not to exceed 350,[280] although, like ESC, its current membership is 222. Its members include regional, local leaders such as mayors and councillors,[281] who elect a President for a two-year term of office. It is divided into eight internal commissions, specialising in various fields. It holds five plenary sessions in Brussels every year.

Like the ESC, the Committee has only weak consultative functions. Along with the ESC, it has no veto power over legislation and it cannot call upon the ECJ under Article 230 to ensure that its functions are respected. In its own publicity[282] the Committee states, 'It is certainly no coincidence that the Committee of the Regions and the concept of subsidiarity were conceived at the same time.' In February 2000, Romano Prodi told members of the Committee that 'In the coming years, the importance of regional authorities will considerably increase…Europe must be built by

---

[279] 'The ESC: a Bridge between Europe and Civil Society' at 7–8.
[280] Once again, post-enlargement membership is set out in the Nice Protocol on Enlargement.
[281] At time of writing the leader of the far right Austrian freedom party, Jorg Haider sits on the Committee as Governor of Carinthia.
[282] http://www/cor.en-int/presentation.

the citizens for the citizens. Who better to get this message across than you (the members of the COR)?'[283] However, there are some reasons for suspecting that the Committee may not live up to Prodi's expectations, nor to more general expectations as to its capabilities regarding pluralism and legitimacy. Its membership is determined by national governments, and although some have left this to the regions themselves, others, such as France and the UK, have exercised strong control. Committee membership also includes municipal as well as regional representation, both of which may be pursuing different and conflicting interests. Furthermore, as Keating and Hooghe allege, 'From the outset, it was highly politicised, not so much on a right-left basis as a north-south one.'[284] These critical comments suggest that the Committee has not, contrary to the claim in its own publicity material, yet 'reached cruising speed'.

THE EUROPEAN OMBUDSMAN

This body was introduced by the Maastricht Treaty, as part of its citizenship provisions. It is governed by Article 195 EC and by the Statute of the Ombudsman.[285] The Ombudsman is appointed by the European Parliament for the Parliament's five-year term. It is based in Strasbourg, and the current (and first) incumbent is Jacob Soderman of Finland. It is a full-time, independent position, with the same rank as judges of the ECJ.

The Ombudsman has two functions: to receive and to investigate complaints from EU citizens[286] concerning maladministration by any Community institution or body;[287] and, secondly, the Ombudsman may conduct own initiative inquiries into suspected maladministration.

The Ombudsman publishes annual reports detailing complaints as well as its own initiative investigations. In 1999[288] the Ombudsman received 1,577 complaints (of which 70 per cent were outside its mandate as they did not concern EC institutions). If the Ombudsman finds maladministration, the matter is referred to the institution concerned which has three months to respond. The institution concerned is obliged to supply the Ombudsman with information and give access to files although they may refuse on 'duly substantiated grounds of secrecy'.[289] After considering this response the Ombudsman sends a final report to the Parliament and institution concerned, as well as informing the person who lodged the complaint. Of the complaints which were investigated in 1999, 27 closed with a critical remark to the body

---

[283] Ibid.

[284] See M Keating and L Hooghe, 'By-passing the nation state? Regions and the EU policy process' (1996) in J Richardson (ed.) *European Union: Power and Policymaking* (Routledge, 1996).

[285] OJ 1994 L113/15.

[286] Or any national/legal person residing/having a registered office in the member states.

[287] With the exception of the CFI and ECJ acting in their judicial capacity.

[288] 1999 report of the Ombudsman.

[289] Member states must also supply information if necessary unless such information is covered by national laws on secrecy.

concerned and 62 were settled by the institution in the applicant's favour. The Commission was the major focus of complaints: 163 out of 206. Many of these were complaints about lack of transparency – lack of information and the provision of inaccurate information being the most frequent allegations.

However, the Ombudsman has no formal powers to correct maladministration, and instead is dependent on the cooperation of the institutions, and the undesirable nature of bad publicity. The criticism has been made[290] that, so far, the Ombudsman has adopted an overly narrow, legalistic and rule-based understanding of mal-administration which limits the Ombudsman's usefulness.[291] Adam Tomkins suggests that while Ombudsmen 'can be the most wonderful and exciting actors on the administrative law stage providing a (cheap) guardian of the little man, with no restrictive standing requirements, the European Ombudsman has been too cautious in his approach, too deferential in his approach to European institutions, especially over the issue of transparency'.[292]

Let us hope that the Ombudsman will take a wider approach to maladministration in future.

EXECUTIVE AGENCIES

It is very common to find executive agencies in most western polities, including the EU. 'Agency' is a general, rather than a specific term, and may be applied to all sorts of bodies, inspectorates and offices.[293] There are various reasons for the growth of agencies: one is simply the growing burden of regulation in the modern world, which has made it difficult for official institutions to accomplish everything them-selves. Another reason is the necessity of having some bodies in place which are able to take a longer-term approach to regulation than governments, which are neces-sarily short-termist in their orientation. The insulation of regulators from the policy process is thought to enhance their regulatory commitments.[294]

---

[290] See A Tomkins, 'Transparency and the Emergence of a European Administrative Law' in Yearbook of European Law (OUP 1999–2000), 34.

[291] See also R Rawlings, 'Engaged Élites: Citizen Action and Institutional Attitudes in Commission Enforcement' (2000) 6 ELJ 44.

[292] Tomkins op. cit. at 52.

[293] The term agency is defined by the American *Administrative Procedures Act* of 1946 as 'a part of gov-ernment that is generally independent in the exercise of its functions and that by law has authority to take a final and binding action affecting the rights and obligations of individuals, particularly by the char-acteristic procedure of rule-making and adjudication'.

[294] The literature is well-established, see for example: M Shapiro, 'The problems of independent agen-cies in the United States and the European Union' (1997) JEPP 276; M Everson, 'Independent Agencies: Hierarchy beaters?' (1995) 1 ELJ 180; A Kreher, 'Agencies in the European Community – a step towards administrative integration in Europe?' (1997) 4 JEPP 225; G Majone, 'Cross-National Sources of Regulatory Policy-making in Europe and the United States' 11 Journal of Public Policy 79; G Majone and M Everson, 'Institutional reform: independent agencies, oversight, co-ordination and procedural control' in O De Schutter, N Lebessis and J Paterson (eds) *Governance in the European Union* (European Commission: Forward Studies Unit, 2001).

These reasons apply in the EU, in which the late 1980s and 1990s saw a growth in the establishment of executive agencies.[295] These include the European Environment Agency, established in 1994 and based in Copenhagen; the Office for Harmonisation in the Internal Market (Trade Marks and Designs) established in 1994 and in Alicante; the European Monitoring Centre for Drugs and Drug Addiction, also established in 1994 and in Luxembourg; the European Agency of the Evaluation of Medicinal Products, established in 1994 and in London, to name but a few.

However EU agencies are constrained in what they may do. According to the *Meroni* case,[296] decided by the ECJ in the 1950s under the ECSC, but applicable to all three communities, only clearly defined executive powers may be delegated to outside agencies by EU institutions.

The reasons why it might be thought undesirable to delegate to outside bodies are well-established. First, such delegation raises problems for the classic separation of powers doctrine. The creation of institutions, outside of a constitutional framework, which perform all three functions (i.e. legislative, executive and judicial) would seem to be a clear violation of the doctrine. However, in the US context, the Supreme Court, in 'a long and tortuous body of case-law',[297] endorsed the establishment of such agencies on the following basis. The view taken by the Supreme Court was that, if the aim of the doctrine of separation of powers was to prevent the concentration of power in any one body, then the delegation of power to agencies could be seen, not as an example of a dangerous accumulation of power, but rather as promoting the further fragmentation of power, and pluralism under the constitution.

A second traditional objection to delegation to outside bodies has been based on the perceived lack of legitimacy and accountability of such bodies. However, this might be overcome. Executive agencies tend to be overseen by a variety of mechanisms, such as accountability to both institutions and to the public at large. Thus, for example, in the US, the Administrative Procedures Act provides for a complex set of requirements which agencies must follow in their rule-making processes, as well as making extensive provision for judicial review. Such measures might be introduced in the context of the EU.[298]

Nevertheless, within the EU, the *Meroni* doctrine still stands. Agencies in the EU are not potent regulatory authorities with the power to adopt and implement policies. Instead, their main responsibility is to monitor the implementation of EU legislation and to provide information.

---

[295] Although their establishment started much earlier with the European Centre for the Development of Vocational Training established in 1975 in Thessaloniki and the European Foundation for the Improvement of Living and Working Conditions established in 1975 and in Dublin.

[296] Case 9/56 *Meroni* [1958] ECR 133. See also Chapter 3 for a further discussion of *Meroni*.

[297] Majone and Everson op. cit., who cite P Strauss, 'The place of agencies in government: separation of powers and the fourth branch of government' (1984) 84 Columbia Law Review 573; see also M Dorf and C Sabel, 'A constitution of democratic experimentalism' (1998) 98 Columbia Law Review, 267.

[298] See Chapter 3 for a discussion of the feasibility of introducing such measures in the context of comitology.

It has been argued[299] that there is a real need for greater autonomy and policy-making powers for European agencies. There is a lack of administrative infrastructure in the EU, as well as a shortage of resources in the Commission. The Commission, even aided by the comitology process, cannot maintain so much responsibility for overseeing regulation in the EU. As Majone and Everson point out,[300] it was the Antitrust Division of the US Justice Department, rather than the Commission Directorate-General, which discovered the 'vitamin cartel' of EC firms.[301] Furthermore, the Commission is becoming increasingly politicised, with commissioners being overseen by the Parliament, and beginning to look more like a European Government: in such circumstances there is a need for more independent regulation.

However, even if agencies are not yet fully-blown autonomous creatures in the EU, then it is the case that they still play an important role in regulatory networks,[302] and once again, as in the case of comitology, play an important role in the largely unwritten constitutional structure of the EU.

---

[299] Majone and Everson, 'Institutional Reform: independent agencies, oversight, co-ordination and procedural control' at 164.

[300] Ibid. at p 165.

[301] There have been demands made to remove competition policy from the Commission and for an independent European Cartel Office to be set up: see e.g. S Wilks and L McGowan, 'Disarming the Commission: The debate over a European Cartel Office' (1995) 32 JCMS 259.

[302] R Dehousse, 'Regulation by Networks in the European Community; The Role of European Agencies' (1997) 4 JEPP 246; G Majone, 'The New European Agencies: Regulation by Information' (1997) 4 JEPP 262.

3

LAW-MAKING AND DEMOCRACY IN THE EU

EU law is complex, obscure and often incomprehensible. While these features are by no means unique to EU law, they do have the effect of making it inaccessible to its already estranged citizens.

It is perhaps inevitable that EU law should be complex. The evolutionary nature of the EU has ensured this, whereby an original common market has been extended by numerous treaty amendments into a hybrid organisation, sprawling out of its pillar structure into protocols and declarations, nearly incoherent as a result of various consolidations, renumbering and repeals. A lack of a proper constitutional procedure has also ensured that opportunities to create a more coherent, constitutional document have been passed up at IGCs in which politicians and diplomats have preferred ambiguity, and a messy treaty structure, in order to further national interests. The redrafting and simplification of the treaties[1] was conspicuously not on the agenda of the 2000 IGC, and it remains to be seen how 'constitutional' the 2004 IGC will actually be, although the simplification of the voluminous body of Community secondary law has become a pressing concern in the past ten years[2]. In any case, the European Convention on the future of the European Union, set up in March 2002, is considering key issues of constitutional import, but its outcome is as yet unclear.

The first sections of this chapter examine the sources of law and the legislative processes of the EU. The remainder focuses on the crucial issue of the EU's democratic deficit, and the ways in which the EU's convoluted law-making processes have contributed to this deficit.

SOURCES OF LAW IN THE EU

As is well-known, the EU has no explicit constitution. The basic documents of the EU are the treaties and they do, however, exhibit some constitutional characteristics.

---

[1] The Commission concluded that such a project was not realistic for the IGC 2000. See, however, the Florence treaty project on the re-organisation of the treaties: 'A Basic Treaty for the EU: A Study of the reorganisation of the Treaties'.
[2] See discussion below.

They set up the institutions of the EU, allocate certain powers to the EU, and contain references to the rule of law, fundamental rights and democracy.[3] On the other hand, they might seem to depart from constitutions in other ways, for example in their large bias toward economic and commercial law.

However, although the treaties are constitutive of the EU, there is no one document which does this. There are, indeed, a large number of treaties: the treaties which are relevant to each of the Communities – namely the ECSC, EC and Euratom treaties, the Merger treaty, and those which have amended them – the Single European Act, the Treaties of Maastricht, Amsterdam and Nice, not to mention various accession treaties on the arrival of new member states. Additionally, there are the various declarations, protocols and annexes attached to some of these treaties, some of which are of a clear constitutional relevance.[4] These different documents do not fit together in a particularly coherent and orderly way, suffering as they do the effects of various revision and renumberings. Therefore primary EU law is opaque. It exhibits none of the formal presentational clarity of the US Federal constitution or the German *Grundgesetz*.

Naturally, however, these treaties are not the only source of law within the EU. There are various types of 'secondary law'. The EC treaty specifically contains a provision, Article 249, detailing the various types of act by which the EC may legislate. Likewise, the other pillars of the EU, the CFSP and PJCC, also make provision for a further number of law-making instruments.

Article 249 reads as follows:

> In order to carry out their tasks and in accordance with the provisions of this Treaty, the European Parliament acting jointly with the Council, the Council and the Commission shall make regulations and issue directives, take decisions, make recommendations or deliver opinions.
>
> A regulation shall have general application. It shall be binding in its entirety and directly applicable in all member States.
>
> A directive shall be binding as to the result to be achieved, upon each member State to which it is addressed, but shall leave to the national authorities the choice of form and methods.
>
> A decision shall be binding in its entirety upon those to whom it is addressed.
>
> Recommendations and opinions shall have no binding force.

It can be seen that Article 249 does not provide a comprehensive definition of each of these types of legislative act. Nor does it make any distinction between legislation (i.e. *Gesetz*, Act) and administrative acts (*Verordnung*, rule) as do most national legal systems. Thus, merely by looking at the name of an act, one cannot really tell how general, or specific, in nature it is. The following section expands on the terse wording of Article 249.

---

[3] For example, Article 6 TEU, which reads as follows: 'The Union is founded on the principles of liberty, democracy, respect for human rights and fundamental freedoms, and the rule of law, principles which are common to the Member States.'

[4] e.g. those regarding the institutions attached to the Treaty of Nice by way of *The Declaration on the enlargement of the European Union*.

TYPES OF COMMUNITY ACT UNDER ARTICLE 249 EC

Regulations are basically legislative in character and the closest the Community comes to an Act of Parliament. According to the ECJ, 'the Regulation, being of an essentially normative character, is applicable not to a limited identifiable number of persons but rather to categories of persons envisaged both in the abstract and as a whole'.[5] Even so, many, indeed most, regulations are not very general in nature, as they are issued by the Commission, as delegated, implementing legislation, usually in those aspects of EC law such as agriculture, or the common customs tariff, where speedy regulation is necessary because market structures and processes change rapidly, and thus, in practice, it is the substance rather than the form of the measure which is important. Thus, the fact that something is called a regulation has not deterred the ECJ from finding some regulations to be 'disguised decisions', because of their individualised nature.[6] Regulations are also directly applicable, which means that they do not need any acts of implementation by the member states,[7] but instead automatically become part of their legal system. Indeed, according to the ECJ in *Leonesio*,[8] their direct applicability must not be compromised by implementing provisions at national level.

Directives are a feature unique to Community law, and are probably the best known type of Community secondary legislation. Directives differ from regulations in two notable aspects. First, they are not of general application: some are addressed to only one member state, where practices might be divergent from the others. Secondly, they are not directly applicable, because they specifically require implementation. Member states are given a deadline by which to implement their obligations, but have a discretion as to how they choose to do so, an important application of subsidiarity.[9] In fact, directives are the most usual measure used in some areas, such as harmonisation of law, environment, consumer protection, company law, intellectual property and social policy. Although, originally, it seemed that the main intent of the treaty founders was that directives would be used for harmonising divergent member states' laws, more recently they have been used for other purposes, to found new obligations and to establish Community-based structures.[10]

From the wording of Article 249 EC, it might seem that, being addressed to member states, directives could not be invoked by individuals, but this is not so. Under the case law of the ECJ, individuals have been able to invoke directives directly in

---

[5] Joined cases 16 & 17/62 *Confédération nationale des producteurs de fruits et légumes* v *Council* [1962] ECR 471.

[6] e.g. Joined cases 41–4/70 *International Fruit Company* v *Commission* [1971] ECR 411.

[7] Although very occasionally they may do so – as was the case of Regulation 543/69 which introduced the tachograph system – OJ 1969 L77/49. Tachographs are instruments placed in cabs of commercial vehicles to record the driver's time speed and distance.

[8] Case 93/71 *Leonesio* v *Ministry for Agriculture* [1972] ECR 287.

[9] However, in a few cases, member states have very little or no discretion: see e.g. Case 38/77 *ENKA* [1977] ECR 2203. On the other hand, implementing legislation may sometimes impose greater obligations than those required by the Directive: Case 2/97 *societa Iraliana Petroli S, A* v *Borsana Srl* [2001] ICMLR 27.

[10] e.g. the European Works Council Directive 94/45 EC OJ 1994 L254.

their national courts, where the obligations under them have been 'clear, precise and unconditional'.[11] This means that if a member state fails to implement a directive, or does so ineffectively, it may still have force. Inadequate transposition of directives by member states has been one of the main breaches of EC law.[12]

Decisions are not intended to be general in nature but are rather addressed to specific parties – to individuals, companies, to an individual member state, or even to all of these, such as in the case of Council Decision of 1976 approving direct elections of the European Parliament.[13] The addressee must be notified of any decision addressed to it.[14] They may be taken under many areas of EC competence. However, they may also be more general in nature: there has been a growth in the use of decisions from 1986, and these have tended to be 'legislative' decisions taken within the framework of policy programmes, such as Erasmus, Socrates, etc.

Regulations, directives and decisions must comply with certain procedural requirements. So, according to Article 253 EC, they must 'state the reasons on which they are based and shall refer to any proposals or opinions which were required to be obtained pursuant to this Treaty'. Community legislation must also comply with the principle of subsidiarity, under Article 5 EC, which will be discussed in the next chapter. Most EC legislation is now published in the Official Journal. Article 254 EC requires that regulations, directives and decisions which have been adopted in accordance with the codecision procedure shall be published in the Official Journal and that they come into force on the date specified or, in the absence of that, on the twentieth day following their publication. Regulations of the Council and Commission, as well as directives addressed to all member states, must also be published in the Official Journal under Article 254. If they do not comply with these essential procedural requirements then they may be annulled by an action before the ECJ under Articles 230 or 234 EC.[15] All of these are important procedural requirements which have acquired a sort of constitutional status.

Recommendations and opinions, the remaining types of Community act to be mentioned in Article 249 EC, are not binding at all. They do not, therefore, create rights upon which individuals may rely before a national court.[16] On the other hand, they do have persuasive authority. However, they need not go through the complex legislation procedures which are detailed later in this chapter.

Acts *sui generis*

The list in Article 249 is not exhaustive. The ECJ has held that there are legally binding acts which do not fall under any of the above categories. These have usually

---

[11] Case 41/74 *Van Duyn* v *Home Office* [1974] ECR 1337; Case 148/78 *Ratti* [1979] ECR 1629.

[12] See Chapters 9 and 12.

[13] Council Decision 76/787 OJ 1976 L 278/1.

[14] Article 254(1) EC. But the decision need only be published if taken under the codecision procedure.

[15] See Chapters 6 and 10.

[16] Case C-322/88 *Grimaldi* [1989] ECR 4407.

[17] Case 22/70 *Commission* v *Council* [1971] ECR 263.

been described as acts *sui generis*. This was established in the *ERTA* case.[17] These acts *sui generis* are encountered, for instance, in the internal management of the Communities, such as in setting up committees, or formulating rules of procedure, or in the adoption of the budget. The *Noordwijk Cement* case[18] is a good example, in which the ECJ held that, just because a Community act bears a label other than a decision, directive or regulation, that does mean that it is immune from challenge under Article 230. The act in question in *Noordwijk* was a letter from the Commission, informing certain cement companies that their immunity from fines for breach of EC competition law was at an end, which the ECJ held to be reviewable because it changed the position of the companies concerned, and thus had binding legal effect.

Acts under the second and third pillars of the TEU and acts of the Council as an intergovernmental body

Under these two pillars there is little supranationalism, and it is the Council which takes the main decisions, with the other institutions playing a subsidiary role. In the context of the CFSP, Article 14 TEU provides that 'the Council shall adopt joint actions': these are general in nature, and concern the operational scope of action taken by the EU. In contrast, 'common positions' taken by the Council under Article 15 TEU define the approach of the EU to a particular matter of geographical or thematic nature. There are a number of instruments which the Council may adopt for third pillar matters, concerning the PJCC. For example, under Article 34 TEU, the Council may adopt common positions, framework decisions, decisions or establish Conventions.

Occasionally, there are meetings of the 'Representatives of the Member States meeting in Council' which are not provided by the treaty but have developed in practice. Decisions taken during these meetings are not 'decisions' in the sense of binding acts provided for in the treaty. They are often taken in the form of a 'Resolution' and concern acts which are not specified in the treaty but are directly connected with Community activities. They form part of the so-called *acquis communautaire*[19] and all new member states are required to accept them. Such acts are not be confused with certain decisions which must be taken, in accordance with the treaty, by 'common accord' of the governments of member states on certain matters which the treaty has deliberately left within the competence of the member states.[20]

Soft law

Soft law as a concept originated in public international law in the 1970s, partly because of the enormous expansion of activities of international organisations and

---

[18] Cases 8–11/66 *Noordwijk's Cement Accoord* [1967] ECR 75.
[19] Article 2 TEU.
[20] e.g. Articles 223(1), 289 EC, Article 48 TEU.

the ways in which those organisations were making law.[21] Soft law has been described as 'the rules of conduct which find themselves on the legally non-binding level (in the sense of enforceable and sanctionable) but which according to their drafters have to be accorded a legal scope'.[22] Soft law is also attractive to national governments, as it relieves them of the burden of regulating in detail and fits in with the current philosophy of lighter regulation. It offers much greater flexibility: unlike legislation, which is expensive, and follows inflexible proceedings, soft law is much easier to introduce to keep up with changing practices. Also, if unsuccessful, it can easily be withdrawn.[23] Examples of such acts in the EC context include guidelines, conclusions, declarations, communiqués, action programmes, notices which provide guidance on the Commission's policy in a certain field, as well as recommendations and opinions.

Soft law creates an expectation that the conduct of states and international organisations will be in conformity with non-binding rules of conduct. However, soft law can be problematic. For example, in the field of competition law, the Commission issues 'comfort letters', which are assurances that it will not proceed against an undertaking. Because, as soft law, these notices are not binding, they may not be challenged (by, for example, other interested parties, such as competitors) before the CFI.[24] Furthermore, because they do not have the status of formal EC legislation, they do not have to follow the rules laid down in the treaty for Community law-making. This, in turn, makes it difficult to hold those responsible for them to account, which is hardly satisfactory from a democratic point of view.

A hierarchy of norms?

During 1991 IGC, the Commission proposed that a new hierarchy of legal norms should be created, to order the EC's legislative activity in a more comprehensive and coherent way. It was the Commission's intention to abolish the directive, leaving only the treaties, general laws and administrative measures. This would certainly have made things clearer. The member states were unhappy with such a proposal, which they saw as depriving them of the element of sovereignty and subsidiarity provided by directives. However, they did indicate their willingness to consider the appropriateness of such a hierarchy in the declaration attached to the TEU.[25]

---

[21] See e.g. I Sedl-Hohenveldern, 'International Economic Soft law' Hague Recueil 1979-ii.

[22] KC Wellens and GM Borchardt, 'Soft law in European Community Law' (1989) ELR 267 at 285.

[23] See F Snyder, 'Soft Law and Institutional Practice in the EC' in Martin (ed.) *The Construction of Europe, Essays in Honour of Emile Noel* (Dordrecht: Kluwer, 1994). Although perhaps the speed with which soft law can be created or withdrawn is somewhat of a myth. Technical questions (and soft law is often used for the technical) are complex whether they are resolved by legislation or by more informal means. See A Ogus, *Regulation* (Oxford University Press, 1994).

[24] Although courts are beginning to create opportunities to intervene, such as through the doctrine of legitimate expectations, see J Schwarze, *European Administrative law* (London: Sweet and Maxwell, 1992).

Nothing has been done to date. The European Parliament has been pressing for a distinction between legislative measures, which it wants to be adopted in codecision by the Council and Parliament, and administrative measures, which would be adopted by the Commission.[26] Again, nothing has so far come of this.

THE LAW-MAKING PROCESS

The EU has perhaps the most complex legislative system[27] in the world, a truly bewildering variety of legislative procedures,[28] reflecting a growing inter-institutional dialogue and dynamic, but creating great complexity, even more so now, given the provisions on closer cooperation in Articles 43–45 TEU and Article 11 EC, which provide a framework for more flexible initiatives. Petersen and Bomberg have used this striking metaphor to describe EC legislation – they refer to 'an organic accretion of decision making processes: new ones are fastened on old ones in the same way that lichens attach themselves first to a tree, then to other lichens, adding layer upon layer, overlapping but never shedding'.[29]

The Council, Commission and Parliament are all involved one way or another in the law-making process, although the Parliament's role has greatly increased over recent years, transforming legislation in the EC from the intergovernmentalism imposed by the Luxembourg accords, to something approaching a bicameralism along the lines of other political systems, by the late 1990s. However, despite its complexity, the legislative process of the EC has in fact been relatively effective in

---

[25] *Declaration no 16 on the hierarchy of Community Acts.* In this they declared their willingness to examine the issue in the next (1996) IGC.

[26] EP *Resolution containing European Parliament's proposals for the IGC 13 April 2000* (A5-0086/00 Resol. Dimitrakopoulos/Leinen).

[27] For a discussion of law-making procedures, see the following works: P Craig and C Harlow (eds) *Law-making in the EU* (Kluwer, 1998); S Boyron, 'The co-decision procedure: rethinking the Constitutional Fundamentals', in Craig and Harlow (eds) op. cit.; A Dashwood, 'Community Legislative Procedures in the Era of the Treaty on European Union' [1994] 19 ELRev 343; D Earnshaw and D Judge, 'From cooperation to co-decision: the European Parliament's path to legislative power' in J Richardson (ed.) *European Union, Power and policy-making* (Routledge, 1996); J Fitzmaurice, 'An Analysis of the EC's Cooperation Procedure' [1988] JCMS 389; K Lenaerts, 'Some Reflections on the Separation of Powers in the European Community' [1991] 28 CMLRev 11; J Lodge, 'The Single European Act and the New Legislative Cooperation Procedure: A Critical Analysis' [1987] 11 JEI/RIE 5; W Ungerer, 'Institutional consequences of broadening and deepening the Community: The consequences for decision-making process' [1993] 30 CMLRev 71; J Usher, 'The Institutions of the European Communities after the Single European Act' [1987] 19 Bracton Law Journal 64; F Jacobs and M Shackleton, *The European Parliament*; M Westlake, *The Commission and the Parliament* (Butterworths, 1994).

[28] 22 different legislative procedures existed in 1996, as reported by the Commission for the 1996 IGC: *Report for the Reflection Group* OOPEC Lux, and this number excluded delegated legislation and cases where the Council or Commission act alone.

[29] J Petersen and E Bomberg, *Decision-making in the European Union* (Macmillan, 1999) at 20 (a metaphor borrowed, as they acknowledge, from Simon Gage).

developing and passing laws.[30] Indeed, as one recent commentator stressed, 'The Community statute book is voluminous'.[31]

The Commission alone has the right to propose legislation but the Council (sometimes acting jointly with the EP under Article 251) decides whether a particular measure should be adopted. However, other Community bodies do have a means of input into the Commission legislation programme, which they exploit to varying extents. Under Article 208 EC, the Council may request the Commission to undertake any studies and to submit to it proposals. This is also the case for the European Parliament under Article 192 EC. Member states may also stimulate ideas for legislation through the European Council, which will sometimes even require specific measures to be introduced.

Once the Commission has decided to act, a preliminary draft proposal will be drawn up by a Commission working party. This process may take from several weeks to several years. Outside experts will be included in the working group and, until the draft is finalised, it will be very fluid. The voting requirements in the Council as well as the legislative procedure to be followed are dictated by the legal basis[32] of the proposed measure.

TYPES OF LEGISLATIVE PROCEDURE

Most basically, the Commission and Council may act by themselves, without consulting any other institution. This is a throw-back to the earlier days of the Community, when the Parliament, as a mere 'Assembly', played little part in the legislative process. So, for example, under Article 57(2) EC, which concerns the free movement of capital, or under Article 301 EC, concerning decisions to take economic sanctions against third countries, there is no requirement that the Parliament (nor any other minor institution such as ESC) be consulted. However, a practice (with the rather cumbersome name of Luns-Westerwerp procedure, named after those who instigated it) has arisen, whereby the Parliament is at least informally consulted.

Consultation

Until the Single European Act of 1986, this was the basic form of legislative procedure. It required the Parliament, and sometimes other institutions such as ESC, to be consulted on legislative proposals, but their opinion had little, if any, impact on the outcome. However, the ECJ managed to improve the position of the European Parliament, prior to the Single European Act, by its decision in the *Isoglucose* case

---

[30] Although the amount of legislation passed has fallen since the completion of the Internal Market.
[31] T Burns, 'Better Lawmaking? An Evaluation of Lawmaking in the EC' in P Craig and C Harlow (eds) op. cit. at 435.
[32] See Chapter 4 for a discussion of the legal basis of Community acts.

of 1981.[33] The background to *Isoglucose* was that the first direct elections to the European Parliament had been held in 1979 and following the dissolution of Parliament, but before its recommencement, the Council had adopted a piece of legislation without consulting the Parliament, when it should have done so. The ECJ annulled this measure on the basis that, where the treaty requires consultation, the Council could not act without the Parliament's opinion, consultation being 'an essential factor in the institutional balance introduced by the treaty'. It also referred to the 'fundamental democratic principle that peoples should take part in the expression of power through the intermediary of a representative assembly'.[34] However, this noble statement is undermined somewhat by the fact that there is no requirement that the Council actually take account of the Parliament's opinion, nor indeed, give any reasons for rejecting it.[35] Thus, in the context of the Consultation procedure, the Parliament may not force its opinion on the Council as a lower house could on an upper house in most bicameral systems. On the other hand, the Parliament does have the power to delay legislation, as in 1989, when it threatened to delay a Commission proposal to start the first phase of EMU on 1 July 1990, because the Commission, against the Parliament's wishes, would not accept a stronger role for the Committee of European Central Bank Governors.

The TEU introduced consultation of the Parliament into more areas, as consequently did Amsterdam, and, to a lesser extent, Nice.[36] It is still used in areas where the member states wish to retain control, such as agriculture (Article 37), indirect taxation (Article 93), as well as Articles 94 and 308, which provide a general basis for legislation. However, in some areas, such as Article 18, the legislative basis for citizenship rights of free movement, and Article 13, the basis for non-discrimination legislation, consultation has given way to codecision under Article 251 EC, discussed later in the chapter.

Cooperation

The cooperation procedure,[37] originally introduced by the Single European Act, and the first procedure to be set out in a separate treaty article (now in Article 252 EC), involves two readings by the Parliament and gives it the opportunity to propose amendments to draft legislation.[38] In the first reading, the Parliament simply offers its opinion on the proposed measure. If the Council does not accept the Parliament's opinion, it has to submit a reasoned common position. The Council then may adopt

---

[33] Case 138/79 *Roquette Frères SA v Council* [1980] ECR 3333.

[34] Ibid.

[35] See M Westlake, *The Commission and the Parliament* (Butterworths, 1994) at 34.

[36] See, for example, Article 159 EC (economic and social cohesion); Articles 104(14), 107(6), 117 EC (economic and monetary policy).

[37] Article 252 EC.

[38] For literature on the cooperation procedure, see D Edward, 'The Impact of the Single Act on Institutions' (1987) 24 CMLRev 19; R Bieber, 'Legislative Procedure for the Establishment of a Single Market' (1988) 26 CMLRev 711; J Fitzmaurice, 'An Analysis of the European Community's Cooperation Procedure' (1986) 26 JCMS 389; J Lodge, 'The European Parliament – from "assembly" to co-legislature: changing the institutional dynamics' in J Lodge, *The European Community and the Challenge of the Future* (London: Pinter, 1988) (1st edn).

the proposed measure in accordance with the common position, unless the Parliament, within three months, rejects the common position, or proposes amendments on which the Commission can also comment. The Council can only override the Parliament's rejection or amendments if it is unanimous. In fact, in the first ten years of its application, the number of outright rejections of the Council's common position could be counted on the fingers of two hands.[39]

Although it increased the involvement of the Parliament, the cooperation procedure was criticised for having the following weaknesses: that the Council of Ministers could still overrule the Parliament in any case and that the Parliament had been given a dubious benefit in the power to hinder EC legislation (as the Parliament prefers to be seen as a positive force in the legislation process). In fact by 1997, only 21 per cent of Parliament's amendments had been accepted by the Council at the second reading.[40] However, the introduction of the cooperation procedure did instil changes in inter-institutional relationships – for example, greater dialogue between the Council and Parliament, but also between the Parliament and the Commission, which introduced considerable internal reforms in order to accommodate the cooperation procedure – such as the creation of a new unit within the Secretariat-General to deal with relationships with the European Parliament.

Although the Single European Act applied this procedure to only ten treaty articles, these included most areas of single market legislation (two-thirds of the 1985 Internal Market White Paper legislation in all[41]), specific research programmes, certain developments relating to structural funds and environmental legislation, and thus a sizeable proportion of legislation. Although the TEU initially extended the scope of the cooperation procedure, this expansion was curtailed by the Treaty of Amsterdam and the growing focus instead on the codecision procedure. Cooperation is now primarily limited to the enactment of measures related to monetary policy,[42] and has been likened to 'some arcane rite so ancient its origins and purpose have been lost in the mists of time'.[43]

Codecision

Difficulties inherent in cooperation, such as the absence of a parliamentary veto, led to calls for a new legislative procedure. The codecision procedure,[44] introduced by the TEU, marked fairly significant changes in EC decision-making mechanisms and institutional interrelations. In its proposals to the pre-Maastricht IGC, the

---

[39] K St Claire Bradley, 'The European Parliament and Treaty Reform: Building Blocks and Stumbling Blocks' in D O'Keefe and P Twomey (eds) *Legal Issues of the Amsterdam Treaty* (Hart Publishing) 134.
[40] See European Parliament report: *(Co)governing after Maastricht: the European Parliament's institutional performance 1994–1999, Political Series POLI 104/rev. EN.)*
[41] D Earnshaw and D Judge, 'From cooperation to codecision: The European Parliament's path to legislative power' in J Richardson (ed) *Policy Making in the European Union* (London: Routledge, 1996).
[42] Namely, Articles 102, 103, 106 EC, which are still seen as too controversial to allow for greater Parliamentary involvement.
[43] St Claire Bradley op. cit. at 128–9.
[44] Article 251 EC.

Parliament had proposed a form of codecision largely based on Article 38 of its Draft European Union Treaty of 1984,[45] and, to a certain extent, the Parliament's proposals were accepted: quite a triumph. The codecision procedure, in its initial form, was highly complicated (it originally allowed for three readings of draft legislation by the European Parliament), and still retains some of this quality, even after attempts at Amsterdam to simplify it. What follows is a brief summary of codecision and its significance.

Codecision now encompasses two readings by the European Parliament. The first follows the presentation of the Commission's draft proposal to both the Council and the European Parliament. If the Council approves of the Parliament's first reading, it may adopt the act. Should it not, it will communicate its common position, and reasons, back for a second reading. At the second reading, the European Parliament may approve, reject or amend the proposal before it. If it approves or rejects, then its decision is final. If an amendment is proposed, there can be an optional reference by the Council to the Conciliation Committee,[46] which consists of an equal number of representatives from the Council and Parliament. The joint text of the Conciliation Committee is final. Should it fail to reach a joint text, the act will be deemed not to have been adopted.

Initial reactions to the codecision procedure, prior to its amendment at Amsterdam, were critical. Deirdre Curtin's is typical: 'the procedure is formally one of codecision, but with the effective balance of power indisputably weighted toward the Council'.[47] Thus, codecision was perceived as not having solved the problem of the democratic deficit.[48] However, following Amsterdam, the legislative balance seems to have shifted in the Parliament's favour. Principally, Parliament may reject outright the Council's common position at the second reading, thus effectively having the final say in adoption of legislation under this procedure. Parliament at last has some real power.

But has EC legislation necessarily been improved as a result? The Parliament has made some impact: it has strengthened environmental and consumer concerns by setting stricter limits or by the insertion of consumer linked provisions.[49] It has, it would seem, used codecision to try to find an audience among its electorate. Furthermore, it seems to have improved Parliamentary procedures. Even before

---

[45] See R Corbett, *The Treaty of Maastricht* (Harlow: Longman, 1993).

[46] The details of this body's work were established following an inter-institutional conference in Luxembourg in October 1993: see *Inter-Institutional Agreement 25 October 1993* (OJ 1993 C331/1). The Conciliation Committee is supported by the Secretariats of the Council and Parliament and meets in camera.

[47] D Curtin, 'The Constitutional structure of the Union: a Europe of bits and pieces' (1993) 30 CMLRev 17 at 37.

[48] J-C Piris, 'After Maastricht, are the Community institutions more efficacious, more democratic and more transparent?' (1994) 19 EL Rev 449; also A Dashwood, 'Community Legislative Proceedings in the era of the treaty on the EU' (1994) 19 EL Rev 343, for further critical comments.

[49] For example, in the case of the directive on *The protection of consumers in respect of distance contracts*, the EP got the Council to agree on a number of consumer-friendly supplier obligations: (e.g. on telephone calls, the identity of the supplier and the commercial purpose of the call must be made clear at the beginning of any conversation with the consumer). (Source: *(Co)governing after Maastricht: the European Parliament's institutional performance 1994–1999, Political Series POLI 104/rev. EN.*)

codecision, cooperation had led to a better organisation and voting discipline within the Parliament. The Parliament has become more disciplined and streamlined, although it has tended to concentrate its workload into only three of its committees, due to the great use made of codecision by Article 95.[50]

Codecision has worked quite well. It has led to a high rate of adoption of legislation. Out of a total of 379 acts to go through codecision from 1994–9,[51] 166 had been adopted, 179 were under way, 21 had lapsed and only three failed altogether. The Parliament has also been pretty successful in having its amendments adopted by the Council,[52] although they may not always be accepted in the form originally proposed by the Parliament. On the other hand, some measures do take a very long time to be processed through the system, although this may often be due to the time taken by the Council to produce a common position.[53] Conciliation of course adds to the length of proceedings.

The codecision procedure has led to a development of more or less formal contacts between the Council and Parliament through the Conciliation committee.[54] The Commission also has greater contact with the Parliament under codecision, as it is forced to engage the Parliament's committees early in the political process in order to get its legislation accepted. Sometimes European MPs are even involved in the drafting.[55] Accordingly, this has led to the development of a dialogue between these institutions, or rather, has transformed the former Commission/Council dialogue into a 'trilogue', involving the European Parliament, something which was underlined by *The Joint Declaration of the Institutions* of 1999, which urged them to achieve agreement at the earliest possible stage.[56] The ECJ has also underlined the duty of sincere cooperation by which every Community institution is to be heard in accordance with the requirements of the Treaty.[57]

Codecision is now the default procedure for EC legislation. Although large in number, the codecision procedure only applies to those Treaty provisions which

---

[50] The three relevant committees being environment, public health and consumer affairs; economic and monetary affairs and industrial politics; and legal affairs.

[51] *(Co)governing after Maastricht.*

[52] *(Co)governing after Maastricht.*
The number of successful 'codecision amendments' voted during the second (and third) reading were much higher in comparison with the first readings, whereas they are substantially lower in the case of the cooperation procedure. In fact, the proportion of successful second (and third reading) amendments doubled in the case of the Council (from 21 per cent to 46 per cent). Moreover, if one adds to the proportion of accepted second reading amendments by the Council the proportion of 12.5 per cent of joint compromise texts, the total proportion increased to nearly two thirds. Finally the success rate of Parliament's second reading amendments increased more than a third in the case of the Commission (from 43 per cent to 61 per cent). Given this quantitative data of successful amendments, it can safely be said that codecision had a positive impact with regard to Parliament's influence in the making of European binding legislation.

[53] The average length of process of the codecision was just 269 days in 1998, although some acts could take as long as 2,000 days to be adopted: *(Co)governing after Maastricht.*

[54] See D Earnshaw and D Judge, 'The European Parliament's path to legislative power' in J Richardson (ed) *European Union: power and policy making* (Routledge, 1996) at 124.

[55] M Westlake, *The Commission and the Parliament* (Butterworths, 1994) at 17.

[56] Joint Declaration of 4 May 1999 on practical arrangements for the new codecision procedure, OJ C 148 28.5.1999.

[57] e.g. in Case C-204/86 *Hellenic Republic v Council* (1988) ECR 5323.

make specific reference for its use, for example: the free movement of persons, (Articles 40, 44, 46(2), 57(1), 57(2) EC); the internal market with some exceptions (Article 95 EC); research frameworks, environmental strategies, consumer protection, trans-European infrastructure networks, measures for education, culture, public health, measures in the fields of employment and social policy. This list was further increased by the Treaty of Nice.[58] About 25 per cent of proposals from the Commission, up to 1998, were by way of codecision, but it is still not used in sensitive areas such as agriculture, tax harmonisation and trade policy. For the whole range of TEU activities, up to 1998, only 13.2 per cent of Council legislation was by way of codecision.[59] To put this in perspective, however, socio-economic legislation, including environment, health and consumer policies make up only 25 per cent of the total EU output. Thus, in the socio-economic field, codecision plays an important part and the Parliament's input should be seen in a somewhat different light.

It has to be noted, however, that not all legislation under codecision has the importance that the procedure warrants. There are a great many technical texts, such as directives on packaging waste, necessary, but hardly of the first importance in the grand scheme of the EU. The overwhelming majority of codecision texts are based on Article 95, the legal basis for the harmonisation of the internal market. By contrast, Article 49 EC, which concerns the free movement of persons, has been little used as a legal base. The exploitation of the newly introduced Treaty articles has been feeble.[60]

According to the Commission, the distribution of subject matter under codecision has been 'fragmentary and arbitrary',[61] although naturally the Parliament has pushed for a greater application of the codecision procedure.[62] However, it would make sense for there to be a more coherent assignment, preferably in areas where democratic accountability is required, rather than more administrative types of act. Furthermore, even after Nice, unanimity is still required in the Council, for codecision on rights of residence of workers, social security for migrant workers and the rules governing the profession. Perhaps unanimous voting should be abolished in the context of codecision (although the move to QMV is inevitably controversial). The search for agreement among all the member states surely reduces the bargaining powers of the Parliament and Commission and impedes constructive dialogue. On the other hand, QMV and codecision have completely different political dynamics. The Parliament does not work along the national lines. There are also different political majorities in the Parliament and Council at present, namely, mostly to the left of centre in the Council and right of centre in the Parliament, which also invariably affects the negotiating strategies of the two institutions.

---

[58] It now applies to seven further provisions which have changed from unanimity to QMV: Articles 13, 62, 63, 65, 157, 159 and 191.
[59] *(Co)governing after Maastricht.*
[60] But note that the amended version of the equal treatment directive is by way of codecision, based on Article 141 EC.
[61] Commission *Report on the scope of the Co-decision procedure* EU Bull 7/8 1996, 192.
[62] *Resolution* A4-0102/95 para 29c.

It has been suggested that there are tensions in the way codecision operates.[63] On the one hand, the procedure is presented in the classical manner. A proposal is put forward by the Commission and examined by the European Parliament and Council, which have various tools at their disposal. Boyron refers, in this context, to the range of mechanisms used by Montesquieu to explain and implement his theories.[64] He cited the action of 'la faculté d'empêcher' (the possibility of preventing an action) as well as 'la faculté de statuer' (the possibility of acting or taking a decision). Codecision, in its pre-Amsterdam form, as well as the coopera-tion procedure, was overwhelmingly occupied with the 'faculté d'empêcher', and thus could be explained by the classical means of checks and balances.

However, the inclusion of the conciliation committee into codecision appeared to shift the direction of the procedure, away from a more classical means of legislation, to incorporate instead something more like mediation and Alternative Dispute Resolution (ADR). With this, the emphasis is not so much on stopping other institu-tions, nor on prevailing over them, but rather on trying to reach an agreement which meets with the approbation of all the parties.[65] These tensions between formal and actual practice are symptomatic of the entire EU constitutional framework.[66]

Another troubling aspect of codecision is whether the practice of conciliation can be reconciled with the requirements of democracy. The meetings of the conciliation committee are not open to the public nor could its procedures be described as any-thing like 'transparent'. On the other hand, conciliation can play a very significant role in the achievement of legislation by codecision.[67] However, the real negotiations tend not to take place at conciliation meetings at all (which are often more like assemblies, with up to 100 participants, although not usually including Council rep-resentation at ministerial level, but rather COREPER) but instead through informal contacts.[68] The processes are often so opaque that the actors themselves are often unsure as to where initiatives are coming from, and accountability is impossible in such circumstances. But perhaps what is really important is that negotiations be conducted on the basis of established positions, or at least be traceable if not trans-parent. Conciliation is an example of a worrying trend in EC legislation, which, although increasing the power of the Parliament and thus apparently making the process more democratic, also increases its complexity and opacity and undermines that very increase in democracy. This issue will be explored later in the chapter.

---

[63] E.g. S Boyron, 'The Co-Decision Procedure: Rethinking the Constitutional Fundamentals' (1996) in P Craig and C Harlow (eds) *Law-Making in the EU* (Kluwer, 1998) at 147.

[64] See Boyron op. cit. at 157.

[65] The Council Presidency plays an important role in conciliation.

[66] This point is discussed elsewhere, for example in Chapter 2.

[67] Up until 31 May 1999 the conciliation committee held a total of 71 meetings on a total of 61 pro-posals (ESPCC activity report 1993–1999. Doc PE 230 998).

[68] See e.g. J Peterson, 'Decision Making in the European Union: towards a framework for analysis' (1995) JEPP 69, discussing policy networks. See also Chapter 2.

Assent

This is the procedure which gives to the Parliament the greatest powers and it was first developed by the Single European Act. Under it, a measure may only be adopted if the Parliament gives its assent. The scope of the assent procedure has been expanded from external relations (Article 300 EC) under which the Parliament has the right to reject association agreements with non-EC countries, as well as the accession of new member states, to other areas such as a uniform electoral procedure for the Parliament (Article 190(4) EC), and most recently, the finding of a serious and persistent breach of fundamental rights by a member state (Article 7 TEU). As there are no time limits within which the Parliament must assent, it has a considerable power of delay. Nevertheless, the assent procedure does have one unfortunate consequence for the role of the European Parliament in rule-making. Assent is the authorisation without which a legislative act cannot be adopted by the Council. However, unlike with codecision, with the assent procedure there is no formal structure within which the Parliament and Council can settle their grievances. As the Parliament has the last word, it may risk being blamed for negative decisions.

Legislation and the Social Dialogue

A special procedure, introduced by the treaty of Amsterdam, applies for some social policy matters. The treaty of Amsterdam inserted a mechanism, via Articles 138 and 139 EC, under which the social partners (namely the representatives of management and labour) play a key role in developing social policy and legislation. The role of the social partners is recognised at national level, whereby member states may entrust management and labour with implementation of directives under Article 137(4) EC. Furthermore, under Article 139 EC, contractual agreements adopted by management and labour may be transformed into EC legislation by means of a simplified legislative procedure.

DELEGATED DECISION-MAKING

The formal legislative procedures of the EC have been described. However, to stop here would be to misrepresent decision-making in the EC. As with so much in the EC, practice departs from form. For the great bulk of EC legislation is actually delegated in nature, passed by the Commission, and, as such, does not follow the formal processes set out above.

As the volume of Community legislation has grown in size and become ever more complex, it has become essential to find methods of processing it efficiently. Much of EC action involves technical and context-specific matters, such as those typical of the CAP. In such situations, it is necessary not only to have a good working knowledge of the detailed issues involved, but also to be able to respond swiftly to deal with changes in circumstances, disturbances in the market and so on. If the Council, or Council and Parliament, had to deal with all of these matters through the standard Community legislative procedures, then the channels of Community decision-making would become jammed and the EC bogged down in a wealth of technical detail. Therefore, it was clear, even in the earlier days of the EC, that something would have to be done to deal with decision-making in an efficient manner.

Delegation enables an authority to make efficient use of its power by developing structures to convey some of its competence to another body. Such delegation has proved to be just as necessary in the Community context as in the context of domestic law, where delegated legislation has existed for a long while. However, in the EC context, the sort of delegation that can take place, and to whom, has been carefully circumscribed. There is no general provision dealing with delegated power in the Community context, and, indeed, the requirement in Article 7(1) EC that, 'Each institution shall act within the limits of powers conferred by the treaty' would almost seem to militate against delegation. On the other hand, Article 202 EC gives the Council the power 'to confer on the Commission...powers for the implementation of the rules which the Council lays down...' and Article 211 EC requires the Commission 'to exercise the powers conferred on it by the Council for the implementation of the rules laid down by the latter'. These provisions clearly deal with delegated power.

The practice of delegation has evolved with the European Community, controlled by the ECJ.[69] Delegation to the Commission by the Council is widespread and relatively unproblematic.[70] It enables the Council to get on with the business of general policy-making, while leaving the Commission to implement more specific provisions, a time-consuming but necessary task. Articles 211 and 202 EC set out the framework for this. Such a system seems to rest on an implicit distinction between legislative and executive acts, a distinction which the treaty of course does not make.[71] However, a legislative act might be defined as an act adopted by Community institutions in accordance with the EC decision-making processes, and an executive act as one adopted in order to implement a legislative act, and having as its legal basis a legislative act. Such delegations from the Council to the Commission are subject to the process of comitology, now regulated by Council decisions.[72] The legitimacy of comitology has been subject to quite a serious critique,[73] especially for the possible renationalisation of policy that it involves, given that the members of the committees are appointed by the member states. However, such is the demand for technical expertise in the European Community, that it would simply not be possible for the Commission, a relatively small bureaucracy, to deal with all of the technical matters involved in implementing acts of Community legislation itself.[74] A very wide variety of implementation powers have been

---

[69] For a general discussion, see M Andenas and A Turk (eds) *Delegated Legislation and the Role of Committees in the EC* (Kluwer, 2000). For a focussed discussion on the role of the ECJ see A Turk, 'The Role of the Court of Justice' in Andenas and Turk op. cit.

[70] At least as far as the **principle** of delegation is concerned. For a critique of the practice of comitology which accompanies delegation to the Commission, see below, and also the section on comitology in Chapter 2.

[71] See K Lenaerts, 'Regulating the Regulatory process: "Delegation of Powers" in the European Community in the European Community', (1993) 18 ELRev 23.

[72] Comitology Decision 1999/468/EC OJ L184 17 July 1999.

[73] See Chapter 2 and pp. 135–142 below.

[74] These are numerous. For a long time the majority of Community regulations have been issued by the Commission, but more recently the majority of directives was also issued by the Commission: see R Dehousse, 'Towards a regulation of transitional governance? Citizens' rights and the reform of comitology proceedings' in C Joerges and E Vos, *EU Committees: Social regulation, Law and Politics* (Hart Publishing, 1999) 109 at 113.

delegated to the Commission, including updating of directives to take account of technical developments; management of the market in agricultural products; decisions on the allocation of funding for projects; the formulation and management of research projects; environment; and the management of food aid projects.

The legality of these comitology proceedings was subjected to the review of the ECJ, long before they were put onto a more formal basis by the SEA, in the *Koster*[75] case. The Council had adopted a regulation under Article 37(2) EC, which set out general principles for the common organisation of the market in cereals. The same regulation also provided for detailed rules to be laid down in measures which were to be adopted by the Commission, acting under the management committee procedure. This Council regulation was challenged as involving an unnecessary restriction on the Commission and an interference with its ability to act autonomously. The Court disagreed, holding that, as the management committee itself had no power to take decisions or substitute its judgment as binding for that of the Commission, it could not threaten the Commission's autonomy.[76] The objection had also been made that the delegation from the Council to the Commission was itself unlawful as, under such a delegation, there would be no provision for consultation with the European Parliament, unlike under the basis for the parent measure, Article 37 (2). The ECJ ruled as follows:

> It cannot therefore be a requirement that all the details of the regulations concerning the common agricultural policy be drawn up by the Council according to the procedures in Article 43. It is sufficient for the purposes of that provision that the basic elements of the matter to be dealt with have been adopted in accordance with the procedure laid down by that provision. On the other hand, the provisions implementing the basic regulations may be adopted according to a procedure different to that in Article 43, either by the Council itself or by the Commission by virtue of an authorisation complying with Article 155.[77]

The Court has reiterated that delegation to the Commission is permissible as long as it is a question of detailed implementation, i.e. executive acts, rather than general principles, or legislative acts, that are delegated. However, the line between policy choices and implementation details, is often blurred. Issues that appear to be technical, such as animal feed, can turn out to be surprisingly controversial, as the BSE saga illustrated. Furthermore, the Court has given a broad interpretation to implementation, as has been confirmed in its case law,[78] and most particularly in the *Rey Soda* case, in which the Court stated that in the field of agriculture, the Council might confer on the Commission 'wide powers of discretion and action'.[79]

The Council may also delegate powers to itself, a practice also confirmed in the *Koster* case and subsequently by Article 202 EC. There are advantages for the

---

[75] Case 25/70 *Koster* [1970] ECR 1161.
[76] The procedures on comitology are discussed in further detail in Chapter 2.
[77] *Koster* at para. 6.
[78] e.g. Case 41/69 *Chemiefarma* [1970] ECR 661; Case 16/88 *Commission v Council* [1989] ECR 3457.
[79] Case 23/75 *Rey Soda* [1975] ECR 1279.

Council in doing this, as it enables it to use simpler procedures than those specified in the treaty. Although this has been used in the field of anti-dumping, there are few other cases in which the Council has exercised this right, as the whole point of delegation seems to be to relieve the Council of the burden of implementation. The Court has also been stricter to police such delegations, holding that the Council must 'state its reasons in detail'[80] for such a delegation. Lenaerts has suggested that the reasoning behind the Court's stringency here might be a concern to protect constitutional checks and balances, which are more likely to be upheld if the Commission is the institution dealing with execution of acts. If the Council delegates to itself there is a risk that it may blur the line between legislation and implementation.

The position is different yet again where it is the member states to whom power is delegated by the EC. The member states have been concerned with implementation since the EC's inception, as the EC has had to rely on them to implement much of EC law. National authorities collect duties, impose levies and so on. In this sense, an executive federalism has always operated within the EC (what under German law is called *Vollzugsfoderalismus*). However, an actual delegation of EC power to the member states is not usual. In the *Rey Soda* case this issue was considered.[81] *Rey Soda* concerned the common organisation of the sugar market. This had been dealt with by Council Regulation 1009/67, which delegated to the Commission the power to take measures to prevent disturbances in the sugar market, exercised under the management committee procedure. This delegation was held to be unproblematic. However, the Commission had subsequently passed its own regulation, delegating the power to Italy to take further measures to deal with disturbances in the Italian sugar market. This the Italian government had done by imposing a levy on sugar stockholders. The ECJ held this subsequent delegation to be unlawful as the Commission had no power to delegate wide discretionary powers: at the very most it might delegate only strictly defined powers of execution.

Why has the Court been reluctant to concede to the EC more than the very limited power to delegate to the member states? There are several reasons. One surely is an unwillingness to allow member states to recover any of the authority which they have transferred to the EC.[82] Another reason, however, relates to issues of federalism within the EC legal order. There is a necessity for the clear drawing of boundaries between acts of the EC and acts of its member states, so that it will be clear who should bear the responsibility for any given action. If a delegation of broad discretionary power is made to the member states then this line is blurred.[83]

Where the EC has delegated power to outside bodies and agencies, the Court has been equally strict in its policing role. This was illustrated very early on in the

---

[80] Case 16/88 *Commission v Council* [1989] ECR 2457 at para 10.
[81] Case 23/75 *Rey Soda* [1975] ECR 1279.
[82] See on this point Case 804/79 *Commission v UK*, opinion of AG Reischl at 1087.
[83] See Lenaerts op. cit.; also K Lenaerts, 'Constitutionalism and the many faces of federalism' 38 AM J Comp L 205; also J Temple Lang, 'Community Constitutional Law: Article 5 EEC treaty' (1990) 27 C.M.L.Rev. 645; for an examination of this issue in the US context, see R Stewart, 'Pyramids of Sacrifice? Problems of Federalism in mandating State Implementation of National Environmental Policy' (1977) 86 Yale LJ 1196.

Meroni[84] case, which was decided under the ECSC treaty. It concerned a scheme set up to deal with scarcity of scrap within the ECSC. Two bodies had been formed to run this scheme, although they were in principle, at least, subject to the control of the High Authority in a number of ways. Meroni was a scrap dealer who had refused to cooperate with this scheme and one of his arguments was that it involved an unlawful delegation of powers. The Court accepted this argument, holding that a delegation of powers to an outside body would be permissible only when 'it involves clearly defined executive powers the exercise of which can, therefore, be subject to strict review in the light of objective criteria defined by the delegating authority'.[85] This has permitted the delegation of competences in only very limited circumstances.

Delegation to outside bodies is problematic. It raises issues of the separation of powers and democratic accountability, in so far as it can lead to the creation of bodies which perform all three executive, legislative and judicial functions. On the other hand, it might be argued that delegating power to outside agencies actually contributes to the fragmentation of power, and thus is in line with the pluralism on which the doctrine of separation of powers rests.[86] In any case, the *Meroni* doctrine, given at such an early stage in the Community's history, continues to affect its development in the twenty-first century. The 1990s, in particular, saw the increase in the growth in the establishment of outside bodies dealing with Community matters, such as the European Environment Agency, the European Agency for the Evaluation of Medicinal Products, or the Community Plant Variety Office.[87] However, *Meroni* continues to place limits on the powers which may be delegated to these agencies, so that they tend to have very few, if any, coercive or general powers, and are usually restricted to the provision of information (in itself, however, an important activity).[88] A major fear in the case of agencies is that delegating any greater competences will lead to an undesirable increase in their powers, especially as they are not overseen by a complex web of comitology committees. On the other hand, such agencies have an important function to fulfil, and the Commission (itself an institution without a huge amount of democratic legitimacy) cannot continue to take on all regulatory functions itself.

How may one render delegation acceptable? The suggestion has been made that this may be done by assuring some accountability and due process by the provision of rights of consultation and participation to interested parties.[89] However, accountability and

---

[84] Case 9/56 *Meroni* [1958] ECR 133.

[85] Ibid. at 149–50.

[86] An argument accepted by the US Supreme Court: see P Strauss, 'The place of agencies in government: separation of powers and the fourth branch of government' (1984) 84 Col. LR 573.

[87] See on this M Everson, 'Independent Agencies: Hierarchy beaters?' (1995) 1 ELJ 180; A Kreher, 'Agencies in the European Community – a step towards administrative integration in Europe?' (1997) 4 JEPP 225.

[88] See M Shapiro, 'The problems of independent agencies in the United States and the European Union' (1997) JEPP 276; R Dehousse, 'Regulation by Networks in the European Community: the role of European agencies' (1997) JEPP 247.

[89] On this point see R Baldwin, *Rules and Government* (Oxford: OUP, 1995); R Stewart, 'The reform of American administrative law' (1975) 88 Harvard L.R. 1667; D Held, *Models of Democracy* (Oxford: OUP, 1987) at 254.

legitimacy of decision-making are features which need to be examined across the general spectrum of the EU, an exercise that will be conducted later in the chapter.

Since the Treaty of Amsterdam, which introduced provisions on 'enhanced cooperation', there has been provision in the treaties for only some member states to pursue initiatives.[90] These procedures will be discussed in the next chapter.[91]

In this maze of different procedures and complex legislation it is sometimes easy to lose sight of the need to maintain democratic control over all types of legislation. This issue will now be discussed in some detail.

DEMOCRACY IN THE EU

According to Article 6 TEU, the Union is founded on the principle of democracy. However, previous sections of this book have attempted to illustrate the labyrinthine and unorthodox nature of EU institutions and their law-making processes. As a result of such structures, there is almost universal agreement that the EU suffers from a democratic deficit. Yet, beyond that, regarding the nature of the deficit, or the steps that might be taken to remedy it, the consensus ends. The following section will highlight what this author takes to be the key elements of that deficit, along with some suggestions for improvement, and thus will inevitably be subjective.

An initial difficulty is that there is no agreed definition as to what democracy is, or what it entails. Inevitably then, perceptions of the EU's democratic deficit may vary, according to the concept of democracy one has in mind. The word is Greek in origin, literally meaning 'rule by the people,' but this is not very helpful, as both 'rule' and 'people' are amenable to differing interpretations. Many systems have considered themselves democratic, without allowing all of their members the right to vote: the exclusion of slaves in pre-civil war America, or women in all systems until the twentieth century, being obvious examples. 'Rule' need not necessarily mean taking the decisions oneself, nor imply actual self-government, but may instead denote the selection of rulers, being in a position to influence their decisions, and, possibly, to control them. Although some accounts of democracy stress the importance of certain institutional or structural arrangements (e.g. separation of powers, checks and balances), others look to ideals (i.e. liberty, equality).[92] Schumpeter, in his famous, and very influential, definition,[93] preferred to look to institutions and procedures, rather than the ideals they were supposed to serve. However, he departed from earlier versions by advocating what has been described as a comparative elitist model, writing: 'the democratic method is that institutional arrangement for arriving at political decisions in which individuals acquire the power to decide by means of competitive struggle for the people's vote'.[94] By this account, the achievement of democracy becomes more like the packaging of a commercial product. Importantly, according to the Schumpeterian vision, political

---

[90] Article 11 EC; Articles 43–45 TEU.
[91] See the last section in Chapter 4.
[92] A Birch, *The Concepts and Theories of Modern Democracy* (Routledge, 1993).
[93] J Schumpeter, *Capitalism, Socialism, and Democracy* (Allen and Unwin, 1942).
[94] Ibid.

participation is not an integral part of democracy, and the political sphere is defined narrowly. This might seem to be a diminished account of democracy,[95] and for this reason, not an attractive model for the EU.[96] Christopher Lord,[97] in his recent study, *Democracy in the European Union*, prefers the simpler definition given by Beetham, which mixes the institutional and substantive, and which he describes as getting to democracy's 'irreducible core'. Beetham defines democracy as 'responsible rule according to related principles of popular control and political equality',[98] and this definition will be used as the basis for the discussion in this section.

A connected preliminary issue is that of how the concept of democracy relates to those of transparency, legitimacy and accountability, which are often bandied about in the same context. They obviously do not all mean the same thing, and yet it is often the perceived lack of transparency, legitimacy or accountability of EC processes which are cited as causes of the EC's democratic deficit. I will not seek to define these concepts here, nor probe too deeply their relations to each other, but rather deal with how they have been used in practice, in the critique of the EU, without the hope of giving some comprehensive definition, but at least seeking to draw some conclusions. Perhaps a truly 'democratic' EU is a vain hope, but we may at least be able to have a more transparent, accountable or even legitimate EU.

A yet further initial problem is that the political theory of democracy which has been developed in relation to single countries might in any case be inappropriate in the context of the EU. Perhaps we have to find a new interpretation of democracy for the post-national polity? But the notion of democracy which we deploy may also depend on how we perceive the post-national polity of the EU itself. Many very different interpretations of the EU have been suggested: statist, intergovernmental, regulatory or multilevel governance. Accountability and legitimacy of EU decision-making is less crucial under the middle two theories. Intergovernmentalist institutions are not renowned for their transparency, deriving their legitimacy from sovereign member states, whose own processes are democratic. A regulatory model for the EU, such as that proposed by Majone, also makes less of the need for accountability, which may indeed be detrimental to the efficiency of the regulatory body, efficiency being the very reason why it was chosen in the first place. However, if we wait until we determine what sort of creature the EU is, and thus, how much democracy it needs, we may very well have to wait for a very long time.

A related proposal is that of Joseph Weiler, who has suggested that different models of democracy may in fact be appropriate for different aspects of the EU. In 'European Democracy and its Critique', Weiler suggested that the international features of the EU might be explained through a consociational model, supranationalism by Schumpeterianism, and infranational aspects through neo-corporatism.[99]

---

[95] e.g. C Pateman, *Participation and Democratic Theory* (Cambridge University Press, 1970); P Bachrach, *The Theory of Democratic Elitism: A Critique* (Little Brown, 1967).
[96] Although a Schumpeterian model has been used to explain the EU's supranational aspects, see e.g. J Weiler, ' European Democracy and its Critique' (1995) 4 W Eur Pols 24.
[97] C Lord, *Democracy in the EU* (Sheffield Academic Press, 1998).
[98] D Beetham, *Defining and Measuring Democracy* (London: Sage, 1994).
[99] J Weiler, 'European Democracy and its Critique' (1995) 4 W Eur Pols 24.

According to this suggestion, one model does not fit all. There is some sense to this. However, while some acknowledgement has to be made of the EU's complex structure, the application of different theories of democracy may complicate and further fragment an already overly complex field: there is a lot to be said for applying Occam's razor in this case. A balance has to be struck between looking to solutions appropriate to the complexity of EU governance and avoiding the possible conceptual confusion of a multimodel democratic structure. So, the remainder of this chapter takes the (perhaps simplistic) approach of identifying well-known and generally agreed problems of democracy for the EU, without proceeding further with tortuous questions of definition either of democracy, or of the EU itself.

Thus, in very general terms, the following features of EU governance might be isolated as being unsatisfactory from almost any perspective of democracy. First, that there is ineffective parliamentary control over the political process in the EU. Second, however, to look just to parliamentary control over the legislative process as the key to democracy is too narrow. If we examine some other aspects of the EU which are seen as undemocratic, it is not necessarily the case that increasing parliamentary control will improve the situation. These other aspects include the executive nature of much EC decision-making and the problematic nature of comitology, fast becoming a structural hydra. How may they be rendered more democratic? Third, there is a lack of transparency to the EU's processes. Fourth, there is insufficient citizen participation in, and public debate about, the EU and closely related to this, the absence of much of a feeling of a European identity or identity of citizens with the EU. No doubt further elements could be added, but these four alone are sufficient to question whether the EU has adequate legitimacy, given the tremendous transfer of power which has taken place to it.

INEFFECTIVE PARLIAMENTARY CONTROL

The issue of the democratic nature of the EU was explored in the German *Bundesverfassungsgericht's* (Constitutional Court) *Maastricht* judgment.[100] The German ratification of the Maastricht Treaty had been challenged on the basis that it threatened the constitutionally guaranteed principles of German democracy, in particular Article 20 *Grundgesetz (GG)*, which states that Germany is a democratic federal state and that all state authority is derived from the people, and Article 38, which provides the right to take part in elections to select the government and its politicians. The argument was that these provisions would have been infringed by a large-scale transfer of competences to the EU, if that left national parliaments unable to control the EU process and the EU itself insufficiently developed and lacking the ability to do so. However, the *Bundesverfassungsgericht* found that the treaty did not violate the *Grundgesetz* because the EU could not act beyond the powers given to it by the member states, who remained 'the masters of the treaty'.

---

[100] *Brunner v European Union Treaty* [1994] 1 CMLR 57.

It thus did not deprive national parliaments of any further powers other than those which had already democratically and constitutionally ceded. It also found that the Maastricht Treaty provided safeguards for future development and confirmed to the principle of legal certainty. It stressed that each step of EU integration had to be subject to the German parliamentary process set up by Article 23 GG. Although the *Bundesverfassungsgericht* seemed, in many ways, to be sending out warning notes to the EU, and the ECJ in particular, it perhaps somewhat surprisingly affirmed the democratic role played by national parliaments.

Perhaps the *Bundesverfassungsgericht* was too quick to come to this conclusion. If we look closely at parliamentary control in the EU we might find it wanting. Unless democracy is literally taken to mean self-government by the people – something well nigh impossible in the modern world even if imaginable in the Greek city state or the Rousseauian ideal community – then the people must exercise control through their representatives, the Parliament. However, parliamentary control of decision-making in the EU has traditionally been weak. This weakness has allegedly taken two forms: the relative weakness of the European Parliament and the lack of involvement of national parliaments in EU affairs. If the EU is seen as a development closer to a state then parliamentary control will be important.

To take the European Parliament first. Discussion in the last chapter and previous section should have made clear the *sui generis* nature of the European Parliament. Is the Parliament an important feature of the EU's democratic deficit? For many years, the Parliament was undoubtedly weak. It had rights to be consulted only in some cases, and its members were not even directly elected until 1979. However, its powers have certainly increased. Those devising the Maastricht Treaty considered codecision as a partial solution to the EU's democratic deficit. Parliament now legislates by codecision with the Council of Ministers in a wide array of EC matters, leading to an almost bicameral arrangement. The additional number of cases in which its assent is required has increased with successive treaty amendments. It has also certainly gained in control over the Commission, with its powers of appointment and censure, which it has recently put to real use, something which begins to look like control of the executive. Its budgetary powers have also increased. All of this is positive. However, on the negative side, the Parliament's role in the budget relates to expenditure which has been determined in advance, which has left only limited room for the Parliament to change; it has no right of legislative initiative, and is still excluded from much of the earlier stages of the decision-making process, when agendas are set. There is a difference between simply being able to alter provisions and being able to initiate, shape and adapt legislation. Even when Parliament does have more power to control legislation in codecision, there are still these troublingly undemocratic aspects, for example the opaque and unaccountable nature of conciliation. In spite of the recent comitology decision, and measures which enable the Parliament to have some knowledge of what is going on in committees, comitology still plays a very troubling role, which will be discussed below. Lastly, Parliament has a very minor role regarding the second and third pillars and it generally has very little control over the Council of Ministers, except to the extent to which it may use the assent procedure.

Nor is this shortfall in parliamentary control of the executive made up for by the possibility of control by the national parliaments,[101] in spite of increased rhetoric concerning attempts to increase their role.[102] All EU treaties have, of course, to be ratified by national parliaments. They also have the opportunity to scrutinise draft EC legislation. Under the Treaty of Amsterdam,[103] draft legislation must be circulated to each national parliament at least six weeks before it can be considered by the Council of Ministers. National parliaments may also have some discretion regarding the transposal of directives. In theory, national parliaments could fill in some of the gaps in representation at the European level regarding CFSP and PJCC. However, the participation of national parliaments varies from member state to member state. The Danish *Folketing* for example, plays a significant role, having the power to authorise the negotiating stance of the Danish minister at Council meetings.[104] The Westminster parliament has less control, being unable to work out negotiating positions with its ministers. However, it does scrutinise all Commission proposals and ministers may not agree their position in the Council until scrutiny has been completed in the House of Commons. Furthermore, whenever it finds a matter it takes to be of public concern, it can request a full parliamentary debate.[105] In the UK it has been difficult to schedule debates on less politically sensitive issues, and those that do take place are often short and late at night. There is also no clear line of communication back to the minister who has to pursue the matter before the EC Council of Ministers. To conclude, the power of national parliaments is still limited. In cases of QMV, they cannot prevent a measure being enacted against their wishes. National parliaments also lack expertise and information about the EU and EU measures. The European Parliament has accrued experience through its highly

---

[101] See E Smith (ed.) *National Parliaments as Cornerstones of European Integration* (Kluwer, 1996); P Norton (ed.) *National Parliaments and the European Union* (Frank Cass, 1996).

[102] For example, Declaration No 13 attached to the TEU, *On the role of national parliaments in the European Union*, which states:

> The Conference considers that it is important to encourage greater involvement of national parliaments in the activities of the European Union. To this end, the exchange of information between national parliaments and the European Parliament should be stepped up. In this context, the governments of the Member States will ensure, *inter alia*, that national parliaments receive Commission proposals for legislation in good time for information or possible examination. Similarly, the Conference considers that it is important for contacts between the national parliaments and the European Parliament to be stepped up, in particular through the granting of appropriate reciprocal facilities and regular meetings between members of parliament interested in the same issues.

See also Protocol 13 of the Treaty of Amsterdam on the role of national parliaments in the European Union.

[103] Protocol 13 of the Treaty of Amsterdam on the role of national parliaments in the European Union.

[104] D Arter, 'The Folketing and Denmark's European policy: The Case of an Authorising Assembly' in Norton (ed.) op. cit. above.

[105] P Norton, 'The United Kingdom: Political Conflict, Parliamentary Scrutiny' in Norton (ed.) op. cit.

specialised committees,[106] but the national parliaments lack the time (spending about only 5 per cent of their time on EU affairs). Moreover, national parliaments have special, particular focuses on EU matters, so their part is inevitably partial, fragmented, often reduced to the national interest.

It might be suggested that the democratic lack created by the weakness of national parliaments and the European Parliament in the EU policy process might be compensated by the fact that Council members have (for the most part) been democratically elected in their national constituencies and that democracy is achieved through their part in the decision-making process. They are also legislators and can exercise control over the unelected Commission. This has some normative justification, as the EU derives part of its democratic legitimacy from the states. If the EU is still seen as intergovernmental in nature, then processes for member state control are important. This is also not unusual in federal systems, where states may wield some sort of controlling power: the US Senate is one example, the German *Bundesrat* another.

However, to suggest that sufficient democracy may be derived through the Council would be a mistake, for several reasons. First, Council members need not, for the most part, follow the suggestions of their parliaments, in which case the democratic nature of their vote may be dubious (although this may also be the case in the context of national government). Second, even if they do, if a decision is taken by QMV and a particular Council member did not vote for it at the ballot, then there is nothing democratic as far as that member state is concerned. Third, the Commission still continues to control many of the earlier stages of the decision-making process: it has the right of initiative, it can choose when to place a particular item on the agenda, and so on. This is very important, as the choice, the timing and the drafting of legislation are not value-free activities, but actions involving judgment and political choices. Fourth, the Council is itself a very secretive, undemocratic body. It legislates for the most part behind closed doors, apart from a few meetings it chooses to hold in public, at which, in any case, it would seem that ministers just get up and read prepared speeches. But surely public law-making is one of the essential elements of democracy? However, even if the Council were to become more democratic in its processes, there is then the attendant danger that it would simply pass up more work, which it wished to keep away from the public eye, to the European Council, whose conclusions have been getting more voluminous every year, and whose business encroaches on sectoral Councils. Finally, the ministers of the Council are, in any case, not responsible for much of the legislation – most of the work being done by obscure working groups, committees and COREPER, which are barely accountable and not democratically selected, as described in the last chapter.

There are reasons for the continued limitations on the European Parliament. The EU is not a state and to increase the Parliament's powers might be to run the risk of upsetting the institutional balance, the feature which prevents too much power being accumulated in any one EU institution. However, if codecision were extended still further to cover all EC legislation, then this would be a step in the process of

---

[106] Although the European Parliament does not always have sufficient resources at its disposal, unlike say the US Congress.

enhancing the democratic legitimacy of the EC, if not the EU. Even better if the Parliament were to be given some real right of legislative initiative. This would also enhance the twofold legitimacy on which the EU is supposedly founded, namely its states and its peoples.

However, there are also limits on the capacity of representative democracy to achieve a truly democratic polity, and these limits are experienced just as much at the national, as at the supranational level. Schumpeter was reflecting political reality when he stated that political choices are not the expression of the 'general will' of the people. Elections are merely ways of choosing (or getting rid of) those who govern. In the complex multilevel bureaucracies of modern society, decision-making has been taken more and more from the legislature and instead put in the hands of experts at secondary levels. It is to this perhaps undesirable state of affairs that I now turn.

EXECUTIVE CONTROL OF DECISION-MAKING AND THE PROBLEMATIC NATURE OF COMITOLOGY

Discussions of the democratic deficit in the EU tend to focus on the weaknesses of the European Parliament as one of its major contributors and on parliamentary accountability as its major remedy. While a weak European Parliament may not provide a bulwark of democracy in the EU, it does not, however, follow that strengthening parliamentary control will remedy all. Too great a reliance on the parliamentary democracy model may be misplaced in the context of the polity that is the EU, a polity whose nature is still very much contested. While so much EU decision-making is still regulatory in nature,[107] then it may be that parliamentary control measures are not simply inadequate, but wrong-headed.

This problem surfaces most particularly in the context of comitology, which was discussed in the last chapter. Comitology has been seen as one of the necessary evils of EC governance for many years. It is not disputed that a system for the delegation of powers is necessary in order for the EC to be able to function efficiently. Member states were unhappy to leave delegation solely to the Commission and so the process of appointing their national delegates to committees, which would advise but also contain the Commission in its exercise of delegated power, was born. Although the practice of comitology achieved the approval of the Court at an early stage in the EC's history, in the *Koster*[108] case, it still continues to provoke unease, the comitology decision of 1999 notwithstanding.[109]

Why should unease about comitology matter so much? After all, it is delegated legislation that comitology deals with, and, even if there is a great deal of it, then surely these are technical issues too time-consuming for the general legislature, which takes up its time with the weightier matters of policy and general rules? It matters, because comitology raises the following serious problems. First, delegated legislation is itself

---

[107] G Majone, *Regulating Europe* (Routledge, 1996).
[108] Case 25/70 *Koster* [1970] ECR 1161. See also discussion at pp. 125–9.
[109] Comitology decision 1999/468/EC OJ L 184.

not uncontroversial. There is the practical near impossibility of separating general rules from the implementing technical detail. Even where there seems to be a clear demarcation, and the technical detail is left to the committee, such issues can prove surprisingly controversial, such as the BSE crisis which converted animal feed into a political issue, and conveyed much publicity to the veterinary standards committee.

Furthermore, comitology's processes are notoriously complex, made up of variants and subvariants of different types of committees, with no objective criteria as to which process to be used (this usually depending on the original legislation which gives rise to that comitology process).[110] Even more seriously, comitology is opaque in the extreme, the most obvious example of this lying in the notorious fact of the absence of certain knowledge as to just how many comitology committees exist, and as to who are their members, who are not democratically elected (lending weight to fears that they are made up of closed circles of elites from similarly privileged backgrounds).[111] Comitology has also appeared lacking in adequate control and safeguards. Until recently, there was no effective system for parliamentary scrutiny, the previous inter-institutional agreements being ineffective for this purpose.[112] This made it very difficult for any interested parties to discover what matters were under consideration by comitology committees. Indeed, in the past, the public only had notice of comitology legislation once an actual rule had been adopted. Such opacity leads to a lack of accountability, as bureaucrats cannot be held to account if one simply doesn't know what they are doing. Thus, not only have important political decisions been concealed from democratic scrutiny – a conspicuous lack of openness which conflicts with the principle of democratic legitimacy – but the lack of informed input may diminish the actual quality of the decisions taken.

Thus, the little discussed yet crucial (how would the EC process so much work efficiently without it?) feature of EC institutional structure raises some very considerable problems for the discussion of democracy and legitimacy in the EU. All the more since the EC pillar has taken on yet greater competence through the transfer of third pillar matters of asylum, immigration and free movement of persons to the EC, and thus the ambit of comitology. These are issues which have a potential to make the impact of delegated rule-making very keenly felt by individual EU citizens.

Making comitology more accountable

What responses have been made to the problems raised by comitology? The growing voluminous literature[113] reveals at least four different responses, which will now be discussed in turn.

---

[110] Although the recent comitology decision now provides some guidance.

[111] In 1994 the Parliament refused to release a share of appropriations for committees until the Commission provided them with more information about them: see K Bradley, 'The European Parliament and Comitology: on a road to nowhere' (1997) 3 ELJ 230.

[112] The EP complained that the Commission either failed to send it the relevant documents under these agreements, or sent them too late to be of any use, see Bradley, op. cit.

[113] e.g. C Joerges and E Vos, *EU Committees: Social regulation, Law and Politics* (Hart Publishing, 1999).

The first such response is to claim that the lack of democratic process in comitology does not create a problem for the EU after all, as the whole point of comitology is to provide for efficient decision-making in a context where it is sorely needed and that comitology has succeeded in doing this. Such a response asserts that comitology aids the EC in its regulatory functions and that there is no great need to open up its processes, and that indeed, if we attempt to do so, we risk compromising its efficiency. This approach emanates from those who see the EU mainly as a regulatory body, and suggest that the most difficult policy decisions in the EU are technical rather than political.[114] Aside from the fact that such an assessment of the EU seems inadequate in this day and age – with EMU, and moves toward a common foreign and security policy, it just does not seem accurate to characterise the EU as only regulatory in nature – this view actually proves to be more complex than at first sight, and to incorporate a need for some control. Even the more vigorous proponents of this view still tend to acknowledge that there should be some sort of controls on the experts. Majone, for example, has suggested that, while self policing mechanisms are already present in the system, there is a need to cross-check, to build complementary and overlapping checking systems, 'instead of assuming that control is necessarily to be exercised from any fixed place within the system'.[115] Thus, although this might not require control by the European Parliament, it still could include quite cumbersome checks, strict procedural requirements and judicial review: indeed Majone goes so far as to recommend that the EU adopt something like the US Administrative Procedures Act, a requirement which would actually prove pretty strenuous and will be discussed in the next section.

Related to the first view is a second, which sees comitology as 'deliberative' in nature.[116] Joerges and Neyer see comitology as a fine example of the sort of deliberative processes recommended as essential to democracy by, for example, Juergen Habermas and Hannah Arendt. While Hannah Arendt may seem a long way from networks of national civil servants, sitting round a table in Brussels discussing technical details, Joerges and Neyer point to the quality of the comitology process and the decisions which it produces, which are a result, not of the formal legislation process, but civic, informal discussion and interaction between participants: the sort of deliberation promoted by Habermas and Arendt. Consensus in comitology meetings is the norm (so much so that the Commission is often content itself to suggest the apparently constraining regulatory procedure).[117] Furthermore, comitology members, while they may gain some democratic legitimacy in being appointed by their member states, are in fact free from their direct political control, and thus

---

[114] G Majone, *Regulating Europe*.

[115] Ibid. at 39.

[116] C Joerges and J Neyer, 'From Intergovernmental Bargaining to deliberative Political Processes: The Constitutionalising of Comitology' (1997) 3 ELJ 271.

[117] R Dehousse, 'Towards a Regulation of Transitional Governance: Citizens' Rights and the Reform of Comitology' in Joerges and Vos op. cit.

manage to avoid the parochial concerns of nation states, and their blindness to non-nationals. Such an order may be worthy of what Habermas writes about in this context as *Anerkennungswurdigkeit* (worthy of recognition).[118]

There are problems with deliberative democracy as a paradigm for the EU, and these will be discussed further below.[119] However, there are also immediately apparent flaws to the Joerges and Neyer view, notwithstanding its importance in drawing attention to the fact that, however complex and opaque comitology may be, it functions well, mainly by consensus. The first troubling aspect of the Joerges and Neyer view is elitism, nothing new in Community law (nor in political philosophy, having been recommended by Plato, in the shape of the philosopher kings of the *Republic*), indeed flourishing since Monnet's time. Monnet's confidence in the elite of the Commission may have been misplaced, but at least we know a fair amount about the Commission and its staff by now.[120] Very little is known about those who make up the comitology committees, their backgrounds, how much they have in common and how these shared world views inform their preferences. Perhaps there is so much consensus in comitology just because those who participate are like-minded? More empirical research is needed before a ringing endorsement of the Joerges-Neyer thesis becomes possible.

The next suggested remedy to the problems of comitology is a horse of a different colour indeed, as it requires a much greater opening up of comitology by means of greater parliamentary control. Parliamentary control of comitology was lacking in the earlier days of the EC, although grew in momentum in the late 1980s and 1990s. Until the so-called *Delors–Plumb* agreement (named after the two presidents of the respective institutions) of 1988, the Parliament had no right even to have sight of comitology proposals. Even after Delors–Plumb, the Commission was tardy in sending these, and in 1994 the *Modus Vivendi*[121] resulted in an agreement by the Commission to send the Parliament all comitology papers. In the Commission *Undertaking* of 1996, this was increased to all draft committee agendas, and records of votes taken in management and regulatory committees. The Comitology decision of 1999 improved the Parliament's situation still further by giving the Parliament the right to all agendas, draft measures, lists of authorities and organisations to which the comitology committee representatives belong.[122] The Comitology decision has also given the Parliament formal powers in the comitology process, by allowing it to request the Commission to reexamine its proposal (Article 8) and the Council to reconsider the Parliament's suggestions (Article 5). However, perhaps most importantly, the Parliament has no right of veto over comitology decisions: the Commission and Council are not bound by the positions that the Parliament takes. So, although progress has been made, the Parliament is still lacking in control over

---

[118] For a discussion of some of these points, see G Schaefer and A Turk, 'Government by Committee: the Role of Committees in European Policy-making' EIPA working paper which can be found at http://eipa-nl.com.

[119] At the end of the chapter.

[120] See e.g. F Duchêne, *Jean Monnet* (New York: Norton, 1994) discussed in Chapter 1.

[121] *Modus Vivendi between Parliament, Council and Commission* [1996] OJ C 102/1.

[122] Comitology decision Article 7(3).

the comitology process, in comparison with, say, its right of veto in the codecision procedure or its growing control over the Commission.

However, even if the Parliament had greater control over comitology, it is doubtful whether it would be very well placed to exercise it. How could it possibly process all the information which it received? Not only does it lack the time and resources to process all the comitology documents which it currently receives, but it also lacks the expertise. Furthermore, increasing surveillance of comitology committees by parliamentary committees just seems to add to the bureaucratic nightmare. Perhaps it would be best if Parliament were able to step in, and demand a hearing in relevant cases? However, even more efficient monitoring by the Parliament might not be satisfactory. After all, scrutiny by MEPs could be unsatisfactory to European citizens, who might actually feel that, in the absence of a European demos, their interests were better served by a comitology national than by an MEP from the other side of the EU.[123] This last point illustrates one of the double binds of democracy in the EU: even an effective form of democratic, representative, parliamentary democracy may be unsatisfactory in the absence of any effective support for that institution by the European populace. This issue is a taxing one which will also be discussed in the next section.

The last remedy under consideration here, for the disease from which comitology suffers, is that which suggests importing greater due process rights into the whole comitology process, by, for example, giving interested parties earlier notice of comitology measures, a chance to participate in the process themselves, and access to judicial review, should the measure ultimately fail them in some legally recognised way. The cornerstone of such a suggestion is usually the demand for the EU to issue some sort of equivalent to the US Administrative Procedures Act, which provides considerable rights for interested parties and will be discussed shortly.[124] While it is certainly true that comitology has been forced to become more transparent as a result of recent developments, most especially the 1999 Comitology decision (for example, EC proceedings that enable citizens to access Commission documents also apply to comitology documents;[125] the Commission is now required to publish a list of all comitology committees and to prepare an annual report on them;[126] and from 2001, the Commission must establish a public register containing references to all documents transmitted to the European Parliament) there is no **right** of participation as such. Thus, unlike in the US, the public have no right of immediate access to draft measures, they cannot submit comments, nor be present at hearings.

It has been argued[127] that in the US, the administrative procedures of notice and comment on administrative rule-making have proved to be a very significant device in fostering accountability to the legislative branch. Thus under the US

---

[123] See Dehousse op. cit.
[124] Administrative Procedures Act 1946; see for a discussion of this F Bignami, 'The Administrative State in a separation of Powers Constitution: Lessons for European Community Rule Making from the US': Harvard, Jean Monnet working paper 5/99.
[125] By way of Article 7(2) of the Comitology decision.
[126] Comitology decision Article 7(4).
[127] Bignami op. cit.

Administrative Procedures Act, the public have the right to be informed of a rule through its publication in the governmental official journal, the federal register; interested individuals may submit comments, the agency in question must justify the rule and judicial review is available to police those administrators who exceed their powers or who produce 'arbitrary and capricious rules'. In the US, the courts took their role seriously, engaging in so-called 'hard look' judicial review, whereby they proved themselves willing to get involved in the technical merits of policy choices of the administration. Judicial review was enlarged by the fact that the rules of standing had been liberalised and, thus, a whole range of private attorney-generals was created to police the operation of the administration. Such a situation might well assist the European Parliament, which suffers from inadequate resources to scrutinise comitology effectively. This sort of development has, after all, taken place before in the EC, in the context of the doctrine of direct effect, developed by the ECJ to enable private citizens to aid the enforcement of EC law against recalcitrant states and so lighten the Commission's burden.

The creation of more due process and participatory rights certainly has its attractions, not just in the policing of comitology, but also in the requirement it could place on the Community administration to reason its decisions as effectively as possible in the shadow of judicial challenge and also in the prospect of a dialogue developing between members of civil society – more deliberation, but of a somewhat different sort, to that extolled by Joerges and Neyer. Naturally an increased proceduralisation and juridification of the administration also has its defects. In the US this has taken the form of deceleration in the speed of administrative rulemaking, while those in charge aim to create review-immune measures. It has led to what has been called 'ossification' of the process.[128] As creating review-immune measures is in any case impossible, it has also led to an increased juridification of the process, as more and more claims are brought to court. A further problem is that giving rights of participation does not necessarily create universal access as certain groups, namely those which have the greatest resources, will tend to dominate the process.

How might these dangers work out in the context of comitology in the EU? Do they make the call for an Administrative Procedures Act pointless? To be sure, ossification of the process is just the danger that writers such as Joerges or Majone warn of. The challenge of designing an administrative process which is accountable, fair, and yet efficient, is so difficult as to be well-nigh impossible. Nor could one have faith that if comitology were to be opened out, it would not become dominated by large interests: Brussels is already dominated by multinationals, who have far greater resources than the small businesses, consumer groups and environmental concerns, and so on, who also try to get their voices heard. However, importantly, part of the success or failure of an Administrative Procedures Act in the EU would depend on the reaction of the courts. US parties have shown themselves to be willing litigators and suspicious of bureaucracy. In the EU, there may be less mistrust of technocracy (although this may be a vain hope after the Commission debacle of 1999). US courts

---

[128] e.g. P Verkuil, 'Rulemaking Ossification – A Modest Proposal' (1995) 47 Administrative Law Rev 453.

have also engaged in quite intense judicial review. This is not the case in the EU, at least where review of **Community** action is at issue.[129] The ECJ and CFI have shown themselves unwilling to censure policy choices made by the institutions, and particularly unwilling to 'second guess' those choices where wide discretion is involved as in the context of, for example, the CAP.[130] (This is in marked contrast to the situation where member state actions have been under review, a distinction which might be justified on grounds of the threat posed to the internal market by non-compliant states, but possibly also just an example of double standards in the ECJ and CFI, and an example of a noted 'preference for Europe'.) On the other hand, the Community courts would need to give effective protection to procedural rights. So far, they have recognised such rights, but in the context of individual cases, without any general framework within which to apply them. In this context, some sort of Administrative Procedures Act might be welcomed.

Therefore, an examination of some possible remedies for the problem of comitology and its democratic lack fails to provide any watertight solutions. Indeed, it reveals the problems and paradoxes on which the undemocratic nature of comitology rests. To be efficient it must not be too vulnerable to judicial challenge, which is, however, one of the necessary corollaries to its increased transparency and accountability. On the other hand, increasing parliamentary control raises the spectre of overwhelming the Parliament and also removing perhaps one sort of democratic accountability (that of member state control) for another, that of the Parliament, which may prove less attractive to a demos-less European people.

The constitutionalising (or not) of comitology?

Perhaps to speak of democratising comitology is to take a wrong turning. It may be that comitology is an administrative process and that to make it acceptable we have not to look at constitutional solutions of democracy and parliamentary accountability, but instead to measure its legitimacy in terms of its results, its levels of expertise and efficient outcomes. However, such a contention immediately raises two further points, pulling in different directions. An immediate reaction to this claim is that, if comitology is administrative in nature and that constitutional concerns are inappropriate to it, why then so is the EU polity, a claim made by those who stress the regulatory dominance of the EC, such as Majone.[131] Such a claim was considered in Chapter 2 and rejected on the basis that the EU is far too complex and rich a structure to be merely administrative or regulatory, even if we do not acknowledge its 'constitutional' nature. However we choose to describe the EU polity, the democratic nature (or lack of democracy) of its processes are important, and cannot be dismissed by characterising comitology as administrative.

A further point, veering off in another direction, is that administrative law, including Community administrative law, does not just serve the God of efficiency.

---

[129] See Chapter 10.
[130] See Case 78/74 *Deuka* [1975] ECR 421 and Chapter 10, section on grounds of review.
[131] A point that was considered in Chapter 2.

More and more, to be viable, it must serve other needs, and be seen to be aware of having fair processes, of individual rights, of acknowledging its accountability. These features look somewhat constitutional (however we may define this hugely contested subject) and thus it seems that the democracy, or not, of comitology is necessarily an issue of the first importance.

It still might be argued however, that, administrative or not, comitology should not be constitutionalised, a point that is made by Joseph Weiler.[132] Weiler sees comitology as simply operating outside of the classic paradigm of constitutionalism (which he, in this context, characterises as premised on a polity, institutions, boundaries and constitutional courts as border patrols). The ECJ has applied a constitutional framework to comitology, and this has not been beneficial according to Weiler. This is because he sees it as having privileged the issues of the function and power of comitology, as well as its ontological boundaries, and thus the ECJ has felt able to give it a clean bill of health. If, instead of being concerned with constitutional categories, the ECJ had been concerned with how comitology really operates, it would have looked to the lack of certain features – equality of access, transparency of its proceedings – rather than delegation and attribution, and seen the unsatisfactory nature of it. One may agree with Weiler's conclusion without agreeing with his methodology. Institutional structures, boundaries and democratic accountability play their part in constitutionalism and comitology is now so embedded in EU institutional structures that it may well have become 'constitutionalised', even if much of it is administrative in nature. However, comitology certainly merits far greater scrutiny.

TRANSPARENCY AND SIMPLIFIED LAW-MAKING

Transparency started to become a focus of concern in the early 1990s, around the time of the Maastricht treaty.[133] Transparency is often defined as openness, but in fact it is more than that, as it also comprises simplicity and comprehensiveness. It also plays its part in making decision-makers more accountable. There are several reasons for this growing focus on transparency. For some time, there had been an awareness that Europe needed to become more approachable to its citizens, an awareness which had come to being in the 1980s with the Adonnino report and its attempt to create a 'People's Europe'. However, this recognition became more urgent as the EC began to accumulate more powers at the expense of its member states, starting with the Single European Act and continuing with the TEU. If the EC was to have competence in areas that were formally the preserves of its member states and national legislatures, then it became necessary for it to be able to justify to its peoples this transference, which certainly would not be possible if its law-making processes were obscure and mysterious, as well as undemocratic. Furthermore, the Danish 'no vote' to the first Danish referendum, as well as the French *petit oui*,

---

[132] J Weiler, 'Epilogue: "Comitology" as Revolution – Infranationalism, Constitutionalism and Democracy' in Joerges and Vos op. cit.
[133] e.g. 1993 *Inter-Institutional Declaration on Democracy, Transparency and Subsidiarity*.

and the challenging language of the German constitutional court in its judgment on the Maastricht treaty, sent warning signs to the EU institutions about the lack of satisfaction with its processes. Something had to be done to make Europe more acceptable to its citizens. Transparency, and the right to information which it comprises, have been perceived as important aspects of democracy and the strenuous process of making the EU more democratic.

According to Article 6 TEU, as already mentioned, democracy is one of the fundamental principles of the EU. A necessary component of effective democracy is that citizens should have sufficient information about what the EU has done and is planning to do. The processes by which these decisions are taken should also be intelligible. With this information, citizens can evaluate the performance of those who are making the decisions, as well as being able to play some part themselves. According to the ECJ, '... the transparency called for by European Councils, in order to allow the public "the widest possible access to documents"... is essential in order to enable citizens to carry out genuine and efficient monitoring of the exercise of powers vested in the Community institutions'.[134] In a speech given at the Humboldt University in Berlin,[135] the European Ombudsman, Jacob Soderman, interpreted transparency as comprising three elements: first, that the processes through which public bodies make decisions should be understandable and open; second, that the decisions themselves should be reasoned; and third, that, as far as possible, the information on which decisions have been based should be made available to the public.

We might add the following normative justifications to the Ombudsman's definition: that transparency serves at least three functions. The first is of a classic liberal nature. It protects individuals from the abuses of authority (and the origin of this justification may be traced to Sweden in the eighteenth century). Second, there is a utilitarian justification. Transparency is also likely to increase the rationality and effectiveness of the decision-making process. Third, transparency may unite openness with active participation.[136] This is linked to a vision of deliberative democracy, stressing the necessity of debate to democracy, rather than classic liberalism, which will be explored in the following section. But to what extent has the EU taken account of these elements?

Ten years on from the Maastricht treaty, with another 'no' vote in another referendum to another treaty on European integration, it can hardly be said that a great deal of transparency has been achieved, in spite of efforts to make the EU more intelligible. Its legislation processes (and the great variety of them) still appear complex and arcane, riddled with obscure committees and obfuscatory procedures. Although it seems to be a clear requirement of democracy that debate and adoption of laws should be carried out in public, the Council of Ministers, for the most part, still legislates behind closed doors. This is unacceptable. On the other hand, to be

---

134 Case T-92/98 *Interporc v Commission (Interporc II)* [1999] ECR II 3521 at para. 39.
135 J Soderman, 'Transparency as a Fundamental Principle of the European Union' (lecture by the European Ombudsman at the Walter Hallstein Institute, Humboldt University Berlin, 19 June 2001).
136 Although this may not always have the intended beneficiaries. In the US for example, the Freedom of Information act has been most used by corporate concerns.

fair, transparency as a fundamental principle is lacking in many national constitutions, in which freedom of information may be heavily circumscribed. Many national governments also act in a complex and obfuscatory way. But they can, of course, be more easily voted out of office if their public do not like what they do.

However, the EU has not been inactive over the past ten years in trying to make its actions more transparent and at least some progress has been made. Provisions on citizenship and subsidiarity were included in the Maastricht Treaty, a recognition that the EU needed to think carefully about its relationship with its member states and their citizens. Nevertheless, there were no specific provisions in the TEU regarding transparency, openness or access to documents.[137] Part of the problem has been that openness has often been perceived as reducing effectiveness. The only reference was to be found in the following declaration, attached to the EC treaty as *Declaration 17*:

> The conference considers that transparency of the decision making process strengthens the democratic nature of the institutions and the public's confidence in the administration. The Conference accordingly recommends that the Commission submit to the Council no later than 1993 a report on measures designed to improve public access to the information available to the institutions.

In line with this, the Commission carried out a survey of national laws and, in 1993, the Council and Commission adopted a so-called 'Code of Conduct' on public access to documents. This Code was implemented by way of decisions which were based on the Council and Commission's powers to take measures of their own internal organisation: these were *Council Decision 93/731* and *Commission Decision 94/90*.[138]

This was all very well but not enough. The Code was not legally binding and the fact that the right to information was to be regulated by the internal rules of EC institutions was regarded as highly unsatisfactory. In *The Netherlands v Council*,[139] the Dutch government sought annulment of Council Decision 93/731 (and the Code) on the grounds that the wrong legal basis had been chosen. It argued that, as the right of access to documents was a fundamental right, instead of determining the principles for public access on the basis of its own discretion, the Council should have followed the normal legislative process, involving the European Parliament. The ECJ, however, did not agree: it held that the Council was entitled to regulate access to documents by virtue of its powers of internal organisation. Although, in his opinion, AG Tesauro described the right of access to information 'a fundamental right', the Court did not do so, noting only 'a trend, which discloses a progressive affirmation of the individual's right of access to documents held by public authorities'.[140] This was a bit disappointing, although it was the first step which the Court took to compile a case law which, little by little, clarified and supported citizens' rights of access to documents.

---

[137] Apart from in the Preambles.

[138] Subsequently amended by Commission Decision 96/567.

[139] Case C-58/94 *The Netherlands v Council* [1996] ECR I-2186.

[140] Ibid. at 2199.

In the *Carvel*[141] case, the Court of First Instance held that the Council and Commission decisions contained enforceable rights for individuals. In *WWF*[142] the Court of First Instance stated that exceptions to the general rule of public access should be construed and applied strictly, in a manner which did not defeat the general objective of transparency. It also imposed a fairly narrow interpretation of the exceptions set out in the Code. In *Hautala*,[143] the CFI referred to 'the principle of the right to information' as a standard for interpreting the access decisions and also held that the institutions must consider whether partial access may be granted to areas not covered by exceptions.

The EC Courts also clarified matters not addressed by the decisions. So, for example, in *Rothmans*,[144] the CFI held that access to documents also covers documents of comitology committees, an important holding. In *Svenska Journalistforbundet*[145] it held that access rights may also concern documents relating to action under the third pillar, as the correct application of Council decisions, rather than those decisions themselves, is still a matter of Community law. In *Bavarian Lager*,[146] the CFI also rejected the idea that documents drawn up for infringement proceedings under Article 226 EC were automatically covered by the exception relating to the public interest and held that the exception for court proceedings applied only to documents expressly drawn up for the purposes of those proceedings.

It is not only the Community courts which have made their mark on the transparency of EU proceedings. The Ombudsman has played an important role and has most certainly been critical of the institutions' record on transparency. In its 1999 report, for example, it noted that 'lack of information or wrong information' is still the most frequent allegation it receives in its complaints (23 per cent).[147] The Ombudsman has produced both decisions and own initiative reports in this area.[148] The issue of the applicability of the Code to third pillar matters in fact came to the Ombudsman first, whose decision[149] was upheld by the Court of First Instance in *Svenska Journalistforbundet*. Other examples of the Ombudsman's decisions may be given: for example, it found the mere reference to 'the fight against organised crime' insufficient as a basis of a rejection of access and also inadequate the fact that a document was alleged to contain 'detailed national positions'.[150] The Commission and Council are, of course, not the only institutions which produce documents which the public may want to see. The Ombudsman produced its own initiative enquiry into the adoption of rules on public access by the institutions other than the Commission or Council, in 1996, which it followed up in 1999. This had the

---

[141] Case T-194/94 *John Carvel and Guardian Newspapers v Council* [1995] ECR II-2765.

[142] Case T-105/95 *WWF v Commission* [1997] ECR II-2765.

[143] Case T-14/98 *Heidi Hautala v Council* [1991] ECR II-2489; also Case T-124/96 *Interporc v Commission* [1998] ECR II 231.

[144] Case T-188/97 *Rothmans International v Commission* [1999] ECR II 2463.

[145] Case T-174/95 *Svenska Journalistforbundet v Council* [1998] ECR II-2289.

[146] Case T-309/97 *The Bavarian Lager Co Ltd v Commission* [1999] ECR II 3217.

[147] The European Ombudsman, *Annual Report for 1999* at 10.

[148] These may be found at the Ombudsman's web site at http://www.euro-ombudsman.eu.int.

[149] Case 1087/96 [1998] EOAR 41.

[150] Case 1057/96 [1998] EOAR 178.

outcome that almost all Community institutions and bodies, including the Court of Auditors, the European Investment Bank and the European Courts, now have their own rules on access to documents. As a matter of good practice Europol also agreed to adopt the Council of Ministers' rules.

In the light of all of this, it has been suggested by some that a fundamental right of public access was emerging as a general principle of Community law.[151] However, if the right of access is a fundamental right then why did the Court in *Netherlands* v *Council* not require a legislative act, if the matter was of such fundamental importance? The answer seems to be that, at that time, there was no legal basis on which the Community could have adopted such an act.

Article 255 EC and its consequences

To debate whether the Community courts had recognised some sort of fundamental right of access to documents is now a rather redundant enquiry, given that the Treaty of Amsterdam introduced Article 255 EC, expressed as a right of access to documents of the European Parliament, Council and Commission. This was supposed to remedy the weakness of existing rules. However, such access was made subject to paragraph 2 of Article 255, which leaves quite a lot of scope for exceptions 'on grounds of public or private interest' in its implementation. Article 255 is also not freestanding. According to Article 255(2) a legal instrument was to be adopted by the Council and Parliament acting under the codecision procedure, in order to give effect to its provisions.

Given that public knowledge, participation and consultation are the keystones of EU transparency, the procedure for the implementation of Article 255 began unfortunately, when the Commission proposed a regulation, without any prior public consultation. Moreover, the draft seemed to be a step backward from the Code of Conduct, being more restrictive in containing new exceptions and a general exclusion of 'texts for internal use'.

Things were to get worse. During the summer of 2000, when Brussels was empty for the holiday season and the European Parliament in recess, the Council itself unilaterally amended its earlier decision on access to documents, through the so-called Solana Decision or 'coup',[152] named after Javier Solana, the General Secretary of the Council, Head of the CFSP and former Secretary-General of NATO, who seemed to have masterminded the action. This involved the amendment of the earlier Council Decision 93/731 on access, to incorporate two new categories of mandatory public interest exception: one based on 'the security and defence of the Union or one of its member states', and the other on 'military or non-military crisis management'. The revised Council decision also completely excluded from the scope of public access any document which had been classified in one of the top three categories of an amended classification system: confidential, secret and top secret. This, Solana had argued, was necessary to maintain the functioning of the CFSP and to satisfy the

---

[151] See e.g. The European Ombudsman Annual Reports.
[152] Council Decision 2000/527 of 14 August 2000, OJ 2000 L212/09.

EU's NATO partners. This apparent act of bad faith on the Council's part (decided on a 12:3 majority vote) certainly seemed to make it more difficult to fulfil the obligations under Article 255. The Council's action appeared in an even worse light when, on the application of Statewatch for access to the amended decision in July 2000, the Council refused its release on the ironic, and very undemocratic, basis that release 'could fuel public discussion on the subject'.[153] This refusal was bitterly received, and challenged by the Dutch government in the CFI along with a separate challenge by the European Parliament.[154]

At this point it seemed likely that agreement on the regulation might not be possible by 1 May 2001, the date required by the Treaty of Amsterdam. The member states themselves were bitterly divided as to the form which the regulation should take, with Sweden taking the most liberal approach to freedom of information and France, Spain and Germany the most conservative, with a variety of positions in between. However, in November 2000, the Parliament adopted amendments to the draft Commission regulation, and a compromise was secured by the Swedish Presidency, after gruelling trilogue negotiations between the Commission, Council and Parliament, and Regulation 1049/2001 on Access to Information was finally adopted on 30 May 2001.

Regulation 1049/2001

There have been different reactions to this regulation: just how important is it in the context of access to information?

According to Article 2(3) of the new regulation, public access will apply to all documents **held** by an institution, not just those drawn up by it, which was a weakness of the previous system. It also expressly applies to the second and third pillars of the TEU. Under Article 11, each institution must maintain a public register of documents, to be operational no later than 3 June 2002. This is very important: the right to information can be rendered redundant if you don't know what it is you are looking for. Article 4 of the regulation, however, contains a rather daunting list of no fewer than nine categories of exception to public access. According to Article 4, for the first five categories[155] the test is whether public access would undermine the protection of the public interest as regards:

—public security,

—defence and military matters,

—international relations,

— the financial, monetary or economic policy of the Community of a Member State,

—privacy and the integrity of the individual, in particular in accordance with Community legislation regarding the protection of personal data.

---

[153] See the comments by Tony Bunyan of Statewatch writing in *Essays for an Open Europe*, European Federation of Journalists, November 2000.
[154] Now probably of historical interest only.
[155] Article 4(1).

For the following three categories[156] the test is whether public access would undermine the protection of:

—commercial interests of a natural or legal person, including intellectual property,

—court proceedings and legal advice,

—the purpose of inspections, investigations and audits.

The last category of exception under Article 4(3) is there to protect a so-called 'space to think'. These are situations in which the institution concerned has not yet taken a decision, in which case:

> Access to a document, drawn up by an institution for internal use or received by an institution, which relates to a matter where the decision has not been taken by the institution, shall be refused if the disclosure of the document would seriously undermine the institution's decision making process, unless there is an overriding public interest in disclosure.

Article 9 of the Regulation deals with sensitive documents. These are documents classified as top secret, secret or confidential, in accordance with the rules of the institution concerned and which protect essential interests of the European Union, or one of its member states, in the areas covered by Article 4(1)(a), notably public security, defence and military matters. These are to be dealt with, for the most part, in the same way as non-sensitive documents, with the following differences: if access is refused, reasons must be given in a way that does not harm the interest protected by the exceptions (Article 9(4)); initial and confirmatory applications are to be handled only by persons with the necessary security clearance to enable them to have knowledge of the documents (Article 9(2)); and the originator of the document, not the institution which holds it, is to make the final decisions as to whether one of the exceptions applies (Article 9(3)). Thus, this represents quite a considerable retreat from the Solana decision of summer 2000.

At time of writing it is difficult to predict what difference this new regulation will make. However, events of the 1990s in the EU do at least seem to suggest a recognition of the growing importance of transparency.

Better law-making

This section has focused on the formal aspects of transparency, i.e. the ability to access Community acts, documents and so on. However, even if one has access to these materials, this does not render them **substantially** transparent. As discussion earlier in this chapter emphasised, Community law is obscure and complex and thus often inaccessible. However, various initiatives have improved its quality. The aim is now to produce fewer, but better-targeted laws, as well as consolidating and repealing them, where possible. Also, deregulation and proportionality review aim to make legislation less intensive, as well as more framework directives and soft law.

---

[156] Article 4(2).

There are many reasons why EU law is not very comprehensible. Some of these relate to the *sui generis* nature of EC legislation. Draft laws may be produced in French (usually by a non-lawyer) but checked by a Commission official whose first language is probably not French, and amendments to this draft will be made in the course of relevant legislative procedures, which will have to be translated into the eleven EC official languages, all of which increases the likelihood of errors. Furthermore, the consensus-based nature of the EC process may mean that the Council is sometimes reluctant to be too precise in the laws it adopts, for fear of reopening the whole process. 'Euro-jargon' is also used quite a lot (after all, why use a term like 'destroyed' when you could instead use the mystifying 'denatured'?) On the other hand, certain concepts are not defined at all. The term 'worker', used in Article 39 EC, famously had to be defined by the ECJ in the *Levin* and *Kempff* cases.[157] EC law is often very technical in nature and frequent amendments have made it difficult to find the relevant text. A further criticism is that there is too much EC legislation and that it tends to be very detailed and prescriptive in nature, which in turn harms economic development.

Law reform entered the agenda in the 1990s, around the time of the Maastricht Treaty, when it became apparent that if the EU were to be brought closer to its citizens, then its laws would have to be made clearer and simpler.[158] Two reports (the Sutherland report and the Brussels report)[159] focused on the technical reform of law, namely better drafting, simplification, codification and consolidation of laws. The Commission also started to produce its annual reports on 'Better Lawmaking'.[160] In 1996, the Commission launched its SLIM initiative (Simpler Legislation for the Internal Market), which looks at specific targeted areas, such as recognition of diplomas. The Molitor report of independent experts (in this case economists) also produced a report on legislation and administrative simplification.[161] The issues of subsidiarity and proportionality also have a bearing on the nature of law-making and will be considered in the next chapter.

The Commission's *White Paper on Governance* of July 2001[162] highlighted and aimed to carry forward some of these law reform initiatives. It identified certain features as necessary to achieve improvements. These included promoting greater use of different policy tools (e.g. regulations, framework directives, guidelines, recommendations, and coregulatory mechanisms: whereby EC action is combined with actions taken by those concerned). The Commission also stressed that proposals for primary legislation should be limited to essential elements, while providing greater scope for implementing measures to complete the technical

---

[157] Case 53/81 *Levin* [1982] ECR 1035; Case 139/85 *Kempff* [1986] ECR 1741.

[158] See for example two declarations of the Edinburgh European Council of 1992: 'Making New Community legislation Clearer and Simpler' and 'Making Existing Community legislation More Accessible' (EC Bull 12, 1992 18–20); also *Inter-Institutional Declaration on Accelerated Working Method for Simple Consolidation* [1995] OJ C43/42 20 February 1995.

[159] Sutherland report of 1992: *The Internal Market After 1992: Meeting the Challenge*; Brussels Programme COM (93) 545.

[160] e.g. 'Better Lawmaking' for 2000, COM (2000) 772 final.

[161] *Molitor Group* report, COM SEC (95) 2125 Final of 29 November 1995.

[162] *European Governance: A White Paper* COM (2201) 428 final.

details of those proposals. A high-profile programme was launched by the Commission to review and simplify Community legislation adopted before 2000, supported by fast track procedures in Council and Parliament for this work.[163] The fact that all legislation adopted up to 2000 was included is alarming: after all, since the early 1990s the Commission has been supposed to be scrutinising EC legislation for its simplicity and necessity; the fact that legislation adopted in the 1990s is to be opened to further such scrutiny suggests that it has not done its job that effectively up until now.

So the quality of EC legislation is at least under consideration and indeed prioritised as a key factor in good governance. But will this bring Community law closer to the citizen? Even if EC legislation is improved in quality and made simpler, the treaties themselves are still untransparent in the extreme, not documents that the European public can relate to, and certainly not really a recognisable constitution for Europe. Much still has to be done to engage the European public with 'their' union, which means including, involving, and giving to European citizens a much greater chance to participate in the building of the European polity.

EUROPEAN IDENTITY AND PUBLIC PARTICIPATION

Parliamentary control, comitology and transparency aside, there is a broader domain to the issue of the democratic 'lack' in the EU. Perhaps we might call this a human domain, although what it involves is really the lack of any such domain. There is a strong feeling that the EU might appear more legitimate if only its citizens felt more included, felt a stronger sense of European identity. As it is, the EU lacks a public space and a civic sense. Indeed, for some writers a European public space has been seen as a near impossibility. As the EU does not have what has been termed a 'demos', a single people, it is suggested that there cannot be a truly European public space, nor a proper democracy at European level. This view derives partly from the views of Carl Schmitt.[164] On this theory, the people of a polity, the demos, or *Volk*, is seen as a concrete, identifiable, ethno-cultural, as well as social psychological, feature. The demos must be an entity possessed of a feeling of shared identity based on a common culture, history, ethnic origin and so on. In Schmitt's words, 'democracy requires, therefore, first homogeneity and second – if the need arises – elimination or eradication of heterogeneity'.[165] For Schmitt, the requirement of homogeneity was essential, and could not be fulfilled by what he dismissively called liberal, 'abstract, logical-arithmetical games' and 'indifferent equality'.[166]

Arguably, Schmitt's conceptual connection between democracy and homogeneity was at the basis of at least some of the reasoning of the German Constitutional

---

[163] *Commission Action Plan for Better Regulation* presented to the Laeken European Council.
[164] C Schmitt, *The Crisis of Parliamentary Democracy* (E Kennedy trans.) (Cambridge Mass: MIT Press 1985) at 9.
[165] Ibid.
[166] Ibid.

Court's Maastricht decision.[167] German constitutional lawyers have consistently upheld the conceptual triangle of 'people-state-constitution', and argued that Europe's democratic deficit needs no remedies, since there is no demos or *Staatsvolk*. On Schmitt's view, parliaments are democratic because they represent the *Volk*. This is not a very attractive view, nor particularly adept to fit the multi-cultural and multi-lingual EU, as it links democracy to the dangerous ties of ethnicity and cultural homogeneity which have sparked so many conflicts in the twentieth century and denied cultural, legal and political entitlements to minorities. A related, but somewhat moderated, view has been taken by Dieter Grimm, who, although distinguishing himself from a Schmittian type of ethno-cultural homogeneity, nonetheless suggested that 'The presuppositions of democracy are development not of the people but the form of society that wants to constitute itself as a political unit. But this presupposes a collective identity.'[168]

Such a reading of democracy has been contested. Above all, most nation states are not (and perhaps never were) unified and homogenous in this way. Does this mean there are no democracies? There is something rather curious about suggesting that only a unified, homogenous demos is capable of giving rise to democratic politics. However, if a European identity is not to be founded on an ethno-cultural basis, then what might it be based on? How else do communities cohere? One way in which they do so is through shared interests. Ernest Gellner has suggested that the modern nation was in fact created to meet the **functional** needs of modernity.[169] If this was so, then it might also be argued that the state can no longer deliver those same needs in a world of globalisation, and that rather, transnational support is needed.[170]

If transnational communities may cohere on the basis of shared interests, then such a commonality probably comes nearest to the sort of classic neo-functionalism which was dominant in the EEC in its early days. However, the linking bond of shared interest may not really instil a strong sense of community, but just a temporary and contingent one. Moreover, if the satisfying of interests is at issue, then there is a danger that people would tend to regard each other as burghers rather than citizens, as other individuals with whom they interact due to some common interest, rather than those which have a right to have their views considered and deliberated. In fact, there is a danger of producing 'market citizenship' at the expense of other, richer conceptions of citizenship.[171] Arguably, this one-sided commonality can play its part in democratic politics, but there is danger that the EU may become severely dysfunctional in the absence of any real public spirit. Such a community brings with it the danger of too much focus on what Derrida termed

---

[167] Maastricht Decision, *Brunner v European Union Treaty* 1 CMLR [1994] 57; see also D Grimm, 'Does Europe Need a Constitution?' (1995) 1 ELJ 282; J Habermas, 'Comment on the Paper by Dieter Grimm: "Does Europe Need a Constitution?"' (1995) 1 ELJ 303.

[168] Grimm op. cit. at 284.

[169] E Gellner, *Nations and Nationalism* (Oxford: Basil Blackwell, 1983).

[170] Gellner op. cit. at 110.

[171] See Chapter 14 on citizenship.

capital rather than **capitale**,[172] too much of a frenetic ethos of competition. It is not for nothing that Articles 81 and 82, which deal with competition in the EC, are the most litigated provisions in the treaty, nor that the focus of selfhood and individualism in the EU tends to be that of the rational economic actor.[173] Can we do any better in promoting some sort of civic identity for the EU?

Jurgen Habermas, in his reply to Dieter Grimm,[174] has suggested that 'Democratic citizenship entails an abstract, legally mediated solidarity among strangers. This form of social integration which first emerges with the nation state is realised in the form of a political socialising community context. What unites a nation of citizens as opposed to a *Volksnation* is not some primordial substrata but rather an intersubjectively shared context of possible understanding.'[175] For Habermas, therefore, a European identity must be rooted in a basis other than ethnic origin if it is to guarantee social integration. Habermas suggests that the ethical and political self-understanding of citizens in a democratic community is, in fact, the result of a circular process which can be generated through legal institutions. Habermas' writing has a procedural bent to it, as it requires a radical participatory democracy. This aligns with the calls of the republicans such as Michael Sandel,[176] who has criticised the liberal constitutional order for facilitating free markets at the cost of the civic community. A genuinely deliberative[177] scheme must look to ways of enhancing popular influence and involvement, and also to solidarity.[178]

How do such theories suggest that a flourishing deliberative democracy may be achieved? At its most abstract, deliberative democracy suggests that common policies are legitimate if they are the result of collective deliberation conducted among rational and free individuals.[179] In this way, the very procedure of articulating a view in public will produce a **reflexivity** on individual preferences. This means that the process itself forces individuals to articulate their reasons and also to think about what constitutes good reasons for others, what Arendt, following Kant, referred to as an 'enlarged mentality'.[180]

---

[172] J Derrida, *The Other Heading* (University of Indiana Press, 1992).

[173] Again Chapter 14 on citizenship.

[174] J Habermas, 'Comment on the Paper by Dieter Grimm: "Does Europe Need a Constitution?"' (1995) 1 ELJ 303.

[175] Habermas op. cit. at 305.

[176] M Sandel, *Democracy's Discontent: America in Search of a Public Philosophy* (Belknap Press, 1996).

[177] Much of the same reasoning may also apply to republican theories. For a republican account and good bibliography, see P Craig, 'Democracy and Rule making within the EC: an Empirical and Normative Assessment' (1997) ELJ 105.

[178] The rhetoric of which is not unknown in the EU: e.g. Article 2 EC refers to cohesion and solidarity, Delors expressed a preference for an EC 'with a social face'. Craig has suggested that the codecision procedure may be said to foster deliberative democracy as it encourages further reflection on initial preferences, in the light of the reaction of others, as exemplified by the Council's adoption of a common position in the light of the Parliament's first reading. Craig op. cit.

[179] See e.g. S Benhabib, 'Toward a Deliberative Model of Democratic Legitimacy' in S Benhabib (ed.) *Democracy and Difference* (Princeton University Press, 1996); see also J Cohen and C Sabel, 'Directly Deliberative Polyarchy' (1997) ELJ.

[180] H Arendt, 'The Crisis in Culture' in *Between Past and Future: Six Exercises on Political Thought* (New York: Meridian, 1961); a similar concept is also to be found in Habermas.

How does all of this work in practice? Surely, if deliberative democracy is to work, then there must be a distinct and stable public sphere in which all of this discussion may take place? Ancient Greece, which provided the paradigm for democracy, at least in its republican form, had just such a forum in the *Agora*. However, the danger of this is readily apparent: it could be taken as suggesting a need for homogeneity of peoples akin to that found in Schmitt's work. Therefore, modern day deliberative democracy looks not to a *res publica*, nor to a 'volonté générale' in the formal sense. Instead it privileges a plurality of modes of association: political parties, but also citizen initiatives, social movements and the like, and suggests that, through this multiple network of interlocking associations, a public conversation will emerge.

Nonetheless, it is still hard to imagine this at the European level. There is clearly no European public space, and the multilingual and complex nature of EU processes hampers the possibility of the development of deliberation. However, if we turn to the call for a plurality of modes of association, then perhaps a Europe-wide deliberative democracy does not look so impossible. Conversations and deliberations are occurring all over the place, in the media, on the internet (fostered by English, which is becoming a universal language, for better or worse), through the networks and committees also discussed in earlier chapters. The Commission's *White Paper on Governance*[181] stressed the need not only for EU institutions to communicate more actively with the general public on EU issues, but also for civil society to play its part, acknowledging that it (i.e. TUs, employers' organisations, NGOs, professional associations, churches and so on) offers 'a real potential to change the debate on Europe's role' as it provides 'a chance to get citizens more actively involved in achieving the Union's objectives and to offer them a structured channel for feedback, criticism and protest'.[182] At an even more concrete level, certain rights could be infused into the decision-making process, such as rights to consultation and participation, for those affected by specific rules. These might even be formalised in the treaty itself.

All this is well and good. If the EU can become more genuinely participatory then that is only a good thing. By giving individuals not only basic civil rights, but also the experience of exercising political rights and addressing issues of public policy, and bringing knowledge and judgment to these, the citizen becomes not just a passive recipient of rights, but an active agent, whose moral development is engaged. Again and again, a discussion of the problems of governance in the EU, especially its democratic deficit, turns up the need for a more participatory deliberative system.

It has become popular to suggest a deliberative or participatory democracy as a remedy for the EU ills[183] and there are well-founded reasons for this. However, this author has reservations about the **completeness** of deliberative democracy as a remedy.

Part of the problem lies in the fact that many deliberative democrats believe that democratic governance can be achieved by process alone. Their belief that this is so

---

[181] *Commission White Paper on Governance* COM (2001) 428 final 25.7.2001.
[182] *White Paper on Governance* at p 11.
[183] e.g. D Curtin, *Postnational Democracy* (Kluwer, 1997).

arises in part from their critique of traditional liberalism, which they see as unsuitable for the EU. Traditional liberalism involves at least some sort of consensus among a constitutional people. Tully[184] has categorised, or stigmatised, this consensus as shared forms of reason, which can generate agreement at least on the constitutional essentials.[185] However, proceduralists, communitarians and republicans have suggested that in conditions of such cultural diversity the liberal consensus is hard to sustain. Instead of the democratic public sphere being extended to a transnational context, they maintain that attempting to do so just leads to fragmentation. They suggest that, instead of the constitution being seen as the pre-condition of politics, political debate itself must become the medium through which a polity constitutes itself, continuing as part of an evolving process of mutual recognition. This, they suggest, fits in with the multidimensional EU, with its diverse and overlapping membership.

There is something unsatisfactory about this. There must additionally be some factor around in which to ground the process. The messy present-day structure of the EU will not do the job. What is needed is a more aesthetic, approachable constitutional document, based on an overlapping consensus.[186] Surely it is possible to achieve such a consensus in the EU context? The member states of the EU share enough by way of liberal democratic values and intellectual culture, which already have force and embedded qualities allowing them to work in a transactional context.[187] Thick, ethno-cultural ties are most certainly not the only way of achieving consensus and constitutional commitment. It is possible for some sort of 'thin identity' to develop on the basis of shared values and a common focus or locus for those values. In such circumstances the modern citizen may well be 'modular', combining many different associations.

Thus, the construction of the EU around civic values needs to reconcile two competing needs.[188] First, the need for a civic identity to rest on a definable core of values which are clearly presented. Second, for those same values to be critically and reflectively defined (this allows for some element of hermeneutics, proceduralism and 'enlarged mentality'). But what is essential is first a clear definition of the shared values. It is one of the themes of this book that, in addition to engaging participation at all levels, and spectrums, of society, it is also necessary to get the **structures** of government right, and indeed republicans themselves have acknowledged this need (as is revealed in the debates shaping the development of the US federal constitution).[189] Institutional design cannot be ignored, but rather must work in tandem with deliberation: complex governance requires fairly complex mechanisms. It is to this latter issue, that of the structures of government, that the next chapter will turn – to look at more classical features of the developing EU constitution – those of the division of powers.

---

[184] See Chapter 15.

[185] J Tully, *Strange Multiplicity* (Cambridge University Press, 1995).

[186] J Rawls, *Political Liberalism* (Columbia University Press, 1993).

[187] But I am not proposing a Schumpeterian democracy, i.e. this cannot be fostered by a top-down model of democracy based on the elite competition inherently exclusionary of ordinary citizens.

[188] C Lord, *Democracy in the European Union* (Sheffield Academic Press, 1998).

[189] See *The Federalist Papers*.

4

THE DIVISION OF POWERS
BETWEEN THE COMMUNITY AND
MEMBER STATES: EMBRYONIC
FEDERALISM?

INTRODUCTION

Thomas Hobbes memorably described sovereign authorities as 'in the state and posture of gladiators and standing guard at the frontiers of their kingdoms'.[1] These gladiators have been forced to retreat as EU law has eroded the frontiers of national sovereignty. The boundaries of EU and national action are unclear, contested, under siege, not always aggressively so, but almost by default.

This chapter aims to delineate the boundaries separating EU from member state action. This is anything but easy, as these boundaries are not very clear. It is difficult to set out with any great precision what is in fact the legitimate scope of EU, and more particularly EC, action: a troubling feature at a time when there is fear of the ever-encroaching effect of the EU on national sovereignty. Although the extent of the EC's competence has been an issue since its inception, it has most recently become 'live' following the prominence given to it by the Treaty of Nice. In the *Declaration on the Future of the Union*, attached to the treaty, the EU set itself the task of establishing a debate 'on how to establish and monitor a more precise delimitation of powers between the European Union and the Member States, reflecting the principle of subsidiarity'.[2] The issue of competences was also specifically set as a subject for consideration by the European convention. This will not be an easy task. One EU specialist commented that most of his time at the Legal Service of the Council had been spent worrying about whether this or that EC action was within the EC's competence.[3]

---

[1] T Hobbes, *Leviathan*, M Oakeshott (ed.), (Oxford: Blackwell, 1946) 83.
[2] *Declaration on the Future of the Union*, Article 5(1).
[3] A Dashwood, 'The Limits of EC Powers' (1996) ELRev at 128.

Nonetheless, despite fears of intrusive 'Brussels bureaucrats', the EC is actually limited in what it can do.[4] Any action taken by the EC must have a legal basis (either in the treaty or in other EC secondary legislation) which must be clearly stated in the preamble to EC legislation. Most importantly, the EC has no general law-making competence, in the sense that national legislatures may have.[5] A constitutional framework, regulating the EC's powers to act, is provided by various articles in the EC Treaty. These are as follows. Article 5(1) EC, inserted by the Maastricht Treaty, provides: 'The Community shall act within the limits of the powers conferred upon it by this Treaty and of the objectives assigned to it therein.' Article 7 EC, after naming the official Community institutions, provides that 'Each institution shall act within the limits of the powers conferred upon it by the treaty.' Articles 5(2) EC, which sets out the principle of subsidiarity, and 5(3) setting out that of proportionality, are also relevant in the context of the exercise of Community's powers, and will be discussed in following sections. Lastly, there is Article 230, which provides that actions taken by EC institutions may be annulled for lack of competence. There are no similar equivalents to be found in the TEU, in the context of the other two pillars, those of the CFSP, and of PJCC. However, action taken under these two pillars is, for the very large part, intergovernmental, requiring the consent of all the states, so unanimity functions much in the way which the Luxembourg Accords did in the past in the EC, as a constraint on an excess of power of the EC.

What none of these provisions does, however, is to specify what exactly the substance of these powers are. There is no express division of powers, no enumeration, in the sense that one would find it in a federal context,[6] and this has created uncertainty. Attitudes towards competence have shifted over the years. In the early days of the EC, most policy-making took place at national level, and the EC institutions were seemingly aware of their limited competence. In the *Algera* case, for example,

---

[4] There is a wealth of literature on the question of EC competences. See e.g. K Lenaerts, 'Constitutionalism and the Many Faces of Federalism' (1990) 38 Am J Comp L 205; D O'Keeffe and P Twomey (eds) *Legal Issues of the Maastricht Treaty* (Chancery, 1994) 13–33; P Craig and C Harlow, *Lawmaking in the European Union* (Kluwer, 1998); TC Hartley, 'Federalism, Courts and Legal Systems: The Emerging Constitution of the European Community' (1986) 34 Am J Comp L 229; Jones, 'The Legal Nature of the European Community' (1984) 17 Cornell Int'l LJ 1; Mackenzie Stuart, 'Problems of the European Community: Transatlantic Parallels' (1987) 36 ICLQ 36; F Mancini, 'The Making of a Constitution for Europe' (1989) 26 CMLRev 595; C Mann, *The Function of Judicial Decision in European Economic Integration* (Martinus Nijhoff, 1972) 288–99; Preece, 'The European Economic Community: International Organisation or Federal State?' (1985) 14 U Queensland LJ 78; J Temple Lang, 'European Community Constitutional Law: The Division of Powers between the Community and the Member States' (1988) 39 No Ire Legal Q 209; J Temple Lang, 'The Development of European Community Constitutional Law' (1991) 25 Int'l Lawyer 455; Tizzano, 'The powers of the Community' in Commission of the European Communities (ed.) *Thirty Years of Community Law* (Office of Official Publications, 1981); J Usher, 'The Scope of Community Competence – Its Recognition and Enforcement' (1985) JCMS 121; H Wallace, 'Europe as a Confederation: The Community and the Nation-State' (1982) 21 JCMS 57; J Weiler, 'Community, Member States and European Integration: Is the Law Relevant?' (1982) 21 JCMS 39.

[5] At least until limited by EC membership.

[6] See e.g. Article 1 section 8 US constitution, which enumerates a series of powers exercisable by Congress. (There is no corresponding list of states' powers but the Tenth Amendment states that they are reserved to the states/people); or Article 73 *Grundgesetz*.

decided under the ECSC treaty, the ECJ referred to the fact that the EC treaty was based on 'the principle of limited competence',[7] and a little later, in *Van Gend en Loos*, in the course of introducing the key constitutional principle of direct effect, the ECJ tempered that introduction by noting that member states had reduced their sovereignty only within 'limited fields'. However, as time passed, this strict approach to the enumeration of powers weakened. By the early 1990s, a broader view of the remit of EC competence was being taken. Jacques Delors referred to the fact that 80 per cent of regulation emanated from Brussels[8] and Koen Lenaerts, in a well-known article,[9] asserted that 'There is simply no known nucleus of sovereignty that the member States can invoke, as such, against the Community.' Thus, there seemed to have occurred what Joseph Weiler has memorably called a 'mutation' in the constitutional architecture of the Community.[10] However, this was what he also termed 'a silent constitutional revolution', given the little attention which this expansion of competences attracted in contrast to other key doctrines, such as those of the direct effect or supremacy of Community law.[11] All the more remarkable, given that this mutation occurred without any treaty amendment.[12]

That a type of expansion of competences did occur seems to be undeniable, and the mechanics of this will be considered below. However, what is also undeniable is that there was a backlash to this expansion in the post-Maastricht years, when the member states reacted to this stealthy growth of Community competence by seeking to impose boundaries on the action which the EC could take. This backlash took several forms: for example, the insertion of the principle of subsidiarity, which requires that decisions be taken at the most appropriate level, by the Treaty of Maastricht; but also by the careful limiting of new EC competences in the Maastricht Treaty so as to avoid giving a harmonisation power in these areas to the EC.[13] Warning messages also seemed to be quite clearly given by the member states, through both their courts, and their political institutions, as to the wisdom of the EC reigning in its competences. The German *Laender*, which felt that powers retained by them were being eroded by the EC, have been particularly vociferous in this respect,[14] but also the German foreign minister, Joschka Fischer, who gave a

---

[7] Cases 7/56. 3–7/57 *Algera* v *Assembly* [1957] ECR 59.

[8] See M Pollack, 'The End of Creeping Competence' (2000) 38 JCMS 519.

[9] K Lenaerts, 'Constitutionalism and the many faces of federalism' (1990) AJCL 205.

[10] J Weiler, 'The Transformation of Europe' in *The Constitution of Europe* (Cambridge University Press, 1999) at 39.

[11] Although one earlyish account was given by C Sasse and H Yourow, 'The Growth of Legislative Power in the European Communities' in T Sandalow and E Stein (eds) *Courts and Free Markets* (Oxford: Clarendon, 1982).

[12] Weiler suggested that it occurred through the use of four techniques, which he listed as categories of mutation – namely, extension, absorption, incorporation and expansion (J Weiler, *Transformation*, 45 *et seq*).

[13] Such as in the fields of education and culture.

[14] See most recently, in this context, the speech given by W Clements, President of Nord Rhein Westphalia, also at Humboldt University, Berlin, available as part of *the Forum Constitutionis Europeae* series at http://www.rewi.hu-berlin.de/WHI. The Laender play a considerable role: they were present at the IGCs and also signed the TEU through the *Bundesrat*.

speech at the Humboldt University, Berlin,[15] stressed the need for a clear delineation of competences. A warning also came from the German Constitutional Court, in its Maastricht judgment of 1993,[16] in which it stressed the limited democratic authority of the EC to extend its powers.

Have EC institutions taken on board these warnings? It might seem that the ECJ has been more cautious than in its 'heroic' earlier years. In *Keck*,[17] it reigned back the scope of Article 28. In its *Opinion 2/94*[18] it held that the EU could not accede to the ECHR on the basis of Article 308 EC (which had previously been used by the EC to justify extensions of competence). More recently it annulled the Tobacco Advertising directive, on the basis that the EC lacked the competence to conclude this directive: the first time that it had ever annulled an EC measure for lack of competence.[19] Nonetheless, we should not get things out of perspective: a recent study[20] concluded that the EC still continues to pass a great deal of legislation and may properly be called what Majone has termed a 'regulatory state'.

THE EXPRESS COMPETENCES OF THE EC

As already stated, there is no specific enumeration, no catalogue of competences of the EC and the member states in the treaties, so an initial problem is simply that of determining what power the EC may legitimately wield. However, Article 3 EC does set out a checklist of EC activities and Article 2 TEU sets out in very general terms what the objectives of the EU are, so it is clear enough that the EU has some competence in the following areas. These are: to create and maintain the internal market; and likewise a common commercial policy to third countries; to preserve competition; develop a common agricultural and transport policy; and to establish an economic and monetary union and single currency. The EC also has specific powers in such fields as social policy, culture, education and vocational training, public health, consumer protection, trans-European networks, industry, research and development, environment and development cooperation. Since the Treaty of Amsterdam it has had competence over some aspects of visas, asylum and immigration. It also has a role in establishing and strengthening economic and social cohesion between the regions.

However, these powers are not exhaustive, nor are they a legal base for Community action, nor do they detail the sort of competence the EC wields in these

---

[15] Speech given by Joschka Fischer on 12 May 2000 as part of the Humboldt speeches on Europe series. Fischer's speech and response to it are available on http://www.jeanmonnetprogram/papers/00/symp.html. William von Humboldt, the founder of the Humboldt university Berlin, is known of his 'Ideas for an attempt to determine the limits of state effectiveness' and thus the Humboldt university was an appropriate location for these speeches!

[16] *Brunner v European Union Treaty* [1994] 1 CMLR 57.

[17] Cases C-267, C-268/91 *Keck and Mithouard* [1993] ECR I 6097.

[18] *Opinion 2/94* [1996] ECR I-1759.

[19] See case C-376/98 *Germany v Council and Parliament* and case C-74/99 *R v Secretary of State for Health ex parte Imperial Tobacco* [2000] All ER (EC) 769.

[20] See M Pollack, 'The End of Creeping Competence' (2000) 38 JCMS 519.

areas. In addition, one must look to other provisions of the EC treaty which set out Community policies and provide both specific, and more general, bases for legislation. However, to gauge the exact limits of Community powers would, as has been remarked upon,[21] be the subject of a doctoral thesis, or, more probably, a lifetime's work.

Some powers are exclusive to the EC, but these are very limited, comprising only the EC's power to define a common commercial policy towards third countries and certain aspects of the common fisheries policy.[22] In such cases the member states may no longer exercise competence, even if the Community does not act. In *Opinion 1/75*[23] the ECJ recognised that, in the field of the common commercial policy, the Community's express powers exclude the exercise of concurrent powers by the member states, except in specific areas where the Community has specifically authorised member states to act,[24] or where existing obligations necessarily have to be carried out by the member states.[25] Unfortunately, it is not particularly clear what exactly is covered by the concept of trade in the context of the CCP; the ECJ has held, for example, that services do not fall within the EC's exclusive competence in the context of negotiations at the WTO.[26]

It is rare for the Community to exercise exclusive competence. Much more usual is the **concurrent** exercise of power by both the EC and member states. Even in agriculture, a field which has been central to the EC since its origins, there has been an interplay of member state and EC powers, allowing member states to act as long as they do not undermine the EC.[27] There are many other specific policies set out in the treaty which permit the EC to take some action, but such action is often carefully circumscribed. For example, in the context of the new competences added by the TEU, care was taken to spell out the limits of competence and to provide that the EC's role was to be ancillary. So we find that Article 149, which deals with education, vocational training and youth, specifically excludes, under Article 149(4), the possibility of any harmonisation by the EC. Similar restrictions apply in the context of culture (Article 151), health (Article 152), and some other policies, in which EC action is limited to incentive measures and cooperation. As Dashwood has commented, 'tight drafting ... would seem to reflect a lack of confidence in institu-

---

[21] Dashwood, op. cit. at 131.

[22] See *Opinion 1/75 (Local Cost Standard)* [1975] ECR 1355, which held that external trade fell within the exclusive competence of the EC. Also, in the field of fisheries, Case 804/79 *Commission v UK* [1981] ECR 1045.

[23] *Opinion 1/75 (Local Cost Standard)* [1975] ECR 1355.

[24] See Case 41/76 *Donckerwolke* [1976] ECR 1921.

[25] See Case 174/84 *Bulk Oil* [1986] ECR 559; *Opinion 2/91 Re ILO Convention* [1993] ECR I-1061.

[26] See N Emiliou, 'The Death of Exclusive Competence' (1996) 21 ELRev 294, commenting on *Opinion 1/94 on Community Competence to Conclude Certain International Agreements* [1994] ECR I-5276; see also *Opinion 1/78 Internal Rubber*, in which ECJ held the Commission's competence was not exclusive because arrangements were financed by the member states; also *Opinion 2/91 Re ILO Convention*, in which the Court held that the exclusive or non-exclusive nature of Community competence depends on the scope of the measures adopted.

[27] See Case 83/78 *Pigs Marketing Board v Redmond* [1978] ECR 2347.

tional self-restraint'.[28] Perhaps this is not very surprising, given the generous view of Community competence taken by the political institutions and by the Court in the 1980s.[29]

As well as specific legal bases for legislation, the treaty also contains more general express bases for action. These are Article 95 (formerly well known as Article 100a) and the residual Article 308 (formerly 235), both under attack for permitting a 'creeping extension' of EC jurisdiction.[30] An extensive interpretation of these provisions was taken in the 1980s, which, however, appears to have been reined in more recently. The division of Community competence into exclusive and concurrent competences is of relevance to the discussion of subsidiarity and will be further discussed below, but for the present it should be underlined that the general view is that Community competence is for the most part held **concurrently** with member states.

IMPLIED POWERS AND ARTICLE 308

The political theory underlying conferred powers is that of limited government. However, this has been undermined by the doctrine of implied powers.[31] The theory of implied powers was originally developed in the constitutional law of the United States,[32] and a current formulation of this doctrine in the US has been stated as follows:

> The exercise by Congress of power ancillary to an enumerated source of national authority is constitutionally valid, so long as the ancillary power does not conflict with external limitations such as those of the Bill of Rights and of federalism.[33]

In fact, the ECJ has taken a pragmatic approach to competences, holding that the EC has competence, not only where expressly granted in the treaty, but also that it has the implied competence to carry out tasks expressly allocated to it.[34]

A significant use made of the doctrine of implied powers by the ECJ in its early days was the introduction of the doctrine of **parallelism**. This doctrine applied to the pressing question of whether powers conferred on the EC regarding its internal competence might also be used to regulate external relations in that field, even although there was no indication in the treaty that they might be so used. The ECJ considered this question in a series of cases which arose in the 1970s, in which it

---

[28] Dashwood op. cit.

[29] e.g. by the Court in cases such as Case 293/83 *Gravier* [1985] ECR 593; or Case 9/74 *Casagrande* [1974] ECR 773, and the discussion in following sections.

[30] See below for a discussion of these provisions.

[31] N Emiliou, 'Implied Powers and the Legal Basis of Community Measures' (1993) 18 ELRev 138–144; Tizzano 'The powers of the Community', in Commission of the European Communities (ed.) *Thirty Years of Community Law* (Office of Official Publications of the EC, 1981).

[32] See *McCulloch* v *Maryland* 17 US (4 Wheat.) 316 (1819).

[33] See L Tribe, *American Constitutional Law* (Foundations Press, 1988) 301.

[34] See: Case 8/55 *Fédéchar* [1954–1956] ECR 292, at 299; Cases 281, 283–5, 287/85 *Germany* v *Commission* [1987] ECR 3203.

gave its opinion on the possibility of the EC entering into certain international agreements,[35] coming to the conclusion that, where the EC has been given powers to achieve a certain objective in its internal system, it has the corresponding external powers necessary for the achievement of this.[36] The doctrine of parallelism is now pretty well-established and several years ago, Dashwood suggested that it should be treated rather like direct effect, which Judge Pescatore termed 'an infant disease' of the Community, namely, something that one should take for granted and no longer worry about.

Article 308

This provides:

> If action by the Community should prove necessary to attain, in the course of the operation of the common market, one of the objectives of the Community and this treaty has not provided the necessary powers, the Council shall, acting unanimously on a proposal from the Commission and after consulting the European Parliament, take the appropriate measures.

Article 308 (formerly better known as 235) constitutes an exceptional provision which may only be used when the treaty has not provided the necessary powers.[37] It has much in common with the 'necessary and proper' clause of the US Constitution,[38] which allows Congress to adopt whatever measures seem appropriate to carrying out its mandates as enumerated in other clauses. The absence of a specific basis is a condition for the use of Article 308, a point that was made by the Court in *Massey Ferguson*.[39] It may, however, also be used where powers exist elsewhere in the treaty, but are insufficient to achieve the Community objective in question.[40]

However, exceptional although the use of this provision might be in theory, the objectives of the EC are very broad, as they are set out in Article 3. Furthermore,

---

[35] These come to the Court by way of an application by the Council, Commission or a member state under Article 300(6). The purpose of Article 300(6) (formerly Article 228(6)) of the Treaty is to forestall complications which would result from legal disputes concerning the compatibility with the Treaty of international agreements binding upon the Community. In order to avoid such complications, the Treaty has established the special procedure of a prior reference to the Court of Justice for the purpose of ascertaining, before the conclusion of the agreement, whether the latter is compatible with the Treaty.

[36] See Case 22/70 *ERTA* [1971] ECR 263; Cases 3,4,7/76 *Kramer* [1976] ECR 1279; *Opinion 1/76 Laying Up Fund* [1977] ECR 741; and most recently *Opinion 2/91 Re ILO* [1993] ECR I-1061.

[37] For further reading see TC Hartley, *The Foundations of European Community Law* (OUP, 1998) 102–108; H Schermers and D Waelbroek, *Judicial Protection in the European Communities* (Kluwer, 1992) 5th edn 342–346; J Schwartz, 'Article 235 and Law-Making Powers in the European Community' (1978) 27 *ICLQ* 614; Tschofen, 'Article 235 of the Treaty Establishing the European Economic Community: Potential Conflicts Between the Dynamics of Lawmaking in the Community and National Constitutional Principles' (1991) 12 Mich J Int'l L 471.

[38] Article 1 section 8 US Constitution: 'The Congress shall have Power to…To make all Laws which shall be necessary and proper for carrying into Execution the foregoing Power, and all other powers vested by this Constitution in the Government of the United States, or any department or Officer thereof.'

[39] Case 8/73 HZA *Bremerhaven v Massey-Ferguson* [1973] ECR 89.

[40] Case 45/86 *Commission v Council (Re General Tariff preferences)* [1987] ECR 1493.

the necessity of Community action has been at the discretion of Community institutions, and often subject to expansive interpretation. This was especially the case
after October 1972, when the European Council took a decision to make full use of
Article 308, as a way of pushing the EEC onward.[41]

In fact, although it should surely be no more than an explicit treaty formulation
of the doctrine of implied powers, Article 308 has led to a radical expansion of
power by the EC. It should certainly not provide the EC with new objectives which
it does not already possess. However, like other provisions in the treaty, Article 308
is textually ambiguous, and the notion of what is an objective is hardly clear cut.
There is a fine line to be drawn between legitimate and illegitimate use of Article 308
(which latter use amounts to *de facto* treaty amendment).

In the early years of the EC, Article 308 was little used and fairly tightly construed
when employed by Community institutions as a basis for legislation. Up until 1975
it was used only a couple of times a year, and, in some years, was not used at all.[42]
Article 308 was used for such things as nomenclature for the common customs tariff (1972), or in matters regarding agriculture where Article 37 (formerly 43) could
not be used as a legal basis. However, in 1975, there was a sharp increase in its use,
and it began to be used for matters such as the instigation of a pilot scheme to combat poverty (1975), and environmental matters, such as disposal of waste oils,
things which were not quite so essential to a traditional common market. In 1976
it was used as a legal basis for the Equal Treatment Directive 76/207. From then on,
use of Article 308 averaged 30–35 times per year,[43] often being used for the environment, in the absence of any specific provisions for environmental legislation in
the treaty. It was also the basis for legislation for the increasingly popular idea of a
'people's Europe': it was the basis for the Erasmus directive which was challenged
in the *Council v Commission* case.[44] Indeed, so wide had been the interpretation of
the Treaty's objectives that Joseph Weiler went as far as to comment, undoubtedly
tongue in cheek, that Article 308 could surely be used to defend the introduction of
a defence policy for the EC, as the common market would surely not be able to function if its member states were occupied.[45]

Indeed, it was not until 1996 that a judicial limit was placed on its use, when the
ECJ held that Article 308 could not be used as a basis for the EC to accede to the
European Convention on Human Rights. In so doing, the Court stated that 'Such
a modification of the system for the protection of human rights in the Community,
with equally fundamental institutional implications for the Community and for the
Member States, would be of constitutional significance and would therefore be such
as to go beyond the scope of Article 235. It could be brought about only by way of

---

[41] See J Weiler, *The Transformation of Europe*, which cites Article 308 as an example of the fourth of
his categories of mutation, expansion, going as far as to call it the 'locus classicus of true expansion', at
p 68.
[42] Figures obtained as a result of a CELEX search conducted by the author.
[43] Ibid.
[44] Case 242/87 *Council v Commission* (Erasmus) [1989] ECR 1425.
[45] See J Weiler in *The Division of Competences in the European Union*, European Parliament DG for
Research Working Document, political series W-26.

Treaty amendment.' This was a somewhat (perhaps the first) restrained interpretation of the EC's human rights jurisdiction and has come under criticism as being too
cautious.[46]

However, if the EC has no jurisdiction to accede to the ECHR, it must be questioned whether Article 308 could have provided it with the competence to enter into
its past (undoubtedly well-respected) actions such as the PHARE and TACIS programmes involving food aid and technical assistance to central European countries.
Could it really be said that such projects were 'necessary in the course of the operation of the common market'? No doubt, the competence to adopt such programmes
has become less of a problem since the SEA and TEU extended the competences of
the EU. Nonetheless, as already mentioned, these extensions were quite carefully
ringfenced, excluding such techniques as harmonisation by the EC.

However, why would it matter if an over-expansive use is made by the EC of
Article 308? After all, Article 308 requires the unanimity of the member states, as
well as consultation of the European Parliament. Legislation cannot be passed under
this provision against the wishes of a country. The answer to this must surely be
that, if Article 308 is used to exceed the existing objectives of the EC, it bypasses the
democratic process for treaty amendment set out in Article N TEU, under which
treaty amendments have to be ratified by the parliaments of the member states (and
in some case referenda required to be held). Such elements of the democratic process
cannot be compensated for by the participation of the European Parliament in the
Article 308 process, which is in any case by way of consultation only, and nothing
like the stronger input which it has through the codecision procedure.

LEGAL BASIS

It is well-established that every EC action must have a legal basis.[47] Following the
institutional changes introduced by the Single European Act and the Maastricht
Treaty, which gave the Parliament an increased role under some law-making procedures, the choice of the correct legal basis for each Community measure came to
play a more important role in institutional politics. The Parliament was keen to protect its prerogatives and to ensure that those legal bases which allowed it the greatest participation were selected. This led to a dramatic increase in litigation before
the ECJ, underlining its role as a **constitutional** court.

The legal bases of Community action to be found in the EC treaty may be divided
into various types. First, there are those in particular policy sectors, such as agriculture, which provide a firm basis for Community action. Second, there are Articles 94
and 95, which can be used for a more general purpose, to regulate the functioning of

---

[46] This case is also discussed in the chapter on human rights.
[47] R Barents, 'The Internal Market Unlimited: Some Observations on the Legal Basis of Community
Legislation' (1993) 30 CMLRev 85; K Bradley, 'The European Court and the Legal Basis of Community
Legislation' (1988) 13 ELRev 379; N Emiliou, 'Opening Pandora's Box: the Legal Basis of Community
Measures before the Court of Justice' (1994) 19 ELRev 488; TC Hartley, *The Foundations of European
Community Law* (OUP, 1998) 108–111.

the internal market. Third, there are specific provisions, such as Article 149 for education, or Article 151 for culture, which provide the EC with a legal basis, but one which is more limited in scope, as it specifically excludes certain types of measure, such as harmonisation. Finally there is Article 308, discussed in the previous section, which is residual. What is clear is that there has been, and still is, a difficult relationship between these general and more specific bases, making the question of choice of legislative base more complex than it might first appear.

This complexity has not been lessened by some of the ECJ's decisions in this area. Certain principles may however be extracted from the case law. First, the ECJ held in *Commission v Council (general tariff preferences)*[48] that 'the choice of the legal basis ... may not depend simply on an institution's conviction as to the objective pursued but must be based on objective factors which are amenable to judicial review'. It is clear that an insufficiently precise statement of the legal basis constitutes an infringement of the requirement relating to the statement of reasons, and hence an infringement of an essential procedural requirement. The adoption of a measure on an incorrect legal basis constitutes a substantive infringement of the treaty. Both will lead to the annulment of the measure.

The use of Article 95 (formerly 100A) is problematic and has perhaps been responsible for the creeping extension of the Community's competences, as it seems to allow a lot of leeway as a basis for legislation. Article 95(1) reads as follows:

> 1. By way of derogation from Article 94 and save where otherwise provided in this Treaty, the following provisions shall apply for the achievement of the objectives set out in Article 14. The Council shall, acting in accordance with the procedure referred to in Article 252 and after consulting the Economic and Social Committee, adopt the measures for the approximation of the provisions laid down by law, regulation or administrative action in Member States which have as their object the establishment and functioning of the internal market.

The wording of Article 95 immediately raises two questions. First, what is meant by 'approximation'? How does approximation legislation differ from action taken by the EC under its common policies, such as free movement? The answer seems to be that action taken under Article 95 must seek to eradicate differences in the law or practice of the member states. The practice in question need not be regulated in all member states of the EU, but must be one in which action at member state level is possible. If the intention is to strike out, and do something independently of the member state, then Article 308 will be the appropriate basis.

The second notable feature of Article 95 is that it may only be used for measures which have as their object 'the establishment or functioning of the internal market'. This requirement may be satisfied in two ways. The measure **may remove disparities between national provisions liable to hinder free movement** (for example, labelling requirements for goods). Alternatively, the measure **may remove disparities liable to create or maintain distorted conditions of competition**. This latter requirement is problematic, as virtually any government measure in the economic or social

---

[48] Case 45/86 *Commission v Council (tariff preferences)* [1987] ECR 1493

sphere may have some impact on the conditions of competition. For example, the number of years which children have in school affects the labour market and may lead to difference in quality of workers which in turn can distort competition: on that basis the EC might have the competence to harmonise education. Alternatively, the length of annual holidays can affect the labour market: could this factor thus lend the EC competence in this area?[49] So it is potentially a very wide condition indeed, allowing for a lot of EC regulation.

How has the ECJ approached Article 95? Although in the *Titanium Dioxide*[50] case, the ECJ seemed to suggest that Article 95 might enjoy priority over specific bases (in this case being the relevant environmental base) in a subsequent case[51] also involving the competing bases of environment and Article 95, it held that, in every case, it must examine the instrument's predominant aim and content, to see where its 'centre of gravity' lay. In the latter case, it found that harmonisation of the internal market had only an incidental effect. As some of these bases (i.e. Article 95 in its current form) allow for much greater participation of the European Parliament than others it is not just the excess of power which is at issue, but also the whole issue of separation of powers or institutional balance.

The leading case on legal basis is now that of *Germany* v *Council* and *Imperial Tobacco*,[52] in which the ECJ annulled the Directive which banned tobacco advertising on the grounds that it had been adopted on the wrong legal basis. This Directive had been adopted by a very narrow margin in the Council and Parliament on the basis of Article 95, after a complicated legislative passage. Indeed, the legal affairs committee of the European Parliament had divided sharply over its compatibility with EC competence. From the very start there was a vigorous lobby which submitted that the directive could not be an internal market measure, but must be a public health measure, in which case the EC did not have the jurisdiction to take this type of action. This assertion seemed to be backed up by the fact that the legislation did seem to have been prompted mainly by public health concerns (this is evident if one looks to the legislative debates) and it had been handled in Council by health ministers. Additionally, the recitals of the directive made quite substantial reference to public health. The problem was that the public health section of the treaty, Article 153(2) EC, specifically excluded harmonisation of the health law of the member states. Challenges were brought to the directive by the tobacco companies,[53] which were found to be inadmissible for lack of standing in a direct action.[54] However, a direct challenge brought by the German government, as well as an indirect challenge referred by the English court, found their way to the Court and were decided together.

---

[49] See, for similar examples, *The Division of Competences in the European Union*, European Parliament DG for Research Working Document, political series W-26.

[50] Case C-300/89 *Commission* v *Council (Titanium Dioxide)* [1991] ECR I-2869.

[51] Case C-155/91 *Commission* v *Council (Waste Directive)* [1993] ECR I-2869.

[52] Case C-376/98 *Germany* v *Council and Parliament* and Case C-74/99 *R* v *Secretary of State for Health, ex parte Imperial Tobacco* [2000] ECR I-8419.

[53] Cases T-172. 175–8/98 *Salamander AG et al* v *European Parliament and Council* [2000] ECR 2487.

[54] See Chapter 10.

During the oral procedure, submissions were made by Imperial Tobacco to the effect that the Court's judgment would decide whether the Community institutions could legislate on any subject matter at all simply by devising theoretical links with the internal market. The argument was made that there was no significant inter-state trade in the EC in many of the advertising products concerned, such as stationary advertising (i.e. billboards and posters, or in local paper) so that the directive exceeded the harmonisation necessary for free movement. It was also argued that the directive could not be justified as necessary to eradicate distortions of competition, as in fact the directive created distortions, by making it more difficult for new products to penetrate the market in the absence of advertising capability. Thus, the internal market elements of the ban on tobacco advertising were simply too minor and uncertain. This was a public health measure and the EC did not have the competence to take this sort of action under the public health provisions.

The ECJ agreed. It found that 'the national measures are to a large extent inspired by public health objectives',[55] going on to state that:

> a measure adopted on the basis of Article 100A must generally have as its object the improvement of the conditions for the establishment or functioning of the Internal Market. If a mere finding of disparities between national rules and of the abstract risk of obstacles to the exercise of fundamental freedoms or of distortions of competition liable to result therefrom were sufficient to justify the choice of Article 100a as a legal basis, judicial review of compliance with the proper legal basis might be rendered nugatory. The Court would then be prevented from discharging the function entrusted to it by Article 164 of the EC Treaty (now Article 220 EC) of ensuring that the law is observed in the interpretation and application of the Treaty.[56]

The Tobacco Directive was therefore invalid as it had been adopted on the wrong legal basis.

So does the *Tobacco Advertising* case clarify the boundaries between the prohibition of an economic activity and its regulation for the purposes of the internal market? If so, where does that boundary lie? It seems that the ECJ answered the question by stating that harmonisation aimed at **rectifying** distortion is in the conditions of competition and can only be justified where those distortions are **appreciable**. In the case of harmonisation to favour free movement, the EC may harmonise national rules which create obstacles to free movement, where the concept of obstacle should be decided in the same way as the Court's case law on fundamental freedoms (i.e. as in *Dassonville*, in that the effects must not be too remote and indirect).

An American case, decided by the US Supreme Court in May 2000, provides a nice contrast with the ECJ's annulment of the Tobacco Advertising directive. Both the ECJ and US cases concern the division of powers between a central authority and component parts, and thus could be said to raise federal issues, in which the US Supreme Court has a longer history of interpretation.

---

[55] *Germany* v *Council* at para. 76.
[56] Ibid. para. 84.

In the US case, *United States v Morrison*,[57] the Supreme Court held that Congress, in passing a federal law, the 1994 Violence against Women Act,[58] had exceeded its power, in basing the Act on the Commerce Clause. The Commerce clause, which is to be found in Article 1 of the US constitution, gives Congress the power to regulate 'commerce with foreign nations, among the several states, and with the Indian tribes'. The Violence Against Women Act had provided a civil remedy for victims of sexual assaults to bring independent civil actions against their assailants. The case involved a Virginia Tech student who claimed she was raped by two football players and who brought the first lawsuit under the law. Congress had attempted to justify basing the law on its constitutional power to regulate interstate commerce (adopting it after four years of hearings) on the ground that women who feared being attacked would be hindered from going out at night, taking public transport, or engaging in other activity that would help them find a job and contributing to the economy. Thus the legal basis of what, on its face, seemed to be a statute which had nothing to do with economic activity, dealing as it did with violence against women, was an unashamedly economic one. This was by no means the first time that Congress's powers under the Commerce Clause had been used in an expansive way: it was used in the 1960s as the basis of Civil Rights legislation, often because federal lawmakers felt that the states had failed to handle problems properly themselves, as was, indeed, felt to be the case in the context of the Violence Against Women Act.

For many years the Commerce clause had been given a broad interpretation. As early as 1824, in *Gibbons v Ogden*[59] Marshall CJ had given a broad construction to the Commerce Clause, stating that the commerce power 'is complete in itself, may be exercised to its utmost extent, and acknowledges no limitations, other than those which are prescribed in the Constitution'.[60] For much of the twentieth century, until 1995, the Supreme Court continued with this broad interpretation of Congress's power under the clause, holding that Congress might regulate under its commerce power 'those activities having a substantial relation to interstate commerce … i.e. those activities that substantially affect interstate commerce'.[61]

Although by no means identical with Article 95 EC, and its concern with the functioning of the internal market, there is a similarity between these two provisions. Both Article 95 and the Commerce Clause seek to regulate economic activity, but in wide and open-textured language. Both had been interpreted with latitude, to admit legislation with no very obvious economic impact. However, in 1995, in the *Lopez*[62] case,

---

[57] *United States v Morrison; Brzonkala v Morrison* [2000] 120 S Ct 1740.

[58] 42 USC s.13981.

[59] *Gibbons v Ogden* 9 Wheat 1, 189. However, Congress did not make use of this power to regulate for over a century.

[60] Ibid. at 196.

[61] *NLRB v Jones & Laughlin Steel Corp*, [1937] 301 US 1, 81 L Ed 893, 57 S Ct 615 in which it sustained labour laws applying to manufacturing facilities.

[62] *United States v Lopez* 514 US 549 131 L Ed 2d 626, 115 S Ct 1624 (1995); see also Jackson, 'Federalism and the Uses and Limits of Law' (1998) 111 Harv L Rev 2180; Gardbaum, 'Rethinking Constitutional Federalism' (1996) 74 Texas Law Review 795; L Lessig, 'Translating Federalism: *United States v Lopez*' 1995 S Ct Rev 125.

the Supreme Court rejected the use of the Commerce clause as a base for Congress's attempt to ban guns near local schools. *United States* v *Morrison* continued to place limits on Congress's power. Speaking for the majority, in a sharply divided 5:4 ruling, Rehnquist CJ started by noting the words of Marshall CJ in *Marbury* v *Madison*: 'The powers of the legislature are defined and limited: and that those limits may not be mistaken or forgotten, the constitution is written.'[63] Rehnquist found that 'Gender motivated crimes are not, in any sense of the phrase, economic activity,'[64] continuing that, 'If Congress may regulate gender-motivated violence, it would be able to regulate murder or any other type of violence.' The four justices in the minority gave a vigorous dissent, addressing the boundary between federal and state power, insisting that the law should be upheld as a valid exercise of Congress's power to deal with an activity that had a substantial effect on interstate commerce. Also, regarding the majority's effort in keeping the federal government out of the traditional business of states, Souter J made the bitter comment that 'the federalism of some earlier time is no more adequate to account for today's economy than the theory of laissez-faire was able to govern the national economy 70 years ago'. Both Souter, and Breyer, in a separate dissent, stressed that 'Congress and not the courts must remain primarily responsible for striking the appropriate state/federal balance.' The majority obviously did not agree, feeling that the Court had an important role in policing the state/federal balance and in striking down federal legislation which they took to disrupt that balance, by foreclosing the states from exercising their own judgment in any area in which they laid claim by right of history and expertise. This case gives us a taste of the sort of problems likely to trouble the EC in the field of competences.

The *Tobacco Advertising* case is constitutionally significant. It is the first case in which the ECJ has annulled a measure taken by the EC on grounds of lack of competence, and thus presents itself as the first full application of the principle of limited powers by the Court. It is also an example of what might be described as the political schizophrenia of the limiting and expanding of EC powers since Maastricht. So, for example, the TEU expanded the competences of the EU, but in some cases in a limited way (e.g. health). Other examples can be given: for example, in the field of human rights, on the one hand, there has been an effort to expand, with the insertion of new provisions in the Treaty, such as the references in Articles 6 and 7 TEU, the proclamation of the Charter on Fundamental Rights, and the recently adopted Race Discrimination directive.[65] On the other hand, the EU's embrace of human rights has not been unambivalent. The Charter is as yet nonbinding, which in itself sends out a message, and the ECJ, as already mentioned, denied the capability of the EC to accede to the ECHR on the basis of Article 308.

The *Tobacco Advertising* case is a first step towards a hard EU constitutional law on competence, a significant recognition of the EU's lack of internal competence to

---

[63] *Marbury* v *Madison* [1803] 5 US 137, 1 Cranch 137, 176 2 L Ed 60.

[64] *Morrison* at 1751.

[65] The race discrimination directive was adopted very quickly indeed by the Council (and probably prompted by the fear of the possible human rights abuses of the new Austrian right wing administration in which Jorg Haider's far right Freedom party participated).

adopt a measure, even a measure which had a great deal of public support. Previous cases have tended to deal with external competences, so the *Tobacco* case is crucial. It might seem that the growth of jurisprudence on the EC's boundaries is reassuring, satisfactory. It signals an important next step in the journey of European integration, a willingness to apply the principle of conferred powers, to set staging points, boundaries, clear demarcation lines, to EC expansion by way of positive law. The logical accompaniment to this jurisprudence would be the drawing up of a list of competences by the next IGC. For others, this path is not so appealing, for reasons which will be discussed in the later sections of this chapter.

PREEMPTION

To speak of the setting of boundaries is to recall solutions visited by federalism, and, more particularly, the doctrine of preemption. Preemption originates in US constitutional law, where the application of laws issued by federal institutions precludes any corresponding regulatory powers of the states.[66] Sometimes legislation will expressly declare its preemptive effect, but a lot of the time this will have to be determined by interpretation and a sizeable body of case law has grown up in the US Supreme Court.[67]

Preemption is a federal concept, which seemed to play no part in the conception of the framers of the EEC treaty, who had international law in mind. However, the doctrine of preemption now does function within EC law.[68] Preemption must take its place as one of the constitutional principles – along with direct effect and supremacy – of EC law. Unfortunately, its application is not very clear cut. If preemption were to apply in a classic way, one would expect member state competences to be reduced as the EC takes more and more actions. But this has not been so. Cross,[69] for example, has referred to the obscurity of preemption as it operates in the EC. So the situation needs to be elucidated somewhat.

The purest, or most extreme, example of preemption is when the EC has exclusive competence. In this case the states cannot act at all, even if the EC has taken no action.[70] The problem however is that such a situation can lead to regulatory gaps,

---

[66] See, for example, L Tribe, *American Constitutional Law* (2nd edn, New York: Foundation Press, 1988) 481; H Maier, 'Preemption of State Law: A Recommended Analysis' (1989) 83 AJIL 832; R Rotunda, 'The Doctrine of Conditional Preemption and Other Limitations on Tenth Amendment Restrictions' (1984) 132 Univ Penn LR 289.

[67] For a discussion of the US Supreme Court's distinction between occupying field and conflict preemption see Tribe op. cit. and *Rice v Santa Fe Elevator Corp* (1947) 331 US 218.

[68] See: for example, for a discussion of preemption in Community law: Waelbroeck, 'The Emerging Doctrine of Community Pre-emption – Consent and Re-delegation' in T Sandalow and E Stein (eds) *Courts and Free Markets* (Oxford: Clarendon Press, 1982); E Cross, 'Pre-emption of Member State Law in the European Community: A Framework for Analysis' (1992) 29 CMLRev. 447; S Weatherill, 'Beyond Pre-emption? Shared Competence and Constitutional Change in the European Community' in D O'Keefe and P Twomey, *Legal Issues of the Maastricht Treaty* (London: Chancery Law, 1994).

[69] Cross op. cit. (1992) CMLRev.

[70] *Opinion 1/75 (Local Cost Standard)* [1975] ECR 1355.

in which no action is taken at all in cases where it may be urgently needed. This severe possible side-effect has been tempered by the ECJ holding that, in such cases, national measures may be permissible with the Commission's authorisation.[71] However, if this is so, it might be concluded that the EC's competence in that area cannot be exclusive, but mixed, if the states are also permitted to act.

The most classic example of preemption, however, is occupation of the field: when the EC has acted, member states no longer can. Even this apparently clear situation is not so straightforward, however. While it may be the case that action by the Community may entail the loss of power for member states, on some occasions it may be more difficult to determine whether member state competence has in fact been completely eroded by Community action. On the one hand, in *Commission v UK (Dim dip)*[72] the ECJ held that a Community directive had totally preempted national competence and had a blocking effect on national competence. However, in the *Jongeneel Kaas*[73] case for example, the ECJ held that a regulation had occupied a neighbouring field rather than the area concerned, and that state action still remained possible. Member state competence may be particularly difficult to assess in those areas in which the Community legislature appears silent on aspects of a subject. How should silence be interpreted? In the *Amsterdam Bulb* case the ECJ interpreted silence as merely silence, not resulting in any preemptive effect on member state action. However, in another case, *Officier van Justitie*[74] it found the opposite to be the case.

Occupation of the field, while it may not lead to regulatory gaps, is, in any case, an example of the sort of total harmonisation which is no longer very popular in these days of a lighter touch in law-making.[75] The EC is much more likely to engage in a more minimal kind of harmonisation, of the kind to be found in a variety of directives, such as those on doorstep selling, or misleading advertisements. These days it is also quite common for the EC to proceed by way of soft law, especially in areas such as health, education, consumer protection and culture. Soft law measures cannot be preemptive, as they are not legally binding in the first place. Furthermore, in the two EU pillars, that of CFSP and PJCC, preemption is not very relevant as the measures are intergovernmental in nature. Therefore, the role played by preemption is hardly straightforward.

---

[71] Case 41/76 *Donckerwolke* [1976] ECR 1921; Also Case 50/76 *Amsterdam Bulb* [1977] ECR 137 (even where Community institutions have failed to act when powers were given to them, member states cannot act unilaterally. They must at the least cooperate with and consult the Commission, since the failure to act may be a deliberate choice of economic policy in an area attributed by the member states to the Community). See also Case 111/76 *Van den Hazel* [1977] ECR 901.

[72] Case 60/86 *Commission v UK* [1988] ECR 3921.

[73] Case 237/82 *Jongeneel Kaas* [1984] ECR 483.

[74] Case 50/76 *Amsterdam Bulb* [1977] ECR 137; Case 111/75 *Officier van Justitie* [1977] ECR 901; see also N Emiliou, 'Subsidiarity: Panacea or Fig Leaf' and S Weatherill, op. cit. both in O'Keefe and Twomey op. cit. for a discussion of these issues, as well as K Lenaerts, 'Constitutionalism and the Many Faces of Federalism' (1990) 38 AJIL 295 at 220; for a discussion of the position regarding the silence of the Congress in the US see Bikle, 'The Silence of Congress' (1927) 41 Harv L Rev 20.

[75] See the discussion in Chapter 3 on the quality of law-making, as well as below, in the section on subsidiarity.

As Stephen Weatherill has commented, 'constitutionally something significant is happening'.[76] What he describes as 'actively multi-functional' legislation is taking place,[77] in which there is a place for national legislation within the framework of EC market regulation. In this way there can still be diversity within unity. This situation is linked to the increasingly fragmented nature of the EC polity, in which there may be flexible cooperation between some but not all member states, a development which is discussed below.[78]

THE FUTURE OF THE UNION AND THE DEBATE ON COMPETENCES

The question of EC competences, and how to regulate them, is, for the time being, a live issue. In February 2001, Clements, the Prime Minister of the German Land, Nord-Rhein Westphalia, gave a speech on the allocation of competences after Nice.[79] In this speech he argued for a new system of division of competences between the EU and member states, quoting the German Foreign Minister, Joschka Fischer, who had controversially, the previous year, called for the same thing in the context of a 'federal' solution for Europe.[80] The question of competences forms a very important part of the work of the European Convention.

If not now, might at least the next IGC, be the time to start drawing up some sort of list or catalogue of competence of the EU and the member states? Such lists are, after all, common in the context of federalism. Federal competences tend to include, for example, those which seem to be in the 'national' interest, such as foreign relations, defence, currency, transport, interstate commerce, indeed those issues relevant to the sovereignty of the central state. A list of concurrent competences may also be set out. So for example, in the context of the US, Article 1 section 8 of the US Constitution defines the competence of Congress, while the Tenth Amendment underlines the fact that everything else is attributed to the competence of the states. Article 73 of the *Grundgesetz*, the German federal constitution, enumerates the powers of the federal government, and also catalogues the concurrent competences of Bund and Laender, while Article 72 sets out structural principles as to the exercise of those competences. Even in the, until recently, very unfederal UK, competence has now been delineated, since devolution to Scotland in 1998. In the Scotland

---

[76] Weatherill op. cit. at 25.

[77] See e.g. Article 95(4) EC, which allows member states to take safeguard measures by way of derogation, on grounds of major needs, such as those referred to in Article 30 EC, or on grounds relating to the protection of the working environment. In order to do this, member states must first notify the Commission, although in fact it has been rarely invoked.

[78] At the end of this chapter.

[79] Clements' speech is available at the Humboldt University Berlin website: http://www.rewi.hu-berlin.de/WHI.

[80] Speech given by Joschka Fischer on 12 May 2000 as part of the Humboldt speeches on Europe series. Fischer's speech and response to it are available on http://www.jeanmonnetprogram/papers/00/symp.html.

Act, the UK reserves to itself the classic state competences (i.e. macro economics, defence, foreign policy) but devolves all others to Scotland.[81]

Delineation of competence might seem a satisfying option, but is nonetheless still problematic. Federalism is by definition unfinished business because many issues cannot be foreseen at the time of the initial bargain.[82] Furthermore, catalogues of competences will always be subject to interpretation, opening the door to all sorts of court challenges. Another problem is the strong centripetal pull often present in existing federal systems.[83]

But lists of competences may seem to have a symbolic attraction. Some imaginative suggestions have been made as to the form which they might take in the EU. Clements, in his recent speech, did not suggest such a bipolar order, but rather a categorising of three types of EC competence: exclusive, fundamental and supplementary. He also suggested augmenting the strength of the subsidiarity principle, and, more controversially, the deletion of Articles 95 and 308 (particularly hated by the German Laender for eroding some of their specific powers). However, Clements also insisted that a recategorisation of EC competences must be taken along with institutional reforms. This is a very important point. Institutional reform is clearly crucial, as the last two chapters have tried to stress. De Búrca[84] has suggested that the evolving dynamic nature of the EU calls into question the possibility of imposing strict constitutional formulae. She sees the possible solution of a list of competences as misconceived, given the essential interdependence of areas of policy in the EU. Unlike in a federal system where there is an overall sense of unity and mutual trust between the various parts, this is lacking in the EU. Therefore rather than focusing on legal lists of competences, de Burca stresses that we should be looking to the question of appropriate institutional design and political culture. This she submits is the best way forward in the multilevel government that is the EU. Nonetheless, there is much to be said for the drawing of clear, positive boundaries. It would prevent another accretion of power to the EU by stealth. Boundaries also have an important symbolic dimension: of containment, definition, identity. This is important in uncertain times.[85]

---

[81] See The Scotland Act c.46 1998, although s.28(7) of the Act specifically refers to the power of the United Kingdom Parliament to legislate for Scotland. Thus the site of primary legislation is shared.

[82] See *The Division of Competences in the European Union*, European Parliament DG for Research Working Document, political series W-26.

[83] Although this has not necessarily been the case in Canada, in which an explicit declaration of the competences of the provinces may have led to some of the present weaknesses: see, for example, R Watts, *Comparing Federal Systems* (McGill and Queensland: McGill University Press, 1999); and less so in the US where recent case law of the US Supreme Court, has reversed the centripetal pull in favour of the states, as for example in the *Morrison* case, discussed above.

[84] G De Búrca, 'Setting Constitutional Limits to EU Competence' Faculdade de Direito da Universidade Nova de Lisboa, Working paper 2001/02.

[85] See the psycho-analytic account given by A Falk in 'Border Symbolism' (1974), Psycho-Analytic Quarterly.

SUBSIDIARITY

Origins and meaning

Another concept which has an important role to play in the delineation (or obfuscation) of boundaries, is subsidiarity. Subsidiarity, such a key word in the EU in the mid 1990s,[86] still merits attention. As it is to be found in Article 5 EC, subsidiarity permits EU institutions to act in areas of concurrent competence 'only if and insofar as the objectives of the proposed action cannot be sufficiently achieved by the Member states'. In the EU context, the principle is a means of determining the appropriate level of action, and is closely related to the concepts of necessity, effectiveness, proportionality, or even good government. It has been promoted as a means of reconciling the conflicting needs of unity and diversity within the EU. It is also seen, along with the principle of proportionality and improved access to documents, as a way of bringing Europe closer to its citizens.[87]

It should be apparent that the EU is itself a complex structure of multilevel governance, in which member states and EU institutions interact in a complicated, symbiotic relationship. When one looks to the activities of EU institutions, be it the Commission, Council, European Parliament, one sees that these do not act in a unitary manner, but that their actions are carried out by groups, committees, shifting networks of individuals, who may be at odds with each other within the one institution. This is perhaps a response to the fact that no single issue can be solved satisfactorily at a single level; the linking of powers seems to be the pattern for the future.

In such circumstances, subsidiarity seems both appropriate and inappropriate. Appropriate, because it purports to address the need to reconcile unity and

---

[86] Here is just a selection of the burgeoning literature on subsidiarity: N Emiliou, 'Subsidiarity: An Effective Barrier against "the Enterprises of Ambition"?' (1992) 17 ELRev 383; TC Hartley, *The Foundations of European Community Law* (OUP, 1998) 111–113; D O'Keeffe and P Twomey (eds) *Legal Issues of the Maastricht Treaty* (Chancery, 1994) 37–83; 'Overall Approach to the Application by the Council of the Subsidiarity Principle and Article 3b of the Treaty on European Union', Annex 1 to Part A of the 'Conclusions of the Presidency', European Council in Edinburgh, 11–12 December 1992. A Toth, 'The Principle of Subsidiarity in the Maastricht Treaty' (1992) 29 CMLRev 1079; K van Kersbergen and B Verbeek, 'The Politics of subsidiarity in the European Community' (1994) JCMS; J Peterson, 'Subsidiarity: A Definition to suit any vision?' (1994) 47 Parliamentary Affairs 117; *Subsidiarity: The Challenge of Change* (Proceedings of the Jacques Delors Colloquium, 1991); G Bermann, 'Taking Subsidiarity Seriously: EC Federalism and US Experience' (1994) 94 Columbia Law Review 331; D Cass, 'The word that saves Maastricht? The principle of subsidiarity and the division of powers within the European Community' (1992) 29 CMLRev 1107; V Constantinesco, 'Who's Afraid of Subsidiarity?' (1992) YEL 33; Cox, 'Derogation, subsidiarity and the single market' (1994) 32 *JCMS* 127; González, 'The Principle of Subsidiarity' (1995) 20 ELRev 355; Kapteyn, 'Community Law and the Principle of Subsidiarity' *Revue des Affaires Européennes* (1991) 35; Kersbergen and Verbeek, 'The politics of subsidiarity in the European Union' (1994) 32 JCMS 215; J Temple Lang, 'What Powers Should the European Community Have?' (1995) 1 European Public Law 97; A Toth, 'Is subsidiarity justiciable?' (1994) 19 ELRev 268; Wilke and Wallace, *Subsidiarity: Approaches to Power-Sharing in the European Community* (Royal Inst of Intern Aff Discussion Paper no. 27, 1990); G de Búrca in 'Reappraising Subsidiarity's Significance After Amsterdam' Harvard Law School Jean Monnet Working Paper 7/99.

[87] See, for example on this, European Parliament constitutional affairs committee report on 'Commission report on Better Lawmaking' EP FINAL A-5–0269/2000.

diversity in the EU. Inappropriate because, in its focus on appropriate levels of action, it might seem to take too simplistic an approach to the complex decision-making patterns of the EU.

Although subsidiarity was the buzz word of the Maastricht Treaty negotiations, it was Pope Pius XI, rather than Jacques Delors, who played a large part in developing subsidiarity as a substantial doctrine of Catholic philosophy. In the papal encyclical, *Quadragesimo Anno*[88] it was stated that:

> It is an injustice, a grave evil and a disturbance of right order for a larger and higher association to arrogate to itself functions which can be performed efficiently by smaller and lower societies.

Such a doctrine implied that social life in modern states had disintegrated mostly because the state had usurped the function of small groups, such as the family. Such thinking had evolved from a particularly Catholic view of organic society, building on the work of Thomas Aquinas and his concern with the relations between Church and State. While Aquinas had, in his writings, implied that the lower level might have to yield to a higher one, he had stressed that this would only be so to promote the general well-being of the whole. In an earlier encyclical, *Rerum Novarum* of 1891, Pope Leo XIII had tried to strike a delicate balance between modern liberal society and *laissez-faire* capitalism, which had produced individualism, undermining a sense of community, and emergent collective socialism which looked to class solidarity and the organic class struggle to achieve social and economic justice. The Catholic view defends the possibility that society may have an objective common good transcending the private goods of individual members (contra the Thatcherite view that there is no such thing as society, only individuals). The Catholic approach makes subsidiarity rely on a strong notion of communitarianism, in which people are united by deep social bonds, whatever these may be, a far step from the *anomie* and displacement which seem to have pervaded late twentieth century society and somewhat difficult to achieve in multicultural societies like the EU. *Quadragesimo Anno* thus built on this earlier Catholic teaching: its thesis can be crudely summarised as the suggestion that small groups should be autonomous and sovereign within a pluralist society, yet united in support of a state which served the common good.

The history of Catholic thought provides us with one of the origins of the subsidiarity principle, but by no means the only one. The focus on the inappropriateness of state action when more localised steps are preferable is also a theme of modern liberal thought, albeit where the focus is on the relationship between the individual and the state, rather than communities and the state. The boundaries of state action are perennial themes in the writings of de Tocqueville and Mill.

It is interesting to compare subsidiarity with federalism as it appeared in the US, where federalism was born of the attempt to protect individual freedom, by the fragmentation of power. They share common ground. The framers of the US Constitution proceeded on the basic belief that individual freedom would be

---

[88] Encyclical Letter, *Quadragesimo Anno* (1931) Pius XI.

advanced by preventing the undue concentration of power in the same governmental hands.[89] The Tenth Amendment of the US Constitution provides that:

> The powers not delegated to the United States by the Constitution or prohibited by it to the States, are reserved to the States respectively, or to the people.

To the extent that subsidiarity promotes diffusion of authority among different levels of government in the EU it can serve as a similar check against political oppression. However, the Tenth Amendment does not express any preference for the particular distribution of power and there are no structures in place in the US which seek to regulate the distribution of competence between the state and federal governments in a way similar to subsidiarity.[90]

As already stated, however, subsidiarity purports to address concerns arising from alienation and *anomie* in modern existence, which may be caused by too fervent an application of liberal individualism. It may also be seen as a response to growing dissatisfaction with the democratic process and an increasing demand for a more participatory type of government, one which is closer to the people, a theme running through this book. In such a way, subsidiarity may become attractive to those not of a Catholic persuasion, but also an entity rather like the planet Neptune, which, before discovery, lurked unseen before known planets, distorting their movements, so that its existence had to be posited to explain their very movements.

In summary, it might be stated that, while subsidiarity may have a specific legal formulation in the context of the EC, which concerns the exercise of competence, it also has a more general meaning, relating to the key questions of political authority, government and legitimacy of government which have been posed by political philosophers and theorists over the years.[91] In fact, it has a sufficiently contradictory panoply of meanings for the contradictions and paradoxes inherent in EU governance. Indeed, as expressed by the French politician Jean Pierre Cot, 'only subsidiarity could manage to put Jacques Delors perfectly in tune with Mrs Thatcher'.[92]

The incorporation of subsidiarity into the EU

Although no specific mention of the word subsidiarity was to be found in the treaties prior to Maastricht, subsidiarity was already operating within EEC law. For example, it could be seen in the approach of the ECJ and Commission to Article 28 (formerly Article 30). *Cassis de Dijon* established the practice of mutual recognition, which ensured that any product marketed in one member state might be sold in any other, subject only to certain requirements which could be demonstrated to serve an

---

[89] See *The Federalist* nos 45, 46.

[90] For a discussion of this issue see G Bermann, 'Taking Subsidiarity Seriously' (1994) 94 Columbia LR. Also H Wechsler, 'The Political Safeguards of Federalism' (1954) 54 Columbia LR 543, 544.

[91] An additional feature must be factored in here. Many discussions of subsidiarity focus only on the relationship between the EU and its member states. However, in an era of globalisation, it must also be questioned whether arenas even above the level of the EU might be the most appropriate for some actions, for example the WTO or NATO. A point made by G de Búrca in 'Reappraising Subsidiarity's Significance After Amsterdam' Harvard Law School Jean Monnet Working Paper 7/99

[92] J Peterson, 'Subsidiarity: A Definition to suit any vision?' (1994) 47 Parliamentary Affairs 117.

objective public interest. An alternative approach to free movement could have been the harmonisation of every last detail of product specification. However, this would not have accorded with subsidiarity and proportionality and would have led to the removal of much regional diversity. The directive provides another example of subsidiarity in action, in that it leaves the form and method of implementation up to member states, so that they choose the methods best suited to their own needs.

More specifically, subsidiarity was being promoted by at least three different groups prior to its appropriation by the Maastricht Treaty in 1992, each drawing from different sources, legal and non-legal. The first was in its familiar guise of Catholic thought, often used by Christian democrats, and already discussed. A second group based its view on German federal thought. Although there is no specific mention of the concept of subsidiarity in the *Grundgesetz*,[93] Article 72 sets out the criteria for the division of concurrent competence between *Laender* and *Bund* and is thus highly relevant.[94] A third, more libertarian (or conservative, in the sense of British politics), emerged in British circles in the 1991 IGC on political union, in which subsidiarity was seen as a principle for limiting the powers of the EC, sanctioning EC action only where necessary to ensure the working of the single market.

However, another different factor which contributed to the inclusion of a specific provision on subsidiarity in the Maastricht Treaty related not to any recognition of the part that it was already playing in EC law, but rather to the very reverse: from a fear that the Community was gaining too much competence at the expense of the member states. The introduction of QMV by the Single European Act had made the Commission bolder in its introduction of legislative initiatives. Member states felt the need to control these initiatives, especially as the SEA had extended Community competence into new areas. Indeed, the cumulative effect of the elements of what Joseph Weiler has termed 'the transformation of Europe', namely the introduction of key constitutional doctrines by the ECJ, such as direct effect and supremacy, as well as the stealthy growth of Community competence by increased use of Article 308, together substantially altered the balance of power between the EC and member states by the late 1980s. This in turn generated new pressures for a doctrine such as subsidiarity, which replaced the unpopular provision in the Dutch presidency draft treaty which referred to 'the EC's federal vocation'.

Legal analysis

(a) Examples of subsidiarity in the treaties

The most obvious place to start is Article 5 EC, inserted by the TEU. Article 5 reads as follows:

> The Community shall act within the limits of the powers conferred upon it by this Treaty and of the objectives assigned to it therein.

---

[93] N Emiliou in 'Subsidiarity: An Effective Barrier against "the Enterprises of Ambition"?' (1992) 17 ELRev 383 claims that the concept was first formulated in German legal thought by Isensee in 1968, who found the principle first to have occurred in the Paulskirchen constitution of 1848.
[94] See below.

In the areas which do not fall within its exclusive competence, the Community shall take action, in accordance with the principle of subsidiarity, only if and in so far as the objectives of the proposed action cannot be sufficiently achieved by the Member States and can therefore, by reason of the scale or effects of the proposed action, be better achieved by the Community.

Any action by the Community shall not go beyond what is necessary to achieve the objectives of this Treaty.

The other key formulation is to be found in Article 1(2) TEU:

This Treaty marks a new stage in the process of creating an ever closer union among the peoples of Europe, where decisions are taken as closely as possible to the citizens.

There are also other provisions in the treaties[95] which are of relevance, as well as the guidelines which have been added by the Treaty of Amsterdam Protocol on the application of the principles of subsidiarity and proportionality.

It will be noted that Article 1 TEU and Article 5 EC provide rather different interpretations of the concept, that in Article 1 being more of a political statement rather than a precise legal definition. This has been elaborated by Bermann as distinction between democratic subsidiarity (or federalism) which relates to the protection of citizens' rights, and that of executive subsidiarity (or federalism) which relates to the protection of executive prerogatives.[96]

Article 5 itself contains three legal concepts, not all strictly concerning subsidiarity. Paragraph 1 concerns the attribution of powers, always a fundamental principle of EC law, and paragraph 3 sets out the principle of proportionality, which has been developed by the ECJ's jurisprudence. Proportionality is a distinct principle, but has come to be linked more and more with subsidiarity.[97] So it is Article 5(2) which is the locus for the legal conception of subsidiarity. This has two major parts. First, that the objectives of the proposed action cannot be sufficiently achieved by the member states, and the second, that the proposed action by reason of its scale and effects can be better achieved by the Community. This leaves much room for interpretation, which will be considered below.

(b) Scope

Much of the discussion of the subsidiarity concept has focused on the nature of the 'exclusive competence' of the Community mentioned in the second paragraph of Article 5 EC. This is perhaps unfortunate. According to Article 5 EC, if the policy falls within the Community's exclusive competence, then the subsidiarity principle will not apply. The difficult question is, of course, what falls within this area, given that, as already discussed, the powers of the Community and member states are not

---

[95] For example: Article 5 ECSC; Article 3 EC; Article 64 EC; Article 126 EC; Article 136(2) EC; Article 149 EC; Article 249(3) EC; Article 308 EC.

[96] G Bermann, 'Taking Subsidiarity Seriously' (1994) 94 Columbia LR 332.

[97] Treaty of Amsterdam, *Protocol on the application of the principles of subsidiarity and proportionality*; see also the Commission's annual reports on 'Better Lawmaking'.

divided up neatly in the treaty. According to the Commission, in a paper[98] presented to the Council and Parliament in 1992, there is no clear, demarcating line of competence, but instead 'blocks of exclusive powers' joined by the common thread of the internal market. This would encompass the four fundamental freedoms, as well as the common agricultural, commercial, transport and competition policies.[99] Newer areas of competence, such as education, environment, vocational training, consumer protection, culture, industry and so on, are less encompassing and not areas of exclusive competence, and therefore areas where the subsidiarity principle might be applied according to Article 5 EC. On the other hand, the ECJ has itself stated that only in very few areas is Community competence exclusive.

Many other commentators have taken a less than absolute view of the Community's competence.[100] The concept of the internal market, if held out as an example of the Community's exclusive competence, is a potentially huge area, granting power to the Community in all sorts of areas. Building regulations, broadcasting laws, the regulation of drugs and pornography, are all capable of having an impact on the functioning of the internal market, but flank it, rather than clearly having internal market objectives. In such cases, the need for **Community**, rather than member state, action is less clear.

The fact of the matter is that the use of the expression 'exclusive competence' is unhelpful, given that there is simply no clear line of demarcation in EC law. The EC tends to have specific delineated powers, rather than exclusive blocks of competence. When it comes to a general assessment, it becomes clear that, while some competences fall clearly within the Community remit, others tend to do so more tangentially. Whether any given area falls within the Community's exclusive competence may well depend on how the objectives of a particular measure are defined. For example, was the Tobacco Advertising Directive a measure truly designed to eliminate distortions of competition within the internal market and thus properly taken under Article 95, or was it more generally concerned with public health? The ECJ found that its true centre of gravity did not concern the elimination of competition in the internal market. This is but an example of the point stressed at the outset of this section: that the EU is a system of multilevel governance and that overlapping spheres of competence, rather than clear blocks of exclusive and non-exclusive competence, are part of this complex plurality of dimensions of governance.

---

[98] Bull EC 10-1992 2.2.1.

[99] A similarly broad view is taken by A Toth, 'A Legal Analysis of Subsidiarity' in D O'Keeffe and P Twomey, *Legal Issues of the Maastricht Treaty* (Chancery Law, 1994).

[100] Steiner and Weatherill, for example, have both been more inclined to the view that, until the Community actually acts, its competence remains concurrent with that of the member states: see S Weatherill, 'Beyond Preemption? Shared Competence and Constitutional Change in the European Community' and J Steiner, 'Subsidiarity under the Maastricht treaty' both in O'Keeffe and Twomey op. cit.

(c) Formal scope of subsidiarity

Article 5(2) EC sets out the legal test to be applied. Unfortunately, this formulation is neither clear nor particularly helpful,[101] even if one adds to it other measures which have, subsequently to the TEU, contributed to the fleshing out of the subsidiarity provisions, such as the Edinburgh Council guidelines of 1992[102] and the Protocol to the Treaty of Amsterdam on Subsidiarity and Proportionality. As stated, Article 5(2) actually sets out two tests: first that the Community should take action 'only if and insofar as the objectives of the proposed action cannot be sufficiently achieved by the Member states' and second, 'can therefore, by reason of the scale and effects of the proposed action, be better achieved by the Community'. These might sometimes dictate different actions.[103] Indeed, the application of subsidiarity to any piece of legislation or issue will often involve a difficult analysis. For example, is the only way to provide for healthy drinking water in all member states the adoption of minimum and enforceable Community standards? Can smoking be effectively discouraged and the internal market sustained only through Community action in the form of a ban on tobacco advertising?

In order to give a clearer account of how these criteria might work in practice, here is an example given by the Commission of how it exercises its right to legislative initiative in conjunction with the principle of subsidiarity. The Commission must explain why Community action is necessary for every draft measure falling within the EC's concurrent competence. In its proposal for a directive of the European Parliament and of the Council on waste electrical and electronic equipment,[104] with regard to the first of the tests in Article 5 (2)[105] the Commission reasoned as follows:

> Different national policies on the management of waste electrical and electronic equipment (WEEE) **hamper the effectiveness of national recycling policies** as cross-border movements of WEEE to cheaper waste management systems are likely.
> Different national applications of the principle of producer responsibility lead to substantial **disparities in the financial burden for economic operators.**

---

[101] It may be compared for example with Article 72 of the German *Grundgesetz*, which divides competence between the *Bund* and *Laender*:

  'I. In the field of concurrent legislative competence the Laender have the power to legislate as long and insofar as the Federation does not make use of its right to legislate.

  II. In this field the Federation will have the right to legislate to the extent that federal legal regulation is needed because:

  1. a matter cannot be effectively regulated by the legislation of individual Lander, or
  2. the regulation of a matter by a Land might prejudice the interest of other Lander or of the people as a whole or
  3. the maintenance of legal or economic uniformity or living conditions beyond the territory of any one Land, necessitates such regulation.'

[102] Conclusions of the Council Presidency 1992.

[103] See R Dehousse, 'Community competences: Are there limits to growth?' in R Dehousse (ed.) *Europe after Maastricht: An ever Closer Union?* (Munich: Law Books in Europe, 1994) and Toth op. cit. on the ambiguity of the two-part test.

[104] (COM(2000) 347).

[105] 'Better Lawmaking' for 2000, COM (2000) 772 final.

Diverging national requirements on the phasing-out of specific substances could have implications on **trade** in electrical and electronic equipment.

For an illustration of the application of the second test in Article 5(2) we may look to the Commission proposal for a Directive of the European Parliament and of the Council on waste electrical and electronic equipment,[106] in which the Commission stressed that action at Community level would make the recycling of certain WEEE economically viable. It stated:

> for various parts of WEEE, recycling **is economically viable only if** large quantities of waste are produced. **According to the principle of economies of scale only a few centralised installations in Europe would process these wastes.**[107]

The Treaty of Amsterdam Protocol guidelines have attempted to develop Article 5 (2). They state that Community action will be appropriate when first, transnational aspects cannot be satisfactorily regulated by member states; second, when state action would conflict with treaty requirements; and third, when action by the Community would have clear benefits of scale. However, this does not add much to the general wording of Article 5(2). The first of these criteria simply raises the question: which cross border effects would be relevant? For example, diverse systems of private law have a transnational impact, but this is surely not an argument for the EU to take on the total harmonisation of private law? The second criterion also raises exactly the sort of problems already mentioned in a discussion of the issue of exclusive competence. For in which areas would member state action conflict with the Treaty? In matters of internal market regulation? But once again, one is left to rely on very general terms, which involve subjective judgments of policy choices as well as values. The third simply uses an expression very similar to the wording of Article 5 itself.

Justiciability

Article 5 is justiciable. Paragraph 13 of the Treaty of Amsterdam Protocol states that 'Compliance with the principle of Subsidiarity shall be reviewed in accordance with the rules laid down in this treaty.' However, there has not been much case law as yet, as, although the concept of subsidiarity has been raised in cases such as those involving the Working Time Directive and the Tobacco Directive, in the latter it was not properly discussed by the Court, which annulled the measure on the grounds of its improper legal basis, and in the former, the Court barely touched on the matter, stating that subsidiarity did not concern the intensity of an act.

However, a proper examination of the test in Article 5(2) would involve the Community Courts in an assessment of legislation which goes beyond strictly legal considerations, to encompass political and economic elements. Determining whether the objectives of measures can be sufficiently achieved by member states surely involves judgments on matters of policy, as well as a subjective assessment of

---

[106] (COM(2000) 347 final.
[107] Bold lettering added by the Commission.

the measure's merits. Much depends on the way in which the Court approaches review for compliance with subsidiarity. It could treat it either as a procedural or as a substantive requirement. Shortly after its introduction into the TEU, George Bermann suggested that the Court treat it as a procedural requirement, which would 'allow the Court of Justice to promote the values of localism without enmeshing itself in profoundly political judgments that it is ill-equipped to make'.[108] In this way, the ECJ's enquiry would be mainly focused on an examination of whether the EU institutions examined the possibility of alternative action at member state level. An alternative assessment, by way of a judgment of the **substantive** merits of Community action, would involve the Court in considering the bases of the institution's assessment and a judgment (or even second-guessing) of its persuasiveness and suitability.[109] In the past, the Court has tended to apply a somewhat expansionist interpretation of the EC's powers, in cases such as *Casagrande* and *Bosman*. On the other hand, the Court has shown itself less expansionist regarding EC competences in more recent cases like *Keck* and *Opinion 2/94*, as well as in its notice on cooperation with national courts in competition matters, itself a positive example of subsidiarity in action.

In the run-up to the Maastricht Treaty, the Parliament proposed a new Article 172A which would enable the Council, Commission, member states or Parliament to require the ECJ to verify whether an act exceeds the power of the EC. This was modelled on Article 300 (formerly 228) in the case of international agreements and its advantage would be that it would offer a sort of pre-facto judicial review. This approach was not adopted and so the issue of subsidiarity will be raised before the Courts through the usual channels of judicial review, after an act has been adopted.[110] In the *Tobacco Advertising* case, Article 5 had been used in the context of domestic proceedings, even though it was stated by the European Council in Edinburgh not to have direct effect.[111]

Implementation

The provisions in the Maastricht Treaty were not the last word on subsidiarity as will already be clear. The European Council in Edinburgh in 1992 set out guidelines[112] on the concept, which were not particularly helpful, but did set the Commission the task of monitoring the observation of subsidiarity as well as

---

[108] G Bermann, 'Taking Subsidiarity Seriously' (1994) 94 Columbia LR 391.

[109] Given these sort of difficulties it is notable that the German Constitutional Court has determined that provisions comparable to subsidiarity in the *Grundgesetz* – Article 72 – are non-justiciable, and that the 'necessity' for federal government legislation in areas of concurrent competence was essentially a political question: see Judgement of April 22 1953, 2 BverfGE 213, 224; Judgement of June 8 1988 78 BverfGE 269, 270; also U Everling, 'Reflections on the Structure of the European union ' (1992) 29 CMLRev 1053, 1071.

[110] Although the tobacco directive was challenged in the UK prior to its implementation in national law.

[111] Although this need not of course affect preliminary rulings as a provision need not be directly effective to be referred to the ECJ. See also, for the application of subsidiarity by national courts, *R v London Boroughs Transport Committee ex parte Freight Transport Association and others* [1992]1 CMLR 5.

[112] Conclusions of the Council Presidency 1992.

submitting an annual report to the Parliament and Council. The guidelines also stated that the Council and Commission should examine every proposal for its relation to subsidiarity and that subsidiarity must form an integral part of decision-making in the EC. They also stated that the Community should legislate only to the extent necessary and that soft law be used wherever possible, thus conflating subsidiarity with the type and extent of law-making, a process that has continued, and was firmed up, by the Amsterdam Protocol.

It is interesting to consider the Commission's reports on subsidiarity. Its 1993 report[113] to the European Council noted the withdrawal of some proposals as a result of the application of the principle of subsidiarity as well as a review of existing legislation. It also conflated subsidiarity with proportionality, treating both it, and the question of shared competence, as matters for consideration under the more general heading of subsidiarity. Much of its report was taken up with the revision of existing legislation, but the Commission stated that it was convinced that 'the real answer to the problem lies in the introduction of a hierarchy of Community norms ... as required by the TEU at the next IGC' (something which has still not been introduced). In the second of its annual reports in 1994,[114] the Commission set out the details of how subsidiarity is taken into account in the legislative process, referring to the compulsory procedure introduced in 1992, whereby all draft proposals had to be reviewed for their compatibility with subsidiarity. It also noted the drop in the amount of legislation proposed, and detailed progress made on the modification of existing legislation. Since 1995, when the Commission presented its report to the Madrid European Council on more effective law-making,[115] the Commission's annual reports on subsidiarity have been part of a broader report on the state of law-making in the EC, to be considered along the general theme of doing less, but doing it better.[116]

By the late 1990s the Commission's approach was changing a bit, partly because the EU had not made particularly effective use of its powers under the JHA and CFSP pillars. As the Commission noted in its report for 1999, under the heading 'A changing background', 'Current events show, first and foremost, that there are **areas in which more Europe is needed**.' The Commission justified this need on the basis of the new provisions in the Treaty of Amsterdam creating an area of freedom, security and justice, which underlined the need for a common European policy on asylum and migration, and for a real European area of justice and crime-fighting at EU level. The Commission also referred to lack of action in the field of foreign and security policy, in which the war in the Balkans had shown how important Community input could be, whether it be help in reconstruction or aid/trade facilities. The Commission stressed that these new needs were not in contradiction to the principle of subsidiarity and continued: 'We have to continue to ask ourselves the ques-

---

[113] Commission report to the European Council on the Adaptation of Community Legislation to the Subsidiarity Principle COM(93) 545 final.
[114] Commission report to the European Council on the Application of the Subsidiarity Principle COM(94) final.
[115] IP/95/1278 22/11/95.
[116] See Chapter 3 for a discussion of Better Lawmaking.

tion whether the proposed action cannot be tackled well enough by the Member States and whether the task should instead be addressed at Community level. The answer will of course depend on circumstances and needs. This is why Article 3 of the protocol on the application of the principles of subsidiarity and proportionality annexed to the EC Treaty (referred to hereinafter as the "Amsterdam Protocol") indicates that subsidiarity is a dynamic concept.'[117]

The discussion of matters such as simplification and better drafting continued. In its 2000 report on *Better Lawmaking*,[118] the Commission noted additional factors that had an impact on the application of the principle of subsidiarity: the Charter of Fundamental Rights, with its focus on diversities which would require more attention on subsidiarity; the issue of enlargement, given that society in applicant countries is even more diverse than that of the current member states; the fact that the application of subsidiarity could never be 'cast in stone', given so many changes in society and that the EU response to subsidiarity must needs change constantly, a fact underlined in the Amsterdam Protocol; the relevance of the debate on good governance and the need to have a greater involvement of civil society. Therefore, not only is subsidiarity a dynamic concept, but also quite clearly an integral part of the current focus on governance in the EU. It illustrates that matters such as the division of power cannot really be separated from issues of democracy, participation and citizenship.

PROPORTIONALITY

Very much linked to subsidiarity in the contemporary debate over competence, allocation of power and governance more generally, is the principle of proportionality. Very roughly defined, it requires a reasonable relationship between an objective and the particular means used (be they legislative or administrative) to attain that objective.[119] It is a principle with a considerable lineage[120] developed in modern times in continental legal systems, especially in France and Germany, essentially as one of the elements of liberal democracy and a means to protect the individual against unnecessary interference by the state.[121] In German law it is known as *Verhaltnismassigskeit* in which context it seems to comprise three elements : suitability, necessity and proportionality *stricto sensu*.[122] Proportionality has functioned

---

[117] Brussels, 3.11.1999, COM(1999) 562 final, Commission Report to the European Council: Better Lawmaking 1999.

[118] Brussels, 30.11.2000 COM(2000) 772 final, Commission Report to the European Council Better Lawmaking 2000 (pursuant to Article 9 of the Protocol to the EC Treaty on the application of the principles of subsidiarity and proportionality).

[119] See G de Búrca, 'The principle of Proportionality and its Application in EC law' (1993) YEL 105.

[120] Perhaps even ancient – note Tridimas, who dates it to ancient times and the Greek dictum '*pan metron aristou*' – T Tridimas, 'Proportionality in Community Law: searching for the appropriate standard of scrutiny' in E Ellis, 'The Principle of Proportionality in the Laws of Europe' (Hart Publishing, 1999) at 65.

[121] See J Schwarze, *European Administrative Law* (London: Sweet and Maxwell, 1992); N Emiliou, *The Principle of Proportionality in European Law* (London: Kluwer, 1996).

[122] Schwarze op. cit.

as a general principle of law[123] for some time in the context of EC law. In *Fedesa*
[124] the ECJ defined proportionality in the following way:

> The principle of proportionality . . . requires that measures adopted by Community
> institutions do not exceed the limits of what is appropriate and necessary in order to
> attain the objectives legitimately pursued by the legislation in question; when there is a
> choice between several appropriate measures recourse must be had to the least oner-
> ous, and the disadvantages caused are not to be disproportionate to the aims pursued.

It is clear that this definition contains the three subsidiary principles that constitute the principle of proportionality in Germany although the ECJ has not always
interpreted the proportionality principle in the same way, nor with the same degree
of intensity.[125] This is because the underlying interests which are protected by the
principle may differ: proportionality has been used to challenge both Community
action and member state action in the Community sphere.[126] When it is invoked as
a ground of review of a particular Community policy then this may involve the balancing of a public interest against a private interest. On the other hand, if it is used
to challenge the compatibility of Community law with national law then
Community interest and national interest will be counterpoised and the degree of
review will be more intense as proportionality will be applied as a market review
mechanism.

It is as a principle governing the exercise of a Community competence that it will
be examined in this section, a role which achieved the status of a constitutional principle with its incorporation into Article 5 (3) EC,[127] in which context it must be seen
as a principle aimed at limiting the expansion of Community action, thus limiting
burdens on member states rather than individuals. It was considered in the *Working
Time Directive* case.[128] In this case the UK had argued that Directive 93/104, which
concerned certain aspects of the organisation of working time, should be annulled,
inter alia, for breaching the principle of proportionality on the grounds that the global restrictions on working time which the directive imposed could not be described
as 'minimum requirements' as warranted by Article 118a (now Article 138), the legal
basis of the directive. They argued that the desired level of protection could have been
achieved by less restrictive means. The ECJ rejected this challenge, on the basis that
'the Council must be allowed a wide discretion in an area which, as here, involves the
legislature in making social policy choices and requires it to carry out complex assessments. Judicial review of the exercise of that discretion must therefore be limited to

---

[123] As established by the ECJ in Case 11/70 *Internationale Handelsgesellschaft* [1970] ECR 1125.
[124] Case C-331/88 *Fedesa* [1990] ECR I-4023, p. 4063.
[125] See F Jacobs, 'Recent Developments in the Principle of Proportionality in European Community Law'
in Ellis, op. cit at 1.
[126] See, for example: Case 11/70 *Internationale Handelsgesellschaft* [1970] ECR 1125; Case 181/84 *ED
& F Man (Sugar) Ltd* [1985] ECR 2889.
[127] See K Lenaerts and P Van Ypersele, 'Le Principe de subsidiarité et son contexte: Étude de l'article 3B
du traité CE' (1994) 30 Cah.dr.eur.3, 61.
[128] Case C-84/94 *United Kingdom* v *Council* [1996] ECR I-5755; see also case C-426/93 *Germany* v
European Parliament [1995] ECR I-3723, an earlier case in which proportionality as a principle governing Community competence was discussed.

examining whether it has been vitiated by manifest error or misuse of powers, or whether the institution concerned has manifestly exceeded the limits of its discretion.'[129] The Court found no manifest error or misuse of powers. Thus the level of review exercised by the Court in this case was fairly minimal.

SUBSIDIARITY, PROPORTIONALITY AND THE GROWING FOCUS ON PROCEDURALISM

There is obviously a close connection between subsidiarity and proportionality, as the Commission has acknowledged in its reports on *Better Lawmaking*, as well as by their linkage in the Amsterdam Protocol. How do they relate? The subsidiarity principle is concerned with whether the EC **should** take action and proportionality with the **means** used when the EC does act.[130] However, the European Parliament has stressed its opposition to the linking of subsidiarity and proportionality in some of the Commission reports. Bermann[131] has also suggested that their linkage may not be so simple, and that proportionality does not simply pick up where subsidiarity left off. A measure may satisfy the requirements of proportionality, in being reasonably related to its objective, and the least burdensome solution while still not satisfying subsidiarity as action may not be necessary at Community level at all. The two may point in the opposite direction. However, it is actually very difficult to differentiate the two, as the objective of an action and the means by which to pursue it cannot be readily separated.[132] It will depend on how and with what degree of specification we define a particular policy issue.

The Amsterdam Protocol places certain requirements on Community institutions regarding subsidiarity, which include the following:

> 9. The Commission should:
> except in cases of particular urgency or confidentiality, consult widely before proposing legislation and, wherever appropriate, publish consultation documents;
> justify the relevance of its proposals with regard to the principle of subsidiarity; whenever necessary, the explanatory memorandum accompanying a proposal will give details in this respect. The financing of Community action in whole or in part from the Community budget shall require an explanation;
> take duly into account the need for any burden, whether financial or administrative, falling upon the Community, national governments, local authorities, economic operators and citizens, to be minimised and proportionate to the objective to be achieved;

---

[129] Ibid. para 58.

[130] An approach taken by the ECJ in the *Working Time Directive* case: Case C-84/94 *United Kingdom v Council* [1996] ECR I-5755. See for a further consideration of this point the Opinion of AG Leger in the case C-84/94 at 5783; see also Lenaerts and Van Ypersele op. cit. and G Strozzi, 'Le Principe de subsidiarité dans le perspective de l'intégration Européen: une énigme et beaucoup d'attentes' 30 RTDE 373 at 379.

[131] Op. cit. Columbia Law review.

[132] See G de Búrca, 'Reappraising Subsidiarity's Significance After Amsterdam' Harvard Law School Jean Monnet Working Paper 7/99.

submit an annual report to the European Council, the European Parliament and the Council on the application of Article 5 of the Treaty. This annual report shall also be sent to the Committee of the Regions and to the Economic and Social Committee.

10. The European Council shall take account of the Commission report referred to in the fourth indent of point 9 within the report on the progress achieved by the Union which it is required to submit to the European Parliament in accordance with Article 4 of the Treaty on European Union.

11. While fully observing the procedures applicable, the European Parliament and the Council shall, as an integral part of the overall examination of Commission proposals, consider their consistency with Article 5 of the Treaty. This concerns the original Commission proposal as well as amendments which the European Parliament and the Council envisage making to the proposal.

12. In the course of the procedures referred to in Articles 251 and 252 of the Treaty, the European Parliament shall be informed of the Council's position on the application of Article 5 of the Treaty, by way of a statement of the reasons which led the Council to adopt its common position. The Council shall inform the European Parliament of the reasons on the basis of which all or part of a Commission proposal is deemed to be inconsistent with Article 5 of the Treaty.

13. Compliance with the principle of subsidiarity shall be reviewed in accordance with the rules laid down by the Treaty.

These provisions reflect a growing focus on the procedural requirements placed on Union institutions.[133] They clearly relate to the debate within political theory, and more particularly theories of governance, as to how the best types of decision-making and participation may be achieved. As a result, subsidiarity requires EU legislative institutions to engage in specific enquiries before concluding that EU action is warranted. This reflects the call for a more consultative, participatory democracy as discussed in the last chapter. Such a decision-making process is also likely to result in greater public trust and member state support. This focus on process in the context of EU legislation reflects a contemporary concern with discursive democracy.[134] Such concerns are to be welcomed, particularly if they result in a shift from interpreting subsidiarity as merely a means of ensuring the most efficient and effective action. For too long efficiency (or lack of it) has been a perennial concern of the EU. However, the more substantial, constitutional dimensions of subsidiarity must not be forgotten. Subsidiarity is not only about the best process, but plays its part in the substantive debate about the nature of the EU constitution and the place of citizens[135] in the EU. If it is to function at all well, all of these aspects must play their part in its implementation.

---

[133] What Grainne de Búrca has called a 'public reason' requirement op. cit. tn 132.

[134] Expressed by writers such as Habermas. For a more detailed discussion see Chapter 3.

[135] Although there is the danger that measures taken to enhance European citizenship might work against subsidiarity: for example, the notion of a European passport might strengthen a sense of European identity and citizenship, but still be better left to the member states.

FLEXIBILITY AND COOPERATION

Whether we call it flexibility, cooperation, variable geometry, or 'opting out', differentiated integration of some sort has always existed within the EU. As examples of such flexibility, we might cite the transitional periods given to new member states in Accession treaties, allowing them some time to adapt to EU laws, or the provisions of EMS and then EMU, which have been applicable to only some member states, or the Schengen accord, only recently brought within the treaty structure. Thus, such differentiated integration is by no means a new phenomenon.[136]

However, it did take on a greater significance and importance in the 1990s. Maastricht provided for a variety of opt-outs and different procedures by way of protocols and treaty procedures themselves, and the issue of differentiated integration became a highly important,[137] although very controversial issue at the 1996 IGC leading to the Treaty of Amsterdam.[138] Indeed, the adoption of the 'enabling clauses' in Articles 40 and 43–45 TEU, and Article 11 EC, if not perhaps of the status of a constitutional moment for flexibility, certainly constitutionalised such principles by adding them to the treaty structure.

Flexibility in integration is likely to become ever more important in the context of EU enlargement, whereby not all partners will be able to move at the same speed, on account of increasing heterogeneity, difference in economic and cultural factors, or perhaps just the still so cumbersome institutional mechanisms of the EU, Nice amendments notwithstanding. Therefore, it seems that that the Union will inevitably be faced with increasingly diverse integration, and may even be unable to sustain homogeneity and communality.

Such developments raise two questions. First, what (legal) mechanisms exist for the member states to take steps to cooperate among smaller groups than full EU membership? And, secondly, what is, and will be, the significance, legal, political, and constitutional, of flexibility of this sort?

The nature of flexibility

Flexibility takes, and has taken, many forms. If we take a general stock-taking of the character of flexibility in the EU, we might, at a basic level, cite the following forms.

---

[136] See, for early examples, R Dahrendorf, 'A Third Europe?' Jean Monnet Lecture (Florence: European University Institute 1979); C Ehlermann, 'How Flexible is Community Law? An Unusual Approach to the Concept of "Two Speeds"' (1984) 82 Michigan Law Review 1274.

[137] See e.g. P Tuytschaever, *Differentiation in European Union Law* (Hart Publishing, 1999); G De Burca and J Scott, *Constitutional Change in the EU: From Uniformity to Flexibility?* (Hart Publishing, 2000); R Harmsen, 'A European Union of Variable Geometry: Problems and Perspectives' (1994) 45 NILQ 109; A Stubb, 'A Categorisation of Differentiated Integration' (1996) 26 JCMS 283; N Walker, 'Sovereignty and Differentiated Integration in the European Union' (1998) 4 ELJ 355.

[138] See e.g. G Gaja, 'How Flexible is Flexibility under the Amsterdam Treaty?' (1998) 35 CMLRev 855; H Koltenberg, 'Closer Cooperation in the Treaty of Amsterdam' (1998) 35 CMLRev 833.

First, we may make a division between those forms of flexibility, or cooperation, which take place within, and those which take place without, the Union's formal institutional framework. In the latter category, we might cite cooperation between two or more member states, ranging from bilateral and diplomatic agreements, such as the Franco-German Cooperation treaty, to cooperation such as that involving the Airbus project, or Eurocorps, or the European Space Agency. Such forms of cooperation take place between member states as sovereign entities, and activities of any sort are permitted, as long as they do not undermine EU objectives, nor compromise those states' obligations as EU members. Then there are other non-EU forms of cooperation, which are nonetheless mentioned in the treaty, such as the Benelux union, specifically allowed by Article 306 EC. An interesting case is the example of the 'Euro' group of finance ministers, which takes place outside of the EU's institutional framework, and was established on the basis of the 1997 Luxembourg European Council conclusions, in the context of the Union's single currency, but is clearly closely linked to provisions in the EC treaty on EMU.

In contrast, there are the mechanisms for flexible development, or enhanced cooperation, which take place **within** the EU institutional framework. These take a variety of forms. There is what might be described as 'pre-defined' enhanced cooperation.[139] This takes place when the treaty, or treaty protocols, or even secondary legislation, sets out the relevant rules and procedures for that form of cooperation. Examples might be given of EMU, or Schengen, which set out detailed rules for the type of action which is to be taken. There are other types of flexible arrangements which take place within the EU such as Article 95 (4) and (5) and 39(3) EC, which permit member states to deviate from certain requirements of the measures for certain reasons, in accordance with certain procedures. There is also the possibility for member states to opt out of individual decisions, such as constructive abstention under the CFSP, or under Article 34(2) (d), which allows for the possibility of certain conventions on cooperation in police and criminal justice matters for a limited amount of time within only some member states.

However, a different, but very significant, type of enhanced cooperation within the EU institutional framework is that of the enabling clauses, introduced by the Treaty of Amsterdam in Articles 40 and 43–45 TEU, and 11 EC. These are very general provisions which enable a group of member states to take action within certain permissible areas, but the details of these arrangements still have to be addressed in the act establishing the cooperation in question. Thus the cooperation is not pre-determined.

Within the EU institutional structure, cooperation has taken place within fields as varied as asylum and immigration, borders, social policy, economic and monetary union, clearly cutting across the divide between high and low politics. However, much attention has been paid to the 'enabling' clauses, whose introduction at Amsterdam proved so controversial, and their potential (not realised at time of writing, when no use has, as yet, been made of them) to pose a serious threat to the coherence of the EU. So they merit more detailed attention.

---

[139] D Galloway, *The Treaty of Nice and Beyond* (Sheffield Academic Press, 2001).

Enhanced cooperation under Title VI TEU

According to Article 43 TEU, 'member states which intend to establish closer coop-eration between them may make use of the institutions, procedures and mechanisms laid down by the EC Treaty and TEU'. However, certain provisos apply. The coop-eration must, for example, be aimed at furthering the objectives of the Union and at protecting and serving its interests. It must respect the treaties and the single institutional framework of the Union as well as the *acquis communautaire* and the measures adopted under other provisions of the treaties. It must also respect the competences, rights and obligations of those states which do not participate and be open for all member states. It may only be taken as a 'last resort'.[140] A further set of requirements is set out in Article 11 EC, regarding enhanced cooperation which is taken specifically under the EC, in particular setting out the procedure to be followed in order to obtain authorisation from the Council for such cooperation. Enhanced cooperation under the EC treaty is ruled out in areas of exclusive Community competence, such as the CAP or the CCP. Notably, the main provision on closer cooperation, Article 43 TEU, is not justiciable and the safeguards operat-ing on closer cooperation take the form of the requirement of authorisation from the Council,[141] before such cooperation can occur.

Quite clearly, these provisions are hedged around with safeguards, reflecting var-ious concerns, such as the need to protect the *acquis*, as well as the position of those less integrationist states which choose not to forge ahead. Given all of these condi-tions and provisions, it is not, therefore, very surprising that the enhanced cooper-ation provisions had not been used at all by the time that the 2000 IGC considered whether or not they should be amended. Thus, as Galloway notes, 'The Conference accordingly found itself in the somewhat surreal position of considering amend-ments to treaty provisions which had never been used, to deal with situations which could not be identified and for no clearly defined objective.'[142] However, it was sug-gested that one of the reasons why the enhanced cooperation provisions had never been used was that the conditions and provisions had circumscribed them so as to make their use impossible.[143]

Changes were made to the enhanced cooperation provisions by Nice. Notably, Nice introduces the possibility of closer cooperation under the second pillar, that of the CFSP, where it had previously not existed, probably because of a perceived need for united action in foreign affairs. However, prior to Nice, under Article 23(10) TEU, it had been possible for a member state to 'opt out' of particular decisions, a sort of constructive abstention, which arguably already applies flexibility. As it now

---

[140] For all of these see Article 43 TEU.
[141] See Article 43 TEU (Article 40a TEU post Nice) and 11(2) EC.
[142] D Galloway, *The Treaty of Nice and Beyond* at 133.
[143] See e.g. S Weatherill, 'If I'd wanted you to understand I would have explained it better: what is the purpose of the provisions on closer cooperation introduced by the treaty of Amsterdam?' in D O'Keeffe and P Twomey (eds) *Legal Issues of the Amsterdam Treaty* (Hart, 1999) for an expression of this view.

stands after Nice, enhanced cooperation under the second pillar is set out in Article 27 TEU, and is very narrow in scope. It only applies in the context of implementation of joint actions and common positions, and matters having military or defence implications are excluded.[144] As Galloway suggests, in this context 'enhanced cooperation' is a bit of a misnomer, as the measures under Article 27 TEU are more akin to 'an implementing measure of an already agreed policy accepted in principle by all member states under which specific tasks are delegated to member states involved in enhanced cooperation'.[145]

The Treaty of Nice has also brought about other changes in the field of enhanced cooperation. It seemed that the member states at Amsterdam had been too cautious and had made enhanced cooperation procedurally difficult to proceed with, for fear of damaging the interest of non-participatory member states. As a result, one of the objectives of the Treaty of Nice has been to make enhanced cooperation easier to launch. Instead of requiring a majority of member states to participate before an initiative may be launched, it will now be sufficient if at least eight countries agree (which would be one third of an enlarged EU of 27 members, although still a majority of the current membership of fifteen). Additionally, in its Amsterdam form, it had been possible for any member state to veto an enhanced cooperation initiative and this has now been removed with qualified majority as the rule. References to enhanced cooperation 'not discriminating among member states' or not affecting the interests of non participating states, have been removed, as these are subjective criteria which could too easily be invoked. On the other hand, Article 43a TEU permits enhanced cooperation only as a last resort 'when it has been established within the Council that the objectives of such cooperation cannot be attained within a reasonable period by applying the relevant provisions of the treaties'.

Attempts were also made at Nice to simplify the presentation of the enhanced cooperation provisions, which were hardly drafted with clarity in mind, as the title of an article by Stephen Weatherill attests.[146] Overall, it seems to be the hope that, in their present form, the provisions will strike a necessary balance between the interests of those states which participate and those which do not. This reorganisation of the provisions recognises the fact that, while they might be seen as an instrument of last resort, an EU of 27 members may simply have to make use of enhanced cooperation in situations where not every member of a larger more heterogeneous EU is able to take part. On the other hand, by strengthening and rationalising the provisions, it has become easier to use them, thus perhaps administering to the fear that, if enhanced cooperation appeared totally unusable, certain member states might have resorted to take initiatives outside of the Union structures altogether. For

---

[144] Article 27(b) TEU.

[145] Galloway, op. cit. at 136.

[146] S Weatherill, 'If I'd wanted you to understand I would have explained it better: what is the purpose of the provisions on closer co-operation introduced by the treaty of Amsterdam?' in D O'Keeffe and P Twomey (eds) *Legal Issues of the Amsterdam Treaty* (Hart, 1999).

example, the possibility of parallel treaties has been contemplated by Jacques Chirac or Joschka Fischer.[147]

The problems of flexibility

Provision for flexibility undoubtedly has certain benefits. It may make it easier for new member states to adapt to the EU regime. It also lessens the danger of splinter groups forming and, more generally, accords with the obvious heterogeneity of the EU, allowing for integration in a lighter manner, rather than the case of 'more Europe'. However, flexibility has undoubted drawbacks as well. These might be summarised as those of complexity, fragmentation of the EU order and a lack of democracy and intelligibility.

A Union of different speeds and initiatives adds yet another dimension to an already complex and Byzantine entity. It also raises issues of boundary disputes and justiciability of the issues concerned. The Community courts have taken on this from time to time, such as in the *UEAPME* case,[148] in which the CFI categorised laws adopted under the Social Policy agreement as 'Community' law. The delimitation of boundaries, already complex enough in the two-dimensional legal space of EU law, becomes even more complex in a multidimensional polity.[149] There are problems of coordinating parallel legal orders. This problem had to be addressed in the EEA agreement, where it was solved by limiting the contribution of EFTA states to decision-making processes. Indeed there is the danger that, by creating so many varying initiatives and institutional structures, the core sense of community, necessary for the continuance of the EU as a cohesive unit, is thereby undermined. Related to this is the danger of the fragmentation of the EU legal order. Then, clearly related to both of these problems is the problem of a lack of transparency, legitimacy and ultimately democracy in such a variegated polity, which becomes ever more far removed from the ordinary citizen and in which the chain of responsibility is evermore difficult to follow.

Constitutionalising issues

Therefore, flexibility presents a danger to the presentation of the EU as a coherent body, as a constitutional polity even – or perhaps not? Is increased flexibility the only way forward, the only way of maintaining the *acquis* in the post national polity, or does it threaten the achievements already made?

---

[147] E.g. President Chirac argued for a pioneer group of member states to move into the fast lane. He also gave a speech on the future of Europe to the German Bundestag in June 2000 in which he advocated creating new structures, including a 'light secretariat'. See also the views set out by the German Foreign Minister in a speech to the Humboldt University Berlin on 12 May 2000.

[148] Case T-135/96 *UEAPME* v *Council* [1998]; see also Case C-170/96 [1998].

[149] For a discussion of these issues see N Walker, 'Flexibility within a metaconstitutional frame in G de Búrca and J Scott (eds) *Constitutional Change in the EU: From Uniformity to Flexibility* (Hart Publishing, 2000) at 10. See also discussion at end of Chapter 1.

A certain structure, as well as stability, seems to be an essential element of any constitution, including the EU constitution. The constitution of the EU lies partly in elements such as adherence to the rule of law, the preservation of the institutional balance, protection of individual rights, all of which require a certain foreseeability and certainty. On the other hand, flexibility may threaten these elements, as outlined in the previous section. However, whether these are true threats may depend partly on how, if at all, we characterise the EU polity (or indeed flexibility).[150] There have been, and continue to be, many competing paradigms for the nature of the EU polity: as a continuation of the Westpahalian state; as a participatory, dialogical democracy; as an intergovernmental entity; as a regulatory unit; or as an example of multilevel governance.[151] Flexibility only truly poses a challenge to the first model, which requires more stability, and perhaps democratic accountability, than the others. Shaw,[152] for example, has seen the possibility of a reconciliation of flexibility and constitutionalism in the processes of deliberative democracy, and she cites the multitextual, intercultural dialogue recommended by Tully,[153] as a means of grappling with the tensions wrought by constitutionalism and flexibility. Shaw suggests that deliberative democratic processes, by their very nature, do not necessarily seek to impose structure, but rather to maintain a conversation, to understand a practice from the other's point of view.[154] This is all very well, and has a certain sense to it, but still surely leaves the danger of collapse and fragmentation already inherent in the EU. In addition to any deliberative conversation that is taking place, there must surely be a strongly defined core, based on common principles and values that delineate the scope of the EU in a way that is clearer than at present. This is surely a task for the next IGC, and the current convention on the future of the European Union.

A FEDERAL UNION?

Throughout this chapter, a question has shadowed the discussion and not been directly answered: how close is the EU to becoming a federal union? Certainly, just the very word 'federal' – in an earlier draft of the TEU – was enough to cause apoplexy in certain quarters in the run up to the Maastricht Treaty, so it has usually been avoided in the EU context. However, if the spectre of the word 'federalism' provoked fear at the Maastricht IGC, it probably should not have done so. Not only may we cite as examples of federal government some of those among the most stable in the world: US (since 1787), Switzerland (since 1848), Canada (since 1867)

---

[150] Walker op. cit. in de Búrca and Scott op. cit.

[151] See E Philippart and M Sie Dhian Ho, 'Flexibility and Models of Governance for the EU' in de Burca and Scott op. cit.

[152] J Shaw, 'Relating Constitutionalism and Flexibility in the European Union' in de Burca and Scott op. cit.

[153] J Tully, *Strange Multiplicity. Constitutionalism in an Age of Diversity* (Cambridge: Cambridge University Press, 1995).

[154] Tully recommends a Wittgenstinian methodology, probably not what the IGC had in mind when it re-formulated enhanced cooperation. See also Chapter 15.

and Australia (since 1901) but federalism has proved sufficiently agreeable to be revived as a political solution in the 1990s (in Belgium, which became a fully-fledged federal system in 1993, in South Africa in 1996, and in aspects of UK devolution, for example).

Aside from mere avoidance of an issue unpalatable to some, there are two reasons why this is a difficult question to answer. The first is that the concept of federalism itself is as complex and contested as those of democracy, sovereignty, constitution, or any others that we have had occasion to deal with so far.[155] As one author recently commented, 'There appears to be no exhaustive list of commonly agreed criteria that a legal order should meet before it can be said to be federal.'[156] The second, very closely related to the first, is that of the complex multidimensional nature of the EU: trying to pigeonhole it within a single concept developed in another age may simply not do it justice. With these two cautionary elements in mind, I shall nonetheless try to draw some conclusions about the EU and federalism, in order to dispel at least some of the shadows which have emerged in this chapter.

It is hard to provide a definition of federalism that is not so vague as to be nearly redundant. Although it has been described, at an already basic level, as the combination of shared rule for some purposes and a regional self-rule for others within a single political system[157] (which would not admit the EU, which lacks a single political system), others have seen the concept of federalism as sufficiently broad to extend beyond the nation state.[158] Lenaerts[159] suggests that federalism might be 'characterised by the existence of a central authority that manages the fields of competence entrusted to it'. In these times of diminished state sovereignty, nation states no longer provide the paradigm for governance, and there are to be found increased interstate linkages of a constitutional federal character, of which the EU might seem to be one.

In the undoubtedly federal US, the following features contribute to, or even comprise, its federalism. A major feature is the division of powers, which is set out in Article 1, section 8 of the US federal constitution, which lists the subject matters which lie under federal authority. In the US, these are mainly concurrent, although those which are exclusively federal prohibit states from legislating on them. Any unspecified residual matter is left to the states. The federal institutions of the US are based on a system of separation of powers, complemented by checks and balances. In the EU, as this chapter should have made abundantly clear, there is no express allocation of powers as is set out in the US constitution. However, competence is

---

[155] For general discussions of federalism see D Elazar, *Federalism: An Overview* (Pretoria: HSRC, 1995); KC Wheare, *Federal Government* (London: Oxford University Press, 1946); WS Livingston, *Federalism and Constitutional Change* (Oxford: Clarendon Press, 1956).

[156] K Lenaerts, 'Federalism: Essential Concepts in Evolution – the case of the European Union' (1998) 21 Fordham Int'l L.J. 746; See also K Lenaerts, 'Constitutionalism and the many Faces of Federalism' (1990) Am J Comp L, 2905.

[157] See R Watts, *Comparing Federal Systems* (Montreal and Kingston: McGill University Press, 1999) at 15.

[158] Unlike the authors of the American eighteenth century papers, *The Federalist*, who envisaged federalism as a means to building up a nation.

[159] K Lenaerts, 'Federalism: Essential Concepts in Evolution,' 765.

divided and there are undoubtedly areas where the states may not act. If the next IGC does follow the German demand for a clearer enumeration of competence, then the EU will start to look more traditionally federal, but even without this, the existence of EU competence is undeniable, and even if there are many areas of uncertain concurrent competence, then this uncertainty also exists within traditionally recognised federal systems.

There are other components of EU law which are indicative of some federal drift: recognition of the doctrines of supremacy, direct effect and preemption, for example. The decision-making processes of the EU, which lend a role both to the member states acting in the Council, but also to peoples of Europe as represented in the Parliament, is also capable of looking federal. Lenaerts has also suggested that the member states' duty of loyal cooperation, in Article 10 EC, reflects a sort of 'executive federalism' in which 'the component entities become agents for the application and enforcement of the policy choices made at the central level'.[160] There are also provisions specifically inserted to protect the identity of the member states, for example Article 6(3)TEU, which provides that 'The Union shall respect the national identities of its member states', an indication of a federal concern with protecting the diversity of the parts.

The second and third pillars of the EU might seem to provide a harder case for federalism, given the amount of intergovernmental decision-making that they involve. However, the CFSP is after all to be a **common** foreign and security policy, constructed according to the principles set out in Articles 11–28 TEU.[161] The Commission and Parliament play some role in this so it is not just intergovernmental: it has the beginnings of some federal interest. Javier Solana, the High Representative of the CFSP, as well as Secretary-General of the Council, holds long-term office, ensuring some sort of consistency beyond the shorter term needs of the member states. In the context of the third pillar, PJCC, although largely intergovernmental, there is also some scope for a more federal type approach. Decision-making is unanimous, and thus in the hands of the member states, but in the implementation of some of these decisions majority voting may be used, and the Commission also has the right of initiative, and the European Parliament the right to be consulted. The Community's democratic deficit may, however, still be seen as a barrier to its being considered a federal form of government, as legitimacy and democracy of the channels of government are very important in this context. The Parliamentary input into the EU and EC is still weak at some levels, as discussed in Chapter 3.

However, it is not just institutional arrangements which are indicative of federalism. Dicey believed that a federal system, if it was to be successful, required a singular state of sentiment among the inhabitants of the countries which it was to unite: 'They must desire union and not desire diversity.'[162] The social forces under-

---

[160] K Lenaerts, ibid. at 766. See also Declaration no 43 annexed to the Treaty of Amsterdam.
[161] For a discussion of the CFSP, see S Douglas-Scott, 'The CFSP of the EU: Reinforcing the European Identity?' in P Fitzpatrick and J Bergeron (eds) *Europe's Other* (Ashgate, 1998).
[162] AV Dicey, *The Law of the Constitution* at 144.

lying federal systems are just as important as its institutional structures. According to WS Livingston, writing in 1956, 'The essential nature of federalism is to be sought for, not in the shadings of legal and constitutional terminology; but in the forces – economic, social, political and cultural – that have made the outward forms of federation necessary.'[163] Most certainly economic forces have made European Union a necessity, and there has recently been a recognition that economics are not enough, and that other features – such as the social and cultural – must link Europeans if Europe is to work. Consequently, the common basis of values is asserted in, for example, the provisions of Article 6 TEU which states that: 'The Union is founded on principles of liberty, democracy, respect for human rights, and fundamental freedoms and the rule of law, principles which are common to the Member States.' Europe lacks a *demos* and there is still little effective support for the EU – but a lack of effective support may also exist in individual states – there may be little support for Westminster in Scotland (even after devolution), little support for Ottawa in parts of Canada, but still linking social, economic and cultural forces and work. This might be the case in the EU too.

However, one should not downplay the role of institutions, nor of formal frameworks either, *pace* Livingston. There is a very complex relationship between institutions and societal behaviour, which is commutative in nature. Common feelings may not only produce federal societies but may themselves in turn be fostered by the institutions and superstructures themselves. There is a continuous interaction. Institutions of the EU could themselves possibly establish and influence feelings of loyalty and engagement with the EU. A comparative study of the world's federal systems (completely beyond the scope of this book) would probably indicate that those which are most successful exhibit both the strong social forces, as well as carefully crafted political institutions, and that these two elements work symbiotically together. No doubt, a carefully crafted constitutional treaty would make the EU feel more 'federal'.

In the end, it surely matters not whether we call the EU a federal system or not. It exhibits enough federal features to satisfy those who are determined to find it federal, and lacks some which would entitle purists to reject the title. It is perhaps simply misplaced to call the EU federal. While the concept of federalism is too rich and contested to be condensed into a simple explanation, it also does not feel quite right as an explanation of the EU, which, as this book has tried to illustrate, is too *sui generis*, too complex, too multidimensional, to fit into any such categorisation. No doubt the EU would benefit from a more clearly delineated enumeration of powers, from a conscientiously drafted, more constitutional-looking treaty, which could clear up many unnecessary uncertainties. But if this were to be the case, it should be so not because the EU needs to be more 'federal', but because it needs to be more meaningful, more intelligible and more authentic to its beleaguered citizens.

---

[163] WS Livingston, *Federalism and Constitutional Change* (Oxford: Clarendon Press, 1956) 1–2.

PART TWO

THE EUROPEAN COURTS, THE NATIONAL COURTS AND THE CONSTITUTION

5

THE EUROPEAN COURTS: LAW, POLICY AND JUDICIAL ACTIVISM

It is not always the case that international courts arouse strong feelings, but this has been so with the European Court in Luxembourg. On the one hand, a former French Prime Minister, Michel Debré, said in 1979, 'J'accuse la Cour de Justice de mégalomanie maladive.'[1] A more measured, but equally vehement, account was given by Margaret Thatcher, in the parliamentary debates on the Maastricht Treaty when she reported that 'some things at the Court are very much to our distaste'.[2] Attacks on it have also been made by the German press[3] and it has been accused of 'revolting judicial behaviour' by the Danish academic, Hjalte Rasmussen.[4]

On the other hand, vibrant though these attacks may be, the European Court has also been ignored, or merely tacitly approved, for long periods of time by lawyers, the media and the academic community alike. Eric Stein gave the now famous description of the Court as being 'tucked away in the fairyland Duchy of Luxembourg and blessed with benign neglect by the powers that be and the mass media'.[5] The European Court thus met with little criticism from academics,[6] or attention from political scientists, even after giving some of its most revolutionary case law. It might seem to have operated by stealth, attracting nothing like the attention given to the US Supreme Court, or to European supreme courts, for much of its history, and thus its influence on the path of European integration is all the more intriguing.

---

[1] Cited by Judge Mancini in *Democracy and Constitutionalism in the European Union* (Hart Publishing, 2000) at 1.

[2] HL Deb 7 June 1993 col 560.

[3] For example by the *Frankfurter Rundschau*: 'Im Zweifel für Europa' 7 December 1992.

[4] H Rasmussen, *On Law and Policy in the European Court of Justice* (Martinus Nijhoff, 1986). Further attacks on the ECJ are considered below.

[5] E Stein, 'Lawyers, Judges and the Making of a Transnational Constitution' (1981) 75 American Journal of International Law.

[6] Rasmussen, op. cit. fn 4, at 266, notes the existence of a 'frequent, close and privileged relationship between the Bench and the legal academic specialists in the study of Community law'.

The role of these judges and advocates-general of the European Court and judges of the Court of First Instance[7] has been seminal in the creation of a European Union, and this in spite of the outwardly uninspiring provisions of the EC treaty which handle its jurisdiction, composition and organisation. This jurisdiction is hard to classify, being unlike that either of an international court or a national supreme court, although sharing some features with both. The ECJ sometimes functions as an international court, as under Articles 226–228 of the EC treaty, whereby enforcement actions may be brought against member states which do not comply with EC law. At other times, their work seems more akin to that of an administrative court, as under Article 230, when exercising a power of judicial review over the acts of legislation of the Community Institutions. This provision was indeed much influenced by French administrative law, and this jurisdiction is now handled largely by the Court of First Instance, which functions very much as an administrative court.[8] Under Article 288, the Court of First Instance also hears actions for non-contractual liability against the Community, a head which has so far not developed into anything like a wide-ranging tortious liability.[9] The Court of First Instance has also traditionally handled cases brought against the Community by its staff, a large volume of work which, however, sometimes produces cases of importance.[10]

The Court of Justice (and CFI in future in some cases)[11] hears preliminary references from the national courts, a jurisdiction discussed in the next chapter which has been of the greatest importance in the development of Community law, and has been seen as a method of federalising or constitutionalising the Treaty.[12]

COMPOSITION AND ORGANISATION

The fifteen judges of each court are all 'chosen from persons whose independence is beyond doubt'. In both courts the judges are appointed for a six-year term and are eligible for reappointment, although they have no guarantee of non-removal,[13] and thus may seem to lack the independence possessed by many judges in national

---

[7] There are currently fifteen judges in each court: 'one judge per member state' according to the wording of Articles 221 and 224 EC. This allows for an increase on enlargement. There are eight advocates general: Article 222 EC.

[8] Mancini, op. cit. fn 1 at 9, describes it as 'a true administrative court'.

[9] For a further discussion of this jurisdiction see Chapter 11.

[10] See Case C-404/92 *X* v *Commission* [1994] ECR I-4737, in which it was held that a Community employee had the right to refuse an AIDS test. Staff cases, however, are very time-consuming and the plan is to remove this jurisdiction from the CFI altogether. Article 225a, inserted by Nice, allows the Council to create judicial panels to hear certain types of action. The *Declaration* in the Final Act of the Nice Treaty calls on the Commission and Court to prepare a draft decision establishing a judicial panel for staff cases as soon as possible.

[11] In specific areas to be determined at a later date by the Statute of the Court: Article 225 EC.

[12] It certainly has something in common with the preliminary reference system to the German (the *Verfassungsbeschwerde*) and Italian constitutional courts.

[13] Article 223 EC. A document for the 1996 IGC suggested a longer unrenewable term for the judges so as to strengthen their independence, but this was not taken up.

supreme courts.[14] However, there are some long records of office at the Court: the current President of the Court, the Spaniard, Rodriguez Iglesias, has been in office since the accession of Spain to the EU in 1986 (but President only from 1994) and the British Advocate General, Francis Jacobs, has been at the Court since 1988. Appointments are staggered so every three years there is a partial replacement of judges so as to ensure continuity.

The judges of both courts come from a variety of backgrounds, some of them political. This was the case with well-known[15] judges, such as Robert Lecourt, who had previously served as French Justice Minister, Pescatore, who was in the Luxembourg Foreign Office, Everling in the German Ministry of Economics and Due in the Danish Ministry of Justice. Hans Kutscher, one-time President of the Court, served in the German Constitutional Court, where appointments are usually made on a political basis, before arriving at Luxembourg. The following Advocates General also had political careers: Lenz served in the German Bundestag, La Pergola in the Italian Cabinet, and Whatelet served for a time as Belgian Justice Minister. However, by 1978, half of the judges and Advocates General had held some sort of judicial office before their appointment in Luxembourg,[16] and some went on to do so again, after leaving Luxembourg.[17] Many also had come from the academic community, an unusual background for a judge in the UK, but not so in continental Europe.

The members of the Luxembourg bench may be less colourful than some of the members of the US Supreme Court, such as Justices Black and Douglas, or more latterly, Scalia, or of national courts, such as the late Lord Denning, but they nonetheless may still create a profile for themselves in, for example, extra-judicial writings of a lively style, such as those of the late Judge Mancini.[18] Appointments to the Court are not high profile affairs, as they are in the case of the US Supreme Court, with its highly publicised Senate hearings on prospective appointees. No member of the ECJ would arrive in Luxembourg with the degree of publicity which, for example, Clarence Thomas of the Supreme Court attracted during the Senate Hearings for his confirmation.

The members of the European Courts in Luxembourg are selected 'by common accord of the governments of the member states'.[19] This is done in private, by way of diplomatic meetings, prompting Judge Mancini to comment that 'few Supreme courts in the western world are so lacking in links with democratic government'.[20] The members of the European Court are supposed to be representative of their respective member states, so that national juridical traditions of the EU may be

---

[14] Who, even if they are not appointed for life, tend to sit for periods of twelve years or more.

[15] Well-known, in at least the sense that these judges have quite frequently written about EU law and their work at the Court.

[16] Although in the first court, that of the ECSC, two of the judges were not legally qualified: Serrarens from the Netherlands, and Rueff from France.

[17] As was the case with Advocate General Rozes, who became President of the French Cour de Cassation, and Gordon Slynn, who now sits in the House of Lords.

[18] Whose writings are in fact referred to throughout this chapter.

[19] Article 223 EC.

[20] Mancini, op. cit. chapter 3. The European Parliament made a resolution in 1995 (OJ 1995 C151/56 23(ii)) arguing that its assent be required for all nominations to the ECJ and CFI. The Court's response was to find this an undesirably unacceptable degree of publicity.

fairly represented,[21] and, although they need not be nationals of the countries they represent, this still carries a risk of too much loyalty to their national background. However, the Court has been regrettably unrepresentative in other ways, namely lacking in participation of women and ethnic minorities. The first female judge of the ECJ, Fidelma Mackem of Ireland, was only appointed in 1999 (although the French Advocate General Rozès sat on the Court from 1979–83)[22] but she has now been joined by Ninon Cloneric, who sits as the German judge, and Christine Stix-Hackl, the new Austrian Advocate General, both appointed in 2000. The first female justices of the CFI were only appointed a little longer ago, on the accession of the new member states in 1995.[23]

Advocates general

There are currently eight advocates general on the court,[24] one appointed by each of the five larger members and the other three appointed on a rotational basis.[25] In the ECJ, one advocate general is assigned to every case. According to Article 222, it is their task, 'acting with complete impartiality and independence, to make, in open court, reasoned submissions on cases brought before the Court of Justice, in order to assist the Court in the performance of the task assigned to it in Article 220'. They have the same status as judges and the same conditions of office. Their role is partly derived from that of the Commissaire du Gouvernement in the Conseil d'Etat, reflecting the influence of French procedure in the earlier days of the EEC. Jean-Pierre Warner, formerly a British advocate general at the Court, suggested that they carry out the role of a court of first instance, ensuring double judicial control.[26] However, surely the most important function of the advocate general is to ensure that a comprehensive overview of the case is provided, given the brevity of the submission made by the parties themselves in court.[27] Thus, after oral argument is over, the advocate general presents their opinion, although they play no part in the deliberations of the judges. The advocate general's opinion is, however, not binding on the

---

[21] Articles 223 and 225 EC.

[22] Unfortunately Madame Rozès is still referred to throughout CELEX, the EU's official full text legal database, as *Mr* Advocate General Rozès.

[23] These were Virpi Tiili, the Finnish judge, and Pernilla Lindh of Sweden.

[24] Pergola was appointed as an extra, ninth advocate general from 1995–2000. He had originally been appointed as a second Italian judge, to make an uneven number at the Court, but on the failure of Norway to ratify the Accession treaty this became unnecessary, and so he was appointed as a short-term extra advocate general instead. Article 222 has been amended by the Nice Treaty to allow the Court of Justice to request the Council to increase the number of advocates general to take account of future enlargements of the EU.

[25] Whose term of office cannot then be renewed.

[26] JP Warner, 'Some Aspects of the European Court of Justice' (1976) 14 SPTL 16. For further contributions on the role of the advocate general see T Tridimas, 'The role of the Advocate General in the development of Community Law' (1997) 34 CML Rev 1349; A Dashwood, 'The Advocate General in the Court of Justice' (1982) Legal Studies 202.

[27] Although this is partly the role of the Juge Rapporteur, see below. As there is no rule of good practice, as in the English courts, requiring parties to cite authorities going against them, the advocate general fulfils a useful function in this regard.

judges, and the Court has sometimes acted against it, as in the early seminal cases of *Van Gend* and *Costa*.[28] The Court is tending, however, to refer to these opinions more and more, sometimes simply relying on them, without giving its own reasoning, as in *Hauptzollamt Hamburg*.[29]

What is certainly the case, is that advocate generals' opinions tend to be far more readable than those of the Court, as well as being more discursive and akin to the Anglo-Saxon style in the nature of their drafting, operating as an exploratory ground for legal concepts and the development of ideas,[30] although, of course, style varies among the various advocates general. AG Jacobs' opinion in the *Konstantinidis* case is a good example of the discursive style. He wrote, in memorable terms:

> In my opinion, a Community national who goes to another Member State as a worker or self-employed person . . . is entitled to assume that, wherever he goes to earn his living in the European Community, he will be treated in accordance with a common code of fundamental values, in particular those laid down in the European Convention on Human Rights. In other words, he is entitled to say 'civis europeus sum' and to invoke that status in order to oppose any violation of his fundamental rights.[31]

In the Court of First Instance, unlike the Court of Justice, there are no advocates general, although judges may act as such if necessary.

Referendaires

The judges and advocates general of the Luxembourg courts have a 'cabinet' staffed by assistants and secretaries. In particular, they have (usually) three legal secretaries who help them in their research on the case and often prepare draft judgments. These secretaries are often referred to by their French title of 'referendaire' (in German they are similarly known as 'Refendar').

These referendaires carry out a function similar to that of law clerks in the US courts, although they are usually at a later stage in their career than the law graduates who people the courts in the States. But they may have just as much influence on the formation of the judge's opinion. This is hard to gauge, however, as, unlike their counterparts in the US, so far none of the Luxembourg secretaries have gone on to write about their time with the Justices.[32] The office of referendaire is thought

---

[28] AG Roemer gave the opinion in *Van Gend*, and AG Lagrange in *Costa v ENEL*. Both were highly skilled and imaginative in style but perhaps inclined toward judicial self-restraint and constructionism. Their style was notably different from a slightly later generation of advocates general: Capotorti, Warner and Reischl.

[29] Case C-59/92 [1993] ECR I-2193 at para 4 where the ECJ stated: 'for the reasons indicated in the Advocate General's opinion of 31 March 1993, the reply to the question put by the national court must be that...'

[30] Which are sometimes, however, not followed up – for example, three advocate generals favoured the direct effect of directives (e.g. AG Jacobs, who gave full reasoning in the *Vaneetveld* case) prior to the Court's ruling against such a concept in *Dori*; see also Chapter 8 of this book.

[31] Case C-168/91 *Christos Konstantinidis v Stadt Altensteig* [1993] ECR I 1191.

[32] See, for example, E Lazarus, *Closed Chambers* (Times Books, 1998): a description of the inner workings of the Supreme Court during his time clerking for Justice Blackmun.

to be a good training, so much so that quite a few of these have gone on to become judges or advocates general in their own time.[33]

PROCEDURE

Procedure in the European Courts reflects the uniqueness of a system comprising eleven official languages, all of which rank equally, and fifteen member states with a wide variety of legal systems: civil law, common law, some unitary and some federal in nature. The Court has at present a very large workload and very little ability to control the type of cases which come its way, as it has no system of filter by way of leave for appeals, such as in the House of Lords, nor docket control, as in the US Supreme Court.[34] Therefore, it cannot be selective, and hears about 400 cases annually,[35] not all of which are of great significance. This has especially become of concern in the case of preliminary references from the national courts, which are discussed in the next chapter.[36]

The Court's rules of procedure are set out in the Statutes of the Court, which are to be found in the protocols to the treaties (which have the same status as the treaties themselves) and in the Court's Rules of Procedure, which are drawn up by the Court and approved by the Council of Ministers. Both were originally based on the rules of the International Court of Justice,[37] reflecting its status as an international court. Written procedure is key, involving only short oral proceedings, a contrast to the Anglo-Saxon notion of a 'day in court', but high flown rhetoric is hardly appropriate in a forum in which the interpreters are more numerous than the judges. A Juge Rapporteur is assigned to every case, preparing a report for the hearing. As the Court has a huge workload it sits in Chambers in order to handle its volume of work; only approximately one in four cases are decided by the full Court.[38] According to Article 221 EC Chambers may consist of three or five judges, although it must sit in a Grand Chamber[39] of eleven judges if a member state or Community Institution insists. Important cases are sometimes heard in Chambers,[40] although it is sometimes suggested that a particular Chamber of the Court is responsible for so-called 'rogue' decisions. The court will sit with all fifteen members in cases of extreme importance. It will usually sit with eleven, and nine is the minimum. In the Court of First Instance, Chambers of three and five are the norm, although, since 1 July 1999, single judges

---

[33] E.g. Advocates General Jacobs and Gulmann were both formerly referendaires, as was Judge Lenaerts of the Court of First Instance.

[34] Which has a yearly docket of about 6,000 cases, but which denies certiorari to all but 5 per cent, on the basis that they disclose no issue of importance or justice.

[35] Figure taken from *Proceedings of the Court of Justice 2001*.

[36] E.g. case C-338/95 *Wiener v Hauptzollamt Emmerich* [1997] ECR I 6495.

[37] See J Schwarze, 'The Origins of the European Court's Statutes and Rules of Procedure' in R Plender (ed.) *The European Court's Practice and Precedents* (Sweet and Maxwell 1997).

[38] *Proceedings of the Court of Justice 2001*.

[39] The Grand Chamber is an innovation of the Nice Treaty: see Article 221 EC. It consists of the President of the Court, the Presidents of the five Chambers and other judges.

[40] Case 241/83 *Rosler v Rottwinkel* [1985] I CMLR 806, which concerned tenancies of immovable property under the Brussels Convention, is such an example.

have been permitted to sit in certain types of cases in order to help with the Court's increasing workload.[41] The case is held in the language chosen by the applicant if a direct action, or that of the referring court if a preliminary reference.[42]

After the advocate general has given their opinion,[43] the Juge Rapporteur prepares a draft judgment for the Court. The Court sits in private to discuss its decision, and, as no interpreters are present, discussions are held in French, the working language of the Court. A majority vote is taken in secret and no dissenting opinions are permitted. As Judge Mancini wrote, a judge who disagrees 'can only grit his teeth'[44] (even worse is the situation of the Juge Rapporteur, who must draft the judgment even if disagreeing with the majority). Contrast this silence in the absence of dissent in the ECJ, with some of the biting dissents which are delivered in the US Supreme Court. A good such example is Justice Scalia's dissent in *Romer v Evans*, in which he referred to the majority opinion as 'so long on emotive utterance and so short on relevant legal citation', as well as being something which 'finds no support in law or logic'.[45] Why are dissents not permitted in the ECJ? Mancini likens the position of the ECJ to that of the US Supreme Court in its early days, suggesting that 'a young court administering and helping to create a new legal order must suppress disagreement in order to enhance its authority by a show of unanimity'.[46] Perhaps this requirement for unanimity is no longer as pressing, and it is time for the Court to do as the German Constitutional Court did some time ago and to allow dissents. This might indicate the 'coming of age' of the Court.

Partly as a result of the requirements of multilinguism and unanimity, the European Court's judgments tend not to be very readable, or, as a well-known work on the Court put it, they often have the 'flatness associated with a Government report'.[47] In complex cases, the Court's reasoning may be especially difficult to follow, as the Court may have been able to secure agreement on some issues only, leaving unclear the basis for its decision. Even if there has not been disagreement, the path of reasoning towards the Court's decision may be difficult to follow. For example, in the seminal case of *Dassonville*, the Court gave no explanation as to why 'all trading rules, either direct or indirect, actual or potential, which hinder the free movement of goods' could be classified as 'measures having an equivalent effect to quantitative restriction', a holding which in fact went against some of the Court's previous decisions, which had required discrimination for the provision to bite.[48]

---

[41] Council Decision of 26 April 1999, OJ L 114 1 May 1999. This applies to cases which do not raise any difficult questions of law and fact, which are of limited importance and which do not involve any other special circumstances. Competition, State Aids and trade cases are excluded in any case.

[42] See Article 29(1) Rules of Procedure for the exceptions to this.

[43] Which may be given in any of the Court's languages, but usually is usually that of the advocate general.

[44] Mancini op. cit. chap. 10.

[45] *Romer v Evans* 116 S Ct 1620 (1996).

[46] Mancini op. cit. at p 167. Mancini also cites an interesting letter in which President Thomas Jefferson, in 1820, castigated the Supreme Court as 'huddled up in a conclave, perhaps by a majority of one, delivered as if unanimous, and with the silent acquiescence of timid or lazy associates, by a crafty chief Judge, who sophisticates the law to his mind by the turn of his own reasoning'.

[47] See Brown and Jacobs, *The Court of Justice of the European Communities* (Sweet and Maxwell, 1995) at 54.

[48] Case 8/74 *Procureur du Roi v Dassonville* [1974] ECR 837.

Judgments are usually drafted in French, which may not of course be the judge's native language, although they will later be translated into all Community languages. The judgments, particularly in the earlier days of the Court, derived much from the French style of drafting, reflecting the prominence of France in the early days of the EC. Thus one would find the judgment to be 'a single Ciceronian sentence...all recited in a long series of subordinate clauses leading eventually to one main sentence, "The Court hereby rules"'.[49] Of course, the influence of other member states has tempered the effect of Francophile procedure: that of German law may not necessarily have improved the drafting style, but it has brought an emphasis on 'general clauses' and fundamental rights, and, since the accession of the common law countries, Britain and Ireland, there has been more questioning of lawyers from the Bench. By 1979, the Court changed its style a bit, no longer using just a single sentence for the most part drafted in the ablative absolute, but this did not necessarily make its judgments more readable. The discursive, even idiosyncratic style of drafting to be found in Anglo-Saxon judgments (of which Lord Denning's famous judgment in *Hinz v Berry*, with the opening line 'It was bluebell time in Kent', is a prime example)[50] is not to be found in the European Court's terse judgments. Consider how the ECJ deals with the emotive issue of abortion in the *Grogan* case. How does it find that abortion can be a service? Surely all sorts of societal, cultural, moral and economic values are involved in such a conclusion, and yet all the Court can come up with in this case is, 'Medical termination of pregnancy, performed in accordance with the law of the State in which it is carried out, constitutes a service within the meaning of Article 60 of the Treaty.'[51] No mention is made of the complicated background that leads to this case being brought before the Court. Contrast this with the striking prose of *Planned Parenthood v Casey*, one of the most recent cases on abortion to come before the US Supreme court, 'Abortion is a unique act. It is an act fraught with consequences for others: for the woman who must live with the implications of her decision; for the persons who perform and assist in the procedure; for the spouse, family and society which must confront the knowledge that these procedures exist, procedures some deem nothing short of an act of violence against innocent human life ...'[52] Does not the prose of the ECJ seem inadequate in comparison?

There also tends to be very little analysis by the Court of its own previous case law. In this way the Court differs from the advocates general, who tend to be more expansive: it is instructive, for example, to compare the fully reasoned opinion of AG Tesauro in *Hunermund* with that of the court in *Keck*,[53] both of which constrain the ambit of Article 28 EC. The ECJ's approach to precedent is not that of the orthodox Anglo-Saxon lawyer:[54] in *Keck*, for example, the Court took an almost gnomic

---

[49] Brown and Jacobs, op. cit. at 52.

[50] *Hinz v Berry* [1970] 2 QB 42.

[51] Case C-159/90 *SPUC v Grogan* [1991] ECR I-4685 at para 2.

[52] *Planned Parenthood v Casey* 112 S.Ct 2791 [1992].

[53] Case C-292/92 *Hünermund* [1993] ECR I-6787; Cases C-267 & C-268/91 *Keck & Mithouard* [1993] ECR I-6097.

[54] See the chapter on preliminary rulings for a discussion of the precedent-like effect of the doctrines of *acte clair* and *acte éclairé*.

approach to precedent, stating that its holding was 'contrary to what had previously been decided', but failing to specify to which cases its holding was contrary. However, what Brown and Jacobs call 'leitmotifs' do occur in case after case – e.g. the *Plaumann*[55] test for *locus standi*. In this way it has been said that 'By constant rehearsals, the Court, like a Welsh choir finds the exact note it wants to sound.'[56]

APPEALS FROM THE CFI

These are governed by Article 225 EC and Articles 49–54 of the Statute of the ECJ. Appeals are on points of law only and must be made within two months of the decision (although may be made by member states and Community Institutions, as well as by the unsuccessful party). If well-founded the ECJ will quash the CFI decision and either give final judgment itself or remit to the CFI. The growing number of appeals and the amount of Court time they occupy has been a matter of concern discussed at the 2000 IGC.

METHODS OF INTERPRETATION

These have played a very important role in the way the European Court functions, and are distinctive from those used under the common law method. English courts, for example, have tended to rely heavily in the past on the so-called 'ordinary' or literal method of interpretation. Thus, Lord Reid stated in *Pinner* v *Everett*, 'In determining the meaning of a word or phrase in a statute the first question to ask always is what is the natural or ordinary meaning of that word or phrase in its context in the statute?'[57] This method is sometimes used by the European Court, but is not ideally suited to its task. The EC texts are often extremely vague and general in their language: unlike British statutes, the treaties provide no definitions of the terms used, there is no glossary. So terms of such generality as 'worker' or 'measure having an equivalent effect to a quantitative restriction' have been left to the Court to decide. Of course, vagueness and generality are nothing new in legal texts, especially in foundational provisions such as the *traité cadre* style drafting of the EC. In the context of the American Constitution, Alexander Bickel commented that 'the major heads of power and of limitation only work, as Marshall said, "the great outlines". "Commerce"... "freedom of speech"... obviously men may in full and equal reason and good faith hold differing views about the proper meaning and specific application of provisions such as these.'[58] There may also be much differing in good faith about the meaning and proper scope of EC law, especially as the vagueness of EC legislation has also been augmented by particular difficulties faced by the EC

---

55 Case 25/62 *Plaumann* v *Commission* [1963] ECR 95 at 107.
56 Brown and Jacobs op. cit. at 54.
57 [1969] 3 All ER 257 at 258.
58 A Bickel, *The Least Dangerous Branch* (New Haven and London: Yale University Press, 1962) pp 36–7.

legislature, whereby a text may be agreed without much agreement on its meaning and scope.[59] Thus, it may have been a deliberate choice to leave the Court to amplify further a difficult subject. As Lord Denning memorably put it, 'the Treaty lacks precision...It uses words and phrases without defining what they mean...All the way through the Treaty, there are gaps and lacunae. They have to be filled by the judges, or by regulations and directives. It is the European way.'[60]

In any case, the Court made it clear from its early days that it was not really about the business of literal interpretation. In the *Humblet* case,[61] decided in 1960, it stated clearly, 'it is not sufficient for the Court to adopt the literal interpretation...' A couple of years later, in a famous passage, it elaborated on the type of considerations which it would regard as sufficient, 'the spirit, the general scheme and the wording of those provisions'.[62] The literal meaning of Article 12 EC, as it then was, a prohibition on the imposition of further customs duties, was clearly going to be insufficient to its aim in *Van Gend* of introducing the concept of direct effect.

If literal interpretation has been thought inadequate to the Court's task, then another method, that of historical interpretation, has not fared much better. By this method, the Court will seek to determine what the legislature originally intended. In England, this was taken to mean not the subjective, but the objective intention of the legislature,[63] ascertainable from the words of the provision themselves. Although in most continental jurisdictions, judges might have recourse to *travaux préparatoires* to enable them to ascertain the subjective intent of the legislature, in England reference to parliamentary debates in Hansard was not permitted until 1993 in the case of *Pepper v Hart*.[64]

Whatever the practice in civil law jurisdictions, the ECJ never engaged much in historical interpretation.[65] Although the requirement to give reasons for all secondary legislation under Article 253 EC may make it simpler to determine what the legislature had in mind, on the other hand, the negotiations for the treaties were kept secret by agreement among the member states. As Professor Pescatore, judge of the European Court, and a member of the Luxembourg delegation which negotiated the EEC treaty, explained in a public lecture in 1963, '...divergent, even conflicting interests may perfectly well underlie a given text...the art of treaty making is part of the art of disguising irresolvable differences between the contracting States.'[66] Controversy over historical intent is a well-known phenomenon in US constitutional interpretation.[67]

---

[59] TC Hartley, 'Five Forms of Uncertainty in European Community Law' (1996) 55 CLJ at 273.

[60] *Bulmer v Bollinger* [1974] 2 WLR 202.

[61] Case 6/60 *Humblet* [1960] ECR 559 at 575.

[62] Case 26/62 *Van Gend en Loos* [1963] ECR 1 at 12.

[63] See *Heydon's case* (1584) 3 Co. Rep 7a.

[64] [1993] 1 All ER 42.

[65] Advocates general, however, have been more willing to refer to preparatory documents; see e.g. Advocate General Roemer in case 6/54 *Netherlands v High Authority* [1954–6] ECR 103.

[66] Cited in Brown and Jacobs, *The Court of Justice of the European Communities* (Sweet and Maxwell, 4th edn, 1995) at p 308.

[67] E.g. R Bork, 'Neutral Principles and Some First Amendment Problems' 47 Indiana Law Journal; A Bickel, *The Least Dangerous Branch* (Yale University Press, 1962); Ely, *Democracy and Distrust* (Harvard University Press, 1980); L Tribe, *Constitutional Choices* (Cambridge, Mass: Harvard University Press, 1985); A Scalia, *A Matter of Interpretation* (Princeton University Press, 1997).

Take the highly contentious issue of whether the founding fathers of the US Constitution wished to outlaw slavery: if so, there is no direct evidence in the Constitution. Divining historical intent is simply no easy task – whose original intent might one be seeking in the context of the EC: that of Jean Monnet, or Walter Hallstein, or the member states negotiating the treaty? How does one elucidate their interests and what can one do in the event of a conflict between the text and their expressed interests?

A good example of the ECJ ignoring intent is the *Chernobyl*[68] case, in which the Court accorded the European Parliament a right of standing before the Court to protect its prerogatives. In so doing, the Court ignored the intentions of the drafters of the Single European Act who, by not having changed the wording of Article 230 (or Article 173 as it then was), presumably had a clear desire not to provide such standing.

CONTEXTUAL AND TELEOLOGICAL INTERPRETATION

The ECJ has not favoured the historical method but it has frequently used contextual interpretation. As the ECJ stated in the *CILFIT* case, 'Every provision of EC law must be placed in its context and interpreted in the light of Community law as a whole…'[69] And so the ECJ will frequently set provisions in their context within the treaty, interpreting them in the light of Articles 2 and 3 of the EC treaty, and of the Preamble, which set out a programmatic, general scheme.

Related to this is teleological interpretation. The term 'teleological' is frequently used for a style of interpretation used by the ECJ, whereby it will interpret that provision on the basis of its **purpose** or **objective**: a method which the Court often uses in order to fill in gaps in the treaty. Use of such methods has been quite openly acknowledged by members of the Court. Hans Kutscher, a former President of the Court, wrote, 'How else should the Court of Justice carry out this function which it has been assigned except by an interpretation of Community law geared to the aims of the Treaty, that is to say, one which is dynamic and teleological?'[70] This methodology is familiar in continental law, where broadly drafted codes often leave quite a lot of gap-filling for the judiciary. Likewise, there are many gaps in the broad *traité cadre* framework of the EC Treaty, many of them intentionally so, as in Article 44, which sets the Council with certain tasks in order to bring about freedom of establishment. As is well known, by 1974 when the *Reyners*[71] case came before the Court, legislation had not been passed, and so the ECJ, in spite of the apparently

---

[68] Case C-70/88 *European Parliament v Council (Chernobyl)* [1990] ECR I-2041.

[69] Case 283/81 *CILFIT v Ministry of Health* [1982] ECR 3415.

[70] Extract from a paper given at a Judicial and Academic conference at the Palais de Justice Luxembourg in 1976. We also find Kutscher's predecessor as president of the Court, Pierre Pescatore, writing along similar lines: 'the rules of Community law fit into a complex of general ideas, of structures, of powers, of legislative and judicial methods, which make it possible, beyond the letter of the unwritten law, to come to grips with the needs of growth and the requirements of effectiveness'. *The Law of Integration* (Leyden, 1974) at 107.

[71] Case 2/74 *Reyners v Belgium* [1974] ECR 631, and see also chapter 18 on direct effect.

conditional wording of Article 44, found a directly effective right of freedom of establishment, necessitated by the objectives of the EC Treaty.

In the *Continental Can* case[72] the Court gave an expansive interpretation to Article 82, to hold that mergers and take-overs could be included within the concept of 'abuse of a dominant position' even though there was no mention of merger control in the EC Treaty. The ECJ held that this was justified, according to 'the spirit, general scheme and wording of Article 86 (as it then was) as well as to the system and objectives of the Treaty', a formula which sounds familiar from the earlier case of *Van Gend*.

A concept also frequently used in this context is that of *effet utile*, whereby the Court has held that the efficacy of Community law would be weakened if it did not interpret EC law in such a way as to fulfil the treaty's objectives. In *Francovich*, for example, the Court stated that 'The full effectiveness of Community rules would be impaired and the protection of the rights which they grant would be weakened if individuals were unable to obtain redress when their rights are infringed by a breach of Community law for which a Member State can be held responsible.'[73]

LAW AND POLICY-MAKING

In spite of an early comment that the ECJ had made only 'a rather modest contribution to the formation of Community policy',[74] the cases mentioned above illustrate that the ECJ has had a considerable role in the development of European integration. The Court's contextual, teleological interpretation of the treaty is clearly a long way from the formalism which some see as the proper role for the courts. For such commentators, the Court's creative contextual interpretation of the treaty is nothing less than judicial legislation in action.[75]

---

[72] Case 6/72 *Europemballage Corp and Continental Can Co Inc v Commission* [1973] ECR 215.

[73] Cases C-6/90 and C-9/90 *Francovich and Others v Italian State* [1991] ECR I-5357 at para 33.

[74] Scheingold, *The Rule of Law in European Integration* (Yale University Press, 1971) at 165. This was not the only early account to be sceptical of the effect of the ECJ. Other early accounts which down-played the role of the Court include J-P Colin, *Gouvernement des Juges dans les Communautés Européennes* (Librarie Général de Droit et de Jurisprudence Générale, 1966); P Hay, *Federalism and supranational organization : Patterns for new legal structures* (Urbana: University of Illinois Press, 1966); AW Green, *Political Integration by Jurisprudence* (Sitjhoff Leyden, 1969); also C Mann, *The Function of Judicial Decisions in European Economic Integration* (The Hague: Nijhoff, 1972). Much later in the 1990s, political scientists of the intergovernmental school were claiming that national governments were still dominating the integration process rather than courts: see e.g. Garrett, 'The Politics of Legal Integration in the EU' (1992) IO 171; also A Moravcsik, 'Preferences and Powers in the European Community: A Liberal Intergovernmentalist Approach' (1993) JCMS 31 at 473.

[75] Other critiques include, A O'Neill and J Coppel, *EC Law for UK Lawyers* (Butterworths, 1994) 21–24; Sir Patrick Neill, 'The European Court of Justice: A case study in Judicial activism' (House of Lords Select Committee on the European Communities, Minutes of Evidence 18th report (HL, 1994–5); I Ward, *A Critical Introduction to European Law* (Sweet and Maxwell, 1996) 64–77. The European Court has been defended in M Cappelletti, 'Is the European Court of Justice "Running Wild"?' (1987) 12 EL Rev 3; J Weiler, 'The Court of Justice on Trial' (1987) 24 CMLRev 555; T Tridimas, 'The Court of Justice and Judicial Activism' (1996) 21 EL Rev 187; A Arnull, 'The European Court and Judicial Objectivity: A Reply to Professor Hartley' (1996) 112 LQR 411; see also now A Arnull, *The European Union and its Court of Justice* (Oxford University Press, 1999).

In his 1986 book,[76] Hjalte Rasmussen accused the Court of engaging in 'a dangerous social evil', by usurping power by its political activism. He highlighted three sets of circumstances in which he thought 'adjudicative lawmaking' occurred. First, where legal provisions give a wide discretion, and, therefore, the Court's interpretation, however seemingly wide, still remains within the textual limits established by the wording of the text, even if inspired by the treaty's spirit of integration. Rasmussen found this sort of interpretation to be 'judicially perfectly justifiable'[77] but also (puzzlingly) an exercise in 'Community policy-making by judicial fiat'.[78] Second, where the treaty was silent, as in the case of supremacy and direct effect, he disapproved of the use of a purposive and contextual interpretation, whereby the Court elicited the concepts of direct effect and supremacy in *Van Gend* and *Costa*. Third, and most heinous for Rasmussen, was the Court's ability to reach a decision despite textual indications to the contrary. This he took to be an 'activism uncontrolled' giving the *Reyners* and *Defrenne II* cases as examples.[79] More recently, in a work published in 1998,[80] Rasmussen further accused the Court of 'federalising' the treaties in disrespect of the 'legal commands of the treaties' texts'.[81] He suggested that the Court was using the 'style and logic of legal argument' and 'the pervasive myth of judicial value neutrality' to 'mask' its policy making,[82] hardly the first time that this charge has been made of courts in action

Hartley is also a stern critic of the Court's 'judicial activism'.[83] For Hartley, a case such as *Chernobyl* involves a deliberate departure from the objective meaning of the treaty.[84] And such conduct, he says, matters, both morally, politically and constitutionally, because it involves a violation of the rule of law as well as an increase of the powers of the EC at the expense of the member states. Further, in response to the argument that EC law is broad and programmatic, Hartley claims that a gap does not exist to be filled merely because a topic is not covered. He is sceptical of the teleological method and reasoning based on supposed *effet utile*, whereby too much scope is left, he suggests, to purposes which the ECJ thinks the authorities **ought** to have had. Thus he is critical of Judge Mancini's claim[85] that 'the preference for Europe is determined by the genetic code transmitted to the Court by the founding fathers', a claim made by Mancini in response to accusations that the ECJ always opted for a 'European' solution.[86] Hartley dislikes the suggestion of the organic which this imparts to the treaty, which he prefers to describe as 'merely words on paper'.

---

[76] *On Law and Policy in the European Court of Justice* (Martinus Nijhoff, 1986).
[77] Op. cit. at 27
[78] Ibid.
[79] Ibid. at 30.
[80] *The European Court of Justice* (Copenhagen: GadJura, 1998).
[81] Op. cit. at 66.
[82] Ibid.
[83] TC Hartley, *Constitutional Problems of the European Union* (Hart Publishing, 1999) chaps 2 and 3.
[84] Hartley op. cit. chap. 2.
[85] Expressed in Mancini in *Democracy and Constitutionalism in the European Union*, at 44, as well as earlier published in a co-authored article with D Keeling, in 57 MLR (1994) 175.
[86] E.g. such as those asserted by the German Press in fn 3.

However, language, even legal language, is a cultural phenomenon, whose interpretation, and often meaning, will change as society evolves. There are few words whose meaning is written in stone. The European Convention on Human Rights has been described more than once by its court as a 'living instrument'.[87] Laurence Tribe suggested (at the outset of his – very long – book *American Constitutional Law*) that:

> How much can be gained by seeking *any* single, unitary theory for construing the Constitution is unclear ... For the Constitution is an historically discontinuous composition; it is the product, over time, of a series of not altogether coherent compromises; it mirrors no single vision or philosophy but reflects instead a set of sometimes reinforcing and sometimes conflicting ideals and notions.[88]

If texts are not to stultify and atrophy their interpretation will surely develop along with that of the society that created them. Thomas Jefferson suggested that if the US did not wish to be ruled by the commands of dead men, then the Constitution should expire naturally every nineteen years,[89] a suggestion which was, of course, never taken up.

A different criticism of the European Court is made by Aiden O'Neill.[90] He shares with Rasmussen the complaint that, while the ECJ started out its existence as a type of administrative court along the model of the French Conseil d'Etat, its history shows its development into a constitutional court along the model of the US Supreme Court, a development which O'Neill claims was not foreseen by the EC treaties, but one which was aided by the Court's expansive reading of Article 220 (formerly Article 164) as well as by its case by case developments based on purposive interpretation, and overuse of concepts such as the principle of effectiveness of EC law. In this way, he claims that the ECJ created a federal legal system not matched by a federal development at political level. And he finds no convincing justification for the Court's behaviour in so doing, rejecting accounts such as Mancini's reference to the constitutional traditions of member states, natural law or the European common legal heritage.[91]

O'Neill makes the particular criticism that the Court has used Article 220, which holds that 'The Court of Justice shall ensure that in the interpretation and application of this Treaty the law is observed' (a very vague and uncertain provision) in a substantive way, taking the expression 'the law' and ascribing to it some higher, unwritten principles in order to claim new grounds of jurisdiction, i.e. by incorporating references to fundamental rights. He likens this to the way the US Supreme Court introduced the notion of 'substantive due process' to the fourteenth

---

[87] E.g. *Tyrer v UK* 2 EHRR 1, where the Court of Human Rights stated at para 31: 'the Convention is a living instrument which ... must be interpreted in the light of present day conditions.'

[88] L Tribe, *American Constitutional Law* (New York: The Foundation Press, 1988).

[89] *The Political Writings of Thomas Jefferson* (eds) Joyce Appleby and Terence Ball (New York, USA: Cambridge University Press, 1999) at 121.

[90] A O'Neill, *Decisions of the European Court of Justice and their National Implications* (London: Butterworths, 1994).

[91] Hartley engages in a similar exercise of rejecting sources for expansionist judicial review, in Hartley op. cit. chap. 3.

Amendment:[92] an interpretation which gives a substantive interpretation to the term 'liberty' in the text which requires the States not to take 'life liberty or property without due process of law'. This reading of the fourteenth Amendment led Justice Holmes, who disapproved of his colleagues using it in this way, to state 'I cannot believe the 14th Amendment was intended to give carte blanche to embody our economic and moral beliefs in its prohibitions.'[93] O'Neill clearly has similar admonitions for the ECJ.

Another commentator, Martin Shapiro, from the other side of the Atlantic, is more sanguine in his discussion of the ECJ's evolution.[94] He finds it unsurprising that the founders of the ECSC and EEC should have been unworried about the prospect of judicial activism, as there had been little experience of it at the time. However, had the Court been designed by comparative constitutional lawyers, rather than international lawyers, they might have taken a warning from the use the US Supreme Court had made of the commerce clause in the constitution.[95]

ACCEPTABLE JUDICIAL ACTIVISM?

The Court has undoubtedly added flesh to the barish bones of the treaty. That much is undeniable. Sometimes it has not only added flesh but clothed it too, as in its expansive case law on equal treatment and pay, or on free movement of goods (perhaps only to unclothe them with the *Keck* decision later). This has often been so because of the inadequacy of the Community legislature which should have been filling out and furthering Community integration itself, but for various reasons was unable to. The ECJ thus continued the pace of European integration.

But litigation creates legal remedies which in turn create further litigants. Back in the 1970s, Judge Robert Lecourt introduced the theme of a 'people's court', an alleged concern for the protection of the weak by the ECJ.[96] Judge Mancini wrote, not intending to be merely rhetorical, 'what citizen of Europe had not been assisted in some way by rulings of the ECJ?'[97] (a glowing reference perhaps slightly marred by the discoveries of the political scientists, Gibson and Caldeira, who found neither a great awareness, nor great support, for the ECJ by the European peoples).[98]

---

[92] This doctrine was introduced into American Constitutional law by Justice Field's dissent in the *Slaughterhouse Cases* (1873) 16 Wall (83 US).

[93] Per Holmes J in *Baldwin* v *Missouri* 1930. It was Holmes who also famously stated, in his dissent in *Lochner* v *New York* (1905): 'The 14th Amendment does not enact Mr Herbert Spencer's Social Statistics.'

[94] M Shapiro, 'The European Court of Justice' in P Craig and G de Búrca (eds) *The Evolution of EU Law* (Oxford, 1999) 321.

[95] Shapiro continues, 'Having created a court because they [the member states] needed a device for resolving the division of powers boundary conflicts, they necessarily got one more major policy participant than they wanted.' Shapiro op. cit. at fn 94, 331.

[96] R Lecourt, *L'Europe des Juges* (Brussels: Bruylant, 1976).

[97] Mancini and Keeling, 'Language, Culture and Politics in the Life of the European Court of Justice' (1995) 1 Columbia Journal of European Law 397 at 412.

[98] Gibson and Caldeira, 'The European Court of Justice: A Question of Legitimacy' (1993) 14 Zeitschrift fur Rechtssoziologie 204–242. In all fairness it must also be said that Mancini lamented the injustice of the lack of access to justice of individual litigants under Articles 230 and 288.

But certainly, the Court's activism, if activism it is (and Dehousse, for example, prefers to describe it as a 'juridification' of the policy process)[99] has been beneficial to some individuals. The ECJ has many times insisted on the importance of 'individual rights', a theme discussed in more detail in other chapters, and in some sense it might be said that individuals have become the 'guardians'[100] of legal integration, because of the uses which they have been able to make of EC law in their national courts. Sometimes actions have been steered by interest groups which follow a determined litigation strategy, such as the Equal Opportunities Commission in the UK, which has handled many of the sex discrimination cases, a feature which explains why so many of the EC's equal treatment cases come as references from the British courts. Sometimes they are 'repeat players'[101] of a commercial sort, such as British Steel, BA and the French companies Leclerc and Denkavit.[102] Perhaps a problem is that a certain type of litigant – usually commercial, but sometimes interest groups – have made much use of EC law and this has sometimes 'skewed' the jurisprudence, producing a certain type of case law and remedy, often focused on the commercial arena.[103] The ECJ has not provided a 'comprehensive' system of remedies, but perhaps one thrown up by the accidents of litigation, especially as the ECJ does not yet have any system of docket control. There is thus a strong line of cases on sex discrimination, but none on race discrimination (an area only truly amenable to the political process since Article 13 was inserted by the Treaty of Amsterdam, and the race discrimination directive based on it), case law on abortion, but only as a commercial amenity, as a possible 'service' under Article 50 EC,[104] case law on human rights, but much of it deriving from an unlikely source of human rights, the Common Agricultural Policy.

Although Mancini is triumphant about the Court's protection of the individual, describing this case law as coinciding with 'the making of a constitution for Europe, its achievements patent to all',[105] others have not been so confident of the effects of the Court's creation. Dehousse gloomily concludes that the ECJ has contributed to the 'depoliticisation' of the political process.[106]

Judges are well aware of the dangers of usurping the political process. This is particularly so in the US, where the Supreme Court has the power to overturn both acts of Congress and the State legislatures, a power highlighted in the controversy of abortion following the Court's 1973 decision in *Roe* v *Wade*.[107] The power wielded

---

[99] R Dehousse, *The European Court of Justice* (Macmillan, 1998) chap. 4.

[100] See J Weiler, 'A Quiet Revolution – The European Court of Justice and its Interlocutors' (1994) 26 Comparative Political Studies at 520, for the use of this phrase.

[101] M Galanter, 'Why the "Haves" Come Out Ahead: speculations on the limits of legal change' (1974) Law and Society, 95–160.

[102] See the discussion of this in M Poiares Maduro, *We, the Court: the European Court of Justice and the European Economic Constitution* (Hart Publishing, 1998) chap. 1, 25–30 and chap. 3.

[103] See C Harlow and R Rawlings, *Pressure through Law* (New York: Routledge, 1992); and also R Rawlings, 'The Eurolaw Game: Deductions from a Saga' (1993) 20 Journal of Law and Society 309.

[104] See for example the *Grogan* case, discussed above.

[105] Mancini op. cit. p 2.

[106] Dehousse op. cit. at 115.

[107] A controversy which has never died down since. Justice Harry Blackmun, responsible for writing the *Roe* opinion, was pursued by hate mail long after the case itself. See e.g. L Tribe, *Abortion: The Clash of Absolutes* (New York: Norton, 1990).

by that Court in the exercise of its powers of judicial review has been subject to much commentary – especially in the light of what Bickel termed 'the counter-majoritarian difficulty'[108] – caused by the fact that judges are not usually elected and have no popular mandate for decisions which go against the will of the elected legislature.[109] However, the ECJ is also not without this power. Decisions such as *Kalanke*, in which the court held that positive discrimination was contrary to the equal treatment directive, threaten popular decisions taken about social practice by elected majorities. It was perhaps an awareness of this danger which caused the Court to limit its *Kalanke* holding in *Marschall* before the member states themselves took the initiative by inserting Article 141(4) in the Treaty of Amsterdam.[110] Judges have made public pronouncements about the dangers of going against popular opinion. In the European context, Judge Koopmans said that courts 'are not designed to be a reflex of a democratic society'.[111] A pronouncement uncannily similar to that of Justice Felix Frankfurter of the US who said that 'courts are not representative bodies. They are not designed to be a good reflex of the democratic society.'[112]

However, the perceived anti-democratic effects of judicial review in the ECJ are somewhat different from those produced in national courts, to the extent that, rather than going against the will of a majority, the ECJ is more likely to decide a case against the position taken by one member state, which will often itself be in a minority, or may not even represent the majority of its peoples. The questions of majorities and minorities in the EU are not straightforward. Thus the counter-majoritarian problem referred to by Bickel takes on a rather different form in the ECJ, leading to decisions which may benefit individuals, but not necessarily at the expense of an overall majority in the EU.

However, if individuals or companies had something to gain from the ECJ's 'progressive' jurisprudence the question still remains why other bodies should go along with it. Why should national courts or the member states for so long have tolerated the ECJ so quietly?

One theory (not incompatible with that which attributes the ECJ's success to the benefits gained by individuals) suggests that it was in the interest of at least some national courts to cooperate – and that they were in fact empowered themselves by so doing[113] – most frequently by the making of preliminary references to the

---

[108] A Bickel, *The Least Dangerous Branch* at 16.
[109] A problem which will surely surface in the UK with the recent coming into force of the Human Rights Act.
[110] Case C-450/93 *Kalanke* (1995) ECR I-3051; Case C-409/95 *Marschall* (1997) ECR I-6363. Article 141(4) reads as follows:

> With a view to ensuring full equality in practice between men and women in working life, the principle of equal treatment shall not prevent any member State from maintaining or adopting measures providing for specific advantages in order to make it easier for the under-represented sex to pursue a vocational activity or to prevent or compensate for disadvantages in professional careers.

[111] Quoted in Mancini op. cit. chap. 1.
[112] *Dennis* v *United States* 341 US 525 (1951).
[113] For an expression of this theory see K Alter, 'The European Court's Political Power' (1996) 19 West European Politics 458; J Weiler, 'A Quiet Revolution' (1994) 26 Comparative Political Studies at 520;

European Court under Article 234, which enabled them to assert themselves against the will of higher domestic courts. This thesis will be explored more thoroughly in the next chapter on preliminary references, but suffice it to say that it is not unproblematic. The theories of individual empowerment and court empowerment are aspects of latter day neo-functionalist theories of integration,[114] which do not provide completely satisfactory answers to the question of why the Court's expansionist jurisprudence should have been for the larger part unresisted.

Perhaps most difficult to explain is the issue of political compliance, what Dehousse calls the 'paradox of compliance'.[115] Why should neither the member states nor the political institutions of the Community raise objections to an ECJ jurisprudence which might result in an encroachment of their powers? One answer might be that, in all of this, the member states of the EU still possessed a lot of control over the decision-making process,[116] certainly until quite recently, through the processes of comitology, unanimity for treaty amendments and the prominence of the European Council in shaping the future of European integration. It has also been the case that some of the Court's more far-reaching decisions have initially been of too low a visibility to create an immediate practical effect or to serve as a target for the media or any popular dialogue. There have been exceptions. Both in France and Germany, public officials have been told on occasion not to apply certain decisions of the ECJ. For example, the ECJ's *Euratom Opinion 1/78*, in which it held that the principle of a single common market applied within the context of the Euratom, as well as the EEC treaty, caused the reaction of the tabling of the *Foyer-Debré Proposition de Loi*[117] in the French *Assemblée Nationale*. This purported to nullify the Court's Euratom opinion, holding that the European Court had no jurisdiction to make rulings on matters of French nuclear concern. In this it resembled some of the declarations on States' Rights made against the opinions of the US Supreme Court, in the early years of its history. What is particularly fascinating is that the proposal proved very popular and was only defeated by government intervention.

Another explanation for general compliance with the Court might be that States have an interest in ensuring that other members of the EC respect the rules: in the

---

A-M Slaughter and W Mattli, 'Europe Before the Court: A Political Theory of Legal Integration' (1993) 47 International Organization 41–76; J Plotner, 'Report on France' in A-M Slaughter, Sweet and J Weiler (eds) *The European Courts and National Courts* (Hart Publishing, 1998); such a theory is contested however by J Golub in 'The Politics of Judicial Discretion: Rethinking the interaction between national courts and the ECJ', (1996) 2 West European Politics 360.

[114] E.g. such as those of Slaughter and Mattli, expressed in 'Europe Before the Court'.

[115] Dehousse, op. cit. chap. 5.

[116] Explored in J Weiler, 'The Transformation of Europe' (1991) 100 Yale LJ 2403.

[117] Tabled in the French Assemblée Nationale, No. 917 of 17 February 1979, named after its draftsmen, Jean Foyer and Michel Debré. One clause states: 'Cette prétendue juridiction en est, hélas! Coutumière s'attachant par une interprétation extensive et déformante des traités à faire entrer dans les fait l'idéologie fédéralisante et supranationale dont plusiers de ses membres sont animées.' So strongly did the draftsmen feel that the proposal went so far as to make it a criminal offence (a 'crime de forfaiture') for anyone holding public office in France to follow the Court's *Opinion 1/78*. Rasmussen notes that this is similar to the post-Vichy legislation which classified collaboration with the German occupation in a similar way (Rasmussen op. cit. at 352).

event of conflict it is necessary to have an impartial enforcer.[118] It was the UK – never usually a state at the vanguard of European integration – which was particularly insistent on the need to introduce a power of sanctions for the ECJ under Article 228 at Maastricht. The need for such enforcement has, of course, not stopped governments from turning against the Court when the mood so took them – the paper prepared on the ECJ under the Conservative administration in 1996 took particular issue with the ECJ's (then recent) rulings on state liability in *Factortame III* – the UK government wished to set a three-year limitation period on the bringing of such actions against the state in the national courts.[119]

It might also be argued that Community institutions did not always have the incentive to go along with the ECJ, but this is questionable. The Commission seems to have been on the whole a powerful ally of the Court from its early days.[120] Further, the Commission has also been careful in the choice of enforcement actions which it has brought before the Court under Article 226, generally eschewing those where there would be little chance of that state's compliance in the event of a judgment against it, thus bolstering the Court's authority.[121] Most of the Court's more contentious judgments have been at the expense of the member states, rather than Community institutions:[122] it has been rare for the Court to have found the Community to be acting in excess of its powers, or to have breached fundamental rights, for example.[123] The Parliament has positively benefited from the Court's jurisprudence on its standing rights. However, within the last decade there have been more general signs of a lesser willingness to tolerate the Court. These are dealt with later in the chapter.

THE IMPORTANCE OF LEGAL REASONING

There may also be another less practical reason why supposedly 'activist' decisions have been met with acceptance, the prevalence of a certain model of legal reasoning, based on a model of formal reasoning and neutrality. Montesquieu described the judge as 'un être inanimé',[124] a being which could only find the law but not create it.

---

[118] For a discussion of this, see Dehousse, op. cit. chap. 5; and Gibson and Caldeira, 'The Legitimacy of Transnational Legal Institutions: Compliance, Support and the European Court of Justice' (1995) 39 American Journal of Political Science 459; M Shapiro, 'The European Court of Justice' in P Craig and G de Búrca (eds) *The Evolution of EU Law*; see also F Scharpf, 'The Joint Decision Making Trap' (1988) 66 Public Administration 239.

[119] UK memorandum to the IGC on the ECJ, July 1996. For a game theory analysis, see Garrett, 'International Co-operation and Institutional Choice' (1992) 46 International Organization 533.

[120] E Stein, 'Lawyers, Judges and the Making of a Transnational Constitution' (1981) 75 American Journal of International Law.

[121] An exception being the second action brought by Cases 24, 97/80R *Commission v France* [1980] ECR 1319, in the context of the notorious 'sheepmeat' regime. See Chapter 12 for a discussion of this case.

[122] One is reminded of another famous saying of Oliver Wendel Holmes: 'I do not think the United States would come to an end if the Supreme Court lost its power to declare an act of Congress void but the Union would be imperilled if the courts could not make that declaration as to the laws of the several states'. OW Holmes, *Law and the Court Collected Legal Papers* (New York: Peter Smith, 1952) at 295.

[123] See Chapter 13.

[124] Montesquieu, *Spirit of the Laws* (Cambridge: Cambridge University Press, 1989) xi, chap. 6.

Combine this with the prevalence of formalism in the nineteenth century (of which the Langdellian orthodoxy that law exists in a remote, abstract world, is a good example)[125] and we have a vision of surprising adhesiveness. In such a vision, judges are seen to be 'doing' law rather than politics. Such a perception of legal reasoning legitimises the work of the courts, which are seen to be adhering to the rule of law. Such an approach is far too simplistic and was already seen as unrealistic in the early nineteenth century: John Austin, a legal positivist but not a formalist,[126] dismissed Montesquieu's view as 'a childish fiction'. Indeed, such formalism seems impossible to apply in the case of EC law, in which such widely drafted, open textured provisions leave much scope for judicial discretion at the very least. However, we should not, as Weiler reminds us,[127] underestimate the compliance pull of the ECJ's jurisprudence based on the formalist approach to law and legal reasoning taken by many still.

Indeed, this doctrinal pull exerted a seemingly strong influence over the academic community's vision of the ECJ until fairly recently, a body of work which the American Martin Shapiro described as 'constitutional law without politics'.[128] However, this abstract formal vision of law is easy to attack and, of course, has been so from many fronts. Political scientists and critical legal scholars have pointed out how a formalistic view of law may be used to 'mask' a political agenda followed by the courts.[129] Law really cannot be a merely formalist exercise, partly because in so many cases it will be impossible to reach a definitive answer merely by the exercise of purely deductive reasoning. European cases are, no less than cases in other jurisdictions, often 'hard cases' – they throw up more than one possible right answer – *pace* Dworkin.[130] As a pillar of the English legal community, Lord Reid, stated, 'in many cases it cannot be said positively that one construction is right and another is wrong...much may depend on one's approach.'[131] Where the law is indeterminate, it will be necessary to make some sort of choice, to exercise discretion in determining which result to take,[132] a second order justification. Very often these types of justification will involve extra-legal considerations. However, it is true that the ECJ will, even in this type of case, often present its decision as simply logical conclusions to certain premises. The *Dassonville* case again provides us with an example – no

---

[125] See the works of Christopher Columbus Langdell, dean of Harvard Law School. The most coherent explanation of Langdell's theory is in his 'Harvard Celebration Speeches' at 3 LQR (1887) 123.

[126] Austin in fact thought that, where necessary, judges should be courageous in their law-making: see Hart, 'Positivism and the Separation of Law and Morals' in HLA Hart, *Essays in Jurisprudence and Philosophy* (Oxford: Clarendon, 1983) at 49.

[127] J Weiler, 'A Quiet Revolution' at 526.

[128] M Shapiro, 'The European Court of Justice' in A Sbragia (ed.) *Euro Politics: Institutions and Policymaking in the New European Community* (Washington DC: The Brookings Institution, 1992) at 143.

[129] E.g. by Burley and Mattli in 'Europe Before the Court'. Rasmussen also makes this point – accusing the Court of 'masking' the political agenda of pursuing integration in *On Law and Policy in the European Court of Justice*.

[130] The 'one right answer' thesis is explored by Dworkin in e.g. *Taking Rights Seriously* (Duckworth, 1977) at 63–65.

[131] *James v Secretary of State* [1972] 1 All ER 175.

[132] See MacCormick, *Legal Reasoning and Legal Theory* (Oxford: Clarendon Press, 1978) at 68.

background justification, no line of reasoning, legal or other is given as to why this particular definition of a measure having equivalent effect to a quantitative restriction is here selected by the Court, any more than the Court sets out its background reasoning to the finding of abortion to be a service in *Grogan*. Cass Sunstein suggests that we need not have full reasoning nor articulation in order to provide the conditions of legitimate adjudication.[133] However, failing to do so sometimes just seems inadequate. Cappelletti's comments on this seem at the very least more honest:

> The profession of the judge requires evaluation and balancing; it means giving consideration to the choice's practical and moral results; and it means employment of not only the arguments of abstract logic, but those of economics and politics, ethics, sociology and psychology. Thus, the judge can no longer hide so easily behind the shield of the law as a clear predetermined, objective norm on which to base his 'neutral' decision.[134]

Law is not neutral. Any court, not just the ECJ, must be involved in controversial decisions, where there is no clear answer, and thus some sort of 'political' decision seems to be taken by the Court. So much of law is indeterminate or incomplete,[135] or even contradictory. The ECJ is no exception to a rhetoric of coherence covering a different, more clouded ideology.[136] Jerome Frank's account, given in the 1930s, is typical, 'At times, indeed [the denial of the fact of judge-made law] seems to resemble an outright benevolent lie, a professional falsehood designed actually to deceive the laity for their own good.'[137]

Perhaps the real complaint is not that the ECJ engages in judicial activism but that it fails to express the sources and grounds of its activism.

THE RETREAT FROM ACTIVISM

Whatever the substance of the charges of activism, it seems that, as the last decade of the last century progressed, the ECJ became more prone to 'self-restraint'. Various examples of this may be cited. The *Keck* decision of 1993 is one, whereby the Court held that, contrary to what had previously been decided, certain types of trading rules would not fall within the ambit of Article 28, thus considerably narrowing the scope of the law in that area,[138] leaving a greater amount of national economic regulation untouched by EC law. In the *Dori* case, contrary to much

---

[133] CR Sunstein, *Legal Reasoning and Political Conflict* (Oxford: OUP, 1996).

[134] M Cappelletti, 'The Law Making Power of the Judge and its Limits: A Comparative Study', (1981) 8 Monash LR 21–22.

[135] See e.g. D Kennedy, 'Form and Substance in Private Law Adjudication' (1976) 89 Harvard Law Review 1685; R Unger, *The Critical Legal Studies Movement* (Harvard University Press, 1983).

[136] See for example the Court's use of a fundamental rights jurisprudence, discussed in Chapter 13.

[137] Frank, *Law and the Modern Mind* (New York: Brentano's, 1930) at 44.

[138] While nonetheless managing to leave it rather uncertain. For criticism of *Keck*, which sees it as retreating from free movement principles: e.g. D Chalmers, 'Repackaging the Internal Market – the

academic urging and urging from some of its own members,[139] the Court refused to extend horizontal direct effect to directives, probably prompted partly by a fear of overreaction from the national courts if it had done so.[140] In its two opinions of 1994 the Court also gave a conservative interpretation of the Community's competences. In *Opinion 1/94* on the WTO, it held that the EC had no exclusive competence in the field of services or intellectual property, either under the common commercial policy or under implied external competences (a contrast with its earlier *ERTA* opinion on the Community's external competence). In *Opinion 2/94* it held that the EC had no jurisdiction to accede to the European Convention on Human Rights as matters currently stood – Article 308 (formerly 235) was insufficient for such a purpose.[141]

Combined with statements made by certain members of the Court, this does give an impression of a greater self-restraint by the ECJ. For example, President of the ECJ, Judge Rodriguez Iglesias, stated in 1996 that the ECJ should act rather as a guardian of the Constitution than as a motor of integration.[142] Mancini also referred to the Court's 'retreat from activism', and described the Court as becoming 'increasingly revisionist in the 1990s'. It has been suggested that this perceived conservatism on the part of the Court might have been prompted by an 'assault on the *acquis communautaire*',[143] or by the threat of political overruling which came with the Maastricht Treaty. For, although Maastricht pushed forward the path of European integration, it constrained the jurisdiction of the Court in some ways. It excluded both the second and third pillars (the Common Foreign and Security Policy and Justice and Home Affairs) from the jurisdiction of the Court for the most part,[144] and appended protocols to deal with the effects of certain judgments of the Court, i.e. the *Barber* judgment, *Grogan* and the provision on Danish second homes.[145] This was hardly the 'benign neglect' previously referred to by Stein.

Although the Treaty of Amsterdam further changed the position somewhat, this was perhaps not always in the Court's favour. Article 141(4) was introduced to overturn the Court's *Kalanke* decision.

Since the Treaty of Amsterdam, the limits to the ECJ's jurisdiction have grown increasingly complex. Although Amsterdam shifted to the EC pillar certain matters concerning justice and home affairs, Article 68 EC limits the EC's jurisdiction in

---

Ramifications of the *Keck* Judgement' (1994) 19 ELR 385; N Reich, 'The "November Revolution" of the European Court of Justice' (1994) 31 CMLR 861.

[139] i.e. Advocate General van Gerven in case C-271/91 *Marshall v Southampton and South West Hampshire Area Health Authority (Marshall II)* ECR 1993; AG Jacobs in Case 316/93 *Vaneetveld* [1994] ECR I-763; AG Lenz in *Dori* itself – Case C-91/92 *Dori v Recreb Srl* [1994] ECR I-3325 at para 43 *et seq.*

[140] See the discussion in Chapter 8.

[141] *Opinion 1/94* [1994] ECR I-5267; *Opinion 2/94* [1996] ECR I-1759.

[142] In a lecture given at the EUI in 1996, published as a Jean Monnet lecture.

[143] Mancini op. cit. at 188.

[144] Article L TEU, subsequently amended by the Treaty of Amsterdam.

[145] Case C-262/88 *Barber v Guardian Royal Exchange* [1990] ECR I-1889; Case C-159/90 *SPUC v Grogan* [1991] ECR I4685; Treaty on European Union Protocol (No 1) on the acquisition of property in Denmark (Official Journal C 191, 29/07/1992 p. 0068).

these matters to references made by national courts of final resort. Furthermore, in what remains of the third pillar, now dealing with Police and Judicial Cooperation in Criminal matters, the ECJ will only have jurisdiction if member states sign up to this. Perhaps even more threatening is the greater use being made of the concept of 'flexibility'[146] (usually meaning enhanced, or closer cooperation), so far rather nebulous and not closely defined. But this closer cooperation involves derogation from the usual pattern of unity and uniformity in EC law, which the Court has been so eager to preserve over the ages,[147] most particularly in the context of references under Article 234. There are also a fair amount of opt-in procedures. An increase in the variable geometry of European integration, although not a new addition by Amsterdam, constrains the operations of the ECJ. This process continued with the IGC of 2000. All in all, this would seem to lead to a fragmentation of the Community, a feature in tune with twenty-first century talk of 'multilevel constitutionalism.'[148] It raises particular problems, such as the meaning of European citizenship in such a context and the issue of how the rule of law, if we wish to use such a term, might operate in such a varied polity.

These changes wrought by recent treaty amendments could be seen as an attempt to assert more control over the judicial branch, even to achieve 'a kind of revenge,'[149] or, if not revenge, then at least a 'more matured and structured role for the Court' in which it will not have 'the freedom of its glory days to interpret EC law into new dimensions, but a different kind of freedom to act within clearer and more obvious confines...'[150] In any case, it seems that the ECJ will no longer have the interpretative autonomy which it has so long possessed in the history of the EC and so jealously guarded.

But if the ECJ's interpretative autonomy is threatened, this is only part of the larger issue of the diffuse nature of the EU generally, which has led Weiler to categorise it as 'feeling the angst of post-modernity – a giant and fragmented at the same time.'[151] EU law adds to the fragmentation of national law, by limiting its sovereignty and coherence, depriving it of the ability to act as the sole sovereign authority within that territory. Mancini links the Court's lack of activism to cultural features, stating that it is 'to do with the decay, stretching well beyond the Community's experience, of idealistic thinking...'[152] Koopmans relates it to a 'loss

---

[146] e.g. General provisions under Title VII TEU (Articles 43–45) and more specific provisions under Article 11 EC and Article 40 TEU. See Chapter 4 for a discussion of these provisions.

[147] See C Lyons, 'Flexibility and the European Court of Justice' in de Búrca and Scott (eds) *Constitutional Change in the EU* (Hart Publishing, 2000); G Gaja, 'How Flexible is Flexibility under the Amsterdam Treaty?' (1998) 35 CMLR 855.

[148] For discussions of differentiated constitutionalism see, e.g., N Walker, 'Sovereignty and differentiated Integration in the EU' (1998) 4 ELJ; Lindahl and Roermund, 'Law without a State?' in Bankowski and Scott (eds) *The European Union and Legal Theory* (Blackwell, 2000). See also the discussion in Chapter 4 and on a European Constitution in the last chapter of this book.

[149] Lyons op. cit. at 108–109.

[150] Ibid.

[151] J Weiler, 'The European Courts of Justice: Beyond "Beyond Doctrine" or the Legitimacy Crisis of European Constitutionalism' in Slaughter, Sweet and Weiler (eds) *The European Court and National Courts* 370.

[152] Mancini op. cit. 187.

of legal optimism'.[153] Perhaps the Court did for too long enjoy too much of a sense of judicial security, nourished by what Rasmussen referred to as 'the existence of the undeniable close ideological kinship between the pro-Community value preferences of the leading academics and those of the Brethren.'[154] This is certainly no longer the case.[155]

Mancini concludes his discussion of the retreat from activism with a famous quote from Alexander Hamilton: 'The judiciary is beyond comparison the weakest of the three departments of power': a quote which apparently so impressed Alexander Bickel that he used an extract as the title of his book on the nature of judicial review, *The Least Dangerous Branch*, as well as prefacing the book with a large section of the quote. But we should not get too carried away: nearly two hundred years later, with the benefit of hindsight, John Hart Ely replied so to Hamilton:

> The Court may be purseless and swordless, but its ability importantly to influence the way the nation has functioned has proved great... It may be true that the Court cannot *permanently* thwart the will of a solid majority, but it can certainly delay its implementation for decades – workmen's compensation, child labor and unionization...and to the people affected that is likely to be forever.[156]

We should also not forget that the same ECJ of the 1990s which was accused of a retreat from activism also produced *Francovich* and *Factortame*, which surely took the purview of EC law, and especially its so-called effective protection of individual rights, much further, so much so that the UK government prepared a memorandum to deal with this topic. Indeed, some of the ECJ's case law on remedies looks forward to a unified, common European system, a provocative notion.[157] Has there really been such a loss of legal optimism recently? Even *Keck* cannot be dismissed as a retreat, given that, as Shapiro comments, 'Once the dragon of open protectionism and discrimination was slain...the ECJ could not go on slaying it over and over again.'[158] The Court is not so much in retreat as complexly motivated. There may be scepticism about European integration in some quarters, distrust of the euro, but the judiciary is not necessarily at its source. Brussels is usually the main target and there has been a *fin de siècle* mistrust of politicians, combined with disappointment, after the heady days of the revolutions of 1989 and 1990 in central, eastern Europe and the former Soviet bloc. As Ely again reminds us in the American context, 'throughout its history the Court has been told it had better stick to its knitting or risk destruction',[159] but this has not materialised. Indeed 'judicial emasculation by way of popular reaction against constitutional review by the courts has not

---

[153] T Koopmans, 'The Role of Law in the Next Stage of European Integration' (1986) 35 International and Comparative Law Quarterly 925 at 928.

[154] Rasmussen, *On Law and Policy in the European Court of Justice* at 266. Little criticism of the Court was to be found in the European law periodicals until recently.

[155] See the articles critical of the Court listed under fn 75.

[156] JH Ely, *Democracy and Distrust: A Theory of Judicial Review* (Harvard University Press, 1980) at 45.

[157] See the discussion in Chapter 9 on remedies.

[158] Shapiro, op. cit. at 341.

[159] Ely op. cit. fn 156 at p. 47.

in fact materialised in more than a century and a half of American experience'.[160] And it is unlikely to do so in the European context.

PRESSING PROBLEMS

Perhaps the most pressing challenges currently facing the European Court, however, are those of a logistical and structural kind, rather than a challenge from the member states or any post-modern angst.

Over the past decade or so, the workload of the ECJ and CFI has been rising at an alarming rate and poses threats to the question of access to justice. Of course, this rise in litigation mirrors the trend in domestic courts generally in the late twentieth century,[161] but has taken an extreme form in the case of Luxembourg, especially in the CFI, set up in 1988 to deal with the particular problem of court overloading. Many reports and commentaries have been written on this problem,[162] suggesting a variety of measures which might be taken to ease the burden on the Community courts, particularly given the ever increasing stream of preliminary rulings and also the prospect of the accession of new member states early this century bringing with them a string of new litigation.

The following types of suggestion have been made in the reports and commentaries. First, that the amount of preliminary rulings be reduced by giving greater responsibility to the national courts. The recommendation was also made that the CFI be given general jurisdiction for direct actions (although cases of 'quasi-constitutional' significance could be left to the ECJ) and that there be an increase in members of the CFI, which tends to have more time-consuming issues of fact to deal with, as well as a system of filtering of appeals from the CFI so that a smaller percentage of cases go on appeal. Another suggestion is that there be set up tribunals of special jurisdiction to take the burden off the Community courts in certain types of cases, such as staff cases, IP, competition and public international law. The ECJ itself suggested that the procedure for amendment of the Court's rules of procedure be amended so that unanimity in the Council no longer be required.

Some of these suggestions were incorporated into the Treaty of Nice. The treaty has given the CFI jurisdiction to hear and determine questions referred for a preliminary reference in certain specified areas, which are to be determined in the Court's Statute at a later date[163] (probably areas in which the CFI already has first instance appellate jurisdiction). Although the suggestion to create specific judicial

---

[160] E Rostow, *The Sovereign Prerogative* (New Haven: Yale University Press, 1962) 165.

[161] e.g. as were pursued in Lord Justice Woolf's enquiries in his paper *Access to Justice* (London: Lord Chancellor's Department, 1996).

[162] One of the earlier ones was produced by Spinelli, who proposed the ECJ as an appellate court in the draft for the new European treaty. Also relevant are: *Report by the Study Group on the Future of the EC judicial System (Due report)* (European Commission, 2000); *Commission contribution on reform of the Community Courts* (IP/00/213); *Contribution of the ECJ and CFI to the IGC* (IGC document CONFER/VAR/3694/0); Presidency report to Feira Council June 2000 chap. 5.

[163] Under Article 225(3) EC, as amended by Nice.

panels was not immediately taken up, enabling clauses, inserted by a new Article 225a, allow the Council to create such panels in specific areas. The 'Declaration to the Final act of the Nice Treaty' also calls on the ECJ and Commission to prepare a draft decision establishing judicial panels for staff cases as soon as possible. Additionally, there has been a rationalisation by the treaty of the provisions relevant to the Courts, which were previously to be found in the treaty, the three Statutes on the Court, the Rules of Procedure, and the 1988 Council decision establishing the Court of First Instance. Article 245 EC, as amended by Nice, and the new Statute of the ECJ, now give the Council the power to amend all provisions (except Article 1) of the Court's Rules of Procedure by a QMV in the Council. This should achieve much greater flexibility and clarity. Finally, the European Parliament has at last been given full rights of standing under Article 230 EC to put it on a par with the Council and Commission.

It is still unclear how the Luxembourg courts will shape up to these challenges in the twenty-first century, especially given the prospect of a much larger EU. How would the Court function with a greater number of judges and languages? Would it not metamorphose from something resembling a court to an assembly? If not, how to preserve the coherence of a great variety of judgments given in chambers? These challenges remain to be dealt with, and no doubt the way in which this is done will have a significant impact on European integration.

6

PRELIMINARY REFERENCES UNDER ARTICLE 234: COOPERATIVE PARTNERSHIP OR PROTO-FEDERALISM?

To give an account of the European courts in Luxembourg is to give only half of the picture. The relationship between those courts and the domestic courts of member states is crucial, not least because, without references made to Luxembourg from those courts, the ECJ would lose up to two-thirds of its case law[1] and the opportunity to give rulings on such fundamental constitutional concepts as the supremacy and direct effect of Community law, and its decisive holdings on substantive EC law; there is scarcely a topic which has not been determined by some reference from the national courts.

Hence it is not surprising to find the procedure under Article 234 (formerly and more familiarly Article 177) described as 'most fundamental' and 'intriguing'[2] as well as being described as the 'keystone' to the 'twin pillars' (of direct effect and supremacy) of the Community legal order.[3]

And yet, the grand architectural metaphors cannot obscure the fact that, at the same time, the procedure under Article 234 is just that, a procedure. But it is one which has been fundamental to the development of EC law, most particularly in the following ways. It has constitutional significance, in that it has, as already mentioned, played its part in the conceiving of the founding principles of EC law.[4] It has also enabled the ECJ to ensure the uniformity and effectiveness of EC law, fundamental in the construction of a new legal order. Supremacy of EC law had been established in *Costa* v *Enel*, but this doctrine alone could not ensure uniformity of interpretation. Issues of EC law could be litigated in domestic courts, and so one national court might interpret

---

[1] Figures taken from Internal Statistics of the ECJ.

[2] D Anderson, *References to the European Court* (Sweet and Maxwell, 1995) at ix.

[3] See F Mancini and D Keeling, 'From CILFIT to ERT: the Constitutional Challenge Facing the European Court' (1991) 11 YEL 2–3.

[4] Namely, *Van Gend en Loos, Costa* v *Enel; Internationale Handelsgesellschaft.*

Article 28, for example, in one way, while another might give it a different interpretation, which would bring about disunity. In another context, the following has been written: '...to subject the highest courts of a State to the authority of the US Supreme Court would deny the State's ultimate sovereignty and incidentally offend proud and sensitive State judges, who gave their primary loyalty to their States and felt at least equal in importance and dignity to the justices in Washington.'[5] The ECJ faced the same problems in its relations with national courts. It did not wish conflicting national interpretations to threaten the uniformity of EC law. On the other hand, it had to be careful in its relations with the higher national courts, for example the Conseil d'Etat and the German Bundesfinanzhof, both as proud and recalcitrant in their rejection of the direct effect of directives as any American state court judges had been of the US Supreme Court's assertion of its authority in the early years of the USA. As it has developed, the preliminary reference procedure has something of the federal to it, in the part which it has played in demarcating the relationship between the national courts and the ECJ, developing a constitutional hierarchy.[6] But its impact has not only been constitutional: as so many cases come to Luxembourg in this way, the ECJ has been able to develop EC substantive law through this medium, deciding key cases on free movement of goods, persons and sex discrimination law.[7]

Nor has it only been a tool for the European Court to use in the furtherance of integration, of the 'certain idée de L'Europe', if one so wishes. It has also been widely used by litigants, who have identified a whole new spectrum of remedies, directly effective and available to them in their national courts under EC law. Indeed, it is the only means by which private parties can challenge national acts which appear to be in breach of EC law, as they cannot challenge national law directly in Luxembourg. But these litigants had to persuade the national courts to use Article 234. And, on the whole, national judges have not been reluctant to do so, working in partnership with the ECJ and perhaps even seeing EC law as a source of empowerment, a role which will be explored later in the chapter. This in turn, has taken the burden off the Commission and Article 226 as a means of ensuring compliance with EC law. In fact, the history of Article 234 provides us with nothing less than a 'record of European integration'.[8]

THE PROCEDURE UNDER ARTICLE 234

Article 234 reads as follows:

The Court of Justice shall have jurisdiction to give preliminary rulings concerning:

(a) the interpretation of the Treaty;

---

[5] A Cox, *The Court and the Constitution* (Houghton Mifflin, 1987) at 63.
[6] The American writer Buxbaum in 1969 described it as a 'federalizing device': R Buxbaum, 'Article 177 of the Rome Treaty as a federalizing Device' (1969) Stanford Law Review 104.
[7] E.g. *Case 120178 Rewe-Zentral AG ('cassis de Dijon')* [1979] ECR 649; Case 53181 *Levin* [1982] ECR 1035; Case 43175 Defrenne v SABENA [1976] ECR 455.
[8] See T de la Mare, 'Article 177 in Social and Political Context' in Craig and de Búrca (ed.) *The Evolution of EU Law* (Oxford, 1998).

(b) the validity and interpretation of acts of the institutions of the Community and of the ECB;

(c) the interpretation of the statutes of bodies established by an act of the Council, where those statutes so provide.

Where such a question is raised before any court or tribunal of a Member State, that court or tribunal may, if it considers that a decision on the question is necessary to enable it to give judgement, request the Court of Justice to give a ruling thereon.

Where any such question is raised in a case pending before a court or tribunal of a Member State, against whose decision there is no judicial remedy under national law, that court or tribunal shall bring the matter before the Court of Justice.

Applications are currently made only to the ECJ, although the Treaty of Nice amended Article 225 to make it possible for certain types of preliminary rulings to be transferred to the CFI.[9] It is the national court, and not the parties, which decides if to make a reference, thus distinguishing it from any kind of appeal procedure. Proceedings are stayed in the national courts until the ECJ gives its ruling which, given current delays, may take some time. The national court must then, on receipt of the ruling, apply it.

The subject matter of the reference

In this context, as elsewhere, the ECJ has not felt the need to stick too closely to the literal wording of the text. It has rather given wide scope to its interpretative power under Article 234, considering anything which forms part of the EC legal order, even if not a treaty provision, nor secondary legislation. Thus, it has held the GATT (now WTO) to fall within its interpretative scope. In *SPI*[10] it held that, although the GATT had been concluded by the member states separately rather than by the EC, and thus could not be considered strictly speaking to be the 'act' of a Community institution, the EC had succeeded to such an international agreement, and therefore the ECJ had the jurisdiction to give a preliminary ruling on its interpretation so as to ensure the uniform interpretation of Community law. This is a good example of the Court's teleological interpretation, justifying its jurisdiction by simply referring to the aim of that jurisdiction: 'to ensure the uniform interpretation of Community law'.[11] Such conduct might be criticised as going beyond what is permitted by the wording of Article 234, and so Hartley, for example, accuses the Court of basing its arguments on the different and (for Hartley) irrelevant point that it is **desirable** that the GATT be covered, otherwise national courts will have the last word.[12]

---

[9] Article 225(3) as amended by the Treaty of Nice reads: 'The Court of First Instance shall have jurisdiction to hear and determine questions referred for a preliminary ruling under Article 234 in specific areas laid down by the Statute.'

[10] Joined cases 267–269/81 *Amministrazione delle Finanze dello Stato v SPI and SAMI* [1983] ECR 801 at 828.

[11] Ibid. at para 15.

[12] T Hartley, *Constitutional problems of the European Union* (Hart Publishing, 1999) chap. 2.

Likewise, the ECJ has held that association agreements with third countries are also covered by the preliminary reference procedure.[13] Indeed, the Court also found that decisions of the body established by the agreement and entrusted with responsibility for its implementation may also be referred.[14] More recently, the ECJ has even held that acts of purely domestic law may be referred if they are based on EC law, again supposedly in the interests of uniformity and consistency, although the matter may be purely internal, such as a national tax law which replicates provisions of an EC tax directive.[15] The ECJ has also been willing to interpret acts which are not legislative in nature at all – such as general principles of law – these were the subject of the reference in *Internationale Handelsgesellschaft*, and are clearly neither treaty provisions nor acts of Community institutions, since they derive from the legal systems of the member states. Nonetheless, the Court has integrated them into the reference procedure.

Interpretation not application

The ECJ's official role under Article 234 is to interpret, rather than to apply national law. This is required by the separate roles and functions of the ECJ and national courts (traditionally thought of as 'separate but equal') under Article 234. However, there is a thin, and apparently moveable, line between these two concepts, or what has been described as a 'formalist fiction.'[16] In some cases, the ECJ sticks to interpretation, giving merely a general statement of a provision's meaning, leaving it to the national courts to apply – as it did in the earlier Sunday trading cases – so in the *Torfaen* case it stated that 'Article 30 of the Treaty must be interpreted as meaning that the prohibition that it lays down does not apply to national rules prohibiting retailers from opening their premises on Sunday where the restrictive effects on Community trade which may result therefrom do not exceed the effect intrinsic to rules of that kind.'[17] This provides an excellent example of the Court's scantiness of reasoning, a feature remarked on elsewhere.[18] This terse statement was hardly the easiest of rulings to apply, and indeed, national courts had great difficulty in applying it, determining whether or not the proportionality criterion (hardly one with which the lower English courts were familiar) had been met. Some found that it was and others not, scarcely promoting the uniformity of Community (nor indeed, national) law. So in *Stoke CC*, where the same issue arose, the ECJ gave a much clearer ruling: 'Article 30 of the Treaty is to be interpreted as meaning that the

---

[13] Case 181/73 *Haegemann v Belgium* [1974] ECR 449.

[14] Case C-192/89 *Sevince* [1990] ECR I-3461.

[15] The so-called '*Dzodzi*' line of cases, named after Cases C-297/88 and C-197/88 *Dzodzi* [1990] ECR I-3763. These are discussed in more detail later in the chapter.

[16] J Cohen, 'The European Preliminary Reference and the US Review of State Court Judgements: A Study in Comparative Federalism' (1996) 44 AM J Comp L 421.

[17] Case 145/88 *Torfaen BC v B&Q plc* [1989] ECR 3851 at para 17.

[18] In chapter 5 on the European Courts. Preliminary rulings are quite typically scant in their reasoning in the operative part. Perhaps because scant reasons offer less opportunity for criticism and more flexibility for future judgments?

prohibition which it lays down does not apply to national legislation prohibiting retailers from opening their premises on Sundays.'[19] This latter is application rather than interpretation,[20] giving credence to the words of Roscoe Pound: 'It is as clear as legal history can make it that interpretation apart from judicial application is impractical, that it is futile to attempt to separate the functions of finding the law, interpreting the law and applying the law.'[21] Such conduct also provides another example of the flexible approach of the Court, although it is, of course, not the ECJ which will invalidate or strike down national law, if this proves necessary, but the national courts. This division of function ensures a uniform interpretation of EC law without the confrontations that might result if the ECJ itself were to be involved in the actual reversal and overruling of national law.

Validity

Questions of the validity of acts of secondary EC legislation may clearly be the subject matter of references. There is nothing in the wording of Article 234 to suggest that lower courts must refer such matters to the ECJ.[22] However, there would be a dreadful confusion and lack of uniformity if national courts did feel able to determine the validity of Community law for themselves. Probably for this very reason, under Article 41 ECSC the ECJ is given the sole jurisdiction to rule on the validity of the acts of the High Authority and Council. In any case, in *Foto-Frost*,[23] the ECJ held that national courts have no authority to declare EC legislation invalid, they must refer such matters to it (although they may declare Community acts valid),[24] stating: 'the requirement of uniformity is particularly imperative when the validity of a Community act is in question.'[25] It also saw its ruling as supported by the fact that an action for annulment of a Community act could only be brought before the European Court.[26]

---

[19] Case C 169/91 *Stoke on Trent CC v B&Q plc* [1992] ECR I 6635.

[20] It should also be noted that the entire case file will usually be forwarded to Luxembourg, rather then merely the questions asked by the national court, and so this will necessarily affect the ECJ's decision.

[21] R Pound, *The Spirit of the Common Law* (1921) at 171.

[22] See below for a discussion of the discretion of the lower courts in making references.

[23] Case 314/85 *Firma Foto-Frost v Hauptzollamt Lubeck-Ost* [1987] ECR 4199.

[24] See for example a recent decision of the Dijon administrative tribunal in which that court held that national courts may dismiss grounds advanced for invalidity if they find them unfounded: *Société BSAD* no97–1250, 5 Jan 99. Furthermore, in *R v Searle* [1995] 3 CMLR 196 the English High Court declared that the *Foto-Frost* doctrine did not preclude them from actually considering the issue of validity and declaring EC legislation valid. It also went on to hold that the Court might limit the effects of a regulation without making a reference. In *Searle*, the defendants had been convicted of breaking sanctions against Serbia by exporting chemicals. They claimed that the EC had the sole jurisdiction to deal with the matter (which it had done by adopting regulations under Article 133 EC). The High Court nonetheless held that conviction and the order on which it was based stood as, under Article 307 EC, EC action was without prejudice to existing international obligations, in this case the UN Charter under which the British order had been adopted. But see also, however, case C-408/95 *Eurotunnel SA v Sea France* [1998] 2 CMLR 293.

[25] *Foto-Frost* at para 15. See also the Report of the Due Working Party on the Future of the European Communities' Court System which recommended amending Article 234 to incorporate the rule in *Foto Frost* into the treaty.

[26] See Chapter 10 for a discussion of acts for annulment.

In *Zuckerfabrik Suderdithmarschen AG*[27] the ECJ laid down criteria for the granting of interim relief pending a ruling from the ECJ under Article 234 on the validity of a Community act. It based these on principles it had already set out for its own jurisdiction to grant such relief under Articles 242 and 243 EC. These were that relief should be granted only if serious doubts exist about the validity of the Community measure (on which the contested national administrative act is based), the case is urgent, and relief is necessary to avoid serious and irreparable harm to the party seeking the relief. Once again, it was important for the uniformity of EC law that the Court provide a common European solution, rather than leaving it to the national courts to devise their own remedies: the ECJ did not feel inclined to respect national procedural autonomy in this instance.[28] In *Atlanta Fruchthandelsgesellschaft*[29] the ECJ held that the *Zuckerfabrik* principles also applied to the grant of **positive** measures. In this case the applicants wished to be granted licences to import bananas pending a ruling on the validity of the Common Banana Regime.[30]

THE PRACTICE OF ARTICLE 234

Ironically enough, the scope of Article 234 itself is not totally clear and has had to be clarified by the ECJ.

'Any court or tribunal of a member state'

As the ECJ has always shown concern to preserve the uniformity of application and interpretation one might expect it to accept references from any national forum which is faced with a point of EC law in need of assistance, to ensure that no rogue interpretations flourish. To some extent it has adopted this view, but it has not gone so far as to accept references from every such forum.

In its adoption of a Community-wide definition, the ECJ has taken national classification to be irrelevant and preferred to adopt a Community interpretation, as stated by Advocate General Reischl in the *Broekmeulen* case:

---

[27] Cases C-143/88, 92/89 [1991] ECR I-415.

[28] The same position has however not been taken in the case of interim relief pending the **interpretation** of EC law. In *R v Secretary of State for Health, ex parte Imperial Tobacco Ltd* (*The Times*, 16 November 1999, QBD) Turner J did not apply the *Zuckerfabrik* criteria. In this case an action had been brought to stop the enactment of domestic regulations banning tobacco advertising pending a ruling on the validity of the Directive on which it was based (see Cases C-376/98 and C-74/99 *Federal Republic of Germany v European Parliament and Council of the European Union, The Queen v Secretary of State for Health, ex parte Imperial Tobacco Ltd and Others* [2000] All ER (EC) 769, in which the Court annulled the Directive). But it was also the case here that the date for the implementation of the Directive (31 July 2001) had not yet been reached.

[29] Case C-465/93 [1995] ECR I-3799.

[30] The ECJ did, however, add that national courts might also take into account repercussions of the interim order on individual national, social and economic interests, as well as the Community interest.

If . . . the term in question [court or tribunal] were to be construed as a reference to national law . . . This would lead eventually to the fragmentation of Community law, which is precisely what the procedure under Article 177 is designed to avoid.[31]

The ECJ's primary concern is whether the body in question exercises a judicial function (established fairly early on in its case law, in *Politi v Italy*)[32] which of course raises nice issues as to how and when this occurs. The system of courts administration in the member states of the EU is largely based on common principles, although influenced by different legal concepts. All sorts of adjudicatory bodies exist in the member states, not all of which have judicial status under national law. Is an adversarial procedure necessary for a body to be 'judicial'? Must it have some public degree of recognition? Thus, for example, the Appeals Committee for General Medicine of the Netherlands, itself part of a professional body and not considered to be a court or tribunal under Dutch law, was held by the ECJ in *Broekmeulen*, to be a 'court or tribunal'. The ECJ's reasoning seemed to be based on the fact that the Committee enjoyed a significant degree of official recognition and carried out a public function – decisions were delivered after an adversarial procedure and were considered to be final.[33]

The key factors which the ECJ will look for (detailed in the *Vaassen*[34] case and known as the '*Vaassen* criteria') seem to be that the body in question should have official recognition, be independent and permanent, make binding decisions on legal rights and obligations, involve a *lis inter partes*,[35] the rules of procedure and evidence and not just be a purely advisory or investigatory organisation, nor be part of the legislature or executive.

However, in *Nordsee v Reederei Mond*,[36] the ECJ held that a private arbitrator deriving powers from the arbitration contract of private parties could not make a reference. *Nordsee* might at first seem hard to reconcile with the need for uniform interpretation of Community law. However, in *Nordsee*, much importance seems to have been attached to the fact that this tribunal was not a permanent body, with compulsory jurisdiction conferred by the State.[37] The ECJ was also probably fearful of a floodgate of litigation arising from unnecessary preliminary references brought about by the whim of private parties creating arbitration fora, rather than questions necessary to resolve the dispute. So it has sought to draw the line here.

In *Corbiau*, the ECJ refused a reference from the Director of Taxation for Luxembourg, on the basis that he was not an independent authority, but rather

---

[31] Case 246/80 *Broekmeulen v Huisarts Registratie Commissie* [1981] ECR 2311 at 2328 paras 16 and 17.

[32] Case 43/71 *Politi v Italy* [1971] ECR 1039.

[33] Case 246/80 *Broekmeulen v Huisarts Registratie Commissie* [1981] ECR 2311.

[34] Case 61/65 *Vaassen* [1965] ECR 261 which concerned an arbitration tribunal which settled disputes of the mining industry pension fund. Although set up privately it had ministerial approval and adversarial procedure – the ECJ held that it was a judicial body for the purposes of Article 234.

[35] Although in Case C-54/96 *Dorsch Consult* [1997] ECR I 4961, this was held not to be an absolute requirement.

[36] Case 102/81 *Nordsee v Reederei Mond* [1982] ECR 1095.

[37] Although in *Nordsee* the Commission had argued that arbitration as such, rather than the individual arbitrator, was a permanent institution in the legal system.

in charge of the revenue departments which had made the very decision contested.[38] Hence he did not exercise an appropriately **judicial** function. Likewise references will be declined from bodies which act in a purely administratory or advisory capacity.[39]

The body in question must also be a court or tribunal of a 'member state'. This does not cover international courts, such as the European Court of Human Rights,[40] where some sort of reference procedure might have been useful either way,[41] although the prospect of the delay caused by a reference from one international court to another is disconcerting. However, the ECJ held recently that the Benelux Court of Justice (which applies the rules common to those states) could make references.[42]

In the *de Coster*[43] case, AG Colomer undertook a through review and critique of the ECJ's definition of a national court or tribunal, in the course of determining whether the College Juridictionnel de la Région de Bruxelles was such a court. Colomer found the ECJ's criteria to be too flexible and insufficiently consistent, that too many of the *Vaassen* criteria had been relaxed, with such vague outlines 'that a question referred for a preliminary reference by Sancho Panzo as governor of the island of Barataria would be accepted'.[44] While a broad definition might have been justified earlier in order to further the uniform dissemination and application of Community law, it now simply hindered the work of the ECJ. He therefore proposed that the concept be redefined to include only references from bodies which were part of the national court system, with very limited exceptions for other bodies whose decisions were final.[45] Following this definition he did not find the body at issue in the case in question to qualify. He, however, urged the ECJ to refer the case to the full court, given the importance of clarifying the definition of court or tribunal.[46]

---

[38] Case C-24/92 *Corbiau* [1993] ECR I-1277. In Case C-134/97 *Victoria Film* [1998] ECR I 7023, the Court held that the Swedish Revenue board was not a court or tribunal, even though it derived from statutory origin and had the power to deliver binding decision. But this was not a final decision and the ECJ held that the Board performed an essentially administrative function.

[39] Thus the ECJ held that the Paris Bar Council, deciding on admission to the profession (Case 138/80 *Borker* [1980] ECR 1975) and the Italian *Corte dei Conti*, which was essentially checking results of administrative activity (Case C-192/98 *Azienda* [1999] ECR I-8583 and Case C-440/98 *Rai* [1999] ECR I-8597), were held not to exercise a judicial function (see also Joined cases C-110/98 to C-147/98 *Gabalfrisa et al.* [2000] ECR I-1577; C-407/98 *Abrahamsson* [2000] ECR I-5539; C-195/98 *Osterreichischer Gewerkschaftsbund* [2000] ECR I-1049).

[40] But note *Matthews* v *UK* [1998] 28 EHRR 361 under which the European Court of Human Rights has held itself entitled to review EC law: see Chapter 13 for a discussion of this case.

[41] See e.g. K Lenaerts, 'Fundamental Rights to be included in a Community Catalogue' (1991) 16 EL Rev. 367, who proposes a reference procedure from the ECJ to the ECHR.

[42] Case C-337/95 *Parfums Christian Dior* [1997] ECR I 6013. See also Cases C-100/89 *Kaefer and Procacci* v *France* [1990] ECR I-4667, in which a reference was accepted form the Tribunal Administratif in Tahiti (French Polynesia) and Case C-355/89 *DHSS* v *Barr and Montrose Holdings* [1991] ECR I-3479 in which a reference was accepted from the Isle of Man (not part of the UK); see also Case C-171/96 *Pereira Roquer* v *Governor of Jersey* [1998] ECR I-4687.

[43] Case 17/00 *de Coster* [2001] ECR 000.

[44] Ibid. AG Colomer at para 16.

[45] Ibid. paras 85 *et seq*.

[46] The case was not, however, referred to the full court, but to the fifth chamber, which did not give a particularly full consideration of the matter – case C-17/00 *de Coster* [2001] ECR 000.

WHEN TO REFER

The reference is made by the national court and not by the parties themselves. Under Article 234 (2), it will make a reference where 'a decision on the question is necessary to enable it to give judgement'. This may happen in two different sets of circumstances. First, there are those courts which **may** refer: which include all national courts or tribunals save those of last instance. The second category concerns these latter, i.e. 'a court or tribunal of a member state against whose decision there is no judicial remedy under national law'. Under Article 234 (3), these courts **must** make a reference if a decision on the question is necessary in order to enable it to give judgment.

Courts which *may* refer

For a national court to make such a reference the matter must be raised and the national court must consider a decision on the question necessary for it to give judgment. We may look at these cases from two different perspectives: those of the national courts themselves, and that of the ECJ.

The national courts

For a long time the ECJ seemed content to leave the decision of whether to refer up to the courts, refraining from interfering with their exercise of discretion. Left to their own devices, national courts formed their own sets of guidelines.[47] Lord Denning, never reticent, issued his well-known guidelines in *Bulmer* v *Bollinger*,[48] given at an early stage of UK membership. These were quite detailed in nature, hardly inciting courts to refer,[49] reminding courts to 'decide the facts first', 'not to overload the Court', and to consider the timing and expense of a ruling, as well as its difficulty and importance. These did not go without criticism, as they seemed to limit the discretion of the national courts to make a reference.[50] Some twenty years later, in *ex parte Else*,[51] Bingham MR suggested that 'the appropriate course is ordinarily to refer the issue to the Court of Justice unless the national court can with complete confidence resolve the issue itself'.

---

[47] Although it is not the practice for courts in some EU legal systems to issue such guidelines, and as far as I am aware, no such principles have been set out by the courts in France, Germany, Belgium and Italy.

[48] *HO Bulmer Ltd v J Bollinger SA* [1974] 2 WLR 202.

[49] Craig suggests that the *Bulmer* guidelines cannot actually be separated from Lord Denning's personality and his traditional view of sovereignty in cases such as *Felixstowe* and *McCarthys v Smith*: per P Craig, 'Report on the United Kingdom' in Slaughter, Sweet and Weiler (eds) *The European Court and National Courts* (Hart Publishing, 1999) 195.

[50] e.g. F Jacobs, 'When to Refer to the European Court' (1974) 90 LQR 486.

[51] *R v International Stock Exchange, ex parte Else* [1993] QB 534. See also *Customs and Excise Commissioners v ApS Samex* [1983] 1 All ER 1042; and *R v Plymouth Justices, ex parte Rogers* [1982] 3 WLR 1, for more liberal accounts than those of Lord Denning on the need of the courts to make a reference. See also *R v Secretary of State for Home Department, ex parte Vitale* [1996] 2 CMLR 587; *CCE and AG, ex parte Shepherd Neame* [1999] 1 CMLR 1274.

Bingham's warning that national courts should refer unless they have 'complete confidence' in resolving the issue themselves places the burden on the courts to refer, a very different approach from that of Lord Denning.[52]

The ECJ's approach to national court discretion

For some time, the ECJ adopted a general rule of non-enquiry into the national courts' decision to make a reference. It made no attempt to set out any criteria to guide national courts on their discretion to refer cases, happily leaving the matter to these courts.[53] Long ago, in *Salgoil*[54] it held that Article 234 was based on a distinct separation of functions between national courts and the Court of Justice and that the ECJ had no jurisdiction to take cognisance of the facts nor criticise the national courts' reasons for action.[55] It found that the national court, with its direct knowledge of the facts of the case, was in the best position to determine whether a preliminary ruling was necessary in order to enable it to give judgment.[56] In *Rheinmuhlen*, it emphasised this freedom: 'national courts have the widest discretion in referring matters to the Court of Justice . . .'[57]

So the ECJ's attitude to the national courts seemed to be a very friendly one. In 1963, in *Da Costa*, a national court referred a question identical to that already referred in *Van Gend*, but this did not prevent the ECJ from accepting it; on the contrary, it stated that 'Article 177 always allows a national court, if it considers it desirable, to refer questions of interpretation to the Court again'.[58] The ECJ was cooperative, even in those cases where it appeared that the national courts had 'botched' the reference. So that in *Costa* v *ENEL*, where the reference was less than perfectly formulated, the ECJ held that it had the power to extract the questions relevant to EC law.

The fact was that the preliminary reference procedure was somewhat slow to get started, and few references were made in the early years of the EEC. Mancini's story, of champagne corks popping when the first preliminary reference[59] was received in

---

[52] Although, in *R* v *MAFF, ex parte Portman Chemicals* [1994] 3 CMLR 18 (QB), Brooke J stated, '. . . I do not have complete confidence that I can resolve the issue myself' – a good example of the national courts disregarding Lord Bingham's guidelines but went on to say, 'I am very much influenced by the fact that both MAFF and the applicants want me to make a decision to avoid the time and cost of a reference to Luxembourg' (at 25) – thus illustrating the pressures which the extreme delays in Luxembourg place on national courts. He went on to construe the provision itself but did look at different language versions of the directive as well as adopting a purposive stance – thus at least showing a desire to follow the methodology of the European Court.

[53] The nearest that it got was in Cases 36 and 71/80 *Irish Creamery Milk Suppliers Association* [1981] ECR 735, in which it set out guidelines for good practice but did not appear to take these very seriously – failure to follow them would certainly not render the reference inadmissible.

[54] Case 13/68 *SpA Salgoil* v *Italian Ministry for Foreign Trade* [1968] ECR 453.

[55] In stating this, the ECJ was simply paraphrasing what it had already said in *Costa* v *ENEL*.

[56] Case 83/78 *Pigs Marketing Board* v *Redmond* [1978] ECR 2347.

[57] Case 166/73 *Rheinmuhlen-Dusseldorf* [1974] ECR 33.

[58] Joined cases 28–30/62 *Da Costa* v *Nederlandse Belastingsadminstratie* [1963] ECR 31. The ECJ did however hold that there was no need for it to give a new interpretation to Article 12 (as it then was) – see below.

[59] In Case 13/61 *De Geus* v *Bosch* [1962] ECR 45.

Luxembourg, is probably not fanciful.[60] The ECJ itself took the initiative, inviting state court judges to Luxembourg to learn more about Community law and after that, there seemed to be a sharp rise in preliminary references from those courts.[61] As Craig and de Búrca put it, for the earlier years of the Community at least, the ECJ's approach seemed to be 'Come one, Come all'.

However, by the late twentieth century, references were not sparse, as in the 1960s. They accounted for a substantial amount of the ECJ's case law, and, as they built up, more and more delays occurred in their disposal. And they were not all seemingly of the first importance. In such a situation, over-referring might actually lead to incoherence. The *Wiener* case is a good example. It concerned the world-shattering issue of whether the term 'nightdresses' used in the Common Customs Tariff[62] was restricted solely to garments intended to be worn as night wear, or whether it might be interpreted as covering products which, while they could be worn in bed, need not be so. A very similar issue had been recently decided by the ECJ in a previous reference.[63] Was it really necessary for the already hard-pressed ECJ to be involved in such relatively minor issues? AG Jacobs thought not in *Wiener*. Although he commended the spirit of cooperation between the ECJ and national courts, he stressed that this approach 'has the drawback of attracting a virtually infinite number of questions of interpretation' such that even the existence of a previous very specific ruling might not obviate the need for further references. He therefore suggested that the only appropriate solution would be a greater measure of self-restraint on the part of national courts, stating that 'A reference will be most appropriate where the question is one of general importance and where the ruling is likely to promote the uniform application of the law throughout the European Union. A reference will be least appropriate where there is an established body of case law which could be readily transposed to the facts of the present case; or where the question turns on a narrow point considered in the light of a very specific set of facts and the ruling is unlikely to have any application beyond the instant case.'[64]

Compelling though AG Jacobs' arguments may seem, they have not been adopted by the Court, which has so far failed to take any steps to curb the national courts' discretion – even in the most heavily litigated sectors – although it may not be able to do so for much longer, given the ECJ's problems with overloading. However, it has sometimes rejected references, suggesting that it would not allow its general rule of non-enquiry to be abused. The first such time was the case of *Foglia v Novello*,[65] where the Court refused to entertain a reference concerning the repayment of French taxes (allegedly contrary to EC law) payable under a private contract for the delivery of Italian wine to France. The ECJ rejected this on the basis of the 'artificial nature' of the dispute 'arranged by the parties in order to induce the Court to give its views on certain problems of Community law which do not correspond to an

---

[60] F Mancini, *Democracy and Constitutionalism in the European Union* (Hart Publishing, 1999) chap. 3.
[61] H Rasmussen, *On Law and Policy in the European Court of Justice* (Martinus Nijhoff, 1986) at 247.
[62] Case C-338/95 *Wiener v Havptzollant Emmerich* [1997] ECR I-6495. s 60.04 B IV b 2bb of the 1985 Common Customs Tariff.
[63] Case C-395/93 *Neckermann Ersand* [1994] ECR I-4027.
[64] Wiener, Per AG Jacobs at para 20.

objective requirement inherent in the resolution of a dispute'.[66] It would not give what amounted to an 'advisory opinion'. In other words, it felt that it was not here dealing with 'a case or controversy'.[67]

But it may be difficult to determine whether proceedings are spurious. As Bebr comments, 'Who may say with any certainty that the plaintiff entertained the action seriously or whether he merely sought to obtain a decision in a test case which although of negligible interest to him, raised a question of principle?'[68] It would be very difficult for the ECJ to determine that the proceedings are artificial without assessing the facts (not necessarily yet clear in domestic litigation), a factor which in any case falls outside of the Court's jurisdiction. In *Foglia*, the Court apparently felt able to identify the artificial nature of the dispute by the fact that remedies available under French law to contest the tax had not been used, but such features will not always be present.

In cases such as *Foglia* the ECJ exercises a power of review over the way in which national courts exercised their discretion, a departure from its earlier, *laissez-faire* case law. But does this endanger the cooperative relationship between the ECJ and national courts on which the whole procedure is based and which the ECJ has so often itself stressed?[69] Nonetheless, *Foglia* found favour with some commentators. Wyatt,[70] for example, highlighted the fact that other procedures under the EC Treaty (namely Articles 226–228) contained certain pre-trial safeguards for member states, which did not exist if their legislation were attacked indirectly through the national courts. Wyatt also compared the situation in the US, where there is a clear constitutional objection to advisory opinions, based on the fact that it is the very capacity to give **judgments** which characterises a body as a court, which is rationalised as a facet of the separation of powers between executive and judiciary.[71] Rasmussen is another supporter, seeing *Foglia* as presenting a good new docket-controlling law, pointing out that it took the US Supreme Court 130 years to develop the doctrine of certiorari.[72] Another problem is the fact that preliminary rulings are binding on national courts: how can this be the case if they are sometimes advisory?

In any case, the Court seemed unwilling to invoke the *Foglia* principle for some while. Attempts to do so by protesting the spurious nature of the proceedings in the subsequent cases of *Rau* and *Vinal v Orbat* failed.[73] But things have subsequently changed yet again and the Court has shown itself as much more willing to review

---

[65] Case104/79 *Foglia v Novello (I)* [1980] ECR 745.

[66] case 244/80 *Foglia v Novello (II)* [1981] 3045 at 3063, para 18.

[67] The term used in the US for the requirement of a genuine dispute between the parties.

[68] G Bebr, 'The Existence of a Genuine Dispute: An Indispensable Precondition for the Jurisdiction of the Court under Article 177 EEC Treaty' (1980) 17 CMLRev 525 at 530–2.

[69] See A Barav, 'Preliminary censorship? The Judgement of the Court of Justice in *Foglia v Novello*' (1980) ELRev 443.

[70] Wyatt D, 'Foglia (No 2): The Court Denies its Jurisdiction to Give Advisory Opinions' (1982) ELRev 186.

[71] See *Muskrat v United States* 219 US 346 (1911).

[72] Rasmussen, *On Law and Policy* at 491.

[73] Case 46/80 *Vinal v Orbat* [1981] ECR 77; Case 261/81 *Rau v De Smedt* [1982] ECR 3961; Case C-150/88 *Eau de Cologne & Parfumerie Fabrik v Provide* [1989] ECR 3891.

the contents of a reference.[74] It has done so in at least three sets of circumstances, other than those in which it perceives there to be no genuine dispute, although the boundaries between these are quite fluid.[75]

First, it will refuse a reference where it considers it to be irrelevant to the substantive action, as in the case of *Meilicke*.[76] In this case, the ECJ was asked to give a ruling on a theory developed by the German courts as to the compatibility of non-cash contributions of capital with the Second EC Banking Directive. It declined, stressing that it was not for the ECJ to give advisory opinions on hypothetical questions. In fact, it seems that the action had been orchestrated by the plaintiff, a German lawyer who wanted to test out the acceptability of his particular theory of non-cash contributions,[77] a factor which was not really at stake in the main action.[78] The Commission had suggested that the ECJ might reformulate the questions so as to cover only matters of contention, but this would have been a very large step as, although the ECJ had reformulated questions previously, it had never done so regarding a question which had not been asked at all and did not cover the real issues put by the national court.[79] In *Lourenco Dias* the ECJ declared that 'If it should appear that the question raised is manifestly irrelevant for the purpose of deciding the case the Court must declare that there is no need to proceed to judgement.'[80]

Second, the ECJ will reject a reference if it comes with an insufficient, or incoherent, factual or legal background. In *Telemarsicabruzzo*, the national court had done a very peremptory job with the order for reference which the Commission had described as 'particularly laconic' and as giving 'sparse detail of the elements of law and fact such as to make it impossible to identify the purpose of the questions referred and thus to comprehend their meaning and scope'.[81] The ECJ therefore ruled that there was no need for it to give a ruling on the questions submitted. In so doing, it went against the opinion of AG Gulmann who did not think that the reference should be declined, but did suggest that the Court might give greater guidelines as to how references might be framed. He did, however, agree that it would be unsatisfactory for the ECJ to have to extract from other documents, such as the parties' observations (the case concerned a particularly complex issue of competition law), the information on the factual and legal background which should have been provided in the Court's reference, as such an enquiry would be demanding in terms

---

[74] See, T Kennedy, 'First Steps Towards a European Certiorari' (1993) 18 ELRev 121; D Anderson, 'The Admissibility of Preliminary References' (1994) YEL 179.

[75] See the opinion of AG Lenz in Case C-415/93 *Union Royale Belge des Sociétés de Football Association v Bosman* [1995] ECR I-4921 for an exhaustive review of the case law up to that date.

[76] Case C-83/91 *Meilicke v ADV* [1992] ECR I-4871.

[77] The work concerned being *Die verschleirte Sacheinlage; eine deutsche Fehlentwicklung* (Stuttgart, 1989) for those interested.

[78] Case C-83/91 *Meilicke* [1992] ECR I-4871 at para 5.

[79] *Meilicke* at 4903.

[80] Case C-343/90 *Lourenco Dias* [1992] ECR I-4673 at para 20. See also cases C-18/93 *Corsica Ferries* [1994] ECR I-1783; C-428/93 *Monin* [1994] ECR I-1707.

[81] Joined Cases 320–322/90 *Telemarsicabruzzo* [1993] ECR I-393.

of resources and carry a risk of errors.[82] The case also provides another example of the ECJ's failure to observe the 'fiction' of interpretation and not application: if it really had just been concerned with interpretation, surely it would not have been so concerned to have had a fuller possession of the facts?[83]

These are pertinent reasons and since then, the ECJ has declined many more references on the same grounds as in *Telemarsicabruzzo*, either by judgment, or by order even, being unwilling to spend good time drafting a judgment.[84] However, in *Vaneetveld*,[85] another case in which the reference was less than satisfactorily drafted, AG Jacobs made strong arguments as to why the Court should accept the reference, which it did, and in so doing, stressed the singular nature of cases such as *Telemarsicabruzzo* and *Monin* and *Banchero*, competition law cases, which are characterised by complex legal and factual backgrounds. But in less complex cases, such as the one at hand, the usefulness of the ECJ's response to the national court's questions is undoubtedly an important criterion. This is still in line with the spirit of Article 234 and the Court's earlier case law, as it continues the cooperative nature of Article 234, avoiding formalism, while focusing on the usefulness of the answers which can be provided. This approach, which seems to be one of common sense, has been adopted by other advocates general. As AG Lenz summarised the situation in *Bosman*, 'The thinking behind all these cases is obvious. The Court of Justice can as a rule give a useful answer to questions put by a national court only if it knows the circumstances of the national proceedings.'[86]

Third, there are other types of cases where the Court has declined a ruling, usually where it feels that to hear the case would be an abuse of procedure. So, for example, in *Mattheus*, it found an action inadmissible concerning conditions for accession of new member states.[87] Some writers[88] have preferred to classify this decision as the development of a political question doctrine, namely refusing to rule on matters so sensitive that they fall outside the Court's jurisdiction, an approach

---

[82] Opinion of AG Gulmann in *Telemarsicabruzzo* at 417.

[83] See also G Bebr, 'Development of Judicial Control of the European Communities' (1981) 9.14 at 432, who writes: 'A meaningful, serviceable preliminary reference must necessarily be facts orientated.'

[84] See e.g. Case C-57/92 *Banchero I* [1993] ECR I-1086; Case C-386/92 *Monin automobiles* [1993] ECR I-2049; Case C-378/93 *La Pyramide SARL* [1994] ECR I-3999 (Order); Case C-458/93 *Saddik* [1995] ECR I-511; Case C-422/98 *Colonia Versicherung* [1999] ECR I-1279; Official Journal C 136, 15/05/1999 at 4; Case C-176/96 *Lehtonen* [2000] ECR I-2681, for just some of the recent cases in which the ECJ has rejected a preliminary reference on the grounds that the national court had failed to define sufficiently the factual and legal background to the dispute.

[85] Case C-316/93 *Vaneetveld* [1994] ECR I-763.

[86] *Bosman* at 673.

[87] Case 93/78 *Mattheus* [1978] ECR 2203. In this case, two parties had concluded an agreement regarding a market survey on Spanish and Portuguese products, terminable if accession of either country proved impracticable in law, a question which they had agreed should be decided by the ECJ. Some writers (e.g. Rasmussen op. cit. at 488) choose to classify this as an example of the Court refusing to involve itself in political questions, while others prefer to see it as the Court refusing to interfere with unfinalised decision making (those countries had not yet acceded). This latter interpretation was adopted by the Court itself in *Lourenco Dias* where it characterised the *Mattheus* decision as the refusal or relating to measures not yet adopted by the EC institutions.

[88] e.g. Rasmussen, *On Law and Policy in the European Court of Justice* at 486–488; D Anderson, 'The Admissibility of Preliminary References' (1994) 14 YEL 179–202.

taken by courts in domestic jurisdictions.[89] The ECJ will also reject the reference if it feels that the appropriate form of action has not been adopted, stressing that if the applicant would have had access to a direct action under Article 230 in the ECJ then they should have done so.[90]

Should one be critical of this more recent line of case law? On the one hand, it is undeniable that the Court has recently been flooded with references, resulting in grave delays, and any decrease in unnecessary ones can certainly be welcomed. On the other, the promulgation of the *Meilicke* and *Telemarsicabruzzo* jurisprudence seems uncertain and sometimes unsatisfactory. After *Meilicke* and its like, it is still uncertain whether the ECJ would accept a national reference regarding a 'test' or constitutional case, if there were no underlying dispute, if such as cases were permitted in national law. In *Leclerc-Siplec*, for example, AG Jacobs noted obvious similarities to the background in *Foglia*, but declared that if national law permitted non-hostile litigation then the ECJ should respect its procedural autonomy, something which the ECJ has been willing to do in other areas of procedure (e.g. on time limits, although there were times during the 1990s when it seemed willing to take a more interventionist approach). In *Leclerc-Siplec* the French government, which submitted written observations in these proceedings and was represented at the hearing, had not objected to the procedure nor suggested that it had been prevented from defending the contested decree as a result of the way in which the litigation had been conducted.[91] The ECJ accepted the reference.

In this context, the notion of access to justice is a real and critical one. Advocate General Darmon in *Corbiau* insisted that applicants should not be denied their right of access to a court.[92] Perhaps the greatest danger lies with those cases where the ECJ declines to accept a reference on the basis of inadequate factual or legal background.[93] These do not concern an abuse of proper procedures, nor a professed reluctance to give advisory opinions, but may involve very real issues of EC law, as noted by AG Gulmann in *Telemarsicabruzzo*. Why should the Court be so

---

[89] Relevant cases in US law on the political question doctrine are *Colegrove* v *Green*, (1946) 328 US 549 in which the US Supreme Court declined jurisdiction in a case concerning a protest by an Illinois voter against the apportionment of electoral districts. However, this was later overruled in *Baker* v *Carr* 369 US 186 (1962) in which the Supreme Court held that it could review congressional reapportionment and the mere fact that a suit sought protection of a political right did not mean that it was non-justiciable. This last was reworked more thoroughly in *Goldwater* v *Carter* (1979) which concerned a challenge brought against the President's unilateral termination of a mutual defence treaty. The Supreme Court held that it had no jurisdiction to deal with this question (see the opinion of Powell J). Although the political question doctrine has been more thoroughly litigated in the US courts (and may be even more so after the November 2000 presidential elections!) there is still no clear definition of it: one commentator stated that a political question is simply one which is 'too hot to handle' (per M Shapiro, *Law and Politics in the Supreme Court* (London: McMillan, 1964) at 184).

[90] Case C-188/92 *TWD Textilwerke* v *Germany* [1994] ECR I-833; Case C-178/95 *Wiljo* v *Belgian State* [1997] ECR; see also D Wyatt, 'The relationship between actions for annulment and references for validity after *TWD Deggendorf*' in Lonbay and Biondi (eds) *Remedies for breach of EC Law* (Chichester, 1997).

[91] Case C-412/93 *Leclerc-Siplec* v *TF1 Publicite SA* [1995] ECR I-179.

[92] Case C-24/92 *Corbiau* [1993] ECR I-1277.

[93] See e.g. D O'Keeffe, 'Is the Spirit of Article 177 under Attack? Preliminary References and Admissibility in *Scritti di Honore di Giacomo Mancini*, (Milan: Giuffre, 1998).

restrictive here? It is certainly true that inadequate information does pose a risk of error as well as an increase in the Court's workload. Joliet[94] also suggested that the Court was prompted by concern for docket control in an era of burgeoning case-loads, but such an action risks undermining the preliminary reference procedure and the relationship between the Courts. Opinion is divided between those who do not wish to jeopardise the relationship between the ECJ and national courts,[95] and those who now think that the time is now ripe for some sort of admissibility criterion, or certiorari, to be introduced into the Court's procedure. It is true that it is very hard for the ECJ to say no to another court; this situation is not the same as a party applying for leave to appeal. On the other hand, the delays caused by the backlog of cases to be heard may result in a greater denial of justice.

The *Dzodzi* jurisdiction

The Court's refusal of certain references also seems puzzling given that, recently, in a parallel but very different line of cases, it seems to have been willing to expand the remit of the preliminary reference procedure by admitting references which it certainly had no need to. These arise under the so-called '*Dzodzi*' jurisprudence.[96] *Dzodzi* concerned the application of Community law rules on the free movement of persons to a purely internal situation, traditionally an area of law which the EC will not enter. However, in this case, under Belgian law, Community law rights had been extended to situations concerning the third country national spouses of Belgians, who could establish no connection between their case and Community law at all. The Court nonetheless accepted jurisdiction, declaring that 'it is manifestly in the interests of the Community legal order that, in order to forestall future differences of interpretation, every Community provision should be given a uniform interpretation irrespective of the circumstance in which it is applied'.[97]

Just as the Court seemed to be ignoring the advice of its advocates general when declining jurisdiction in cases such as *Meilicke*, so it ignored many of its advocates general in these cases.[98] The Court, however, chose not to reconsider its 'generous' assumption of jurisdiction in *Leur-Bloem*.[99] And so, finally, the advocates general seem to have given up on the battle to decline jurisdiction in such case. In

---

[94] R Joliet, 'Co-opération entre la CJCE et les juridictions nationales' (1993) Journ. Trib 1.

[95] eg Anderson, who states that 'to erect further barriers to the admissibility of preliminary references could alienate national judiciaries, and would risk sending a notable success story into reverse' Anderson op. cit. at 202. See below for a discussion of reforms of the preliminary ruling procedure. See also O'Keeffe op. cit., who writes, 'If the Court's work-load is the problem, the solution would appear to be the reform of the Court's own working methods to make them more efficient.'

[96] E.g. Case 166/84 *Thomasdunger* [1985] ECR 3001; Joined cases C-297/88 and C-197/88 *Dzodzi v Belgian State* [1990] ECR I-3763; Case C-231/89 *Gmurzynska-Bsher* [1990] ECR I-4003; Case C-88/91 *Federconsorzi* [1992] ECR I-4035; Case C-28/95 *Leur-Bloem* [1997] ECR I-4161.

[97] *Dzodzi* at para 2.

[98] See e.g. the comments of AG Tesauro in Case C-346/93 *Kleinwort Benson Ltd v City of Glasgow* [1995] ECR I-615. See also A Gagliardi, 'The Right of Individuals to invoke the provisions of mixed agreements before national courts: a new message from Luxembourg' (1999) 24 ELRev.

[99] Case C-28/95 *Leur-Bloem* [1997] ECR I-4161, see also G Betlem (1999) 36 CMLRev commentary on *Leur-Bloem* and *Giloy* at 1656.

Schoonbroodt, for example, another case in which a member state (in this case Belgium) applied EC law to a purely internal situation, AG Jacobs simply referred to the Court's judgment in *Leur-Bloem*, stating 'However, the Court has held that it has jurisdiction under Article 177 of the Treaty to interpret Community law provisions in situations where, as in the present case, the facts being considered by the national court are outside the scope of Community law but those provisions have been rendered applicable by domestic law.'[100]

Accepting references in situations of reverse discrimination

Another related line of cases are those which involve so-called 'reverse discrimination': where a member state national is disadvantaged, because they cannot invoke Community law, in a situation in which an EC national from another member state would be able to do so, an increasingly common situation in those areas in which EC law has outstripped domestic law in the remedies which it provides. Some member states have dealt with this problem by providing that the application of EC law is to be extended to domestic situations in order to avoid unreasonable discrimination.[101] As has been noted[102] these situations require the consideration of a hypothetical factor, namely the treatment of the situation as if it would be covered by Community law. Will the ECJ be willing to give a preliminary ruling in such cases, or will it treat them as falling outside of the scope of Community law? In some ways, these cases are similar to *Dzodzi*, in that they apply EC law to domestic situations, but they do so, not by specific national legislation, but by a rule of general scope, namely the principle of equality.

In *Angonese*[103] these sorts of issues arose. Mr Angonese had been rejected from his job application with a private employer on the ground that he did not possess a 'patento', a certificate of competence in Italian and German, specific to the province of Bolzano, although he was actually completely bilingual in both languages. He contested this as discrimination under Article 39.[104] However, Mr Angonese was an Italian national, so it was difficult for him to find, in these circumstances, any connection with Community law. He tried to rely on the fact that he had studied other Community languages in Vienna, suggesting this provided a sufficient connection.

---

[100] Case C-247/97 *Marcel Schoonbroodt, Marc Schoonbroodt and Transports AM Schoonbroodt* [1998] ECR I-8095; see Case C-456/98, also *Centrosteel Srl v Adipol GmbH* [2000] ECR I-6007. Opinion of Mr Advocate General Jacobs.

[101] See Judgment of the Italian Constitutional Court ruling in 1997 that such a difference on treatment was prohibited by the Italian Constitution; also see A Adinolfi, 'The Judicial Application of Community law in Italy' (1998) 35 CMLRev 1325; also Case C-132/93 *Steen Deutsche Bundespost* [1994] ECR I-2715 in which Article 3(1) of the Grundgesetz was invoked before the Arbeitsgericht. The principle of equality was also accepted by the French courts in Joined Cases C-321/94 to 324/94 *Pistre* [1996 ECR I-2343; see also G Betlem, (1999) 36 CMLRev 177 for a discussion of the application of the principle of equality by the Dutch courts.

[102] See S Kaleda, 'Extension of the preliminary rulings procedure outside the scope of Community law: The Dzodzi line of cases', (2000) EIOP at http://olymp.wu-wien.ac.at/eiop/ texte.

[103] Case C-281/98 *Angonese v Cassa di Risparmio di Bolzano SpA* [2000] ECR I-4139.

[104] The certificate could only be obtained after examination at a language centre at one place in Bolzano.

The ECJ found the action admissible. It stressed the cooperative nature of the pre-liminary ruling procedure, stating that the rejection of a reference was to be regarded as exceptional. However, the Court made no reference to *Dzodzi*, nor did it in fact give any justification of what it took to be the basis of its jurisdiction here. However, as has been suggested,[105] 'the acceptance of jurisdiction in *Angonese* indi-cates that the Court is, in principle, prepared to exercise the jurisdiction in the situ-ations involving a reference by the rule or practice of a general scope, aimed at the elimination of reverse discrimination'. Groups of cases like *Telemarsicabruzzo* and *Meilicke* on the one hand, and *Dzodzi* and *Angonese* on the other, send out contrary messages: that the ECJ wants to cooperate with national courts and that it does not. At present they seem almost impossible to reconcile.

Notes for guidance on references by national courts

In any case, following an increase in inadequately drafted references over the last decade, late in 1996 the Court issued its own notes for guidance for national courts in this matter in order to avoid problems caused by cases like *Telemarsicabruzzo*.[106] Paragraph 6 of this Notice states that the order for reference should contain a state-ment of reasons 'which is succinct but sufficiently complete to give the Court . . . a clear understanding of the factual and legal content of the main proceedings', stress-ing that, in particular, the order should contain a statement of the facts, an expos-ition of applicable national law, a statement of the reasons which prompted the national court to make the reference and, where appropriate, a summary of the par-ties' arguments. The Notice does not, however, provide that a failure to do this will result in the reference being inadmissible, a fact of which national courts may not be aware. The Notice also states that it is for guidance only, having no binding effect in the national courts. So it adds very little, if anything, to the Court's existing case law. Quite recently, the Court also adopted a preliminary check on admissibility as part of new procedure. On receipt at the Court's registry a check is made to ensure that the subject matter of the reference arises out of a real dispute, not 'contrived' proceedings, that it falls within the Court's jurisdiction and that the questions are relevant and that the factual and legal context is clearly set out. The fact that much effort was spent on preliminary rulings at the 2000 IGC suggests that these provi-sions have certainly not dealt adequately with these problems.

THE OBLIGATION TO REFER UNDER ARTICLE 234(3)

According to this provision, courts against whose decisions there is no judicial rem-edy under national law must make a reference where a decision on the question is

---

[105] Kaleda in EIOP op. cit. p. 6.
[106] *Notes for Guidance By National Courts For Preliminary Rulings, Proceedings of the Court 34/96, 9 December 1996.* See also the UK *Practice Direction of the Supreme Court* which adopts the Guidance of the ECJ.

necessary in order to enable the court to give judgment. Interestingly, fewer references are made this way than under the discretionary procedure.[107]

What sorts of courts fall within Article 234(3)? It may sometimes be obvious when a court is one of final resort, e.g. the House of Lords. But a classic illustration of the problems that may arise in this area is the issue of whether the Court of Appeal, should both it and the House of Lords have refused leave to appeal, would fall under Article 234(3).

It is generally stated that there are two theories on this matter, the abstract and the concrete theories.[108] Under the abstract (or institutional) theory, the only bodies to fall within Article 234(3) are those whose decisions may never be appealed. This would cover courts such as the House of Lords. On the other hand, the concrete (or functional) theory stipulates that whether or not a court is covered by Article 234(3) depends on whether that body is subject to appeal in the case in question. So this would cover the Court of Appeal, in the example cited above, and even lesser courts in some cases. Such an approach is obviously better geared towards the comprehensive legal protection of the individual.

The jurisprudence of the ECJ does not make this issue entirely clear. *Costa* v *ENEL* might seem to support the concrete theory. In that case, a reference was made by the *giudice conciliatore*, an Italian magistrate whose decisions are unappealable in certain minor cases. The ECJ stated, 'national courts against whose decisions, as in the present case, there is no judicial remedy, must refer the matter to the Court of Justice.'[109]

Even if the concrete theory is acceptable, the position of the Court of Appeal is still problematic and the English courts seem to veer towards acceptance of the abstract theory. Leave to appeal will not be given until the end of the case, when it will be too late for that court to make the reference to Luxembourg. In the *Chiron* case, Lord Justice Balcombe summarised the situation as follows:

> If the Court of Appeal does not make a reference to the ECJ, and gives its final judgement on the appeal, then the House of Lords becomes the court of last resort. If either the Court of Appeal or the House of Lords grants leave to appeal, then there is no problem. If the Court of Appeal refuses leave to appeal, and the House of Lords is presented with an application for leave to appeal, before it refuses leave it should consider whether an issue of Community law arises which is necessary for its decisions . . . and is not acte clair. If it considers that a reference is requisite, it will take such action as it may consider appropriate in the particular case.[110]

Another difficult position is that of the national judge hearing an application for interim relief. If a question of EC law is raised in interlocutory proceedings is a

---

[107] For example, in the UK by the end of 1995, seventeen references had been made from the House of Lords, but 79 from the High Court (Internal Statistics of the ECJ).

[108] See e.g. Craig and de Búrca op. cit. at 412, Hartley, *Foundations of European Community Law* (OUP, 1998) at 272.

[109] Case 6/64 *Costa* v *ENEL* [1964] ECR 585 at 592.

[110] *Chiron Corporation* v *Murex Diagnostics ltd* [1995] ALL ER (EC) 88 at 93. However, the House of Lords failed to refer this question to the ECJ. In *Trent Taverns* v *Sykes* [1998] EU LR 571 the Court of Appeal held that it was not subject to Article 234(3) and that the right to petition the House of Lords for leave to appeal **was** a judicial remedy.

national court bound to make a reference to the ECJ if its decision is unappealable in the national legal order? The German *Oberlandesgericht* referred this question to the ECJ in the *Hoffmann La Roche* case. The ECJ held that a national court would not be bound under Article 234(3) to make a reference during interlocutory proceedings even where the interim procedures were not appealable provided that each of the parties would be able to institute proceedings on the substance of the case and that the question of EC law could be referred at that later stage.[111] In other words, there must still be an opportunity to refer.

Acte clair/acte éclairé and the creation of European precedents

In the *Da Costa* case, a Dutch court referred to the ECJ a question almost identical to that which had already been referred in *Van Gend en Loos*. As already discussed, the ECJ did not reject the reference in this case, although it did simply restate its judgment in *Van Gend*, adding that the authority of the interpretation already given by the Court under Article 234 had rendered the question unnecessary to answer again and thus emptied it of substance. This would especially be the case, it said, where a question was raised which was materially identical with a question already subject to a preliminary ruling in a similar case.[112] This might be described as *acte éclairé*. Craig and de Búrca suggest that *Da Costa* initiated a system of precedent,[113] encouraging national courts to apply earlier rulings. This makes a lot of sense. It might seem pointless to refer to the ECJ points which have already been decided. This principle was later extended in the *CILFIT* case, in which it held that there would be no need to make a reference if previous decisions of the ECJ had already dealt with the point of law in question, even though the questions at issue were not strictly identical,[114] although it did state that the national court might still make a reference in those circumstances if it really wished to do so. This was a signal from the ECJ for national courts to rely on its prior rulings, something which then places the ECJ in a more hierarchical relationship with the national courts. It also turns it into a multilateral rather than bilateral relationship, since any national court may rely on a previous ruling.[115] This last point was further underlined in the *ICC* case, in which the ECJ held that if it had already declared a Community act void then national courts should rely on that judgment; thus its rulings would have an *erga omnes* effect.[116]

The ECJ in *CILFIT* also stated that a national court would not be bound to make a reference if the EC provision in question were clear and free from doubt:[117] a ruling which seemed to be approving the doctrine of *acte clair* sometimes used by the French courts. AG Capotorti in *CILFIT* had denied the relevance of *acte clair* to

---

[111] Case 107/76 *Hoffmann La Roche v Centrafarm* [1977] ECR 957 at 973.
[112] Joined Cases 28–30/62 *Da Costa* [1963] ECR 31.
[113] Craig and de Burca op.cit. at p 415.
[114] Case 283/81 *CILFIT* [1982] ECR 3415 at 3429 para 13.8.
[115] See Craig and de Burca, *EU Law* (OUP, 1998) chap. 11 for this argument.
[116] Case 66/80 *ICC* [1981] ECR 1191.
[117] *CILFIT* para 16.

Community law. He dismissed its relevance because he saw the doctrine of *acte clair* as originating from a very different set of circumstances under French law.[118] He also suggested that the theory failed to stand up to closer scrutiny, as it was inconceivable for any provision to be applied without the need to interpret it. As the literary theorist, Stanley Fish, has expressed it: 'The point is a simple one: All shapes are interpretively produced, and since the ends of interpretation are themselves unstable – the possibility of seeing something in a "new light" and therefore of seeing a **new** something, is ever and unpredictably present – the shapes that seem perspicacious to us now may not seem so or may seem different tomorrow.'[119] Furthermore, he found that the French courts had misused the *acte clair* doctrine in the context of EC law in any case.[120] Thus, he concluded that, if recognised under EC law, its effect would be in substance 'to deprive the third paragraph of Article 177 of any meaning'.[121]

Indeed, any encouragement from the ECJ to regard preliminary rulings as precedents raises sensitive issues. Not the least of these is the problem posed for the separation of powers, most particularly in civil law jurisdictions, which resist the notion that judicial authority may bind future cases.[122] However, the ECJ does seem to attribute binding precedent to its judgments: consider *Keck,* for example, a ruling given after a preliminary reference: 'Contrary to what has been previously decided . . .'[123] Furthermore, at least some of the French courts appear to attribute a de facto *erga omnes* effect to preliminary rulings, as was the case with the Cour de Cassation in the *Café Jacques Vabres* case,[124] in which it referred to previous rulings of the ECJ as binding.

However, in *CILFIT* the Court also qualified the doctrine of *acte clair* by stating that, before it could be applied, 'the national court or tribunal must be convinced that the matter is equally obvious to the courts of other Member States and to the Court of Justice'. They should bear in mind that 'Community legislation is drafted in several languages' each of which is equally authentic and that 'legal concepts do not necessarily have the same meaning in Community law and in the law of the various member States'.[125] Surely it would be difficult for any provision to satisfy these

---

[118] *Acte clair* apparently emerged because the French legal system entrusts the interpretation of international treaties exclusively to the executive (often the Ministry of Foreign Affairs) merely allowing courts to apply them. In these circumstances French courts developed the doctrine to restrict the role of the executive, retaining themselves the power to determine whether or not broad differences of interpretation in fact existed. See Opinion of AG Capotorti *CILFIT v MOH* [1981] ECR 3432 at 3435.

[119] S Fish, *Doing What Comes Naturally: Change, Rhetoric and the Practice of Theory in Literary and Legal Studies* (Oxford: Clarendon, 1989) at 302.

[120] e.g., he cited the Conseil d'Etat, the principal body to apply the theory, as early as 1967 finding Article 30 (as then was) *acte clair* in *Syndicat Nationale des Importeurs Francais en produits Laitiers* 27/1167 Recueil Lebon 1967 41; also notoriously in *Cohn Bendit* 22/12/78 Recueil Lebon 1981.

[121] *CILFIT* at 3437.

[122] See e.g. Lipstein, 'The Doctrine of Precedent in Continental law with Special Reference to French and German Law' 28 J Comp Legis & Int'l L (1946); Toth, 'The Authority of Judgement of the European Court of Justice: Binding Force and Legal Effects' 4 YEL 1 (1984); although section 3(19) of the European Communities Act provides for the binding effect of ECJ judgments in British courts.

[123] Joined cases C-267 and C-268/91 *Keck and Mithourd* [1993] ECR I 6097.

[124] Judgment of 24 May 1975 [1975] 2 CMLR 336.

[125] *CILFIT* at paras 18–19.

requirements? The ECJ also stated that 'Finally every provision of Community law must be placed in its context and interpreted in the light of the provisions of Community law as a whole, regard being had to the objectives thereof and to the state of its evolution at the date on which the provision in question is to be applied.'[126] This is surely a very daunting task – especially so in the case of dynamic criteria such as the 'state of evolution' of EC law, which if applied, would seem to rule out the possibility of *acte clair* altogether, as it would suggest that the interpretation of a provision is always evolving and thus never stable or clear, a view akin to that of AG Capotorti.

Some of these criteria were applied in the recent *Skatteministeriet*[127] case, a reference from the Danish court in which the interpretation of Council Directive 69/335 on indirect taxation on the raising of capital was at issue. The defendant had tried to argue that only the Danish version of the directive should be followed, as, under this, duty was payable only on disposal on the Stock Exchange. Other language versions, however, did not make this restriction, indicating that duty would be payable on the transfer of shares by any means. The defendant submitted that individuals could only be expected to rely on provisions in their native language (an understandable point) and should not be expected to compare the Danish version with other language versions. This interpretation was rejected by AG Alber, who looked to other language versions, holding that where several versions diverged from one another, the interpretation could not be based solely on the Danish version. He suggested that the court would have to give a uniform interpretation by reference to the purpose of the measure.[128]

CILFIT had been subject to quite a lot of commentary and criticism. One criticism was that the *CILFIT* criteria were too easily manipulated by national courts, encouraging them to decide too many difficult points for themselves and thus jeopardising the uniform application of the treaty.[129] Sometimes this has been the case, indicating a tense, even antagonistic relationship between the ECJ and national courts, rather than the cooperative one which is so often alluded to. Some higher courts, such as the French Conseil d'Etat and German Constitutional Court, have rarely made references, a policy which Karen Alter has described as 'don't ask and the ECJ can't tell'.[130] Little may actually be done to remedy such wilful resistance to the ECJ. In theory, the Commission might bring an action under Article 226 EC

---

[126] *CILFIT* para 20. However, AG Jacobs warned national courts against interpreting *CILFIT* as imposing a duty on national courts to examine Community provision in every Community language: Case C-338/95 *Wiener* [1997] ECR I 6516, and it is indeed the case that not even the ECJ appears to follow its own *CILFIT* principles assiduously in this regard.

[127] Case C-236/97 *Skatteministeriet v Aktieselskabet Forsikringsselskabet Codan* [1998] ECRI 8679.

[128] In this he was followed by the Court which declared: 'It must also be pointed out that the need for a uniform interpretation of the language versions requires, in the case of divergence between them, that the provision in question be interpreted by reference to the purpose and general scheme of the rules of which it forms part' (Case C-449/93 *Rockfon* [1995] ECR I-4291, para 28, and Case C-72/95 *Kraaijeveld and Others* [1996] ECR I-5403, para 28).

[129] See e.g. A Arnull, 'The Use and Abuse of Article 177' (1989) 52 MLR 622. See also D Anderson, op. cit. (fn 1) at 6–047-052.

[130] K Alter, 'The European Court's Political Power' (1996) 19 West European Politics 458.

against the state whose courts fail to make the reference, but the Commission has always stated its reluctance to do this,[131] and no such action has yet been taken. In some countries, such as Germany, failure to make a mandatory reference breaches domestic administrative law.[132]

In *Cohn-Bendit*, the Conseil d'Etat used *acte clair* to avoid an obligation to refer, holding 'directives cannot be cited by nationals of these states against specific administrative actions'. This was clearly contrary to the case law of the ECJ, namely *Van Duyn*, in which case, the interpretation of Article 189 (now 249) could hardly be said to be clear. Thus it would seem that the Conseil d'Etat's definition of an *acte clair* was not one which is clear, but rather one to which it wants to give its own interpretation. As M Genevois, Commissaire du Gouvernement at the Conseil d'Etat observed, 'How could it be maintained that there is not the slightest doubt as to the interpretation of the EEC treaty when the interpretation which seems evident is contrary to the interpretation of this treaty provision by the European Court . . . ?'[133] However, the Conseil d'Etat went on to deny the direct effect of directives in two further decisions,[134] and in this was followed by the German Bundesfinanzhof,[135] both acting in clear defiance of fundamental principles of EC law under the pretext of *acte clair*. These actions, of course, did not spring from nowhere, but rather from an intense dislike of the ECJ's finding that directives could have direct effect, something some have interpreted as an overt 'political' act. Certainly the positing of the direct effect of directives was a large step in the furthering of European integration and the 'constitutionalising' of the treaty. The Conseil d'Etat was reacting by protecting the national interest against what it perceived as an invalid assertion of the primacy of EC law. So Article 234 played its part in the developing constitutionalising of the treaty. However, by the late 1980s, the Conseil d'Etat modified its position, appearing to recognise that directives could have direct effect.[136]

More recent examples of a somewhat wilful use of *acte clair* can be found among quite a few other higher national courts. They include a decision of the Italian *Corte di Cassazione*, in which it construed a provision of Council Regulation 1035/72, finding it *acte clair*, although the ECJ had never given a ruling on it.[137] Another concerns the German *Bundesverwaltungsgericht*[138] (Federal Administrative Court) which rejected the application of female officers to join the armed forces combat

---

[131] See Commission reply of 30 January 1970 to written question No 349/69 OJ 1970 No C20 p 4, since reaffirmed several times. See also Schermers and Waelbroeck, *Judicial Protection in the European Communities* (Kluwer, 1991) at ss 540–542.

[132] And also Article 101(1) *Grundgesetz* (Basic Law), the 'gesetzliche Richter' provision.

[133] Extract translated by G Bebr, in 'The Rambling Ghost of Cohn-Bendit: Acte Clair and the Court of Justice' (1983) CMLRev at 442.

[134] *Société Sovincast* 27 November 1980 and *Société Civil Centre Internationale* 25 February 1981.

[135] In its decision of 16 July 1981 EuR (1981) 442.

[136] This change came about in the following cases: *Compagnie Alitalia* CE 3 February 1989; *Nicolo* CE 20 October 1989; *Boisdet* CE 24 September 1990; *SA Rothmans et SA Philip Morris* CE 28 February 1992.

[137] Decision of the Corte dei Cassazione of 7 May 1999 no 4564.

[138] Decision of the Bundesverwaltungsgericht of 20 May 1999 1 WB 94/98. See also the decision of the Belgian Cour d'Arbitrage of 30 September 1999 in which it partially annulled the Belgian law which transposed the EC directive 98/43 prohibiting tobacco advertising, without acceding to the requests of the parties to refer the matter to the ECJ and before the ECJ had itself determined the validity of the Tobacco Advertising Directive.

units' driving school, without making a preliminary reference. It did so on the basis of its reading of Article 12a(4) of the *Grundgesetz*, precluding women from bearing arms, which it found to be in accordance with EC Directive 76/207. This was an interpretation which the ECJ would have been unlikely to share as, in July 1998, following a reference from the Hannover Administrative court on a similar question, the ECJ responded with its judgment of 11 January 2000 in *Kreil*,[139] making it clear that it took a contrary view to the Federal Administrative Court. Nor is the House of Lords free from an apparently over zealous application of *acte clair*. In *British Fuels* v *Baxendale*[140] that court held that an employee who had been dismissed by an undertaking immediately before it had been taken over had no contract with the transferee. Lord Slynn led the House of Lords in this judgment, finding it *acte clair* that there was no such contract under the Acquired Rights Directive. It would seem, however, that the situation could not have been so *acte clair*, given that the ECJ had recently held in *Dethier*,[141] that in such a situation the contract of employment could be regarded as still extant. Such examples of senior courts failing to make references when they seem to take a contrary position to those of the ECJ are troubling, but perhaps inevitable, given the pride and self-regard of the higher national judiciary, as high now as in Thomas Jefferson's day in the description given at the outset of this chapter.

However, not everyone takes a negative view of *CILFIT* and the *acte clair* doctrine. Rasmussen argues that one should not take the *CILFIT* ruling at face value. He suggested that it might actually reduce the number of cases decided by the highest national courts without recourse to Luxembourg by its clever use of a deliberately beguiling structure.[142] Similarly, Mancini and Keeling, in a well-known article, construed it as part of a necessary dialogue with national courts, in which the ECJ was doing no more than paying 'lipservice' to the doctrine of *acte clair*. They preferred to characterise *CILFIT* instead as subtly displaying 'an acute understanding of judicial psychology'. In this way, they suggested that the Court 'hoped to induce the supreme courts to willingly use the mechanism for judicial co-operation'.[143] It is true that *CILFIT* was decided at a sensitive time for the ECJ's relationship with some of the higher national courts. The French Conseil d'Etat had completely refused to make a reference in the *Cohn-Bendit* case, a refusal that did not relate to any position taken by the French court on which EC law was *acte clair*.[144] By giving tacit approval to *acte clair*, the ECJ was deferring a little way to such national courts. But this also had advantages for the ECJ. It could remove unnecessary drags on the ECJ's time brought by unnecessary references – with the inherent risk of the development of an inconsistent national line of case law – but the system becomes more efficient overall. Delegation to the national courts, which

---

[139] Case C-285/98 *Kreil* [2000] ECR I-69.

[140] *British Fuels* v *Baxendale* [1999] 2 AC 52 HL.

[141] Case C-319/94 *Dethier* [1998] ECR I-1061.

[142] H Rasmussen, 'The European Court's acte clair strategy in CILFIT' (1984) 9 EL Rev 242 at 249.

[143] Mancini and Keeling, 'From CILFIT to ERT: The Constitutional Challenge Facing the European Court, (1991) 11 YBEL at 4.

[144] See G Bebr, 'The Rambling Ghost of Cohn-Bendit' (1983) 20 CMLRev 439.

become 'community courts', is seen as necessary in an overstretched community and mirrors developments elsewhere, such as in the field of competition law.

OTHER TYPES OF PRELIMINARY REFERENCE

Article 234 is not the only procedure for referring a matter to Luxembourg from the national courts. The Treaty of Amsterdam amended Article 35 TEU so as to introduce a new procedure, giving the ECJ the jurisdiction to give preliminary rulings on the validity and interpretation of framework decisions, decisions and on the interpretation of conventions and measures implementing them under that Title (i.e. Title VI: Police and Judicial Cooperation). However, this procedure is somewhat limited in nature: only courts of member states which have made a declaration accepting the jurisdiction of the court may make references, and if the member state so chooses, it may restrict referring courts to those of final instance: 'against whose decision there is no judicial remedy under national law'.[145] As with the former Justice and Home Affairs pillar prior to its amendment by the Treaty of Amsterdam, the ECJ has been largely excluded from control of the third pillar, as have the national parliaments, and therefore large areas of policy are removed from democratic control.

Similarly, the ECJ has always taken preliminary references on the Brussels Convention on Jurisdiction and Judgments of 1968[146] but, once again, only from courts of last instance. These policy choices send out various messages about perceptions of the European Court: a reluctance to entrust too many issues to its jurisdiction, and ambivalence about past success of the preliminary reference procedure, as well as a fear of overloading it.

Article 68, Title IV of the EC treaty, dealing with visas, asylum, immigration and other provisions on the free movement of persons, provides that Article 234 'shall apply to this Title'. However, it applies in a somewhat watered down form. Again, only courts of final instance may make the references, and in any case, the ECJ is excluded from ruling 'on any measure or decision taken pursuant to Article 62(1) relating to the maintenance of law and order and the safeguarding of national security'. Member states and Community institutions may also refer matters under this provision. Thus, in all of these areas, court control remains strictly limited.

THE CHANGING FACE OF ARTICLE 234: THE NATURE OF THE RELATIONSHIP WITH THE NATIONAL COURTS

Political scientists, as well as European lawyers and judges, have investigated, and even become fascinated with, the nature of this relationship. Back in the 1970s, Robert Lecourt, himself a judge of the ECJ, wrote of a 'L'Europe des Juges',[147]

---

[145] Article 35 (3) TEU.
[146] Soon to be replaced by the present draft Brussels Regulation, issued under new Article 68 EC.
[147] R Lecourt, *L'Europe des Juges* (Bruxelles, 1976).

something which sounds rather ominous. But what does this imply? Surely not that the Community dreamed of by Monnet and Schuman had been taken over by an over zealous legal profession, but rather a Europe in which he perceived the courts to have played an important role in the process of integration, simply aspiring to be an example of the rule of law at its best. Lecourt was certainly one of its architects, working hard to encourage national judges to become European judges. The term 'cooperation' is much used to describe the relationship between the ECJ and national courts, we find Clarence Mann using it as early as 1972.[148] Usually the description is of a pleasant, friendly, but nonetheless unequal relationship. The ECJ is usually described with admiration and respect (eulogy even) in this regard. Dehousse, for example, writes of the 'deference with which the Court treats its national counterparts', continuing, 'It is not difficult to imagine that a judge in a rural backwater may find something gratifying in having a direct link to one of the highest European courts'[149] – a relationship he characterises as 'fraternal,' perhaps unfortunately giving the impression that the Europe of judges is rather like an exclusive gentlemen's club. Mancini, too, is quick to praise the demeanour of the ECJ, which 'showed unlimited patience' towards its lowlier national counterparts, using a 'courteously didactic method' connoting this time more of a chivalric ethos.

It does seem that the ECJ became progressively more didactic, distorting this 'friendly' relationship over time as the ECJ became more assertive, for example in its recent case law on rejecting references. Nonetheless, the ECJ has continued to use the language of partnership and cooperation, most likely because it relies on the compliance of the national courts. However, why should national courts accept their role in the partnership?[150] Do they find it as profitable and stimulating as the accounts above suggest? Why should there exist what Weiler refers to as a 'compliance pull'?[151]

It might seem that at least some of them do feel themselves empowered.[152] But what sort of empowerment? After all, different national courts have had different benefits and burdens from EU membership.[153] One example of an increase in judicial power might be provided by the innovation of judicial review into some national courts' jurisdiction, where it previously did not exist. The UK,[154] of course, provides a good example of this: prior to the *Factortame* decision the UK courts had

---

[148] C Mann, *The Function of Judicial Decision in European Economic Integration* (The Hague: 1972).

[149] R Dehousse, *The European Court of Justice* (Macmillan, 1998) at 140.

[150] See Shapiro, surprised at their acquiescence, cited in A-M Slaughter. and W Mattli, 'Europe Before the Court: A Political Theory of Legal Integration' (1993) 47 International Organization 41–76.

[151] Weiler, 'Journey to an Unknown destination: A Retrospective and Prospective of the ECJ in the Arena of Political Integration' 31 JCMS (1993) 417 at 422.

[152] See Weiler, 'Has not power been the most intoxicating potion in human affairs?' Weiler, A Quiet Revolution – The European Court of Justice and its Interlocutors' (1994) 26 Comparative Political Studies; but see also J Golub, in 'The Politics of Judicial Discretion: Rethinking the Interaction between national courts and the ECJ' (1996) 2 West European Politics 360, who suggests that openness of national economy has something to do with amount of references.

[153] See Slaughter and Mattli, op. cit.

[154] But this is also the case with France, where there has recently been a great increase of review by the Conseil Constitutionnel: see A Stone Sweet, *The Birth of Judicial Politics in France* (Oxford University Press, 1992).

no jurisdiction to set aside acts of Parliament as this was prohibited under the doctrine of parliamentary sovereignty. After that reference it was clear that they could, indeed must, in some cases. As Lord Bridge stated:

> Some public comments on the decision of the Court of Justice, affirming the jurisdiction of the courts of member states to override national legislation if necessary to enable interim relief to be granted in protection of rights under Community law, have suggested that this was a novel and dangerous invasion by a Community institution of the sovereignty of the United Kingdom Parliament. But such comments are based on a misconception . . . Thus there is nothing in any way novel in according supremacy to rules of Community law in those areas to which they apply and to insist that, in the protection of rights under Community law, national courts must not be inhibited by rules of national law from granting interim relief in appropriate cases is no more than a logical recognition of that supremacy.[155]

This 'novel and dangerous invasion', if not an open act of empowerment, was at least apparently accepted with complete equanimity.[156] Thus, a more recent generation of UK judges seems to have, if not embraced, at least welcomed, its powers under EC law, resulting in something of a judicial 'sea-change' in the UK: one sees the courts being more willing to interfere with discretionary decisions taken by ministers, e.g. *M v Home Office*,[157] and to do justice to arguments based on rights. This is unlike some of their forerunners, e.g. the judges in the cases of *Henn and Darby, Santillo* and *Marshall*, in which Rasmussen has located 'clear signs of attitudes of self-righteousness and localism pervading some UK judgements'.[158] Other supreme courts may originally have been more recalcitrant: e.g. the Italian Constitutional Court in *Simmenthal*, which insisted that only it had the power to declare domestic legislation invalid, so placing obstacles in the way of the effectiveness of EC law. Likewise it could hardly be said that the Conseil d'Etat, or the Bundesverfassungsgericht, seemed empowered by EC law, rather they often asserted their authority against it, sometimes refusing to implement judgments of the ECJ, as already discussed. However, it is nonetheless very rare for a national court to fail to apply a preliminary ruling. A national court with a mind of its own is much more likely not to refer in the first place.[159]

Karen Alter attributes some of the success of Article 234 to an inter-court competition model.[160] She suggests that 'lower courts found few costs and numerous benefits in making references. They could circumvent the jurisdiction of the higher courts and reopen legal debates that were closed.'[161] So, for example, industrial tribunals in

---

[155] Case C-213/89 *R v Secretary of State for Transport, ex parte Factortame* [1990] ECR I-2433.

[156] See e.g., Craig op. cit., in Slaughter, Sweet and Weiler op. cit., who also urges us to look to the personalities of judges: those such as Woolf, Brown-Wilkinson, Mustill, Slynn and Sedley, who have been willing to take on board European rights and remedies.

[157] See also *M v Home Office* [1994] 1 AC 377.

[158] Rasmussen, *On Law and Policy* at 330.

[159] G Bermann et al., *Cases and Materials on European Community Law* (St Paul Minneapolis: West, 1993) at 248: 'Only in wholly exceptional circumstances have national courts misunderstood the rulings or showed reluctance to implement them.'

[160] K Alter, 'The European Court's Political Power' op.cit. fn 130.

[161] Alter, ibid.

the UK were able to circumvent the Employment Appeals Tribunal and Conservative government policy on employment, going straight to Luxembourg on issues of sex discrimination. On occasion, higher courts might have tried to stop lower ones from making references, as in cases of the restrictive guidelines issued by Lord Denning discouraging references in many circumstances. The Italian Constitutional Court reformulated all issues of the compatibility of national law with EC law as constitutional, hence trying to reserve them for itself, a move that was unsuccessful after the ECJ's judgment in *Simmenthal*. Therefore, partly on account of the actions of lower courts, referring all sorts of cases to Luxembourg, in their capacity as Community courts, EC law expanded into all sorts of areas: questions of payment of university fees, equal treatment of transsexuals, issues of fundamental rights.

Legal culture also cannot be ignored in this context. It is a truism to state that values are embedded in legal systems, but this is nonetheless worth restating, especially in the case of public law, which reflects particular political philosophies, cultural norms, perceived societal roles, functions and duties. The French Conseil d'Etat saw itself as protector of the national interest, so it would be less likely to embrace EC law. The German constitution contains the concept of the *gesetzlicher Richter* (the 'lawful judge'), so German courts, or at least the lower ones, and litigants, would be more likely to rely on it in making references.

Legal culture is also reflected in the types of questions which are referred, which form the subject matter of the dialogue between national courts and the ECJ. They are constructed in various ways, on various levels[162] – depending on whether they are of constitutional importance – i.e. must Parliamentary statutes be set aside under EC law, or on specific issues of EC law: are pyjamas solely to be classified as night garments under the Common Customs tariff? They may be of the confrontational sort ('Banana wars'), or more deferential in nature. They may also be backed up by a strong 'constitutional armoury' as in the case of references concerning fundamental rights emanating from Germany, backed up by references to provisions in the German constitution, or less so, if emanating from an unentrenched constitutional legal system, such as the UK. The extent to which a member state intervenes to make its views known, even in cases where its own conduct is not at issue, will also increase and influence this dialogue.[163] Thus, ultimately, the preliminary reference procedure can be seen as a reflection of the legal, social, political and philosophical culture of the member states of the EU, instilling a richness into the Community legal system.

THE FUTURE

The Due Report[164] described preliminary references as 'undoubtedly the most important issue currently confronting the Community Courts'.[165] The system of ref-

---

[162] de la Mare op. cit., in Craig and de Burca, op. cit. at fn. 8.
[163] The UK, for example, apparently gives its views more than any other member state: ECJ Internal Statistics.
[164] Report by the Working Party on 'The Future of the European Communities' Court System', January 2000.
[165] Ibid. at 11.

erences has experienced an 87 per cent increase in 9 years.[166] The Due report attributes its success to its current distinctive features, but warns that it will have to be ensured that in future the Court is not swamped by a tide of preliminary references.

Various proposals have been made to reform the system, one being that only courts of final instance should entitled to make references. This seems unsatisfactory, given that currently about three-quarters of the existing references come from courts other than those of final instance. Thus, although such a change might stem the tide of references, it would also undoubtedly make excessive inroads into the cooperation and dialogue between national courts and the Community courts. Another proposal is that the member states might set up bodies with devolved powers under EC law to deal with references. However, to do so might jeopardise the uniform application of Community law. It might also be the case, if such a plan were followed, that a problem might be considered by three courts in succession, prolonging proceedings and involving high costs for the member states as well as distorting the national court structure. Alternatively, it has been suggested that the ECJ might be given the power to select those preliminary questions it considered sufficiently important for it to consider, rather than having the national, and in this context, peripheral, courts make the decision. This would be similar to the system of certiorari employed by the US Supreme Court.[167] It has been suggested that it would be difficult to transpose the certiorari system into the EU, which has a very different court structure.[168] Unlike in the US, a hierarchical relationship does not (officially) exist between the ECJ and the national courts,[169] but rather the relationship is (at least supposedly, but surely not always) one of cooperation and dialogue, which might be, according to the Due Working Party, 'upset by such a crude form of selection'.[170] However, the Due report's reference to certiorari as a crude form of selection is puzzling, as it actually enables the Supreme Court to make highly discriminating choices, keeping its workload to the manageable, in a situation not so far removed from that of the ECJ.

On the other hand, it does seem that the national courts should be encouraged to be bolder in applying Community law themselves. The Due report proposed amending Article 234 to give effect to this. So they suggested that courts, other than those of final instance, should be dissuaded from referring matters to the Court of Justice where EC law clearly states what the answer should be, or where the issue raises no real significance for Community law. They also suggested amending the obligation imposed on courts of final instance, so that they are required to refer only questions 'which are sufficiently important for Community law and about whose

---

[166] *Commission contribution on the reform of the Community courts* March 2000 IP/00/213.

[167] See US Judiciary Act 1925.

[168] Due report at 21.

[169] Although see Craig and de Búrca, *EU Law* at 423, for argument concerning the transmutation of the nature of the relationship between the ECJ and national courts.

[170] Due report at 21. Certiorari in its present form was first introduced by the US Judiciary Act of 1925, abolishing access to the Supreme Court as of right. It was introduced as a result of the continued expansion of federal litigation, and also seen as important that the Supreme Court be able to give expeditious and authoritative rulings when cases of far-reaching importance fell within its jurisdiction.

solution there is still real doubt' after examination by the lower courts.[171] The working party did not see this as threatening the uniformity of Community law, as, were it to be the case that courts of final instance gave incorrect answers on questions of Community law, then they suggested that the Commission, in its capacity of guardian of the treaties, could ask the ECJ, without stipulating a time limit, to decide such questions. The working party also thought that the ECJ's 1996 'Information to national courts' on poorly drafted, irrelevant or premature references, might be incorporated into the Court's Rules of Procedure in order to give it more force. They also suggested shifting some types of preliminary reference to the CFI (while recognising the dangers of overloading that court) as well as the better training in Community law of all those involved in the reference procedure, and the making available of a powerful information system to practitioners. In these ways, they thought, national courts might deal more fruitfully with EC law themselves.

In the event, the Treaty of Nice opted to give the Court of First Instance some jurisdiction in the preliminary reference procedure. Article 225 EC was amended to give the Court of First Instance 'jurisdiction to hear and determine questions referred for a preliminary ruling under Article 234, in specific areas laid down by the Statute'. This will take place at a later date and will probably be in areas in which the CFI already has jurisdiction. Article 225(3) also provides that such cases may be exceptionally subject to review by the ECJ 'where there is a serious risk of the unity or consistency of Community law being affected'. Changes were, however, also made by amendments to the Court's Rules of Procedure in July 2000 and February 2001,[172] which concerned preliminary rulings in particular. These introduced a simplified procedure under Article 104(3) of the Rules, whereby the Court may give a decision by order where the question referred for a preliminary ruling is either identical to one on which it has previously ruled; where the answer may clearly be deduced from existing case law; or where the answer to the question admits to no reasonable doubt. Article 54a of the amended rules also permits the Juge Rapporteur or advocate general to request from parties all the information or documents as they deem relevant and they may also ask for additional clarification from the national courts under Article 104(5). The Court has been swift to make use of these new procedures,[173] and, although these amended rules may help in some of the situations described in this chapter, they still do not really address the problem of the flood of cases coming to court.

The first pages of this chapter stressed the importance of preliminary rulings, an importance that is constitutional in dimension. The practice has survived the rebellion of some national courts, but now it must survive the overwhelming growth in references. It may well be that it should follow the practice introduced to the US Supreme Court early last century, and that the time is now ripe for the introduction of some filter mechanism.

---

[171] Due report at 15.

[172] OJ 2000 L 122 and OJ 2000 L 322. See also the Expedited procedure under Article 104a ROP for cases of extreme urgency, used for the first time in case C-189/01 *Jipper* [2001] ECR I-5689 in the context of the foot and mouth epidemic.

[173] Cases C-89/00 *Bicakci* OJ 2001 C95/4 and C-242/99 *Vogler* OJ 2001 C108/1, Cases C-9/01 to C-12/01 *Monnier* OJ 2001 C24512.

7

SUPREMACY, SOVEREIGNTY AND PLURALISM

The Treaty of Rome came into existence in one aspect like any other international treaty – it contained no supremacy clause providing for the supremacy of Community law over that of its member states. The European Economic Community, at its inception in 1957, was to be an international organisation, providing for a set of international obligations, of common but important goals, with which the member states were to comply, within limited fields, and thus the types of supremacy clauses to be found in federal constitutions seemed inapplicable. Forty years on, the concept of supremacy is, itself, in doubt, and the concept of a sovereign state, consigned by some to a bygone era of history, 'a passing phenomena of a few centuries.'[1]

Such radical thoughts are partly prompted by the work of the European Court. The bedrock principle of the supremacy of EC law over national law is a creation of the European Court, dating from the early years of its existence, in what has been described as its 'heroic period'[2] although the issues of supremacy and sovereignty have resurfaced in the 1990s, partly prompted by the challenging jurisprudence of the German Constitutional Court. A key stage in the now near mythic history of the European Union is the case of *Van Gend en Loos*.[3] This was the case which established that provisions of Community law were not just tools of international law, but had direct effect, and thus could be relied upon by individual litigants in their national courts. But if such directly effective provisions of Community law could be pleaded before the domestic courts, then they might conflict with an incompatible provision of national law. How should the domestic courts deal with such a situation? The Court of Justice did not choose to give detailed explication, instead stating, in these now infamous words: 'the Community constitutes a new legal order for the benefit of which the states have limited their sovereign rights, albeit within

---

[1] Neil MacCormick, 'Beyond the Sovereign State' (1993) 56 MLR at 1.
[2] This phrase is used in J Weiler, 'The Transformation of Europe' (1991) 100 Yale Law Journal at 2428, who acknowledges that the phrase was used by 'insiders' of this period.
[3] Case 26/62 *NV. Algemene Transport en Expeditie Onderneming van Gend en Loos v Nederlandse Administratie der Belastingen* [1963] ECR 1.

limited fields, and the subjects of which comprise not only the member states but also their nationals.'[4]

Different member states of course have different constitutional systems, only some of which accord priority to international law over national law. As Advocate General Römer[5] pointed out in *Van Gend*, only the Netherlands, Luxembourg and possibly France would have given priority to international agreements. Detailed consideration came only when the European Court revisited the issue two years later in the case of *Costa v ENEL*.[6] In *Costa*, the court set out a series of arguments pertaining to the supremacy of Community law. The Court started by stressing the comparison between international treaties and the Community which 'by contrast … has created its own legal system'. According to the Court, 'By creating a Community of unlimited duration, having its own institutions, its own personality, its own legal capacity and capacity of representation on the international plane and, more particularly, real powers stemming from a limitation of sovereignty or a transfer of powers from the states to the Community, the Member states have limited their sovereign rights, albeit within limited fields, and have thus created a body of law which binds both their nationals and themselves.' What the European Court does not do[7] is to examine the Constitution of any member state, to see if such a transfer was possible according to that country's constitutional law. The Court also refers to Article 249 of the Treaty to give textual support (in fact the only textual support) to its arguments: this provision, which states that 'a regulation "shall be binding" and "directly applicable in all member states" would be quite meaningless', asserted the Court, 'if a State could unilaterally nullify its effects by means of a legislative measure which could prevail over Community law.' The argument used here by the Court, although rooted in the treaty, is not necessarily a strong one. Article 249 sets out the means by which regulations (and only regulations, not other types of EC law) become binding within national legal systems but does not deal with any questions of priority between EC law and national law.

Perhaps the most interesting aspect of the judgment is its strongly teleological nature. The 'terms and spirit of the Treaty' according to the Court 'make it impossible for the States, as a corollary, to accord precedence to a unilateral and subsequent measure over a legal system accepted by them on the basis of reciprocity. Such a measure cannot therefore be inconsistent with that legal system. The executive force of Community law cannot vary from one State to another in deference to subsequent domestic laws, without jeopardising the objectives of the Treaty . . . '[8] This argument is based on the necessity of ensuring the uniformity and effectiveness of Community law and is one which has been frequently used by the European Court over the years. (It is also interesting to note that, somewhat presciently, AG Lagrange, in his opinion in this case, stated that 'It is certainly true to say that the

---

[4] Ibid. at 12.
[5] Ibid. at 23.
[6] Case 6/64 *Flaminio Costa v ENEL* [1964] ECR 585.
[7] As noted by P Craig and G de Búrca, *EU Law* (2nd edn, OUP, 1998) at 259.
[8] *Costa v Enel* at 597.

EEC Treaty has, in a sense, the character of a genuine constitution, the constitution of the Community.')[9]

History shows us that the ECJ's technique is not unique. Interesting parallels may be drawn between the European Court's development of the doctrine of supremacy of Community law and the US Supreme Court's success in maintaining ultimate control over the federal and state legal systems in the early nineteenth century. This assertion of control on the part of the American court involved a definite vision of the type of association of states which the Constitution had formed, a necessary component of which was the uniform application of federal law. The disputes between the US Supreme Court and the state courts which did not want to accept its authority as the ultimate arbiter of power, have a particular resonance with the German Constitutional court's threats to refuse to accept the European Court's ultimate authority to determine the competence of the Community to act[10] at certain stages of the EC, but the stress placed by the early Supreme Court justices, such as Story or Marshall, on the uniformity of federal law, strike a chord with the European Court's early jurisprudence. In both systems, federal or European court judges have promoted strong central values which have been in conflict with state sovereignty. Like many Europeans today, states' rights advocates in the early years of the US believed in the sovereignty of the states, arguing that, since the validity of the US constitution was based on the consent of the states, the federal government's powers must be subject to the limitations binding the states. In *Martin* v *Hunter's Lessee*[11] Justice Story upheld the jurisdiction of the federal courts over the state (in this case, Virginian) courts, insisting that this could be derived from the need for the uniformity and harmony of decisions on all constitutional matters throughout the country: ' ... the laws, the treaties and the constitution of the United States would be different in different states, and might perhaps, never have precisely the same construction, obligation or efficacy in two states.'[12] These arguments resurface, 150 years later, in *Costa*.

Both courts were motivated by a vision of what they took their new legal order to be, although, in the context of the US and the early days of the EEC, these amounted to different things. The US Supreme Court was dealing with a federal constitution, the ECJ with a traditional multilateral treaty, which did not even enjoy the status of higher law in some of its member states, and which, as a treaty, should have been subject to interpretative canons, such as the presumption that states do not lose their sovereignty; little on which to base the Court's statement that EC law had a 'special and original nature' which could be called into question if it could be overridden by domestic law.

Notwithstanding this, over the next ten years or so, the Court expanded on its declaration of the supremacy of Community law. Regardless of its status (i.e. whether treaty provision, Community legislation or agreement with a

---

[9] *Costa* v *Enel* 605.
[10] See below.
[11] 14 US (1 Wheat) 304 (1816).
[12] Ibid. at 348.

non-Community state) a directly effective Community law provision was to prevail over national law. Even a fundamental constitutional provision could not be invoked to challenge the supremacy of Community law. In *Internationale Handelsgesellschaft*[13] the ECJ used the same uniformity based argument to make this point:

> Recourse to the legal rules or concepts of national law in order to judge the validity of measures adopted by the institutions of the Community would have an adverse effect on the uniformity and efficacy of Community law. The validity of such measures can only be judged in the light of Community law. In fact, the law stemming from the Treaty, an independent source of law, cannot because of its very nature be overridden by rules of national law, however framed, without being deprived of its character as Community law and without the legal basis of the Community itself being called into question. Therefore the validity of a Community measure or its effect within a member state cannot be affected by allegations that it runs counter to either fundamental rights formulated by the constitution of that state or the principles of a national constitutional structure.[14]

The German constitutional court was no happier with this declaration than the Virginia courts had been with Justice Story's insistence on uniformity in 1816, and, just as the Virginia courts (and those of other states) showed their teeth, so a conflictual relationship has continued between the ECJ and the German Constitutional Court.[15] The ECJ has not, however, resiled from this position.

Another case in the supremacy canon is *Simmenthal*.[16] This case well illustrated the practical effects of the supremacy doctrine and its transformational effects on national law. The Simmenthal company imported beef from France into Italy and had to pay a public health inspection fee as prescribed by an Italian law passed in 1970. However, such a charge was contrary to the free movement provisions of the EC Treaty and two Community regulations of 1964 and 1968. The Italian fiscal authorities challenged the Pretore's order of repayment of the amounts with interest on the basis that, first, subsequent Italian law must prevail over Community law and, second, that even if there were a conflict, the matter must first be brought before the Italian Constitutional Court, which was the only tribunal with the authority to declare Italian law unconstitutional. The European Court did not balk at the weight and authority of the national constitutional courts, nor fear their response. As well as stating that Community provisions 'render automatically inapplicable any conflicting provision of current national law but ... also preclude the valid adoption of new national legislative measures to the extent to which they would be compatible with Community provisions' the ECJ held that:

> any provision of a national legal system ... which might impair the effectiveness of Community law by withholding from the national court having jurisdiction to apply

---

[13] Case 11/70 *Internationale Handelsgesellschaft gmbH v Einfuhr und Vorratsstelle fur Getreide und Futtermittel* [1970] ECR 1125.
[14] Ibid. at para 3.
[15] This will be explored more fully below.
[16] Case 106/77 *Amministrazione delle Finanze dello Stato v Simmenthal SpA* [1978] ECR 629.

such law the power to do everything necessary at the moment of its application to set aside national legislative provisions which might prevent Community rules from having full force and effect are incompatible with those requirements which are the very essence of Community law.[17]

So, the lower court, even if not empowered under national law to do so, must give full effect to Community law.

This point was revisited in the *Factortame*[18] case, where the conflict between Community law and national law this time embroiled a fundamental principle of the British Constitution: parliamentary sovereignty. However, the clash of legal systems was further complicated by the fact that the status of Community law itself was not certain, it was only putatively incompatible with national law. The Common Fisheries Policy of the EU allocated fishing quotas to the member states, and on the exhaustion of the Spanish quota, Spanish fishing concerns had turned to England, where, by setting up as English companies, they were able to fish out of the British quota. The British government, becoming aware of this state of affairs, passed the Merchant Shipping Act and Regulations, stipulating residency and nationality requirements for company licence holding to prevent this invasion of the British fishing quota. However, such requirements involve manifold breaches of the Treaty of Rome, namely the prohibition of discrimination on grounds of nationality, as well as the freedom to supply services and freedom of establishment. On the other hand, the quota system of the Common Fisheries Policy seemed itself to be in tatters. Troubled waters indeed. The Spanish fishing concerns applied for interim relief against the application of the English law. The European Court ruled that the doctrine of parliamentary sovereignty could not prevent the English court from providing relief, even if that meant that the courts would have to set aside the application of an English statute (a state of affairs unknown in English law: the last judicial threat to the sovereignty of Parliamentary legislation having occurred, if at all,[19] in the early seventeenth century). The Court justified its reasoning in terms of ensuring the effectiveness of Community law and, although it did not prescribe a new remedy, as Advocate General Tesauro put it, 'the national court is obliged to afford judicial protection to the rights conferred by a Community provision.'[20] Thus, three hundred years of Parliamentary sovereignty came to an end, or at least in so far as Community law was implicated.

CONSTITUTIONALISM, COMPETENCE AND SOVEREIGNTY

In the light of the profound changes wrought by the European Court it is common in this context to read of how the European court has 'constitutionalised' the

---

[17] *Simmenthal*, paras 17 and 22 of the judgment.
[18] *R v Secretary of State for Transport, ex parte Factortame* [1990] ECR 1 2433.
[19] See, for a discussion of this, J Goldsworthy, *The Sovereignty of Parliament* (OUP, 1999).
[20] *Factortame* at 2454.

treaties by, *inter alia*, declaring the supremacy of Community law.[21] Federico Mancini, a judge of the European Court, wrote in 1989 that 'If one were asked to synthetise the direction in which the case law produced in Luxembourg has moved since 1957, one would have to say that it coincides with the making of a constitution for Europe.'[22] The doctrine of supremacy of Community law established in *Costa, Internationale Handelsgesellschaft, Simmenthal* and *Factortame*, is a keystone of the doctrine of European constitutionality. In other case law the ECJ has acknowledged the constitutional status of the treaties, describing them as a constitutional charter in *Les Verts* and its first opinion on the draft EEA agreement. Indeed the latter opinion, *1/91*, is a good illustration of what the ECJ considers to be distinctive about the new legal order. The ECJ described the draft EEA agreement as simply an agreement under Public International law, involving no transfer of legislative sovereignty. The EEC on the other hand, was, according to the court, a new legal order because, in the words of the ECJ:

> The EEA court is to ensure the sound operation of rules on free trade and competition under an international treaty which creates obligations only between parties. In contrast the Court of Justice has to secure observation of a particular legal order and to foster its development with a view to achieving the objectives set out in Article 2 ... 8A ... and 102A ... of the EEC Treaty and to attain a European Union among Member States.[23]

Thus the *acquis communautaire* must not be threatened by a court and treaty which did not pertain to this new legal order.[24]

So even if the EEC did conform to the status of international organisation in its early days (which is unlikely) it has now moved well beyond that.[25] In addition to this incipient and creeping constitutionalism, it is also now difficult to fathom where any remaining core of state sovereignty might reside. The somewhat relentless process of European integration, particularly in its swifter form of the 1980s and 1990s, along with the introduction of qualified majority voting and completion of

---

[21] Weiler refers to the 'constitutionalisation of the Community legal structure' naming the doctrine of supremacy as one key doctrine in the constitutionalising of the treaties. Weiler J, *The Transformation of Europe* at 2413.

[22] F Mancini, 'The Making of a Constitution for Europe' (1989) 26 CMLRev 5933.

[23] *Opinion 1/91, Re a Draft Treaty on a European Economic Area* [1992] CMLR 245 at 272.

[24] A O'Neill points out that the 'essential differences' perceived by the European Court between the European Court and the EEA Court simply rested on repeated judicial assertions (such as those of the doctrines of direct effect and supremacy) rather than any particular differences in the wording of the two treaties. In fact the provisions of free movement and competition are identically worded in the two treaties. A O'Neill, *Decisions of the European Court of Justice and their Constitutional Implications in the UK*, (Butterworths, 1994).

[25] Evidence of this may be found in the fact that the EU treaties may not be amended according to the rules of international law. Under international law parties to a treaty may revoke it at any time, even disregarding provisions in the treaty stipulating a special procedure for amendment and withdrawal – see the Vienna Convention 1968. Although in its early days, the EEC treaty was amended in this way, more recently the ECJ has held that the treaties may only be amended according to Article 48 (1), a statement which would be illegitimate if the EU existed only according to the norms of international law. See P Pescatore, *L'ordre juridique des Communauté européénnes* (Liège: Presses universitaires de Liège, 1975) 62–63.

the internal market, has removed many areas of state competence (as maintained by the 'spillover' concept of functionalist theory).[26] Thus, for example, transfer of competence to the former Justice and Home Affairs pillar resulted in an encroachment of state sovereignty in matters of national security.

Many federal constitutions set out a division of competence between the federal government and its constituent units. While edging toward constitutionality, the EC treaty is silent about the division of competence between the EC and the member states, although of course it allocated the power to act to the EC in certain areas. The division of powers is thus unclear. The ECJ, as might be expected, has developed a jurisprudence regarding the respective competences of the EC and member states, through the development of the doctrines of exclusivity and pre-emption. In some areas, such as the Common Commercial Policy, it has held that the EC is exclusively competent.[27] Elsewhere, there is concurrent competence, and if the EC has not acted in a particular area, the member states may take action. Once the Community does act, however, it assumes exclusive competence within that field: this is the doctrine of pre-emption.[28] However, for the member states, as Lenaerts[29] writes, there is 'no constitutionally protected nucleus of sovereignty'. Even where the residual powers of the member states are expressly recognised in the treaty, such as in Article 30, the ECJ has held that these marked out areas are not constitutionally protected areas of national sovereignty but rather permissible derogations from the principle of free movement of goods, which are only justified if they set out the objectives set out in Article 30.[30]

Another reason why it is difficult to identify a discrete residual area of member state sovereignty is that, even where enumerated in the treaty, the doctrine of implied powers, or widespread use of Article 308 (formerly 235),[31] has been used to push Community competence to the limits. As Weatherill writes, 'it is difficult to envisage the court ever holding a sphere to lie beyond the Community's strict legal competence, once a measure based on Article 235 has invaded that sphere'.[32] The *Van Gend* case referred to the member states transferring their sovereignty within 'limited fields'. However, as Weiler has pointed out, a mutation of Community competence occurred during the 1970s, so that 'no core activity of state function could be seen as still constitutionally immune from Community action . . . but also that no

---

[26] See e.g. LN Lindberg, *The Political Dynamics of European Integration* (Oxford: OUP, 1963), for an example of a neo-functionalist approach to European integration. See also chapter 1.

[27] *Opinion 1/75* [1975] ECR 1355.

[28] See M Waelbroeck, 'The emergent doctrine of Community pre-emption – consent and redelegation' in M Sandalow and E Stein (ed.) *Courts and Free Markets* (1982) Vol. II 548–577; R Bieber, 'On the mutual completion of overlapping legal systems: the case of the European Communities and the national legal orders' (1988) ELRev 147–158; S Weatherill, 'Beyond Pre-emption Shared Competence and Constitutional Change in the European Community' in D O'Keefe and P Twomey (ed.) *Legal Issues of the Maastricht Treaty* (Law Chancery, 1992) 13–33. See also chapter 4.

[29] K Lenaerts, 'Constitutionalism and the Many Faces of Federalism' (1990) 38 American Journal of Comparative Law 205 at 220.

[30] See Case 153/78 *Commission v Germany* [1979] ECR 2555.

[31] For more detailed information on Article 308 see Chapter 4.

[32] Weatherill, op. cit. at n 28.

sphere of material competence could be excluded from the Community acting under Article 235.'[33] Curiously, as Weiler points out, this huge expansion of Community jurisdiction did not ignite major political disputes between EC and member states, a feature which Weiler suggests is partly explicable on the basis that 'the governments of the member states could control each legislative act, from inception through adoption and then implementation'.[34] This expansion in the use of Article 308 occurred before the Single European Act and the introduction of qualified majority voting, so the transfer of competence to the Community did not come at the expense of the member states. However, as Weiler goes on to warn, this mutation of competence posed constitutional dangers to the Community as it did threaten a legal rather than a political consensus. This legal consensus was formed by the relationship of trust between the ECJ and the national courts. Weiler writes, 'The erosion of enumeration meant that the new legal order, and the judicial-legal contract which underwrote it, was to extend to all areas of activity.'[35]

Matters are further complicated by the fact that there is no provision in the EC Treaty for what under German constitutional law is termed *Kompetenz-Kompetenz*: the issue of who shall have the ultimate authority to determine what comes within the sphere of application of federal, or in this instance, Community law. There is, as with supremacy, or the enumeration of competences, no provision for this factor in the EC Treaty. The ECJ has used Article 220 to police the boundaries of Community and member state law but the German Constitutional court, unhappy with this assertion of competence, has claimed this power for itself. In fact, all of the factors discussed above were to provoke an undercurrent of discontent which came to a head with the German Constitutional court's *Maastricht judgment* in 1993.[36]

THE NATIONAL RESPONSE TO SUPREMACY

If a constitutional revolution has taken place, even a quiet[37] one, how have the national authorities responded to this concomitant loss of their sovereignty? Weiler used the expression 'the dual character of supranationalism' some time ago to capture the way in which the development of Community law and its supremacy is the achievement both of the Community institutions and its member states.[38] This section will examine their response, mostly with regard to the reaction of the courts. But first, the reaction of the political authorities will be examined.

---

[33] J Weiler, 'The Transformation of Europe', at 2416.

[34] Weiler ibid. at 2449.

[35] Weiler ibid. at 2452.

[36] The *Maastricht judgment* is discussed further in a later section of this chapter.

[37] The phrase a 'quiet revolution' in the context of loss of sovereignty is used by HWR Wade, 'The Basis of Legal Sovereignty' (1955) CLJ 172 at 187.

[38] J Weiler, 'The Community System: the Dual Character of Supranationalism' (1981) Yearbook of European Law 267.

The political response

In the case of the US, legislative opposition to the jurisdiction of the Supreme Court was as frequent as and even more vehement than the court denunciations. For example, the Kentucky legislature even went as far as to request the governor to inform it 'whether . . . it may be advisable to call forth the physical power of the state to resist the execution of the decisions of the Court'.[39] In 1828 South Carolina introduced its infamous 'nullification' ordinance under which the state could declare a federal government act to be void and not binding in that state. Ultimately, the battles between federal government and state could only be resolved after the Civil War, and not always even then. How could such an extreme response to the ECJ's path-breaking jurisprudence have been avoided within the EC? After all, there had occurred (if one also includes other fundamental innovations, such as the doctrine of direct effect, the introduction of a fundamental rights jurisprudence) what Weiler terms 'a radical mutation of the treaty'.[40] The surprising fact is that the member states so quietly accepted the European Court's extension of its jurisdiction and of the treaties. The fervent reaction of certain British 'eurosceptics' to extensions of EC jurisdiction in the Maastricht Treaty and the British government's desire to control the jurisdiction of the European Court,[41] as well as other examples such as the first Danish 'no vote' to Maastricht, should not lead us to believe that such responses were the norm in the EC's early days. True, de Gaulle had deadened the progress of the EC by insisting on the maintenance of a member state veto through the Luxembourg accords. But the French government (nor any other) was certainly not threatening to nullify the effects of the European Court's judgment through its legislature.[42] And yet, as Weiler again points out,[43] the changes of the 'Heroic Period' of the ECJ, would normally require something akin to a constitutional Convention (i.e. a gathering of delegates) to occur. Weiler's own explanation for the lack of an outraged response from the member states is the very fact that this constitutional revolution was judicially driven, 'thus attaching to itself the deep seated legitimacy that derives from the mythical neutrality and religious-like authority with which we invest our supreme courts'.[44] But Supreme Courts are not always treated with a

---

[39] C Haines, *The Role of the Supreme Court in American Government and Politics 1789–1835* (1973) at 468 cited in S Boom, 'The European Union after the Maastricht Decision; Will Germany be the Virginia of Europe?' (1995) 43 American Journal of Comparative Law 177–226 at 196.

[40] Weiler, 'The Transformation of Europe' at 2437 *et seq.*

[41] On 22 July 1996 the then UK Foreign Secretary, Malcolm Rifkind, published a *memorandum on Proposals to improve the operation of the ECJ*. Rifkind stressed that changes were needed to 'curb the excessive effects of certain court judgements' and also said that 'We are also concerned that the ECJ's interpretation sometimes seems to go beyond what Member States intended when they made the laws. The role of the Court is to interpret existing law, not to make new law.' In response to these words, Sir Leon Brittan, speaking to the Bow Group at the House of Commons, said ' . . . there is no chance of getting any legitimate improvements if when you are asking for them you give the impression that your real intention is to undermine the Court's whole purpose and role.'

[42] Although the *Foyer-Debré Proposition de Loi*, tabled in the Assemblée Nationale as an attempt to nullify the ECJ's *Opinion 1/78*, was only defeated by French Government's intervention: see further the discussion in Chapter 5, and below.

[43] Weiler, op. cit.

[44] Weiler, 'The Transformation of Europe' at 2428.

religious-like authority as the experience of the US Supreme Court in its early days[45] testifies. Perhaps this passive response is also attributable to the idealism of the early years of the EEC, according to which European union seemed to be an essential part of dealing with the heritage of the Second World War. Weiler also points to another possible explanation. The European Court's jurisprudence did not (at this stage of European integration at least) come at the expense of the member states. As the Community at this stage, due in no small part to the work of de Gaulle and the suspension of majority voting in 1966 (to the disgust of many political scientists), proceeded on a largely inter-governmental basis the member states were still very much the 'masters of the treaty'. Supremacy of Community law was not a zero-sum game.[46]

The judicial response

If the political branches of the member state governments largely accepted the supremacy of Community law, their judicial branches have been less willing to do so. The reaction of the national courts is quite complex, complicated by the fact that different member states, of course, have different constitutions and different mechanisms for the reception and application of Community law within their territory. National courts have also tended to recognise the supremacy of Community law as being a product of their own domestic legal orders, rather than a feature of the unique *sui generis* nature of Community law, which is the position which the European Court takes. This interpretation of the primacy of Community law raises problems when Community law conflicts with national constitutions. As the courts see Community law as deriving its authority from their constitution, they are unlikely to accord it primacy to that very same constitution.

The remainder of this section highlights the most important issues and controversies which have arisen between national courts and the ECJ, focusing in particular on the relationship between the German constitutional court and the ECJ which currently raises some of the most interesting and salient problems for European integration.

France

In France, the *Conseil Constitutionnel* has exclusive jurisdiction to review compatibility of France's international commitments, or draft legislation, with the French Constitution. This review is carried out before the measures are introduced into the French legal order and there is no *ex post facto* review of the constitutionality of legislation by the French courts. Once the *Conseil Constitutionnel* establishes that

---

[45] Or even more recently see for example the reaction to *Brown v Board of Education* 347 U.S 483 (1954) in which the Court held that the Equal Protection clause required equal access to education of blacks and whites in segregated schools. Southern state legislatures passed resolutions of 'Interposition and nullification'.

[46] However, the Single European Act and the move to majority voting introduced a different state of affairs which was much less acceptable, setting the scene for the battles of the 1990s.

France's obligations under Community law are compatible with the French Constitution then they become part of French law. However, the French courts may of course consider cases which raise the question of the illegality of French law on the basis that it infringes Community law.

The ordinary courts in France are divided into two separate court systems, with very different traditions:[47] the ordinary courts and the administrative courts which the Victorian jurist Dicey so famously criticised as unnecessary. This bifurcated system produced a bifurcated response to the primacy of Community law, which was accepted in the *Cour de Cassation*, the highest court in the ordinary judicial courts, but not by the *Conseil État*, the supreme administrative court, which finally recognised it only in 1989.[48]

In the *Café Jacques Vabre*[49] case it had been argued that the ordinary French courts could not determine the constitutionality of a French statute and that this could only be done by the *Conseil Constitutionnel* before the legislation in question was passed. The *Cour de Cassation* rejected this argument. The *Vabre* case was a courageous one, especially as it involved considerable expense to the French Treasury. Vabre had imported instant coffee into France from the Netherlands. This coffee was subjected to a higher rate of taxation than that produced in France. Vabre claimed a breach of Article 90 [formerly 95]. It was argued that the courts could not determine the constitutionality of the French statute imposing the tax but this was rejected by the *Cour de Cassation*, which held that EC law constituted a new legal order binding on the national courts. There was a reaction. The ECJ was compared to Stalin's revolutionary courts and the *Cour de Cassation* seen as its accomplice.[50] In 1978 the French National Assembly proposed a law which made it an offence for anyone holding French public office to follow the ECJ doctrine in its *Opinion 1/78* decision.[51] Another measure, the Aurillac Bill was tabled to protect national law against the impact of international treaties but failed when it was blocked in the Senate.[52]

Arguments for the supremacy of Community law did not meet with success in the *Conseil d'État*. In *Semoules*[53] and subsequent cases the *Conseil d'État* held that it was not for the administrative courts to review the validity of legislation and it upheld the legality of subsequent French statutes over Community regulations. As

---

[47] For an account of how the reception of EC law in France was affected, in particular, by differing court traditions, see J Plotner, 'Report on France' in Slaughter, Sweet and Weiler (eds) *The European Courts and National Courts* (Hart Publishing, 1998).

[48] For a more full discussion of the issues discussed in this section see Plotner op. cit.; P Roseren, 'The application of Community Law by the French Courts From 1982 to 1993' (1994) 31 CMLRev 315; Simon and Dowrick, 'Effect of EEC Directives in France: the Views of the *Conseil' d État*' (1979) 95 LQR 376; Simon, 'Le Conseil d'État et les directives communautaires; du gallicanisme à l'orthodoxie' (1992) RTDE 265.

[49] *Directeur Général des Douanes v Société Vabre & Société Weigel, Cour de Cassation* 24 May 1975 [1975] 2 CMLR 336.

[50] Plotner op. cit.

[51] *Foyer-Debré Proposition de Loi.*

[52] *Journal Officiel Assemblée Nationale*, débats 10 October 1980 2634.

[53] *Conseil d'État* 1 March 1968 [1970] CMLR 395.

discussed in the chapter on direct effect, for many years it refused to accept *the* primacy or direct effect of Community directives, most prominently in *Cohn-Bendit*.[54]

Only in 1989 did the *Conseil d'État* move away from this position in the *Nicolo* case.[55] At issue in *Nicolo* was the French statute dealing with elections to the European Parliament which was challenged as being contrary to the EC Treaty. The *Conseil d'État* rejected the French statute as incompatible with the EC Treaty. Here the *Conseil* held that Article 55 of the French constitution, which provides for the primacy in the French legal system of international treaties over national law, enabled the courts, by implication, to review the compatibility of statutes with treaties. Commissaire Frydman pointed out the inconsistency of the *Conseil's* earlier stance, arguing, 'France cannot at one and the same time accept restrictions on sovereignty and uphold the supremacy of its own law before the courts: there is an element of illogicality which, it seems to me, your 1968 decision may have underestimated.' However, Commissaire Frydman's stance was hardly *Communautaire* for he continued, 'I do not think you can follow the European Court in this judge made law which, in truth, seems to me at least open to objection. Were you to do so, you would tie yourself to a supranational way of thinking which is quite difficult to justify, to which the Treaty of Rome does not subscribe expressly and which would quite certainly render the Treaty unconstitutional ... '[56] Frydman therefore suggested that the *Conseil's* decision should be based on Article 55 of the French Constitution, thus rejecting the argument that the primacy of Community law could be derived from the inherent nature of the Rome Treaty itself.[57]

Since *Nicolo* the *Conseil d'État* has gone further and recognised the primacy of directives over statutes in the *Rothmans* and *Arizona Tobacco* cases,[58] in which the *Conseil* also showed a willingness to grant damages to those who suffered loss by governmental action in breach of EC law, thus according with the *Francovich* judgment of the European Court.

The French Constitution was amended so that France could ratify the Maastricht treaty.[59] By a narrow majority, the French people voted in favour of ratification in the referendum, thus showing that enthusiasm for the Community in France was muted, to say the least.

Germany: the 'Virginia of Europe'?

The reception of Community law in the German courts was not much warmer than that given by the *Conseil d'État*, and it is on account of this lukewarm, or even

---

[54] Conseil d'Etat 22 December 1979, 8 Dalloz 1979 at 155.

[55] *Raoul Georges Nicolo* Conseil d'Etat [1990] 1 CMLR.

[56] *Nicolo* at 177, 178.

[57] Such an approach was suggested by Procureur Général Adolphe Touffait of the Cour de Cassation in *Café Jacques Vabre*. The Cour, however, declined to follow his suggestion.

[58] *Rothmans and Arizona Tobacco and Philip Morris* [1993] 1 CMLR 253.

[59] This was held necessary by the Conseil Constitutionnel in Decision of 9 April 1992 [1993] 3 CMLR 345.

sometimes aggressive, reception that one commentator has termed Germany the 'Virginia of Europe'.[60] Indeed, the German Constitutional Court is very much responsible for the resparking of the debate over sovereignty in the 1990s. Accession of Germany to the EEC was based on Article 24(1) of the German *Grundgesetz* (Basic Law) which allowed the *Bund* (federal government) to transfer sovereign powers to an interstate organisation. This provision was interpreted as an expression of 'open statehood'[61] suggesting a break with the concept of the nation state and a possible willingness of the German courts to react positively to the primacy of Community law. This has not been the case, partly because of the fact that, since the Second World War, Germany's constitution, the *Grundgesetz* of 1949, has given particular weight to the protection of fundamental rights and any provision of Community law which conflicts with this constitutional protection of basic rights is unlikely to be welcomed.

The European Court's judgment in *Internationale Handelsgesellschaft*, in which it held that fundamental rights were protected as general principles under Community law, has already been mentioned. But the litigation in that case did not end with the European Court's judgment. The German administrative court (*Verwaltungsgericht*), which was seized with the matter, was still unhappy. It feared that Germany might have transferred to the Community legal system under Article 24(1) the powers to enact laws which would be exempt from any scrutiny, contrary to other obligations in the German constitution, such as the principle of democracy in Article 79. This it feared might lead to a constitutional vacuum as the highest national check would be eliminated. It thus found the Community deposit system to be in breach of German constitutional law and requested a ruling on the matter from the Constitutional Court (*Bundesverfassungsgericht*) as to whether the regulations which provided for the Community's deposit system under the CAP were contrary to the fundamental rights provisions of the *Grundgesetz*.[62]

In this 1974 judgment[63] the *Bundesverfassungsgericht* found that Article 24 could not be used to transfer to the EEC a power to amend an 'essential inalienable feature of the German Constitution' and that it would not abandon its jurisdiction to rule on which transfers of power to the EEC would alter such inalienable Constitutional features. It also stated, in the phraseology which gave its name to the judgment, that fundamental rights were an inalienable feature of the German Constitution, and, given the current state of European integration, *so long as* community protection of fundamental rights did not measure up to the standard of protection under the German Constitution, then Community measures would be subject to the standard set by German law.[64]

---

[60] S Boom, 'The European Union after the Maastricht Decision; Will Germany be the Virginia of Europe?' cf fn 39.

[61] See M Zuleeg, 'The European Constitution under Constitutional Constraints: The German Scenario' (1997) EL Rev at 22; also K Vogel, *Die Verfassungsentscheidung des Grundgesetzes* (Mohr: Tubingen, 1964) at 35.

[62] The *Verwaltungsgericht* decision is reported in [1972] CMLR at 177.

[63] 37 BVerfGE 271 reported in English at [1974] 2 CMLR 540.

[64] Ibid. (italics added). The Court however went on to find that the Community measures at issue were not contrary to German law.

The *Solange I* decision of the *Bundesverfassungsgericht* was subject to much criticism,[65] mainly on the basis that, as in fact the dissent in *Solange I* pointed out,[66] it would have the effect of needlessly jeopardising the uniform application of EC law 'negating the basic idea of European unification'.[67] By 1986 the *Bundesverfassungsgericht* seemed to have modified its position when, in the *Wunsche Handelsgesellschaft*[68] case, it declared that so long as protection of fundamental rights by the EC satisfied German standards then the Constitutional Court would no longer exercise its jurisdiction to review Community measures against the standard of protection in the *Grundgesetz*. This case is, unsurprisingly, referred to as *Solange II*.

In 1992 the *Grundgesetz* was amended and a new Article 23 inserted which states that Germany participates in the development of the European Union to realise a united Europe and that no policy to the contrary shall be permitted under domestic law. Unlike Article 24, which is retained for membership of other international organisations, Article 23 appears to recognise the unique status of the EC, but it also requires that the EU respect democratic, social and federative principles, the rule of law, subsidiarity and fundamental rights equivalent to those in the *Grundgesetz*.[69] This was thought sufficient to enable Germany to ratify the Maastricht Treaty.

But, in 1993, the *Bundesverfassungsgericht* gave a dramatic warning to the European union, regarding future conduct of its affairs, in its so-called *Maastricht-Urteil*.[70] This action was brought by Manfred Brunner, a former official at the European Commission, who challenged the constitutionality of Germany's ratification of the Maastricht Treaty. The basis of Brunner's challenge, or at least the only ground found admissible, was that the Maastricht Treaty violated the 'constitutional democracy' principle in Article 38 of the Grundgesetz, namely, that state authority must emanate from the people under national elections. In order to consider this issue, the *Bundesverfassungsgericht* had to consider the nature of legislation in the EU and the extent to which it is democratic.

Three major issues can be extracted from the court's judgment. First, in an apparent move back to its *Solange I* jurisprudence, the court confirmed that it retained jurisdiction to guarantee fundamental rights protection, albeit 'in cooperation' with the ECJ.[71] This relationship of cooperation is different from that envisaged in Article 234 and new to EC law, being apparently a power of supervision over

---

[65] See e.g. J Frowein, 'Europaisches Gemeinschaftsrecht und Grundgesetz' in Starck (ed.) *Bundesverfassungsgericht und Grundgesetz* (Mohr, 1976).

[66] [1974] 2 CMLR at 564.

[67] Ibid.

[68] *Wunsche Handelsgesellscaft* [1987] 3 CMLR 225 at 265. See also W-H Roth, 'The application of Community Law in West Germany 1980–1990' (1991) 28 CMLR 137 for further discussion of this case.

[69] see M Zuleeg, 'The European Constitution under Constitutional Constraints' (1997) 22 ELRev 19 at 26.

[70] *Brunner v European Union* 89 BVerfGE 155, and reported in English translation in [1994] 1 CMLR 57. 'So-called' after the German expression for the Maastricht Treaty.

[71] [1994] 1 CMLR at 79.

European law-making and case law.[72] Second, with regard to the control of European legislation by the European peoples, the court held that the *Bundestag* retained sufficient control of the EU law-making process: 'the peoples of the individual states provide democratic legitimation through the agency of their national parliaments'. However, the court rejected the simplistic view of the European Parliament as a panacea for the democratic deficit in the EU, holding that democracy required an exchange of ideas among peoples and that communication among parties and interest groups at European Parliament level was not sufficient to fulfil the democratic mandate of ideas at European level. As the Council of Ministers was not popularly elected nor transparent in its decision-making processes, democratic legitimacy could only be achieved through the national parliaments. In fact, the Court's vision of democracy was quite singular. According to the Court, only the nation state was capable of being the guarantor of freedom, law and democracy. This view is certainly questionable and has already been discussed in this book.[73]

Third, the *Bundesverfassungsgericht* also considered whether Article 38 was violated because transfer of competences to the EU was insufficiently precise and certain. In particular, it considered whether either the principles of direct effect or implied powers render the nature of EU acts insufficiently foreseeable, and it cited Article 308 as an example of the transfer of competences to the EU without treaty amendment. If there were an open-ended transfer of power to the EU without approval by the national parliaments then Article 308 would be violated. The court, however, held that the transfer of powers was sufficiently clear. The EU was not a federal state (*Bundesstaat*) but a federation of states (*Staatenbund*) deriving its authority from the member states which remained the 'masters of the treaties' (*Herren der Vertage*).[74] However, in one of the widely reported aspects of the judgment, the court held that there were absolute limits to the competences that might be transferred to the EU (this flowed from the 'democratic principle').[75] It thus reserved the power to review Community legislation to ensure that it fell within the boundaries of permissibly transferred powers.[76] This last point was of crucial importance as it asserted the right of the Constitutional Court, rather than the ECJ, to police the division of power between the EU and the member states, or put more technically, that it had the *Kompetenz-Kompetenz*, namely the competence to

---

[72] Zuleeg suggests that this aspect of the case is in conflict with an earlier opinion given by the First Senate of the Court on women's work at night (Case C-345/89 *Stoekel* [1991] ECR I-4047 at 4067) in which the first senate accorded precedence to the ECJ as safeguarder of human rights: Zuleeg, 'The European Constitution under Constitutional Constraints' at 28.

[73] See Chapter 3.

[74] Compare this to the judgment of Justice Story in *Martin* v *Hunter's Lessee*, mentioned above, who stated 'the constitution of the United States was ordained and established, not by the states in their sovereign capacities, but emphatically as the preamble of the constitution declares, by "the People of the United States"' (at 324). In fact Story's proclamation had uncertain historical foundation. A later commentator writes, 'If anything is clear beyond peradventure in the history of the United States, it is that the Constitution was established by the States, acting through Conventions authorised by the legislatures thereof, and not by "the people of the United States" ... ' W MacDonald, *Jacksonian Democracy* (1906).

[75] [1994] 1 CMLR at 105.

[76] [1994] 1 CMLR at 91.

determine the competence of European law-making institutions. This was a major blow to the supremacy of Community law.[77] It was also untenable for the uniformity of Community law as it raised the prospect of a Community law being found *ultra vires* by the German Court but valid elsewhere, just the lack of harmony which the European Court alluded to in its early jurisprudence.

Thus the Court's assertion of jurisdiction over the constitutionality of EU law went beyond the fundamental rights which were at issue in the earlier *Solange I* litigation: any future legal acts which exceeded the competence of the EC would not be binding in Germany. Therefore, the court ruled not just on the matter of Germany's current competence to ratify the Maastricht Treaty but also on future matters of EU competence, and as Neil MacCormick writes, 'the (German) court thus left a marker, a line drawn in the sand, indicating there might be future challenges that it would uphold if European organs should adopt an unduly expansionist view of their competences'.[78]

Thus, prospects for a confrontation between the German constitutional court and the EU remained uncertain. In its *Television Directive* judgment[79] the Second Senate of the *Bundesverfassungsgericht* rejected a request to declare the Directive inapplicable in Germany. The German Lander considered that broadcasting fell within their jurisdiction and challenged the European Commission's powers to legislate in this area, especially when it aspired to introduce quotas for non-European broadcasting. But the German federal government had assented to the Directive in the Council of Ministers. The Second Senate of the *Bundesverfassungsgericht* held that in disputes between the Bund and the Lander, acts of Community institutions were not subject to constitutional review and the priority of Community law with regard to national law was confirmed.[80]

However, the recent controversy over bananas has the potential to be far more damaging: as one commentator suggests, 'will Europe slip on Bananas?'[81] It seems surprising, and perhaps even indicative of one sceptical view of Europe, which sees the EU endangered and demeaned by internecine squabbles over green pounds, prawn cocktail crisps or straight cucumbers, that European law might be threatened by such a marginal subject as bananas. However, as Everling reminds us, quarrels over bananas were in existence even at the origins of the EEC when there was a conflict over the source of banana imports into the EEC which was only solved by the

---

[77] Although the Court first made such an assertion in the earlier *Kloppenburg* case [1988] 3 CMLR 1 at 13, where it stated that the member states were the masters of the treaty.

[78] N MacCormick, 'The Maastricht Urteil: Sovereignty Now' (1995) ELJ 259 at 260.

[79] 92 BVerfGE 203 [1995].

[80] Since its amendment, Article 23 of the *Grundgesetz* regulates the rights and duties of the federation and the Lander. See Zuleeg op. cit. at 33 and M Herdegen, 'After the TV Judgement of the German Constitutional Court: Decision making within the EU Council and the German Lander' (1995) 32 CMLRev 1369.

[81] U Everling, 'Will Europe Slip on Bananas? The Bananas Judgement of the EECJ and the National Courts' (1996) 33 CMLRev 401. See also Rabe, 'Ausgerechnet Bananen' (1996) NJW, 1320; N Reich, 'Judge Made Europe à la Carte: Some remarks on recent conflicts between European and German constitutional law provoked by the Bananas litigation' (1996) 7 EJIL 103; S Peers, 'Taking Supremacy Seriously' (1998) 23 ELRev 146.

Protocol on Bananas.[82] Forty years on, however, new rules on bananas have become essential, as the member states apply different systems regarding the import of bananas, thus partitioning the markets, a situation which is incompatible with Article 14 EC. Therefore, by means of Regulation 404/93, the Council organised a common market in bananas, to the great consternation of German importers, who claimed the new regime favoured ACP producers at the expense of Latin American producers, from whom the German importers received their supplies at preferential rates. As Everling again notes, 'in the view of German lawyers, the Bananas regulation seemed to justify all the insinuations and distrust underlying the *Maastricht* judgment of the *Bundesverfassungsgericht* with regard to the rule of law and fundamental rights in the Community'. The German government challenged this regulation on the basis that it violated the vested right of the German traders, as did the individual traders, whose claims were, however, dismissed in Luxembourg for lack of standing.[83] The ECJ, however, found no violation of the principle of proportionality, nor of fundamental rights, by the regulation, nor any breach of the GATT.[84] This judgment has been severely criticised, mainly on the basis that it would be difficult to imagine a clearer discrimination between operators according to Article 34 [formerly 40(3)] than that accepted by the Court, and that the Court misapplied the principle of proportionality by submitting it to the discretion of the EC institutions, thus reducing judicial control to minimum. Therefore, Everling comments that 'in face of this regrettable part of the judgement, one cannot exclude that the question will once more arise whether the Court takes rights seriously'.

Aggrieved German importers then brought a variety of actions in the German courts, perhaps the most interesting and threatening for EC unity being those which challenge the ECJ judgment upholding the validity of the regulation as well as the regulation itself[85] – which matter was referred to the *Bundesverfassungsgericht*, thus giving that court a chance to exercise the jurisdiction it threatened in its *Maastricht* judgment. The applicants also referred the matter to the dispute settlement body of the World Trade Organisation (WTO), which held that other aspects of the regulation violated the WTO. The 'imbroglio'[86] of the banana wars, which has involved

---

[82] U Everling, 'Will Europe Slip on Bananas?' at 401.

[83] See e.g. Case C-257/93 *Leon Van Parijs v Council and Commission* [1993] ECR I-3335; subsequent indirect challenges via a reference from the German courts were also dismissed: Cases C-465/93 and 466/93 *Atlanta Fruchthandelsgesellschaft I and II* [1995] ECR I-3761 (whose action for damages was also dismissed by the European courts). In Case C-68/95 *T Port GmbH & Co. v Bundesanstalt fur Landwirtschaft* [1996] ECR I-6065 the ECJ held that where it was asserted that the Commission had failed to act, by failing to grant further import licences, the ECJ had the exclusive jurisdiction to determine this matter, although it did expand the procedural protection available to individuals in this situation: see Peers op. cit. at n 81 *supra*.

[84] Case C-280/93 *Germany v Council* [1994] ECR I-4973 at 5061–5070.

[85] Another action was brought by the German government against the Council in the ECJ regarding the discrimination in the regulation against importers of bananas from certain Latin American countries. In this case, the ECJ showed itself a little more flexible in its approach, holding that the regulation discriminated against certain importers: Case C-122/95 *Germany v Council* [1998] ECR I-973.

[86] U Everling, 'Will Europe Slip on Bananas?' at 403.

over twenty separate cases before the Luxembourg courts,[87] continued for some time, with the attendant danger that a declaration of inapplicability by a German court would violate the supremacy and uniformity of Community law, thus presenting a scenario in which Germany would truly be 'the Virginia of Europe'. Furthermore, if the German courts were to decide on the application of Community law according to their own criteria it also seemed possible that the courts of other member states would follow suit.

Further wars of a different kind also continued, between jurists Dr Gunter Hirsh, a member of the ECJ, who warned that if the *Bundesverfassungsgericht* disregarded ECJ judgments then 'Proceedings will be brought against Germany for breach of Treaty obligations' and Paul Kirchhof of the *Bundesverfassungsgericht*. Kirchhof described his role rather alarmingly as that of 'a swing bridge operator', whose job it was to ensure that 'nothing untoward' crosses over to the German side from the EU.[88] However, if the attitude of the *Bundesverfassungsgericht* is dangerous, then the ECJ itself is not faultless.[89] Although still a young court, the ECJ no longer has the primary role of its earliest years, to further European integration above all. As the European Court has been taking on more and more attributes of a constitutional court, so it has been suggested that its task must be to ensure a 'balanced equilibrium between the competences, rights and functions of the institutions, Member States and citizens'.[90] Fairly recent judgments, such as *Keck* or *Dori*, suggest the Court's awareness of this responsibility but unfortunately some of its earlier bananas judgments do not follow in this tradition. Weiler[91] characterised the relationship between the *Bundesverfassungsgericht* and ECJ as a 'conversation of two superpowers' employing the Cold War MAD metaphor. The striking down of a Community law by the German court would be so hazardous as to render its usage unlikely, given the possible 'domino' effect of such an action and the constitutional crisis which it would precipitate. Fortunately, the danger of such folly seems to have reduced recently. Already in its *T Port* judgment[92] the ECJ had stated that provisions of the banana regulation could be used to protect fundamental rights of traders, so that a claim might be brought in Luxembourg as well as in Karslruhe. In two subsequent cases,[93] the ECJ assessed certain aspects of the banana regime and in so doing engaged in a much more intensive scrutiny of EC agriculture policy than usual.[94] In these cases, it seemed to be offering a compromise to the German

---

[87] In 1996, apart from the actions already mentioned above, fifteen cases were pending before the ECJ, some of them concerning the share of the banana quota of the new member states which had joined the EU after the Regulation was passed; there were also seven actions pending before the CFI. Everling comments that the amount of proceedings before the German courts and those of other member states was unknown.

[88] European Information Service, European Report, Nov 9 1996.

[89] However, fault of course also lies with the Community institutions and member states, which did not spot the flaws in the banana regulation in time

[90] Everling op. cit. at 436; Everling 'Zur Föderalen Struktur der Europäischen Gemeinschaft', *in Festschrift für Karl Doehring* (1989) 179 at 196.

[91] J Weiler, 'The Reformulation of European Constitutionalism' (1997) 35 JCMS 97.

[92] Case C-68/95 *T Port* [1996] ECR I-6065.

[93] Case C-364/95 *T Port* [1998] ECR I-1023 and Case C-122/95 *Germany v Council* [1998] ECR I-973.

[94] See Chapter 10 on judicial review, under grounds of review.

constitutional court and trying to avoid a conflict. This seems to have worked, as in 2000 the Second Senate of the *Bundesverfassungsgericht*[95] found a claim brought against the EC banana regime inadmissible on the grounds given in its *Solange II* judgment, that while EC protection of fundamental rights remained satisfactory, action of the review of secondary EC acts in the German courts was inadmissible. So the war seems to be over, for the present at least.

However, setting aside the antagonistic and combative metaphors, Weiler sees the present situation as not necessarily regrettable, for it leads us to a more poly-centred view of constitutional adjudication, forcing greater conversation between the ECJ and its national constitutional counterparts. Maybe, suggested Weiler, the German court's warnings would force the ECJ to take competences seriously, just as in the 1970s it was forced to take rights seriously. In the *Tobacco directive* case,[96] in annulling an EC directive for lack of competence, it seems to have done just that.

Italy

Similar conflicts have arisen in the Italian courts, although of less stridency. Under Article 11 of the Italian Constitution limitations of sovereignty are permitted where 'necessary to an arrangement which may ensure peace and justice between nations'. However, the Italian courts have not accepted supremacy of Community law unconditionally. In *Frontini*[97] the applicant argued that a Community regulation which increased the levies applicable on the import of cheese into Italy was unconstitutional, as, under Article 23 of the Italian Constitution, charges could be imposed only by statute. As regulations are directly applicable under Article 249 (189) of the EC Treaty, he argued the Treaty must therefore be incompatible with the Constitution, and the statute which provided for Italian membership of the Community, unconstitutional. The Italian Constitutional court noted that 'by Article 11 ... limitations of sovereignty are allowed solely for the purpose of the ends indicated therein, and it should therefore be excluded that such limitations of sovereignty ... can nevertheless give the organs of the EEC an unacceptable power to violate the fundamental principles of our constitutional order or the inalienable rights of man'. The Court continued by stating that 'if ever Article 189 had to be given such an aberrant interpretation, in such a case the guarantee would always be assured that this Court would control the continuing compatibility of the Treaty with the above mentioned fundamental principles'.[98] Thus we see the Italian court taking a very similar approach to that of the *Bundesverfassungsgericht*, and indeed it appears that the *Frontini* case was one of the sources of inspiration for the German court.[99]

---

[95] BverfG 2 BvL 1/97 7.6.2000.

[96] See Chapter 4 for a discussion of this case.

[97] *Frontini v Ministero delle Finanze* [1974] 2 CMLR 372.

[98] *Frontini* at 384. However, the Court ruled out the possibility that a question on the consistency of a single EEC Regulation with constitutional fundamental rights could ever be raised before it.

[99] see Gaja, 'New Developments in a Continuing Story: The Relationship between EEC Law and National Law' (1990) 83 CMLRev 95 at 93.

By 1984, however, in *Granital*[100] the Italian Constitutional Court was more accepting of the idea that the Italian courts should ignore Italian legislation which conflicted with directly effective EEC measures. However, as Petriccione comments, the basis of the Italian court's decision was that national law and Community law were to be kept conceptually distinct.[101] In addition, Petriccione continues, the Constitutional Court itself reserved the right to deal with conflicts between EC law and fundamental principles, such as inalienable rights. Under this interpretation, an ordinary judge would not be able to disapply conflicting national legislation – this would be the remit of the Constitutional Court only – an approach in conflict with the ECJ's ruling in *Simmenthal*.

In *Fragd*,[102] the Constitutional Court, held itself unwilling to take the sort of conciliatory approach adopted by the German courts in *Solange II*. *Fragd* was a continuation of litigation which had gone to the European Court,[103] which was itself a replay of the maize cases such as *Roquette*,[104] and thus part of a cycle of cases concerning agricultural property rights as complex and long running as the banana wars saga. In *Fragd*, the Italian Constitutional Court held that a rule of Community law could be inapplicable in Italy if it infringed fundamental human rights. This case goes much further than its *Frontini* ruling for, here, the Court showed that it would be willing to test the consistency of individual provisions of Community law with fundamental rights protected in the Italian Constitution.[105]

United Kingdom

As the UK does not have a written constitution, it could not become a member of the EEC by means of a constitutional amendment such as Article 24 of the German *Grundgesetz*. UK membership was introduced instead by Act of Parliament, the European Communities Act (ECA) of 1972, which also, given that the UK takes a dualist approach to international law such that treaties do not immediately take effect within the domestic legal system, gave internal effect to EC law. Otherwise, as Lord Denning made clear, 'Even though the Treaty of Rome has been signed, it has no effect, so far as these courts are concerned, until it is made an Act of Parliament.'[106] However, just as fundamental provisions of the German and Italian constitutions, such as protection of basic rights and the principle of democracy, were to present problems for the reception of Community law in Germany and Italy, so did the fundamental keystone of the British constitution, the sovereignty of Parliament, threaten the reception of Community law in the UK. Blackstone famously wrote that 'The power and jurisdiction of Parliament, says Sir Edward Coke, is so transcendent and absolute, that it cannot be confined, either for causes

---

[100] *Granital v Amministrazione delle Finanze* [1984] 756, English translation [1984] 21 CMLRev 756.
[101] Petriccione, 'Italy: supremacy of Community law over national law' (1986) 11 EL Rev 320.
[102] Decision 232 of 2 April 1989 (1989) 72 RDI 103.
[103] Case 33/84 *Fragd* [1985] ECR 1605
[104] Case 145/79 [1980] ECR 2917; Case 109/79 *Maiseries de Beauce v ONIC* [1980] ECR 2883.
[105] See Gaja op. cit. at n 99 at 95.
[106] *McWhirter v Attorney General* [1972] CMLR 882 at 886.

or permissions, within any bounds.'[107] Although an English court had claimed in 1610 in *Dr Bonham's case*[108] that the English common law could 'controul acts of Parliament . . and sometimes adjudge them to be utterly void' this claim[109] did not survive the constitutional upheavals caused by the Glorious Revolution of 1688 and the expulsion of James II and VII, and Parliamentary sovereignty was a foundational principle for writers on the English Constitution such as Blackstone, Austin and Dicey.

A central provision of the ECA is thus section 2(4) which provides for the supremacy of Community law in the UK by requiring that any British 'enactment passed or to be passed' should be subordinated to directly effective Community law. Section 2(1) provides for the direct effect of Community law in the UK. However, the English courts initially held that s 2(4) contains a rule of interpretation: that Parliament is presumed not to intend to override Community law, unless Parliament states clearly and expressly that it intends to do so. Lord Denning stated in *McCarthys v Smith*, 'Unless there is such an intentional and express repudiation of the treaty it is our duty to give priority to the treaty.'[110] In *Garland v British Rail Engineering*, Lord Diplock, citing s 2(4) of the ECA stated, 'it is a principle of construction of United Kingdom statutes, now too well established to call for citation of authority that the words of a statute passed after the treaty has been signed and dealing with the subject matter of the international obligation . . . are to be construed, if they are reasonably capable of bearing such a meaning, as intended to carry out the obligation and not to be inconsistent with it'.[111]

However, as Craig and de Burca point out, the *Garland* approach of 'harmonious construction' of national law rather than the direct application of EC law leads to problems where the national courts are required to implement directly effective law.[112] The *Marleasing* case requires that courts ensure the effectiveness of EC law by interpreting national law in the light of the wording and purpose of the relevant EC law. In *Duke v Reliance*,[113] Lord Templeman was of the view that the requirement in s 2(4) to interpret domestic law in accordance with EC obligations did not apply where EC law was not directly effective (in this case because a directive was being asserted against a private party). However, in *Litster v Forth Dry Dock Co Ltd* and *Pickstone v Freeman's*,[114] the House of Lords interpreted domestic law in conformity with EC law which was not directly effective, even where the construction went against the literal meaning of the statute. In *Webb v Emo*, the House of Lords interpreted the Sex Discrimination Act so as to comply with the ECJ's interpretation

---

[107] Blackstone, *Commentaries on the Law of England* (16 edn, Butterworths, 1825) Vol I Bk. 2 160–1.
[108] [1610] 77 ENG Rep 646 at 652 (CP 1610).
[109] This reading has been questioned by J Goldsworthy, *The Sovereignty of Parliament* (OUP, 1999).
[110] [1979] 3 ALL ER 325.
[111] *Garland v British Rail Engineering Ltd* [1983] 2 AC 751.
[112] Craig and de Búrca *EU law* (Oxford, 1998) at 284–5. See also P Craig, 'Report on the United Kingdom' in A-M Slaughter, A Stone Sweet and J Weiler (eds) *The European Courts and National courts* (Hart Publishing, 1998).
[113] [1988] AC 618.
[114] *Litster v Forth Dry Dock* [1990] 1 AC, 546 *Pickstone v Freeman's* [1989] AC 66.

of the 1976 Equal Treatment Directive, notwithstanding the fact that the Court of Appeal had considered that such an interpretation would amount to a distortion.[115]

Thus the English courts had found techniques to deal with problems caused by the doctrine of supremacy, although they still derived the authority to apply directly effective law in the UK from s 2(4) of the ECA rather than the case law of the European court. Their thinking was still not highly 'Europeanised'. By 1990, for example, a survey showed[116] that *Costa v ENEL*, the keystone case on supremacy of Community law, had been cited in only four cases by the English courts. Prior to *Factortame*, the idea that the judiciary might disapply an Act of Parliament seemed to be unthinkable – as Lord Donaldson MR stated in the early stages of the *Factortame* litigation, 'Any attempt to interfere with primary legislation would be unconstitutional.'[117] The English courts' recognition of their ability do so, and their subsequent disapplication of the Merchant Shipping Act in the *Factortame* case thus represented a major shift in the constitutional order in the UK. This shift is illustrated by the opinions of Lord Bridge at different stages of the *Factortame* litigation. Prior to the reference to Luxembourg, when the interlocutory application first came to the House of Lords, Lord Bridge stated, 'I am clearly of the opinion that as a matter of English law, the court has no power to make an order which has these consequences.' But in his judgment following the ECJ ruling he said, 'Thus there is nothing in any way novel in according supremacy to rules of law ... and to insist that, in the protection of rights under law, national courts should not be inhibited by rules of national law from granting interim relief.' As O'Neill points out, this statement is somewhat disingenuous: if the matter was so clear, why the need for a reference to Luxembourg?[118]

In this way, EC law has given the UK courts the power to reclaim powers denied them perhaps since the seventeenth century and the House of Lords seems to have become master of the UK constitution. This may constitute a 'quiet revolution' in the UK constitutional order, abolishing the concept of Parliamentary sovereignty which has held sway for at least the past 300 years[119] but this result does not necessitate a change in the way that jurists approach the issue of sovereignty. A traditional approach has been to locate the rule concerning sovereignty at the apex of a legal system, on the basis of its fundamental status. The source of authority for this basic rule is usually perceived as being, at least in part, extra-legal, as it would be paradoxical if authority could be assumed by acting on the very power to be

---

[115] *Webb v Emo Air Cargo (No 2)* [1996]; *Roquette v French Customs* 2 CMLR 990.

[116] i.e. see the Lexis search carried out by Aiden O'Neill – see A O'Neill, *Decisions of the ECJ and their Constitutional Implications* (Butterworths, 1994) at 39.

[117] [1989] 2 CMLR 353 (CA) at 397.

[118] O'Neill op. cit. at 43; the parochialism of the English courts in making the reference to Luxembourg is also criticised in Gravells, 'Disapplying an Act of Parliament' (1989) PL; see also Craig, 'Report on the United Kingdom' in Slaughter, Sweet and Weiler op. cit., fn 112.

[119] Although it is perhaps questionable whether the effect of *Factortame* may be construed in this way. Lord Bridge attributed the courts' duty to disapply the Merchant Shipping Act to s 2(4) of the ECA thus applying the traditional interpretative approach to international obligations.

conferred. Thus Wade[120] for example suggested that the basic rule of a system could only be altered by revolution, whether it be 'quiet and legal', or real, and probably noisy, unpleasant and so on, such as the events concerning the execution of Charles I, after which the seat of sovereignty changed, to incorporate a kingless parliament. The constitutional changes wrought by EC membership thus constitute a quiet revolution. No kings have been beheaded. However, this approach is expressed as a type of legal positivism, and is characterised by key features of the positivist approach: legal system seen as hierarchy, with some basic norm, or rule of recognition at its apex, which identifies law from non-law. This is a highly conceptual method although it asserts itself as descriptive in approach, which aims to isolate the legal from the moral, along with identifying the institutions or sources from which law originates.[121] What this approach does not do is to take a substantive and normative approach to the question of law and legal system. It is arguable that the changes wrought by the existence of EC law have rendered this approach unworkable and that therefore the question of supremacy of EC law requires that we not only rethink the matter of sovereignty in practice, i.e. where is sovereignty actually located, but also the legal theory which accompanies or underlies the case and statute law and commentary usually discussed in this context. This transformation is the legacy of European law and will be discussed in the next section.

SOVEREIGNTY, CONSTITUTIONALISM AND LEGAL THEORY

If the ECJ has been working hard at constitutionalising the treaties, their superordinate, supreme status is simply not accepted by many, not least the member state legal orders themselves. From *Van Gend*, in which the member states urged the ECJ to proceed cautiously, reminding the Court that it was dealing with a treaty, to the *Bundesverfassungsgericht's* recent strident challenges to the supremacy of EC law, the member states have persisted in considering their own legal orders as sovereign. As De Witte comments, 'the (national supreme) courts tend to recognise the privileged position of Community law, not by virtue of the inherent nature of Community law, as the Court of Justice would have it, but under authority of their own legal order'.[122] Thus, the Conseil d'Etat attributed the supremacy of EC law to Article 55 of the French Constitution, and Lord Bridge, in the House of Lords, attributed the same supremacy to s 2(4) of the ECA. According to the ECJ, EC law rests at the pinnacle of the legal order but according to most member states, their own constitutions, or principles such as Parliamentary sovereignty, occupy that position. Thus, there is a clash of two constitutional visions. This difference of opinion matters as there is no authoritative manner (in law at least) for resolving

---

[120] H Wade, 'The Basis of Legal Sovereignty', (1955) CLJ 172. See also J Salmond, *Jurisprudence* (10th edn, Stevens, 1947) at 155.

[121] See e.g. Kelsen, *The Pure Theory of Law* (Massachusetts: Smith, 1989); Hart, *The Concept of Law* (Oxford: Clarendon 1961); J Raz *The Concept of a Legal System* (Oxford: Clarendon Press, 1980).

[122] B De Witte, 'Community law and National Constitutional Values', (1991) 2 Legal Issues of European Integration at 4.

conflicts such as the Banana wars: a situation which leads to a lack of legal certainty and a loss of confidence in the European legal order.

What therefore is the nature of the legal order in the contemporary EU? This is a foundational question of legal theory, but one with vital, practical effects for contemporary Europe. To answer this question satisfactorily, it would appear that we would now have to move beyond the sort of theorising about law and legal systems which has been popular for centuries and was constitutive of a modernist way of thinking.

At one time, the notion of sovereignty was all important in explaining how (legal-political) authority worked. At the apex of any system was said to be a sovereign authority, an uncommanded commander free from external and internal constraints, whose orders were obeyed by a populace, backed up by force if necessary. This theory of legal and political obligation stems from the seventeenth century, and, as MacCormick explains, this commitment to the absolute nature of sovereignty may be partly explained by the uncertain nature of the times, exemplified by the Thirty Years War and the English revolution.[123] The writings of authors such as Hobbes or Bodin were thus partly engendered by concern about the fragmentary nature of the state and a concomitant need for certainty, a foundation in uncertain times. Foundationalism also inhered in other areas of thought at that time, for example in Descartes' search for a certain basis to our knowledge in clear and distinct ideas. The concept of sovereignty has endured – through, in more certain times, the command theories of Bentham and Austin, to, in once more uncertain times, the sovereign nation state still proclaimed in the EU. But although few of those who protest the sovereignty of the state would turn to Austin or Hobbes for support, many would, unconsciously perhaps, adhere to a theory such as that of HLA Hart,[124] based on a Rule of Recognition – the fundamental criterion for identification of those rules which make up a legal system – applied by the officials of that system, or Kelsen's[125] *Grundnorm*, a presupposed basic norm at the foundation of a legal system, from which all other norms derive their validity. Thus, a great deal of legal theory (and fact) is based on the idea of law as **hierarchical system**. In the UK many still identify Parliamentary sovereignty as the basis for the English legal system. EU law is not necessarily regarded as a threat to sovereignty, or as a mutation of the rule of recognition, as such a theory might explain EU law as a devolved or delegated power under the ECA which might be revoked if Parliament so chose. Likewise, the *Bundesverfassungsgericht*'s denial that *Kompetenz-Kompetenz* rests with the EU can be seen as the assertion that the arrangements under the German constitution and the hierarchy of supremacy under that constitution have not been altered by membership of the EU.

These views are, of course, not shared by the ECJ, which places EU law above state law in the hierarchical order. But the jurisprudence of the ECJ does not neces-

---

[123] N MacCormick, 'Beyond the Sovereign State' (1993) 56 MLR 1; see also N MacCormick, *Questioning Sovereignty* (Oxford: OUP 1999).
[124] Hart, *The Concept of Law* (Oxford: Clarendon, 1961).
[125] Kelsen, *The Pure Theory of Law.* (Mass., Smith 1982)

sarily involve a shift in legal paradigms. Within this interpretation, the supremacy of EC law can be accommodated within e.g. Kelsen's system, which accorded priority to international law, in a unified, hierarchical system,[126] or even, with some contortion, within Hart's concept of law. But in real life, the contortion is all too visible and the idea of member states as delegates of, or subordinate to, the EU seems in many ways legally and politically undesirable and inaccurate.

Thus, neither of these two constitutionalisms is satisfactory, as pointed out by a number of commentators.[127] Indeed, preservation of the hierarchical sovereignty paradigm just seems to perpetuate in legal theory the Cold War scenario of the clash of two courts envisioned by Weiler in the context of the banana wars. MacCormick rejects the idea that there can be one overarching hierarchical system, thus denying the ability of the positivism of Hart or Kelsen to account for the contemporary European legal order, although he does not necessarily reject the notion of the systematic nature of law. MacCormick's suggestion is to identify 'the legal order in the complex interaction of overlapping legalities which characterise contemporary Europe'. The reality of contemporary Europe, suggests MacCormick, is a plurality of interacting systems, 'distinct but interesting'.[128]

Part of the problem surely lies in the belief that a solution to the nature of the European constitutional question can be found by legal doctrine. Eleftheriadis doubts the ability of the European Court to assert the sovereignty of the new legal order of European law by its own pronouncements alone. This, he writes, 'begs the constitutional question' because, 'if the doctrine of supremacy changes the basis of validity, then it cannot be subject to a test of validity. As a result it **cannot be legally valid**'.[129] In other words, theories of law which bind the system within a determinate limit cannot have anything to say about the legality of that limit. This is part of the broader query into what makes **law**, as opposed to a particular system, valid. What makes a validating source authoritative? Any ultimate basis of validity cannot be explained in terms of the system itself. [130]

Instead, we have to look to some substantive assessment whereby we can assess the ECJ's claims on behalf of the EU legal order. This, as Eleftheriadis suggests, 'can be evaluated and justified only by substantive criteria related to constitutionalism and the rule of law. It cannot be reduced to a matter of formal reasoning.'[131]

---

[126] Kelsen, *Principles of International Law* (Berkeley and LA: University of California Press, 1967).

[127] N MacCormick, 'Beyond the Sovereign State'; N MacCormick 'The Maastricht Urteil: Sovereignty Now' (1995) ELJ 259; *Questioning Sovereignty*; P Eleftheriadis, 'Aspects of European Constitutionalism' (1996) 21 ELRev at 37; P Eleftheriadis, 'Begging the Constitutional Question' (1998) JCMS; M Kumm, 'Who is the final arbiter of Constitutionality in Europe?' (1999) 36 CMLRev 351.

[128] MacCormick, 'Beyond the Sovereign State', at 5.

[129] P Eleftheriadis, 'Aspects of European Constitutionalism' (1996) 21 ELRev at 37.

[130] For Derrida, the origin of authority is 'a violence without ground', a logical aporia. J Derrida, 'Force of Law: The Mystical Origins of Authority', in Cornell (ed.) *Deconstruction and the Possibility of Justice* (New York: Routledge, 1992) at 14; see also Goodrich who describes the source of legal authority as 'hidden' and 'obscure', P Goodrich, *Reading the Law* (Oxford: Basil Blackwell, 1986) at 62.

[131] Eleftheriadis, op. cit. fn 129 at 42.

This recognition is not new. As Craig[132] points out, the doctrine of parliamentary sovereignty in the UK does not stand alone: those who advocated it in its earlier days backed it up by reasoned arguments in its favour, which are now overlooked by those who fervently protest its continued application. Blackstone argued for the sovereignty of Parliament as a check against government, within a system of checks and balances, so that 'every branch of our civil polity supports and is supported, regulates and is regulated by the rest'.[133] Dicey partly justified arguments for parliamentary sovereignty on the basis of the normative argument that the elected parliament (even if not by universal franchise) represented the will of the people and therefore should be able to implement it and was also unlikely to act against the wishes of those from whom its authority derived. As an accurate description of the constitutional legal order at that time these arguments are probably inaccurate, but as an attempt at a normative justification they are significant, an attempt at a principled, normative support for a constitutional system. In similar fashion, the *Bundesverfassungsgericht* offered up a justification for the sovereignty of the German state and its own assertion of its *Kompetenz-Kompetenz*. In the *Maastricht Urteil* the supreme status of the German constitution was argued on the basis of the *demos* or *Staatsvolk* of the German state;[134] as Europe did not have a demos in this sense the German Court argued that the pinnacle of the constitutional order could not lie with the European legal order. An equally principled but contrasting argument was presented by the framers of the American Constitution, who did away with the idea of a sovereign, indivisible body politic, instead creating an entirely new power centre by the balancing of powers; 'Power must be opposed to power, force to force, strength to strength, interest, as well as reason to reason, eloquence to eloquence, and passion to passion.'[135]

How might a European constitutional order be justified? One justification might be found within the same old hierarchical paradigm described above. The supremacy of Community law might be asserted within a monistic legal order on the basis of the value of a European polity which extended the rule of law to the supranational legal order, thus avoiding wars and clashes between nation states, while preserving the benefits of legal certainty and regularity which adhere to the rule of law. This interpretation would still be based on a hierarchy of norms, but would provide for a legal order without statehood. However, this justification, while it might have appeared appropriate in the early years of the EEC, simply fails to do justice to the complex reality of the Europe of the twenty-first century. On the one hand, a justification which accorded simple supremacy to EU institutions, without looking to enrich fundamental rights protection, democratic accountability, citizenship and so on, fails to present any attractive arguments for that supremacy. On the other, it fails to recognise the fact that state power is far more multidimensional and

---

[132] P Craig, 'United Kingdom Sovereignty after Factortame' (1991) YEL 236 *et seq.*; also Craig 'Report on the United Kingdom' in Slaughter, Sweet and Weiler (eds) op. cit. fn 47.
[133] Blackstone, *Commentaries on the Law of England* (16th edn, Butterworths, 1825) vol. 1 book 2 155.
[134] [1994] 11 CMLR.
[135] John Adams, quoted in Z Haraszti, *John Adams and the Prophets of Progress* (Cambridge, 1952) 219.

extensive than mere legal sovereignty, and by clinging to sovereignty still ignores other important aspects of power which may be enhanced by an apparent transfer of competence, i.e. the 'productive' relationship of cooperation between the ECJ and *Bundesverfassungsgericht*. Furthermore, as an argument for the democratic legitimacy of the EU, such a justification is unsatisfactory. What is wanted is a justification which would combine the advantages of European union with the protections of the modern democratic state: – fundamental rights, democratic accountability, a rich sense of citizenship and so on – the sort of revolutionary thought which prompted the framers of the US Constitution to 'split the atom of sovereignty'[136] and argue for, and introduce, divided power and federalism. To continue the metaphor, rather than splitting the atom, contemporary Europe might seem to have to take a **molecular** approach such as MacCormick's notion of a plurality of interacting systems.

On a more theoretical level, this is also more satisfactory. The foundationalism inherent in the hierarchical positivist approach to sovereignty is a key feature of the modernist approach, which seeks an all-encompassing systematising approach to its subjects. Such an approach is rejected, for example, by postmodernism, which repudiates the totalising approach to law as a system which imposes coherence and order through rules of recognition or grundnorms where none is alleged to exist. In this way, legal orders become constructed concepts and the European Union is no exception. A plurality of legal orders (if even 'order' here can be safely used) whose boundaries are unclear, broken and whose ultimate basis for authority is uncertain seems to be a more appropriate characterisation of today's EU.

The only problem is that such a characterisation presents the EU as fragmented and perhaps also undesirably incoherent, the antithesis of a unifying positivist vision. EU citizens need a map to find their way, not only through the plurality of legal orders, but also through the disorganised sprawl of EC law itself. Supremacy may be a constitutional principle, but EC law must surely be worthy of that supremacy. The need for a normative justification remains, in an era when such justifications are often suspect. It is the task of today's EU to find such a justification.

---

[136] Per Kennedy J in *US Term Limits Inc* v *Thornton* Sct (1995) 514 US 779 at 838: 'Federalism was our Nation's own discovery. The Framers split the atom of sovereignty. It was the genius of their idea that our citizens would have two political capacities, one state and one federal, each protected from incursion from the other.'

8

DIRECT EFFECT: FOUNDATION OF
THE CONSTITUTIONAL ORDER?

In 1963 the European Court decided a case which transformed the nature of Community law, as well as its relationship with national law. This case was *Van Gend en Loos*,[1] perhaps the most written about case in the 'canon' of EC law.[2] On the facts it seemed unremarkable. A Dutch court referred to the ECJ a case brought by the Van Gend en Loos company, which had challenged the imposition on it of an increased customs duty[3] by the Dutch Customs and Excise as contrary to Article 25 [previously 12] of the Treaty, which prohibits the introduction by member states of any new customs duties on imports or exports from other EEC countries. Van Gend argued that Article 25 could be enforced in the national courts. The Dutch court specifically asked whether individuals could 'lay claim to individual rights which the courts must protect'.

The suggestion that EEC law might give rise to individual rights which could be invoked in the national courts could not be derived from the specific provisions of the treaty. Nothing in the EC treaty specifies that individually enforceable rights can be derived from international obligations imposed on the member states. The Netherlands government submitted that interpreting Article 25 in this way would be contrary to the intentions of its drafters.[4] In this they were backed up by Advocate General Roemer, who wrote: 'it is in my opinion doubtful whether the authors, when dealing with a provision of such importance to customs law, intended

---

[1] Case 26/62 *NV Algemene Transporten Expeditie Onderneming van Gend en Loos v Nederlandse Administratie der Belastingen* [1963] ECR 1.

[2] The late Judge Mancini went as far as to write that ' ... if the EC still exists 50 or 100 years from now, historians will look back on Van Gend en Loos as the unique judicial contribution to the making of Europe', G Mancini, *Democracy and Constitutionalism in the European Union* (Hart Publishing, 1999) at 40.

[3] The Netherlands implemented a Benelux protocol which reclassified the chemical in question, urea-formaldehyde, and imposed a higher duty.

[4] A view supported by international law, which stresses the importance of the will of the parties in Treaty interpretation: see Winter, 'Direct Applicability and Direct Effect; Two Distinct and Different Concepts in Community law' 9 CMLRev 425 (1972). See also Articles 31 and 32 Vienna Convention on the Law of Treaties.

to produce the consequences of an uneven development of the law involved in the principle of direct application, consequences of which do not accord with the essential aim of the Community.'[5] Three member states (Belgium, the Netherlands and Germany) also argued that breaches of Article 25 could be enforced under Articles 226–228 of the Treaty, reinforcing the view that the EEC Treaty should be seen as a contract between states.

The judges of the European Court did not choose to follow these submissions. The EEC Treaty, it stated, was 'more than an agreement which merely creates obligations between the contracting states'. Where did the Court find support for this view? It pointed to the preamble of the Treaty 'which refers not only to governments but to peoples' as well as finding it 'confirmed more specifically by the establishment of institutions endowed with sovereign rights, the exercise of which affects member states and also their citizens'. From this it went on, in one of the most frequently quoted passages of EC law, to state:

> The conclusion to be drawn from this is that the Community constitutes a new legal order of international law for the benefit of which the states have limited their sovereign rights, albeit within limited fields, and the subjects of which comprise not only Member States but also their nationals. Independently of the legislation of Member States, Community law therefore not only imposes obligations on individuals but is also intended to confer upon them rights which become part of their legal heritage. These rights arise not only where expressly granted by the Treaty, but also by reason of obligations which the Treaty imposes in a clearly defined way upon individuals as well as upon the Member States and upon the institutions of the Community.[6]

The textual support for the creation of this 'new legal order' is rather thin. In addition to referring to the preamble, the Court cited Article 234 as evidence for its claim that individuals could invoke EEC law in their national courts. They also looked to the European Parliament and Ecosoc as a source of citizen empowerment. This was somewhat hopeful in 1962, as the Parliament was not then even directly elected and Ecosoc continues to be appointed by governments. But the Court's approach to legal interpretation is indicated by an earlier passage in its judgment, in which it said that 'To ascertain whether the provisions of an international treaty extend so far in their effects it is necessary to consider the spirit, the general scheme and the wording of those provisions.' The ordering of these sources indicates the Court's priorities and its willingness to engage in teleological interpretation of the Treaty, a fact which may baffle lawyers from a common law background used to more literal styles of interpretation. But this disposition to look to the spirit of the Treaty meant that the Court could transform provisions which were intended to guide actions of member states and Community institutions into fundamental freedoms which can be invoked by parties before their national courts. And, in this way, the EEC was transformed from a regional free trade community into a 'new legal order'. Had this not been the case, according to Stein, 'It is safe to say, with the benefit of hindsight, that had the Court followed the Governments, Community law

---

[5] *Van Gend* at 19–24.
[6] *Van Gend* at 12.

would have remained an abstract skeleton, and a great variety and number of Treaty violations would have remained unresolved and unredressed.'[7]

For Pierre Pescatore, a former judge of the Court, the fact that individuals must be visualised as being subjects of Community law 'is the consequence of a democratic ideal, meaning that in the Community, as well as the modern constitutional state, governments may not say any more what they are used to doing in international law: '*L'Etat, c'est moi*.'[8] But this particular realisation of a democratic ideal also illustrates the political character of the Court's judgments and its inclination to interpret the treaty in a different way from that originally envisaged by the founding member states: in this case in a constitutional mode, rather than a traditional international law interpretation. In this way it resembles the conjuring act of *Marbury* v *Madison*,[9] by which Chief Justice Marshall of the US Supreme Court introduced judicial review into US constitutional law, despite its absence from the text of the Constitution. The lofty characteristics of *Van Gend* are, however, belied by its subject matter: tariff classification, a subject which is hardly world shattering, and may explain the 'benign neglect'[10] of the Court's early jurisprudence. This provides an example of how the apparently 'neutral mould of law' helps to mask the political implications of the Court's decisions.[11] And the political implications would be considerable.

However, the Court's acknowledgement of the direct effect of EEC law was not perhaps as original as is sometimes suggested.[12] In countries which take a monist approach to international law, treaties may be directly enforceable (or in American terminology 'self-executing') without the need for incorporation. Several countries in the EEC took this approach.[13] Furthermore, it seems that the Court drew con-

---

[7] See E Stein, 'Lawyers, Judges and the Making of a Transnational Constitution', [1981] 75 American Journal of Comparative law, 1 at 6.

[8] P Pescatore, 'The Doctrine of Direct Effect: An Infant Disease of Community Law' (1983) 8 EL Rev 155 at 158.

[9] *Marbury* v *Madison* [1803] 5 US 137, 1 Cranch 137, 176 2 L Ed 60.

[10] Per Stein op. cit. at 1.

[11] See W Mattli and A-M Slaughter, 'The Role of National Courts in European Integration', in A-M Slaughter, Sweet and J Weiler (eds) *The European Courts and National Courts* (Hart Publishing, 1998).

[12] Already in 1960, the ECJ had said of the ECSC treaty that it 'contains rules capable like rules laid down by the national legislation of being directly implemented in the member states': Case 20/59 *Italy* v *High Authority* [1960] ECR at 339.

[13] Including the Netherlands. Claes and de Witte trace Dutch support for the direct enforcement and application of international treaties to Grotius' seventeenth-century treatise *Mare Liberum*, basing it on the need of a small country for open borders: Claes and de Witte, 'Report on the Netherlands', in A-M Slaughter, Sweet and J Weiler (eds) *The European Courts and the National Courts* (Hart Publishing, 1998) at 189. Indeed de Witte and Claes, op. cit., suggest that the truly radical actor in *Van Gend* was not the ECJ but the Dutch referring court. In countries such as the UK or Italy, treaties have to be incorporated by Act of Parliament. However, equally radically, in 1962, an Italian court had already ruled that the EEC Treaty had direct effect, in *Societa Biscotti Panettoni Colossi di Milano* v *Ministero del Commercio* [1963] CMLR 133 at 139. See also Jackson, 'Status of treaties in Domestic Legal Systems' (1992) 86 Am. Jo. Int. L. 310. In the US context see Marshall CJ's definition of a self-executing treaty in *Foster &Elam* v *Neilson*, 27 US (2 Pet.) 253, 314, (1829). Developments in international law had also predated the ECJ's introduction of direct effect. See the opinion of the Permanent Court of International Justice, the Hague, *Jurisdiction of the courts of Danzig*, Advisory Opinion no 15 March 3 1928, Publications of the Permanent court, Series B.

siderable inspiration from the Commission in finding Article 25 to be directly effective. The idea of the Community as a 'new legal order' originated with the legal service of the Commission, which also suggested that EEC law must be supreme over national law as a necessary corollary to direct effect.[14] In this way, as Advocate General Lagrange recognised in the *Costa* case,[15] the EEC Treaty could be treated as a constitution, rather than another example of international law. This, however, did not seem obvious to everyone in 1962, not least Advocate General Roemer – a 'prisoner' of traditional doctrine – in *Van Gend*, who stood the assertion on its head, denying the possibility of direct effect on account of the lack of a supremacy clause. The Court in *Van Gend* chose not to follow him, and a year later affirmed the supremacy of EEC law in *Costa*.

Pescatore, as well as looking to direct effect as a democratic ideal, also stresses its technical and practical nature. When will a provision of EC law be found to possess direct effect? In *Van Gend*, the Court seemed to set three conditions. It stated that 'The wording of Article 12 contains a clear and unconditional prohibition which is not a positive but a negative obligation' which was 'not qualified by any reservation on the part of the states which would make its implementation conditional upon a positive legislative measure enacted under national law.'[16] According to some commentators[17] this is simply justiciability. However, Pescatore went on to comment that 'This means that "direct effect" of Community rules in the last analysis depends less on the intrinsic qualities of the rules concerned than on the *possumus* or *non possumus* of the judges in the different member states, on the assumption that they take these attitudes in a spirit of good will and with a constructive mind.'[18]

If Pescatore's interpretation is correct, there was certainly a good quantity of *possumus* as well as a highly constructive approach by the Court to the direct effect conditions of *Van Gend*. *Reyners*[19] is a good example. Reyners, a lawyer of Dutch nationality, had been refused permission to practise at the Belgian Bar, although he had qualified in Belgium. He argued his case in the Belgian courts, relying on Article 43, which provides for freedom of establishment throughout the Community.

---

[14] See E Stein, op. cit., at 24. Stein also questions why the Belgian and Dutch legal establishment, often at the forefront of European integration, argued against direct effect. Stein suggests that they were reluctant to abandon hallowed constitutional principles. But abandon them they did. See also Chapter 7 on Supremacy.

[15] Case 6/64 *Costa* v *ENEL* [1964] ECR at 605.

[16] *Van Gend* at 13. The requirement of a negative obligation was soon dropped: see the *Reyners* case below.

[17] P Pescatore, 'The Doctrine of "Direct Effect": An Infant Disease of Community Law' (1983) 8 EL Rev 155. Prechal, however, gives a somewhat more complex definition of direct effect as 'the obligation of a court or another authority to apply the relevant provisions of Community law, either as a norm which governs the case or as a standard for legal review': S Prechal, *Directives in European Community Law* (Oxford: OUP, 1995) at 276; see also the discussion later in this chapter on the complexity of direct effect.

[18] Pescatore op. cit. at 177.

[19] Case 2/74 *Reyners* v *Belgium* [1974] ECR 631. See also Case 57/65 *Lutticke* [1966] ECR 205 where the ECJ found Article 90 directly effective even although it imposed a positive rather than a negative obligation.

However, the objective of Article 43 was to be achieved by a general programme, overseen by the Council of Ministers, which would harmonise national rules on training or qualifications for the professions by means of Community legislation. Thus it might seem that Article 43 was clearly dependent on further action and not an unconditional provision which conferred rights on individuals. The Court still found Article 43 to be capable of direct effect. It held that Article 43 'imposes an obligation to attain a precise result, the fulfilment of which had to be made easier by, but not made dependent on, the implementation of a programme of progressive measures'. The Court found a core principle of non-discrimination on grounds of nationality, which was directly effective, and could be directly invoked by Reyners. Therefore, a provision which at first sight appears to be positive in character, imposing legislative obligations, was transformed by the Court into a clear negative prohibition, capable of direct effect. This approach would, of course, not help every applicant who wished to plead the freedom of establishment. Without further legislation, discrepancies between member state professional requirements remained in place. If Reyners had been a Belgian who had qualified in Holland, and wished his Dutch qualifications to be recognised in Belgium, a right of non-discrimination on grounds of nationality would not have helped him. This type of situation has only been remedied more recently with the introduction of directives 89/48 and 92/51, which provide for a general system for the recognition of higher education diplomas awarded on completion of professional education and training.

In a similar way, the Court held, in the *Defrenne*[20] case, that Article 141 which states that 'Each Member State shall ... maintain the application of the principle that men and women should receive equal pay for equal work' was capable of direct effect. The Belgian government had failed to take any steps to ensure the application of this principle, to the detriment of Gabrielle Defrenne, an air hostess with Sabena, the Belgian national airline, who claimed a number of grounds of discrimination, including pay, in comparison to her male steward colleagues. At first sight Article 141 does not appear to satisfy the criteria for direct effect: as Advocate General Trabucchi put it in the *Defrenne* case, 'the form of words used ... may seem vague and the meaning of the word "principle" itself not to be very specific'.[21] However, as Trabucchi continued, 'the purpose of the rule is nevertheless clear: to prohibit any discrimination to the detriment of women with regard to pay.'[22] The Court agreed with him. It drew a distinction between direct and overt discrimination and indirect and disguised discrimination, holding that Article 141 was capable of direct effect in the former case, even if 'certain cases involve the elaboration of criteria whose implementation necessitates the taking of appropriate measures at Community and national level'.[23] Importantly, the *Defrenne* case is also an illustration of horizontal effect, i.e. a provision which can be invoked by one individual against another. In this respect the Court did not follow the Commission, which

---

[20] Case 43/75 *Defrenne v Sabena* [1976] ECR 455 2 CMLR 98.
[21] *Defrenne* at 486.
[22] Ibid.
[23] *Defrenne* at para 19.

would have limited direct effect to the public sector.[24] It also follows that some provisions, as pointed out by Pescatore, may simultaneously have and not have direct effect. For example, there is a core or inner circle to Article 141, which can be applied to purely direct discrimination which can be detected on a purely legal analysis. But such a core principle is none the less wide ranging, capable of being applied to situations of part-time work[25] and so transforming Article 141 into a valuable tool in sex discrimination suits. As Pescatore writes, direct effect is an example of '*l'art du possible*', as will be illustrated later in the case of directives. Indeed, so worried did the member states seem about what might be possible that, in Article 34 TEU, they explicitly denied the direct effect of framework decisions in third pillar matters.

DIRECT EFFECT OF INTERNATIONAL AGREEMENTS

Where the direct effect of international agreements, rather than the EC Treaty, is at issue, the ECJ has been somewhat circumspect in its approach. Although the ECJ professes to apply the same conditions of direct effect as in the case of internal law, case law in this area has not been very coherent. In the *International Fruit* case,[26] the Court applied the direct effect criteria and found that the relevant provision of the GATT was not directly effective. However, in the *Bresciani*[27] and *Kupferberg*[28] cases, it found the relevant international provisions to be directly effective, although it is not really clear why these cases produced different results. It would seem to be the case that the Court has applied the conditions for direct effect more strictly in the case of international agreements. However, its reasons for doing so are not particularly transparent. It seems to have continuously found the GATT not to be directly effective. This is understandable, as the rules under the GATT are not unconditional and quite flexible: direct effect seems out of place in a set of rules characterised by flexibility. The WTO, the successor organisation of the GATT, however, underwent many changes, and the question of its direct effect was uncertain. In *Portugal* v *Council*[29] the Court had a chance to rule on its capacity for direct effect. Although the ECJ recognised that, when compared with the 'old' GATT, the WTO had undergone significant changes, it argued that the WTO agreements were still based on the principle of negotiations and 'reciprocal and mutually advantageous arrangements', and thus not capable of direct effect. Thus the ECJ has chosen not to depart from its case law first established in *International Fruit*.

---

[24] Articles 81 and 82 are also horizontally directly effective. See also Case 36/74 *Walrave & Koch* v *Association Union Cycliste Internationale* [1974] ECR 1405 and Case C-415/93 *Bosman* [1995] ECR I-4921 regarding the direct effect of Articles 48 and 52. In Case C-281/98 *Angonese* v *Cassa di Risparmio di Bolzano SpA* [2000] ECR I-4139, the Court found Article 39 to be capable of direct effect.
[25] See e.g. Case 96/80 *Jenkins* v *Kingsgate* [1981] ECR 911 and *McCarthys* v *Smith* [1979] 3 All ER 325.
[26] Cases 21 & 22/72 *International Fruit Company* [1972] ECR 1219.
[27] Case 87/75, *Bresciani* [1974] ECR 129.
[28] Case 104/81 *Kupferberg* [1982] ECR 3659.
[29] Case C-149/96 *Portugal* v *Council* [1999] ECR I 8395.

DIRECT EFFECT OF DIRECTIVES

Finding provisions of the treaty capable of direct effect is all very well, but not always useful, as a huge amount of Community regulation proceeds by secondary legislation. If this is not capable of direct effect, individuals will be disempowered. Is EC secondary legislation capable of direct effect?

Regulations may be similar to primary legislation, i.e. normative in nature, and they rarely leave the member states a discretion as to implementation. They are already stated to be 'directly applicable' in Article 249 [formerly 189] of the Treaty. 'Directly applicable' sounds suspiciously similar to direct effect and, indeed, the Court often uses these expressions interchangeably. However, it is suggested that 'directly applicable' is best understood as meaning that a regulation automatically becomes part of the law of the land, without the need for further implementation, whereas direct effect has the meaning given above, i.e. capable of giving rise to individual rights enforceable in the national courts, or justiciability.[30] Regulations may sometimes be directly effective, if they satisfy the criteria laid down in *Van Gend*, and were held to be so in the *Leonesio*[31] case. In *Grad*,[32] the Court held that decisions too can be directly effective, even although they are not referred to in Article 249 as being directly applicable, stating, 'It would be incompatible with the binding effect attributed to decisions by Article 189 to exclude in principle the possibility that persons affected may invoke the obligation imposed by a decision.'

It was a short and perhaps inevitable step from the ruling in *Grad* to the decision in *Van Duyn*[33] that directives were capable of having direct effect. A short step, but a very controversial ruling. Ms Van Duyn was a Dutch national who had come to the UK to take up employment with the Church of Scientology. She was refused entry into the UK on grounds of public policy. The British government regarded scientology as socially harmful (although it was not a banned organisation in the UK).[34] She protested that her exclusion was contrary to Article 39 of the treaty, which provides for the free movement of workers. She also sought to rely on directive 64/221 which regulates measures taken by member states which exclude or expel persons on grounds of public health, policy or security. This appears to leave a large amount of discretion to the state in its application of the provision and thus to preempt its direct effect. However, Ms Van Duyn claimed that, under this directive, such measures had to be based exclusively on her 'personal conduct' which she claimed did not cover her membership of the Church of Scientology. The UK contested her action, claiming that directives could not be directly effective.

---

[30] Also see Winter, 'Direct Applicability and Direct Effect' for a fuller discussion of this topic; see also Lenz, Tynes and Young, 'Horizontal what?' (2000) 25 ELRev 509 for a fuller interpretation of the doctrine of direct effect.

[31] Case 93/71 *Leonesio v Italian Ministry of Agriculture* [1972] ECR 293.

[32] Case 9/70 *Franz Grad v Finanzamt Traunstein* [1970] ECR 825.

[33] Case 41/74 *Van Duyn v Home Office* [1974] ECR 1337.

[34] Parliament had debated the matter in 1968, concluding there was no power to ban it – this was described by Advocate General Mayras as 'one of the consequences of a liberal government'.

The UK's rejection of the direct effect of directives was understandable and the text of Article 249 seems to confirm it. If directives were directly effective, what would there be to distinguish them from regulations, and yet Article 249 defines them quite differently. According to Article 249(3) directives are only binding on member states, which therefore would appear to be the only addressees of a directive. Also, as directives are only stated to be binding as to the result to be achieved, it would also seem that effects for individuals follow only from the national implementing measures. Furthermore, at the time of *Van Duyn*, directives did not have to be published.[35] Thus an applicant's chance of establishing a legal right derived from a directive seemed to depend on the rather fortuitous point of whether they were aware of its existence, which seemed undesirable on grounds of legal certainty.

The European Court did not find these arguments convincing and found directive 64/221 to be directly effective. It used three arguments, none of which is very persuasive, but which illustrate the Court performing 'perhaps the most striking example of its teleological method of interpretation'.[36] First, it said, it would be incompatible with the binding effect attributed to a directive by Article 249(3) to exclude in principle their direct effect. As there are many EC laws which are binding at interstate level without being directly effective this is not a very strong argument, although it was at least one based on the text of the treaty. Second, the Court said that the *effet utile* (useful effect) of the measure would be weakened if individuals were prevented from relying on it in their national courts. This argument is frequently cited by the Court, and has become a thread running through subsequent case law on remedies. However, this was surely not a textual argument but rather a rule of interpretation which requires preference to be given to the construction which gives a legal provision it fullest effect.[37] Third, the Court also referred to Article 234 of the treaty, which allows national courts to refer questions of Community law to the ECJ, as implying that those acts may be invoked by individuals in their national courts. Again, this is not a strong argument, as Article 234 is not restricted to the interpretation of binding or directly effective provisions. In fact this last line of reasoning was swiftly abandoned by the Court.

Writing of the *Van Duyn* case Wincott has referred to 'a breathtaking radicalism which often amounts to judicial legislation ... (whereby) less convincing arguments are dropped and more convincing alternatives found'.[38] However, the reasoning of the Court in *Van Duyn*, although controversial, was not revolutionary. It did not emerge from thin air. As in *Van Gend en Loos*, the ground had already been prepared. Everling, himself a former judge of the European Court, reminds us that the Court's case law was preceded by a lively debate in academic writing which

---

[35] Since Maastricht all regulations and directives must be published in the Official Journal: Article 254 (2) EC.

[36] Stein, op. cit. at 22.

[37] See S Prechal, *Directives in European Community Law* (Oxford: Clarendon Press, 1995) at 249.

[38] D Wincott, 'The role of law or the rule of the ECJ?' (1995) JEPP at 591.

prepared the way for its decision.[39] Those who argued for direct effect suggested that the arguments presented against it above were formalistic. Moreover, they could employ the moral argument that direct effect would strengthen the legal protection of individuals as well as integration. Ironically, Ms Van Duyn's position was not strengthened by the ruling, as the Court held that the British government's interpretation of Article 3 of the directive was justified. So this case seems to provide an example of the Court's rights rhetoric, rather than its substance.

Five years later in the *Ratti*[40] case, the Court added another argument for the direct effect of directives, which has been advocated by some as the most convincing ground. It was based on an estoppel-like notion, according to which a member state should not be able to rely on its own failure to implement a directive, and was first proposed to the Court in the *Enka*[41] case by the British Advocate General Warner. In *Ratti*, the Court held that 'a member State which has not adopted the implementing measures required by the directive in the prescribed period may not rely, as against individuals on its own failure to perform the obligations which the directive entails'.[42]

This argument has been seen to be the most satisfactory by many writers. Pescatore[43] cites it as the *'motive véritable'* of the Court and it has also been invoked by several advocates general.[44] It is frequently invoked by the Court but has not been without detractors, especially in recent years, and criticism of it will be considered later.

Therefore, by the late 1970s, the principle of the direct effect of many provisions of Community law seemed well established. As will be seen, this principle was not always accepted by the national judiciary, which is unsurprising given the radical nature of the concept. In fact, the introduction and expansion of the doctrines of direct effect and supremacy has led to the 'constitutionalisation' of the treaty, a perennial theme of this book. As well as serving as a keystone in the constitutional architecture of the EC, Craig[45] suggests that direct effect has served distinct but overlapping functions. Two of these are worth considering in further detail. First,

---

[39] U Everling, 'Zur Direkten innerstaatlichen Wirkung der EG Rechtlinien: Ein beispiel richterlicher Rechtsfortbildung auf der Basis gemeinsamer rechtsgrundsatze', in Borner (ed.) *Einigkeit und Recht und Freiheit* (Koln: Carl Heymann, 1984).

[40] Case 148/78 *Ratti* [1979] ECR 1629 at para 22 of the judgment.

[41] Case 38/77 *Enka* [1977] ECR 2203 at p 2203. Given the equitable origins of estoppel its introduction by AG Warner is unsurprising. However, a similar concept exists in German law, the 'Auspragung des Grundsatzes von Treu und Glauben', i.e. the expression of the principle of good faith. See e.g. Nicolaysen 1984 p 386. In Case 190/87 *Moorman* [1988] ECR 4686, the ECJ referred to Article 10 EC as another basis for the direct effect of directives.

[42] *Ratti*, at para 22. In *Ratti*, the Court also made the important qualification that a directive may not be directly effective until the period for its implementation has expired, ' ...it is only at the end of the prescribed period and in the event of the Member State's default that the directive ... will be able to have the effects described in the answer to the first question.' (para 43).

[43] P Pescatore, 'L'effet des directives communautaire: une tentative de démythication' (Dalloz Chronique, 1980) at 171.

[44] e.g. AG Slynn in Case 8/81 *Becker* [1982] ECR 53; Case 152/84 *Marshall I* [1986] ECR 723; AG Mischo (Case 80/86 *Kolpinghuis* [1987] ECR 3969); AG Lenz (Case 103/88 *Costanzo* [1989] ECR 1839; AG Darmon (Case 190/87 *Moorman* [1988] ECR 4689).

[45] P Craig, 'Once Upon a Time in the West: Direct Effect and the Federalisation of EEC Law' (1992) 12 OJLS 453 at 454.

direct effect may be used as a means of enforcing Community law. Second, it has been used in a quasi-legislative way – as Ian Ward writes, 'the development of the direct effect jurisdiction reveals the European Court creating for itself a tripartite role...a judiciary, a legislature and an executive all in one.'[46]

AN ENFORCEMENT FUNCTION

Although there are procedures in Articles 226–228 (formerly Articles 169–171) enabling the Commission to proceed against member states in breach of their treaty obligations, such a procedure will not always be a desirable way of enforcing Community law. If the Commission took action against every treaty breach or failure to implement a directive, it would be overwhelmed; it simply does not have the manpower to cope. Furthermore, the Commission may also find it politically undesirable to proceed: it may be trying to push forward an important legislative initiative within the Council which may be jeopardised by the threat of an Article 226 action. Indeed, even if the Commission decides to pursue Article 226 actions vigorously, this may not have the desired effect. As Mancini and Keeling note, multiplication of Article 226 procedures may result in a sort of vicious circle which undermines its deterrent effect: 'The greater the number of actions, the less probable it is that the member States will succeed in executing the resulting judgements; the more cases of non-compliance, the less credible becomes the organ whose decisions are thus disregarded...'[47] In contrast, by declaring the possibility that treaty provisions and directives can be directly effective, the Court, in the words of Robert Lecourt, a former President of the ECJ, creates a number of 'auxiliary agents for the Community'.[48] This, of course, was recognised by the Court in *Van Gend*, when it stated, 'the vigilance of individuals concerned to protect their rights amounts to an effective supervision in addition to that entrusted by Article 169 and 170 to the diligence of the Commission and Member States.'[49] It also meant that all sorts of disputes could be referred to the ECJ which would never have arisen under direct action by the Commission or a member state. In this way political pressure is taken off the Commission and the burden of enforcing Community law is shifted to the national courts,[50] which have sanctions[51] and the power of the State behind them

---

[46] I Ward, *A Critical Introduction to European Law* (Butterworths, 1996) at 56.

[47] Mancini and Keeling, 'The Constitutional Challenge Facing the European Court', 11 Yearbook of European Law, 1–13 at 10. For an example of this state of affairs see the *Sheepmeat* case, where France stated that it would not comply with the Court's judgment until the Council introduced a new regime to support French farmers: Case 232/78 *Commission v France* [1979] ECR 2729.

[48] R Lecourt, *L'Europe des Juges* (Brussels: Bruylant, 1976) 307.

[49] *Van Gend*, at para 16.

[50] And, indeed, not just the national courts but also the national **administration**, as the ECJ decided in Case 103/88 *Costanzo* [1989] ECR 1839 that the administration must apply directly effective provisions in the same way as national courts. See also case C-431/92 *Grosskrotzenberg* [1995] ECR I 2189 and Case C-224/97 *Ciola* [1999] ECR I 2517.

[51] Unlike the ECJ, which could not impose fines or sanctions until Article 228 was amended by the Maastricht Treaty.

to enforce compliance. Such a shift to national court actions also transforms them into Community courts and creates something closer to a federal system. It also ensures that judges, lawyers and maybe even some individuals, will 'internalise' Community law, seeing it as part of their own legal system, thereby adopting toward it the 'critical reflective attitude' which HLA Hart[52] maintained was the key to the existence of a legal system. In this way, some of the argument over the hierarchy of Community law, discussed in the chapter on supremacy, might be avoided.

Although this is an effective means of ensuring European integration, it can also be presented in an attractive democratic light. For, by giving individuals a role in the enforcement of European law, it gave them an apparent stake in European integration, as the individuals endowed with rights of *Van Gend en Loos*, in the same way that the US Bill of Rights has been enforced by individual suits. This, Dehousse suggests, 'has fostered a kind of undeclared alliance between private litigants and pro-integration forces'.[53] The suggestion has been made that this has contributed to the integration process, through what Dehousse terms 'some sort of invisible hand mechanism' whereby individuals do not protect only their own interests but also contribute to ensuring the effectiveness of Community law.[54] This suggestion might seem to be supported by the fact that the amount of Article 234 references overtook the number of Article 226 actions in the 1970s, thus indicating a greater reliance on the national courts as a means of enforcing EC law. Therefore, it might seem, European integration and the protection of individual rights have gone hand in hand.[55]

Two further points have to be made, however. First, which was the greater impetus behind the ECJ's development of direct effect: the protection of individual rights, or an effective enforcement function? This question resembles one which might be posed of the Court's initial motives in positing a doctrine of human rights for the EC in the *Internationale Handelsgesellschaft* case and others.[56] It is common to find enthusiastic support for direct effect as a democratic ideal – Mancini's accolade is typical: 'The effect of *Van Gend en Loos* was to take Community law out of the hands of politicians and bureaucrats and to give it to the people. Of all the Court's democratising achievements none can rank so highly in practical terms.'[57] However, if the effective enforcement of EC law could be dressed in the more acceptable language of rights[58] or the democratic ideals referred to by Pescatore, this might imply

---

[52] HLA Hart, *The Concept of Law* (Oxford: Clarendon, 1961).

[53] R Dehousse, *The European Court of Justice* (Macmillan, 1998) 49–51.

[54] See also neo-functionalist theories of integration which attempt to explain the Court's activism as prompted by various interest groups, e.g. A.-M. Slaughter and W Mattli, 'Europe Before the Court: A Political Theory of Legal Integration' (1993) 47 International Organization 41–76.

[55] e.g. R Dehousse, *The European Court of Justice* at 47; Lecourt, *L'Europe des Juges*, at 308.

[56] See Chapter 13.

[57] Mancini, cited in European Law Brief, November 1998.

[58] Although directly effective provisions need not necessarily create individual **rights**. They can be broader, as directly effective provisions can be invoked for other purposes: see S Prechal, 'Does Direct Effect Matter?' (2000) 37 CMLRev, who also notes the problems experienced in Germany as a result of regarding the creation of an individual right as an implicit condition for direct effect. She sees this as a result of the German focus on *Individualrechtsschutz*.

a certain amount of cynicism in the ECJ's use of the doctrine, sincere though Pescatore or Mancini may be in their praise.[59] Some support for this proposition might be gathered from the Court's Article 230 and 288 case law, which has not shown the Court over ready to use the language of rights protection where it is Community institutions which are being challenged. Second, one might question just how effective this protection of individual rights has been. There are significant limitations placed by EC law itself as to the judicial protection that can be offered by the national courts; these will be considered below.[60] Additionally, the effectiveness of such a system depends on the good relationship between the ECJ and national courts. Although some commentators, such as Karen Alter, see the success of EC law as built on a political alliance between the European Court and national courts,[61] relations have not always been good, as will be illustrated below. This has threatened both the enforcement function and the democratic ideal.

PROMPTING LEGISLATION

The second function performed by the doctrine of direct effect is that of acting as a legislative catalyst in times of inaction by the political institutions, as is well illustrated by *Reyners* and *Defrenne*. At times when the Community legislation process is proceeding slowly, courts can step in. Weiler[62] has described the ECJ's methodology in this context as normative supranationalism, distinguishing it from decisional supranationalism, which he defines as the institutional framework and decision-making process in which Community policies and legislation are promulgated and executed. In contrast, normative supranationalism is concerned with 'the relationships and hierarchy which exist between Community policies and legal measures of the Member States'.[63] At the time of *Defrenne* and *Reyners* decisional supranationalism was not functioning effectively. The complex and cumbersome nature of Community legislation in the early years of the EEC, which required unanimity in voting, as well as a totalising approach to harmonisation, which attempted to regulate even the most intricate aspects of a given field, meant that progress was inevitably very slow.[64] It is in this context that the ECJ's contribution was vital. As Craig[65] notes, in *Reyners*, the Court adopted a legislative role. The ECJ

---

[59] There is also the question of whose rights are being enforced – most EC actions are brought by major corporations, rather than individuals.

[60] These are limitations as to the provisions of EC law which are capable of direct effect, as well as the bodies against which they may be pleaded. Further limitations will be considered in the field of remedies in the next chapter.

[61] K Alter, 'The European Court's Political Power' (1995) 19 West European Politics 458.

[62] J Weiler, 'The Community System: The Dual Character of Supranationalism' (1981) 1 YEL 267.

[63] Ibid. at 271.

[64] Sharpf has characterised the inability of the political institutions to move beyond the status quo in policy: Sharpf, 'The Joint Decision Trap: Lessons from German Federalism and European Integration' (1988) 66 Public Administration 239.

[65] P Craig, 'Once Upon a Time in the West: Direct Effect and the Federalisation of EEC Law' (1992) OJLS at 453.

'functions as a surrogate legislature when the "real" legislature is unable to perform the tasks assigned to it'.[66] The member states would not, or could not, take the necessary steps to enact Community legislation on the freedom of establishment and so the Court developed its own brand of normative supranationalism, by making use of the direct effect and supremacy of EC law, thus ensuring that this area of Community policy could be taken forward. The Commission reacted to *Reyners* by withdrawing a number of draft directives, which were now obsolete, and declared that it would in future focus on the coordination of rules governing the admission to, and practice of, the professions (although it was not until the aftermath of a later Court decision, *Cassis de Dijon*, that the political institutions of the Community began to consider that they should change the way that they legislated).

Others have preferred to see this type of action by the Court as providing a catalyst for legislation, rather than usurping the legislative role. Thus, writing about Article 28 in the context of the *Cassis de Dijon*[67] decision (in which the direct effect of Article 28 was not at issue but the ECJ appeared to be taking fairly radical action to effect the free movement of goods), Alter and Aitsahalia[68] suggest that, by introducing the concept of mutual recognition into the debate, the Court provoked political responses to its decisions which did radically change the harmonisation process. In any case, what is not disputable is that the Court has acted as a catalyst in situations where the political process has been stalled.

Most commentators have seen the Court's action as much needed progress and have been happily uncritical of the Court's methodology. However, for Mary Volcansek, what is remarkable about the Court's law-making has been 'the almost total lack of criticism and virtual sycophantic praise of the Court's actions'.[69] As such it has seemed to be a case of 'constitutional law without politics'.[70] One exception to this favourable consensus has been Hjalte Rasmussen, for whom the European Court's methodology constitutes 'the most grave judicial policy involvement'.[71] Rasmussen complains of the *Reyners* case that 'It is activism to substitute the existence of a right of establishment to a legislative power in order to provide for such a right'[72] going on to cite Alf Ross's warning against judicial activism that 'the judge shall not be like the Homeric king who received his *themistes* direct from Zeus, or like the Oriental Cadi who makes his decision out of an esoteric wisdom.'[73] This, according to Rasmussen, is exactly what the ECJ was doing in a case like *Reyners*. Rasmussen has a point. The direct effect judgments are highly 'political' in the sense of being as much prompted by a certain agenda as by a solid textual foun-

---

[66] Craig, op. cit. at 464–5.

[67] Case 120/78 *Rewe-Zentrale AG v Bundesmonopolverwaltung fur Branntwein* [1979] ECR 649.

[68] Alter and Aitsahalia, 'Judicial Politics in the European Community: European integration and the pathbreaking Cassis de Dijon decision' (1994) 24 Comparative Political Studies 536.

[69] Volcansek, 'The European Court of Justice: Supranational Policy-Making', in Volcansek (ed.) *Judicial Politics and Policy Making in Western Europe* (London: Cass, 1992).

[70] Per M Shapiro, 'The European Court of Justice' in A Sbragia (ed.) *Euro-Politics* (Washington DC: The Brookings Institution, 1992) at 93.

[71] H Rasmussen, *On Law and Policy in the European Court of Justice* (Martinus Nijhoff, 1986) at 29.

[72] Ibid.

[73] A Ross, *On Law and Justice* (London, 1958).

dation. However, it is somewhat naive to dismiss this as illegitimate. While legal interpretation should attempt fidelity to the textual source and coherence with precedent and the *acquis communautaire*,[74] very often texts are ambiguous, or so general as to admit more than one interpretation. In such 'hard cases' the legislative intent may be unclear, the legal materials highly indeterminate, and much of EC law is like this. In *Reyners*, the ECJ were not so 'squarely disrespectful of the textual indications found in the constitutional document'[75] as Rasmussen suggests. Although Article 43 did not appear unconditional in the sense of the *Van Gend* criteria, the *Reyners* case was in fact a straightforward situation of discrimination, in which the absence of legislation was not critical. Likewise, the principle of equal pay in Article 141 is also expressed in such abstract, general terminology as to give rise to several interpretations. The approach taken by Ross or Rasmussen is too formalist, assuming that legal texts are capable of rigid, inflexible interpretation. This is simply not the case, especially with the vague *traité cadre* which is the EC Treaty. The 'objective regularity' posited by Ross in 'On Law and Justice'[76] is a very elusive entity. Over a hundred years of constitutional scholarship in the USA has not succeeded in providing a theory of judicial interpretation acceptable to all,[77] in the context of the similarly abstract principles of the Bill of Rights. But to be wary of formalism does not mean that one is totally uncritical of the Court's approach. To say that the Court has been dealing with abstract, ambiguous texts is not to endorse every decision made by the Court. It is just to say that the text does not deliver a determinate right answer every time.

DELIMITING DIRECT EFFECT

However, the Court did draw some limits to the principle of direct effect. It had continued to emphasise the distinction between regulations and directives in its case law, even if this distinction was not very transparent. However, in the *Marshall*[78] case in 1986, it gave a ruling which made one distinction between these two types of legal provision very clear. Directives may not impose obligations on individuals. They do not, to use what for a long time has been the accepted terminology, possess horizontal direct effect.[79]

---

[74] As proposed by Ronald Dworkin, an acceptable interpretation must 'fit' and 'justify' the practice. R Dworkin, *Law's Empire* (Fontana, 1986).

[75] Rasmussen op. cit. at p 29.

[76] Ross op. cit. at 18.

[77] See e.g. A Bickel, *The Least Dangerous Branch* (Yale University Press, 1962); JH Ely, *Democracy and Distrust* (Harvard University Press, 1980); A Scalia, *A Matter of Interpretation* (Princeton University Press, 1997).

[78] Case 152/84 *Marshall v Southampton & Southwest Hampshire Area Health Authority (Teaching) (Marshall I)* [1986] ECR 723.

[79] As with the issue of direct effect of directives this question had been discussed in academic literature, as well as by advocates general, before the court actually gave its ruling. See e.g. Easson, 'Can Directives Impose Obligations on Individuals?' (1979) 4 ELRev 69; see also AG Reischl in *Ratti* (cited at fn 40) and Slynn in *Becker*, (cited at fn 44).

Helen Marshall, a dietician working for Southampton Area Health Authority, had been required to retire at 60, although, under the written policy of the Authority, male workers were able to continue until 65. Such a discrepancy was permitted by the 1975 Sex Discrimination Act, which excluded matters relating to retirement from its scope. Ms Marshall claimed this breached Article 5(1) of the Equal Treatment Directive 76/207. Although Ms Marshall won her case, in that the Court held that the differing retirement ages breached Article 5(1) of the Equal Treatment Directive, the Court and the Advocate General made it very clear that directives could not impose obligations on private applicants. The reasons given by the Court and the advocate general were somewhat different. Advocate General Slynn reasoned on the grounds that, first, directives are addressed to member states and not to individuals, second that a directive did not have to be notified to an individual and was only published in the Official Journal by way of information and third, that giving horizontal effect to directives would totally blur the distinction between directives and regulations. The Court simply based its reasoning on the text of Article 249(3) holding that, since according to this paragraph the binding nature of a directive exists only in relation to the member state to which it is addressed, a directive may not of itself place obligations on an individual. This latter ground does not seem to be a very strong argument, and is out of line with other Court judgments on direct effect, such as the *Defrenne* case, where the ECJ was quite willing to find Article 141 directly effective, notwithstanding that it is addressed to member states, rather than individuals. Such a focus on the exact wording of the Treaty has also not been held conclusive by the Court elsewhere, when it has been willing to look to the spirit, aim and *effet utile* of Community law.

In *Marshall I* the Court also held that an individual may rely upon a directive against the State, regardless of whether the State is acting as public authority or employer. The consequence of this ruling is that, for example, a private employee may not rely on a directive but a state employee may. The ruling has been attacked as provoking unjust and anomalous situations, particularly in the field of labour law, where the scope of the Equal Treatment Directive has been reduced. The decision also led to the necessity for an impossibly rigorous definition of the State which proved very difficult to apply in case law.

THE CONCEPT OF THE STATE

In *Marshall I* Advocate General Slynn had suggested that the member states themselves should determine what constituted a 'public body'. Such an approach would no doubt have resulted in a lack of uniformity throughout the EC and it was not long before the ECJ made its own attempt at a definition. In *Foster v British Gas*, the applicant sought to rely on the Equal Treatment Directive against British Gas. But was British Gas (at that time unprivatised) a public body against which the directive could be enforced? The matter was referred to the ECJ by the House of Lords. Advocate General Van Gerven linked the concept of the state to the estoppel justification of directives, looking for some responsibility of the public body in the enforcement of the directive: 'I think the answer is this: [direct effect] may extend as far as "the State" ... has given itself powers which place it in a position to decisively influence the conduct of persons – whatever their nature, public or private, or their sphere of activity – with regard to the subject matter of the directive which has not been implemented correctly.'[80] His approach was not followed by the Court, which held that a directive might be used against a body which was 'subject to the authority or control of the state or has special powers beyond those which result for the normal relations between individuals'.[81] The Court went on to rule in paragraph 20 of the judgment that 'a body whatever its legal form, which has been made responsible, pursuant to a measure adopted by the State, for providing a public service under the control of the State and has for that purpose special powers beyond those which result in the normal rules applicable in relations between individuals'.

The ECJ's approach in *Foster* has been criticised as 'remarkably silent upon the solution to the problem of categorising the extent of state involvement in public life'.[82] The Court's approach is also not really fair, as a body in the position of British Gas could hardly be responsible for implementing the Equal Treatment Directive. When the case returned to the House of Lords, it held that British Gas met the test set by the Court of Justice, as by statute it was responsible for supplying a public service which was under control of the state and British Gas had special powers beyond those applicable in normal relations between individuals. The reactions of other English courts have been unpredictable. In *Doughty* v *Rolls-Royce*[83] the Court of Appeal found that Rolls-Royce, when a nationalised industry, although under the control of the state, did not provide a public service. But in *Griffin* v *South West Water*[84] the High Court held that a privatised utility can be considered an emanation of the state according to the *Foster* test. More recently, in *NUT* v *St Mary's School*[85] the Court of Appeal took a flexible approach to the *Foster* definition and held that the concept of an emanation of the state should be 'broad' and that the governing body of a voluntary aided school was an emanation of the state. Such a broad interpretation seems to undermine the arguments against horizontal direct effect, given that the aim of the *Marshall I* judgment seemed to be that obligations imposed by unimplemented directives should only be placed on those who were in a position to implement them in the first place, and this can hardly be said of South West Water or a primary school. These entities become 'liable by association'.[86] The estoppel justification is surely out of place used against such defendants. It would have been fairer and more straightforward to have accorded horizontal effect to directives.

---

[80] Ibid at para 18.
[81] Case C 188–89 *Foster v British Gas plc* [1990] ECR I-3313 at 3339.
[82] E Szyszczak, *Foster v British Gas* (1990) 27 CMLRev 859 at 868. See also Curtin, 'The Province of Government: Delimiting the Direct Effect of Directives in the Common Law Context' (1990) 15 EL Rev 195.
[83] [1992] ICR 538.
[84] [1995] IRLR 15.
[85] [1997] 3 CMLR 630.
[86] Per Steiner, 'From Direct Effect to Francovich' (1993) EL Rev 10.

However, when the ECJ was given a second opportunity to do this, in *Faccini Dori*,[87] the Court, despite the contrary pleadings of Advocate General Lenz, declined. Some commentators blame too strong a focus on the estoppel basis of direct effect as the foundation for the *Marshall I* judgment. By the *Faccini Dori* case, the Court was proposing estoppel as the main basis for direct effect of directives, which, it stated, 'seeks to prevent the State from taking advantage of its own failure to fully comply with Community law'.[88] Although it had appeared in the earlier case law that the Court said that it followed from the binding nature of directives and their useful effect that a member state might not plead their failure to implement them, this justification receded in the later case law. To place so much weight on an estoppel theory is undesirable, as this appears to change the nature of the Court's approach to the Community legal order, reducing direct effect to a side effect of the member state's inaction, rather than a capacity of a legal provision in the first place.

However, in *Dori*, other factors were also at play. By the early 1990s, when *Dori* was decided, the Court was able to point to an alternative remedy against the defaulting state in damages which it had introduced in the *Francovich* case.[89] Political factors were also at issue – the ECJ was urged by most member states in *Dori* not to depart from its *Marshall I* jurisprudence – pressure which it was likely to take seriously, given the refusal of some national courts to accept the doctrine of direct effect of directives, a feature which will be considered in the next section.[90]

POCKETS OF RESISTANCE[91]

France

> Historically the European Court of Justice has been able to achieve a remarkable relational feat: despite the integrationist radicalness of its doctrinal construct, with few exceptions the Court managed to hegemonize the EC interpretive community and to persuade, co-opt, and cajole most, if not all, other principal actors to accept the foundations of its doctrine and of its position as the final arbiter of constitutional determinations for the Community.[92]

This section considers those courts which formed 'pockets of resistance' to the hegemony of ECJ doctrine. Direct effect has not been as problematic as supremacy in the national courts. However, ascribing direct effect to directives caused very real

---

[87] Case C-91/92 [1994] ECR I-3325.

[88] Ibid.

[89] See below: member states' continued opposition to horizontal direct effect is actually rather surprising, given that since *Francovich*, this leaves the State open to increased financial liability.

[90] The *Dori* case was also in line with the Court's 'conservative' ruling in *Keck*, and its reluctance to extend EC competence, even in the case of fundamental rights in *Opinion 2/94*.

[91] The expression used by Joseph Weiler in 'A Quiet Revolution: The European Court of Justice and Its Interlocutors' (1994) 26 Comp. Pol. Stud. 510, 521–22.

[92] Weiler, 'A Quiet Revolution' at 517.

problems in some jurisdictions, which has belied the perceptions of some members of the Court as to their relations with national courts.[93] The position in France was perhaps the most extreme. Although in the *Vabre*[94] case of 1975 the Cour de Cassation had accepted the supremacy of Community law and did not object to the direct effect of directives, the Conseil d'État, the French Supreme Administrative Court, did not take such an equable approach. In *Semoules*[95] and subsequent cases, as already discussed,[96] the Conseil d'État held that it was not for the administrative courts to review the validity of legislation and it upheld the legality of subsequent French statutes over Community Regulations. The Conseil d'État also for many years refused to accept the primacy or direct effect of Community directives. *Cohn-Bendit*[97] is a good example of this attitude.

Cohn-Bendit was a case of its day: Danny *'le rouge'* Cohn-Bendit, a student at the Paris-Nanterre University where the troubles of 1968 originally arose, was one of the ringleaders of the student uprisings of May 1968. The French Minister of the Interior issued him with a deportation order (he was a German citizen) on the basis that Cohn-Bendit's presence in France was contrary to *ordre public*. Cohn-Bendit left France but in 1975 wanted to return when he was offered employment. The Minister refused to revoke the deportation order and did not give any reasons. Cohn-Bendit challenged this in the Paris Administrative court arguing that it infringed his right under Article 39 of the EC Treaty, which gives Community citizens a right to enter other member states to take up employment there. The rights under Article 39 are, however, limited on grounds of 'public policy, public security or public health'. But Cohn-Bendit additionally claimed that his rights under directive 64/221, which constrains the way the public policy proviso in Article 39 may be invoked, had been infringed, in that Article 6 of the directive states that the applicant must be given reasons for the decisions, unless this would be detrimental to state security. The Paris Administrative Court made a reference to the European Court under Article 234 for interpretation of these provisions but the Minister appealed against the order of reference to the Conseil d'État. The Conseil d'État allowed the Minister's appeal on the basis that directives did not have direct effect, and thus Cohn-Bendit could not rely on directive 64/221 in the Administrative Court. A reference to obtain a ruling on the interpretation of directive 64/221 was thus irrelevant and redundant.[98] As the doctrine of the direct effect of directives, and indeed of this particular directive 64/221, had been clearly established by the

---

[93] See e.g. the highly optimistic comments of K Lenaerts, 'Some thoughts on the interaction between judges and politicians in the EC' (1992) 12 YEL 1.

[94] *Administration des Douanes v Société 'Cafés Jacques Vabre' et SARL Weigel et Cie* [1975] 2 CMLR 336.

[95] Conseil d'État 1 March 1968 [1970] CMLR 395.

[96] In Chapter 7 on Supremacy.

[97] Conseil d'État 22 December 1978, Dalloz 1979 at 155.

[98] As expressed by Pescatore: 'But this request never reached the Court. There had been an appeal to the Conseil d'État by the Minister of the Interior and the request of the Tribunal had disappeared in a mysterious way. Thus the Conseil d'État said the final word without the European County ever having had a chance to give a ruling on the issue': P Pescatore, 'The Doctrine of Direct Effect: an Infant Disease?' at 169.

European Court by then in *Van Duyn*, the Conseil d'État was acting in deliberate contravention of the former court, challenging its authority and the scheme of Community law generally. Such action perhaps explains the reluctance of the ECJ to take the direct effect of directives any further.

The Conseil d'État's action also rendered whole tranches of Community law inapplicable in French administrative courts, if not the ordinary civil courts. In the aftermath of *Cohn-Bendit*, the European Parliament recommended, and the European Commission considered, an action against France under Article 226 for failure of a member state to meet its treaty obligations. However, this never occurred and only in 1989 did the Conseil d'État move away from this position in the *Nicolo* case.[99]

In fact, it was in France that the integration of EC law experienced some of the greatest difficulties. In a sense this is puzzling. After all, the original integrationist impulse in Europe owes much to French initiatives and, as French law takes a monist approach to international law, the reception of EC law into national law should have been comparatively straightforward. However, it would seem that two factors in particular contributed to the problematic relationship between French law and national law. First, the traditionally Parliament-centred nature of French government, which stresses domestic legislation as representing the 'common will'. This has meant that the French courts have been unwilling to apply EC law when it conflicts with statute law. Second, as Plotner[100] suggests, the differing approaches of the Cour de Cassation and Conseil d'État may be explained by the different traditions and social contexts of these courts as well as by the different career paths of the judges. While the Cour de Cassation is the highest French civil court with, as its main task, the adjudication of individual law suits, the Conseil d'État most frequently deals with public authorities.[101] As such it has been more aware of provoking a strong governmental or parliamentary reaction by 'Euro friendly' decisions. In 1962 General de Gaulle had even considered terminating the Conseil d'État after its *Canal* decision.[102] So Conseil d'État judiciary were aware they must tread carefully. Its judges were also trained differently, and instilled with the notion of 'national interests' likely to be inimicable to European law, a feature absent from the preoccupations of the Cour de Cassation, which was more concerned in its judgments to facilitate commerce and protect individual rights: it had long seen itself as a bulwark against arbitrary state action. The Cour de Cassation was also well aware that if the French business community were unable to rely on directives they would

---

99 *Raoul Georges Nicolo* Conseil d'État [1990] 1 CMLR.

100 Plotner, 'Report on France', in A-M Slaughter, Sweet and J Weiler (eds), *The European Courts and National Courts* (Hart Publishing, 1998) 41 at 55 *et seq.*

101 For an account of the Conseil d'État, see M-C Kessler, *Le Conseil d'État* (Armand Colin, 1968); J-P Negrin, *Le Conseil d'État et la vie publique en France depuis 1958* (PUF, 1968); Lochak, 'Réflexion sur les fonctions sociales de la responsabilité administrative ' in J Chevallier, (ed.) *Le Droit Adminstratif en mutation* (PUF, 1993).

102 Conseil d'État, 19 October 1962, Rec Lebon 552. In this case the Conseil d'État invalidated an order given by General de Gaulle to establish a special military court to deal with crimes committed in Algeria. The Conseil d'État, being the oldest French court, is not mentioned in the Constitution and is thus more prone to dissolution.

suffer in comparison with other European competitors. French business might move its head offices elsewhere.

Another relevant and connected factor is that of judicial empowerment. The Conseil d'État was seen as being the most senior of France's supreme courts and its judiciary, selected from France's elite École National d'Administration, seemed to perceive themselves as such. The Cour de Cassation judiciary, on the other hand, had worked their way up through the French court system. If it felt itself as second to the Conseil d'État, then EC law appeared to offer a way to redress this.[103] As Alter suggests, 'different courts have different interests vis-à-vis EC law... national courts use EC law in bureaucratic struggles between levels of the judiciary and political bodies, and thereby inadvertently facilitate the process of legal integration.'[104]

By the later 1980s the Conseil d'État was standing alone in its resistance to EC law. In 1986, in *Solange II*,[105] the German *Bundesverfassungsgericht* held that it would no longer control the constitutionality of Community acts, so long as the level of protection of human rights at Community level was comparable to that under national law. Furthermore, the 1992 initiative and the Single European Act put European integration very clearly back on the agenda. The internal market would not function efficiently if EC law were not fully integrated into French law and if the 300 directives of the White Paper were not enforceable in the French courts. Discrimination against French citizens, who could not rely on Community directives in the administrative courts, was highly undesirable. The national government began to put pressure on the Conseil d'État.[106] However, Plotner cites a final reason for the shift of approach in the attitude of the Conseil towards directives. This was the appointment of Conseiller Galmot to the ECJ in 1982. Until then, Conseillers had been appointed as advocates general in Luxembourg, but in 1982, the French government made a shift, partly because it was troubled by the number of instances in which the Court had failed to follow the advocate general's opinion. By appointing a Conseiller as judge they were hoping to influence the Court more directly. However, when Yves Galmot left Luxembourg in 1988 he said, 'I can assure you that after six years in Luxembourg, I, as a Conseiller d'État, will never again see the French Public law as before.'[107] One year after his return, the Conseil gave its *Nicolo* decision. According to this decision, Article 55 of the French Constitution enabled treaties to prevail over national law. However, as the Commissaire du Gouvernement pointed out in *Nicolo*, 'It cannot be repeated often enough that the

---

[103] Furthermore, as noted by Plotner, Touffait, the public prosecutor, was a fervent Europeanist, a friend of Teitgen, who made use of the ECJ's teleological interpretative techniques. In 1976 he went to Luxembourg as a judge but his Euro friendly approach undoubtedly influenced the Court. Plotner, op. cit. at 60.

[104] K Alter, 'Explaining national court acceptance of the ECJ', in Slaughter etc. op. cit. at 24.

[105] BVerfG 22/10/86.

[106] In 1988 the Prime Minister asked the Conseil to undertake 'a synthetic reflection on the possibilities of increasing the effort of adaptation of the French domestic law to the Community exigencies. 'Letter from the Prime Minister 21 November 1988' quoted by Plotner op. cit. at p 66.

[107] European Court of Justice, 'Aperçu des travaux de la Cour de Justice et du Tribunal de premier instance des Communautés Européennes en 1988 et 1989' (Luxembourg, Office des Publications Officielles 1990) p 191, cited in Plotner op. cit. at p 69.

era of the...supremacy of internal law is now over. International rules of law, particularly those of Europe, have gradually conquered our legal universe...'[108] In 1992, in *Rothmans and Philip Morris*[109] the Conseil d'État went further. These tobacco companies had submitted that the French law under which the government had a monopoly to fix retail prices for tobacco products was contrary to an EC directive of 1972. The Conseil d'État agreed, and, assimilating directives to international conventions, held that they could take priority over national law. The Conseil also awarded damages, thus falling in line with the ECJ's *Francovich* jurisprudence. Thus the era of the Conseil d'État's isolation seemed to be over.

Germany

In Germany, the *Bundesverfassungsgericht* is the most senior court and its interpretations bind other courts, even other supreme courts. It has not always accepted the supremacy of Community law willingly, as has been discussed in Chapter 7, although it has been little troubled by direct effect.

However, some other German courts have, at one time or another, struck out on a limb with regard to direct effect. In a 1981 decision the Federal Tax Court rejected the position of the ECJ on the direct effect of directives,[110] explicitly supporting the position of the Conseil d'État[111] on this matter. The German Court was responding to previous jurisprudence of the ECJ on turnover tax which had led to severe political difficulties in Germany, with 300,000 claims for tax refunds. In 1985 in the *Kloppenburg*[112] case, the Federal Tax Court again rejected the direct effect of directives. In these cases one sees the Federal Tax Court struggling to maintain its own legal authority: Judge Voss, at one time a judge of this court, argued that given the development of EC tax law, 'the Chamber of the Bundesfinanzhof, that is the judges who are in charge of VAT jurisdiction, would hardly be needed any more'.[113] In *Kloppenburg*, without making a reference to the ECJ, the Federal Tax Court held that directives could never have direct effect, as according to Article 249, national legislation is needed to give them the force of law in the member states. It also cited the *travaux préparatoires* of the EC Treaty in which the German government had stated that directives could not impose an obligation on an individual without national legislation. The Federal Tax Court also held that the power to legislate in the field of turnover taxes had not been transferred to the EC under Article 24(1) of

[108] Frydman, *Raoul Georges Nicolo*, 1990 CMLRev, vol 1 73–191. As Karen Alter points out, the role of Commissaire du Gouvernement is not a government advocate but a member of the Conseil d'Etat who assists the Conseil by giving opinions (it was this office which was in part the inspiration for the role of Advocate General in Luxembourg). K Alter, 'The European court's political power' (1996) 19 West European politics, 458–487.

[109] *Rothmans & Philip Morris* [1993] 1 CMLR 253.

[110] BFH, *Decision of 16 July 1981*, 16 EuR 442.

[111] Ibid. at 443.

[112] Bundesfinanzhof, *decision of 25 April 1985* (VR 123/84) Entscheidungen des Bundesfinanzhofes 143 383.

[113] R Voss, 'Federal Republic of Germany: National Report' in Schermers, Timmermans, Kellermann and Stewart (eds) *Article 177 Experience and Problems* (Amsterdam, 1987) 239–252.

the German *Grundgesetz* (Basic Law) apparently interpreting Article 24(1) of the *Grundgesetz* to allow a transfer of power to an international organisation only in so far as the future development of that institution was foreseeable, a type of reasoning which foresaw that of the Constitutional Court's *Maastricht* decision, as well as displaying some unease about the development of Community law. Both of the Federal Tax Court decisions were subjected to severe criticism[114] on the basis that they clearly disregarded the exclusive competence of the European Court under Article 234.[115] The Federal Tax Court's act of disobedience was brought to an end when in 1987 the *Bundesverfassungsgericht* ruled[116] that the Federal Tax Court's failure to make a preliminary reference violated the right to a lawful judge (*gesetzliche Richter*)[117] under Article 101(1) of the German *Grundgesetz*. The Tax Court's decision was therefore annulled.

These problems perhaps go some of the way to explaining why the ECJ did not develop a doctrine of horizontal direct effect of directives in *Marshall* or in *Dori*, when the opportunity arose again. It did not wish to see its authority flouted by further acts of insurrection in the national courts. Although, for some national courts, accepting direct effect and supremacy proved enormously empowering, enabling them to develop judicial review of national legislation where previously none had existed, elsewhere, as in the case of the Conseil d'État, or German Tax Court, EC law seemed to threaten and disrupt the very existence of national law, particularly those disciplines such as administrative, tax or family law which are very much the preserve of national policies and values.

INDIRECT EFFECT

There was dissatisfaction with the Court's rulings on lack of horizontal direct effect. Some of this emanated from the Court itself, for example Advocate General Jacobs in the *Vaneetveld*[118] case, who, after listing the reasons why it was difficult to restrict the justifications of direct effect to cases brought against the state, went on to suggest, 'In general however, it seems to me that directives, whose very object is that rights should be conferred on individuals, and that obligations should be

---

[114] E Millarg, 'case note to BFH decision of 16 July 1981' (1981) 16 EuR; S Magiera, 'Die Rechtswirkungen von EG-Richtlinien im Konflikt zwischen Bundesfinanzhof und Europaischem Gerichtshof' 38 DOV 940 (1985); C Tomuschat, 'Nein und abermals Nein' (1985) 20 EuR.

[115] A competence which the *Bundesverfassungsgericht* has also been willing to deny on occasions, wishing to preserve *Kompetenz-Kompetenz* to itself: see Chapter 7 on Supremacy.

[116] *Bundesverfassungsgericht*, decision of 8 April 1987 (2 BvR 687/85) [1988] 3 CMLR 1.

[117] This section of the German Constitution guarantees everyone the right to have their case heard in a lawfully constituted court having jurisdiction: a provision which would seem to have no exact equivalent in English Law. The *Bundesverfassungsgericht* had already held in *Solange II* (*Wünsche Handelsgesellschaft* [1987] 3 CMLR 225) that the ECJ is a 'lawful judge'.

[118] Case C-316/93 *Vaneetveld* [1994] ECR I-763. See also Advocate General Van Gerven in Case C-271/91 *Marshall II* and Advocate General Lenz in *Faccini Dori*, who similarly urged the horizontal direct effect of directives. See also T Tridimas, 'Horizontal Direct Effect of Directives: a Missed Opportunity?' (1994) ELR 621.

conferred on individuals, should be enforceable at the suit of the plaintiff unless the legitimate expectations of the defendant would thereby be defeated...'[119] But this did not change the Court's mind.

If the result of holding that directives could have no horizontal direct effect seemed unfair and uncertain, the ECJ at least did something to remedy this by introducing the concept of indirect effect. This requires national courts to interpret national law in the light of non-directly effective provisions of directives.[120] This doctrine was introduced in the *Von Colson* and *Harz* cases[121] (which predated *Marshall*) both of which concerned the Equal Treatment Directive. The applicants, both women, had applied for posts in the German prison service and had been rejected. The German Labour Court held that they had been discriminated against on grounds of sex, but under German law the only compensation they were entitled to was for their travel expenses. The ECJ referred to the member states' obligation under Article 10 of the EC Treaty to 'take all appropriate measures...to ensure fulfilment of their Community obligations'. The ECJ held that this obligation also bound the Courts of the member states and so the German courts had to interpret German law so as to ensure an effective remedy as required by Article 6 of the Equal Treatment Directive. As the ECJ stated, 'It is for the national courts to interpret and apply the legislation adopted for the implementation of the directive in conformity with the requirements of Community law, in so far as it is given discretion to do so under national law.'[122] This has become known as the principle of indirect effect, and is an early example of the Court relying on Article 10 to enforce Community law. Article 10 has been described by Ward as 'the sort of spiritual and essentially vacuous clause that is more commonly found in constitutional orders such as that of Nazi Germany or the Soviet Union'.[123] Notwithstanding its highly general character, it has been relied on more and more by the Court in the field of remedies,[124] and will be further discussed in the next chapter.

However, the scope of the *Von Colson* ruling was not clear. Would it also apply as between private parties, or in the case of national legislation not intended to implement a directive? These matters were raised in the *Marleasing*[125] case, the most radical of the Court's decisions on indirect effect. In this case, the plaintiff company was seeking a declaration that the articles of association of the defendant company were void as a sham transaction carried out to defraud their creditors. This was a valid base for nullity of a company under the Spanish Civil Code but the defendants argued that this matter was now dealt with under EC directive 68/151, which gave an exhaustive list of situations in which nullity might be invoked, which did not

---

[119] *Vaneetveld* at para 34.
[120] Although the principle is not restricted to directives: see Case C-322/88 *Grimaldi* [1989] ECR 4407 and Case C-165/91 *Van Munster* [1994] ECR I-4661.
[121] Case 14/83 *Von Colson v Land Nordrhein Westfalen* [1984] ECR 1891 and Case 79/83 *Harz* v *Deutsche Tradax* [1984] ECR 1921.
[122] *Von Colson* at para 28.
[123] I Ward, *A Critical Introduction to European Law* (Butterworths, 1996) at 65.
[124] It was also posited as a basis for direct effect of directives in Case 190/87 *Moorman*, see fn 44 above.
[125] Case C-106/88 *Marleasing SA* [1990] ECR I-4135.

include lack of cause. This directive had not been implemented in Spain. The Court first affirmed its *Marshall* ruling that directives cannot impose obligations on private parties. However, it then went on to reiterate its *Von Colson* holding that national courts must interpret national law in the light of the wording and purpose of the directive in order to achieve the result of the directive. Thus, the principle of interpretation could be applied as between private parties, with the perhaps unfortunate result in the instant case that it bolstered an apparently rather shoddy defence. This is a very extensive ruling: Hartley goes as far as to suggest that 'this however would no longer constitute interpretation – it would create horizontal direct effect under another name'.[126]

Are there any limits which may be placed on the national courts' duty of interpretation? *Kolpinghuis Nijmegen*[127] were the subject of criminal proceedings for breach of EC directive 80/777 on water purity which had not been implemented by the Dutch authorities. In this context, the ECJ stated that 'a directive cannot, of itself and independently of a national law adopted by a member state for its implementation, have the effect of determining or aggravating the liability in criminal law of persons who act in contravention of the provisions of that directive'.[128] Therefore it would seem that the *Von Colson* principle may not be used against the legitimate expectations of individuals.

Alec Stone Sweet interprets the jurisprudence of direct effect as an instance of 'a particular type of relation between the European and national courts: a working partnership in the construction of a constitutional "rule of law" community'. Thereby national judiciaries are empowered '(even without a referral) to interpret national rules so that these rules will conform to EC law, and to refuse to apply these rules when they do not'.[129] But this was a constitutional dialogue in which some courts would not always participate. The English courts have suffered some problems with this duty of 'harmonious interpretation'. Unlike some of their counterparts in the Conseil d'État, the English judiciary experienced no problems recognising the direct effect of directives, but their indirect effect was another matter. As many English judges simply viewed s 2(1) of the ECA as placing an interpretative duty on the courts with regard to directly effective Community law, this did not leave much room for an interpretation of EC law which is not directly effective. Such interpretations simply proved too much for the judiciary in some cases, especially as judges versed in the common law method tend to reason their decisions in judgments in which the relevant European materials are discussed at length, a feature which requires the interpretive obligation to be very transparent.[130] This problem was especially severe where the domestic courts were asked to interpret

---

[126] TC Hartley, *The Foundations of European Community Law* (Oxford: OUP, 1998) at 213.
[127] Case 80/86 [1987] ECR 3969.
[128] At para 14.
[129] Sweet, 'Constitutional Dialogues in the EC', in Slaughter *et al.* op. cit. at 308.
[130] As the House of Lords stated in *Duke v Reliance* [1988] AC 618, 'the European Court of Justice in the *Von Colson* case did not assert power to interfere with the method or result of the interpretation of national legislation by national courts' (at 639).

national legislation not passed to implement EC law. In *Duke* v *Reliance*[131] the House of Lords was asked to interpret s 6(4) of the Sex Discrimination Act to comply with the Equal Treatment Directive. Ms Duke had been forced to retire at 60 whereas her male colleagues were able to continue working until the age of 65. She could not rely on the directive directly as Reliance were a private company. The House of Lords held that the Sex Discrimination Act was passed before the directive and therefore could not have been intended to give effect to it, stating, 'It would be most unfair to the respondent to distort the construction of the 1975 Sex Discrimination Act in order to accommodate the Equal Treatment directive.'[132] However, following *Marleasing*, it would also seem that it is immaterial whether any national law at issue was intended to implement the directive.[133] However, the House of Lords took a similar position in *Finnegan* v *Clowney*.[134] This concerned the Sex Discrimination (Northern Ireland) Order 1976 which was passed after the Equal Treatment directive. It had not, however, been passed to implement the directive. Lord Bridge stated, 'to hold otherwise would be…effectively eliminating the distinction between Community law which is of direct effect between citizens of member states and Community law which only affects citizens of Member States when it is implemented by national legislation'.[135]

On the other hand, in *Pickstone* v *Freeman's* and *Litster* v *Forth Dry Dock*, the House of Lords showed itself more willing to engage in a purposive construction[136] and was able to achieve a result compatible with EC law in a case in which UK legislation was implementing the Equal Treatment Directive. However, in *Webb* v *Emo*[137] the House of Lords stated, 'As the European Court of Justice said, a national court must construe a domestic law to accord with the terms of a directive in the same field only if it is possible to do so.'[138] This would not be the case if the national court was forced to 'distort' the meaning of the domestic law.[139]

In any case, the wide reading of *Marleasing* was reduced by the ECJ itself in *Wagner Miret*.[140] There, the ECJ held that national courts must strive 'as far as possible' to interpret domestic law to achieve the result intended by the directive, but where this was not possible, an action against the State in damages might lie instead. However, on the more specific issue of the imposition of obligations on individuals, the most recent case law of the ECJ is uncertain. In *Arcaro*,[141] a case in which the

---

[131] [1988] AC 618.

[132] *Duke* at p 639. Such an interpretation also compromises the spirit of legitimate expectations.

[133] *Marleasing*, however, did not result in the imposition of an obligation on a private party.

[134] [1990] 2 AC 407.

[135] Ibid. p 416. See E Szyszczak, 'Sovereignty: Crisis, Compliance, Confusion, Complacency?' (1990) EL Rev 480, for a critical view of these cases.

[136] *Pickstone* v *Freeman's* [1989] AC 66; *Litster* v *Forth Dry Dock* [1988] ECR 3057.

[137] [1993] 1 WLR 49 HL.

[138] Ibid., at 60.

[139] However, following a preliminary reference to Luxembourg, the House of Lords found that it was able to interpret the Sex Discrimination Act in accordance with the ECJ's ruling in the Equal Treatment directive.

[140] Case C-334/92 *Wagner Miret* [1993] ECR I-6911.

[141] Case C-168/95 *Criminal Proceedings against Luciano Arcaro* [1996] ECR I-4705.

defendant faced criminal proceedings for discharging dangerous substances, the ECJ stated,

> However, the obligation of the national court to refer to the content of the directive when interpreting the relevant rules of its own national law reaches a limit where such an interpretation leads to the imposition on an individual of an obligation laid down by a directive which has not been transposed, or more especially, where it has the effect of determining or aggravating, on the basis of the directive...the liability in criminal law of persons.

Following *Arcaro*, it might seem that EC law imposes no requirement to interpret national law in such a way as to impose on an individual an obligation laid down in a directive which has not been transposed.

TOWARDS A HORIZONTAL DIRECT EFFECT OF DIRECTIVES

If one turns to other recent case law the strength of the *Marshall I* prohibition does not seem so clear, with the Court at least seeming to uphold an 'incidental' horizontal direct effect, which has the capacity for an impact on individuals. In *CIA Security International*,[142] the ECJ held that CIA could rely on a directive in a libel action brought against a party relying on national law incompatible with the directive. CIA, a Belgian manufacturer of alarm systems, was suing two of its competitors in the security field for unfair trading practices on the basis that they had libelled CIA's product. Their advertising had highlighted the fact that CIA's alarm did not comply with Belgian law. However, the domestic regulations which it was said to breach should have been notified to the Commission under EEC directive 83/189. The ECJ held that failure to notify rendered the national law inoperative. As a result CIA's competitors were unable to raise the defence in the libel action that their advertising had been based on fact. This case has been interpreted as giving horizontal direct effect to directives. The result was certainly detrimental to the other companies involved; although it did not actually impose an obligation on the defendants, it did require them to change their trading practices. On the other hand, the EEC directive at issue did not actually impose any obligation on private individuals, so perhaps it is best seen as an example of incidental direct effect. However, Lord Hoffmann, in the House of Lords in *Seymour-Smith*,[143] certainly thought *CIA Security* distinct, on the basis that it was a case 'in which, unusually, the issue in litigation between private parties was whether, as a matter of public law, the manufacturer was doing something unlawful'.[144] The ECJ gave no indication in *CIA Security* that it intended to depart from previous jurisprudence and Advocate General Elmer also indicated that he saw no incompatibility. The ECJ continued

---

[142] Case C-194/94 *CIA Security International* [1996] ECR I-2201.
[143] *R v Secretary of State for Employment, ex parte Seymour-Smith and Perez* (1997) 2 All ER 273.
[144] *Ex parte Seymour-Smith*, per Lord Hoffmann at 277. Such a distinction has been explored elsewhere: see e.g. S Weatherill, 'Breach of Directives and Breach of Contract' (2001) ELRev 177.

with the approach of *CIA Security* in two subsequent cases: *Ruiz Bernaldez* and *Panagis Parfitis*.[145]

However, in *Lemmens*,[146] decided in June 1998, it seemed to limit the scope of *CIA*. Lemmens was trying to challenge a conviction for drunk driving. The breathalyser used to obtain evidence for his conviction was approved by the government but the national regulations specifying the use of this equipment had not been authorised by the Commission, as required by an EC directive. Lemmens tried to rely on *CIA Security*, which seemed at least superficially similar, but the ECJ, while agreeing that the national procedures should have been notified, held that this 'did not have the effect of making it impossible for evidence obtained by means of such apparatus…to be relied upon against an individual'.[147] Member states had argued in *Lemmens* that the relevant directive was designed to promote trade and should not be applied in cases where the free movement of goods was not at issue, an approach which had motivated the ECJ itself in *CIA Security*, where the internal market was at issue.

More recent case law seems only to have confused matters further. In *Unilever Italia*[148] the Court seemed to be extending yet further the circumstances in which unimplemented directives might be applied to cases involving private parties. The *Unilever* case concerned the same directive as that at issue in *CIA* – directive 83/189 (now replaced by directive 93/94) – which requires member states to notify draft technical regulations to the Commission and not to apply them until the Commission has approved them. Unilever had supplied olive oil to Central Foods, which rejected it on the grounds that it was not labelled in accordance with an Italian law notified to, but not yet approved by, the Commission. Unilever argued that Italian law should not be applied and sued Central Foods for the price of the oil. On a reference to the ECJ, that court held that Italian law should not be applied,

---

[145] The ruling in Case C-129/94 *Rafael Ruiz Bernaldez* [1996] ECR I-1829 had the incidental effect of placing an obligation on a third party, in this case an insurance company, to compensate the victim of the defendant drunk driver. No such obligation existed under national law, but an EC directive required such compensation. Finally, in Case C-441/93 *Panagis Pafitis* [1996] ECR I-1347 the enforcement of a directive against a provision of national law affected the position of a bank and its shareholders, who were relying on domestic law. The outcomes of these cases seem to suggest a measure of 'passive' horizontal direct effect which does not amount to a positive obligation, a concept which was suggested by J Stuyck and P Wytinck in a comment on the *Marleasing* case in (1991) 28 CMLRev 205. See also J Coppel, 'Horizontal Direct Effect of Directives' (1997) 28 ILJ 69, and P Slot, 33 CMLRev (1996) 1035. These cases seem to blunt the rule against horizontal direct effect in *Marshall* and *Dori*.

[146] Case C-226/97 *Johannes Martinus Lemmens* [1998] ECR I 3711.

[147] Ibid.

[148] Case C-443/98 *Unilever Italia SpA v Central Foods SpA* [2000] ECR I-7535; see also for similar types of case: Case C-13/96 *Bic Benelux v Belgian State* [1997] ECR I 1753; Case C-180/95 *Draempaehl* [1997] ECR I-2195. For a commentary on this series of cases see Lackhoff and Nyssens, 'Direct Effect of Directives in Triangular Situations' (1998) 23 ELRev 397; Hilson and Downes, 'Making Sense of Rights' (1999) 24 ELRev 121; Lenz, Tynes and Young, 'Horizontal What? Back to Basics' (2000) 25 ELRev 509; Dougan, 'Disguised Vertical Effect' (2000) 59 CLJ 586; S Weatherill, 'Breach of Directives and Breach of Contract' 26 (2001) ELRev 177. For a more general commentary on the many facets of direct effect, and its relationship to rights, see Edward, 'Direct Effect, the Separation of Powers and the Judicial Enforcement of Obligations' *Scritti in Onore di Giuseppe Federico Mancini* (Giuffre, 1998); Ruffert, 'Rights and Remedies in European Community Law: A Comprehensive View' (1997) 34 CMLRev 307; Van Gerven, 'Of Rights, Remedies and Procedures' (2000) 37 CMLRev 501.

as to do so might hinder trade in products not complying with it. The ECJ seemed to view this case as in line with its earlier ruling in *CIA*. The result, however, was that Central Foods was forced to pay, and an unimplemented directive had a very powerful impact on a private party. The ECJ stipulated that its holding in *Unilever* was not incompatible with its denial of horizontal direct effect. However, it is becoming more and more difficult to find a coherent distinction[149] between the denial of horizontal effect and the allowing of incidental effect, much less a justification for it. In this context, Weatherill has commented that it is 'troubling that the ECJ finds itself justified in loading immense constitutional significance on to such a narrow distinction'.[150] It surely remains difficult to predict when national regulations will be inapplicable and thus the scope of 'incidental horizontal direct effect' remains more uncertain than ever.

Thus, over fifteen years since *Von Colson*, the doctrine of indirect, or even incidental, effect causes more problems of legal certainty than ever. If an applicant wishes to enforce an unimplemented directive against a private party it is difficult to predict whether domestic courts will uphold domestic law or EC law: this may well depend on whether the courts feel able to reconcile national law with differently, or flexibly, worded Community law. Part of the problem is that the concept of direct effect has undergone a gradual development which has resulted in a broadening of its scope. Initially, following *Van Gend*, direct effect was often seen as the creation of rights which the courts must protect, but later it came to be associated with the broader concept of 'invocability', which allows for a greater diversity of the effects which direct effect may produce.[151] Indeed, Prechal goes as far as to suggest that 'at a certain moment, when Community law comes of age, direct effect can do more harm than good'.[152]

Things would be much simpler if directives had horizontal direct effect. As Advocate General Lenz pointed out in *Dori*, it is unsatisfactory that 'individuals should be subject to different rules depending on whether they have comparable legal relations with a body connected with the State or with a private individual'.[153] Furthermore, an action against the State in damages is clearly a poor alternative. It requires the plaintiff to bring two sets of proceedings either simultaneously or successively, quite possibly in different courts with different procedural rules. As Advocate General Jacobs noted in *Vaneetveld*, this can 'hardly be compatible with the requirement of an effective legal remedy'.

---

[149] Such attempts have of course been made – one is based on finding such cases as CIA to be of a quasi-administrative nature – see e.g. Lord Hoffman in *Seymour-Smith*; another seeks to draw a distinction between using Community law as a shield (in which case it is possible for there to be some incidental effect) and as a sword (in which case it is not); another such attempted distinction has been the use of Hohfeldian juridical correlatives, whereby it has been suggested that the success of an action depends not only on the type of EC right at issue, but also on its juridical correlative: see Hilson and Downes fn 148 op. cit. for this type of analysis. However, none of these attempted elucidations is functionally perfect, as there is always case law which simply does not fit.

[150] Weatherill fn 148 op. cit. at 183.

[151] S Prechal, 'Does Direct Effect Still Matter?' (2000) 37 CMLRev 1047.

[152] Ibid. at 1068.

[153] Advocate General Lenz at para 5 *Dori* opinion.

CONCLUSIONS

Within the field of direct effect, several interlocking themes emerge. First, the need to protect rights, cited by the Court as a prime motivation in *Van Gend*. The Court's reading of the treaty in this way undoubtedly had a huge impact. Treaty provisions which originally appeared no more than building blocks in a free trade community became, in the language of the Court, fundamental freedoms and have been litigated to great effect. Without direct effect, neither *Cassis* nor *Dassonville* would have been decided and the Court's impact on an economic constitution would have been much diminished. The combination of direct effect and Article 234 enabled individuals and companies to make significant use of EC law for their own purposes to combat protectionist trade practices or unequal pay. This would not have been possible if state breaches of EC law were litigated only by the Commission or member states under Article 226 which does not accommodate private parties. Thus, protection of EC rights has seemingly worked in tandem with the acceptance and cooperation of national courts, which is the second leitmotif of this area.

A broad consensus on European integration seems to have prompted national courts to cooperate with the ECJ and enforce directly effective European law within their own jurisdiction, even if the ECJ's methodology and purposive interpretation did not command their full support. For some national courts, the inception of EC law was empowering, lending them greater influence than they might have expected to wield. For other courts, relations with the ECJ were uneasy, as the direct effect doctrine appeared to carry with it implications for national constitutional law. As the pressure has built on national courts to provide 'effective' remedies for breaches of EC law, the relationship has perhaps further strained and this will be considered in the next chapter.

However, mention of 'effective' protection introduces a third theme: to what extent has the direct effect jurisdiction been motivated by individuals' rights and to what extent has its impetus been that of enforcement – to render EC law effective? Sometimes the Court itself does not seem sure, particularly in more recent case law, where, prompted by Article 10, the Court has used these concepts interchangeably. The distinction between these two concepts may not usually make a large difference to the outcome of the case, but the difference in language signals a shift from an ethical approach, which takes Community citizens, and their rights,[154] seriously, to one in which law enforcement is the imperative.

The final theme is the 'constitutionalising' of the treaty. This theme is not new. Back in 1962, Advocate General Lagrange recognised the constitutionalising features of the Treaty of Rome. Direct effect clearly does have federalising, constitutionalising implications. It transforms EC law from the international mode into something more akin to federal law. The rhetoric of 'rights', whether in this context, or that of fundamental rights, also affirms the constitutional mode. At one and the

---

[154] Although, as footnoted earlier, most EC litigants are not individual citizens, but corporate litigants: see Harding, 'Who goes to Court in Europe? An Analysis of litigation against the European Community' (1992) ELRev 105.

same time, citizens are given a role in the new legal order and the treaty becomes more than just a treaty.

However, this constitutionalising, when so heavily a creation of the Court, does not come without a loss. Without the jurisprudence of the ECJ, the Treaty of Rome would not be transforming into a constitution. But, having been so, there has been a 'juridification' of the policy process. As such, developments tend to have been incremental, *ad hoc* and pragmatic, such as in the advances and retreats in the saga of indirect effect. Until, and indeed if, the political institutions of the EC attain more legitimacy and effective support, this 'juridification' looks set to continue for some years.

9

REMEDIES IN THE NATIONAL COURTS: THE EFFECTIVENESS OF EC LAW ON TRIAL

The field of remedies may seem peripheral to the huge terrain of EC law, the end product of a binary and exclusive division between substance and procedure. A superficial impression is that, while the EC has created much new substantive law (i.e. competition rules, environment, discrimination law and so on) it has not been active in creating new procedural law, which has been left up to the national legal orders. As ever, superficial impressions are misleading. Although initially ignored, the field of remedies in the national courts has become crucial: a battleground for the protection of rights, the effectiveness of EC law and the search for justice.

The story of the development of remedies for breach of EC law in the national courts is (unsurprisingly) one of a sometimes uncomfortable interaction of different legal cultures. Because Community law does not lay down rules of procedure to govern its enforcement in the national courts, the role played by those courts in enforcing it is crucial. Their cooperation is required by Article 10 (formerly 5) of the EC treaty,[1] which imposes an obligation of solidarity on national authorities in respect of Community law. This has meant that national courts must conduct themselves as Community courts.[2] Advocate General Tesauro suggested that 'Community law should now be seen as a routine component of the rules rather than an exotic excrescence upon the national legal order.'[3] But this conjunction is not always harmonious. National judiciaries, often virtually unskilled in EC law (in the earlier days of the EC at least) have had to give direct effect to Community law, to interpret national law in conformity with it, and to provide remedies in the national courts to ensure that it is effective. And the burden on the national courts

---

[1] As established in Case 14/83 *Von Colson* [1984] ECR 1891.
[2] I Maher, 'National Courts as Community Courts' (1994) 14 Legal Studies 226.
[3] G Tesauro, 'The Effectiveness of Judicial Protection and Co-operation between the Court of Justice and the National Courts', *Festkrift til Ole Due: Liberum Amicorum* (1994) 355, 373.

to do this has increased as individuals and companies have become more aware of the uses of Community law, especially after the well publicised 1992 programme.

Indeed, the subject of remedies is vital, for effective judicial process goes to the heart of EC law, issuing economic and constitutional imperatives: 'Economic, in that market integration presumes the uniform application of Community law across the Internal Market. Constitutional in that citizens are entitled to expect that Community rights are fully respected within national legal systems.'[4]

Although, in principle, matters of procedure are for the national courts, the ECJ has laid down two essential requirements: Community law must not be treated less favourably than comparable national claims[5], and there must be an effective remedy for the enforcement of Community law; this latter requires that the national rules must not be framed in such a way as to render virtually impossible or very difficult the exercise of the rights conferred by EC law. These principles were established long ago in the cases of *Comet* and *Rewe*[6] and confirmed in a series of subsequent cases. Thus, as long as adequate remedies were available in the national courts the ECJ was happy to respect national procedural autonomy in this matter. In *Comet*, the ECJ held:

> In the application of the principle of co-operation laid down in Article 5 [10] of the Treaty, the national courts are entrusted with ensuring the legal protection conferred on individuals by the direct effect of the provisions of Community law…It is for the national legal order of each Member State to designate the competent courts and to lay down the procedural rules for proceedings designed to ensure the protection of the rights which individuals acquire through the direct effect of Community law.[7]

However, national procedural autonomy, while it may leave the provision of remedies to those who know their legal system best, has the effect of damaging the uniformity of Community law. Very different remedies may be available in the courts of different member states, thus prejudicing individual rights, legal certainty and justice, as well as the authority of Community law.[8] On the other hand, the harmonisation of legal remedies seems an unimaginably large project, 'perfectly in line with building pyramids and cathedrals'.[9] Procedural law – issues such as burden of proof, standing rules, the rules of evidence or limitation periods – as much as any other branch of the law, is reflective of and emanates from a particular legal culture

---

[4] E Szyszczak, 'Making Europe more Relevant to its Citizens: Effective Judicial Process' (1996) 21 ELRev at 352.

[5] This point raises the difficult but relatively unexplained issue of what constitutes a similar action of a domestic nature. See J Steiner, 'How to make the action suit the case' (1986) EL Rev 102, and the opinion of AG Jacobs in case C-312/93 *Peterbroeck* [1995] ECR I 4599 paras 20–27 for a discussion of this issue.

[6] Case 45/76 *Comet* [1976] ECR 2043 and Case 33/76 *Rewe* [1976] ECR 1989.

[7] *Comet* at 2043.

[8] So, for example, recovery of social welfare benefits owed under a breach of EC discrimination law may be possible in one jurisdiction but not in another, owing to differing limitation periods. Limitation periods vary greatly from state to state. In Belgium, the limitation period for an action in damages is 30 years but in most other member states it is much shorter. However, the Courts' own case law on such things as time limits sometimes appears contradictory: compare the cases of *Emmot* and *Steenhorst Neerings* discussed below.

[9] Per P Lindblom, 'Harmony of the Legal Spheres' (1997) European Review of Private Law, 11. Nonetheless, such a project has been contemplated: see the discussion at the end of this chapter.

and society. It is closely connected with constitutional and administrative law and legal philosophy. The infiltration of a uniform European standard may play havoc with a delicate balance, such as that set between legal certainty and fairness in the case of time limits. Procedural law is also, as Kahn-Freund comments, '...tough law. All that concerns the technique of legal practice is likely to resist change.'[10]

INROADS INTO NATIONAL PROCEDURAL AUTONOMY

In a series of cases, however, the ECJ gave a clear message as to the importance of ensuring the effectiveness of Community law in the face of restrictive rules of national law. In *Simmenthal*,[11] the ECJ stated that if the Italian Constitutional Court had the sole jurisdiction, as it asserted, to set aside national law in conflict with Community law, this would impede the application of Community law and protection of Community law rights in the Italian courts. Referring such cases to the Italian Constitutional Court would involve lengthy, costly, complex proceedings which would deter individuals from seeking to enforce their rights under Community law.[12] National procedural autonomy must give way and the ordinary courts must, therefore, set aside incompatible national law. Thus, in *Simmenthal*, the supremacy and the effectiveness of Community law intersect, requiring immediate enforceability in the national courts. Little, however, is said of individual rights, the *raison d'être* of *Van Gend*, the emphasis being as much on effective judicial protection, which comes to be used more or less interchangeably with individual rights in subsequent case law.

Van Gerven notes a transition in the Court's terminology from the subjective rights of *Van Gend*, through rights *simpliciter* to a stress on remedies after the accession of the new common law legal systems in 1973.[13] Did this new membership have such an impact on the Court's approach?[14] While it may be interesting to recall Dicey's[15] tirade against continental declarations of rights as valueless in comparison with the Anglo-Saxon stress on remedies derived from decided cases, it is hardly clear that the ECJ had in mind an inductive, Anglo-Saxon legal methodology. The main motivation seems to have been bringing member states to book: 'effective judicial protection is...used more to exact obedience from Member States than to protect citizens'.[16] In *Von Colson* the ECJ seemed to combine both rationales by

---

[10] O Kahn-Freund, 'On Uses and Misuse of Comparative Law' (1974) MLR 1 at 20.

[11] Case 106/77 *Amministrazione delle Finanze dello Stato v Simmenthal* [1978] ECR 629.

[12] As suggested in *Simmenthal* by AG Reischl at p 653.

[13] W van Gerven, 'Bridging the Gap between Community and National Laws: Towards a Principle of Homogeneity in the Field of Remedies' (1995) CMLRev, 679–80.

[14] This is the view taken by Ruffert, 'Rights and Remedies in Community Law' (1997) CMLRev 307, who suggests that EC law has followed the common law's focus on remedies rather than those legal systems, such as German law which focuses on rights.

[15] AV Dicey, *Introduction to the Law of the Constitution* (1885).

[16] R Caranta, 'Judicial Protection Against Member States: a new *jus commune* takes place' (1995) 32 CMLRev, 713 at 710.

stating that the remedy must be such as to guarantee real and effective judicial protection and must have a real deterrent effect.

In *UNECTEF v Heylens*,[17] a case in which a Belgian football trainer's Belgian diploma was not recognised in France, the ECJ found a fundamental rights origin to effective protection. Article 6 of the European Convention on Human Rights (ECHR) has had a huge impact on the procedural law of member states. The ECJ drew upon the right to an effective judicial remedy under Articles 6 and 13 of the ECHR, which it held to encompass both the right to a judicial hearing and the requirement to give reasons. Thus a decision rejecting a claim under Community law must enable a person 'to defend that right under the best possible conditions'.[18]

In *Factortame*,[19] the ECJ also sought to remedy the perceived inadequacy of protection of Community rights in the national courts. The applicants had challenged, by way of judicial review, the compatibility of the UK Merchant Shipping Act with Community law. The ECJ stressed the importance of the effectiveness of Community law, holding that:

> the full effectiveness of Community law would be just as much impaired if a rule of national law could prevent a court seized of a dispute governed by Community law from granting interim relief in order to ensure the full effectiveness of the judgement to be given on the existence of the rights claimed under Community law. It follows that a court which in those circumstances would grant interim relief, if it were not for a rule of national law, is obliged to set aside that rule.[20]

Such a strong emphasis on the principle of effectiveness might seem like an abandonment of the principle of national procedural autonomy and the dictation by the ECJ of a new Community remedy. But Advocate General Francis Jacobs suggests that *Factortame* '...was not in legal terms revolutionary...Judicial protection of Community rights would clearly have been inadequate, indeed illusory if, pending the delivery of its final judgement following a ruling by the Court of Justice, the Divisional Court had been unable to grant interim relief to prevent the party seeking such relief from incurring irremediable damage.'[21] In a parallel ruling in *Zuckerfabrik*[22] the ECJ held that domestic courts might temporarily suspend national measures based on allegedly invalid *Community* acts in cases of urgency to prevent an applicant suffering serious and irreparable harm, pending a reference to the ECJ.

In fact, it would seem that it is in this area, in the need for national courts to provide effective remedies for breaches of EC law rights, rather than in any loss of

---

[17] Case 222/86 [1987] ECR 4097.
[18] Ibid. at para 15.
[19] Case 213/89 *The Queen v Secretary of State for Transport, ex parte Factortame* [1990] ECR I-2433.
[20] Ibid. at para 210.
[21] F Jacobs, 'Enforcing Community Rights and Obligations in the National Courts', in Biondi and Lonbay (eds) *Remedies for Breach of EC Law* (Wiley, 1996).
[22] Case C-143/88 and C-92/89 *Zuckerfabrik Suderdithmarschen* [1990] ECR I-415. See also Case C-465/93 *Atlanta Fruchthandelsgesellschaft gmbH* [1995] ECR I-3761.

Parliamentary sovereignty, that the true importance of *Factortame* is to be found.[23] The ECJ relied in part on Article 10 EC to support its conclusions. One may note how, as the ECJ became more activist in developing the field of remedies, Article 10 took on greater prominence in its reasoning.[24] As Article 10 seems to have been drafted as a declaration of political intent rather than to create any binding obligations, this was a conscious manipulation of a vague and bland treaty article indicating the attention that the ECJ now gives to the national judicial function, a function which is constitutional in nature because it flows from the basic treaty principle in Article 10.[25] In this way, national administrative procedures and the law of remedies become constitutionalised by EC law. So Caranta, for example, prefers to describe the ECJ's efforts in this area as the evolution of a constitutional *jus commune*.[26]

AG Jacobs has also referred to a 'constructive dialogue'[27] between the ECJ and national courts. However, the relationship between Luxembourg and the national courts has not always been 'constructive'. Some courts have been very unwilling to turn to the ECJ for help in resolving constitutional difficulties. Sometimes it has been the ECJ's dictation of a new judicial remedy which has been responsible for the constitutional difficulty, as in the Conseil d'État's refusal to recognise the direct effect of directives. In any case, the obligation under Article 10 surely works both ways, requiring the ECJ to cooperate and to engage in dialogue with the national courts.[28] This requires a sensitive approach to the constraints of national procedural law. In this way, national judges are more likely to 'internalise' the elements of EC law and less likely to see it as something imposed upon them from above, by a twentieth Century supranational mutation of the sovereign of legal positivists such as Bentham or Austin.

The ECJ continued its interventionist approach in *Dekker* and *Cotter and McDermott*.[29] In *Dekker*, the applicant had been refused a job on the ground that she was pregnant. The ECJ held that Dutch law could not require Dekker to prove fault on her employer's part before her claim could succeed, holding, 'It must be observed that, if the employer's liability for infringement of the principles of equal

---

[23] See Ross, 'Refining Effective Enjoyment' (1990) 15 EL Rev 476 at 478; Douglas-Scott, 'The Factortame case: Fishing in Troubled Waters' (1991) King's College Law Journal 14; Curtin, 'Directives: the Effectiveness of Judicial Protection of Individual Rights' (1990) 27 CMLRev 709.

[24] See Jacobs and Klarst, 'The Federal Legal Order: the USA and Europe compared – a Judicial perspective' in M Cappelletti *et al.* (eds), *Integration through Law* (Berlin: de Gruyter, 1985).

[25] J Temple Lang, 'Community Constitutional Law: Article 5 EEC Treaty' (1990) 27 CMLRev 645; Temple Lang, 'The Duties of National Courts under Community Constitutional Law' (1997) 22 ELRev 3; J Temple Lang, 'The duties of cooperation of national authorities and courts under Article 10 EC: two more reflections' (2001) 26 ELRev 84.

[26] R Caranta, 'Judicial Protection against member states: a new Jus Commune takes shape' (1995) 32 CMLRev 703.

[27] F Jacobs, in Lonbay and Biondi op. cit. at 33–4.

[28] See e.g. C Harlow, 'Francovich and the problem of the disobedient state' (1996) 2 ELJ 199. This point is also made by AG van Gerven, who writes of the 'continuous interplay' between the courts in (1995) CMLRev 679.

[29] Case C-177/88 *Dekker* [1990] I ECR 3941; Case C-377/89 *Cotter and McDermott* [1991] ECR I-1155.

treatment were made subject to proof of a fault attributable to him...the practical effect of those principles would be weakened considerably.'[30]

In *Dekker*, the national rule did not discriminate, nor did it make it impossible to exercise the Community law right. It simply made it more difficult. This was enough to set it aside. In *Cotter and McDermott* the ECJ gave an even stronger ruling. The applicants relied on directive 79/7 to claim the same entitlement to social welfare benefits as similarly situated men. The Irish Supreme Court had rejected their claim on the basis that it would offend the principle of unjust enrichment as they might receive allowances for dependants for which their husbands had already claimed. The ECJ held that 'married women are entitled to those increases even if in some circumstances that will result in double payment of the increases'.[31]

In *Rewe* and *Comet*, in which the ECJ first established the principles of effectiveness and non-discrimination, the ECJ accepted the right of the member states to impose reasonable time limits in the interests of legal certainty.[32] However, in subsequent cases, the ECJ's attitude began to change and it became more willing to dictate to national courts how they should deal with matters. If national procedural law appeared to conflict with the principle of effectiveness then national law would have to give way. In *Emmot*[33] the applicant had been denied the claim to four years worth of equal benefits under the Equal Treatment Directive because she failed to make her claim within a three-month period from the date on which the grounds arose as specified by Irish law.[34] The ECJ held that because the directive had not been properly transposed into Irish law the time limit did not apply. The justification here seems to be the estoppel reasoning again: until individuals have clear knowledge of their right to bring an action, the state should not be able to rely on national time limits to bar it. Mrs Emmott's claim was surely meritorious, but not all applicants could plead injustice in such a situation. Many litigants are commercial operations with a wealth of legal advice; in such situations they are well-placed to know of the existence of EC directives.[35]

A similarly wide ruling was that of *Marshall II*,[36] in which the ECJ stated that EC law requires that women who had been forced to retire earlier than men in contravention of Article 141 EC should receive 'full and adequate compensation' irrespective of any national procedures setting a ceiling on the compensation

---

[30] *Dekker* at para 24.
[31] *Cotter and McDermott* at para 22.
[32] *Rewe* para 5, *Comet* para 17. This had the result that huge discrepancies in national time limits were permitted to stand.
[33] Case C-208/90 *Emmot* [1991] ECR I-4269.
[34] This delay was partly prompted by the fact that she had been told by the Irish Department of Social Welfare to await the outcome of *Cotter and McDermott*.
[35] See e.g. M Hoskins, 'Tilting the Balance' ELRev 1996 at 371. Hoskins' view that 'Ideally the ECJ should overturn the decision in *Emmott*' (op. cit. at 371) was typical of many. Some resistance to *Emmott* has been shown in the national courts: see *Downer v Onyx* [1995] 1 CMLR 559; *Tate v Minister for Social Welfare* [1995] 1 CMLR 825; *R v Customs and Excise, ex parte Eurotunnel* [1995] CLC 392.
[36] Case C-271/91 *Marshall v Southampton and South West Area Health Authority II* [1993] ECR I-4367.

available.[37] *Marshall II* had a considerable financial impact. Actions were brought by female members of the armed forces who had been dismissed on becoming pregnant, in breach of the ECJ's *Dekker* ruling. Given that *Emmott* had abolished the statutory time limit, actions continued to be brought and by 1996 £55 million compensation had been paid out.[38] It has been suggested that the ECJ would have been wise to take the approach that it took in *Defrenne v Sabena*[39] in the context of Article 141 EC, namely the American practice of prospective overruling, whereby the new rule can be applied only to cases arising after the judgment introducing it. Such an approach, however, would not protect those whose rights under EC law had been infringed by governments. However, it will not always be clear to government when it is in danger of infringing EC law, i.e. where the ECJ's case law itself is unclear. In these sorts of case, a liability to pay large sums of money does seem unfair, a problem which will be further discussed in the context of state liability.

GROWING CAUTION?

Therefore, the case law presents us with strong rulings in favour of the effectiveness of Community law, and also perhaps indicates the impatience of the ECJ with the national courts' failure to develop new rules. However, more recent case law suggests a shift in approach, with the ECJ setting a limit on the intrusiveness of EC law into national procedural law. In some cases, the ECJ even seemed to suggest that *Emmott* had been overruled and that limitation periods were a matter for domestic law.[40] In *Steenhorst Neerings* and *Johnson*,[41] which concerned limits on claims for arrears of benefits, the ECJ held, unlike its ruling in *Emmott*, that Community law did not preclude reliance on national time limits even where the relevant directive had not been properly implemented into national law. In *Fantask*,[42] both AG Jacobs and the ECJ suggested that *Emmott* should be confined to its special circumstances, interpreting it as a ruling that could be explained by the requirements of equity and the principle of good faith.

In *Peterbroeck* and *Van Schijndel*[43] the ECJ came to apparently contradictory rulings in an attempt to strike a balance between the need to respect national procedural autonomy and enforcing EC law. In *Van Schijndel* the applicants challenged

---

[37] And so Mrs Marshall finally received compensation thirteen years after her original law suit.

[38] See S Fredman, 'A Difference with Distinction: Pregnancy and Parenthood Reassessed' (1996) 110 LQR 220, 222.

[39] Case 43/75 *Defrenne v Sabena* [1976] ECR 455.

[40] See e.g. particularly Case C-188/95 *Fantask* [1997] ECR 6783; also Case C-128/93 *Fisscher* [1994] ECR I-4583; Case C-261/95 *Palmisani* [1997] ECR 4025; Case C-62/93 *BP Supergas* [1995] ECR I-1883; see also A Ward, 'Effective Sanctions in EC Law: a Moving Boundary in the Division of Competence' (1995) 1 ELJ.

[41] Case C-338/91 *Steenhorst -Neerings* [1993] ECR I-5475 and Case C-421/92 *Johnson* [1994] ECR I-5483.

[42] Case C-188/95 *Fantask*, [1997] ELR 6783.

[43] Case C-312/93 *Peterbroeck* [1995] ECR I 4599; Cases C-430 and 431/93 *Van Schijndel* [1995] ECR I 4075.

compulsory membership of a Dutch pension scheme. On appeal to the Hoge Raad to have the judgment of a lower court quashed they argued that the court should have raised the issue of the compatibility of the scheme with Community law of its own motion. Under national law this was only possible if it did not require a new examination of the facts. On a reference to Luxembourg, the ECJ held that an independent application of the law by the court would only be required if this would also be the case in a purely domestic dispute. After finding that the Dutch rule of judicial passivity could be justified on the basis of principles common to the member states – the rights of the defence, concern with legal certainty, the proper conduct of procedure and relations between the State and the individual – the ECJ concluded that the rule was not an excessive restriction on the effectiveness of Community law.

However, in *Peterbroek*, where similar points of procedure were at issue, the Court found the inability of a national court to raise points of Community law of its own motion to be objectionable.[44] These two initially incompatible rulings seem to be explicable on the basis of the European Court's introduction of a purposive approach. AG Jacobs suggested in *Van Schijndel*[45] that any conflict between EC and national law must be resolved by a balancing exercise between interests served by national rules and the effectiveness of Community law. Especially important will be the court's perception that the principle at issue is part of the legal heritage common to the member states. Prechal[46] suggests that this looks rather like a transplant of the ECJ's *Cassis de Dijon* rule of reason from the field of free movement of goods to that of remedies.[47] But will such an approach work in the field of remedies? It could certainly prompt the referral of many more procedural rules to Luxembourg, an undesirable consequence in an ECJ already awash with Article 234 references.[48] Referral does not necessarily bring clarity, as the outcomes of *Peterbroek* and *van Schijndel* illustrate. On the other hand, failure to refer may leave too many national rules as they stand. Apparently self-evident national procedural rules may not always have a good justification. However, in the case law since *Van Schijndel* the ECJ has not applied an elaborate rule of

---

[44] See, for example, M Hoskins, 'Tilting the Balance: Supremacy and National Procedural Rules' (1996) ELRev 365 at 372–6, who sees the judgments as involving too great an intrusion into procedural autonomy. Others see them as enhancing the application of EC law by the national courts – for example, Szyszczak and Delicostopoulos, 'Intrusions into national procedural autonomy: the French paradigm' (1997) ELRev 141. See also F Jacobs, 'Enforcing Community Rights and Obligations in the national courts: striking the balance' in Lonbay and Biondi op. cit; G de Burca, 'National procedural rules and remedies: the changing approach of the Court of Justice' in Lonbay and Biondi op. cit. 41; and L Flynn, 'Taking Remedies too seriously: National Procedural Autonomy in the European Court of Justice', (1996) *The Irish Jurist* at 129.

[45] At para 18.

[46] S Prechal, 'Community Law in National Courts: the Lessons from *van Schijndel*' 1998 35 CMLRev 681 at 690.

[47] There are precedents for this, i.e. *Comet* and *Rewe*, where the Court held that national time limits could be justified by the principle of legal certainty and *Steenhorst-Neerings*, in which limits on social security benefit were held justified by the requirements of good administration and the financial equilibrium of the social security scheme: see fn 35 p 691 in Prechal.

[48] L Neville Brown, 'National protection of Community Rights: Reconciling Autonomy and Effectiveness', in Lonbay and Biondi op. cit. 68.

reason in every case.[49] All in all, the purposive test appears to do little for legal certainty and clarity while hardly helping national courts.

In *R* v *Secretary for State for Social Security, ex parte Sutton*,[50] the ECJ also seemed to retreat from an aggressive enforcement of the principle of effectiveness. Mrs Sutton had been refused invalid care allowance on grounds that she had reached retirement age. She claimed this breached directive 79/7 which implements the principle of equal treatment in the field of social security. The Social Security Commissioner upheld her claim and Mrs Sutton claimed interest on arrears of benefit on the basis of Article 6 of the directive (which requires member states to introduce measures to enable persons wronged by the failure to implement the principle of equal treatment to pursue their claims by the judicial process). Given the likeness of this case to *Marshall II*, which concerned the similarly worded Article 6 of directive 76/207, one might have expected the ECJ to rule that full compensation included interest, but it did not. It distinguished *Marshall*, which it saw as concerned with reparation for discriminatory dismissal, from *Sutton*, which it saw as concerned with the right to receive interest on social security benefits, something which it perceived as not compensatory in nature and thus not part of the right to equal treatment. This might seem to run counter to the Court's earlier case law on effectiveness, creating the impression, as Szyszczak suggests, that 'as quickly as the Court began to assert the supremacy of Community law over national procedural rules it has begun a hasty retreat'.[51]

In *Levez* v *Jennings (Harlow Pools) Ltd*,[52] a case involving a sex discrimination claim brought under Article 141 EC and Directive 75/117, the ECJ held that 'it is for national courts to ascertain whether the procedural rules intended to safeguard rights derived from Community law were safeguarded under national law and complied with the principle of equivalence'. It continued that 'the principle is not to be interpreted as requiring member states to extend their most favourable rules to all activities brought in the field of employment law'. In order to assess equivalence, national courts should consider 'the purpose and essential characteristics of allegedly similar domestic actions'. This again indicates a less interventionist approach than some of the Court's previous case law. The problem is that there seem to be no coherent principles linking the case law discussed so far. One may find highly technical explanations for individual cases but they are hard to reconcile with each other, a situation not well disposed to provide certainty, nor equality of remedies in the internal market.[53]

---

[49] See also, Case C-246/96 *Magorrian* [1998] ECR I-38; case C-441/93 *Panagis Pafitis* [1996] ECR I-1347; and Case C-192–218/95 *Comateb* [1997] ECR I-165 in which the ECJ did not seem to be examining the rationale for the national rules at all.

[50] Case C-66/95 [1997] ECR I-2163.

[51] E Szyszczak, 'Making Europe more Relevant to its Citizens' (1996) ELRev 352.

[52] Case C-326/96 *Levez* v *Jennings (Harlow Pools) Ltd* [1998] ECR I 7385.

[53] Although in the circumstances of the particular case, the ECJ found that a national two-year time limit could not be applied against the applicant. For other cases, indicating a more 'hands-off' approach by the ECJ, see Case C-231/96 *EDIS* [1998] ECR I 4951; Cases C-10–22/97 *IN.CO.GE* [1998] ECR I 6307 and Case C-189/98 *Criminal Proceedings against Nunes* [1999] 2 CMLR 1403; see also A Biondi, 'The European Court of Justice and certain national procedural limitations: not such a tough relationship' (1999) 36 CMLRev 1271; R Crauford-Smith, 'Remedies for Breaches of EC law in National Courts: Legal Variation and Selection' in P Craig and G de Burca, *The Evolution of EU Law* (Oxford: OUP, 1999).

However, applicants such as Ms Sutton might have an alternative claim in damages against the State. In this way their rights might still be protected without disturbing the balance between individual rights and the collective interest in legal certainty.[54] This type of alternative claim will now be considered.

STATE LIABILITY IN DAMAGES

The introduction of state liability in damages for loss to individuals caused by the state breaching EC law is the most drastic example of the intrusion of EC law into national remedies. There is nothing in the EC Treaty as to the liability of member states to injured parties for breaches of EC law. Although the ECJ had pointed out as early as 1960 in *Humblet*[55] that a judgment against a member state under Article 228 EC might serve as the basis for liability under national law for private parties, it was thought that the matter was governed by national law.[56] However, in 1991 the ECJ intruded further into the procedural autonomy of the member states, as well as increasing the pressure on the states to implement directives, in the *Francovich*[57] case. Francovich and Bonifaci had been employed by companies which became insolvent and they brought proceedings in the Italian courts for arrears of unpaid salary owed to them under directive 80/987, which harmonised member state laws relating to protection of employees' salaries in event of their employer's insolvency. Unfortunately, Italy had taken no steps to implement this directive, in spite of being found in breach of the treaty by the European Court in 1989.[58] As Advocate General Mischo commented in *Francovich*, 'Rarely has our court had to give judgement in a case where the loss caused to individuals concerned by the failure to implement a directive has been as scandalous as here.'[59] The applicants argued that the directive had direct effect. Alternatively they claimed compensation for the loss they had suffered. The Italian court made a preliminary reference to the European Court. The ECJ held that directive 80/987 could not be directly effective as the provisions relating to the arrangements which made the state guarantee the unpaid arrears were insufficiently specific. Therefore the applicants could not rely on it.

However, the ECJ did find that a member state is liable for damage caused to individuals for breaches of the treaty. It found this principle of liability to be 'inherent in the treaty' (para 35) and derived it from the following features of EC law. First, the autonomy of EC law and its ability to create rights for individuals: it specifically cited *Van Gend en Loos* (para 30). Second, it referred to the requirement that

---

[54] See comments of AG Jacobs in *Fantask*.
[55] *Humblet v Belgium* [1960] ECR 559; See also Case 181/82 *Roussel* [1982] ECR 389.
[56] And national law was not well able to deal with the matter: see *Bourgoin SA v Ministry of Agriculture, Fisheries and Food* [1986] QB 716, where the English Court of Appeal struggled to find an appropriate procedure in national law to remedy loss caused to a turkey farmer by the government's breach of Article 28, twisting misfeasance in public office and breach of statutory duty into contortions before failing to find a remedy.
[57] Cases C-6, C-9/90 *Francovich and Bonifaci v Italy* [1991] ECR I-5357.
[58] Case 22/87 *Commission v Italy* [1989] ECR 143.
[59] *Francovich* at para 1.

national courts give full effect to individual rights under Community law as illustrated in *Simmenthal* and *Factortame*. It followed that 'the full effectiveness of Community rules would be impaired and the protection of the rights which they grant would be weakened if individuals were unable to obtain compensation when their rights are infringed by a breach of Community law for which a member State can be held responsible' (para 33). The Court found further foundation for the principle of liability in Article 10 EC (para 36) under which member states are required to take all appropriate measures to ensure fulfilment of their obligations under Community law. Among such measures, stated the Court, was the obligation to nullify the consequences of a breach of Community law.

The sources given by the Court for state liability in *Francovich* tend not to be derived from explicit treaty provisions, and, for the legal purist, are little more convincing than those offered in its early direct effect case law. The effectiveness argument is based on policy grounds and ignores the existence of Articles 226–228. The by now inevitable reference to Article 10 provides at least a treaty base, but one which is hardly closely related to the principle of state liability in damages. Once again it seemed that the Court had left itself open to the charge of judicial lawmaking and the undermining of the rule of law.[60]

The ECJ also laid down three specific conditions for the establishment of state liability in damages for failure to implement a directive, or the incorrect implementation of a directive. First, the result prescribed by the directive must involve the grant of rights to individuals; second, those rights must be identifiable according to the provisions of the directive and third, there must be a causal link between the breach of the state's obligation and the harm suffered by the injured parties.[61]

Therefore, the much cited need to protect individual rights and to ensure full effect of Community law are the basis of state liability as laid down in *Francovich*.[62] The *Francovich* ruling has a clear constitutional significance. Establishment of state liability in damages has been characterised as the high point in the evolution of the principle of primacy from a general principle of constitutional law, to a specific obligation on national courts to provide full and effective remedies for the protection of Community law rights.[63]

Francovich clearly requires national law to apply the principle of state liability even where an equivalent remedy does not exist under national law. Such a 'cross-infection' of national law by EC law, as Harlow terms it, departs from the ECJ's earlier insistence on the procedural autonomy of the national courts. *Francovich* does,

---

[60] E.g. C Harlow, 'Francovich and the problem of the disobedient State' (1996) ELJ; Sir Patrick Neill QC, *The European Court of Justice: a case study in Judicial Activism*, published as evidence before the House of Lords sub-committee on the IGC conference, session 1994–95 18th report (HL paper 88) 218–245, in which Neill is particularly critical of *Francovich*.

[61] *Francovich* para 40.

[62] Ironically, Francovich's rights were not in the end protected: in Case C-479/93 *Francovich II* [1995] ECR I-3843 it was held that employees whose employer is not subject to procedures to satisfy collectively the claims of creditors were not covered by directive 80/987.

[63] See e.g. T Tridimas, 'Member State Liability in Damages for Breach of Community Law: An Assessment of the Case Law' in J Beatson and T Tridimas, *New Directions in European Public Law* (Hart, 1998).

however, help overcome the negative effects of *Marshall I*. A remedy under *Francovich* is fairer than pleading direct effect against a body with no direct responsibility for implementing directives, such as privatised utilities, and usually more predictable than indirect effect, which may require some tortuous judicial interpretation. Again, the ruling did not come out of the blue, it was preceded by academic debate.[64] The timing of *Francovich* was also significant. The internal market was to be achieved by 31 December 1992, mainly by the implementation of over 300 directives. But there were problems with carrying this out, as member states neglected to implement some of them.[65] In 1989, 26 Article 226 actions were brought for the second time.[66] *Francovich* thus provided an alternative means of enforcement.

FURTHER CLARIFICATION

However, the Court did not make the **scope** of the remedy in damages clear. It remained uncertain after *Francovich* whether there would be state liability for breaches of Community law other than non-implementation of directives and, if so, whether fault, negligence or some other standard would be required before liability could be established. Could there be state liability for damage caused by primary legislation given that many national jurisdictions refused to recognise such liability? It was also unclear whether liability would exist only with regard to provisions of Community law which were not directly effective.[67]

In *Brasserie du Pêcheur* and *Factortame III*[68] the ECJ provided some clarification of the basis of, and conditions for, state liability in damages. Brasserie du Pêcheur was a French brewery which sought to recover damages lost during the period when it was forced to stop exporting its beer to Germany because of the German beer purity laws. Germany was later found to be in breach of Article 28 of the treaty. In the continuing *Factortame* saga, Spanish fishermen, who had already succeeded in establishing that the Merchant Shipping Act breached Article 43 of the treaty, sought at least £30m damages for the lost time in which they could not fish in British waters.

These cases, unlike *Francovich*, concerned not inaction, but rather illegal action, under Community law. The ECJ did not consider this distinction to be an obstacle

---

[64] E.g. N Green and A Barav, 'Damages in the national courts for Breach of Community Law' [1986] YEL 55; J Temple Lang, 'The duties of national courts under the constitutional law of the European Community", 1987 Lasok Lecture (1987, Exeter), pp 27–8.; D Curtin, 'The Effectiveness of Judicial Protection of Individual Rights' (1990) 27 CMLRev 709.

[65] A general problem in international law: see R Higgins, 'Accountability and Liability: the Law of State Responsibility', in *Problems and Progress, International Law and How we Use it* (Oxford: Clarendon, 1994). But Allott denies that there is any justifiable basis for state liability in international law: P Allott, 'State Responsibility and the Unmaking of International Law' (1988) 29 Harv Int LJ 1.

[66] European Commission: *7th report on Monitoring and Application of Community law* [1990] OJ C 232/1. See chapter 12 for a discussion of Article 226.

[67] See e.g. Ross, 'Beyond Francovich' (1993) 56 MLR 55; Steiner, 'From Direct Effect to Francovich: Shifting Means of Enforcement of Community Law' (1993) 18 EL Rev 3, for a discussion of these issues.

[68] Cases C-46/93 *Brasserie du Pêcheur SA v Germany* and Case C 48/93 *R v Secretary of State for Transport, ex parte Factortame Ltd and others* [1996] ECR I-1029.

to recovery. The German government had argued that a general right to damages could only be created by legislation but the ECJ did not accept this. It held that it had the power to rule on such a question under Article 220 of the EC treaty 'in particular by reference to the fundamental principles of the Community legal system, and . . . general principles common to the legal systems of the member states.'[69]

The reference to 'principles common to the member states' in the judgment is rather optimistic, given that it is very difficult to identify such common principles.[70] In fact, the reference to Article 220 is a rather blunt acknowledgement of the Court's law-creating role in this case. Article 220, like Article 10, is an aspirational, declaratory principle often relied upon by the Court to provide authority for its law-making.

The Court did seek an additional justification other than the reference to the principle of effectiveness which it had made in the *Francovich* case.[71] It linked the principle of state liability to the liability of the EC under Article 288, an approach which had been suggested by Advocate General Mischo in *Francovich*, but not followed by the Court. The Court in Factortame stated:

> the conditions under which the State may incur liability for damage caused to individuals by a breach of Community law cannot, in the absence of particular justification, differ from those governing the liability of the Community in like circumstances. The protection of rights which individuals derive from Community law cannot vary depending on whether a national authority or a Community authority is responsible for the damage.[72]

In its case law under Article 288 the ECJ has held that the Community legislature will only be liable in the case of 'a sufficiently serious violation of a superior rule of law for the protection of the individual', a famous formula developed in the *Schöppenstedt* case.[73] This has been interpreted in subsequent case law to require a 'manifest and grave disregard of the limits on the exercise of its powers'.[74]

Following *Factortame III* and *Brasserie du Pêcheur* the conditions for liability appeared to be as follows: (i) the rule of law infringed must have been intended to confer rights on individuals; (ii) a manifest and serious breach has occurred; (iii) there must be a direct and causal link between the breach of the obligation by the State and the damage suffered by injured parties.[75] It is the second of these

---

[69] Ibid. at para 27.

[70] See Advocate General Leger's observations in Case c-5/94 *Hedley Lomas* [1996] ECR I-2533 at 2579. However, there is a consensus on some aspects, namely strict liability, fault and the duty to mitigate. See J Schwarze, 'European Administrative Law' (Sweet and Maxwell 1992); A Barav, 'Damages in Domestic Courts for Breach of Community law by National Authorities' in *Non Contractual Liability of the European Communities* Schermers, Heukels and Mend (ed.) (Dordrecht, 1988).

[71] Advocate General Tesauro added a further contractarian justification in his Opinion in *Factortame*, by suggesting liability arose for legislative acts which were in breach of obligations which member states had themselves agreed under the treaty, at para 39.

[72] *Factortame III* at para 42.

[73] See Case 5/71 *Aktien-Zuckerfabrik Schöppenstedt v Council* [1971] ECR 975. See also Chapter 11.

[74] Joined Cases 83 and 94/76 *Bayerische HNL* [1978] ECR 1209 para 12.

[75] This is assumed to be left to national courts to decide on the facts. However, doing so might result in a 'renationalisation' of liability: see Tridimas, in J Beatson and T Tridimas, *New Directions in European Public Law* (Hart Publishing, 1998) at 17.

conditions – that of the serious breach – which is the most important and has occasioned problems for courts in subsequent cases which will be discussed below.

A SLIDING SCALE OF LIABILITY?

This alignment of the conditions of Community and State liability may seem well and good. However, the conditions set under Article 228 have made it very difficult in practice for an applicant to recover damages from a Community institution. The requirement of 'a sufficiently serious breach' of Community law has been interpreted very strictly.[76] These stringent conditions seem to have been partly prompted by the ECJ's wish to avoid a flood of actions for damage caused by Community legislation in the highly discretionary field of the common agricultural policy and liability has thus been made exceptional. In such cases, the EC is acting as primary legislator. Moreover, traders to whom this type of legislation is likely to apply are very often operating with a known level of risk in any case.

On the other hand, member states frequently have less discretion when acting within the field of Community law, as they are confined by higher ranking norms of Community law. Failing to implement a directive is a flagrant breach of EC law: the State has no discretion as to **whether** it enforces a directive, only as to the way it does so. Liability in such instances should therefore be less exceptional, a point made by Advocate General Leger in *Hedley Lomas*,[77] who suggested that state liability should not have the same foundations as the liability of the EC. The Advocate General also continued that 'it would be somewhat paradoxical to align state liability for breach of Community law with Article 288(2) rules which are judged to be unsatisfactory, unduly stringent and affording insufficient protection for the right to effective judicial relief'.[78] Another Advocate General, Van Gerven, while recognising that 'in the case of discretionary (mostly legislative) powers on the part of the Community or national Public Authorities liability is less likely to arise', was critical of the apparent application of the strict *Schöppenstedt* test in cases which did not involve states in policy choices. This he thought was likely to lead to the 'virtual immunity for any kind of conduct on the part of the legislature which does not fly in the face of Community law'.[79]

It remained unclear after *Factortame III* and *Brasserie du Pêcheur* whether the manifest and serious breach would be applicable in all types of case – notably to those types of case which did not involve choices of legislative policy. As the

---

[76] See Case 5/71 *Aktien-Zuckerfabrik Schoppenstedt* v *Council* [1971] ECR 975, see Chapter 11. Very few applicants have ever succeeded in getting damages in this way.

[77] Case C-5/94 *R* v *Ministry of Agriculture, Fisheries and Food, ex parte Hedley Lomas* [1996] ECR I 2533.

[78] Ibid. But perhaps the ECJ might begin to apply Article 288(2) more strictly against Community institutions, now that it has acknowledged the parallel between non-contractual liability and the liability of the EC. See also, for a hint of such an approach, for example, Case C-352/98P *Laboratoires Pharmaceutiques Bergaderm* [2000] ECR I-5291, discussed in Chapter 11.

[79] Van Gerven, 'Bridging the Unbridgeable: Community and National Tort laws after Francovich and Brasserie' (1996) ICLQ 518.

misgivings of Advocate Generals Leger and Van Gerven illustrate, to make no distinction would be to ignore an important difference between the situation in which a member state is implementing Community law, as in *Francovich*, and one in which it has a number of possible options, i.e. where it has some discretion. Where states have some discretion, liability is less straightforward and there is a great need for clear principles of state liability. The nearest the ECJ came to offering guidance in *Factortame III* was in its consideration of the concept of a 'sufficiently serious breach' where it held that the following matters could be taken into account:

> the clarity and precision of the rule breached, the measure of discretion left by that rule to the national or Community authorities, whether the infringement and the damage caused was intentional or voluntary, whether any error of law was excusable or inexcusable, the fact that the position taken by a Community Institution may have contributed towards the omission, and the adoption or retention of national measures or practices contrary to Community law.[80]

On the other hand, Van Gerven has suggested 'a sliding scale' of liability 'from a mere breach...such as a clear-cut (inexcusable and unjustifiable) violation of a precise obligation such as in Francovich...to a breach committed in the execution of wide discretionary powers...'[81]

The ECJ has not subsequently employed Van Gerven's terminology of a sliding scale but it seems to have made a distinction. Liability is most straightforward in cases where a member state commits a breach in circumstances in which it has no discretion at all, such as in *Dillenkofer*,[82] in which the German government had totally failed to implement directive 90/314, which provided for the financial compensation of those whose package holiday provider had become bankrupt. In this context the Court, contrary to the arguments of several member state governments which argued that there should be liability for non-implementation only in the case of serious breaches of Community law, held that non-implementation *per se* was sufficient to incur liability.

Liability will also be fairly automatic when a member state has very limited discretion. In *Rechberger*,[83] the ECJ found the Austrian government's implementation of directive 90/314, the same as at issue in *Dillenkofer*, to be manifestly incompatible with the directive, as Austria had not only provided a later date from which claims could be brought than under the time limit for implementation, but also failed to provide an adequate level to protection: this therefore constituted a suffi-

---

[80] *Factortame III* at para 56.

[81] Van Gerven op. cit. at 518. Van Gerven also makes a more specific distinction of types of state breach, including breach of duty *simpliciter* (obligations which are incapable of being misinterpreted); breach by misinterpretation of vague, open-ended, sometimes unwritten general principles in which case the ECJ may decide to limit the temporal effects of its interpretative judgment; breaches committed in the exercise of broad discretionary powers: Van Gerven, in op. cit. p. 21. See also a similar classification by Browne-Wilkinson L in *X v Bedfordshire* [1995] 2 AC 633 in the context of national law.

[82] Cases C-178–9/94, 188–190/94 *Dillenkofer and others v Federal Republic of Germany* [1996] ECR I-4845.

[83] Case C-140/97 *Rechberger v Austria* [1999] ECR I-3499.

ciently serious breach. In *Hedley Lomas*[84] the ECJ confronted a breach of a specific treaty article, namely Article 29. In 1990 the British government had imposed a ban (an administrative rather than a legislative act) on the export of live animals to Spain on the grounds that it believed[85] that Spanish abattoirs had not complied with EC Directive 74/577[86] (which required animals to be stunned before slaughter) and, therefore, that animals were suffering unnecessarily. The British government claimed that this export ban was justified under Article 30 EC, which permits member states to restrict exports on public policy, public morality and the protection of health and life of animals. The problem is that EC harmonisation legislation, such as Directive 74/577, usually preempts national action under Article 30, unless harmonisation is not complete. Hedley Lomas had applied for an export licence for sheep and had been refused. They brought proceedings in the English courts for damages. The ECJ found that the ban was not justified. Although the Court considered that there was a significant risk that the directive had been violated,[87] it went on to say that 'member states must rely on trust in each other to carry out inspections on their respective territories' and not unilaterally adopt measures to deal with putative breaches of EC law by other member states.[88] Furthermore, it also found that this breach by the UK was sufficiently serious to give rise to liability in damages, 'where at the time it committed the infringement the member State in question was not called upon to make any legislative choices and had only considerably reduced, or even no, discretion, the mere infringement of Community law may be sufficient to establish the existence of a sufficiently serious breach'. Where there was no discretion, as here, because the Community directive preempted any national action, any violation of Community law would result in liability.

Where there is some discretion, liability will be less automatic. In the *British Telecom* case[89] BT sought annulment of domestic regulations implementing directive 90/351 on public procurement in the utilities sector, which had been transposed into English law by means of the Utilities Supply and Works Contract Regulations 1992. BT claimed these regulations wrongly implemented the directive, with the result that BT had been financially disadvantaged. The ECJ held that the relevant provisions of Article 8(1) of the directive were insufficiently clear and reasonably capable of the interpretation given to it by the UK in good faith and thus that the government's error was excusable. The Court stressed the link between state liability and Article 288(2) holding that 'in the transposition of Directives, a restrictive approach to state liability is justified'. Its reasoning was 'the concern to ensure that the exercise of legislative functions is not hindered by the prospect of actions for damages whenever the general interest requires the institutions or member states to adopt measures which may adversely affect individual interests',[90] a decision no doubt greeted by EU

---

[84] Case C-5/94 *R v Ministry of Agriculture, Fisheries and Food, ex parte Hedley Lomas* [1996] ECR I-2553.
[85] In fact, it seems that the only evidence was to be found in press reports.
[86] Council Directive 74/577 on stunning of animals before slaughter [1974] OJ L 316/10.
[87] Moreover, the directive did not lay down any Commission procedures for monitoring compliance.
[88] *Hedley Lomas*, at para 19.
[89] Case C-392/93 *R v HM Treasury, ex parte British Telecommunications plc* [1996] ECR I-1631.
[90] *Ex parte British Telecom* at para 40.

governments with relief.[91] It would seem that, in this case, the division usually made under Article 234 between interpretation, which is for the ECJ, and application, which is left for the national courts, collapsed, perhaps indicating that this was a case in which the ECJ felt the national courts needed guidance. In a similar vein, in the *Denkavit*[92] case, the Court held that faulty implementation of a directive did not give rise to liability because the incorrect interpretation taken by Germany had also been used by almost all other member states, following discussions with the Council while the Directive was being adopted.[93]

It would appear, therefore, that a sufficiently serious breach must always be established. However, where there is non-implementation, or omission, a sufficiently serious breach will automatically be established. In other situations, negligence will be implicit in the manifest and grave requirement.

Two recent cases involve the misapplication of a directive by national authorities. In *Norbrook Laboratories* v *MAFF*[94] the applicants had applied for marketing authority for a veterinary medical product and had suffered loss as a result of national requirements which infringed directives 81/851 and 81/852. The ECJ held that these directives did confer rights on individuals but left it to the national courts to determine whether the breaches concerned were sufficiently serious to warrant recovery. In *Brinkmann Tabakfabriken* v *Skatteministeriet*[95] the Danish authorities had erroneously committed the heinous error of classifying a tobacco product as a 'cigarette' rather than 'smoking tobacco' for tax purposes. This involved the misapplication rather than the non-implementation of a directive, in this case directive 79/32.[96] According to Advocate General Jacobs, this did not involve a serious breach of EC law as the Danish authorities' interpretation of the directive was not untenable or in bad faith and was shared by other member states and the Commission. The ECJ held that, in these circumstances, the Danish government was not bound to compensate the manufacturer. This is in line with *Denkavit* and *ex parte BT*: a member state is not liable for an erroneous interpretation of Community law where the provision in question does not rule out such a reading. Finally, in *Klaus Konle* v *Austria*, which concerned action by the Austrian land of Tyrol under the EC Accession treaty, the ECJ held that apportionment of state liability was a matter for the division of powers under the Austrian constitution, rather than a matter for the ECJ to determine.[97]

---

[91]   P Craig, 'Once More unto the Breach: The Community, the State and Damages Liability' (1997) 109 LQR 67 at 87.

[92]   Cases C-283, 291 & 292/94 *Denkavit International* v *Bundesamt für Finanzen* [1996] ECR I-5063.

[93]   In past case law the ECJ has held that discussions in the Council of Ministers have no legal status unless actually expressed in the legislation. Here it would seem, however, that such discussions may be used to establish excusable error of a member state in the context of an action for damages.

[94]   Case C-127/95 *Norbrook Laboratories* [1998] ECR I-1531.

[95]   Case C-319/96 *Brinkmann Tabakfabriken* [1998] ECR I-5255.

[96]   On taxes other than turnover taxes which affect the consumption of manufactured tobacco.

[97]   Case C-302/97 *Klaus Konle* v *Austria* [1999] ECR I 3099; see also Case C-424/97 *Haim* [2000] ECR I-5123.

THE INTRUSIVENESS OF THE EUROPEAN NORM

The introduction of a European remedy in damages intrudes on the assumptions and traditions of national law. First, there is the problematic introduction of **state** liability, particularly in the case of legislation, a cause of action unrecognised in most Community legal systems prior to *Factortame III*. Most domestic legal systems have worked on the presumption that government is a special case, that the ordinary rules of tort liability, for example, cannot apply when government is the defendant. In spite of Dicey's[98] stipulation that government should not be treated any differently from the average citizen (in any case untrue when he wrote it) government has always been subject to differential treatment. Government, unlike private citizens, supposedly acts for the benefit of the community. Its activities are, or should be, intended for the general welfare of society and thus should not be unduly restricted. Discretionary conduct will often not be actionable.[99] Public interest may have to prevail over private rights. The development of the remedy of State liability seems to cut through this, privileging private rights under European law.

If the European Court's introduction of a 'Euro-remedy' is to have credibility, it must have a sufficient justificatory foundation. But this is what it seems to lack. One of the problems prompted by the ECJ's now complex jurisprudence in this field lies in the difficulty of providing just such a coherent justification for such liability. This reflects the absence of a solid theoretical basis.[100] Is the purpose of State liability deterrence, or perhaps even punishment of the unlawful State, or is such liability intended to compensate the victims of the State's unlawful action, an approach which is also capable of protecting individual rights?

On this matter, there is a division of opinion in the academic community. On the one hand, Steiner sees state liability as deterrence, writing 'the prospect of liability to **all** parties suffering damage as a result of their failures to implement Community law would provide States with a powerful incentive to comply with their Community obligations'.[101] However, there are problems with a deterrence-based approach, as highlighted by Harlow, in an important and highly critical article, *Francovich and the Problem of the Disobedient State*.[102] The focus of Harlow's complaint seems to be that *Francovich* type state liability certainly cannot be justified in terms of a punitive/deterrence theory. The ambiguous nature of EC legislation, the difficult division of responsibility between State and region, as well as the problems involved in transferring the liability in sanction in French administrative

---

[98] 'With us every official, from the prime Minister down to a constable, is under the same responsibility for every act done without legal justification as any other citizen.' AV Dicey, *Introduction to the Law of the Constitution* (1885) at 187.

[99] See *Anns v Merton LBC* [1978] AC 728 for a distinction between policy and operational decisions; but also *Murphy v Brentwood* [1990] 2 All ER 908. See also T Weir, 'Government Liability' [1989] Public Law 40.

[100] See R Cass, 'Official Liability in America', in Bell and Bradley (eds) *Governmental Liability: A Comparative Survey* (UKNCCL 1991) at 111 who makes a similar point regarding official liability in the USA.

[101] J Steiner, 'From Direct Effect to Francovich' (1993) EL Rev 9.

[102] (1996) 2 ELJ 1999.

law[103] into the EC arena make it problematic for the State to be in a position to control conduct for which it will ultimately be responsible. This will be the case, for example, in a State in which power has been devolved to regional entities, such as in Belgium or Germany.[104] Alternatively, the failure to implement, or wrongful implementation, may be inadvertent, resulting from the ambiguous and complex nature of EC legislation, as in the *British Telecom* case.[105] Harlow, therefore, prefers to look to a rights-based justification of state liability, writing:

> A sensible 'rights-based' response to the problem of Francovich would have been to fashion a discrete remedy at EC level and ideally administered by the CFI for breach of a right protected by EC law. Such a solution would more accurately reflect the wording of Article 178 EC, which speaks of 'compensation for damage'. It would acknowledge a tradition which stretches back, according to Judge Edward, to the Aquilian concept of 'uncovenanted loss – loss for which equity demands compensation as opposed to loss which must be regarded as an ordinary risk of commercial life.'[106]

Such a principle is indeed to be found in every member state, e.g. in Articles 14 and 34 of the German *Grundgesetz* or the French principle of *égalité devant les charges publiques*, which is essentially equitable in character. It has been invoked in the US as a justification for damages liability for a state law which violates the Constitution, 'to interpose the federal courts between the States and the people, as the guardian of the people's federal rights'.[107] It is also seen by many as the foundation of tort liability, involving the notion of corrective justice: 'From a rights oriented standpoint then, the role of the tort system is to perform "corrective justice" in order to preserve entitlements against wrongful infringement.'[108]

Members of the ECJ have suggested such a basis, such as Advocate General Tesauro, in his Opinion in *Brasserie*, who saw such a solution as reflecting 'a shift of emphasis, at least in the more advanced legal systems, from the conduct of the perpetrator of the damage to the rights of the injured party'.[109] Protection of individual rights is, of course, the rhetorical leitmotif running throughout the ECJ's case law on direct effect and remedies.[110] But such an approach, based on the content of

---

[103] Harlow writes, 'It is probable that French administrative law, in which liability undoubtedly contains an element of sanction, provided the pattern for the ECJ's sanctions theory of liability. Before this road was travelled, however, attention should have been paid to the special position of the French Conseil d'Etat.' C Harlow, 'Francovich and the problem of the disobedient state' at 11. Harlow locates the singular position of the Conseil d'Etat partly in its special role as the conscience of the executive and in its powers of regulatory control over administrative authorities. Harlow op. cit. 12. See also M-C Kessler, *Le Conseil d'Etat* (Armand Colin 1968); J Chevallier (ed.), *Le Droit administratif en mutation* (PUF, 1993).

[104] See de Winter and Laurent, 'The Belgian Parliament and European Integration' (1995) 1 J of Legislative Studies 75 at 87, cited by Harlow op. cit. at p 15.

[105] See Chapter 3 of this book, for an account of EC lawmaking.

[106] Harlow, op. cit. at 13; D Edward, 'Is there a Place for Private Law Principles in Community Law?' in Schermers, Curtin and Heukell (eds) *Institutional Dynamics of European Integration* (Martinus Nijhoff, 1994) at 122.

[107] *Mitchum v Foster* 407 US 225 (1972) at 242.

[108] D Rosenberg, 'The Causal Connection in Mass Exposure Cases: a Public Law Vision of the Tort System' (1994) 97 Harvard Law Review 851.

[109] *Brasserie*, Opinion of AG Tesauro at para 12.

rights found in EC legislation, has not been articulated clearly by the Court in its case law on remedies, where it has issued ambiguous and conflicting rulings in the area of indirect effect, for example, and refused to reverse its *Marshall* ruling in *Dori*.[111]

A rights-based liability is problematic. If such liability is not to raise Cardozo's spectre of 'liability in an indeterminate amount for an indeterminate time to an indeterminate class' then which rights should be protected? What types of loss should be compensated? Some important rights, such as liberty or physical integrity, may justify protection by the courts in many circumstances. Their breach provides a strong argument for corrective justice. These rights have been traditionally compensated as, for example, in the famous eighteenth century cases *Wilkes* v *Wood* and *Entick* v *Carrington*,[112] in which John Wilkes successfully sued the government for trespass on the basis of illegal search warrants.

Some domestic legal systems place a cap on liability by requiring that the law at issue itself creates private rights rather than providing for the public welfare. So, for example, under English law, the failure to perform a statutory duty is actionable at the instance of members of a protected class.[113] In this way the English courts construed Article 82 EC as creating a statutory duty for the benefit of persons affected by the abuse of a dominant position.[114] In German law the *Schutznorm* theory, whose academic roots[115] stretch back to the beginning of the twentieth century, is generally accepted by administrative courts and academic writers. Under this theory, in order to determine whether a *subjektives Recht* has been granted, one has to interpret the relevant statutory provision to see whether it aims at the protection of individual interests, and thus whether it is a protective norm, a *Schutznorm*. The ECJ's *Schöppenstedt* test under Article 288(2) appeared to acknowledge some sort of *Schutznorm* test, by requiring the law breached to be for the protection of the individual.[116]

Where there is no special recognition given to individual interests, national legal systems have proceeded with care. This has been especially the case where pure

---

[110] See e.g. J Coppell, 'Rights, Duties and the end of Marshall' (1994) 57 MLR 859.

[111] See Chapter 8 on Direct Effect.

[112] *Wilkes* v *Wood* (1763) 2 Wils KB 203, *Entick* v *Carrington* (1765) 2 Wils KB 275.

[113] See *Lonrho* v *Shell (No 2)* [1982] AC 173, 185 and R Buckley, 'Liability in Tort for Breach of a Statutory Duty' (1984) 100 LQR 204.

[114] In *Garden Cottage Foods Ltd* v *Milk Marketing Board* [1984] AC 130 they were to construe Article 86 [82] in this way. However, in *Bourgoin* v *Ministry of Agriculture Fisheries & Food* [1986] QB 716, the Court of Appeal held that Article 30 [28] merely imposes a duty in the public interest not to impose measures impeding trade between member states.

[115] See Buhler, *Die subjektiven öffentlichen Rechte und ihre Schutz in der deutschen Verwaltungsrechtsprechung* (1914); Jellinek, *System der subjektiven öffentlichen Rechte* (2nd edn 1905). See also s 823 (2) BGB. For a modern interpretation see BS Markesinis, *The German Law of Torts* (3rd edn 1994); Ruffert, 'Rights and Remedies in Community Law' (1997) CLMRev 307.

[116] For an account of this test see Chapter 11 of this book.

economic interests are at stake.[117] Community law has not, however, always followed this cautious position and the ECJ has been more willing to acknowledge economic interests as rights, often as fundamental ones. This may be partly because of the predominantly economic character of the Community legal order, which is a liberal, property-based system: a paradigm of the market type which has dominated modernist thought but whose origins can be traced to Roman law, with its concept of *dominium* where goods and slaves could be freely exchanged by economic actors.

This ability to identify rights, particularly when they are of an economic nature, may confound the domestic lawyer. In *Bowden* v *South West Water*,[118] the English courts struggled with state liability in the context of an action brought by a mussel fisherman who claimed his livelihood was damaged by discharge of sewage into the sea from a sewage works owned and operated by South West Water. Those parts of his claim which were based on European directives (quality of bathing water, shell-fish waters directive and urban waste water directive) had been struck out at first instance by Carnwath J who found 'nothing in either which could possibly be said to entail the grant of rights to shell-fishermen'. Some of these EC claims were reinstated by the Court of Appeal which, notwithstanding the 'surprise of the common lawyer' conceded that the ECJ had in its past case law found that these directives had created rights and obligations for individuals.[119]

National courts are unlikely to find it easy to determine what sorts of interest will qualify as a right to satisfy the state liability test. Van Gerven suggested that directly effective law will create individual rights but, as the value of state liability may lie in its application in situations where the relevant EC law is not directly effective, there must be some other means of establishing whether rights are generated. There seems to be no clear test. As with state liability in damages, the problem lies in the lack of a coherent theoretical basis. The concept of a right is uncertain and contested. Some theorists suggest that rights must involve the exercise of autonomy, the ability to waive the right in question.[120] Others insist that they be correlated with clear duties and involve interests which must be protected,[121] which tends to beg the question, of precisely what interests need protection. However, given that a typical incidental effect of recognising something as a right is that compensation becomes payable for its violation, the ECJ should be cautious. The spectres of vast damages claims, such as the £30 million *Factortame* suit, rise to haunt contemporary European government. In the light of this complex interplay of justification and national legal principle one is almost inclined to agree with Harlow's castigation of

---

[117] See *Spartan Steel and Alloys Ltd* v *Martin* [1973] QB 23 discussed by Van Gerven, who, in 'Bridging the unbridgeable: Community and National Tort laws after Francovich and Brasserie' ICLQ (1996), compares four cases on economic loss from four jurisdictions, contrasting the position under French, Dutch, English and German law, concluding that French and Dutch law take a more victim friendly approach. See also discussion below.

[118] *Bowden* v *South West Water Services Limited* [1999] 3 C.M.L.R. 180 CA.

[119] See also *Gloag and Son Ltd.* v *Welsh Distillers* [1998] 2 CMLR 203; *Consorzio del Prosciutto di Parma* v *Asda Stores Ltd* [1998] 2 CMLR 215 for a similar examination by the English courts.

[120] See HLA Hart, *Essays on Bentham* (Oxford: 1982) essays 7 and 8 for an example of this view.

[121] See N MacCormick, 'Rights in Legislation' in Hacker and Raz (eds) *Law, Morality and Society* (Oxford: Clarendon1977).

the ECJ as 'selfish' in imposing state liability and her further admonition that 'The door opened in Francovich should have been firmly slammed.'[122] A rights based liability, even with a more adequately developed conceptual basis, is likely to be as controversial and troublesome as a punitive/deterrence one. Harlow suggests that we should follow the circumspection of other jurisdictions in providing a remedy in state liability in damages, citing the reluctance of the European Court of Human Rights, the US Supreme Court and the Canadian Supreme Court to use damages as a remedy for unconstitutional activity.[123] Indeed, Harlow's own perhaps rather negative preference seems to be ultimately not for a remedy in damages at all, but for the ECJ to show more interest in alternative dispute resolution and look to 'patient negotiation rather than obedience'.[124]

However, this is surely too negative a conclusion, for several reasons. First, many of these state breaches are flagrant violations of binding EC obligations. In such cases, the deterrence element has substance. Patient negotiation in the context of Article 226 has not always worked. Firm sanctions are sometimes needed. Furthermore, in less straightforward cases, the ECJ's own case law has determined that state liability is not always automatic. Third, national courts may apply the *Francovich* and *Factortame* criteria strictly,[125] so we should perhaps not be too haunted by the spectre of vast damages awards.

MORE QUESTIONS

Uncertainty lingers as to the ambit of the remedy in damages. However, most of this uncertainty is caused, either by the lack of clarity and precision of European law, or by the difficulties of grafting a European remedy on to national procedural law. The following examples give a flavour of the sort of problems courts will face.

Damage

A question which has already been touched on concerns the type of damage which should be recoverable. Should all actual damage be compensated? This was usually the case on those rare occasions when an applicant succeeded under Article 288(2),

---

[122] Harlow op. cit. at 29.

[123] Harlow op. cit. pp 19–20; see also Mas, 'The Right to Compensation under Article 50', in MacDonald, Matscher and Petzold (eds) *The European System for Protection for Human Rights* (Martinus Nijhoff, 1993); JH Ely, 'That Due Satisfaction may be made: the Fifth Amendment and the Origins of the Compensation Principle' (1992) 36 Am J of Legal History 1; Mullan, 'Damages for Violation of Constitutional Rights – a False Spring?' (1995) 6 National J of Constitutional law 105.

[124] Harlow op. cit. at 33; see also F Snyder, 'The Effectiveness of EC Law: Institutions, Processes, Tools and Techniques' (1993) 56 MLR 19–54, who also proposes such a role for the ECJ. See also T Weir, 'Government Liability' (1989) Public Law, for suggestions on alternative compensation for wrongful governmental activities.

[125] Even in the case of such a flagrant beach as *Francovich*, the applicant did not succeed in their national courts.

as in the *Mulder*[126] case. On the other hand, the ECJ has refused to compensate in cases where damage has not exceeded normal entrepreneurial risks.[127] In the *CNTA* case the ECJ stated that 'the system of compensation cannot be considered to be tantamount to a guarantee for traders against the risks of alteration of exchange'.[128] In such a case, risks are 'normal' and 'loss caused by such errors is part of business and compensated by the prices charged'.[129] Recovery for economic loss is in any case a thorny issue; many believe that these losses should be left to the market to resolve.[130] However, the effect of *Factortame III* is to introduce a general right to compensation for economic loss which is unavailable in many legal systems of the EU, such as England. Most European states limit recovery for pure economic loss as distinct from physical damage, but, under EC law, it is economic loss which is most likely to be suffered, as was acknowledged in *Brasserie*.[131] In principle, economic loss is recoverable, provided it is not purely speculative.[132]

It may be that the extent of compensation, i.e. whether full or partial, will depend on the function served by the rule in question.[133] In *Francovich*, the directive secured payment of a specified amount of salary arrears, therefore compensation had to be for that full amount. In *Marshall II*, where the ECJ stressed the need for full and adequate compensation, it had to be equivalent to the alternative remedy of reinstatement of the victim of discrimination. On the other hand, if the damage does not exceed the boundaries of normal business risks, it may remain uncompensated.

Status of the remedy

A further question concerns the status of the remedy in damages. Is it available as a free-standing, autonomous remedy, independently of whether the applicant has pursued other available remedies? Or must it be a residuary action? In German law, for example, the recovery of damages is precluded where the applicant has 'deliberately or negligently failed to avert loss by seeking another remedy'.[134] Advocate General Tesauro in *Factortame III* thought that the member states 'cannot be reasonably debarred from making actions for damages dependent on a previous action for annulment having been brought'.[135] He drew a parallel with liability of the Community under Article 288, where he took the action for damages to be ancillary,

---

[126] Joined cases 104/89 and 37/90 *Mulder and Heinemann* [1992] ECR I-3061 paras 23–36. See discussion in Chapter 11.

[127] Cases 83, 94/76 *Bayerische HNL* [1978] ECR 1209 at para 6.

[128] Case 74/74 *CNTA v Commission* [1975] ECR 533.

[129] Schermers, Curtin and Heukell (eds) *Institutional Dynamics of European Integration* at xi.

[130] See R Epstein, *Simple Rules for a Complex World* (Harvard University Press, 1995) at 109.

[131] At para 87.

[132] See Cases 56/74 *Kampffmeyer* [1976] ECR 711 para 6.

[133] Van Gerven ICLQ op. cit. who takes this view.

[134] Article 839(3) German Civil Code.

[135] *Factortame III*, at para 104. AG Tesauro also drew support from the *Mulder* case, in which the ECJ held that there was 'a general principle common to the legal systems of the member states to the effect that the injured party must show reasonable diligence in limiting the extent of his loss or risk having to bear the damage himself'. Joined Cases C-104/89 and C-37/90 *Mulder v Council* [1992] ECR I-3061 at 3136 (para 33); see also Case 238/78 *Ireks-Arkady GmbH v Council* [1979] ECR 2955 for an application of this principle by the Court.

as evidenced by the ECJ's portrayal of it in *Wagner Miret* as 'an individual's last resort'.[136] Therefore, if an action concerns sex discrimination, for example, it should be brought against the employer in the labour courts and not against the State in the public law arena. The Rule of Law would be undermined if private parties could disregard their Community obligations secure in the knowledge that the State will underwrite responsibility. In this way, liability is simply cast on the party with the most resources.[137] However, in *Comateb*[138] the ECJ seemed to be drawing limits to the national courts' power to require the applicant to avert or limit loss by seeking another remedy, when it held that 'traders may not be prevented from applying to the Courts…irrespective of whether the charges have been passed on'.[139] The *Sutton* case also suggests that the remedy in damages exists independently of other remedies, as the ECJ admitted the possibility of recovery of interest even though Mrs Sutton would not have been able to recover this under the directive. This view was backed up by AG Jacobs in *Fantask*, who interpreted *Comateb* and *Sutton* as recognising that repayment claims and damages actions may coexist as independent remedies and what is recoverable under each may differ.[140]

Private actions

An offshoot of state liability may be the possible development of an action in damages against private individuals. Is an action in damages against, e.g. a company, for anti-competitive behaviour in breach of Articles 81 or 82 a realistic possibility? In *Banks v British Coal*[141] in which it was alleged that British Coal (a private company) had engaged in anti-competitive behaviour, Advocate General van Gerven said, 'The general basis established by the Court in the *Francovich* judgement for state liability also applies where an individual infringes a provision of Community law to which he is subject, thereby causing loss and damage to another individual.'[142] But litigating EC law in national courts against private parties has not proved straightforward. In the *Garden Cottage*[143] case the English courts struggled to find an appropriate translation of Article 82 into the context of domestic remedies much in the same way as they had done in the context of state liability in *Bourgoin* in pre-*Francovich* days.

In *Courage v Bernhard Crehar*[144] the ECJ was in no doubt about the theoretical availability of damages for breach of Article 81(1). It justified its reasoning by stating that national courts must ensure that EC rules take full effect. Would an action in damages lie against an individual for breach of a non-directly effective directive, or in the context of a treaty article such as Article 28 which binds the state rather

---

[136] Case C-334/92 *Wagner Miret* [1993] ECR I-6911 at 6932 para 23.
[137] E Szyszczak, 'Making Europe More Relevant' (1996) 21 ELRev 351, at 361.
[138] Case C-192/95 to 218/95 *Société Comateb* [1997] ECR I-165.
[139] Ibid. Contrast *Ireks-Arkady* in the context of Article 288(2) supra.
[140] Jacobs at para 82 *Fantask*.
[141] Case C-128/94 *Banks v British Coal Corp* [1994] ECR I-1207.
[142] Ibid. In that case, however, the ECJ found the relevant provisions of the ECSC treaty not to be directly effective.
[143] *Garden Cottage Foods v Milk Marketing Board* [1983] 2 All ER 770 (HL).
[144] Case C-453/99 *Courage v Bernhard Crehar* [2001] ECR I-6297.

than individuals? This seems highly unlikely given the concern of the ECJ in recent case law such as *Arcaro*, to avoid imposing obligations on individuals. On the other hand, if the focus of future developments is on the effective protection of EC rights, then one might expect to see further developments in this area.

Back to national procedural autonomy?

In *Brasserie du Pêcheur* and *Factortame III*, the ECJ laid down common EC conditions governing the nature of the breach giving rise to state liability in damages. What the Court has not done, however, is to provide guidelines for other aspects of state liability, such as damage, causation and the other issues raised in previous paragraphs. In the *Sutton* case, the ECJ stated that 'while the right to reparation is founded directly on Community law ... the national law on liability provides the framework within which the State must make reparation for the consequences of the loss and damage caused, provided always that the conditions laid down by national law relating to reparation of loss and damage must not be less favourable than those relating to similar domestic claims and must not be so framed as to make it virtually impossible of excessively difficult to obtain reparation'.[145] However, while national law governs these areas of procedure, what will be the case is that there will be differences in treatment and thus inequality in remedies from member state to member state. Further control by the ECJ seems quite unlikely. However, if not the Court, might there not still be room for legislative action harmonising the conditions for recovery? This will be considered in the next section.

A NEW *JUS COMMUNE?*

Procedural disparities distort the internal market just as much as differences in substantive law. As Jolowicz writes, 'Distortion is bound to occur if the mode of litigation, with all that implies both by way of procedural techniques and by way of their implications for costs, delays, appeals, enforcement of judgements and so on, varies substantially from one place to another.'[146] Given the problems involved in maintaining and developing an effective damages action in the national courts of the EC, might it not be preferable to look to harmonisation of EC remedies? Academic and practitioner literature contains many calls for rationalisation or 'procedural purification'[147] as if this area of EC law had somehow become replete with foreign bodies.

The EC's political institutions have turned their minds to this. In 1983, in the Sieglerschmidt report, the European Parliament resolved 'emphatically that the uniform, complete and simultaneous application of Community law in all member states is a fundamental pre-requisite for the existence of a Community governed by

---

[145] Case C-66/95 *R v Secretary of State for Social Security, ex parte Sutton* [1997] ECR I-2163.
[146] Jolowicz, introduction to M Storme and others (ed.) *The Storme report on the approximation of judiciary law in the European Union* (Dordrecht/Boston/London: Kluwer and Martinus Nijhoff 1994) at xiii.
[147] per Ross, 'Beyond Francovich' (1993) 56 MLR 55 at 69.

the rule of law'.[148] Twenty years on, the outcome of a case may still be determined by the national procedural rules applicable. Factors such as the role of the judge (whether active or passive)[149] *locus standi*, amendment of pleadings, or rules permitting the introduction of new facts, vary greatly from country to country. In the absence of at least some minimal uniformity, there will be no internal market as far as litigation in the EC is concerned.

Nonetheless, writers such as van Gerven, Schwarze and Caranta[150] have for some time written about an *ad hoc* federalism or convergence of European law. Most of these writers point to a core area of administrative law and judicial protection where this *rapprochement* is taking place. Caranta for example suggests, '. . . the subject now shows a remarkable coherence, which allows the observer to trace the development of a set of rules that should be common to all the Member States, and thus replace pre-existing domestic rules. That is to say that a new *jus commune* is slowly taking place, and that great emphasis is now laid on remedies.'[151]

This activity in the field of remedies at European level may also have a beneficial effect on purely domestic remedies. Currently, it is perfectly possible for two quite different sets of procedural rules to operate – one in the field of EC law and one under national law – a situation which may lead to reverse discrimination under national law, which may not set such stringent requirements for effective remedies. However, in *M v Home Office*,[152] the House of Lords broke new ground by holding that there would be jurisdiction against the Crown in a purely internal situation, a decision clearly influenced by its *Factortame* decision. Lord Slynn, speaking at the Frankfurter Buchmesse, stated that he considered it to be 'one of the most absorbing questions of the interaction of the ECJ and the national judge' how the latter can or will 'adjust to bringing into his own legal system ideas fixed in the Community crucible'.[153]

This convergence and cross-fertilisation is for the most part seen as desirable. In this way, to paraphrase Zweigert and Kötz, who extol the benefits of comparative law, legislators are able to legislate better for their own jurisdiction, and lawyers

---

[148] EP Doc 1-1052/82.

[149] Although the English adversarial system has been subject to some modifications recently. See *Access to Justice Final Report to the Lord Chancellor* by the Right Honourable Lord Woolf, 1996, as well as the New Civil Procedure Rules 1999.

[150] W van Gerven, 'Bridging the Gap between Community and National Laws: Towards a Principle of Homogeneity in the Field of Legal remedies?' (1995) CMLRev 679 and 'Bridging the Unbridgeable: Community and National Tort Laws after Francovich and Brasserie' 45 ICLQ (1996) 507; J Schwarze, 'Tendencies Towards a Common Administrative Law in Europe' (1991)16 El Rev 3 and *European Administrative Law* (London, Sweet and Maxwell 1992); R Caranta, 'Judicial Protection against member states: a new jus commune takes place' (1995) CMLRev 703; see also C Timsworth, 'Things Fall Apart: The Harmonisation of Community Judicial Procedural Protection' (1997) 22 ELRev 291; B Markesinis, 'The Gradual Convergence' in Markesinis (ed.) *Learning from Europe and learning in Europe* (1994).

[151] Caranta, op. cit.

[152] [1993] 3 WLR 433.

[153] 'The Court at Luxembourg through the eyes of a national judge'; see also Sir Thomas Bingham, 'There is a world elsewhere: the changing perspectives of English law' 41 ICL (1992) 513. See also I Ward, 'The Anomalous, the Wrong and the Unhappy: UK Administrative Law in a European Perspective' (1994) NILQ.

interpreting their own domestic laws may draw on solutions found elsewhere.[154] However, as the 1994 Storme report on *The Approximation of Judiciary Law in the European Union* (a group of experts set up by the European Commission in 1990)[155] noted, there are particular problems connected with the unification of procedural law. Kahn-Freund's characterisation of procedural law as 'tough law' has been noted already, but the Storme report stressed the particularly national character of procedural law which was 'fraught with political overtones', forming 'part of the prerogative of the sovereignty of the State ... and as such the structural expression of national sovereignty'.[156] Nonetheless, the report recommended the setting of the Community's sights on approximation of procedural law. In 1995 the Council adopted a Resolution on the effective and uniform application of EC law and of remedies.[157] Provisions on civil cooperation (which were originally dealt with in the third pillar of the TEU) were also introduced into Article 65 of the EC treaty by the Treaty of Amsterdam, although these concern private international law matters for the most part.

Not everyone is as willing as the members of the Storme Committee to look to greater unity. It is certainly true that codification, if it took place, would be very time-consuming, involving national systems in a potentially stultifying process, which would deny them the chance to develop their own procedural system where necessary. Alternatively, partial harmonisation would increase complexity by maintaining a two-tier system with inevitable gaps and overlaps. At its worst, this could lead to 'disintegration' at national level.

Perhaps the most extreme approach to harmonisation is taken by Pierre Legrand, who is vehemently opposed to convergence, whether by *ad hoc* judicial harmonisation, or by the introduction of a European civil code.[158] Legrand's objection is based on a perceived fundamental distinction between civil law and common law. He asserts that these systems are based on two distinct *mentalités*, which share no unitary rationality or morality. Legrand's view contrasts with that of comparativists such as Markesinis or Zweigert and Kötz, who suggest that, although legal systems may conceptualise problem situations differently, the functional solution to such problems tends to be similar. For Legrand, however, the functional level (i.e. that of rules) only presents the surface image of a legal system. If we wish to know more of a system's deep structures, we need to look beyond neatly organised rules to Law's sub system.

---

[154] Zweigert and Kötz, *An Introduction to Comparative Law*, trans T Weir (Oxford: OUP, 1998 3rd edn).

[155] M Storme and others (ed.) *Approximation of Judiciary Law in the European Union* (Dordrecht/Boston/London: Kluwer and Martinus Nijhoff, 1994). A report which according to Timsworth 'is rather chaotically organised; and it appears not to have attracted much further attention from either the Commission itself or in other quarters': Timsworth op. cit. fn 150 at 303. See also P Lindblom, 'Harmony of the Legal Spheres' 1997 European Review of Private Law 11, who is equally critical.

[156] Storme report p 31.

[157] OJ 1995 C 188/1.

[158] See P Legrand, 'European Legal Systems are not converging' 1996 ICLQ at 52, and 'Against A European Civil Code' (1997) MLR 44. See also D Caruso 'The missing view of the cathedral: the private law paradigm of European legal integration' (1997) 3 ELJ 3; H Collins, 'European Private law and the cultural identity of states' (1995) 3 European Review of Private Law 353.

In Montesquieu's words 'it is not the body of the laws I am looking for, but their soul'.[159] Instead, Legrand urges us to follow Levi-Strauss's advice to embrace the habits and customs of a culture, its true epistemological foundations. In this way we will be able to unravel the cognitive structure underlying a legal system.

According to Legrand, if we examine this deeper level, it is by no means clear that European legal systems are converging. Legrand considers a variety of different features, such as the nature of legal reasoning; the significance of systematisation; the character of rules; the role of facts; the meaning of rights and the presence of the past and concludes that there are irreconcilable differences between the common law and the civil law worlds. For example, according to Coke, 'the common law... consisteth upon so many, and almost infinite particulars',[160] but according to Legrand, 'In the civil law tradition, on the contrary, the aim is to rapidly remove any trace of the circumstances and to establish an idea or concept'.[161] Furthermore, unlike the civil law system, which 'goes beyond the raw classification of case law decisions around salient facts to become a system of institutions capable of transcending disputes to move away from factual immediacies' common law reasoning is inductive and empirical in nature and cannot be axiomaticised. Indeed, for Legrand, by linking these two legal worlds, the European Community has dramatised their cognitive disconnections, highlighting 'the difficulties involved in achieving mutual understanding between [different groups of lawyers] given that each one views the others within the meanings constructed in its own language'.[162] Thus Legrand concludes, 'the ambition of a European *concordantia* is (and must be) a chimera...European Legal systems are not converging.'[163]

Legrand's argument is a radical one. It seems to rest partly on an extreme form of relativism: the assertion that, because there is no universal rationality, therefore discourse or understanding between two different cultural systems is impossible. A new *jus commune* is ruled out on the basis of the incommensurability of 'deep' values underpinning different legal worlds, as well as the damage and violence that assimilation brings with it. But Legrand underplays the extent to which intercultural dialogue takes place and understanding is possible. Moreover, Legrand's arguments also are based on the premise that the legal cultures of the EU states are coherent within themselves.[164] However, any one culture is itself already fragmentalised or pluralised so that a legally unitary society is not derived from a homogenous life-world as Legrand suggests.

The coming of a new age *jus commune* may not be as imminent as advocates of procedural harmonisation suggest but neither is it an impossibility. Differences exist, and some should be respected and maintained: indeed the history of EC law is the history of the learning of this lesson.

---

159 Montesquieu, *De L'esprit des Lois* at 1025.
160 Edward Coke, *The Preface to the Reader* 1 Co Rep I at xxvii.
161 P Legrand, 'European Legal Systems are not converging' at 71.
162 B Jackson, 'Ius Gentium, Ius Commune, European Law', in B Jackson and D McGoldrick (eds) *Legal Vision of the New Europe* (London: Graham and Trotman 1993) (1993) at 34.
163 Legrand at 81.
164 C Joerges, 'The Impact of European Integration on private law as a rationalisation process and as a contest of disciplines' (1995) 3 Eur Rev of Private Law 175 at 183.

PART THREE

DIRECT ACTIONS: A LACK OF INDIVIDUAL JUSTICE?

10

CONTROLLING THE COMMUNITY INSTITUTIONS: JUDICIAL REVIEW

INTRODUCTION

Justice demands that the Community should be legally accountable for its actions and so the law promulgated by EU institutions is subject to review by the European courts, whose task, under Article 220 of the EC Treaty, is to see that 'the law is observed'. This involves a variety of judicial procedures. Under Article 230, the Court may review the legality of Community acts other than recommendations or opinions. Article 232 mirrors this provision where it is unlawful Community **inaction** which is under review. Article 241, the so-called plea of illegality, allows for the nullification of certain unlawful acts, and under Article 288(2) action may be brought to recover damages caused by the Community under its non-contractual liability.[1]

These articles of the Treaty may be used, depending on the provision, by member states, individuals and companies, or the EU institutions themselves. They involve the Community Courts in procedures which are overly recondite and formal, as well as quite diverse in nature. Article 230 may take on the character of administrative law, constitutional/institutional law, or international law, depending on who is doing the challenging – individuals, EU institutions or member states – or on the type of act which is being attacked. The same is true of Article 232, whereas Article 241 may only be used by 'privileged applicants', i.e. member states or institutions. Article 288(2) is a sort of hybrid private/public law action, involving damages claims brought by individuals against institutions, but the act which causes the damage may be of a basically tortious nature or it may actually be a legislative act.

Such a variety of actions of course illustrates the oft cited '*sui generis*' nature of Community law, but hardly provides a transparent system of legal remedies for the European citizen, should they wish to litigate in 'their' court. Moreover, these provisions do not offer the level of individual protection which a first look at the Treaty might suggest. In this respect, the Court has departed from case law where it showed itself eager to ensure the 'effective protection' of EC rights in the national courts

---

[1] This procedure is discussed in Chapter 11.

and, in so doing, has been (gently) castigated on a number of occasions.[2] Its case law has also proved to be contradictory and confusing, particularly in the area of Article 230.[3] Indeed, it is difficult to discern what motives underlie this disappointing jurisprudential approach, as will be considered shortly.

Harold Laski observed that constitutional law is unintelligible if not understood as an expression of the economic system which it was designed to serve.[4] However, much writing on EU public, and particularly judicial review, law[5] still proceeds as if the Court's decisions in this area were cocooned from the political and economic imperatives involved in the running of the EU. This makes some of the Court's case law in this area almost unintelligible, particularly in the field of standing to sue, where, to plagiarise the expression of an American judge, 'standing is a...word game played by secret rules'.[6]

ARTICLE 230 (FORMERLY 173): THE COMMUNITY LEGAL ORDER AND THE ACTION FOR ANNULMENT

In its post-Nice form, Article 230 reads as follows:

> The Court of Justice shall review the legality of acts adopted jointly by the European Parliament and Council, of acts of the Council, of the Commission, and of the ECB other than recommendations or opinions, and acts of the European Parliament intended to produce legal effects vis-à-vis third parties.
>
> It shall for this purpose have jurisdiction in actions brought by a Member State, the European Parliament, the Council or the Commission on the grounds of lack of competence, infringement of an essential procedural requirement, infringement of this Treaty or of any rule relating to its application, or misuse of powers.
>
> The Court shall have jurisdiction under the same conditions in actions brought by the Court of Auditors and by the ECB for the purpose of protecting their prerogatives.
>
> Any natural or legal person may, under the same conditions, institute proceedings against a decision addressed to that person or against a decision which, although in the form of a regulation or decision addressed to another person, is of direct and individual concern to the former.

---

[2] E.g. Mancini and Keeling, *Democracy and the European Court of Justice* (1994) 57 MLR at 188; Advocate General Slynn in Case 246/81 *Lord Bethell v Commission* [1982] ECR 2277 at 2299.

[3] See below.

[4] H Laski, *A Grammar of Politics* (1925); see also Harlow and Rawlings, *Law and Administration* (Weidenfeld, 1984) at 1.

[5] There are notable exceptions, i.e. H Rasmussen, *On Law and Policy in the European Court of Justice* (Martinus Nijhoff, 1986) and 'Why is Article 173 interpreted against private plaintiffs?' (1980) 5 EL Rev at 112; as well as the writings of Joseph Weiler. More recently, writers have inquired into the policy reasons for much of the Article 230 case law: e.g. Paul Craig in Craig and de Búrca, *EC Law* (1995); Craig P, 'Legality, Standing and Substantive Review in Community Law' (1994) 14 OJLS 507; and Carol Harlow, 'Towards a Theory of Access for the European Court' (1992) YEL 213. However, generally the field of remedies in EC law has been treated in a rather insular way, in contrast to other branches of EU law, such as competition or social law.

[6] Per Harlan J (dissenting), *Flast v Cohen* 392 US 83, 129 (1968).

The proceedings provided for in this Article shall be instituted within two months of the publication of the measure, or of its notification to the plaintiff, or, in the absence thereof, of the day on which it came to the knowledge of the latter, as the case may be.

'The rule of law requires not only that a court be able to deal with all the violations of legal rules but, in addition, that all injured parties be entitled to adjudication of their grievances.' So wrote Sheingold, in his study of the European Court in its early days.[7] It can hardly be said, nearly 40 years later, that the European Court has provided ready access to 'all injured parties', partly, no doubt, from the prudential fear of being overwhelmed by suits. For some commentators,[8] given the structure of the Treaty of Rome (i.e. primarily an international law document in *traité cadre* form), it is amazing that Article 230 allowed individuals any right of access at all. However, the scope of EC law has widened since its early days, with the changes of the Single European Act and the Maastricht and Amsterdam Treaties, and the ambit of EU law has expanded to include citizenship of the union and the protection of fundamental rights. Thus, even if it were true that the inclusion of an individual right of judicial review in 1957 was a privilege for such litigants, this is no longer the case in an age in which access to court is considered an important legal right. And therefore it is worrying that rights of access of individuals and companies before the European courts have barely improved since its early days.[9]

What does 'judicial review' mean in the context of Article 230? A well-known example of judicial review is that in which an individual brings an application claiming that certain legislation infringes their constitutional rights, such as the action brought by Johnson[10] in the US Supreme Court who claimed that his conviction for burning the American flag in public infringed his right to free speech under the first amendment of the US constitution,[11] or that brought by Brunner in the German Constitutional Court, who claimed that ratification of the Maastricht Treaty by the German government infringed his rights under the German constitution.[12] But in some member states of the EU such judicial review of primary legislation is not possible (i.e. the UK, unless, following *Factortame*, EC law is at issue, or France, where only the Conseil Constitutionel may preview legislation). In these jurisdictions, judicial review is properly confined to acts of the **administration**, such as the procedure under Order 53[13] of the English Supreme Court.

Although it is not possible to draw direct comparisons with domestic law, because reviewable acts under Article 230 correspond neither to primary nor secondary legislation in national law (a regulation may be extremely general in nature, such as Regulation 1612/68 concerning the free movement of workers, or highly specific,

---

[7] S Sheingold, *The Rule of Law in European Integration* (Yale University Press, 1965).

[8] E.g. Stein and Vining, 'Citizen Access to Judicial Review of Administrative Action in a Transnational and Federal Context' in F Jacobs (ed.) *European Law and the Individual* (North Holland, 1975).

[9] Compare e.g. *Plaumann* or *Calpak* with *Campo Ebro* or *Po Delta*. These cases are discussed below.

[10] *Texas* v *Johnson* 491 US 397 (1989).

[11] However, citing American constitutional law as providing a paradigm example of judicial review, is problematic, given the contested origins of the validity of review under the US Constitution in *Marbury* v *Madison* 5 US (1 Cranch) 137 (1803).

[12] *Brunner* v *European Union Treaty* [1994] 1 CMLR 57.

[13] Now Part 54 of the Rules of Civil Procedure 2000.

such as some of those passed under the CAP, and thus more like an individual administrative act), Article 230 has proved in practice to be an unhappy compromise between these two types of judicial review. Individuals (or more likely corporate litigants) may not challenge regulations where they are truly general in nature, even if those measures involve a gross breach of their rights by, for example, violating the principles of non-discrimination and proportionality.[14] So we plainly do not have the sort of judicial review which courted the attention of so many commentators, such as Bickel, Ely, Tribe and Dworkin in the context of the US Supreme Court,[15] although of course the European Court has been judicially active in a way which would have bothered at least some of those authors in the context of its dealings with the national courts, and its development of substantive Community law.[16]

On the other hand, the standing rules for natural and legal persons are limited, even where the measure is of a more individuated nature – the applicant has to show that they are 'individually concerned', a test which is extremely hard to satisfy. So, even in the context of specific measures, akin to administrative acts, the standing rules are tighter than they would be under many systems of national administrative law, allowing little in the way of group actions.

A reviewable act

In any case, regardless of the applicant's standing, there must first be a reviewable act. Not all Community acts are susceptible to judicial review: recommendations and opinions are expressly excluded by Article 230. However, reviewable acts are not confined to regulations, directives or decisions (those types of act characterised as having binding force according to Article 249, which details the type of acts the Community institutions may pass 'to carry out their task'). Instead, all acts which are binding, or designed to have legal effects, may be reviewed by the Court. This broadens the field considerably, as illustrated by the *ERTA*[17] case, which involved one of the many Community inter-institutional battles. The Commission (piqued by, as it thought, being left out of negotiations) challenged a Council resolution aimed at coordinating negotiation procedures for a European Road Transport Agreement, on the basis that this procedure was not in accordance with the Treaty. The Council argued that the objective of these proceedings was simply the expression of a voluntary coordination and thus could not be reviewable under Article 230. The Court disagreed, holding that the proceedings were designed to lay down a course of action 'binding on both the institutions and the Member States and that the proceedings had definite legal effects.[18] In holding the act to be reviewable, the Court also supported the Commission in its struggle for power with the Council.[19]

---

[14] For consideration of the European court's fundamental rights jurisprudence, see Chapter 13.
[15] A Bickel, *The Least Dangerous Branch* (New Haven, 1962); L Tribe, *American Constitutional Law* (New York, 1988); Dworkin R, *Freedom's Law* (Oxford, 1996).
[16] For further examples see Chapter 5 of this book.
[17] Case 22/70 *Commission v Council* [1971] ECR 263.
[18] Ibid. at paras 53 and 54.
[19] Noted by I Ward, *A Critical Introduction to European Law* (Butterworths, 1996) at 62.

However, it may not always be clear whether a particular act does produce legal effects. Community acts are taken in a wide variety of circumstances, in varying forms. The enforcement of EC competition law by the Commission, which involves a mass of complex rules and procedures, often running to many stages, has supplied much of the case law in this area, reflecting the strong economic thrust of the EC until recently, and the corporate character of most of its litigants. An initial comparison of two superficially similar cases illustrates the problems. The *Cimenteries*[20] case involved the Commission's attempts to deal with potentially huge cement cartels in the early days of the EEC. 74 companies had entered an agreement called the Noordwijk's Cement Accord, dividing up the cement market by quota. Such activity potentially infringes Article 81(1) of the EC Treaty, which prohibits agreements between undertakings which restrict competition in the common market. Under Regulation 17/62 such agreements must be notified to the Commission, which may fine the undertaking concerned, or grant an exemption under Article 81(3), if it finds the agreement economically beneficial. Article 15(5) of Regulation 17 provides that undertakings shall enjoy immunity from fines from the time of notification of the agreement, but Article 15(6) provides that such immunity will cease once the Commission has informed the undertakings after a preliminary examination that the agreement appears to violate Article 81(1). From that point, those undertakings operate the agreement at their own risk. The Société Anonyme Cimenteries had notified its agreement in 1962 and received a letter from the Commission under Article 15(6) which they then challenged under Article 230. The Commission argued that the letter contained no more than an opinion and was not legally binding. The court disagreed, stating that: '...the said measure affected the interests of the undertakings by bringing about a distinct change in their legal position. It is unequivocally a measure which produces legal effects touching the interests of the undertakings concerned and which is binding on them. It thus constitutes not a mere opinion but a decision.'[21]

Therefore, the Court looks at the substance and nature of the act, to see whether it produces legal effects, rather than what it is called. However, in the *IBM* case,[22] the Court held that 'in principle an act is open to review only if it is a measure definitively laying down the position of the Commission or the Council on the conclusion of that procedure, and not a provisional measure intended to pave the way for a final decision'.[23] IBM had tried to challenge a statement of objections by the Commission, stating that IBM were in potential abuse of a dominant position contrary to Article 82 of the Treaty. The Court held that the statement could only be

---

[20] Cases 8–11/66 *Re Noordwijk's Cement Accord* [1967] ECR 75.

[21] *Cimenteries* at p 91. At time of writing, Regulation 17/62 is in the process of being reformed: see commision proposal for a regulation on the implementation of rules on competition laid down in Articles 81 and 82 EC, COM (2000) 582 final.

[22] Case 60/81 *IBM* [1981] ECR 2369; see also Cases C133, 150/87 *Nashua Corp v Commission* [1990] ECR I-719.

[23] *IBM*, para 10.

challenged in the course of the review of the final decision.[24] In *Coca Cola*, the CFI recently held that the mere finding by the Commission of a dominant position (for the purposes of Article 82 EC), even if likely in practice to influence the policy and future commercial strategy of the company concerned, had no binding legal effect.[25]

A large body of cases are also brought by complainants in competition cases who wish to challenge under Article 230 the rejection of their complaint by the Commission. Complainants are an important source of information for the Commission in its pursuit of abuses of EC competition rules and they have certain rights in the investigation of complaints. These types of cases are a good illustration of how Community action can be hard to categorise, bordering on the formal/informal, its legal effects uncertain. The Court of First Instance has attempted to rationalise these very problematic procedures, setting out rather complex rules regarding what can be challenged.[26]

The Commission's increasing tendency to proceed by way of 'soft law' is also causing problems for Article 230. In Edinburgh, in 1992, the European Council[27] agreed that the EC should proceed with the least intrusive type of act wherever possible, an application of the subsidiarity principle in policy-making. But soft law notices and communications may be harder than they appear. In the *Air France* case,[28] there was no written act at all, but a statement by a Commission spokesman (as it was in this case) that the Commission had no jurisdiction under the Merger Regulation[29] to examine the acquisition of one airline by another. The CFI held[30] that the 'act' had a definitive nature, since it had been made public and confirmed

---

[24] IBM wanted to challenge this statement before the substance of the case was dealt with on the basis that its arguments against the statement of objections (namely that the statement of objections lacked clarity, that the Commission had not followed the correct procedure and that the proceedings were an extra territorial application of EC competition law and thus contrary to international law) were independent of its case on the merits.

[25] Cases T-125/97 T-127/97 *Coca Cola* [2000] ECR II-1733.

[26] Case T-64/89 *Automec v Commissison* [1990] ECR II 367 at paras 45–47 and repeated in other cases since. Basically, first, the Commission receives the complaint and decides whether to proceed, but as the Commission takes no formal action there is nothing at this stage which can be attacked by the complainant before the Court. Certain formal legal steps are taken in stage two. If the Commission decides not to proceed with the complaint it may communicate this to the complainant by way of an 'Article 6 letter' (the procedure is provided in Art 6 of regulation 99/63. The letter is sometimes referred to by the Court as a notice) setting out its reasons and giving the complainant time to respond within a time limit. The Court held in the *Automec I* that such a letter is not a decision or other legal act challengeable before the Court but the complainant can, by way of Art 232, compel the Commission to send it such a letter (see e.g. Case 125/78 *GEMA v Commission* [1979] ECR 3173). In the third stage the Commission takes account of any response that the complainant may have made to the Art 6 letter and this may end with a final decision by the Commission rejecting the complaint. If so this decision can be challenged in Court.

[27] Edinburgh Council conclusions on transparency of decision making; Interinstitutional declaration on democracy, transparency and subsidiarity of 25 October 1993. See also the discussion on law-making in Chapter 3.

[28] Case T-3/93 *Air France v Commission* [1994] ECR II-121.

[29] Council Regulation 4064/89 [1989] OJ L 395/1 on the control of concentrations between undertakings.

[30] *Air France* at para 43 of the judgment (p 149) relying on case 60/81 *IBM v Commission*.

the Commission's position beyond all doubt.[31] Similarly, in *France v Commission*[32] the Court held that a 'Commission Communication on an Internal Market for Pension Funds' was a binding act, as it imposed new obligations on member states, and so should have been founded on a specific legal basis in the treaty. This conclusion was supported by the fact that the Commission had previously submitted a proposal for a directive in this field which had been withdrawn following failure to reach agreement in the Council, thus strengthening a suspicion that the Commission was trying to introduce this measure through the back door. On the other hand, in a more recent action brought by France the ECJ took a stricter view. France had brought an action for the annulment of a decision allegedly adopted by the Commission not to repeal its act lifting the British beef ban. France asserted that the existence of a such a decision was revealed by statements by the Commissioner responsible and by a decision of the College to send France a letter of formal notice for its failure to comply with the act lifting the ban. The Court found the French action inadmissible on the basis that neither the statement nor the letter of formal notice constituted a reviewable act.[33]

In another *France v Commission*[34] case, France sought to annul an agreement between the Commission and the US government in the field of competition law. This agreement had been made to help solve ever-growing problems which had arisen by the concurrent application of both parties' competition law to international business operations. By this agreement, both parties agreed to cooperate by, for instance, allocating enforcement between the jurisdictions, or requesting the other to investigate on its territory activities which might affect the other party. The agreement was signed in Washington in 1991 by Sir Leon Brittan, then EC Competition Commissioner. France attacked this agreement on the basis that the Commission had no jurisdiction to conclude the agreement under Article 300 EC which, although it allows the Commission to negotiate such agreements, only empowers the Council to **conclude** them. Was this an act susceptible to annulment under Article 230? It would be strange if the Court of Justice had the power to annul the agreement itself, which is a bilateral binding treaty of international law.[35] However, the Court upheld the French government's plea but declared void, not the agreement itself (a binding agreement in international law) but the prior decision of the Commission authorising Sir Leon Brittan to conclude the agreement.[36] Nonetheless,

---

[31] However, there has been some criticism of this decision. Greaves, for example, suggests that the Court's ruling is too uncertain and that the ruling of the Court of Justice in *BASF* is to be preferred (on the basis that, in that decision, the ECJ identified some essential factors – reasons to be given for the decision, complete text of the act adopted – which should exist before the act can be classified as a decision): R Greaves, 'The Nature and Binding Effect of Decisions under Article 189' (1996) 21 EL Rev at 16.

[32] Case C-57/95 *France v Commission* [1997] ECR I-1627.

[33] Case C-514/99 *France v Commission* [2000] ECR 000.

[34] Case C-327/91 *France v Commission* [1994] ECR I-3641.

[35] However, the Court has held, in the context of an Article 234 reference to interpret Community measures, that agreements concluded with third countries are acts of the Institutions of the Community within the meaning of Article 234(b), Case 181/73 *Haegeman Srl v Belgium* [1974] ECR 449).

[36] The position was subsequently regularised by a decision of the Council and the Commission of 10 April 1995.

it might be questioned whether these cases are compatible with Article 7 of the EC Treaty which states that 'Each institution shall act within the limits of the powers conferred upon it by this treaty.'

The author of the act

Not only must the act produce legal effects in order to be reviewable, but it must also be adopted by an appropriate Community institution or body. According to Article 230, these are acts adopted jointly by the European Parliament and Council, acts of the Council, acts of the Commission, acts of the European Central Bank and acts of the European Parliament.[37] Acts of bodies which are not Community institutions, such as the European Council, cannot be annulled.[38] If the decision is one adopted by the member states acting as representatives of their governments, rather than as the Council of Ministers, the decision will not be a Community act and thus not reviewable under Article 230. This situation can, however, be difficult to determine.[39]

Prior to the TEU, Article 230 only applied explicitly to the Commission and Council, but the Court held that the acts of the European Parliament could also be reviewed by the ECJ in the *Les Verts* case.[40] In this case, the European Green Party sought to challenge a decision of the Bureau of the Parliament, which allocated campaign funds for the 1984 European Parliamentary elections on the basis of the share of votes which those parties had achieved in the last set of elections. This prejudiced parties like the Greens which had not taken part in the last round. The Court held that the Parliament's acts produced significant legal effects and thus, 'An interpretation of Article 173 which excluded measures adopted by the European Parliament from those which could be contested would tend to a result contrary both to the spirit of the Treaty as expressed in Article 164 and its system.'[41] *Les Verts* did not meet with universal approval. Hartley, for example, is extremely critical, arguing

---

[37] Furthermore, acts of a Community institution need not be adopted pursuant to the legislative provisions of the Treaty in order to be susceptible to challenge, as the *ERTA* case established. Moreover, if a Community institution has the power to take legally binding decisions but decides to delegate that power to another institution then the Court will be able to review the acts of the delegate (see e.g. Cases 32–3/58 *SNUPAT* v *High Authority* [1959] ECR 127 and Chapter 3 for a discussion of this topic).

[38] Case T584/93 *Roujansky* v *European Council* 1994 ECR II 585 and also Case C-25/94 *Commission* v *Council* [1996] ECR I-1469.

[39] As Joined Cases C-181 and C-248/91 *Parliament* v *Council and Commission (Bangladesh)* [1993] I ECR 3685 illustrates. In this case the Parliament sought to annul a decision taken by the member states to provide humanitarian aid to Bangladesh on the basis that this was an act of the Council which had budgetary implications and thus should have been adopted under Article 272 of the EC Treaty. The Council objected that this was an act of the member states rather than the Council and therefore not within the scope of Article 230 and the Court agreed. It was an exercise of the collective competence of the member states, rather than an EC act.

[40] Strictly speaking, the first such cases were brought under the ECSC treaty, as Article 38 ECSC specifically allows for an action to review to be brought against the Parliament. These were actions brought by Luxembourg against the Parliament on the occasion when the Parliament moved its plenary sessions and committees from Luxembourg to Strasbourg and Brussels. Case 230/81 *Luxembourg* v *Parliament* [1983] ECR 255. Case 294/83 *Parti Ecologiste 'Les Verts'* v *European Parliament* [1986] ECR 1339.

[41] Ibid. at para 23.

that the Court ignored 'the distinction between what law ought to be and what it is – a distinction fundamental to the western concept of law'.[42] Hartley's distinction may be fundamental to one western tradition – the positivism of Hart, Austin or Kelsen, who aspired to describe law as an autonomous system, distinct from morality and politics – but the separation of law and morality is not considered fundamental by those who see the law as inevitably reflecting the political and moral judgments of its creators.[43] Moreover, what is 'the law' in this context? Merely the wording of Article 230 or, more expansively, 'the law' referred to in Article 220, which must be observed by the institutions? In justifying its judgment, the Court stated that '…the general scheme of the Treaty is to make a direct action available against "all measures adopted by the institutions…which are intended to have legal effects…"' The Court reasoned that the Parliament was not originally mentioned in Article 230, as it originally had only powers of consultation and political control, rather than the ability to adopt binding measures. But it concluded that it was never intended that the Parliament be immune from suit where it had the ability to adopt binding measures, i.e. under Article 95 ECSC Treaty, as evidenced by the fact that it was not immune to actions for annulment under Article 38 of that the ECSC Treaty. Craig suggests another rationale – that the Court wished to emphasise the fact that the Community was open to all shades of political party, and in that sense representative of European opinion. Borrowing a phrase from John Hart Ely, Craig and de Búrca argue that the Court was willing to use its own power to ensure that the democratic system was not used by the 'ins' to exclude or prejudice the 'outs'.[44]

LOCUS STANDI

Locus standi, or more simply, standing, is much the most complex and difficult aspect of Article 230, and has provoked considerable case law. In the US, where standing is rather more liberal (at least as far as review of administrative decisions is concerned) a well-known academic testified to Congress that the concept of standing 'is among the most amorphous in the entire domain of public law'.[45] This statement rings just as true of *locus standi* for direct actions in the Community courts.[46]

---

[42] TC Hartley, *The Foundations of European Community Law* (Oxford: Clarendon Press, 1994) at 87–88.

[43] E.g. critical legal theorists, natural lawyers or Ronald Dworkin, to name but a few.

[44] Craig and de Búrca (eds) *EU law* (Oxford: OUP 1998) at p 486 fn 68. JH Ely, *Democracy and Distrust: A Theory of Judicial Review* (Harvard University Press, 1980).

[45] Per Professor Freund, hearings before subcommittee on constitutional rights of the committee on the Judiciary, 89th Congress, 2nd session, 498 1966.

[46] See e.g. A Ward, *Judicial Review of the rights of private parties in EC Law* (Oxford: OUP, 2000). For a recent example of the denial of standing see joined cases T-175/98, T-178/98–177/98 *Salamander et al v European Parliament and Council* [2000] ECR II-2487, in which the applicant companies were denied standing in an action brought to annul the tobacco advertising directive.

Privileged applicants

The Court's international law origins are clear in Article 230(2) whereby an action may be brought by a member state, the Council, the Commission or the Parliament. These are known as privileged applicants, and much of the litigation conducted by them under Article 230 tends to be constitutional in nature, such as the action for the annulment of the tobacco advertising directive brought by Germany on the basis that the EC had exceeded its competence.[47]

Until the Treaty of Nice, the Parliament could only bring actions for the purpose of protecting its prerogatives as is still the case for the court of Auditors and the ECB. This provision was added to Article 230 by the TEU to reflect the Court's judgment in the *Chernobyl*[48] decision, as prior to then, the Parliament had no standing under Article 230 at all. In *Chernobyl*, the Parliament applied to annul a Council Regulation taken under the Euratom treaty establishing the permitted level of radioactive contamination of foodstuffs following the nuclear disaster of Chernobyl. The Parliament's argument was that the measure should have been taken under Article 95 (then Article 100A) of the EC Treaty instead, which gave the Parliament greater rights in the legal process through the cooperation procedure. The Court followed the opinion of Advocate General Van Gerven,[49] who spoke of a 'Parliament under tutelage' as an affront to the rule of law. The Court also stated, 'Observance of the institutional balance means that each institution must exercise its powers with due regard for the powers of the other institutions. It also requires that it should be possible to penalise any breach of that rule which might occur.'[50] Hartley has been as critical of this case as of *Les Verts*, writing 'it is hard to imagine a clearer example of changing the law while supposedly interpreting it'.[51] However, there was surely a clear justification for the solution in *Chernobyl*, that the Court aimed to create procedural protections for the democratically elected Parliament, so as to maximise the Parliament's input into the Community law-making process (which was even smaller prior to Maastricht and Amsterdam than at present) and thus help minimise the 'democracy deficit'.[52]

This may be so: the EC certainly needs to do all it can to remedy its democratic deficit. Nonetheless, the concept of a Parliament with standing is somewhat alien, given that parliamentary procedure is not designed for litigation, and opinion in parliament is fragmented and expressed through discussion and debate. Nevertheless, since *Chernobyl*, the Parliament has not been slow to litigate, chal-

---

[47] See Chapter 4, for a discussion of this case.

[48] Case C-70/88 *Parliament* v *Council* [1990] ECR I-2041.

[49] And that of Advocate General Darmon, in the earlier *Comitology* case (Case 302/87 *European Parliament* v *Council (Comitology)* [1988] ECR 5615), who unlike the Court itself in that case, opined that the Parliament should have the jurisdiction to challenge the comitology decision.

[50] *Chernobyl* at para 22.

[51] Hartley op. cit. at p 88.

[52] This is of course similar to that used to justify the Court's reasoning in *Les Verts*, namely that democracy demands equal opportunity of access of all political parties to the electoral process.

lenging acts which it feels that the Council has adopted on the wrong legal basis, even if it does not disagree with the substance of those acts.[53]

Non-privileged applicants

Article 230(4) reads as follows: 'Any natural or legal person may, under the same conditions, institute proceedings against a decision addressed to that person or against a decision which, although in the form of a regulation or a decision addressed to another person, is of direct and individual concern to the former.'

Thus, under this tortuously worded section natural or legal persons may only challenge measurers which are either:

(a) decisions addressed to themselves;

(b) decisions in the form of a regulation which are of direct and legal concern to them;

(c) decisions addressed to another person which are of direct and individual concern to them.

Not only does the wording of Article 230(4) restrict the range of measures which may be challenged, but the Court has also applied this measure very restrictively, if not always consistently: even members of the Court have attacked the Court's restrictive approach to Article 230.[54] In this respect the Court has certainly not lived up to the opinion of one of its first Advocates General, Lagrange, who, in its early days, ironically as it now seems, wrote that the Court 'has tried to open its forum as much as possible to private persons'.[55]

As Feldman has commented,[56] the standing of citizens before the courts in public law cases reflects more than just a bare legal rule, but rather 'the rights and responsibilities of citizenship and the relationship between electors, legislatures, executives, courts and the disenfranchised'.[57] Feldman suggests that 'prevailing ideas of democracy and constitutionalism shape the capacity of private citizens to use forms and procedures of public law'. In the case of Article 230, limited standing rights would seem to reflect, on the one hand, the unwillingness of the Court to become involved in reassessing legislation (very often measures under the CAP or customs tariff,

---

[53] E.g. Case C-295/90 *Students' Rights of Residence Directive case* [1992] I ECR 4193; C-316/91 *Fourth Lomé Convention* [1994] I ECR 625 ; C-187/93 *Waste Case* [1994] I ECR 2857; but also the *Bangladesh Case*, where, although it failed to show that its prerogatives had been infringed, the Parliament did succeed in getting the Court to examine the substantive issues and to find illegality.

[54] E.g. W Van Gerven, 'The Legal Protection of Private Parties in the Law of the European Economic Communities' in F Jacobs (ed.) *European Law and the Individual* (North Holland, 1976) 1; Mancini and Keeling, 'Democracy and the European Court of Justice' (1994) 57 MLR 175 at 188; Slynn in Case 246/81 *Lord Bethell v Commission* [1982] ECR 2277, who argued that 'natural and legal persons should have a wider right of challenge before the Court in regard to activities of the Commission'.

[55] M Lagrange, 'The Role of the Court of Justice of the European Communities as seen through its case Law' (1961) 26 Law and Contemporary Problems 403.

[56] D Feldman, 'Public Interest Litigation and Constitutional Theory in Comparative Perspective' (1992) 55 MLR 1.

[57] Feldman op. cit. at 44.

which are the objects of a large part of Article 230 challenges) which has a strong discretionary component, and thus usurping the Commission and Council,[58] and on the other, an underdeveloped approach to the rights to legal redress of European citizens whose interests are affected by the ever increasing impact of European legislation. It does not seem to have taken their citizenship very seriously.

(a) Decisions addressed to themselves

A typical example might be a company wishing to challenge a decision finding it to be in breach of the EC competition rules. Such cases are generally unproblematic as far as standing is concerned, although they may raise problems of admissibility regarding the status of the act, i.e. whether it is a reviewable act, which has already been considered.

(b) Decisions in the form of regulations[59]

It is virtually impossible for an individual to challenge a true regulation. This is in line with the law of many EU member states, in which it is not possible for an individual to challenge general legislation. But what is a true regulation?[60] According to Article 249 EC, 'A regulation shall have general application. It shall be binding in its entirety and directly applicable in all Member States.' In contrast, Article 249 provides that 'A decision shall be binding in its entirety upon those to whom it is addressed.' In *Confédération Nationale des Producteurs de Fruits et Légumes* v *Commission*[61] the Court elaborated on these provisions in the following way: 'The essential characteristics of a decision arise from the limitation of the persons to whom it is addressed, whereas a regulation, being essentially of a legislative nature, is applicable not to a limited number of persons, defined or identifiable, but to categories of persons viewed abstractly and in their entirety.'

However, Article 249 is descriptive only, and does not instruct the Community institutions which type of measure should be used to implement a particular policy. Instead, instructions are contained in specific provisions of the Treaty, but, in a significant number of cases, this choice is left to the institutions themselves, with the result that the distinction between regulations and decisions has become blurred. Many EC policies (especially the highly regulated field of the CAP) are implemented by directly applicable regulations which have a considerable impact on individuals (e.g. raising levies or decreasing subsidies) but which are in many ways more akin

---

[58] This motivation is reassessed below.

[59] Article 230 only refers to regulations and decisions but individuals can also challenge directives if they can show them to be decision-like in nature. The leading case is C-298/89 *Government of Gibraltar* v *Council* [1993] ECR I-3605.

[60] M Hedemann-Robinson, 'Article 173 EC, General Community Measures and Locus Standi for Private Persons: Still a Cause for Individual Concern?' (1996) 2 European Public Law; see also J Schwarze, *European Administrative Law* (Sweet and Maxwell, 1992) at 251–2.

[61] Cases 16–17/62 [1962] ECR 471.

to administrative than legislative measures. The ECJ has, however, made it hard for non-privileged applicants to challenge such measures.

Calpak v *Commission*[62] shows just how difficult this can be. In this case the applicants sought annulment of a regulation which concerned production aids for Williams pears preserved in syrup. This regulation restricted the amount of aid granted to processors to 105 per cent of the amount they had produced the previous year. The applicants considered this test less favourable to them than the previous test which had calculated aid on the basis of average quantity of production over three years. This later seemed to be a fairer way of quantifying aid as the quantity of pears preserved in any year depended on the size of the crop: when the crop was heavier it would be more profitable to preserve pears. In the 1978/79 marketing year, Italian production of Williams pears was extremely low, and the applicants had processed only a small quantity. The applicants submitted that undertakings which processed Williams pears during 1978/79 marketing year formed a closed and definable group, the members of whom were identifiable to the Commission when it adopted the contested regulation.[63] This argument was rejected by the Court, which found their application inadmissible, holding: 'In fact the measure applies to objectively determined situations and produces legal effects with regard to categories of persons described in a generalised and abstract manner. The nature of the measure as a regulation is not called in question by the mere fact that it is possible to determine the number or even identity of the producers to be granted the aid which is limited thereby.'[64]

As Craig notes,[65] the Court in *Calpak* pointed out the reason for allowing individuals to challenge measures in the form of a regulation. This was to prevent Community institutions from being in a position, merely by choosing the form of a regulation, to exclude an application by an individual which concerns them directly and individually.[66] By clever drafting it would have been possible for the Community to immunise its measures from challenge, especially given the discretion left to the institution as to its choice of measure, mentioned above. Thus, the Court said, the choice of **form** cannot change the nature of a measure. But Craig criticises this test as, rather than looking behind form to substance, it comes perilously close to looking behind form to form.[67] It will always be possible to draft a measure so that it satisfies the abstract terminology test, even if the measure in fact only applies to a few individuals, as in *Calpak* and many other cases.

Somewhat inconsistently, however, the Court has not always taken this approach. It has also applied a 'closed category' test. In such cases, an applicant will succeed

---

[62] Joined Cases 789 and 790/79 *Calpak* v *Commission* [1980] ECR 1949.

[63] As Advocate General Warner noted, there were only 38 processors in the Community, fifteen in France and twenty-three in Italy: *Calpak* at 1967.

[64] This 'abstract terminology' test was also applied in other cases: e.g. Cases 103–109/78 *Beauport* v *Council and Commission* [1979] ECR 17; Cases 162/78 *Wagner* v *Commission* [1979] ECR 3647; Case 45/81 *Alexander Moksel* v *Commission* [1982] ECR 1129.

[65] Craig 'Legality, standing and substantive review in community law' (1994) 14 OJLS 507 at 514.

[66] *Calpak* para 7.

[67] Craig op. cit. OJLS at 515.

if it can be shown that the measure in question, although framed in general and abstract terms, applies only to a closed category of persons. In *International Fruit* v *Commission*,[68] the applicant was challenging a measure in the form of a regulation by which the Commission granted applications to import apples from non-member states. Importers had to apply in advance for a licence from their national authorities who would then pass on those details to the Commission which would decide the applications in question. Thus the regulation covered only a limited or closed category: those who had applied for a licence the previous week. The Court found the application admissible (holding that the relevant provision was in fact a bundle of decisions) and later adopted the same approach in some other cases.[69] However, the Court of First Instance has more recently returned to the abstract terminology test and been less reluctant to find applications admissible.[70]

(c) Decisions addressed to another person

In this context the word 'person' is a bit misleading. It is often the case that the disputed decision will be addressed to a member state rather than another individual or company.[71] Generally the member state concerned will have requested authorisation from the Community to do something: to levy a duty on imports or exports of a particular product, for example, and it is that situation which the applicant challenges. In such cases, the applicant does not have to overcome the hurdle of establishing that the measure is not a normative act, but they have the equally difficult obstacle of establishing that they are **directly and individually concerned** as required by Article 230(4).

Direct concern

Direct concern requires that there be a direct causal connection between the contested act and its effect on the applicant. If there has been any intervention between the passing of the measure and its effect on the applicant, capable of breaking the causal link, then the applicant is unlikely to be directly concerned. This will especially be the case where a member state is given discretion to implement a measure.[72] In the recent *Salamander* case,[73] the CFI held that the applicants were not directly concerned by the tobacco advertising directive, which they sought to

---

[68] Cases 41–4/70 *International Fruit Company* v *Commission* [1971] ECR 411.

[69] Case 100/74 *Cam* v *Commission* [1975] ECR 1393; Case 88/76 *Exportation des Sucres* v *Commission* [1977] ECR 709; Case 123/77 *UNICME* v *Council* [1978] ECR 845; 138/79 *Roquette* [1980] ECR 3333.

[70] E.g. *Campo Ebro*, see discussion below. However, in case T-32/98 T41/98 *Netherlands Antilles* v *Commission* [2000] ECR II-201, the CFI did find the applicant entitled to challenge a regulation on the basis that, although it was a measure of general nature, the applicant was individually concerned as the Commission had been obliged to take account of the applicant's particular situation.

[71] Unless the applicant is a complainant in competition cases, as in e.g. *Metro*, discussed below.

[72] See Case 222/83 *Municipality of Differdange* v *Commission* [1984] ECR 2889, also Case T-244/00 *Co; llre Teorantel* v *Commission* [2001] ECR II-1275.

[73] Joined Cases T-172/98, T-175–177/98 *Salamander et al* v *European Parliament and Council* [2000] ECR II-2487.

challenge, as it left to member states a power of assessment, or discretion. However, generally, direct concern is easier to establish than individual concern, which will now be considered.

Individual concern

The following scenario is typical of the sort of problems raised in this context. Imagine that the subsidy for butter is increased (as an attempt to relieve the EC of its tedious 'butter mountain'). As a result, margarine producers complain that their sales are affected.[74] Who may bring a legal challenge against it? Who has a legitimate interest in this decision? Margarine producers in the EC? Consumer groups? In the US, a wide approach to the question of standing (in administrative law at least) has been taken under section 10 of the Administrative Procedure Act which states: 'A person suffering a legal wrong because of agency action, or adversely affected or aggrieved by it...is entitled to judicial review thereof.'[75] The European Court has certainly not progressed this far in its interpretation of 'individual concern'. Lord Diplock's explanation of the requirement for standing in judicial review was 'to prevent the time of the court being wasted by busybodies with misguided or trivial complaints or administrative ardour...'[76] However, it may be difficult to secure agreement as to whether a particular individual is in fact a busybody.[77] Arnull cites Lord Rees-Mogg, who sought a declaration under English law that the UK could not ratify the Maastricht Treaty[78] (and whose standing to do so was not contested by the Secretary of State) as a possible problem case for 'busybodyhood'. The problem is that tests limiting standing involve normative judgments identifying those 'concerned' in a way courts wish to recognise. And the Community Courts have not wished to recognise very many.

Indeed, the Community Courts seem to have attempted to deal with the problem of individual standing by simply seeking to exclude nearly everyone. The case that is usually cited in this context is *Plaumann*,[79] an early decision of the ECJ. Plaumann, an importer of clementines, wished to challenge a decision of the Commission addressed to the German government, which refused the government's request to suspend duties on clementines imported from third countries. The Court, after stating that the provisions of Article 230 'must not be interpreted restrictively' then went on to produce a restrictive test for individual concern:

---

[74] A scenario in fact very like that which gave rise to the *Deutsche Lebensmittelwerke* (Case 97/85 [1987] ECR 2265) case in which the ECJ did not find the margarine producers' claim admissible.

[75] Although US case law has not abandoned the requirement for a material interest as *Sierra Club* v *Morton* 405 US 727 (1972), in which an environmental group tried to assert claims on behalf of the natural environment failed: also see C Stone, *Should trees have standing?* (Los Altos: CA Kaufmann, 1974); L Tribe, *Ways not to think about plastic trees* (1974) 84 Yale Law Journal 1315.

[76] *R v IRC, ex parte National Federation of Self Employed and Small Businesses Ltd* [1982] AC 617 (HL) at 643.

[77] Arnull, 'Private applicants in the action for annulment under Article 173' (1995) 32 CMLRev 7 at 10.

[78] *R v Secretary of State for Foreign and Commonwealth affairs, ex parte Lord Rees-Mogg* [1993] 3 CMLR 101.

[79] Case 25/62 *Plaumann* [1963] ECR 95.

Persons other than those to whom a decision is addressed may only claim to be individually concerned if that decision affects them by reason of certain attributes which
are peculiar to them or by reason of circumstances in which they are differentiated
from all other persons and by virtue of those factors distinguishes them individually
just as in the case of the person addressed. In the present case the applicant is affected
by the disputed decision as an importer of clementines, that is to say, by reason of a
commercial activity which may at any time be practised by any person and is not therefore such as to distinguish the applicant in relation to the contested Decision as in the
case of the addressee.

Therefore, the individual must show a particular suffering, although the Court
does not specify which characteristics 'peculiar to them' will suffice to establish
individual concern. However, from decided case law, it seems that the following
effects are not sufficient: showing that your business interests were adversely
affected (*Plaumann*), nor that you have been affected more severely than other
traders (*Calpak*). Neither it seems will the fact that the applicant's identity was
known to the Commission when the measure was passed. Even establishing that
you were the cause of the measure will not necessarily do the trick, if the measure
is to take effect subsequently and thus affect others, if only theoretically. The
Plaumann test certainly does not seem to have been designed with the protection
of individuals in mind. Craig has been very critical of the test, suggesting that it is
economically unrealistic: 'If there are only a very limited number of firms pursuing
a certain trade this is not fortuitous, nor is the number of those firms likely to rise
overnight...if there are two firms in the industry this is because they can satisfy
the current market demand...The argument that...importing clementines can be
undertaken by any person is...unconvincing...'[80] The test may also be criticised
on conceptual grounds, as suggested by Advocate General Roemer in the *Eridania*
case. Roemer thought it mistaken to take account of the future effect of a decision
(as the Court appears to, by categorising a measure as general because others
could, potentially, still enter the class in future) since, if this were the case, it would
never be possible to claim individual concern in relation to a measure which had
permanent effect, even though at the time it was made the decision affected only
one firm.[81]

The test for individual concern is very similar to the closed category test mentioned in the last section, so that if an applicant can establish that they are a member of a closed category they have little difficulty in showing they are individually
concerned. *International Fruit*, mentioned above, provides an example of such a situation.[82]

What is notable about the case law on *locus standi* so far, is that, unlike in the
case of a reviewable act, the court is unwilling to consider the particular **effect** of a
measure on the individual applicant. In the *Cimenteries* case, the Court was willing
to categorise the Commission 'letter' as a decision, because it affected the applicant's

---

[80] Craig op. cit. at 509.
[81] Cases 10 and 18/68 *Societa 'Eridania' Zuccherifici Nazionali v Commission* [1969] ECR 459, 492.
[82] See also Case 112/77 *Toepfer v Commission* [1978] ECR 1019.

situation. In contrast, when considering standing, the Court shows a remarkable reluctance to consider an effects based test. The fact that the applicants in *Calpak* or *Plaumann* were more severely affected than others is irrelevant.

A MORE LIBERAL CASE LAW?

The cases described so far obviously adopt a very restrictive approach to standing. However, most recent commentators on Article 230 have separated the case law into two groups: the former comprising cases mainly concerned with the CAP, of the sort described above, and the latter involving a group of so-called 'quasi-judicial' decisions[83] within the field of competition law, anti-dumping procedures and state aids.

If the challenge is of the former kind, it might typically allege a breach of Article 34(2) EC, which prohibits discrimination between producers and consumers in the EC in the common organisation of agricultural markets. Article 34(2) also provides that the CAP shall be limited to pursuit of objectives in Article 33. However, the objectives set out in Article 33 are wide-ranging in nature and may collide with each other. They include increasing agricultural productivity; stabilising markets; assuring availability of supplies; and reasonable prices for consumers. In executing the CAP, the Commission and Council may have to make difficult discretionary choices, which may not always please all concerned. The ECJ does not want to be continually reassessing the discretionary choices made by other institutions, otherwise it would be swamped, so it employs very strict tests of standing.

However, in the 'quasi-judicial' cases, the Community institution concerned (usually the Commission) is involved in a procedure of an inquisitorial nature, for example the determination of whether a given undertaking has breached Article 81(1) of the EC Treaty by acting in an anti-competitive way. The key feature which distinguishes these cases from those described in the preceding paragraphs is that, rather than involving discretionary decisions which are typically taken under the Common Agriculture Policy, these decisions involve predominantly issues of fact and law. The parties challenging these decisions have also very often played some sort of part in the proceedings and in these cases it seems to be easier to demonstrate standing to challenge a decision resulting from that process, sometimes characterised as rights of 'due process'.[84]

The distinction made between these two types of case is a valid one, but does it justify the Court's far more restrictive approach in the CAP cases? It would seem not. Just because, in general, CAP cases involve broad discretionary decisions, does not mean that an applicant does not have a compelling case in many particular instances. This point is supported by the amount of challenges which, initially failing under Article 230 for lack of *locus standi*, are successfully brought to measures under an Article 234 preliminary reference, such as the *KSH*[85] case. *KSH* resulted

---

[83] This term is used by Hartley op. cit. at 378.
[84] See R Stewart, *The Reform of American Administrative Law* 1975 88 Harv LR 1667.
[85] Case 101/76 *KSH v Council and Commission* [1977] ECR 797.

from the EC's isoglucose disaster, in which the Community had taken steps to deal with the EC 'sugar mountain'. So the Community authorities imposed a crippling levy on isoglucose, a product in competition with sugar. This made production uneconomic and the Dutch firm, KSH, was forced into liquidation. The number of isoglucose producers in the EC was very small (about six) and unlikely to increase as some of their technology was protected by patents. The Community authorities involved were probably aware of their identity. However, the Court ruled that the measures were true regulations and that KSH had no *locus standi*. Is this case fair? Are the circumstances so distinguishable from *Extramet*, discussed below?

Competition, state aids and anti-dumping cases

A case frequently cited is *Metro* v *Commission (No. 2)*[86] in which the Court held that the applicant had standing to challenge a Commission decision addressed to another undertaking, SABA, granting exemption from Article 81(1) to SABA's distribution system of its electrical products. Metro had been refused admission to SABA's system and had complained to the Commission that SABA was breaching Article 81, by operating a selective distribution system. The Court found Metro's action admissible. The Court's reasoning was partly based on the fact that complainants have a special status, with certain procedural rights under Article 3(2)(b) of Regulation 17/62. If the Court had applied the *Plaumann* test, their action would surely have failed, because the persons affected by the decision were an open category – those self-service wholesalers of electrical goods who wished to handle SABA's products.

The ECJ has taken a similarly broader approach in the fields of state aids[87] and anti-dumping, holding that involvement in the procedure leading to the adoption of an act may be of relevance in establishing the applicant's *locus standi*. Dumping occurs when goods are imported into the Community at a price below that of the same goods in their home market, thus threatening the market position of producers in the Community. This is normally remedied by an anti-dumping duty imposed on the imported product by way of regulation. Anti-dumping measures are in principle acts of general application which concern all imports of the product from the country concerned. They do not apply to specific persons, although the names of certain companies may appear in their text.[88] If one adhered to the strict view that they are regulations, then individuals who were not mentioned in the act would not have standing and this would be particularly harsh on complainants who participated in the procedure and had a right to complain under the basic regulation. They would in effect be deprived of their right to complain if they could not challenge the Commission's response. On the other hand, a finding that the anti-dumping measures

---

[86] Case 26/76 *Metro v Commission* [1977] ECR 1875.

[87] Case 169/84 *COFAZ v Commission* [1986] ECR 391.

[88] As did those of the major producers in the *Japanese ball-bearings* Case 113/77 *NTN v Council* [1979] ECR 1185; Case 118/77 *ISO v Council* [1979] ECR 1277; Case 119/77 *Nippon Seiko v Council and Commission* [1979] ECR 1303; Case 120/77 *Koyo Seiko v Council and Commission* [1979] ECR 1337; Case 121/77 *Nachi Fujikoshi v Council* [1979] ECR 1363.

were in fact decisions would mean that they were all being adopted in the wrong form and thus voidable. In order to find its way out of this dilemma, the Court has tended conveniently to overlook the decision/regulation distinction and instead focus on individual concern. In *Timex* v *Council and Commission*[89] the Court held that anti-dumping regulations were legislative in nature and scope, inasmuch as they apply to traders in general,[90] but went on to state that the regulation was 'a decision which is of direct and individual concern to Timex',[91] and thus Timex had standing: it had participated in the investigation, and the duty had been fixed with regard to the effect of the dumping on Timex (the only British manufacturer).[92]

However, until the *Extramet*[93] case, it seemed that importers of dumped products would not have standing to challenge anti-dumping regulations. The ECJ seemed to take the view that importers could use the alternative means of Article 234 to challenge the regulation by bringing a national action against the agency collecting the duty. The national court could then make a reference under Article 234. But, in *Extramet*, decided in 1991, the Court took a new step. Extramet was a company importing calcium from China and the former Soviet Union. Following a complaint from the Electrometallurgy trade association, the Commission imposed anti-dumping duty on those imports and Extramet challenged it. In hearing Extramet's action, the Court held that Extramet had established the existence of a set of factors which differentiated it as regards the regulation from all other traders. These factors were that the applicant was the largest importer in the Community and the end user of the product. The applicant was also to a large extent economically dependent on imports of the product as the only supplier of the product within the Community was its main competitor and unwilling to supply it. In these circumstances, not allowing Extramet standing would have amounted to a denial of justice.[94] Of course, the same arguments could have been applied in *Calpak*, *Plaumann* and *KSH*, but were not, by the Court.

A new direction?

Was the approach in *Extramet* to be limited to anti-dumping, or at least 'quasi-judicial' cases? If so, it was becoming ever harder to reconcile the Court's cases in competition law with other areas. In *Codorniu*,[95] the Court showed a willingness to be more flexible outside of the charmed 'quasi-judicial' circle. *Codorniu v Council*

---

[89] Case 264/82 [1985] ECR 849.
[90] *Timex*, para 12.
[91] *Timex*, para 16.
[92] In Joined Cases 239 and 275/82 *Allied Corporation* v *Commission* [1984] ECR 1005, the Court held that 'measures imposing anti-dumping duties are liable to be of direct and individual concern to those producers and exporters who are able to establish that they were identified in the measures adopted by the Commission or the Council or were concerned in the preliminary investigations' (para 12). Subsidiaries of producers named in anti-dumping regulations were also held to have individual concern in Case 113/77 *NTN Toyo Bearing Company Limited and Others* v *Council* (1979) ECR.
[93] Case C-358/89 *Extramet* v *Council* [1991] ECR 1-2501.
[94] N Neuwahl, 'Article 173 Paragraph 4 EC: Past, Present and Possible Future' (1996) 21 EL Rev at 27.
[95] Case C-309/89 *Codorniu* [1994] ECR I-1853.

in fact concerned the CAP. A Spanish producer of sparkling wine sought annulment of a provision in a regulation concerning the word *cremant*, a designation of quality to sparkling wines which satisfied certain criteria. One of these was that the wine had to have been produced in France or Luxembourg. The regulation was subject to a five-year transitional period before it came into effect. However, the applicant had used the label '*Gran cremant*' for its product (quality sparkling wines known as *cava*) for years and it had registered the trade mark '*Gran Cremant de Codorniu*' in Spain in 1924. Did *Codorniu* have standing under Article 230 to challenge the regulation?

Advocate General Lenz[96] pointed out the discrepancies in the Court's jurisprudence. If the abstract terminology test were applied then the measure in question had to be treated as a regulation because it was worded generally so that it applied to all future sparkling wine producers.[97] However, if the Court were to apply the more liberal competition and anti-dumping case law, and to focus on specific effects of the regulation on Codorniu, a very different conclusion would be reached, and Lenz suggested that the ECJ adopt the latter route. He proposed a twofold test. First, the applicant would have to show it belonged to a fixed group of persons which could not be enlarged after adoption of the measure in question. In *Codorniu* this was satisfied by belonging to a closed class of traders affected by the five-year transitional period. Second, the applicant would have to show that the contested measure had a specific impact on their own situation. This was difficult for Codorniu to maintain, as the regulation applied to all potential future traders. AG Lenz suggested it would be sufficient if Codorniu showed that the measure had special economic effects for it which distinguished it from rest of those affected in the same way as if it had been the addressee of a Decision, and he thought this was satisfied by Codorniu's special market position in being the single largest producer of *cremant* sparkling wine in the EC, as well as of two-thirds Spanish *cava* wine. Before the Court gave judgment in *Codorniu* Advocate General Van Gerven endorsed the Lenz opinion in *Abertal* v *Commission and Council*.[98]

Unfortunately, the judgment of the Court in *Codorniu* lacks the scope of reasoning and proceeds rather more cautiously than Advocate General Lenz, probably because of disagreement among its members. It held that Codorniu had *locus standi* but it is unclear whether it agreed with the second part of Lenz's test. In fact, the Court started rather discouragingly for the applicant by repeating that the legislative nature of a measure was not called into question by the fact that the number or identity of those to whom it applied could be identified. But, somewhat incompatibly, the Court then continued, 'By reserving the right to use the term *cremant* to

---

[96] Ibid. at 1869.

[97] A previous similar case, *Binderer*, had been decided on that basis. Binderer, a wine merchant had enquired of the Commission whether he could use a German expression to market wines produced in Hungary and Yugoslavia. He was told he could, but the Commission then passed a regulation prohibiting the use of the words in question. Binderer's challenge failed, as the Court held he lacked *locus standi*: not even the fact that he had previously consulted the Commission was sufficient to single him out according to the Court. Case 147/83 *Binderer* v *Commission* [1985] ECR 257.

[98] Cases C-213/91 and C-264/91 [1993] ECR I-3189.

French and Luxembourg producers, the contested provision prevents Codorniu from using its graphic trade mark . . . It follows that Codorniu has established the existence of a situation which from the point of view of the contested provision differentiates it from all other traders.'[99] The Court then quashed the contested provision for breach of the principle of non-discrimination.

There has been a lot of discussion about the possible meaning and effect of the *Codorniu* decision. First, it has been suggested that the Court's reasoning implies that one need only show individual concern and need no longer show that the contested regulation is also a decision. Furthermore, the test for individual concern seems to have been relaxed, a particularly serious impact on the applicant's business now being regarded as sufficient, even if it is a measure which apparently affects the market generally.[100]

But the Court offers little guidance as to how to assess the impact of legislation on individuals to determine whether they are individually or just generally concerned. This lack of guidance makes *Codorniu* of limited value as a precedent. It is also unwise to assume that the Court fully accepted Lenz's opinion, particularly given that, although it had two years to consider the Advocate General's opinion, there was no reference to it in their judgment.[101]

The Court of First Instance has tended not to carry forward the *Codorniu* approach in its more recent decisions. This is unsurprising, given the lack of guidance offered by that case. Indeed, some of its recent case law seems inconsistent with *Codorniu*.[102] In *Campo Ebro*, the CFI held the applicants were affected in the same way as any other existing or future traders in the Community sugar market, despite the fact that they had protected the product by patent registration and licensing. The CFI also seemed to reject the possibility of using economic criteria to show that, by virtue of the measure's effect on their business (as in *Extramet*), they were individually concerned. The fact that the applicants could be described as being in a uniquely disadvantaged competitive position was insufficient as far as the Court was concerned.

Representative groups, pressure groups and public interest actions

Groups are very active within the framework of EC law (e.g. in lobbying the Commission and Parliament) and yet the rules of standing under Article 230 make

---

[99] *Codorniu* paras 19–23.
[100] E.g. Arnull, op. cit.; Hedemann-Robinson, op. cit.; J Usher, 'Individual concern in general legislation: 10 years on' (1994) EL Rev at 637.
[101] Arnull, op. cit. at 39–40, highlights the unusual delay before judgment was delivered: the application was launched in October 1989, Advocate General Lenz gave his opinion in October 1992, and the Court did not deliver judgment until May 1994 (a total of four and a half years overall, when direct applications take on average two years); see also Arnull 'Private applicants and the action for annulment since *Codorniu*' (2001) 38 CMLRev 7.
[102] E.g. Case T-83/92 *Zunis Holdings SA v Commission* [1993] ECR II 1169; Case T-472/93 *Campo Ebro Industrial SA v Council* [1995] ECR II 421.

no special provision for this. The *Fruit and Vegetables*[103] case seems to block the way to a class action in the ECJ. A trade association sought associational standing to challenge a Council Regulation which abolished quantitative restrictions on the import of fruits and vegetables. The ECJ would not accept that the group could, in its capacity as a representative of a class of tradespeople, be individually concerned by a general measure. This would:

> result in the grouping, under the heading of a single legal person, of the interests properly attributed to the members of a category, who have been affected as individuals by genuine regulations, and would derogate from the system of the treaty which allows application for annulment of private individuals only of decisions which have been addressed to them...[104]

This seems objectionable for a number of reasons. In the US, class actions are defended in terms of judicial economy and efficiency:[105] to discourage group actions is inefficient. Second, it is unfair. Multinationals and monopolies which are more able to show individuation are strengthened at the expense of small companies and individuals, who are deprived of the mutual support needed to win complex court cases. Finally, the *Fruit and Vegetables* decision is a temptation to present a set of decisions in regulatory form and so protect them from judicial review, exactly what the Treaty drafters did not desire and apparently recognised as a danger by the Court in *Calpak*. A more appropriate test might be whether the measure was 'aimed at' the victim.[106] If it was, then, however many victims exist, they should be individually and directly concerned.

The BEUC (*Bureau Européen des Unions des Consommateurs*) has played an important role in challenging Community law. This is partly because it has often been a participant in EC competition proceedings and thus able to challenge Community acts under the Court's more liberal case law. In *BEUC v Commission*[107] BEUC actually based its claim to standing on the argument that consumer interests were best expressed by a representative body. BEUC had been involved in anti-dumping proceedings and wanted to challenge anti-dumping regulations subsequently imposed on imports of audio cassettes from the Far East, on the basis that the regulations did not make room for representative groups. The ECJ held the action admissible on the basis that BEUC was 'directly affected' by the Commission decision, but went on to find against BEUC on the merits.

But outside of the competition law field, more recent case law of the CFI is not encouraging to group actions, even where it appears that the applicants have some sort of procedural rights. In *Associazone Agricoltori della Provincia di Rovigo*

---

[103] Cases 16, 17/62 *Confédération Nationale des Fruits et Producteurs des Fruits et Légumes* v *Council* [1962] ECR 471.

[104] Ibid.

[105] S Yeazell, 'From Group Litigation to Class Action' (1980) 27 *University of California Law Review* 767.

[106] A test used in the English case of *Lonrho v Shell Petroleum Co Ltd* (*No. 2*) [1982] AC 173 per Lord Diplock.

[107] Case C-170/89 *Bureau Europeen des Unions des Consommateurs (BEUC)* v *Commission* [1991] ECR 5709.

v *Commission (Po Delta)*[108] the applicant associations of agriculturists challenged a Commission decision which approved the Italian government's plans for protecting the environment in the Po region funded by the EU. The Court found that none of the provisions put the Commission under a duty to take account of the particular situation of the applicants before granting financial assistance and thus they did not have standing as they were not affected differently from all the other residents in the Po Delta.[109]

In *Greenpeace v Commission*,[110] Greenpeace challenged a Commission decision addressed to Spain which granted aid under the EC Regional Aid Development Fund to build two power stations in the Canary islands. Greenpeace challenged the measure on the basis that the projects did not comply with Community environmental policy and also that the Spanish government had commenced construction without the appropriate Environmental Impact Assessment (EIA).[111] The CFI found the action inadmissible, holding that none of the applicants (residents of the Canaries, Greenpeace International, local environmental and tourist associations) had individual concern. The CFI also refused to take account of the applicants' point that their interests were environmental rather than economic, and thus that the *Plaumann* test should not apply. Greenpeace argued that it was individually concerned by virtue of its particularly important role in the process of legal control by representing general interests shared by a number of individuals in a focused and coordinated manner. As in *Po Delta*, the CFI refused to draw any distinction between the interest of individual applicants and representative associations, holding that only if an association represents a closed category of persons could it be granted standing.

On appeal to the ECJ, Greenpeace contended that special attention should be paid to the fact that the environment is a common good and that the usual test did not take this into account. They also claimed that the right to be informed and consulted in an EIPA procedure gave them a special status. In a brief judgment, the ECJ held that the CFI had not erred in denying Greenpeace *locus standi*. These decisions met with a lot of criticism. Most authors suggested that special consideration was needed, as environmental matters are usually difficult to relate to a personal interest. Several suggestions for changes in the standing rules have been made. One is that made by the applicants themselves, in the *Greenpeace* case, who proposed a new test for individual concern. This was that an association should be recognised as having *locus standi*, where its objectives concern environmental protection and one or more of their members are individually concerned by the contested Community decision.

---

[108] Case T-117/94 [1995] ECR II-455.
[109] See also T-219/95R *Danielsson v Commission* [1995] ECR II 3051, in which the CFI rejected an application for interim measures brought by residents of Tahiti (a *département outre-mer* of France and thus falling within the jurisdiction of the EC treaty) who were concerned about the Commission's refusal to apply Article 34 Euratom to French nuclear testing in the Pacific Ocean. Their application was rejected as the applicants were not affected in any way which differed from the other inhabitants of Tahiti.
[110] Case T-585/93 *Stichting Greenpeace Council v Commission* [1995] ECR II-2205.
[111] As required by Council Directive 85/337.

In any case, the approach of the Community Courts in *Greenpeace* may be usefully contrasted[112] with that of the English courts in *R v HMIP and MAFF ex parte Greenpeace*,[113] which arose out of facts concerning British Nuclear Fuel's operations at Sellafield. Greenpeace were seeking judicial review of HMIP/MAFF's authorisation to BNF's emission of waste. Otton J first held that the leave stage should filter out those applicants who had no interest, but that the question of whether the applicant had a **sufficient** interest should be left for the substantive hearing. At this later stage, he held that the Court had a discretion to be exercised with reference to matters of fact and law. Relevant factors in determining whether an applicant had a serious interest would include the nature of the applicant, the extent of the applicant's interest in the issue, its ability to mount a serious challenge and the ease with which other persons could mount a challenge. In his judgment Otton J took into account Greenpeace's international reputation stating that: '...with its particular experience in environmental matters, its access to experts in the relevant realms of science and technology (not to mention law) the applicant is able to mount a carefully selected, focused, relevant and well argued challenge' – an example of the approach conspicuously not adopted by the CFI.

However, in the *Perrier*[114] cases, the CFI did recognise that the applicant works councils were individually concerned, as they constituted a closed category which was clearly defined at the time of adoption of the decision. The applicants had also been given the express right to submit observations in the administrative procedure[115] and the CFI held that the action was admissible in so far as it was brought to ensure protection of their procedural guarantees. To this extent the case is in line with the previous 'more liberal' decisions. However, this was a pyrrhic victory, as the CFI held that as they were not **directly** concerned by the measure their application must be dismissed in its entirety.

The demand for wider access

This restrictive case law can be set against the fact that wider rights of access to the court are being demanded by public interest groups. As many of these groups are well-versed with US administrative procedure[116] this demand may increase. The

---

[112] As evidence that the European Courts are not alone in their strict approach to standing, the *Lujan* case, a decision of the US Supreme Court, may also be cited. Where constitutional suits are brought in the federal courts, the applicant must show that they have a 'case or controversy' under Article III US Constitution. In this case, an American environmental association with a particular interest in protecting animals, challenged a ruling by the Secretaries of the Interior and Commerce for failing to consult regarding endangered species. The Court dismissed the application, holding that they were 'seeking relief that no more directly and tangibly benefits [the plaintiffs] than it does the public at large...does not state an Article III case or controversy'. *Lujan v Defenders of Wildlife* (1992) 112 S Ct 2130. See also A Scalia, 'The Doctrine of Standing as an essential element of the Separation of Powers' (1983) 17 Suffolk UL Rev 881; Parker 'Standing to litigate abstract social interests' (1995) Col J tr L.

[113] [1994] 4 WLR 352.

[114] Cases T12/93 and T96/92 *Comité central d'Enterprise de la Société Générale des Grandes Sources v Commission* [1995] ECR II-1247.

[115] By virtue of Article 18(4) of Council regulation 4064/89.

[116] Which has more liberal standing rules than US constitutional law.

European Court of Justice has been accused in the past of 'revolting judicial behaviour.'[117] Perhaps one way to offset this impression of haughtiness might be to develop machinery for effective public interest representation in the European Court. But there are few signs of this happening yet.

Why should group or representative actions be unpopular? Those arguing against associational standing sometimes maintain that the 'Hohfeldian' claimant (i.e. an individual having a concrete 'claim right' correlative to a distinct obligation in another person or entity)[118] is best placed to prosecute cases, because they have a concrete claim, not an ideological one, as may be the case with associations.[119] Others disagree, arguing that associations may have longer-term interests than the Hohfeldian claimant, for precisely the sort of reasons that were given by Otton J in the *ex parte Greenpeace* case. Moreover, greater flexibility in group standing would protect smaller companies and individuals, which at present suffer in comparison to larger concerns.[120] The Community Courts seem, however, bound to a conservative view of standing based on the protection of a legal right, or the showing of special damage, rather than a more liberal approach which would allow a citizen's action to be brought on the basis of a public interest in ensuring that public bodies keep within their powers. However, elsewhere, outside of the European Court, the predominant trend in the case law reflects a more liberal approach going beyond the protection of legal rights and injury in fact,[121] and a progressive relaxation of standing rules in both common-law and civil districts. So, in the UK, in *R v SS Employment, ex parte EOC*,[122] it was held that the EOC had standing to challenge the compatibility of an Act of Parliament with Article 141 of the EC Treaty. This trend is reflected in other jurisprudence, e.g. US, France, and, to a lesser extent, in Germany.[123]

In a series of important articles in the 1970s, American writers put in issue the function of courts in deciding public law cases, suggesting that, in such cases, courts should be seen as serving a wider role than the traditional dispute resolution function assigned to them in the classic positivist theory of law. Public law disputes may be seen as essentially polycentric in character, because third party interests and a

---

[117] H Rasmussen, *On Law and Policy in the European Court* (Martinus Nijhoff, 1986).

[118] Following the work of Wesley Hohfeld, *Fundamental Legal Conceptions* (Yale University Press, 1919).

[119] See e.g. M Tushnet, 'The Sociology of Article III: a response to Professor Brilmayar' (1983) 93 Harv L Rev 1698.

[120] Harding ('The private interest in challenging community action' (1980) 5 ELRev. at 116) cites two types of strategy: the repeat player phenomenon, involving repeated litigation by one company, such as Roquette Frères, the French isoglucose manufacturer (Case 34/74 *Roquette v France* [1974] ECR 1217; Case 26/74 *Roquette v Commission* [1976] ECR 677). The other strategy is the 'saga,' which involves systematic attack on a particular Community policy from one or more losers. In the nine years covered by his survey Harding identified several sagas such as isoglucose, tomato concentrate and fisheries policy.

[121] See Law Commission consultation paper No 126 (1992) *Administrative Law: Judicial review and Statutory Appeals*.

[122] [1994] 2 WLR 409.

[123] It seems that the strict approach taken in Germany influenced the European Court in its early days: Fromont, 'L'influence du droit français et du droit allemand sur les conditions de recevabilité du recours en annulation devant la Cour de Justice des Communautes européennes' (1966) 2 RTDE.

possible wider public interest are also involved. In this way, decisions taken by the courts in these contexts are similar to decisions taken by administrators and legislators. A consequential need for interest representation before courts was noted.[124]

Stewart, the author of one such influential article, explains the American relaxation of standing requirements as partly judicially inspired. He writes: 'Increasingly the function of administrative law is not the protection of private autonomy but the provision of a surrogate political process to ensure the fair representation of a wide range of affected interests in the process of administrative decisions. Implicit in this development is the assumption that there is no ascertainable, transcendent public interest but only the distinct interests of various groups and individuals.'[125] Such an approach implies expanded judicial function. This may be contrasted with the tests of 'special damage' or 'private legal right' which denote a more quietist model for the judiciary.[126] However, on a more cautionary note, as Harlow suggests, we should not see the growing phenomenon of public interest (even if it is a phenomenon which has yet to reach the Community Courts) as an unmitigated good, as it is liable to blur the political/legal boundary.[127] It is for this reason that, in the US, the concept of constitutional standing is often presented as an integral part of the separation of powers and checks and balances: it restricts the power of the judiciary to control the legislature and executive. This is why there is a requirement that the applicant have a case or controversy under Article III US of the Constitution in order to bring suit.[128] The trick is surely to strike a balance, to allow sufficient group action to represent important public interests which would otherwise go unrepresented, but not to upset the EC institutional balance.

It might be argued that pluralist representation of the public interest in the EU is ensured by the access of the privileged applicants to the ECJ. But states may intervene for reasons which may have little to do with the 'public' interest as such, e.g. as in the case of the UK to argue against integrationist interpretations of EC law. Such an example is given by the '*Butterbuying cruises*'[129] cases, where the UK supported the classic view that treaty enforcement is a matter for member states. Some have suggested that a less self interested view might develop. France sees itself as promoting a 'long term vision of the EC' but academic writers do not necessarily accept this claim.[130] Alternatively, it has been suggested that the Commission operates as a sort of *amicus curiae*, but although the Commission perceives itself as disinterested it is widely viewed as supporting the Court's integrationist strategy, and in any case, it has been discredited since its mismanagement fiasco of 1999.

---

[124] See Feldman op. cit.; Harlow 'Towards a Theory of Access for the European Cost of Justice' (1992) 12 YEL 213.

[125] Stewart, op. cit.

[126] See Cane, *Standing, Legality and the Limits of Public Law* (1981) PL.

[127] See A Cox, *The Role of the US Supreme Court in American Government* (Oxford: OUP, 1976).

[128] Parker op. cit.

[129] Case 158/80 *Rewe Handelsgesellschaft Nord gmbH v Hauptzollamt Kiel* [1981] ECR 1805.

[130] E.g. H Rasmussen, *Law and Policy* 283–8, cites series of cases showing France supporting EC agricultural policies.

Critical conclusions

Is it simply unrealistic to expect the Court to allow wider access? Article 230 is clearly restrictive in its wording and at successive intergovernmental conferences the member states have foregone the opportunity to increase access to the Court.[131] Harding, writing in 1980, suggested that 'Article 173(2) itself, taken together with Article 189, does not and probably never was intended to hold out much hope to private plaintiffs in the case of measures not actually addressed to them.'[132] But this view is a question of interpretation. A wider reading of Article 230 would have been open to the Court, and indeed, it has engaged in such a reading in such cases as *Les Verts* and *Codorniu*.

Although it is indeed the case that not all member states permit review of primary legislation by administrative or constitutional courts, it could certainly be argued that the European Court, which has been so active in constructing an individual right to challenge the constitution of national laws in national courts,[133] should submit the EC to a similar democratic discipline.

Judicial review in EC law certainly diverges from the traditional European pattern where general executive regulations are usually susceptible to review at the suit of individuals in administrative courts.[134] But in the ECJ an individual may challenge only an individual administrative act by which they are directly affected. Thus, jurisprudence of the Court is already narrower than a typical administrative court. It is sometimes argued that collateral review permitted under Articles 230, 288 or 241 provides a substitute. But such indirect access is hardly the same thing as direct, and is in any case problematic.[135]

The status of the ECJ has clearly changed since its early days. It is now seen as a constitution builder and its ranking alongside natural supreme courts is generally accepted. Its maturation into a federal constitutional court is also evidenced by its increasing interest in human rights. But all this has taken place within a serious democracy deficit. Rasmussen tried to explain the ECJ's limited approach to standing on the basis of its long term project in reshaping the Court into a high court of appeals. Rasmussen suggests that for the Court, this outweighs citizens' interest in direct access. But there are problems with Rasmussen's thesis, given that restrictive access under Article 230 means that more cases are referred under Article 234, where the ECJ has even less in the way of 'docket control'. Furthermore, most individual cases of judicial review go to the CFI, which has no status as an appeal court.

Feldman suggests that the scope for citizens to use judicial processes to advance public, political ends gives a discernible indication of social and legal attitudes to politics, the rights and responsibilities of citizenship and the relationship between

---

[131] E.g. at the IGC leading to the Treaty of Amsterdam, where the member states ignored even the Court's own plea for wider access under Article 230.

[132] C Harding, 'The Private Interest in Challenging Community Action' (1980) 5 EL Rev 354, 355.

[133] See Chapter 7.

[134] J Schwarze, *European Administrative Law* (Sweet and Maxwell, 1992).

[135] This fact has been clearly acknowledged by the European Court itself, in *Foglia* v *Novella* and *TWD*: see Chapter 6.

electors, legislatures, executives, courts and the disenfranchised. If this is so, what messages are the Community Courts sending out? One of a lack of justice and of disenfanchisement. As an alternative to this unattractive message, it is suggested that there are two types of situation in which there should be a presumption in favour of standing.[136] First, where a right to participate in the administrative process leading to the adoption of the contested act has been conferred by the legislation.[137] This type of situation has sometimes been taken by the ECJ, most particularly in the 'quasi-judicial cases'. However, it would be nice if the Court would extend its case law on standing beyond this, particularly in cases such as the environmental, to take into account the participation of interested parties and groups in environmental matters. In this way the Courts would be going further down the road towards recognising the sorts of participatory democracy rights discussed in Chapter 3. The second situation is where an important legal question has been raised and there is no real prospect of it being raised again if the action is not allowed to continue.[138] Occasionally, it seems as if the ECJ has adopted this approach,[139] but again there are more instances where it should do so. Only if this is the case, will the Community Courts really strengthen their democratic credentials and be seen to be taking their citizens seriously.

GROUNDS OF REVIEW

For most of this chapter, the focus has been on individual *locus standi*. One might get the impression that this is all there is to Article 230, and that, once established, the rest is plain sailing. This is understandable, as much of the Article 230 case law does concern standing. However, there are other prerequisites to a successful claim. One is the observance of time limits under Article 230: two months from 'the publication of the measure, or of its notification to the plaintiff, or, in the absence thereof, the day on which it came to the knowledge of the latter as the case may be'. This does not leave litigants much time to sit around.

Moreover, it is not enough, of course, simply to be able to show that your claim is admissible: you have to be able to show that there is a substantive ground of review, a reason why the Community act in question should be annulled. These are set out in Article 230(2) which states that actions for annulment may be brought on the grounds of 'lack of competence, infringement of an essential procedural requirement, infringement of this Treaty or of any rule of law relating to its application, or misuse of powers'. These grounds of review also apply in other types of challenge (such as the plea of illegality under Article 241, or actions referred from the national courts by the preliminary reference procedure).

---

[136] Arnull op. cit. fn 77 at 11.

[137] See Evans and de Smith, *Review of Administrative Action* (1980) at 413; Stewart, 'The Reformation of American Administrative Law' (1975) 88 Harv LR 1667 at 1670.

[138] This type of situation was proposed by the JUSTICE/All Souls review, *Administrative Justice: Some Necessary Reforms* (1988).

[139] E.g. in *Extramet*, or *Les Verts*.

The four grounds of review specified in Article 232(2) have their origin in French administrative law and there is quite a lot of overlap between them. The third ground, that concerning an infringement of the treaty or any rule of law relating to its application, is so broad that it could possibly cover all of the others. Indeed, the European Court will often not specify which of the grounds is their basis of annulment.

(1) Lack of competence

Every EC act must have its basis in the treaty. The EC has no general competence, unlike national parliaments. Under this heading, it will often be a Community, institution or member state, rather than an individual, who has brought the claim. Pleading a lack of competence is rather like the claim for *ultra vires* in English administrative law. It is rare for the European Courts to annul a Community act for lack of competence, although it is not uncommon for it do so because they have the wrong legal basis.[140] Until quite recently both the Community institutions and the Community Court tended to take a wide view of the Community's competence.[141] This is supported by provisions in the treaty, such as the implied powers clause of Article 308, which seem to provide the EC with wide scope for action. So apart from in the case of powers delegated to an institution,[142] it was rare for the Court to find that an institution had exceeded its competence. However, in 2000, the Court found the Community to have exceeded its power in adopting the tobacco advertising directive, and annulled it in an action brought by tobacco companies and the German government.[143] It has also sometimes found the Commission to have exceeded its powers, as in the case brought by France against the Commission,[144] in which the Court held that the Commission lacked the competence to issue a Community provision for the liberalisation of the market in pension funds.

(2) Infringement of an essential procedural requirement

A good deal of procedures exist under EC law, for example under the treaty (the requirement to give reasons under Article 253 EC), under secondary legislation (requirements to consult certain committees) or under general principles of law (such as the requirement of *audi alterem partem*). Each EC institution also has its own internal rules of procedure. Not every EC procedure infringed, however, will constitute a reason for annulment. Article 232 specifies that it must be an 'essential' requirement (again this feature is taken from French administrative law). Hartley suggests that the reason for insisting that the requirement be essential is that 'to

---

[140] In which case, it is likely to be annulled for breaching the third of the grounds of review: that of infringing the treaty, or any rule of law relating to its application.
[141] See the discussion in Chapter 4.
[142] Discussed in Chapter 3.
[143] *Germany v European Parliament* (C376/98) [2000] ECR I-8419.
[144] Case 57/95 *France v Commission* [1997] ECR I-627.

invalidate an act for an insignificant procedural defect would unduly hamper legislative activity and would encourage excessive formalism and red tape...On the other hand, not to annul for any formal defect at all would be detrimental to good administration and would prejudice the rights of individuals.'[145] However, as Hartley rightly points out, compromise has the disadvantage of uncertainty: how is one to tell if a procedure is sufficiently 'essential'? Just by looking at the procedure, one often cannot tell how essential it is, nor how serious the consequences of not observing it would be. Hartley's suggestion is that we look to the procedure's **function**. Sometimes this function may have a determining effect on the final content of the act. This may be so if there is a failure to consult another body. Such duties are often set out in primary legislation, such as the requirement to consult Parliament, which the ECJ held to derive from the 'fundamental democratic principle that peoples should take part in the exercise of power...through the intermediary of a representative assembly'.[146] Sometimes, however, the procedure has a function that, while unlikely to have an effect on a measure's final content, may still be crucial. This is so, for example, in the case of the duty to give reasons, which has the functions of enabling an enacting authority to specify its objectives, the courts to exercise their function of review, and individuals to defend their rights, as well as lending a greater general transparency to the Community process. Indeed, at its most ambitious, the giving reasons requirement might be seen as, by requiring disclosure of the factors relevant to the measures adoption, also increasing the ability of interested parties to participate in the policy making process.[147]

Thus, the Court has held the following procedural requirements to be essential: the requirement to grant a hearing;[148] the requirement to consult – this includes the duty to consult not only the Parliament, but also other bodies, such as scientific committees. In the *Angelopharm*[149] case, the Court held that it was important for the Commission to make use of increased scientific expertise, and that its failure to consult the scientific committee on cosmetology regarding the Cosmetics directive constituted a breach of an essential procedural requirement. Other requirements deemed 'essential' by the Court include internal procedures, for example in the *BASF*[150] case, in which the Court insisted that the Commission must follow its own procedures in order for its decisions to be valid. The duty to give reasons is also quite clearly essential. In *Germany v Commission*,[151] the Court stressed the nature of this duty. The German government had applied to import a large quantity of wine from outside the EC. It intended to distil it for domestic consumption. The Commission rejected its application for an import licence, with only the meagre explanation that 'information that has been gathered indicating that the production of wines of this nature within the Community is amply sufficient'. The Court held

---

[145] TC Hartley, *The Foundations of European Community Law* (Oxford: Clarendon, 1998) at 412.
[146] Case 138/79 *Roquette* [1980] ECR 3333.
[147] See M Shapiro, 'The Giving Reasons Requirement' (1991) University of Chicago Legal Forum.
[148] Case 17/74 *Transocean Marine Paint* [1974] ECR 1063; see also Case C-315/99 P *Ismeri Europa v Court of Auditors* [2001] ECR I-5281.
[149] Case C-212/91 *Angelopharm* [1994] ECR I-171.
[150] Case C-137/92 P *Commission v BASF* [1994] ECR I-2555.
[151] Case 24/62 *Germany v Commission* [1963] ECR 63.

that such a statement was simply inadequate: the statement of reasons should pro-vide the opportunity to all interested parties of 'ascertaining the circumstances in which the Commission had applied the Treaty'. Although the Court has not required the EC to give complete disclosure of all issues of fact and law relevant to a measure's adoption, it has at least held that the reasons given must be sufficient to help interested parties to defend their rights before Court.[152]

(3) Infringement of the treaty or any rule of law relating to its application

This is a very broad ground indeed. It covers the treaties, but also any 'rule of law relating to its application'. What does this mean? The Court has held that it encom-passes all rules of Community law other than those in the treaties. The most com-monly pleaded such rules are general principles of law and fundamental rights.[153] Those most commonly used, and most successfully pleaded, as reasons for the annulment of an act, are the principles of proportionality, non-discrimination and legal certainty and this section will focus only on these three.[154] Chalmers defines, and links, these three as having the function of imposing 'a substantive rationale upon the authority. They are there to ensure that, after all the other checks, it does not exercise its power in a capricious or arbitrary manner.'[155] They are also consti-tutional standards which underpin the Community legal order and the Court will frequently refer to them.

Proportionality

This principle is derived from German administrative law, where it is known as *Verhältnismassigkeit*, but it is also seen as underlying the values in the *Grundgesetz*, the German Constitution.[156] The principle of proportionality requires that a meas-ure be no more heavy-handed than necessary. It operates as a bulwark against state interference. As it has developed in German law, the proportionality principle has three requirements: first, that the measure must be the most suitable means of achieving the objectives of the administration; second, that the measure must be nec-essary for the achievement of the objective; and third, that the measure must be that which imposes the least interference on individual interests.[157] The principle has found a place in EC law for some time; indeed, according to Schwarze, it 'should at all times be regarded as the overriding principle seeking to restrict the scope of the

---

[152] Cases 209–215 & 218/78 *Van Landewyck v Commission* [1980] ECR 3125.

[153] See Chapter 13 for a discussion of fundamental rights.

[154] Others are discussed in the chapter on fundamental rights.

[155] D Chalmers, *EU Law* (Ashgate, 1998) at 414. See also T Tridimas, *General Principles of EC Law* (Oxford, OUP 1999).

[156] See N Emiliou, *The Principle of Proportionality in European Law* (Kluwer, 1996); J Schwarze, *European Administrative Law* (Sweet and Maxwell, 1992).

[157] See J Schwarze, *European Administrative Law*; also G de Burca, 'The Principle of Proportionality and its application in European law' (1993) 13 YEL 113.

Community rules which impose duties'.[158] The proportionality principle is stated in Article 5(3) EC, regarding the intensity of institutional action, where it has a close relationship to the principle of subsidiarity, also to be found in Article 5.[159] But, for a long time, the Court has been highlighting its relevance for the economic law of the EC, as a ground of annulment of legislation. In *Germany* v *European Parliament and Council* the ECJ stated, 'In order to establish whether a provision of Community law complies with the principle of proportionality, it must be ascertained whether the means which it employs are suitable for the purpose of achieving the desired objective and whether they do not go beyond what is necessary to achieve it.'[160] Much of the CAP has, in practice, involved the imposition of taxes, levies or subsidies and the principle of proportionality has often been prayed in aid as a reason to attack such measures. In the *Bela Muhle (Skimmed Milk Powder)* case,[161] the Court found that it had been disproportionate to require farmers to buy animal feeding stuffs containing skimmed milk, which had displaced the cheaper soya, as a method of dealing with the Community milk mountain.

Legal certainty

This is a very broad concept, which is to be found in nearly every legal system of the world. It is part of the EU's commitment to the Rule of Law. It first made its appearance in Community law in the case of *SNUPAT* v *High Authority*,[162] but takes a variety of forms in EC law. One such is the principle of **non-retroactivity** of law. This requires, to use slightly convoluted language, that no rule be applied to the completed effects of a situation occurring prior to the date at which the rule was promulgated (although it may apply to their future effects).[163] The rule operates in an almost absolute manner in the context of criminal law, although sometimes exceptions have had to be made elsewhere. This was the case, for example, in the case, in the isoglucose saga, *Amylum* v *Council*,[164] in which the removal of a production support levy had caused catastrophic damage to producers of isoglucose.[165] The EC re-imposed a levy by way of a regulation, which had to have retroactive effect in order to meet its objective, namely to remedy the effects of the first invalid measure which had removed the levy, and also, to provide relief to the producers.

Another aspect of the principle of legal certainty is that of the protection of **legitimate expectations**. This, again, is derived from German law, in which it is known as *Vertrauensschütz*, from which it might more accurately be translated as a principle of legitimate 'confidentiality' and in which it seems to be specifically connected with

---

[158] Case 114/76 *Bela Muhle* [1977] ECR 1211.
[159] For a discussion of proportionality in this context, see Chapter 4.
[160] Case C-233/94 [1997] ECR I 2405.
[161] J Schwarze, op. cit.
[162] Cases 42 & 49/59 *SNUPAT* v *High Authority* [1961] 109.
[163] Case C-331/88 R v *MAFF ex parte Fedesa* [1990] ECR I-4023.
[164] Case 108/81 *Amylum* v *Council* [1982] ECR 3107.
[165] See Chapter 11 on damages for greater details.

the notion of good faith.[166] This principle of legitimate expectations has been found at work in Community economic law, specifically the CAP, in which it has been held that the common organisation of markets should not proceed in such as way as to defeat legitimate expectations. In the *Efisol* case, the CFI referred to the right of legitimate expectations as extending to 'any individual who is in a situation in which it is apparent that the Community administration, by giving him precise assurances, has led him to entertain justifiable expectations'.[167] However, it seems that precise assurances need not actually be given personally to the applicant. In the *Sofrimport* case[168] it was held that the applicants had legitimate expectation because of the EC's general duty to take into account the interests of those with 'goods in transit' even although they had not made a personal assurance in this case. Indeed, the mere undertaking of a certain course of conduct may be sufficient to give rise to legitimate expectations, as is illustrated by the *Mulder*[169] case. In this case, in order to deal with overproduction in the milk market, the EC had been encouraging farmers to stop producing milk for a while. However, the EC then took action inconsistent with this, by introducing a subsequent system which penalised those farmers who had set aside their land from milk production, effectively excluding them from the milk market entirely. The Court held that this was a breach of those farmers' legitimate expectations. Some writers have even gone as far as to suggest that even just a change in policy may be sufficient to give rise to legitimate expectations.[170] However, the Community courts do not seem to have taken this approach, holding that the EC must have freedom in which to legislate and make policy, and that the prudent trader should take this into account and accept some risk of regulatory change.[171]

A final dimension of the principle of legal certainty is that of **clarity**. This requires that the law should not be unpredictable, unclear or inconsistent. This is connected to transparency, but also to the protection of individual freedom: that the law should be sufficiently clear so that individuals should be able to plan and conduct their affairs without interference.

Equality and non-discrimination

This is another crucial and much litigated principle. However, it is not necessarily straightforward. Equality is a relative concept and, far from requiring that all be treated equally, may actually require unequal treatment.[172] Even if we apply a formal standard of equality, requiring that like cases be treated alike, the notion of what is a 'like' case in the first place is one that may be highly subjective in nature.

---

[166] See also Case T-115/94 *OPEC* v *Austria* [1997] ECR II 39 at para 93.

[167] Case T-336/94 *Efisol* v *Commission* [1996] ECR II-1343.

[168] Case C-152/88 *Sofrimport* v *Commission* [1990] ECR I-2477.

[169] Case 120/86 *Mulder* [1988] ECR 2321.

[170] Paul Craig, for example, in 'Substantive Legitimate Expectations in Domestic and Community Law' (1996) 55 CLJ 289 at 299; see also E. Sharpston, 'Legitimate Expectations and Economic Reality' (1990) 15 ELRev 103.

[171] Case 265/85 *Van den Bergh* v *Commission* [1987] 1155.

[172] J Schwarze, *European Administrative Law* 552; see also R Dworkin, 'Reverse Discrimination' in *Taking Rights Seriously* (London: Duckworth, 1977) at 223 for a discussion of the principle of equality.

Thus, the ECJ's statement, in the *Assurances du Crédit*[173] case, that equality need not be extended to persons or firms in 'objectively different' situations, can only beg the question, as the term 'objectively different' is hardly self-defining.

The principle of equality features in various aspects of EC law: it prohibits discrimination on grounds of nationality under Article 12 EC and also appears as a general principle and legal basis for non-discrimination in Article 13; it requires equal pay for men and women in Article 141; and in Article 34(3) (formerly Article 40) prohibits discrimination among producers and consumers in the field of agriculture. In this last context, the principle was used as another ground of annulment of the skimmed milk regime which had been set up in the *Bela Muhle* case. The benefits of this regime had been felt by dairy farmers, who were in over-production, but the livestock breeders suffered as a result. This was discrimination.

The principle of equality was more recently applied to the international trade law of the EC in the context of the banana war cases, although the framework agreements on bananas were largely upheld by the Court.[174]

(4) Misuse of powers

This is the fourth of the grounds of review under Article 232 and little used. Its origins lie in French administrative law, in the concept of *détournement de pouvoir*, although it tends to feature in most legal systems. A misuse of power basically consists of adopting a measure for purposes other than those for which it was intended, i.e. in having an improper purpose.

It is very hard to succeed on this ground. Whether an act has an improper purpose, or whether there has been bad faith, may be highly subjective and very hard to prove, especially as the Court has required this to be shown 'on the basis of objective, relevant and consistent indications'.[175] Institutions do not usually choose to leave evidence of their bad faith lying around. Those cases in which the principle has succeeded, and there are few, have tended to be staff cases.[176]

THE INTENSITY OF JUDICIAL REVIEW

All four grounds above would appear to raise only questions of **law**, and not of review of the **facts** or the **merits** of the measure in question. Indeed, the European Court exercises only 'limited jurisdiction' in judicial review of Community acts, whereby it is restricted to reviewing the objective legitimacy of a measure, namely, whether it is in conformity with the treaty or other rules. The European Courts have

---

[173] Case C-63/89 *Les Assurances du Crédit v Council* [1991] ECR 1799 at 1848.
[174] E.g. Case C-122/95 *Germany v Council* [1998] ECR I-973; Case C-364–365/95 *T Port GmbH* [1998] ECR I-1023.
[175] Case C-323/88 *Sermes* [1990] I-3027.
[176] Cases 18 and 35/65 *Gutmann v Commission* [1966] ECR 103; Case 105/75 *Giuffrida v Council* [1976] ECR 1395. For recent examples (again staff cases) of success, see Case T-84/98 *C v Council* [2000] ECR staff cases II-0497, and T-223/99 *Dejaiffe v OHIM* [2000] ECR staff cases II-1267.

the power to annul a measure but may not substitute their own decision in its place. The notion of 'limited jurisdiction' is another import from French administrative law. The limited nature of review was made explicit in the context of the ECSC Treaty, Article 33 of which states that 'the Court may not examine the evaluation of a situation resulting from economic facts or circumstances in the light of which the High Authority made its decisions or recommendations, except where the High Authority is alleged to have misused its powers or has manifestly failed to observe the provisions of the treaty or any rule of law relating to its application'. There is no corresponding provision in the EC Treaty, but the European Courts have been very limited in their exercise of judicial review.[177]

Therefore, although the power of judicial review would appear to hand the Luxembourg bench a very powerful instrument for supervising the EU's political organs, in fact, the European Courts have made surprisingly little use of this power (in assessing the actions of Community institutions at least). Indeed, the European Court has been especially reluctant to engage in heavy-handed review in those areas of economic law in which the treaty has given the EC a lot of discretionary power. Some provisions, such as Articles 33, 34 and 37 EC, which set out the objectives of the CAP, are framed in a very general way and also have a capacity to clash with each other. Article 33 EC requires an agricultural policy legislative measure to comply with broad treaty instructions to increase agricultural produce, ensure a fair standard of living, stabilise markets, assure availability of supplies and ensure supplies reach consumers at reasonable prices. In this context, the Commission and Council have had to deal with economic difficulties and serious disturbances in the market (expressions which in any case are again broad, and subject to differing interpretations). In such cases, the Court has been willing for the most part to let the choices of the Commission and Council stand, and has rarely sought to re-evaluate their decisions.[178] As the Court stated in the *Deuka*[179] case, '... the Commission enjoys a significant freedom of evaluation both as regards the taking into account of possible factors of disturbance and in choosing the means to deal with them...when examining the lawfulness of the exercise of such freedom the courts cannot substitute their own evaluation of the matter for that of the competent authority, but must restrict themselves to examining whether the evaluation contains a patent error or constitutes a misuse of power.'

Therefore, although general principles of law, particularly proportionality, would seem to provide the Court with justification for *de novo* review, inviting the Court to substitute its own judgment for that of the administrative agency, in practice review has been very limited in such cases.[180] When applying the principle of

---

[177] This may be contrasted with the 'hard look' judicial review often applied by US courts in administrative law; for a comparison see F Bignami, 'The Administrative State in a Separation of Powers Constitution: Lessons for European Community Rulemaking from the United States', Harvard Jean Monnet Working Paper No. 5/99, http://www.jeanmonnetprogram.org./papers/ 99/990501.html.

[178] Although Case 106–107/63 *Toepfer* [1965] ECR 405 provides an example of a case in which they did so.

[179] Case 78/74 *Deuka* [1975] ECR 421.

[180] See for a commentary on this G de Búrca, 'The Principle of Proportionality and its Application in European law' (1993) 13 YEL 105; C Vajda, 'Some Aspects of Judicial Review within the Common

proportionality, the Court has held that the measure in question must be 'manifestly' inappropriate or disproportionate.[181]

The Court has been equally deferential in other areas where complex economic choices have to be made, such as state aids or mergers.[182] However, where there is less discretion, such as in areas of competition law, the Court has been more willing to engage in substantive review and to substitute its own judgment for that of the Commission. It has also not shown itself to be remotely shy of subjecting the actions of national authorities to very strict scrutiny indeed, using very creative methods of interpretation to construct a constitutional jurisprudence which has been examined elsewhere in this book.[183]

Perhaps, however, the attempt to maintain a distinction between legal, formal review and a substantive review on the merits is in any case doomed, if it is used by the Community Courts as an attempt to escape involvement in political and economic questions. Francis Snyder, in his analysis of the operation of the CAP, provides a critique of the view which sees the European court's role in judicial review of Community action as being deferential to the institutions' large discretion.[184] If such an approach is supposed to steer the Court away from 'political' involvement, he suggests, it is bound to fail, and will do so without giving the Court the benefit of an analysis of all the background factors which led to the taking of the decisions in the first place. He illustrates this point by an analysis of the *Bela Muhle* case, a product of the EC's attempt to deal with the large skimmed milk mountain. This concerned a highly controversial aspect of Community policy: the delimitation of legally permissible ways in which agricultural surpluses can be controlled. On this matter, the political institutions, the Court and the companies and other groups involved, took different views. Snyder is critical of the way in which the Court, while having the last word, ruled out a wide-ranging enquiry, and in so doing, abstracted the specific legal issues from the complex political and economic background to the case. By taking such a narrow focus, the Court excluded the important connection between CAP law and politics, agricultural production, food marketing and multinational companies, all of which were of critical importance to the determination of the legal principles of proportionality and non-discrimination. As Snyder explains, the reason why skimmed milk was higher in price than soya was because of the strength of the oil seed crushing industry, which had succeeded in ensuring that soya could be imported into the EC free of any levy. The ECJ, however, simply took for granted this background structure of power. Snyder stresses

---

Agricultural Policy – Part II' (1979) 4 ELRev 341; E Sharpston, 'Legitimate Expectations and Economic Reality' (1990) 15 ELRev 103; M Herdegen, 'The Equation of the Principles of Equality and Proportionality' (1985) 22 CMLRev 683.

[181] See Case C-331/88 *R v MAFF, ex parte Fedesa* [1990] ECR 4023.

[182] See Sharpston op. cit. for a consideration of the Court's application of the principle of legitimate expectations in these fields.

[183] In Chapters 7, 8 and 9.

[184] F Snyder, *New Directions In Community Law* (Weidenfeld and Nicolson, 1990); see also the article by Professor Mertens de Wilmars, Judge, and subsequently President, of the ECJ, 'The Case Law of the Court of Justice in Relation to the Review of the Legality of Economic Policy in Mixed-Economy Systems' (1982) LIEI 1.

that the ECJ, in focusing only on the legal outcome of the legislative process, failed to look sufficiently into its economic and political context. However, *Bela Muhle* was perhaps an unusual case, in that the ECJ did actually annul the act in question. When it came to an action for damages brought by the farmers, for losses caused by the increased cost of animal feed, the Court was unwilling to find that the institutions had committed a 'sufficiently manifest and grave breach' of Community law for there to be EC liability for damage caused by the regulation in question.[185]

ACTIONS UNDER ARTICLE 232 FOR FAILURE TO ACT

It is important that there be judicial control not only in the case of unlawful actions by Community institutions, but also in those cases in which they violated their obligation to act. Both the treaties and secondary legislation impose duties on EC institutions to carry out the objectives of the EC. For example, one such is Article 71 EC, which requires the Council to introduce legislation to implement certain aspects of a common transport policy. On its failure to do so the Parliament brought an action based on the Council's failure to act.[186] Article 232 sets out the conditions under which an action may be bought against a Community institution for its failure to act.

Article 232 (formerly Article 175)

Should the European Parliament, the Council or the Commission, in infringement of this Treaty, fail to act, the Member States and the other institutions of the Community may bring an action before the Court of Justice to have the infringement established.

The action shall be admissible only if the institution concerned has first been called upon to act. If, within two months of being so called upon, the institution concerned has not defined its position, the action may be brought within a further period of two months.

Any natural or legal person may, under the conditions laid down in the preceding paragraphs, complain to the Court of Justice that an institution of the Community has failed to address to that person any act other than a recommendation or an opinion.

The Court of Justice shall have jurisdiction, under the same conditions, in actions or proceedings brought by the ECB in the areas falling within the latter's field of competence and in actions or proceedings brought against the latter.

The first paragraph gives standing to all member states and Community institutions, including the European Parliament, to challenge a failure to act by the Community, and the third paragraph covers the standing of non-privileged applicants. Paragraph 2 sets out the procedure to be followed before such an action may be brought before the Court. In the *Chevalley* case,[187] the Court stressed the **unity** of procedures under Articles 230 and 232, stating that 'the concept of a measure capable of giving rise to an action is identical in Articles 173 and 175 as both principles merely prescribe

---

[185] See Chapter 11 on damages.
[186] Case 13/83 *Parliament v Council* [1985] ECR 1513.
[187] Case 15/70 *Chevalley v Commission* [1970] ECR 975.

one and the same method of recourse'. In which case, it would seem that it will be just as difficult for individuals to obtain relief under Article 232 as under Article 230. Somewhat less facetiously, the unity principle would seem to require that, if an act could be challenged by a party under Article 230, then the failure to adopt that act should be reviewable under Article 232.

The three crucial issues under Article 232 are, first, what sorts of omissions are reviewable; second, the vexed question of *locus standi*; and third, as to the nature of the procedure set out in the second paragraph.

What omissions are reviewable?

For Article 232 to apply, the applicant must be challenging an actual omission and not an actual refusal to act, which the Court has characterised as a negative decision, which may be actionable under Article 230.[188] If the unity principle set out by the Court in *Chevalley* is correct, then only those types of omission having **legal effects** should be reviewable, given that only such measures are reviewable under Article 230. As far as natural and legal persons are concerned, this is the case, and the wording of Article 232(3) makes clear that they may not bring an action regarding recommendations or opinions. There is some authority, however, that privileged applicants may bring an action regarding the failure to adopt **any** kind of act: this is what the wording of Article 232(1) states, and the Court, in its *Comitology*[189] decision, suggested that the Parliament might bring an action for the failure to adopt a non-binding act.[190] For an omission to be reviewable, there must be an obligation for the institution concerned to act in the first place. Thus, the failure of the Commission to bring enforcement proceedings against a member state is not a reviewable omission, since the Commission is under no duty to take such proceedings in the first place.[191]

Locus standi

There will be no problem with privileged applicants, which have *locus standi* under Article 232(1). However, the position is not so straightforward with natural and legal persons. Article 232(3) states that the institution concerned must have 'failed to address to that person any act other than a recommendation or opinion'. Once again, a unity of procedures under Articles 230 and 232 would suggest that non-privileged applicants should be directly and individually concerned by the act that the institution has allegedly failed to enact. This would seem to be the case, although the Court has not stated so explicitly in the context of the EC treaty. In *Bethell*

---

[188] Case 42/71 *Nordgetreide v Commission* [1972] ECR 105; Cases 10, 18/68 *Eridania v Commission* [1969] ECR 459.

[189] Case 302/87 *Parliament v Council (Comitology)* [1988] ECR 5615.

[190] See also Toth, 'The Law as it stands on the Appeal for the Failure to Act' (1975) 2 LIEI 65.

[191] Case 48/65 *Lütticke v Commission* [1966] ECR 19; Case 247/87 *Star Fruit Co v Commission* [1989] ECR 291.

v *Commission*,[192] Lord Bethell, a Euro-MP, was attempting to force the Commission to take action against European airlines on account of their anti-competitive practices. The Court held Bethell's actions under both Articles 230 and 232 inadmissible. He had no legitimate interest in this matter and, according to the Court, could not succeed in showing that the Commission had failed to adopt, in relation to him, a decision which he was legally entitled to claim. In the *ENU*[193] case, an action under the Euratom Treaty, which has a provision equivalent to Article 232 EC, the Court held that the applicant should be directly and individually concerned.[194]

Procedure

A special procedure must be followed before an action for failure to act may come to court. According to Article 232(2) the action will only be admissible if the institution has first been called upon to act.[195] The applicant must make it clear what action is required. The institution concerned then has two months in which either to act, or to define its position. What does this curious expression mean? The function of the definition of position is to make the nature of the omission clearer. However, the Court has not been particularly clear in this context. For example, in the action brought by the European Parliament against the Council concerning its failure to establish a common transport policy, the President of the Council had responded to the Parliament's request to define its position by simply acknowledging that the transport policy was incomplete and detailing the steps that had been taken to date. The Court held that this did not constitute a definition of position.

The definition of position encompasses a decision refusing to act.[196] However, the definition of position need not itself be a reviewable act, provided that 'it is the prerequisite for the next step in a procedure which is to culminate in a legal act'. This somewhat convoluted statement was made by the Court of First Instance in the *Guerin*[197] case. In this context, the CFI held that the Commission could be compelled to adopt what is known as an 'Article 6 letter', which is a letter in which the Commission states that it is minded not to pursue a complaint. An Article 6 letter is not final, however, but a stage in a procedure which will lead to a definitive decision not to pursue a complaint, which is a reviewable act.[198] Indeed, Article 232 has proved

---

[192] Case 246/81 *Bethell* v *Commission* [1982] ECR 2277.

[193] Case C-107/91 *ENU* v *Commission* [1997] ECR I-1329.

[194] Although note the CFI's subsequent more equivocal opinion, in the context of the EC Treaty, in Case T-277/94 *AITEC* v *Commission* [1996] ECR II-351.

[195] Although there is no time limit set in Article 232, this should be within a reasonable time: Case 59/70 *Netherlands* v *Commission* [1971] ECR 639.

[196] Which may then be a reviewable act for the purpose of Article 232.

[197] Case T-186/94 *Guerin Automobiles* v *Commission* [1995] ECR II-1753.

[198] See also Case C-72/90 *Asia Motor France* v *Commission* [1990] ECR I-2181; and Case T-64/89 *Automec Srl* v *Commission (Automec I)* [1990] ECR II-367. In Case T-24/90 *Automec* v *Commission (Automec II)* [1992] ECR II-2223 the CFI held that a complainant is entitled to a reviewable act. Thus Article 232 is very useful as a means of forcing the Commission to undertake an investigation; see also the discussion on *Automec*, earlier in this chapter, under Article 230 at fn 26.

important in the field of competition law, in which complainants have managed to invoke it in order to require the Commission to take action on their complaints.

If the institution concerned fails either to define its position or to take action the applicant has two months to bring the case before the Court. If the institution, however, does define its position, then according to the *Lutticke*[199] case, this will bring Article 232 proceedings to an end, although the applicant might be able to challenge the definition of position, as a reviewable act under Article 230, if they have standing.

Under Article 233, an institution whose unlawful failure to act has been declared contrary to the treaty is required to take remedial action to comply with the Court's judgment. This may not, however, be the action which the applicant had required.[200]

INDIRECT CHALLENGE UNDER ARTICLE 241 (FORMERLY 184)

This states that:

> Notwithstanding the expiry of the period laid down in the fifth paragraph of Article 230, any party may, in proceedings in which a regulation adopted jointly by the European Parliament and Council, or a regulation of the Council, of the Commission, or of the European Central Bank is at issue, plead the grounds specified in the second paragraph of Article 230 in order to invoke before the Court of Justice the inapplicability of that regulation.

As already discussed earlier in this book, much Community legislation is delegated. Thus, it may gain its legal basis, not from the treaties, but from another act of Community legislation, usually a regulation. However, this situation presents applicants with problems if they wish to challenge an individual act addressed to them on the basis that the act from which it derives its authority is invalid. They cannot challenge a normative act directly, and will probably be out of time to do so, even if they had standing. Article 241, sometimes known as the 'plea of illegality'[201] provides a means of indirect challenge to Community legislation. Its object is to ensure that illegal, 'parent' Community acts can be attacked through the medium of their implementing (Community or national) measures. It may be used in the context of direct challenges under Articles 230 and 232 (although not in the course of indirect challenges in the national courts).[202] It is thus not a free-standing action but dependent on other proceedings. The provision is designed to benefit individual applicants

---

[199] Case 48/65 *Lutticke* v *Commission* [1966] ECR 19.
[200] Case 13/83 *Parliament* v *Council (Common Transport Policy case)* [1985] ECR 1513, in which the ECJ held that it was for 'the Council to introduce the measures which it considered necessary'.
[201] After the French legal concept, the *'l'exception d'illégalité'*.
[202] Cases 31 and 33/62 *Wohrmann and Lutticke* v *Commission* [1962] ECR 501. However, such indirect challenges may be brought through the preliminary ruling procedure under Article 234, which allows national courts to refer to the ECJ questions concerning the 'validity and interpretation of acts of the institutions of the Community'. National courts may not hear a direct challenge to Community legislation, so they must refer the matter to the Court in Luxembourg.

rather than privileged applicants who always have *locus standi* to challenge any reviewable act directly.[203]

What types of act may be subject to an indirect challenge? Article 241 specifies a **regulation** of the Council, Commission, European Parliament and Council, or European Central Bank. However, as with Article 230, it is not the form of the act, but its **substance**, which is decisive. This fact was illustrated by the *Simmenthal*[204] case. The applicant sought to challenge a decision addressed to the Italian government, in which it, Simmenthal, was directly and individually concerned. Simmenthal claimed that the parent measure, which was a general notice of invitation to tender, on which the decision had been based, was invalid. The ECJ held that, since the notice was a general act, normative in substance, it therefore produced similar effects to a regulation and thus could be challenged.

According to the wording of Article 241, it would seem that the scope of indirect challenge has been deliberately limited to general measures. Part of the justification for this seems to be that, as individuals and companies are unable to challenge general measures through Article 230, they should have the chance to do so in the context of other proceedings, where the legality of the prime measure they are challenging depends on the validity of its parent measure. However, the case law makes it all somewhat more complex. Despite the wording of Article 241, it would seem that some **individual** measures may also be challenged indirectly. Although the addressees of an individual act may not challenge it indirectly, through Article 241, in the ECJ,[205] it would seem that a person who is not an addressee of an individual act and does not have *locus standi* to challenge it directly may challenge indirectly in the national court. It used to be thought that a person not an addressee of an individual act, but who had direct and individual concern, might nonetheless be able to challenge the measure indirectly.[206] However, the more recent *TWD*[207] case made it clear that this is not so. The background to this case was that a German company had been given aid by the German authorities but the Commission had found this aid to be incompatible with the common market by means of a decision addressed to the German government. TWD could have challenged this decision directly in the Community Court, as it would have been directly and individually concerned. However, it chose not to do so. The German government then took a decision requiring repayment of the aid. The company did however, challenge this measure in the German courts, partly on the basis that the original Commission decision was

---

[203] Case 135/93 *Spain v Commission* [1995] ECR I-1651, which settled a long controversy on this matter. In Case 32/65 *Italy v Commission* [1966] ECR 389, AG Roemer suggested that member states should have the same rights as other applicants because, in addition to the fact that Article 241 is expressed in general terms (it refers to 'any party'), it is also the case that member states may not have challenged the measure directly because its defaults were not apparent until it was applied in a particular case. However, the ECJ failed to deal with this point, and it remained unresolved until *Spain v Commission*.

[204] Case 92/78 *Simmenthal v Commission* [1979] ECR 777.

[205] Case 21/64 *Dalmas v High Authority* [1965] ECR 175.

[206] Case 216/82 *Universität Hamburg* [1983] ECR 2771; Case 133–6/85 *Walter Rau v BALM* [1987] ECR 2289.

[207] Case C-188/92 *TWD Textilwerke Deggendorf Gmbh v Germany* [1994] ECR I-833; see also Case C-178/95 *Wiljo NV v Belgium* [1997] ECR I 585.

invalid. The German courts made a preliminary reference to the ECJ and the ECJ held that no indirect challenge could be made since the company could 'without any doubt' have challenged the measure under Article 230.'[208] This might seem somewhat unfair; however, the Court seemed particularly keen to uphold the balance of remedies under the treaty. Thus, it would seem that a party directly and individually concerned by an act may not challenge that act indirectly, either in the Community court, or in the national courts.

Applicants cannot challenge just any regulation somehow connected with another measure. There must be a more specific relationship between the two. Although it may not be necessary for the regulation to form the legal basis of the subsequent measure, it must be the case that the regulation must be applicable either directly or indirectly to the subsequent measure,[209] a rather unclear formula apparently signifying that there must be a real connection between the subject matter of the application and the normative measure whose legality is being challenged; indeed, in *Salerno v Commission and Council*[210] the ECJ went as far as to suggest that the measure in question must have the regulation as its **legal basis**.

The effect of a successful indirect challenge is that the regulation will be declared inapplicable and any subsequent act based upon it void.[211] If the challenge has come by way of a preliminary reference from the national courts then other national courts should also regard the measure as void.[212]

CONSEQUENCES OF A FINDING OF INVALIDITY

Article 231 states that:

> If the action is well-founded, the Court of Justice shall declare the act concerned to be void.
>
> In the case of a regulation, however, the Court of Justice shall, if it considers this necessary, state which of the effects of the regulation which it has declared void shall be considered as definitive.

If it is a regulation which is found to be invalid and subsequently declared void, then it will be void *erga omnes*, i.e. for everyone, including third parties. However, Article 231(2) also clearly gives the Court the opportunity to declare only part of the measure in question void and to keep other parts in place.[213] As one well-known commentator recently remarked, 'The Court has accepted the principle that a challenged act, like a curate's egg, may be bad in part only.'[214]

---

[208] But see now Case C-408/95 *Eurotunnel SA v Sea France* [1997] ECR I-6315, in which *TWD* was not applied; see also M Ross, 'Limits on using Article 177 EC' (1994) 19 ELRev at 640.

[209] Case 32/65 *Italy v Council and Commission* [1966] ECR 398.

[210] Cases 87, 130/77 22/83 and 9, 10/84 *Salerno v Commission and Council* [1985] ECR 2523.

[211] Although the act may be valid for the past: Case 145/79 *Roquette* [1980] ECR 2917.

[212] Case 66/80 *ICC* [1981] ECR 1191.

[213] See in this regard, Case 17/74 *Transocean Marine Paint v Commission* [1974] ECR 1063.

[214] L Neville Brown and T Kennedy, *The Court of Justice of the European Communities* (Sweet and Maxwell, 2000) at 162.

However, the treaty goes further than just giving the Court the power to declare a measure void or voidable. Article 233 EC also gives the Court the power to require an institution to comply with its judgment by taking certain steps.[215] This could, for example, require the elimination of any effects the measure might have had, or require that the institution concerned not adopt an identical measure. However, if an act is annulled on formal grounds (i.e. because of an inadequate, or no, statement of reasons) then it will be permissible for the institution to re-enact it, using the correct procedure.[216] What it seems that the Court may not do, is to devise a detailed order suitable for dealing with the losses which the applicants have suffered from unlawful conduct. As the Court stated in the *Pfloeschner* case, 'The Community judicature may not, when upholding an application for annulment, dictate to the institution from which the contested measure emanated what action is to be taken in consequence of the judgment; it must confine itself to referring the matter back to the institution concerned in view of the fact that it is the institution which adopted the contested act that must take the necessary measures to comply with the judgment.'[217] In the context of access to information, the Court has held that it had no authority to order the release of documents held by the Commission, even if they had been unlawfully held.[218] From the applicant's point of view, this may be less than satisfactory, yet another example of the often inadequate nature of the judicial review of Community acts.

---

[215] Article 233:

> The institution or institutions whose act has been declared void or whose failure to act has been declared contrary to this Treaty shall be required to take the necessary measures to comply with the judgement of the Court of Justice.
>
> This obligation shall not affect any obligation which may result from the application of the second paragraph of Article 288.
>
> This Article shall also apply to the ECB.

[216] Case 110/81 *Roquette* v *Council* [1982] ECR 3159.
[217] Case T-285/94 *Pfloeschner* v *Commission* [1995] ECR II 3029.
[218] Case T-126/96 *Interporc* v *Commission* [1998] ECR II 231.

11

CONTROLLING THE COMMUNITY INSTITUTIONS: ACTIONS FOR DAMAGES

INTRODUCTION

The EC, just as much as its member states, subscribes to the principle of the rule of law. So much is stated in Article 6 TEU. However, if this is to be more than a declaratory statement, then the EC must be seen to be governing according to the law, which requires both the freedom of the individual from arbitrary power and the subjection of the Community administration and its officials to requirements of the law. Thus, the transfer from the member states to the Community of (once limited) powers has been accompanied by a system of checks and balances on those powers, as well as judicial protection for individuals, should the Community exceed those powers at their expense.

In the context of the EC Treaty, important and quite sophisticated mechanisms have been included to control the administration. These are Articles 230, 232 and 241 (considered in the last chapter) and Articles 235 and 288, which provide individuals with a remedy in damages for harm caused to them by a Community institution. Thus the power has been given to the Community courts (now principally the Court of First Instance)[1] to control the functioning of the administration. In so doing, it ensures that the EC acts within the limits of its powers, as well as protecting individual rights, for, as Lord Mackenzie-Stuart, a former judge at the ECJ once stated, 'Community law is as much concerned with the protection of rights as with the imposition of obligations.'[2]

But has the Court given effective protection to individuals' rights in applying Article 288? The articles themselves are tersely worded and the Court has had to put flesh on them, as with so many other areas. In so doing, the Court has faced the

---

[1] The Court of First Instance now has exclusive jurisdiction to hear all claims for compensation against the Community brought by individuals.
[2] Mackenzie-Stuart, 'The "non-contractual" liability of the EEC' (1975) 12 CMLRev 493 at 94.

problems encountered by all systems of administrative law, namely, how to strike a fair balance between discretion of the administration and its accountability? How should the Court hold EC institutions with wide-ranging discretionary powers accountable without unduly fettering their discretion, or assuming the role of the decision maker itself? How may the Court avoid the danger of being seen to pass judgment on a Community policy?

The case law under Article 288 reveals the difficulties which the Court has faced in this context (as indeed does the case law on *locus standi* under Article 230). Although there has not been a great deal of jurisprudence in this area (indeed the court's jurisprudence could be described as almost retarded) the Court does seem to have performed this balancing act in a way which has ensured that, while a high level of protection exists in principle, it has rendered that protection almost nugatory by a strict application of the criteria required to bring those mechanisms into play. In other words, in applying the law, it appears to have come down too strongly on the side of the EC.

COMMUNITY LIABILITY

Community non-contractual liability (essentially tortious) is governed by Article 235 (ex 178) EC and Article 288 (ex 215(2)) which, in a conspicuously sparse and vague manner, read as follows:

> Article 235
>
> The Court of Justice shall have jurisdiction in disputes relating to compensation for damage provided for in the second paragraph of Article 288.
>
> . . .
>
> Article 288
>
> (2) In the case of non-contractual liability, the Community shall, in accordance with the general principles common to the laws of the Member States, make good any damage caused by its institutions or by its servants or agents in the performance of their duties.

Therefore, the Community is liable, at least in principle, for any damage that it causes. Such damage may be caused either by the Community's institutions (a *faute de service*, to use the French terminology which the ECJ itself employs), whereby the responsible institution is sued, or by its employees (a *faute personelle*) whereby the Community is liable by way of vicarious liability.

According to Article 288(2), it is the task of the Community courts to determine liability 'in accordance with the general principles common to the laws of the Member states'. Although, according to Fines,[3] this formulation reflects 'the desire of the founders of the treaty to establish a fundamental common law by using comparative methods,' the general consensus among commentators is that the framers did not intend the Court to engage in a comparative law exercise, but rather to

---

[3] F Fines, 'A General Analytical Perspective of Community Liability' in T Heukels and A McDonnell, (eds) *The Action for Damages in Community Law* (Kluwer, 1997) 11 at 13.

empower the Court to 'develop a European standard of liability through the concretisation of general legal principles,'[4] taking into account 'the objectives of the Community and the particularities of its institutional structure'.[5] There are, within the EC member states, no common principles governing state liability in tort and thus this reference to 'general principles' has been likened to a 'diplomatic formula'.[6] As AG Gand stated, the ambiguity of these words was no doubt intentional.[7] Therefore, the comparative exercise is a difficult one. Where it cannot find any principle 'common to the Member states' the Court has drawn from those that do exist to develop a system suitable to the EC. The Court may even, in the context of Article 288(2), apply rules not to be found in any legal system. The European courts therefore have the opportunity, at least, for quite a constructive approach.

It should be noted that the relevant law is that of **public** tort liability, as the EC is a public authority.[8] While under the French legal system there is a separate system of public administrative tort law, in most member states of the EU, liability of public authorities in tort is governed by the same principles as the liability of private individuals (although, as special rules apply to public authorities, inevitably the law is quite different).

In some respects, it might appear that provision for non-contractual liability is quite generous. The applicant has a five-year limitation period in which to bring the action.[9] Moreover, this time will not begin to run until all the requirements for liability have materialised. Furthermore, there are no restrictive requirements regarding *locus standi*. Unlike under Article 230, there is no requirement that the applicant establish direct and individual concern for the action to be admissible. However, as will be discussed, these favourable aspects are more than compensated by the restrictive way in which the Court has developed an Article 288 jurisprudence.

---

[4] Grabitz, 'Liability for Legislative Acts,' in H Schermers, T Heukels and P Mead (eds) *Non-Contractual Liability of the European Communities* (Dordrecht, 1988).

[5] Per AG Roemer in Cases 63–69/72 *Werhan v Council and Commission* [1973] ECR 12.

[6] Lagrange, 'The non-Contractual Liability of the Community in the ECSC and the EEC' 3 CMLR (1966) 10 at 32.

[7] In Cases 5, 7, 13–24/66 *Kampffmeyer v Commission* [1967] ECR 317.

[8] See AG Roemer in Case 25/62 *Plaumann* [1963] ECR 95 at 116–17: 'reference to the national law of a member state . . . can only mean a reference to the national law on administrative liability and not to the general law on compensation'. However, more recently it has been suggested that private law has invaded Article 288, for example in the principles for the calculation of damages: see D Edward and W Robinson, 'Is there a Place for Private Law Principles in Community Law' in Heukels and McDonnell op. cit.

[9] According to Article 43 of the EC Statute of the Court of Justice (which is annexed by way of protocol to the EC Treaty); see M Broberg, 'The calculation of the period of limitation in claims against the EC for non-contractual liability' (2001) 26 ELRev 275.

ELEMENTS OF LIABILITY

These are straightforward and similar to those applied in domestic tort law. In order for an action in damages against the Community to be well-founded, there must be:

(a)　a wrongful act or omission imputable to the Community;[10]

(b)　damage to the claimant;

(c)　a causal link between these two.

WRONGFUL ACTS IMPUTABLE TO THE COMMUNITY

Although the Court has rarely examined the concept of fault, or set out any guidelines determining what it deems wrongful behaviour, it is implicit in the case law that there must be some sort of fault for the Community to be liable under Article 288(2). There is no strict liability. The ECJ has not yet accepted the French doctrine of *égalité devant les charges publiques*[11] (equal apportionment of public burdens), or the similar German concept of *Sonderopfer*,[12] whereby a public body may be strictly liable where a citizen suffers exceptional or abnormal damage as a result of a policy measure in the public interest.[13] Such a principle was considered in *Compagnie d'Approvisionnement*, but the claims lost on other grounds, and in *Dubois v Commission and Council*,[14] in which a customs official argued that the completion of the internal market had put him out of work.

The wrongful act alleged must be an act ascribable to the EC. The institutions covered are not only those mentioned in Article 7 EC, but also Community related bodies, such as the European Environment Agency and the European Central Bank.[15]

However, the actual concept of a wrongful act is extremely wide, including all sorts of things, from the sort of torts that individuals may commit, through administrative acts, to legislative acts intended to have legal effects. Omissions may also be covered (provided that there was a duty to act in the first place). Further examples are detailed below, under three separate sub-categories:

---

[10]　However, where the wrongful act concerned is normative or legislative in nature, rather than being an individual administrative or factual act, the Court will apply a more stringent test, requiring the act not merely to be wrongful, but to involve a sufficiently serious breach of a superior rule of EC law: see below.

[11]　For an example, see the judgment of the Conseil d'Etat in the *Couiteas* case, Recueil Lebon 1923, 789.

[12]　Now apparently losing its force in German law: see Schmitt-Kammler, 'Das "Sonderopfer": ein lebender Leichnam im Staathaftungsrecht?' NJW (1990) 2515.

[13]　Although neither does the ECJ seemed to have entirely ruled out such a doctrine. See Case T-184/95 *Dorsch Consult* [1997] ECR II 351; see also Cases 9, 11/71 *Compagnie d'Approvisionnement v Commission* [1972] ECR 391.

[14]　Case T-113/96 *Dubois v Commission and Council* [1998] ECR II 125; see also regarding the ECSC Treaty Case T-120/89 *Stahlwerke Peine-Salzgitter* [1991] ECR II 2779.

[15]　This has been accomplished by secondary Community legislation, treaty amendment etc. See, for example, Case C-370/89 *SGEEM and Etroy v European Investment Bank* [1992] ECR I-6211.

(a)   negligent acts;

(b)   failures of administration;

(c)   the adoption of wrongful legislative acts.

(a) Negligent acts by servants of the Community in the pursuit of their duties

The Community may be vicariously liable for those wrongful acts of its employees (*fautes personelles*) providing that it can be shown that they were acting in the course of their duties. The ECJ has taken a fairly restrictive approach: this is illustrated by the case of *Sayag* v *Leduc*.[16] Sayag was an engineer with Euratom, who took Leduc (who was not an EC employee) around the Euratom installations at Mol in Belgium. He used his own private car, but was given a travel order by Euratom to cover his expenses. In the course of a traffic accident they were injured. The question was as to whether Leduc should sue Sayag in the national courts, under his own personal liability, or whether Sayag was liable as a Community servant, because he had been on official business at the time. The Belgian Cour de Cassation made a preliminary reference to the ECJ, which, following AG Gand, held that '...the Community is only liable for those acts of its servants which, by virtue of an internal and direct relationship are the necessary extension of the tasks entrusted to the institutions', continuing that 'A servant's use of his private car for transport during the performance of his duties does not satisfy the condition referred to above.'[17] Therefore, it is only in exceptional circumstances that the EC will be liable, for example *force majeure*, or circumstances of overriding importance, such as that in which, without the servant's use of a private car, the EC would be unable to carry out the tasks entrusted to it.

In *Leussink-Brummelhuis* v *Commission*,[18] on very similar facts, the Community was found to be liable. In this case, the claimant had been involved in a traffic accident while driven round by a Community employee. But unlike *Sayag*, the car was owned by the Commission and the ECJ found that the Commission had been negligent in maintaining the car: it had 'failed to exercise the diligence required'[19] and thus was liable. Similarly, in the case of *Grifoni* v *Euratom*[20] the claimant, who worked for a an Italian construction company which was carrying out a contract for Euratom in Italy, had been injured while working at the Ispar research centre in Italy. He had not been wearing a safety harness as required by Italian law. The ECJ found the EC liable for its failure to comply with Italian law on industrial safety.

Generally, however, liability of the Community for acts of its employees is narrower than that of most of its member states. In *Sayag*, AG Gand carried out a

---

[16] Case 9/69 *Sayag* v *Leduc* [1969] ECR 329.

[17] Ibid. at 335–6.

[18] Cases 169/83 and 136/84 [1986] ECR 281.

[19] Ibid. at para 15.

[20] Case 308/87 *Grifoni* [1990] ECR I-1203.

comparative survey of the original six states, finding that liability was wider in all of them but Germany. Hartley[21] has suggested that it is difficult to see any justification for such a narrow concept of vicarious liability as evinced in *Sayag*, and it does seem hard to see what reason the Court might have had in construing liability so narrowly, apart from a perhaps understandable, but not very justifiable, desire to protect the Community from too many claims.

However, if the EC is not found to be liable, it will usually be possible to sue the employee in the national courts under their domestic law. Community employees are immune from suit for acts performed in the course of their official capacity.[22] However, it is unlikely that they will be immune if the EC itself has not been found liable.

(b) Administrative acts

What are administrative acts?[23] They might be defined as acts by which the administration applies general rules in individual cases or otherwise exercises its executive power in an individual manner.[24] The case law of the Court has not been very highly developed regarding liability for administrative acts. Many types of malfunction of the administrative system[25] may constitute a *faute de service*. Examples of breaches of good administration might be the failure to adopt provisions; the failure to supervise officials or outside agencies and bodies when functions are delegated to them; the failure to obtain all relevant facts before taking a decision; or the taking of decisions based on erroneous or irrelevant facts – indeed the types of actions which English lawyers would label 'maladministration'. However, not every deviation of the standard of good administration will constitute a wrongful act for the purpose of Article 288(2): what is required is some sort of blameworthiness, whereby the act in question is not excusable in some way. So, for example, in the case of *Richez-Parise v Commission*[26] the applicants had been given incorrect information by the Commission as to their pensions and had resigned as a result. The information had been given on the basis of an interpretation which the Commission had no reason to believe was erroneous at the time, However, subsequently, the Commission realised that its validity was doubtful, although took no steps to inform the applicants. The ECJ held that the initial information did not constitute a wrongful act and was excusable, but that the failure to correct it did constitute a *faute de service*.

---

[21] TC Hartley, *The Foundations of European Community Law* (Oxford: Clarendon Press, 1998).

[22] Under the *Protocol on Privileges and Immunities of the European Communities*, Article 12(a).

[23] See M Van der Woude, 'Liability for Administrative acts in Heukels and McDonnell (eds) op. cit.

[24] Grabitz, 'Liability for Legislative Acts' in Schermers, Heukels, Mead (eds) *Non-Contractual Liability of the European Communities* (Dordrecht, 1988).

[25] There is probably a legal duty on Community institutions to carry out their actions in a sensible and efficient manner, i.e. a duty of good administration: see Chapter 2 for the discussion of the possible emergence of this duty in the context of the reform of the Commission. Article 41 of the 2000 Community Charter of Fundamental Rights stipulates a citizen's right to 'good administration'.

[26] Cases 19, 20, 25, 30/69 [1970] ECR 325.

In a later case, *KYDEP* v *Council and Commission*,[27] the ECJ stressed that EU institutions are only liable for omissions in this context where there is a breach of a duty to act resulting from a provision of EC law. If, therefore, the institution concerned is acting under a wide discretion, it will be difficult to establish liability for omissions.

On the other hand, in the *Fresh Marine*[28] case, the CFI recently awarded damages for the first time in an anti-dumping case. In principle, anti-dumping measures constitute legislation[29] but the CFI held that, where the Commission has little or no discretion, then the mere infringement of Community law will be sufficient to establish liability. In *Fresh Marine*, the Commission had failed to take account of corrections to clerical errors in determining whether an undertaking given by Fresh Marine had been complied with: this was sufficient to establish liability.

Another such rare example of a case resulting in the award of damages to an individual, and also a case with striking facts, is *Adams* v *Commission*.[30] Adams had worked for the Swiss pharmaceutical giant, Hoffman La Roche, and, after requesting confidentiality, had provided the Commission with documents which showed that Hoffman La Roche had violated EC competition law. The Commission brought proceedings against Hoffman La Roche and the company was fined. Hoffmann La Roche was able, however, on the basis of the internal codes of documents which Adams had sent to the Commission, to establish the identity of Adams as the informant. By then Adams had ceased to work for them, but he took the somewhat imprudent step (he was by then living in Italy) of returning to Switzerland, where he was arrested under Swiss industrial espionage laws and placed in solitary confinement and interrogated. His wife was also interrogated and committed suicide. Adams was convicted and given a suspended sentence, following which he sued the Commission for damages. His claim succeeded (although was reduced by 50 per cent due to his contributory negligence in returning to Switzerland). The ECJ held that the Commission was bound by a duty of confidentiality (Article 287 EC imposes confidentiality obligations which apply in particular when a complainant has requested anonymity) which they had violated, in particular, by not warning Adams that Hoffmann La Roche was planning to prosecute him.

(c) Liability for wrongful acts having legal effects

This is the most significant category of cases under Article 288(2) and constitutes an area in which the Court has developed special rules, largely unique to the Community. They concern cases in which legislative, or semi-legislative, measures are taken which involve a degree of discretion on the decision maker's part, for example the decision to impose a levy on certain producers. Such decisions are normative in nature, and necessarily involve more than one person. A great many of

---

[27] Case 146/91 [1994] ECR I-4199.
[28] Case T-178/98 *Fresh Marine* [2000] ECR II-3331.
[29] See below for a discussion of the Community's liability for legislative action.
[30] Case 145/83 [1985] ECR 3539.

them concern the CAP, and the EC's mistakes, or gaffes, in dealing with the common problem of over-production. In such cases, the ECJ has held that the EC may be liable, despite the general nature of the act. In this respect EC law is unlike most systems of national law, where liability for legislation is very unusual. However, it has proved very difficult for applicants to succeed in their claims.

There will, in any case, be no liability for actions regarding the treaty (itself a normative document, with much scope for discretion) as the *Dubois* case,[31] mentioned above, illustrates. Dubois had claimed that his business as a customs agent had suffered 'an almost total and definitive cessation of its activities', resulting in huge losses of millions of francs, following the removal of customs checks on borders at the completion of the internal market. The Court held there could be no liability under primary Community law.

This is not the case with secondary legislation, such as regulations, or even directives and decisions, which may also be normative in their effects. However, it was thought for some while that, in order to succeed in a damages claim, the act in question had first to be annulled. Plaumann,[32] the unfortunate importer of clementines, had failed in his claim under Article 230 for lack of *locus standi*. He then brought a claim for compensation, and failed yet again, because the ECJ held that it could not, by way of actions for compensation, take steps that would nullify the legal effects of decisions which had not been annulled. Some years later, this decision was reversed in the *Lutticke*[33] case, in which the ECJ held that the action for damages under Article 288(2) was an **independent** form of action, with a particular purpose to fulfil, and thus could be brought, even if an action for annulment had been found inadmissible.[34] (A bit of a pyrrhic victory, however, as Lutticke's case failed on the merits.)

The two actions under Article 230 and Article 288 are independent and quite different in nature. For example, Article 230 is in essence what the Germans would call a '*Gestaltungslklage*', geared toward the alteration of a legal position, but Article 288 is what would be termed a '*Leistungsklage*', namely, an action directed at obtaining compensation.[35] The former is designed to challenge the objective legality of a Community measure, whereas the latter is intended to operate in situations involving necessarily a subjective element: the awarding of damages to rectify a particular wrong that has taken place *inter partes*.[36] Or, as AG Dutheillet de Lamothe characterised it, the action for damages is in essence the exercise of a subjective right and implies a direct relationship between the individual and the EC.[37]

---

[31] Case T-113/96 [1998] ECR II 125.

[32] Case 25/62 *Plaumann* [1963] ECR 95.

[33] Case 4/69 *Lutticke* v *Commission* [1971] ECR 325.

[34] This is the case for administrative acts as well as for legislative acts: Joined Cases T-480 and T-483/93 *Antillean Rice Mills and Others* v *Commission* [1995] ER II-2305.

[35] Toth, *Legal Protection of Individuals in the European Communities* Vol 2 (North Holland 1978) at 118.

[36] P Mead, 'The Relationship between an Action for Damages and an Action for Annulment: The Return of Plaumann?' in Heukels and McDonnell op. cit. fn 3.

[37] In Cases 9–11/71 *Compagnie d'Approvisionnement* [1972] ECR 391 at 411.

The 'Schöppenstedt' formula

Although the absence of annulment of a legislative act is not a bar to an action for damages under Article 288, this does not mean that the latter types of action are generally successful, as the ECJ has been very restrictive in the test which it has set for the liability of legislative acts. However, unlike under Article 230, in the context of Article 288, it has tended to reject claims on the basis of material grounds, rather than at the admissibility stage.

That the Court should nonetheless have been restrictive is perhaps hardly surprising, as most legal systems tend not to allow liability for damage caused by legislative acts. As AG Darmon stated in *Vreugdenhil II*, 'In many, if not all of the Member states . . . The liability of the legislative authorities . . . is governed by stricter rules (than in the case of administrative authorities) with in particular a requirement of unusual and specific damage, or is quite simply non-existent.'[38] This restrictive approach is for policy reasons. Such actions tend to involve decisions which are taken in the public interest, involving all sorts of activities, and naturally involve quite a lot of discretion on the part of the public authority. While public authorities should be kept in check by judicial review, it is quite another thing to require them to pay out damages, in the absence of any bad faith on their part. Indeed, it has been argued that to do so would fetter the executive process and place a very large burden on public authorities.[39]

However, the Court did rule in *Schöppenstedt*[40] that the EC could be liable for its legislative acts. Unfortunately, it failed to give any useful elaboration of its reasons for doing so. However, if we look to the reasoning of AG Roemer in the same case, we may see that he at least concluded in favour of liability chiefly on the ground that parliamentary control in the EC was deficient. He also resorted to the familiar principle that provisions relating to the protection of rights should not be interpreted restrictively.

However, in cases involving legislative acts, unlike individual acts, it is not sufficient if the EC failed to act lawfully. Where the action involves a legislative measure involving choices of economic policy, the ECJ has held there will be no liability unless there is 'a sufficiently serious breach of a superior rule of law for the protection of the individual'. This is known as the '*Schöppenstedt*' formula after the case[41] in which the issue was litigated, although the ECJ actually formulated the test, in the form stated above, in another case, *Bayerische HNL*.[42] The *Schöppenstedt* test involves three principal elements:

(a) A legislative measure involving choices of economic policy

Legislative measures are those which lay down general rules which apply to indefinite categories of persons. For the purposes of the *Schöppenstedt* test, they must be

---

[38] Case C-282/90 *Vreugdenhil v Commission (Vreugdenhil II)* [1992] ECR I-1937 at 1958.

[39] For an example of this view see e.g. C Harlow, *Compensation and Government Torts* (Sweet and Maxwell 1982) at 100.

[40] Case 5/71 *Aktien-Zuckerfabrik Schöppenstedt v Council* [1971] ECR 975.

[41] Ibid.

[42] Cases 83, 94/76 [1978] ECR 1209 para 4.

discretionary, but this is hardly difficult to satisfy, as most legislation involves some discretion or other. They usually take the form of regulations but could be direct-ives.[43] The majority of legislative measures will involve choices of economic policy (since the EC was for so long principally an economic community). However, the fact that an applicant has been permitted to challenge a measure directly under Article 230 does not necessarily establish that it is not legislative in nature.[44]

(b) A breach of a superior rule of law for the protection of the individual

There is no specific definition of what makes a rule of law 'superior' for this purpose, although it is implicit in the Court's case law that such rules tend to be general principles such as equality, proportionality, fundamental rights, as well as the fundamental freedoms, and the Court has been reasonably liberal in this area.

Most of these tend to be for the benefit of the individual in any case. The require-ment that they benefit individuals derives from the German *Schütznorm* doctrine. According to this doctrine, a *Schütznorm* is a legal norm protecting a subjective public right of the injured party, which is intended not only to protect individuals in general, but also a specific circle of individuals to which the claimant belongs.[45] However, *Vloeberghs*[46] provides an example of a case where the ECJ did not find a general rule to be for the benefit of the individual. Vloeberghs brought an action for damages against the High Authority, based on an alleged breach by the High Authority of the free movement of goods (the goods in question being coal). However, the ECJ held that the relevant principle was not there to benefit coal importers, thus they could not rely on it. Another such example is the *Vreugdenhil* case, in which an action to recover damage caused by an invalid EC action adopted in breach of the division of powers between the EU institutions failed. The ECJ held that the concept of institutional balance was not designed to benefit the individual.[47] This seems somewhat unsatisfactory. Traditional constitutional theory posits the separation of powers, or in the Community context, the institutional balance, as a structural feature with the purpose of preventing misuse of power, very much for the benefit of citizens, albeit not a subjective right in the sense of a *Schütznorm*.

---

[43] In Case C-298/89 *Gibraltar v Council* [1993] ECR I-3605, the ECJ held that directives usually con-stitute 'a form of indirect regulation or legislative measure'.

[44] Joined Cases T-480/93 and 483/93 *Antillean Rice Mills v Commission* [1995] ECR II-2305. However, this seems somewhat illogical: surely a measure cannot be legislative for the purposes of one article but not another, when the definition of a legislative measure is the same under both? See A Arnull, 'Liability for Legislative Acts' in Heukels and McDonnell, at 136, who seeks to explain this discrepancy by sug-gesting that the description of the act as legislative under Article 230 is becoming irrelevant: what mat-ters, he suggests, is whether there is direct and individual concern. (He explains this as a result of the Court's decisions in *Extramet* and *Codorniu*.)

[45] See Grabitz, 'Liability for Legislative Acts' in Schermers and Heukels and Mead (eds) *Non-Contractual Liability of the European Communities* (Dordrecht, 1988) at 6.

[46] Cases 9 and 12/60 [1961] ECR 197.

[47] Case C-282/90 *Vreugdenhil v Commission* [1992] ECR I-1937.

(c) The breach must be 'sufficiently serious'

This is the most significant aspect of the *Schöppenstedt* formula and extremely difficult to establish, as is illustrated by the *HNL* case.[48] This case resulted from the over-production of milk in the EC which had led to the creation of a skimmed milk mountain.[49] To get rid of it, the Council passed a regulation obliging animal feed producers to purchase skimmed milk from intervention agencies, to replace soya as a source of protein. However, skimmed milk was more expensive, so the farmers had to pay more. The farmers brought actions, and, in the course of a preliminary reference from one of these actions in the national courts, the ECJ had held the regulation to be invalid on the basis of a violation of the principles of proportionality and non-discrimination.[50] They then brought an action for damages. They had no difficulty in satisfying the first two limbs of the *Schöppenstedt* formula, but was the breach committed by the Community authorities sufficiently serious? The ECJ held not, stating that in the legislative field, involving wide discretion, there would be no liability unless the institution concerned had 'manifestly and gravely disregarded the limits of the exercise of its powers'.[51] This was not the case here, stated the Court, for the following reasons. The measure affected a wide category of persons, namely all buyers of animal protein feed. The price increase had only a limited effect on production costs, which was insignificant in comparison with increases caused by fluctuations in world prices. Moreover, the effect on profits did not exceed the normal level of risk inherent in these activities. Therefore, for all of these reasons, the Court held that the breach was not sufficiently serious. From the *HNL* case, it would seem that, for liability to arise, there must be a serious effect on the applicants' interests, and it would also seem that the applicants themselves must form a small group.

In a case that followed shortly after *HNL*, the *Dumortier Frères* case,[52] the applicants were exceptional in being among the few to be successful in their claim for damages against a Community institution. The applicants were quellmehl and gritz producers, substances used in baking and brewing. To a certain extent, these substances are exchangeable with starch and thus in competition with it. Starch had benefited from EEC subsidies, as had quellmehl and gritz. However, the EC then removed the subsidies from quellmehl and gritz. The regulation by which it had done this had been found invalid in an earlier case,[53] as the ECJ found that it breached the principle of equality, and the Council restored the subsidies. However, it only did so from the date of judgment. The applicants wanted this to be backdated and they applied for compensation in a separate action. Was the Council's breach, according to the *HNL* test, a 'manifest and grave' one? Somewhat surprisingly, the

---

[48] Cases 83, 94/76 *Bayerische HNL (second Skimmed Milk Powder)* [1978] ECR 1209.

[49] For a different view of the skimmed milk saga, see F Snyder, *New Directions in Community Law* (Weidenfeld, 1990) at 19 *et seq*.

[50] In Cases 114/76 *Bela Muhle* [1977] ECR 1211 and 116/76 *Granaria* [1977] ECR 1247.

[51] *HNL* at para 5.

[52] Cases 64 and 113/76 *Dumortier Frères* [1979] ECR 3091.

[53] Case 117/76 *Albert Rückdeschel* [1977] ECR 1753.

ECJ held that it was. The ECJ's reasoning was not particularly clear, but the following factors seemed to weigh: that the applicants were a small and clearly defined group; and that the loss went beyond the level of risk inherent in their business. However, although their claim was successful and the Court held that the extent of their damages should be based on the amount of subsidy which they should have received, the ECJ reduced their damage to the extent that they failed to mitigate it, by failing to pass on their loss to their customers.[54]

On the basis of *Quellmehl and Gritz*, it might have been thought that the applicants in the contemporaneous *Isoglucose* cases[55] would have been successful. These cases arose out of the EC's disastrous isoglucose fiasco. Isoglucose is a substance which competes with sugar and is used, as is sugar, in sweets, jams and drinks and so on. By 1976 it posed a threat to sugar, which was in surplus, in the form of a sugar mountain the size of the skimmed milk and butter mountains. The EC took steps to deal with sugar over-production and did so by imposing a huge levy on isoglucose production, to prevent it from providing successful competition to sugar. This levy had a disastrous effect on isoglucose production. The isoglucose producers, who were a small and clearly defined group, numbering only a few EC wide, suffered catastrophic losses; for example, one of them, the Dutch firm, KSH, went into liquidation. On a preliminary reference to the ECJ from the English courts, the measures imposing the levy had been annulled, again on the basis of the principle of equality, and the levy was withdrawn. However, the producers wanted compensation for their huge losses. Their claim failed. Although they were a very small group indeed, and had suffered 'manifestly unequal treatment', whose impact was catastrophic, the ECJ held that the error concerned was not of such gravity that it could be regarded as 'verging on the arbitrary'. This last involved the introduction of a new requirement, but unfortunately the Court's reasoning as to why it was imposing the test was very sparse, probably indicating that the Court was divided. Thus, after *Isoglucose*, there seemed to be two elements required to found a successful damages claim. First, the requirement of an impact on the applicants, as well as that they form a small group, and second, a factor concerning the nature of the breach, in this case imposing a requirement of irrationality which was almost impossible to surmount.

However, since then, the Court has appeared to relax its attitude, no longer seeming to require that the breach be verging on the arbitrary: in, for example, *Stahlwerke Peine-Salzgitter* v *Commission*, and *Sofrimport*.[56] In *Sofrimport*, the applicants succeeded in their claim, the basis of the Court's reasoning was that they formed a closed group, namely 'a restricted group which could not be extended after the contested measures had been imposed' and that also, the Commission had 'failed completely to take the applicants' interests into account'.

---

[54] This is discussed further below.
[55] Cases 116 and 124/77 *Amylum NV and Tunnel Refineries Ltd v Council and Commission* [1979] ECR 3497.
[56] Case C-220/91 P *Stahlwerke Peine-Salzgitter v Commission* [1993] ECR I-2923; Case C-152/88 *Sofrimport* [1990] ECR I 2477.

The still more recent *Mulder*[57] case provides another example of at least a partially successful claim. This case again concerned measures taken by the EC to deal with over-production of milk. A premium was given to farmers if they did not market milk over a five-year period. The EC, however, additionally introduced milk quotas, under which a production levy on milk was payable by those farmers who produced more than their quota. Their quota was based on a certain year specified in the regulation, but the system failed to take account of those farmers who had produced no milk during that year due to their undertaking under the premium system. Therefore, they received no quota. In the course of a preliminary ruling,[58] the ECJ had held the measure imposing the quotas to be invalid, on the basis of a breach of legitimate expectations. The Council then passed another regulation allocating specific 'reference quantities' calculated at 60 per cent of production in the year prior to that in which they had stopped producing milk. This was also held to be invalid by the ECJ. The applicants thereafter sought compensation for both the period of the original regulation, during which they had been totally denied a milk quota, and also for the period during the second regulation when they had been permitted a quota at 60 per cent. In the former they succeeded and the Court held that the Council had 'failed to take account of the specific situation of a clearly defined group' and that their loss was 'not foreseeable as falling within the normal level of economic risk' – thus it was a grave and manifest breach. However, the applicants were not successful in their second claim: the court held that in setting the quota at that level, the Council had not committed a sufficiently serious breach.

Interestingly, in the *Mulder* cases, although the group was clearly defined, it was not small. Indeed, it was so large that the Council had to deal with the issue of compensation by way of another regulation.[59]

Following *Mulder* then, the law would seem to be that two tests are applied in order to determine if a breach is sufficiently serious. First, regarding the nature of the breach. It must be manifest and grave: the *HNL* test is still good law, and it must not be justifiable. The second concerns the effects on the applicants. The harm must go beyond the normal level of risk inherent in the claimant's business, in other words it must be unforeseeable. An applicant may be able to establish such an effect if it can show that it belonged to a class which had been singled out for special treatment but ignored when the contested measure was adopted. In this case they can argue that the special treatment accorded them a legitimate expectation which was then ignored.[60] However, following *Mulder*, it would seem that it is not necessary that applicants form a small group. There is also no longer a requirement that the breach be verging on the arbitrary. The *Mulder* saga finally came to an end with the ECJ's judgment in January 2000,[61] whereby it fixed the actual amount of compensation to producers of milk products.

---

[57] Case C-104/89, C 37/90 *Mulder v Council and Commission* [1992] ECR I-3061.
[58] Case 120/86 *Mulder v Minster van Landbouuw en Visserij* [1988] ECR 2321.
[59] Regulation 2187/93 OJ 1993 L 196/94.
[60] See E Sharpston, 'Legitimate Expectations and Economic Reality' (1990) 15 ELRev 103.
[61] Cases C-104/89 and C-37/90 *Mulder* [2000] ECR I 203.

However, as the *Mulder* chapter closed, another opened, with the *Bergaderm* case,[62] in which the ECJ sought to unite its Article 288(2) jurisprudence with that of state liability under *Francovich* and *Factortame III*, a unity which some had thought to be a long time coming. The ECJ held in *Bergaderm* that the concept of a 'sufficiently serious breach' must be interpreted in the same way with regard to EC institutions as it had been for member states in the *Factortame III* jurisprudence, and that protection of individual rights under EC law could not vary depending on whether it was a national authority or an EC institution which was responsible. Therefore, where a Community institution had reduced discretion in legislative matters, a mere infringement might amount to a sufficiently serious breach. This should make it easier, in principle,[63] for individuals to recover where the legislative act in question does not involve a wide amount of discretion.[64]

Conclusions on *Schöppenstedt*

Many try but only few have succeeded. When AG Tesauro wrote his opinion in *Brasserie du Pêcheur* in December 1995[65] he noted that, by then, only eight awards of damages against EC institutions had ever been made. Although, since 1995, several more awards of damages have been made, these have tended to be made in the context of administrative failures, rather than legislative acts.[66] Does the award of so few judgments in damages against the EC mean that many applicants have been left without a remedy?[67] It is true that applicants may be, or have been, able to proceed in national courts and get an offending measure annulled through a preliminary reference to Luxembourg. However, it is not possible to obtain damages in the national courts where the wrong in question is attributable to the EC. Steiner[68] has suggested that, in such circumstances, the best solution would be for the speedy provision of interim relief, through the national courts, in order to render the offending measure inoperative. She also suggests that, if the damage is due to a lawful act, then perhaps in exceptional circumstances, the ECJ might be persuaded to introduce strict liability by way of the French doctrine of *'égalite devant les charges publiques'*. So far, neither the ECJ nor the CFI has shown any great inclination to do so.

Naturally, the explanation for the Court's extremely cautious attitude in the context of legislative acts is its fear of floodgates of litigants.[69] As the ECJ stated in the

---

[62] Case C-352/98P *Laboratoires Pharmaceutiques Bergaderm* [2000] ECR I-5291.

[63] It did not assist the applicants in the *Bergaderm* case, as their application for damages caused by the Commission's directive on cosmetics (which they claimed was not legislative in nature) was dismissed.

[64] See the judgment of the CFI in its *Fresh Marine* case, cited above. See also Chapter 9 for a discussion of state liability.

[65] Joined Cases C-46/93 and C-48/93 *Brasserie du Pêcheur v Germany* and *The Queen v Secretary of State for Transport, ex parte Factortame* [1996] ECR I 1029.

[66] E.g. as in Case T-203/96 *Embassy Limousines v European Parliament* [1998] ECR II-4239.

[67] See C Stefanou and H Xanthaki, *A Legal and Political Interpretation of Article 288(2) of the Treaty of Rome: The Individual Strikes Back* (Aldershot Dartmouth, 2000) for a critical account of the individual protection afforded under Article 288(2).

[68] J Steiner and L Woods, *EU Law* (Blackstone Press 2000, 7th edn).

[69] See Lord Wilberforce in *Anns v Merton LBC* [1978] AC 728, HL, for the policy reasons for not doing so.

HNL case, 'the legislative authority, even where the validity of its measures is subject to judicial review, cannot always be hindered in making its decisions by the prospect of applications for damages whenever it has occasion to adopt legislative measures in the public interest which might adversely affect the interests of individuals.'[70] Most domestic legal systems of the EU do not award compensation for damages caused by primary legislation. However, such a justification assimilates normative acts of the EC to member state legislation. Such an assimilation can be questioned. EC normative measures, and most particularly regulations, are hybrid in nature; their purpose and legal effect resembles that of statutory laws, but their origin may well be like that of national secondary legislation, especially in those cases where the European Parliament has little say, which is especially so in the field of agriculture, which most of the Article 288 cases concern. Therefore a straightforward comparative law approach is out of tune with establishing Community liability. Yet the Court has, at least until recently (and it remains to be seen how liberally *Bergaderm* will be applied) maintained a formal approach, requiring the same restrictive conditions, whatever the characteristics of the economic measure and the scope of the discretionary power.

Non-contractual liability is a highly problematic area of law, in which the Court may be embroiled in weighing the often conflicting interests of securing adequate flexibility in decision-making of the administration and protecting individuals who may be adversely affected by such decisions. Although flagrant abuse of power or other clearly illegal legislative action should not go unchecked, in cases of lesser infringements, the right path is less clear cut. Just how complex is this field is illustrated by Snyder's commentary on the skimmed milk saga case, *Bela Muhle*, in his book, *New Directions in Community Law*.[71] Snyder highlights the multi-dimensional politico-legal background. *Bela Muhle* concerned the delimitation of legally permissible ways in which agricultural surpluses can be controlled. The ECJ took a narrow focus, but, in its own way, was also making economic policy.

In the case of individual, rather than legislative, acts, there is no danger of a floodgate of claims and the Court can afford to be more generous in its approach. The Court has always applied a less stringent test regarding individual acts. However, the ECJ has not always been as cautious as it might have been of the differences between these two types of situation, a feature which was mentioned by AG Tesauro in *Brasserie*, when he considered the transportation by the ECJ of the legislative act test under Article 288 into the field of state liability under *Francovich*.[72]

DAMAGE AND CAUSATION

The other two essential ingredients for a successful action under Article 288 are the establishment of damage and causation.

---

[70] *HNL* at para 49.
[71] F Snyder, *New Directions in Community Law* (Weidenfield, 1990) at 19 *et seq.*
[72] Discussed further below, but again now see *Bergaderm*.

Damage

The concept of 'damage' is nowhere defined in the treaty. The treaties do require the Communities to make good 'any damage', but the Court does seem yet again to have taken a restrictive approach. It will generally require the damage to be certain, specific and quantifiable.[73] However, the Court has relaxed these requirements to the extent that the EC may be liable if the loss is 'imminent and foreseeable with sufficient certainty:[74] this enables a claimant to challenge a normative Community act as soon as it has taken place in order to prevent further damage and in so doing escape the rigours of Article 230.

Many of the cases brought under Article 288 are economic in nature, and the Court will award damage for economic loss.[75] In *Kampffmeyer*,[76] for example, the applicants had been forced to break their contracts as a result of unlawful EC action. They were able to recover damage for cancellation fees and lost profits on the contracts already concluded, although this was reduced very considerably, to 10 per cent of their losses, due to the inherent risks of the transactions concerned. In the *CNTA* case,[77] the applicants were held entitled to compensation caused by currency fluctuations, which the EC had been responsible for exposing them to, but were unable to recover their anticipated profits.

The ECJ has also made it clear that there is a general duty to mitigate (derivable from principles common to the member states) and that damages will be reduced if the applicants fail to do so. They applied this duty to mitigate in the *Gritz and Quellmehl* case in which they held that it encompassed a duty to pass them on to a third party.[78] This requirement has been quite severely criticised.[79] Not only is it very difficult to prove to what extent price increases did, or could have, compensated for lost refunds, but also this requirement places an unreasonable duty on the injured party. While some reasonable action in minimising losses can be expected from any ordinary citizen, it might seem that the Court has gone too far here. Such a requirement makes innocent third parties, or the public at large, bear the costs of illegal Community action: this rests somewhat uneasily with the established principles of liability which require the tortfeasor to make good the consequences of wrongful conduct.

The ECJ has also been willing to make awards for types of damage other than economic loss, such as damages for anxiety and hurt feelings, where, for example, EC employees have been wrongfully dismissed or unfairly treated.[80] Generally, the onus to prove damage lies with the injured party. The Court

---

[73] Toth, 'The Concepts of Damage and Causality in Non-Contractual Liability' in Heukels and McDonnell op. cit. 179.

[74] Cases 5,7, 13–24/66 *Kampffmeyer v Commission* [1967] ECR at 317.

[75] Unlike in some of the member states where it is difficult to obtain such damages.

[76] Case 5,7,13–24/66 *Kampffmeyer* [1967] ECR 245.

[77] Case 74/74 *CNTA SA v Commission* [1975] ECR 533.

[78] *Quellmehl and Gritz* Case 238/78 *Ireks-Arkady v Council and Commission* [1979] ECR 2955.

[79] Toth, op. cit.

[80] See Cases 7/56, 3–7/57 *Algera v Assembly* [1957] ECR 59.

dictates a high standard of proof: the evidence furnished has to be both conclusive and verifiable.[81] As in many areas of economic activity, success or failure results from an interplay of contributing factors. The exact injury caused by one act may be hard to quantify and prove conclusively. Indeed, many applications have been dismissed on grounds of insufficient evidence.[82]

Thus, although the Court's willingness to grant declaratory judgments in principle, along with compensation for pure and immaterial economic loss, indicate that it might have been possible for the Court to offer a high degree of protection for individuals, however, overall, as should be evident, the Court has not been so generous regarding damage.

Causation

The ECJ has also taken a restrictive approach to causation. Once again, it has not laid down clear guidelines. However, it has made it clear that any damage caused must be **a sufficiently direct consequence** for wrongful EC action. This may be very difficult to establish, especially in the economic and commercial field in which the cause of an event can be traced to many matters. The liability of the Community will naturally be excluded or limited where the injured party has been entirely or partly the author of their own misfortunes.[83]

CONCURRENT LIABILITY

Although this chapter discusses EC liability, Community law is very often implemented by national authorities rather than directly by the EC. There are a great variety of schemes of shared administration. Citizens therefore deal with national authorities such as intervention agencies, and it is to these bodies that they must pay levies which may be unlawful, or may be refused subsidies which are due. One may not proceed against both the Community and national authorities in the same forum and so the question therefore arises as to which forum claimants should use for litigation. If a claimant is dealing with national bodies' actions, should they not proceed in their national courts, proceeding by way of tort, or restitution (quasi-contract)? The case law in this area is somewhat confusing.

The ECJ considered this issue in the *Kampffmeyer* case.[84] This case was the successor to the *Toepfer*[85] case, which was discussed in the last chapter. It will be remembered that the applicants in this case were German grain dealers, who had been refused permits to import maize from France into Germany. When the import ban had been lifted, the levy on imports was increased and they had to pay an

---

[81] Case 26/74 *Roquette Fréres v Commission* [1976] ECR 677 at 688.
[82] Toth op. cit. at fn 73.
[83] Case 145/83 *Adams v Commission* [1985] ECR 3539 at 3592.
[84] Cases 5,7, 13–24/66 *Kampffmeyer v Commission* [1967] ECR 317.
[85] Cases 106 and 107/63 *Toepfer v Commission* [1965] ECR 405.

additional sum. They had succeeded in getting the levy annulled in *Toepfer* (one of the rare such cases in which they succeeded in establishing *locus standi* under Article 230). However, in their second claim, they wanted to have the levies they had paid to the German authorities returned (a claim in restitution) and they also wanted compensation for the contracts which they had had to cancel, a tortious claim. The applicants had commenced proceedings in the German courts, but these had been stayed, pending a decision by the ECJ. The ECJ then, however, also stayed its proceedings in order to give the German courts a chance to determine whether the national authorities were liable. The ECJ thus seemed to be taking the view that any EC liability was subsidiary to that of the German authorities. This was not a particularly satisfactory decision. The ECJ had subscribed to a principle of exhaustion of domestic remedies, appearing to place any financial risk on the member states and thereby leaving the EC free for any incentive to act legally.[86] Alternatively, it risks placing the burden of double litigation, a very expensive burden, on the applicants. The applicants did eventually succeed in gaining compensation from the national courts, nine years later.

In the *Haegeman*[87] case, a Belgian importer sought restitution of damages which it claimed had been unlawfully levied on the import of wine from Greece. The ECJ stated that the collection of duties was for the national authorities (although they had subsequently been paid into Community coffers) and thus, in order to recoup them, the applicants should proceed in the national courts.

However, in three subsequent cases,[88] the ECJ itself admitted claims for sums unlawfully withheld from the applicants, without requiring them first to proceed in the national courts.

In the light of the foregoing, admittedly rather unclear authorities, the following tentative conclusions regarding concurrent liability might be suggested.[89] First, if one is claiming the return of sums unlawfully paid to the national authorities, then one should proceed in the national courts, even although the sums may have been paid on into Community funds. *Haegeman* might be cited as authority for this. Second, if one is claiming sums unlawfully withheld by a national authority then one may bring proceedings in either court.[90] Finally, unliquidated damages may be claimed only in the ECJ, on the basis of *Dumortier*, for example. In this respect, Steiner[91] has suggested that *Kampffmeyer* is wrong in requiring an applicant to proceed first in the national courts. All of this is still rather confusing, but, essentially, the choice of court seems to rest on whether one is pursuing a quasi-contractual

---

[86] D Chalmers, *EU Law* (Ashgate, 1998) at 580.

[87] Case 96/71 *Haegeman* [1972] ECR 1005.

[88] Cases 9 and 11/71; *Compagnie d'Approvisionnement* [1972] ECR 391; Case 153/73 *Holtz* [1974] ECR 675; and Case 74/74 *CNTA* [1975] ECR 533.

[89] See P Oliver, 'Joint Liability of the Community and the Member States' in Heukels and McDonnell; also A Meij, 'Article 215(2) EC and Local Remedies' in Heukels and McDonnell; also W Wils, 'Concurrent Liability of The Community and member states' (1992) 17 ELRev 191; Steiner and Woods, *EC Law* (Blackstone, 2000 7th edn), Chapter 33.

[90] Cases 9 and 11/71; *Compagnie d'Approvisionnement*; Case 153/73 *Holtz*; and Case 74/74 *CNTA*.

[91] Steiner and Woods op. cit. at 565.

claim, or a tortious claim.[92] It would indeed be fairer if the ECJ would recognise a system of joint and several liability, whereby the applicant could choose in which forum to sue, with defendants receiving a contribution from each other.[93] In any case, the current system runs the risk of leading to disharmony regarding the European court structure, as, if one is claiming damages directly from the EC, one will proceed directly in the CFI. However, if one proceeds in the national courts, they, in any case, may decide to make a preliminary reference to Luxembourg, in which case the matter will go to the Court of Justice and there will be a danger of two courts considering the same matter under different actions, which may lead to confusing and contradictory results.[94]

COMMUNITY NON-CONTRACTUAL LIABILITY AND MEMBER STATE LIABILITY UNDER *FRANCOVICH*

In developing the principle of state liability in damages for breach of EC law, the ECJ, in the *Factortame III* and *Brasserie du Pêcheur*[95] cases, utilised the principles of EC liability under the *Schöppenstedt* test, as AG Mischo had earlier suggested they do in his Opinion in *Francovich*. This was generally welcomed as providing a unity of remedies for claimants, whether damage had been caused to them by member states breaching EC law, or by EC institutions themselves.

However, there has been some criticism of the incorporation of the *Schöppenstedt* test into state liability, on two different grounds. First, on the basis that the *Schöppenstedt* test has been applied very restrictively by the Court. If applied inflexibly in the arena of member state liability, it would not result in a high level of protection for individuals. Second, on the basis that not every state breach of EC law, which causes damage to individuals, involves legislative choices with a high degree of discretion. Sometimes states have very little discretion at all, in which case a less restrictive test would seem to apply.[96] In *Brasserie*, however, the ECJ confirmed that the *Schöppenstedt* test would apply in the arena of state liability, but did at least also introduce some criteria whereby the national courts might assess whether the breach were 'sufficiently serious'. For example, it stated that 'the clarity and precision of the EC rule breached, the measure of discretion left by that rule to the national or Community authorities, whether the infringement and the damage caused was intentional or voluntary, whether the error of law was excusable or non-excusable',[97] should be taken into account. This, at least, gave some room for manoeuvre to the national courts in their assessment of the nature of the breach.

---

[92] Meij op. cit. at 284.

[93] In this respect see P Oliver, 'Joint Liability of the Community and Member states' in Schermers *et al.* (eds) *Non Contractual Liability of the European Communities* (Dordrecht: Martinus Nijhoff, 1988).

[94] D Chalmers, *EU Law* 581.

[95] Joined Cases C-46/93 and C-48/93 *Brasserie du Pêcheur* v *Germany* and *The Queen* v *Secretary of State for Transport, ex parte Factortame* [1996] ECR I 1029.

[96] As in *Francovich* itself, which involved the failure by the Italian government to implement a directive.

[97] At para 56.

Nonetheless, some writers have found it regrettable that the ECJ has failed to look further afield than *Schöppenstedt* in applying its Article 288 jurisprudence in the context of state liability. For example, Walter Van Gerven[98] has suggested that, had the ECJ looked beyond *Schöppenstedt*, it would have been able to have defined, and differentiated, the liability conditions for breach by member states according to the type of situation involved. Van Gerven, along with Van der Woude, has instead argued for the application of the *Schöppenstedt* test only to legislative acts involving choices of economic policy and that for other types of state liability, the ECJ should recommend the classic test under Article 288, namely, that it should be illegality, rather than the seriousness of the breach, which is the determining factor. In this way, member states would not have the possibility of escaping liability in matters in which they have very little discretion. In its *Bergaderm* decision of 2000, the ECJ seemed to be taking on board some of this criticism.[99]

CONCLUSIONS

In spite of an increasing amount of claims, Article 288 has proved itself to be an action with a very low success rate. Although it would seem that, in principle at least, the Court has developed mechanisms for protecting individuals – including some which are more generous than those provided under national law, such as liability for pure economic loss, or liability for normative acts – the Court has in fact been generous in principle only. In its enforcement of Article 288, the Court has all too often stopped short of awarding damages. Even if an applicant has been given judgment in their favour, the Court has very frequently not awarded full damages: Adams had his damages reduced by 50 per cent for contributory negligence, Kampffmeyer's were reduced to 10 per cent of the claim due to their speculative nature and in *CNTA* the claimants failed to recover anything at all, in spite of a judgment in their favour. It might be argued that these judgments nonetheless turn on the facts and are not out of kilter with accepted principles of tort law. It is also true that the Court must be aware of its effect on the administrative system, lest it be subject to the complaint that it will deter officials from making law, or that the Court itself might end up dictating the financial priorities of government. Nonetheless, the Court's approach seems harsh and has been subjected to criticisms.

These critiques have taken a variety of forms. One is that it is all very well to hold up the ECJ's doctrine of liability of legislative acts as an advance on the position in most of its member states, but that this misses the point, as the EC is not like its member states, and that it still, due to the weaknesses of the Parliament, lacks strong democratic control: the reason given by AG Roemer in *Schöppenstedt* for the introduction of legislative liability in the first place. Another criticism is that, by failing to allow full recovery, the ECJ is ruling out 'dual vigilance' of the very sort that it

---

[98] W Van Gerven, 'Taking Article 215 seriously', in Beatson and Tridimas (eds) *New Directions in European Public Law* (Hart Publishing, 1998).

[99] Van der Woude, 'Liability for Administrative acts under Article 215(2) EC' in Heukels and McDonnell op. cit. at 109.

introduced with the doctrine of direct effect. Such a small prospect of success deters individuals from exercising their role as watchdog. The vigilance of individuals is needed as a check on Community institutions.

Another pertinent critique is that the Court has been too keen to protect the freedom of economic action of the EC, at the expense of individual interests. In so doing, it has failed to provide relief for unfortunate effects of unsatisfactory policies. This stands out in contrast to the Court's concern to protect individuals from being denied effective protection of their EC rights by the **member states,** and has something in common with the critique made by Coppell and O'Neill[100] of the ECJ's development of a human rights jurisprudence, which they castigate as instrumental in function and as applying different standards to member state acts and to Community acts.

Walter Van Gerven has provided another critique, which is that the ECJ has paid too little regard to the general principles common to the member states in its development of an Article 288 jurisprudence. In so doing, it has not only ignored the wording of Article 288 itself, but acted in defiance of at least four reasons why it should have looked more avidly to the member states for a development of its jurisprudence. He gives the following reasons as to why the Court should have been more assiduous in developing a comparative approach. First, a policy based argument: if the Court wishes to pursue a creative function in developing EC law then it must look systematically for common legal ground: this would be an example of 'subsidiarity in action'. Second, a specifically legal need to strengthen those elements which preserve homogeneity in the face of diversity. Third, economic: for economic actors to function efficiently, legal disparities need to be kept to a minimum. Last, a cultural justification: according to Article 151 EC, the Community 'shall contribute to the flowering of the cultures of the member states'. In ignoring all of these factors, the Court has been all too willing to construct a *sui generis* case law of liability in damage, which has resulted in a denial of individual justice. Indeed, the late Judge Mancini, in his famous article, referred to Article 288 as one of the areas in which the Court had let the individuals down (the other, he thought, was the restrictive standing requirement applied in Article 230).[101]

Article 288 is one of the essential safeguards in the EC legal order for maintaining the rule of law in an EC in which the democratic element is still lacking. It should not be applied with too much caution. In 1975, Lord Mackenzie-Stuart compared the non-contractual liability of the Community to the early nineteenth-century map of Africa: 'The coast is shown; we see the deltas of the great rivers; but where they lead and where they have their sources are as yet uncharted.'[102] The reference to the discovery of Africa was perhaps unfortunate, given the brutal and imperialistic way in which the nineteenth-century European powers exploited Africa, with no regard for individual rights or other cultures. Let us hope that the European Courts will take a more sensitive approach to their relatively uncharted field.

---

[100] J Coppell and A O'Neill, 'The ECJ: Taking Rights Seriously?' (1992) 29 CMLRev 669.
[101] F Mancini, *Democracy and Constitutionalism in the European Union* (Hart Publishing, 1999) Chap 3.
[102] Lord Mackenzie-Stuart, 'The non-contractual liability of the EEC' (1975) 12 CMLRev 493 at 512.

12

CONTROLLING THE MEMBER STATES

INTRODUCTION

In April 2000, Internal Market Commissioner Frits Bolkestein lamented: 'After years of progress, it is disheartening to see the difference deepening between those who implement Internal Market rules and those who delay their implementation.'[1] The 2000 issue of the single market scoreboard indicated a disappointing, uneven record of implementation of internal market directives.[2] Ironically, this happened only shortly after the member states had set themselves the challenge at the Lisbon Summit, in March 2000, of speeding up reform and establishing a fully operational internal market. Things do not seem to have got any better. A year later, Bolkestein followed up his earlier comments by saying that he was 'particularly disappointed' in the poor performance in the year since Lisbon.[3]

This discrepancy between ideal (a 'fully operational' internal market) and practice (a piecemeal, fragmented record of implementation of measures) is indicative of the relation of the member states to the EU. On the one hand, in a certain sense, they constitute the EU, setting the agenda at Council meetings such as Lisbon, as well as taking a large part of the responsibility for the implementation and enforcement of EC law. On the other, the EC has an undeniable autonomy and logic of its own and unruly member states can seriously impede its progress and efficiency. So a central problem for the EU has always been the tension which exists between it and its member states.[4]

---

[1] Quoted in the Commission's Internal Market Scoreboard for 2000, the full text of which is available on the European Commission's Internal Market website at: http://europa.eu.int/comm/internal_market/ enb/update/score.

[2] Ibid.

[3] Commission Update on the Internal Market: Internal Market Strategy April 2001. In May 2001, the Commission was dealing with c.1800 infringement cases for breaches of Internal Market law. (Source: Single Market Scoreboard for 2001.)

[4] U Everling, 'The Member States of the EEC before their Court of Justice' (1984) ELRev at 215.

One of the Commission's well-known roles is that of 'guardian of the treaties'. Article 211 charges it with ensuring that 'the provisions of this Treaty and the measures taken by the institutions pursuant thereto are applied'.[5] And so the EC treaty contains certain provisions specifically designed to enable the Commission to deal with the problem of non-compliance by the member states. The first, and most important, is Article 226, which enables the Commission to take action against member states in breach of EC law and if necessary bring them before the ECJ. Additionally, there are other more specialised procedures, perhaps the most notable of which is Article 7 TEU, whereby the voting rights of a member state which has committed a serious and persistent breach of human rights or the principles of liberty, democracy and the rule of law, may be suspended under a special procedure (although it is actually the Council which makes this determination). Other, perhaps less striking, enforcement procedures in the EC treaty include that in Article 88(2) which deals with member states which fail to comply with a decision that state aid is illegal; Article 95(9) concerning illegal national measures which derogate from the harmonisation process; Article 298 concerning improper national invocation of derogation on national security; and Article 104, which enables the Commission to monitor the national budgetary situation.[6]

This chapter will be mainly focused on the general procedure for infringements contained in Article 226, the basics of which can be briefly stated. The procedure divides into an administrative and judicial stage, although the latter is rarely used. In the former stage the Commission will contact the member state concerned, giving it a chance to respond and try to resolve the matter, through various stages of formality, a process which may take some time.[7] If this fails, the Commission may instigate the judicial stage, bringing the matter before the Court of Justice, which may give judgment against the member state. This process was strengthened by the Maastricht treaty, which enabled the ECJ to impose pecuniary sanctions on member states which do not comply with its judgments.

Article 226 constitutes a considerable advance on standard procedures under international law, by virtue of the introduction of the prosecutorial function of the Commission and mandatory jurisdiction of the Court of Justice. But, given the importance of this procedure, it is perhaps surprising that Article 226 remains

---

[5] This function was emphasised by Declaration 19 attached to the Final Act of the Maastricht Treaty, paragraph 2 of which reads:

> 'The Conference calls on the Commission to ensure, in exercising its powers under Article 155 [now 211] of this Treaty, that Member States fulfil their obligations.'

There is also the Declaration on the Implementation of Community Law annexed to the Maastricht treaty, requiring the member states to transpose EC law fully and adequately.

[6] In addition to these EC provisions, there is also Article 35(7) TEU, which gives the Court of Justice jurisdiction to rule on any dispute between member states and the Commission regarding interpretation or application of conventions established under Article 34(2)(d). There are also further specialist procedures provided for in secondary internal market legislation: e.g. in the field of Public Procurement; or in the Compliance Directive; or Directive 83/189 which sets out a special procedure for supervising the conformity of new national technical rules with EC law; and Directive 92/59 on the Protection of Heath and Safety.

[7] This procedure is dealt with in more detail below.

somewhat obscure, a rather unknown and uninvestigated treaty article. Not a great deal has been written about it and most of that dates from some time ago.[8] Much of the procedure seems shrouded in obscure administrative practice – both of the member states and the Commission, whose recent attempts at transparency have only partially opened up the procedure.[9] As the Article 226 procedure is, for the most part, instigated following particular complaints made to the Commission, this is frustrating for those who made the complaints, if they are not adequately informed as to why the Commission has chosen not to proceed with their complaint. This is especially so where the Commission's disregard of the complaint seems arrogant, high-handed or even deferential to biased political interests.[10] As well as the procedure often appearing obscure and incoherent, such a lack of clear, transparent proceedings is also problematic at a constitutional level, as disregard of law by public bodies, such as the Commission, or national authorities, threatens individual rights and also the principle that holders of public office be accountable to citizens for their actions. And, in addition to raising issues of the relation of European citizens to public authorities, the enforcement of Community law by the Commission also raises the following more obvious (in this context) matters: the question of the balance of power between the Commission and member states; the question of how and why the Commission proceeds against infringements (i.e. does it prefer negotiation to prosecution?); and also the relationship of centralised enforcement to decentralised enforcement (i.e. by the national courts) of Community law. All of these issues will be dealt with in the following pages.

TYPES OF VIOLATION

What types of infringement are likely to trigger the Article 226 process? Article 226 refers to the member states failing 'to fulfil an obligation under this Treaty'. This covers a wide range of possibilities.

The most obvious is that of failing to implement a directive, or doing so improperly. The *Francovich* case[11] arose not only because the Italian government had failed

---

[8] Exceptions are A Gil Ibanez, 'A Deeper Insight into Article 169,' Harvard Jean Monnet papers 1998; A Gil Ibanez, *The Administrative Supervision and Enforcement of EC Law* (Hart, 1999); R Rawlings, 'Engaged Elites, Citizen Action and Institutional Attitudes in Commission Enforcement' (2000) 6 ELJ 4; Mastroianni, 'The Enforcement Procedure under Article 169 of the EC treaty and powers of the European Commission: Quis Custodiet Custodes?' (1995) 1 EPL 535; see also H Audretsch, *Supervision in European Community Law* (Amsterdam, 1986); A Dashwood and R White, 'Enforcement Actions under Articles 169 and 170 EEC' (1989) 14 ELRev 388; U Everling, The Member States before their Court of Justice (1984) EL Rev 215; A Evans, 'The Enforcement Procedure of Article 169: Commission Discretion' (1979) 4 ELRev 442; A Barav, 'Failure of Member States to Fulfil their Obligations under Community Law' (1975) 12 CMLRev 369; and more generally, F Snyder, 'The Effectiveness of Community Law: Institutions, Processes, Tools and Techniques' (1993) 56 MLR 19.

[9] See the discussion below.

[10] See discussion of the *Newbury Bypass* case below.

[11] Considered in Chapter 9.

to implement a directive,[12] but had also failed to comply with the European Court's finding of an infringement in that case, a state of affairs which AG Mischo found to have caused 'scandalous' loss to individuals. Non-implementation was especially a danger in the run up to the completion of the internal market of the 1992 programme, given the number of measures to be introduced. However, as early as 1977, the Commission took the decision to proceed invariably against non-transposition, so it has been a priority for quite some while. Although by 1992, the member states were actually making quite good progress, as we can see, if we look to the Commission's annual report of that year,[13] with most of the White Paper directives implemented, by the end of the decade things have not improved, indeed they are worsening, as the single market scoreboard cited at the beginning of this chapter illustrates. According to this, 13 per cent of all internal market directives in force by 15 April 2000 (194 out of 1,489) were still not implemented in all member states, with some states far worse offenders than others.[14] Particularly serious was the late application of older directives, whose implementation deadline had expired before 1998. Therefore the Commission set the member states the task of bringing down the implementation deficit to less than 1.5 per cent by the end of the year.[15] This deficit in implementation is especially serious in the light of the EU's specific objective of realising the EU as an information society, given that not one of the five directives related to information society services had been fully implemented across the EU in mid 2000. Compliance continues to be a problem for the EU in the new millennium.

Other violations of EC law

These are obvious sources of infringement actions and have given rise to some familiar case law. Member states may find all sorts of devious ways to protect their national markets and so the Commission has to be vigilant. One such example is *Commission v UK*,[16] in which the UK was found to be in breach of Article 28 of the Treaty for having placed an import ban on poultry meat and eggs. This was supposed to prevent the spread of the highly infectious Newcastle disease, a danger which the UK certainly took seriously, having introduced a compulsory slaughter policy in the case of infected domestic poultry. However, the UK ban also coincided with the increase in imported turkeys from France, which were cheaper than domestic produce (having benefited from French subsidies) and thus attractive fare for UK consumers. The government had been under considerable pressure from the press

---

[12] Directive 80/987 harmonising national laws in relation to protection of employees' salaries in the case of employers' insolvency.

[13] Commission 10th Annual Report on the Monitoring and Application of Community Law. These reports are produced on a yearly basis in response to a requests made by the European Parliament (Resolution of 9 February 1983).

[14] The Commission's 17th and 18th Annual Reports on the Monitoring and Application of Community Law (2000 and 2001) revealed France, Greece and Italy to be particular offenders.

[15] Single market scoreboard 2000, see fn 1. This seemed to be having some impact – as the Commission's 18th report noted, although this seems to have been mainly due to the acceleration by the Commission of the proceedings for giving formal notice.

[16] Case 40/82 *Commission v UK* (Re Imports of Poultry Meat) [1982] ECR 2973.

and other sources to reduce these imports. Moreover, the timing of the ban just so happened to prevent the import of turkeys in the run up to Christmas, when an overwhelming majority of the imports took place. There was no evidence that these imports were infected. When the case finally reached the ECJ, it found that the ban was a disguised restriction on trade, not proportionate to the dangers caused by the disease but rather to protect the domestic market.

Member states also find other ways of keeping out imports. The Germans strictly adhered to their *Reinheitsgebot*, a law of 1617 on the purity of beer, banning the import of foreign beers which did not adhere to such strict standards. However, the Commission proceeded against this, finding it to be a way of protecting the German market. In *Commission v Germany*,[17] the ECJ found the law to be incompatible with free movement of goods. (However, the Bonn Minister responsible concluded his acceptance of the judgment by commenting that he believed that 'all good Germans will still drink German beer'.)[18]

Sometimes the breach concerned is that of the more general obligation of cooperation in Article 10 of the Treaty, increasingly used by the Commission in this context,[19] especially where the state concerned fails to respond to the Commission's request for information, or does so in an excessively dilatory way, in the earlier administrative stage of the proceedings.[20] (The Commission may also be discharged from bearing the burden of proof in infringement proceedings[21] if the state fails to cooperate in this way.) Article 10 is also coming to play a new important role in the context of state inaction in the face of illegal activity by private parties, as in *Commission v France*, which is discussed below.

Breaches not attributable to central government

There are also several situations in which a state may breach the treaty, even if the central government itself committed no act of infringement.

(a) Constitutionally independent branches of the state

The state will be held responsible for these even if the body concerned is considered to be a 'constitutionally separate' institution. In *Commission v Belgium*,[22] the government claimed to have done all it could to secure enactment of a law repealing a discriminatory tax in breach of Article 90, but the legislature simply failed to pass it. The government tried to plead *force majeure*, claiming there was nothing they could do, but this failed. The Court's position seems to be that the actual defendant

---

[17] Case 178/84 *Commission v Germany (Re Beer Purity Laws)* [1987] ECR 1227.
[18] Quoted in K Middlemas, *Orchestrating Europe* (Fontana, 1995) at p 337.
[19] See J Temple Lang, 'The Duties of National Authorities Under Community Constitutional Law' (1998) 23 EL Rev 109.
[20] See e.g. Case 96/81 *Commission v Netherlands* [1982] ECR 1791 in which the Netherlands failed to provide adequate information in the context of breaching the bathing water directive.
[21] See below.
[22] Case 77/69 *Commission v Belgium* [1970] ECR 237.

is the state and not the government, and that the legislature is just as much a branch of the state as the government. The same goes for regional, or local, authorities.

The present position, however, might seem unsatisfactory. Why should the administration be held responsible for acts of a separate body over which it may have no control, which is especially so in the case of federal states? The justification seems to be based on principles of international law, in which states are the relevant actors, but this seems anomalous in the self-proclaimed 'new legal order' of EC law, which departs from international law in so many ways. This situation may also give rise to different types of breach within one infringement action, making it difficult for the Commission to proceed against both. Take, for example, a situation like that in the *Fratelli Costanzo*[23] case. This concerned tenders for public works contracts, and the applicant alleged that the municipal authorities had not complied with the provisions of the relevant directive. As it turned out, Italy had not implemented this directive. However, the ECJ held that the administrative and municipal authorities are under the same duty as the national courts to apply directives and to refrain from applying inconsistent provisions. So in this situation, it would seem that there are in fact two obligations of a different sort: one for the State to implement the directive in the first place and the other for the local authority to apply directly effective provisions of a non-transposed directive. And surely the State is not best placed to defend both types of non-compliance here? It would make more sense if the Commission were to deal directly with the region concerned with violating EC Law.[24]

(b) The judiciary

According to the traditional theory of the separation of powers the judiciary is a separate branch of government. Can the state be held responsible if the national courts violate EC law? This is not such a far-fetched possibility as it has sometimes been the domestic courts which have put up the biggest resistance to EC law witness the warnings given to the ECJ by the *Bundesverfassungsgericht* in the context of fundamental rights and supremacy, or the downright disobedience of the *Conseil d'État* in the matter of the direct effect of directives.[25] This issue was raised in the *Bouchereau* case,[26] in which AG Warner suggested that, while judicial error could not be treated as a breach, action could be taken where a national court deliberately disregarded EC law.[27] So far the Commission has been ambivalent in its approach to this matter. It instituted proceedings against Germany following the *Bundesverfassungsgericht's* judgment in *Internationale Handelsgesellschaft* (in which the German court disagreed with the Court of Justice on the interpretation of

---

[23] Case 103/88 *Fratelli Costanzo SpA v Commune di Milano* [1989] ECR 1839.

[24] Although in a very few cases, Council regulations do allow for direct relations between the Commission and the regional administration, but these are very limited: e.g. Council Reg. (EEC) No 2088/85 concerning the integrated Mediterranean programme (OJ 1985 L 197/1).

[25] See Chapters 7 and 8 for a discussion of these matters.

[26] Case 30/77 *Bouchereau* [1979] ECR 1999.

[27] In this he was citing AG Gand in Case 77/69 *Commission v Belgium* [1970] ECR 237.

fundamental rights) but then dropped the action and proceeded no further. It took no action against the Conseil d'État following its disregard of the direct effect of directives in *Semoules*.[28] So it seems unlikely that the national courts will prove to be the subject matter for future Article 226 cases.

(c) Private parties

On the other hand, private parties are likely to cause States more headaches by their actions. It would certainly be unfair to hold member states responsible for all violations which occur within their jurisdiction, as it would be impossible for them to deal with them all. But it is clearly established that if the State exercises some degree of control, then it will be held responsible for breaches by non-State actors, however the body in question describes itself, even if it is a quasi-autonomous, or autonomous, actor. This was held in the '*Buy Irish*'[29] case in which the Irish government set up a distinct semi-private Irish Goods Council in order to give Irish customers information about how they might exercise their preference for Irish goods, a measure which would clearly violate Article 28 if adopted by the government. As it was, the ECJ held that the government had a sufficient degree of control over the Goods Council for it to take responsibility for the breach of the treaty. (Other defences put forward by the Irish government fared no better, including the rather curious claim that Article 28 could not have been violated as the campaign had not worked and sales of foreign imports had increased during this period. The ECJ was unimpressed, holding that the test for impeding the free movement of goods laid down in the *Dassonville* case only required a 'potential' hindrance to trade.[30])

The State will also have to accept responsibility for the actions of private actors if it was in a position to prevent or terminate violations of the treaty caused by them. This was established in *Commission* v *Greece*[31] and confirmed more recently in the important case of *Commission* v *France*.[32] This latter case arose from events which seem typical of the unfortunate squabbles which have chequered the EC's history. It concerned long-standing protests and violent actions committed by French farmers against agricultural products from other member states, in particular strawberries from Spain, which were apparently seen as a great threat to the French strawberry market. These protests often took the form of violence against lorry drivers and vandalism of their loads as well as destruction and pillaging of foreign products in French shops. These were no spontaneous outbursts but well organised by a group of French farmers who called themselves 'Co-ordination Rurale'. The French government could not, of course, be held responsible for these acts of vandalism, but the Commission was of the opinion that the government had not been as vigilant as it might have and had continually failed to put a stop to the protests: they had been

---

[28] *Semoules* (Conseil d'État) [1970] CMLR 395.
[29] Case 249/81 *Commission* v *Ireland* ('Buy Irish') [1982] ECR 4005.
[30] Case 8/74 *Procureur du Roi* v *Dassonville* [1974] ECR 497.
[31] Case 68/88 *Commission* v *Greece* [1989] ECR 2965.
[32] Case C-265/95 *Commission* v *France* (*Spanish Strawberries*) [1997] ECR I 6959.

in a position to predict when these outbreaks would occur and even when police had outnumbered demonstrators at some of these occasions, the police had taken no action. So the Commission brought an action under Article 226, on the basis of the government's breaches of Article 28 and 10 of the EC treaty (the latter being relevant because the Commission claimed that France had failed to adopt the 'necessary and proper measures'). The ECJ found that such a failure to act was just as likely to obstruct intra-Community trade as a positive act,[33] and held that the measures that were taken by the French government had been 'manifestly inadequate to ensure freedom of intra-Community trade'.[34] It also held that, although member states 'retain exclusive competence as regards the maintenance of public order and safeguarding public security,' the ECJ nonetheless had the jurisdiction to verify whether the measures adopted by the State were appropriate for ensuring the free movement of goods.[35] When the Court gave its judgment in December 1997, this case was seen as a victory and also a reprimand to states who plead inability to deal with troublesome demonstrators. It also showed the use which could be made of Article 10, already increasingly used in the context of competition law in Articles 81 and 82. But the case also raised problematic tangential issues, such as the question of whether it might be preferable to regard Article 28 as directly effective, at a time when other free movement articles, such as Article 39 are increasingly regarded as so.[36] It also raises the issue of whether importers who had suffered damage as a result of these demonstrators might be able to commence a *Francovich* action in damages against the government.[37]

France had still not complied with the judgment at the end of 1998, which was in any case a bad year for France, as in that year more infringement proceedings were set in motion against France than any other member state. But France was closely followed by Italy, Greece and Belgium, which were also causing the Commission concern. Although it would seem somewhat extreme to speak in terms of a 'North–South' divide in terms of compliance in the EU,[38] some states have an undeniably poorer record in conforming with EC law than others, as is evidenced by the single market scoreboard report of 2000.

DEFENCES

How may States seek to defend themselves? Unsuccessfully, if that does not seem too frivolous an answer. Virtually all of the defences availed of by the states fail in the ECJ, a factor which partially explains the Commission's high success rate at

---

[33] Ibid. at para 31.
[34] Ibid. at para 52.
[35] Ibid. at para 33.
[36] See, in the context of Article 39, Case C-281/98 *Angonese v Cassa di Risparmio di Bolzano SpA* [2000] ECR I-4139.
[37] See Chapter 9.
[38] Which is suggested by Trevor Hartley in *Constitutional Problems of the European Union* (Hart Publishing, 1999) chapter 6.

prosecuting Article 226 actions. The following examples are defences which have been tried, and for the most part failed.

(a) Administrative difficulties/economic problems

These sorts of argument do not work. They were used by the Belgian government as a reason for failing to transpose directive 80/778 on the quality of drinking water by the appointed time.[39] The government pleaded that it had done all that it could, but the cost and complexity of construction works at the water station needed to supply the town of Verviers with water in conformity with the directive (as well as being the responsibility of one of the Belgian regions) was of such a complexity that they would need longer to complete. As this argument was made four years after the expiry of the implementation period it seemed unlikely to succeed and indeed it did not. The Court stressed that Article 226 is an objective process and the government's good faith or honest attempt to implement a law may be irrelevant, as it is the Commission's task to ascertain whether an infringement, and not a deliberate wronging, has taken place.

(b) EC law itself is illegal

This argument generally does not work unless the act concerned is so defective as to be deemed non-existent, as in the case of *BASF*.[40] Again, the ECJ has been quite definite about the function of Article 226, which is to give a declaration that the member state concerned has violated the treaty and not to provide judicial review of EC law. As the Court pointed out in *Commission* v *Greece*,[41] member states are privileged applicants under Article 230 and have already had their opportunity to bring an action for judicial review

(c) Another member state is in breach

This is a recognised defence under international law.[42] However, it does not work in the context of Article 226. As the Court stated long ago in *Van Gend*, the Community legal order constitutes a new legal order and this is distinct from international law. So are its procedures.

(d) *Force majeure*

At last we have a recognised defence, but it is rarely used successfully. The leading case is *Commission* v *Italy*.[43] The Italian government had failed to compile its statistical

---

[39] Case C-42/89 *Commission* v *Belgium* [1990] ECR I 2821
[40] Case C-137/92P *Commission* v *BASF* [1994] ECR I 2555.
[41] Case 226/87 *Commission* v *Greece* [1988] ECR 3611.
[42] For an example of a case where this defence was attempted see Case 78/76 *Steinicke and Weinlig* [1977] ECR 595.
[43] Case 101/84 *Commission* v *Italy* [1985] ECR 2629.

returns for goods carried by road as required by directive 78/546. This was not surprising initially, as the Italian Data Processing Centre had suffered a bomb attack in 1978 and its vehicle register had been destroyed. The government was thus unable to make its returns on time, a claim which seemed reasonable enough. However, by 1982, the Ministry of Transport was still unable to give the slightest indication of the date from which returns would be made. While the ECJ accepted that the bomb attack did constitute a *force majeure*, it held that its effect could only have lasted a certain time. If the Italian administration had shown a normal degree of diligence in replacing the equipment it would not still have been giving it as a reason in 1982. Therefore it could not rely on the event to justify its continued failure years later.

PROCEDURE

The process under Article 226 can be long and drawn out, not the swiftest way of dealing with disputes, but this is because it serves other functions in addition to the prosecutorial and litigious, which will be discussed below. As already mentioned, it has two stages, the administrative and the judicial. The former may itself be divided into two further stages: the informal (or non-contentious) and the formal.

(a) Informal administrative

At this stage the Commission considers information about infringements, which comes from a number of sources, an important element of which is complaints. It then informs member states of these allegations and hears their response. Informal though this may be, most cases are actually dealt with at this stage,[44] although usually without any publicity. They may often be dealt with at so-called 'package' meetings with national civil servants, at which a whole variety of matters are dealt with, including the violation at hand, which may be part of a bargaining process between member state and Commission.

(b) Formal administrative

This is known as the formal stage but it has to be said that there are very few formal rules applying as to procedures or deadlines, a factor which has adverse effects on legal certainty and will be discussed later. This commences when the Commission sends a letter of formal notice (what was often called a '169 letter' after its old numbering). This letter sets out the Commission's case against the member state, giving it a chance to explain its action and is often in short summary form. Following this, the state concerned submits its observations. If the matter is not then resolved, the Commission issues a more formal document called a 'reasoned opinion' which is much more detailed than the earlier letter of formal notice, although it may not con-

---

[44] As is evident from the figures given in the Commission's annual reports on the monitoring and application of EC law.

tain any new allegations. If the Commission wishes to introduce new claims it must start a separate Article 226 action. On the other hand, the Commission has a discretion as to whether it issues such a reasoned opinion at all,[45] and its failure o do so will not be an act subject to judicial review under Article 230.[46] The existence of such discretion was underlined in the *Commission* v *UK*[47] case, in which AG Darmon stressed that the Commission's motives in bringing the action were irrelevant, continuing, 'the decision whether or not to bring an action against a Member State... is in any event in the entire discretion of the Commission, as guardian of the treaties.'[48]

There are no time limits imposed as to when the Commission may issue its reasoned opinion. It is up to the Commission to act when and if it wants, and there exist no guidelines, legislation or case law from the ECJ. However, member states must be given a reasonable time to respond and to right their behaviour. The two weeks allotted by the Commission to Belgium to abolish its university fee, the 'minerval', (found to be contrary to EC law in *Gravier* v *City of Liége)*[49] was held, unsurprisingly, to be too short a period by the Court.

The Commission has recently been issuing more reasoned opinions, which it takes to be the result of its quicker and stricter action following its internal reforms of 1996.[50]

(c) The judicial stage

If the member state takes no action to remedy the breach, the Commission may refer the matter to the Court, although, once again, no time limits are given within which it may do so, providing that it has given the state a reasonable time to comply with its reasoned opinion. On the other hand, even if the breach has ended before the Court gives judgment, this will not necessarily terminate the judicial stage.[51] Some breaches may, by their very nature, be short in duration, yet it may be necessary to have a ruling on their legality. The Commission bears the burden of proof in the Court proceedings,[52] although this may be discharged, where, for example, the state fails to provide any, or sufficient, information, or where it pleads a derogation under e.g. Article 30 of the treaty.[53] The Court's judgment at this stage is declaratory only, and may not specify in detail what the State should do to remedy its breach, thus often leaving the government in doubt. However, few cases go to judgment, and

---

[45] Cf. Evans, op. cit. at fn 8, for a discussion of this point.
[46] See e.g. Case 48/65 *Lutticke* v *Commission* [1966] ECR 19; Case 247/87 *Star Fruit* v *Commission* [1989] ECR 291.
[47] Case 416/85 *Commission* v *UK* [1988] ECR 3127.
[48] Ibid. at para 9.
[49] Case 293/83 *Gravier* [1985] ECR 593.
[50] Cf. Commission's 16th Annual Report on the Monitoring and Application of Community law, which states that the number of reasoned opinions in 1998 was up by 102 per cent. The Commission's internal reforms are discussed below.
[51] Case 7/61 *Commission* v *Italy (Pork Imports)* [1961] ECR 317 at 326.
[52] Case C-347/88 *Commission* v *Greece* [1990] ECR I 4747.
[53] E.g. Case 174/82 *Officier van Justitie* v *Sandoz* [1983] ECR 2445.

those which do are usually won by the Commission:[54] this is because so many of the breaches have been dealt with in the earlier non-litigious stages. On the other hand, those cases which do go to judgment are often important high profile cases, such as the German beer purity case, or the UK turkeys case, already mentioned.

As the ECJ seemed to be quite burdened by its judicial workload in this area, not to mention others, there have been proposals to reform the procedures under Article 226. One such was made by the Due Working Group,[55] which proposed making the Commission responsible for adopting binding decisions in such cases and leaving member states who dispute the decision to bring annulment actions in the ECJ. However, the provisions in Articles 226–228 EC were left untouched by the Treaty of Nice. This does not, however, mean that the issue of the reform of the infringement procedure has been dropped, as will be discussed later in this chapter.

INTERIM MEASURES

These are not an integral part of Article 226 but are often used in conjunction with it. Article 243 provides that 'The Court of Justice may in any case before it prescribe any necessary measures.' Initially, there seemed to be doubt as to whether the Court had the jurisdiction to make such an order in an action against a member state. However, *Commission v UK*[56] removed these doubts. The UK had introduced a subsidy scheme for pig producers without getting Commission approval. The Commission decided that the scheme was not compatible with the treaty and issued a decision under Article 88 EC (under a special enforcement procedure used in the case of state aids) requiring the UK to terminate the procedure forthwith, which the UK did not do. The Commission then brought an enforcement action under the special procedure for state aids, in the course of which it also applied for interim measures. The Court readily granted them (although the Advocate General doubted the Court's jurisdiction to do so).

The Court in fact has wider powers under Article 243 than under Article 226, as it can actually specify what the state must do to conform. In *Commission v UK*,[57] it was established that three conditions must be satisfied before interim measures will be granted. First, the Commission must demonstrate a likelihood of success in the main action, at least a prima facie case. Second, the case must be urgent. Third, the Commission must be able to demonstrate irreparable damage to the Community interest. Thus in the *FYROM* case,[58] in which Greece had unilaterally imposed sanctions on the former Yugoslav Republic of Macedonia (FYROM), in breach of the

---

[54] As is again evidenced by the Commission's annual report figures for the 1990s.
[55] *Report by the Study Group on the Future of the EC Judicial System (Due report)*: see Chapter 5 for other Due recommendations.
[56] Cases 31 53/77 R *Commission v UK* [1977] ECR 921.
[57] Ibid.
[58] Case C-120/94R *Commission v Greece* (FYROM) ECR I [1994] 3037. For a recent example see Case T-17/00 *Willi Rothley* [2000] ECR II-2085.

common commercial policy (alleging that country's ambitions on Greek territory), the ECJ refused the Commission's application for interim measures against Greece, on the grounds of lack of urgency. Another difficulty is that the Commission may only ask for interim measures once the pre-litigation procedures are completed.[59]

ACTIONS BY MEMBER STATES

This procedure, brought under Article 227, is the sister action to Article 226, in which the member state, rather than the Commission, brings the matter before the Court of Justice. Before the accusing state can do this it must first bring the matter before the Commission, which is required to deliver a reasoned opinion within three months. If it fails to do so, the member state may commence proceedings before the Court of Justice. As it is rather unpleasant to have states suing each other in a Community supposedly based on peace and comity, unsurprisingly, the procedure is scarcely ever used. Perhaps, equally unsurprisingly, one of the few occasions on which it was used was an action brought by France against the UK, in which France claimed that the UK had adopted fishing conservation measures contrary to the treaty.[60]

SANCTIONS

States do not always comply with the Court's judgments. *Francovich* would not have arisen if they did. The Commission's annual report on the monitoring of the application of EC law for 1998 gave a long list of ECJ judgments still unimplemented, some dating back as far as 1988.[61] In the *French Vessels* case the Court gave a judgment against France in 1974. Over twenty years later in 1996 it gave another judgment regarding the same subject matter, as France had not complied with the earlier judgment.[62] A further French case[63] is another good example. This arose out of the Community's unsuccessful 'Sheepmeat' regime, a reorganisation of the market which proved particularly unsatisfactory as far as the French were concerned. France thus continued to ban the import of British lamb from the UK despite having a judgment against it for doing so.[64] This being the case, the Commission commenced another action against France, in an attempt to enforce the previous judgment, also asking the Court for interim measures. However, the ECJ refused, stating that to do so would only be to repeat its previous judgment. The Court clearly

---

[59] Article 83 (1) ECJ Rules of Procedure.
[60] Case 141/78 *France* v *UK* [1979] ECR 2923. The Court went on to give judgment against the UK. In May 2000 an action (Case C-388/95 *Belgium* v *Spain* [2000] ECR I-3123) brought by Belgium against Spain concerning Spanish rules for the bottling of Rioja wine was dismissed by the ECJ.
[61] E.g. judgment given against France in the Wild Birds case (Case 252/85 *Commission* v *France* [1988] ECR 2243) cited in the annex to the Commission's 16th Annual Report on the Monitoring and Application of Community law.
[62] Cases 163/73 *Commission* v *France* [1974] ECR 359 and C-334 /94 *Commission* v *France* [1996] ECR.
[63] Case 24, 97/80R *Commission* v *France* [1980] ECR 1319.
[64] Case 232/78 *Commission* v *France* [1979] ECR 2729.

felt in a somewhat powerless position, as it did not want its dignity to be eroded in what it presumably took to be the likelihood of another unsatisfied order against France. This left France in a good bargaining position to continue its demands from the Commission for support for its sheep farmers. And it succeeded. The ban was finally lifted after the UK gave some concessions in return for a budget rebate.[65]

With these difficulties no doubt in mind, the member states decided in the Maastricht Treaty to introduce a provision for sanctioning member states which disregard ECJ judgments, notwithstanding reservations about such a concept in some quarters (such as those of AG Tesauro, who challenged the whole idea of monetary sanctions, stating that he failed to find any support for the concept of fining the state, either in national law or in international law).[66] Article 228 now sets out the relevant provisions. Before an application for pecuniary sanctions can be made in court, the Commission must go through the whole process under Article 226 again (this time, the breach of EC law being of course the failure to comply with a judgment of the ECJ): namely, it must issue a letter of formal notice, give the state a chance to respond and then issue a reasoned opinion. Only after that may it apply to the Court.

The provisions in Article 228 are not particularly clear. Article 228 (2)ii provides for two different types of sanction: a lump sum and a periodic penalty, without defining either, nor does the treaty give any guidelines as to their use. However, common sense dictates that a **lump sum** is a one-off payment and a **periodic penalty** is a recurring sum. Nor does Article 228 give any guidance as to when which of these penalties can be used. The Commission has, however, issued a memorandum as to their use.[67] This states that the Commission will, on referring the case to the ECJ, give its view as to the type of penalty and amount thereof. According to Point 4 of the memorandum the Commission considers a periodic penalty to be the most appropriate, although this does not mean that it will never request a sanction in the form of a lump sum.[68] A decision as to the amount of the sanction will be calculated, according to Point 5, on the basis of the seriousness of the injury, its duration and the need to ensure that the penalty acts as a deterrent. Additionally, the Commission adds in Point 6 that the infraction's seriousness will depend on the importance of the Community rules infringed and the effects of the infringement on general and particular interests, further stating that breaches such as those of the principle of non-discrimination or of fundamental rights, or the fundamental freedoms of the EC Treaty, will always be regarded as serious.

The treaty gives no guidance as to how the exact amount of the fine may be calculated, nor does it provide a legal basis for adopting legislation to do so, as does

---

[65] See F Snyder, *New Directions in Community Law* (Weidenfield, 1990) for a general discussion of the Sheepmeat regime.

[66] Tesauro, 'La Sanction des infractions au droit communautaire' in Curtin and Heukel (eds) *Institutional dynamics of European integration: essays in honour of Henry Schermers* (vol II) (Martinus Nijhoff, 1994) at 489.

[67] Commission memorandum 96/C 242/07 on applying Article 171 (as it then was). This memorandum also fails to define the two sanctions.

[68] This might be requested, for example, if the breach has been terminated at the time of judgment.

Article 83 in the case of competition law.[69] Once again this is left to the Commission's discretion, and it has elaborated on how it will exercise this in a further non-binding act, this time a communication issued in 1997.[70] According to this, the Commission will start with a basic sum of 550 euros per day, which will be multiplied by two factors, according to the seriousness and duration of the breach. To achieve deterrence the result will be multiplied by a further sum based on the ability of the relevant state to pay.[71]

By 1998 the Commission had taken several decisions to propose fines, some of which were referred to the Court. A large part of these concerned violations of environmental law; however, most states responded to these moves by rapidly coming into line, either before the case was referred to Court, or shortly after.[72] The first hearing concerning the request for a member state to be ordered to pay a periodic penalty did not take place until *Commission v Greece*[73] in 1999. This concerned a judgment previously given by the ECJ against Greece in 1992, in which it held that the Hellenic Republic had violated obligations in the Waste Directive, specifically those on toxic and dangerous waste disposal, a fact which had become all too obvious by the existence of an uncontrolled dumping site in the Kouropites river in Chania, Crete. The Commission initiated proceedings in 1997 asking for a periodic penalty of 24,600 euros per day. Various problems came to light in the course of the application, including the important issue of the purpose of sanctions: namely, are they actually administrative or penal in nature? This question was addressed by the Advocate General,[74] whose closely reasoned opinion is worth citing in some detail. He first noted, however, that the work of the ECJ in reviewing the Commission's proposal was limited to verifying the facts, ascertaining whether the Commission had committed a manifest error of assessment and to the observation of the principles of proportionality and equality. He then continued by considering that the task of enforcing judgments against member states could easily have been left to the Council of Ministers, which could, for example, have used devices to suspend votes in the Council, and he cited such comparable procedures in other international organisations. Thus, the European Court of Human Rights leaves enforcement to the Committee of Ministers[75] and judgments of the International Court of Justice may be enforced by the Security Council.[76] Given that the EU had chosen to depart from these diplomatic channels, what functions could these sanctions be said to serve? He perceived the sanctions as administrative in nature, their objective being to get states to comply as quickly as possible, rather than as criminal sanctions.

---

[69] Under which Regulation 17/62 (Article 15 of which deals with penalties) was enacted.

[70] [1997] OJ C63/2.

[71] This is based on the member state's GDP and ranges from a scale of 1 of Luxembourg to 26.4 for Germany. Thus the maximum daily penalty payable by Luxembourg would be 30,000 euros whereas it would be a much larger sum of 791,293 euros for Germany.

[72] Commission 16th annual report on Monitoring and Application of Community law.

[73] Case C-387/97 *Commission v Greece* [2000] ECR I-5047.

[74] Opinion of Advocate General Ruiz-Jarabo Colomer of 28 September 1999. He concluded by reducing the fine to 15,373 euros per day.

[75] Article 54 ECHR.

[76] Article 54 UN Charter.

Therefore, he considered that sanctions were best seen as an issue of enforcement of judgments,[77] citing comparative European law, in particular Article 888 of the German Code of Civil Procedure, the *Zwangsvollstreckung*, which specifically declares its aim to be not penal but to compel enforcement of the judgment in question. He also warned of the difficulties that could arise in applying a quasi-criminal procedure to member states – for instance, would all criminal procedural protections, such as the presumption of innocence, have to apply to the state – a possibility which he found to be counter-intuitive. The ECJ gave its judgment on 4 July 2000.[78] It held that a periodic penalty would be most appropriate in this case and set three criteria for application: the duration of the infringement, the degree of seriousness and the ability of the member state to pay. Their application would depend on the effect on public and private interest and the urgency of the matter. As this was a particularly serious breach the Court set the fine at 20,000 euros per day from 4 July 2000.[79]

A last question remains on the issue of sanctions. If their task is perceived to be greater efficiency in the enforcement of judgments, will they achieve this?[80] Would the case brought against France in the context of the *Sheepmeat* regime have turned out differently if the Court then had the power to award sanctions? Is France more likely to prevent its disaffected rural population from protesting against foreign produce as a result? The *Commission v France (Spanish strawberries)* judgment discussed earlier was still unimplemented by the end of 1998.[81] What if a member state simply refuses to pay the penalties? How could they be forced to do so? Their powers in the Council of Ministers might be revoked, or various payments from the EU withheld, but the state concerned might then respond by withholding its budget contributions, which, if that state were considerable enough, could bring the EU to the sort of standstill achieved by de Gaulle prior to the Luxembourg Accords. In such extreme situations, the EU could do nothing but resort to the usual diplomatic channels and procedures used under international law, thus illustrating the continuing problems of enforcement in an international community.

INCOHERENCE OF PROCEDURE

Analysis of Articles 226–228 reveals a lengthy, cumbersome procedure with several problematic traits: first, lack of clear rules, second, a lack of transparency and, third, a lack of coordination in both the Commission and national administrations in dealing with enforcement actions.[82] There seems to be no clear enforcement

---

[77] At para 33 of his Opinion.

[78] Case C-387/97 *Commission v Greece* [2000] ECR I-5047.

[79] These are paid into the Commission's own resources account.

[80] By 31 December 2000, in spite of paying over a considerable sum of money, Greece had still not taken measures to comply with the original judgment.

[81] Commission 16th Annual Report.

[82] A fact which is discussed in some detail in Gil Ibanez, op. cit. at fn 8. Ibanez questioned a number of officials in both administrations and sets out their responses in his paper.

policy. There is little in the way of legislation or guidelines and what does exist usually takes the form of internal rules of the Commission. The absence of clearly prescribed rules on things such as time limits, or calculation of sanctions, has meant that the Commission has been able to choose a form of rules to suit itself. There has been little publicity of the Article 226 procedure: reasoned opinions were not even published until recently and access to them was usually refused to third parties. Even the Commission described this as a degree of confidentiality that was perceived as 'excessive'.[83] Following complaints to the European Ombudsman[84] the Commission has now taken to issuing press releases in at least some cases at this stage.

The third form of incoherence listed above concerns arrangements for coordinating infringement actions While each Directorate-General tends to work independently of others (some of which are very independent, such as Competition DG, formerly DG IV) it is the General Secretariat along with the legal service which is the central coordinating body in infringement proceedings. So there can sometimes be a lack of communication. The same can be said of the national administrations.[85] All, as might be expected, have different ways of responding to Commission investigations. However, it usually seems to be the case that while one national unit is in charge of the administrative stage, another takes control of the judicial stage, should things come to that. In four of the member states, including the UK, these units actually belong to different state entities.[86] So there is again a risk of contradictory policy. National administrations also complain of a lack of information, delay and short deadlines imposed on them by the Commission. All in all, it is hardly surprising that states win so few enforcement actions in the ECJ. However, the Commission did try to improve its internal procedure in 1996, with its programme for improving efficiency and transparency in infringement proceedings.[87]

THE COMMISSION'S DISCRETION

This is clearly a notable element in the Article 226 procedure.[88] The Commission has discretion as to whether to commence proceedings at all, whether to issue a reasoned opinion, whether to take the matter to Court, whether to bring the matter back to Court again if the initial judgment is not complied with and further discretion as to the amount of fine that is applied for.

---

[83] Commission 14th Annual Report.
[84] See below.
[85] See Gil Ibanez op. cit. at fn 8.
[86] e.g. in the UK the Cabinet Office, the Treasury Solicitor and the Foreign Office are all involved, with the inevitable ideological differences.
[87] Discussed below.
[88] See in particular Mastroianni, op. cit. at fn 8.

This high amount of discretion, amounting to what might be described as 'selective enforcement,'[89] might seem to be on the one hand unsurprising. Although a selective enforcement of EC law might appear to conflict with the Commission's role under Article 211, it is obviously the case that the Commission could not pursue every infringement; it simply lacks the resources. If it did, the introduction of direct effect in the *Van Gend* case, enabling the 'private' enforcement of EC law, carried out in the national courts, might not have seemed so necessary. It might be also be argued that the enforcement of law is always politicised, involving the exercise of choice and competing values.[90] The Commission is, to be sure, a 'political' body (indeed conceived by Jean Monnet as the 'Platonic embodiment of Community spirit')[91] one of whose important functions is to defend the Community interest, so it will prioritise those cases necessary to do this. On the other hand, the Commission, although it may possess political objectives, lacks democratic legitimacy and the politics of its members do not necessarily correspond with those of the Community's more democratic institution, the Parliament, nor those of the member states. Thus, such discretion in enforcement is troubling.

The history of the enforcement of Article 226 could roughly be divided into three stages. In the early days of the EC the Commission proceeded sparingly with Article 169, as it then was, and this cautious usage was criticised by the ECJ in *Defrenne* v *Sabena*,[92] – which went as far as to state that if the Commission had done its job properly in the first place, female workers in the EC would not have suffered such widespread discrimination.[93] The second stage began with a decision taken by the Jenkins Commission in 1979 to prosecute failure to transpose directives more vigorously and in 1984 the Commission began to present annual reports to the European Parliament on the monitoring and application of EC law. Third, after the 1992 watershed and the decline in the volume of new legislation, the Commission has become more selective and specialised procedures have also been created to deal with certain types of infringement.

The Commission always seems to prioritise the implementation of directives. It also rates highly the enforcement of the single market, public procurement, and the environment. It will also take seriously any breaches that produce any important negative effects on EC goals, as well as infringements implying fraud on Community funds.[94] However, the Commission is not always consistent in this selective enforcement policy. Sometimes it is simply easier for it to pursue the smaller infringements

---

[89] Much has been written on selective enforcement, e.g., Brigham and Brown, *Policy Implementation: Penalties or Incentives?* (Beverly Hills: Sage, 1980); Davis, *Discretionary Justice: a Preliminary Enquiry* (Urbana: University of Illinois Press, 1977); Shumavon and Hibbeln (eds) *Administrative Discretion and Public Policy Implementation* (New York: Praeger, 1986); Jowell, *Law and Bureaucracy: Administrative Discretion and the Limits of Legal Action* (New York: Dunellen, 1975).

[90] See Snyder op. cit. at fn 8.

[91] See Mancini, *Democracy and Constitutionalism in the European Union* (Hart, 1999) at 3.

[92] Case 43/75 *Defrenne v Sabena* [1976] ECR 415 at paras 72–3 p 484. Fewer than 30 169 judgments had been given at that stage.

[93] Ibid. at para 73.

[94] Commission decision 30/7/96 (unpublished and cited by Gil Ibanez op. cit. fn 8. The Commission prosecution policy may also be seen in its annual reports.)

and to leave the more significant ones, where political reasons might militate against too tough an approach.

Dissatisfaction with the Commission's approach to its discretion was recently very evident in the *Newbury* case.[95] This stemmed from the Commission's failure to bring Article 226 proceedings against the UK for the UK's failure to carry out an environmental impact assessment before authorising the Newbury bypass. There was discontent in particular over the lack of transparency involved: the Commission did not inform the complainants as to why it was terminating the case and the quality of reasoning given by the Commission for terminating its investigation into what were clearly politically sensitive projects seemed inadequate. The complainants thus lodged complaints about this with the European Ombudsman as well as petitioning the European Parliament, suggesting that the Commission had been influenced by political factors. In response the Commission simply stated that it had complete discretion in the matter, an approach hardly likely to appease the complainants, and it added that complainants under the Article 226 procedure do not possess any special procedural rights, unlike those in other sectors such as competition or anti-dumping procedures. Therefore, it stated, there had been no maladministration.

The Ombudsman was, however, unimpressed, and responded by stating that it was precisely in such circumstances of unfettered discretion that the ability of the Ombudsman to hold an investigation was critical, adding, 'it appears that the procedure currently used by the Commission causes dissatisfaction among European citizens, some of which regard the Commission … as arrogant and high-handed.'[96] Contrary to the Commission's claims, the Ombudsman found there to have been maladministration in the event of the Commission's issuing of a press release stating that it would not issue proceedings against the UK, before it had even notified the complainants of this fact. The Ombudsman also stipulated that the Commission must give its reasons to the complainants for not proceeding.[97]

So unimpressed was the Ombudsman by the Commission's behaviour in this area that it decided to proceed with its 'Own Initiative' enquiry into the general workings of Article 226, noting in particular the Commission's withdrawal from high-profile, politically sensitive, infringement proceedings in the environmental field, as well as the dwindling number of complaints to the Commission generally, which suggested a lack of confidence in the Commission's procedures.[98] However, it concluded its enquiry[99] by finding no maladministration, although suggested that the Commission should create more procedural rights as a matter of good administrative behaviour.

---

[95] See Kunzlik, 'The Enforcement of EU Environmental Law: Article 169, the Ombudsman and the Parliament' (1997) EELRev at 46, for a detailed discussion of this case.

[96] Ombudsman's ruling of 29 October 1996 p 9.

[97] Ibid. p 10.

[98] These fell by 14 per cent from 1995 to 1996, a fact which the Commission itself preferred to ascribe to an improvement in the enforcement and implementation of EC law by member states (in its 14th Annual Report). However, as the Commission noted two years later in its 16th annual report, the number of complainants had risen quite substantially again by the end of 1998. Surely the Ombudsman's reservations and the Commission's optimism cannot both be right!

[99] 303/97/PD.

The conclusion must be somewhat tentative: that the Commission lacks a transparent enforcement policy, relying greatly on its own discretion. However, this does not mean that the Article 226 procedure should be seen as absolute and arbitrary. Discretionary power need not be dictatorial power. There are limits and the Commission should act constitutionally and in good faith. And, to be fair, some progress has been made: the Commission introduced some reforms in 1996 as a result of the Ombudsman's enquiries and also as a result of repeated requests from the European Parliament regarding delay, incoherence and lack of transparency.[100] Since then, the Commission has attempted to improve its internal procedures and publicity has become the general rule for decisions to issue reasoned opinions. Referrals to the ECJ and termination of decisions are often also announced as press releases[101] (before 1996 this was the exception rather than the rule). In 1998 the Commission evaluated the operation of its reformed working methods[102] and decided on a yet further range of measures aimed at the faster handling of cases, greater transparency and better relations with complainants. Since April 1998 it has held fortnightly meetings devoted specifically to the application of Community law, enabling it to process violations far more quickly.[103] Perhaps most importantly, the Commission has attempted to give complainants a role in the infringement procedure: registration of the complaint, respect for confidentiality, information for the complainant and the possibility of making views known before a decision is taken to close the case. It has also commenced a codification of current administrative practices to ease contacts with complainants.[104]

EFFECTIVENESS

Article 226 probably works best when it functions with the cooperation of the member states, when there could even be described as some sort of 'partnership' with them. In 1966 Scheinman described the relationship between the Commission and member states as 'bureaucratic interpenetration',[105] and more recently the vocabulary of partnership has appeared throughout the EU in this context.[106] The Sutherland Report suggested the development of a partnership between the member states and Commission to help the latter to apply EC law.[107] The Article 226 procedure should not be seen as too adversarial or prosecutorial in character. Although

---

[100] These are listed in the 14th annual report on the monitoring and application of Community law 1996 COM/97/0299 final/ at p 9 *et seq.*

[101] Since January 2001, these have also been announced at the Commission's Europa website.

[102] The evaluation is to be found in doc SEC (1998) 1733 and also discussed in its 16th annual report.

[103] Gil Ibanez however suggests there is still the need for some sort of new legal instrument, such as a European Administrative Enforcement Act. Gil Ibanez, op. cit. at fn 8.

[104] See Commission 18th Annual report on monitoring the application of Community Law (2000) Com (2001) 309 final.

[105] L Scheinman, 'Some Preliminary Notes on Bureaucratic Relations in the EEC' (1966) 20 IO 751.

[106] E.g. 'partenariat' is appearing in French dictionaries as well as in Spanish, e.g. *Le Grand Robert de la Langue Français* vol 7 1985, Le Robert (ed.), Paris.

[107] Sutherland report: 'The Internal Market after 1992: Meeting the Challenge'.

it might seem easy to characterise the Commission as enforcer and states as non-compliants, the states, of course, are members of the Council of Ministers and sit in committees in the comitology process.[108] The Commission cannot function without them. Therefore, it must work with them, whether in partnership, or through 'networks', which is becoming somewhat of a buzz term.[109] Litigation is not the only means the Commission uses to ensure effectiveness of EC law, indeed negotiation should perhaps be regarded as its main form of dispute settlement.[110] After all, most violations by member states are dealt with in this way. But there are problems with negotiation. There is the risk of too many over-powerful government interests prevailing, of a lack of publicity and a too informal nature of the agreement with a concomitant lack of procedural safeguards. Administrative policy making has its drawbacks and disadvantages. Therefore there will always be high-profile cases like the Spanish strawberries dispute in *Commission* v *France*.

There is also perhaps a gap between what the Commission can do and what EU citizens expect it to do. There may be a misunderstanding by the public of the Commission's enforcement function: a lack of public understanding would be after all nothing new in the EU. There is a danger, noted by the Commission in its 14th Annual Report for 1996, that the Commission be seen as capable of solving every individual situation, as a kind of Community Supercourt. But the object of Article 226 is to induce a member state to come back in line with Community law and the citizen is not a party to this procedure, which cannot help their personal situation at all. Citizens can instead rely on Community law in the national courts and have their rights under Community law secured there.[111] The public enforcement function of the Commission works in tandem with the private enforcement of Community law in the national courts, a function described elsewhere in this book.[112]

However, as Rawlings has observed,[113] there is also the sense of a lack of responsibility in the Commission's conduct of infringement proceedings, which is underlined by the attitude which it has displayed to complainants. The Commission's conduct in this context is likely to be scrutinised all the more closely after the mismanagement debacle of 1999. Some commentators, such as Ibanez,[114] have suggested that the citizens' lot might be improved by the introduction of a European Administrative Procedures Act, along the lines of the American version. This is by no means the first time that such a suggestion has been made.[115] However,

---

[108] See Chapters 2 and 3 for a discussion of this.

[109] See R Buxbaum, 'Is Network a Legal Concept?' (1993) 149/4 J Instit & Theoret Econs 689; W Powell, 'Neither Market nor Hierarchy: Network Forms of Organisation' (1990) 12 Res in Org Behaviour 303; H Kassin, 'Policy Networks and EU Policy Making: A Sceptical View' (1994) 17 W Eur Pols 15. See also the discussion of networks in chapter 2.

[110] See the discussion in Chapter 2.

[111] The Commission in its 16th Annual Report proposed to publish a new complaint form in the OJ, also including information on how individuals can obtain redress in the national courts.

[112] In Chapters 7, 8 and 9.

[113] Rawlings op. cit. fn 8 at 25.

[114] Ibanez op. cit. fn 8.

[115] See Chapters 2 and 3 for a discussion of its relevance in the context of comitology.

such an innovation might prove to be too inflexible for the realities of Article 226. What is really needed are further practical improvements to the lot of complainants, although some improvements have been made. The European Ombudsman complained in a recent speech[116] that the Commission has never accepted the obvious implications of citizenship and citizenship rights for proceedings under Article 226, and went as far as to suggest that complainants should be made parties to proceedings under Article 226. Even if is not possible to implement this suggestion, another suggestion by the Ombudsman made in its recent *Thessaloniki Metro* decision[117] does seem plausible. This was that the Commission should consider adopting a procedural code for the treatment of applicants along the lines of Article 41 of the Community Charter of Fundamental Rights.[118] This would make some sense. If the European Union wants to be seen to be taking its citizens at all seriously, then at least this would be a start.

---

[116] 'The citizen, the rule of law and openness', Speech by Jacob Söderman, European Ombudsman, European Law Conference, Stockholm, 10–12 June 2001.

[117] Case 995/98, decision of 30 January 2001.

[118] Relevant sections of Article 41 read as follows:

1. Every person has the right to have his or her affairs handled impartially, fairly and within a reasonable time by the institutions and bodies of the Union.

2. This right includes:

– the right of every person to be heard, before any individual measure which would affect him or her adversely is taken;

– the right of every person to have access to his or her file, while respecting the legitimate interests of confidentiality and of professional and business secrecy;

– the obligation of the administration to give reasons for its decisions.

This would go further than the current codification of administrative rules embarked on by the Commission: see above at fn 104.

PART FOUR

THE DEVELOPING
CONSTITUTION

13

THE EU AND HUMAN RIGHTS

The turn of the century European Union manifests an obsession with human rights,[1] citizenship, democracy, justice and constitutionalism. The language of European integration has been colonised by a vocabulary of rights, identity, freedom, participation and membership, shifting concepts such as 'market partitioning' and 'harmonisation' to a more or less peaceful co-existence, no doubt in what has been seen as a need to 'personalise integration'[2] as well as, of course, an attempt to increase democracy in the EU. The roots of this shift go back some time to early efforts to create a 'People's Europe'[3] and (weakish) institutional attempts to articulate a greater consciousness of fundamental rights in the EU, but, in spite of its most recent brainchild, the EU Charter of Fundamental Rights,[4] its fruit remains unripe.

It is commonly assumed that this growing 'humanisation' of the discourse of the European Union is beneficial, an effective and valuable means of lessening the EU's democratic deficit and of bringing the EU closer to the citizen. The protection of rights stands in the way of an over-deference to pragmatic considerations, such as economic efficiency. But the appeal and power of these unquestionable and sacred contemporary obsessions, fundamental rights, also endures on account of their present perceived status as a universal remedy for the ills of millennial Europe. As Klaus Gunther has written, 'We realise that the European history of human rights is written in blood. And it goes on...'[5] Recurrences of racism and xenophobia in the EU – the murder of Stephen Lawrence, the burning of Turkish houses in Germany, the despoiling of Jewish graves in France – are unpleasant reminders of this brutal, violent history. Gunther continues by suggesting that 'a human right is the rejection

---

[1] In this chapter, the expressions 'human rights' and 'fundamental rights' will be used interchangeably, although there are of course definitional distinctions.
[2] J Lodge, *The European Community and the Challenge of the Future* (Pinter, 1993) at 377–8.
[3] See for example, the debate on 'special rights' at the Paris summit of 1974 and later the Adonnino committee's work on a 'People's Europe' in the 1980s (Suppl Bull EC 7/85).
[4] Discussed later in the chapter.
[5] K Gunther, 'The Legacies of Injustice and Fear: A European Approach to Human Rights and their Effects on Political Culture' in Alston (ed.) *The EU and Human Rights* (Oxford: OUP, 1999) at 127.

of a concrete historical experience of injustice and fear, caused by actions of the State'.[6] A right is also the affirmation of human dignity, liberty and moral autonomy.

But the allure which rights have for us is also premised on a more fundamental problematic than that of contemporary Europe, one that is importantly rooted on a psychological level. This allure derives from their assurance of quelling the anxiety and despair which is part of human subjectivity[7] or the human condition. At a time when the EU faces testing challenges of deeper and wider integration, identity and resurgent nationalism this panaceic promise is enticing, but, ultimately, may be unredeemed.

FUNDAMENTAL RIGHTS AND CITIZENSHIP IN THE EU: THE GROWTH OF AN IDEA

Why has it taken 45 years to produce this current level of obsession within western European integration? The fact that fundamental rights were not a pressing concern in the early EEC may be gleaned from the very little space allotted to this subject in early textbooks.[8] The reasons for this lack of attention are embedded in the EU's history, and are similar to the explanation as to why there was no Bill of Rights in the original draft of the American Constitution,[9] when it was thought that the federal government would be insufficiently powerful to require a bulwark against its powers in the form of guaranteed rights. The EEC Treaty started out as an economic treaty, of limited ambitions, with the aim of creating a common market. It was originally modest in nature, partly no doubt because of the failure of the draft Political and Defence Union treaties[10] due to the refusal of General de Gaulle to countenance perceived attacks on French national sovereignty. There were no sections on fundamental rights or citizenship because the EEC founders did not think this relevant to

---

[6] Ibid. Gunther also suggests that human rights operate as performatives, as articulations of suffering. But Gunther's view may of course be contrasted with sceptical views, in existence since Bentham's dismissal of natural rights as 'Nonsense on Stilts' in the late eighteenth century. And, of course, it is not only state action which violates human rights.

[7] See e.g. R Salecl, *The Spoils of Freedom* (Routledge, 1994), and also S Zizek, *The Sublime Object of Ideology* (Verso, 1989) as well as, ultimately, J Lacan, *Ecrits* (London: Tavistock, 1977).

[8] Not so very long ago, Kapteyn and Verloren's *Introduction to the Law of the European Communities* (Kluwer, 1989, 2nd edn) devoted just four pages out of 900, Lasok and Bridge, *Law and Institutions of the European Communities* (Butterworths, 1987, 4th edn) 4 pages out of 500 and the first edition of Hartley's *The Foundations of European Community Law* (Oxford: Clarendon Press, 1981) seven pages out of 546 (although to be fair, Hartley allots another ten pages to general principles of law). Contrast to this the 2nd edition of Craig and de Burca, *EU Law* (OUP, 1998), which devotes 54 pages to fundamental rights and another 22 (in a separate chapter) to general principles.

[9] A Bill of Rights was not included in the original Constitution because it was thought that individual freedom would be best protected by the structural features of the US Constitution. So, prior to the Amendments, Alexander Hamilton observed, 'the Constitution is, itself, in every rational sense, and to every useful purpose, a Bill of Rights' (*Federalist Paper* No. 84). But of course a Bill of Rights was added to the US Constitution just a few years later, unlike in the EC.

[10] In which human rights had a prominent role: Stein and Vining, 'Citizen Access to Judicial Review of Administrative Action in a Transnational and Federal Context' in F Jacobs (ed.) *European Law and the Individual* (North Holland, 1976).

a treaty with mainly economic aspirations. (The European Convention on Fundamental Rights was also of course already in existence and probably thought sufficient to operate as a 'Bill of Rights' for Europe.) The scope of the Treaty of Rome has, however, come to extend far beyond purely economic matters – as some of the EEC's founders intended. The reference in the preamble to an 'ever closer union' of Europe's peoples surely signified that the Rome treaty was merely the starting point for European integration.[11]

EU law today covers many fields capable of having a human rights dimension. Cases have been heard by the ECJ concerning the freedom of expression (*Connolly*), the right to property (*Hauer*) and the right to equal treatment of transsexuals (*Grant*).[12] The ever expanding competence of the EU into areas traditionally within the preserve of state sovereignty has ensured that the issue of the breach of fundamental rights by the Union is not merely a theoretical possibility. However, in spite of this, the EU has only very recently, in December 2000, proclaimed its own (non-binding) Charter of Rights, and it continues to lack a general competence in the field of human rights. There are still relatively few references to such rights in the body of EU law, even after treaty revisions of the Single European Act, Maastricht, Amsterdam and Nice. European citizens thus have little idea what their rights are, even although they possess quite a few of them under European law.

The most important references are the following. Article 6(2) of the Maastricht Treaty states that 'The Union shall respect fundamental rights, as guaranteed by the European Convention on Human Rights and as they result from the constitutional traditions common to member states as general principles of Community law.'[13] The Treaty of Amsterdam added a new paragraph by way of Article 6(1) TEU, which states that 'The Union is founded on the principles of liberty, democracy, respect for human rights and fundamental freedoms, and the rule of law, principles which are common to the Member States.' These provisions are backed up by a sanctions procedure, also introduced by the Treaty of Amsterdam into Article 7 TEU, whereby a member state's rights may be suspended if it engages in 'a serious and persistent breach...of principles mentioned in Article 6(1).'[14] These are the general references to human rights. Previous attempts have also been made by the political institutions of the EU to improve the protection of fundamental rights. But, numerous

---

[11] Indeed, even the original treaty was not restricted to purely economic matters, as the provisions on the health and safety of workers, as well as equal treatment, in the original treaty illustrate. But the absence of any concrete reference in the EEC treaty to human rights is surprising, given that even the 1948 Brussels treaty on WEU, which is concerned with military cooperation, affirms its signatories' 'faith in fundamental human rights, in the dignity and worth of the person'. On the other hand, very few international treaties did so refer. The 1945 Preamble to the UN Charter was almost the first to do so, the first being the German and Polish Convention on Upper Silesia of 1922.

[12] These cases are discussed below.

[13] This provision is in fact a formulation drawn from the case law of the ECJ, as will be discussed below.

[14] Article 7(2) TEU. This provision is only to be used in extreme circumstances. The Treaty of Nice however amended Article 7, to allow for a slightly more graduated response. Under the post-Nice Article 7(1) there is a new procedure for determining whether there is a 'clear risk of a serious breach' of human rights. This provision operates as a sort of 'early warning system' and may be determined by a majority of the Council, unlike the determination of an actual breach under Article 7(2), which still requires unanimity.

although these are, they are not legally binding, amounting to little more than declarations of intent from the institutions concerned.[15] The most recent of these is, of course, the Charter of December 2000.

In April 1994, the Council of the European Union referred to the European Court of Justice the issue of the possible accession of the EU to the European Convention on Human Rights, raising in particular the issue of the competence for the EC to do this. However, such a move seems to have been ruled out, at least for the time being, following the Court's negative opinion given in 1996.[16]

A floating concept?

These recent treaty provisions may be the main general references to human rights in the treaties but they do not exhaust the sources of human rights for the European Union. What, however, is undoubtedly the case, is that protection of fundamental rights in the EU has evolved in an *ad hoc*, incremental way, making a comprehensive overview very difficult to generate.

First, the ECJ has played an important role in the development of a fundamental rights jurisprudence for the EC. Although in early cases (the so-called 'sins of youth')[17] the European Court of Justice rejected any applications based on alleged breach of fundamental rights by the EEC institutions, by the late 1960s and early 1970s it was forced to acknowledge such claims and to offer protection to individuals who asserted that the EEC was infringing their fundamental rights.[18] But it did so, the popular history goes, not because of any great love for the noble ideas of human rights, but rather because the European Court feared that if it did not, some member state courts, particularly the constitutional courts of Germany and Italy, would refuse to accord supremacy to EEC law if they found it violated fundamental rights in their own constitutions. Anything was preferable to that, so the

---

[15] The following measures have been passed:

—European Parliament Resolution April 4 1973: 'concerning the protection of fundamental rights of Member States' citizens when Community law is drafted.'

—Joint Declaration of Parliament/Commission/Council April 5 1977, stressing the importance of fundamental rights and respect for those rights.

— European Parliament Resolution November 16 1977: 'on the granting of special rights to citizens of the EC.'

—'Declaration on Democracy' of Heads of State and Government meeting as the European Council in Copenhagen April 1978: 'to ensure that the cherished values of their legal, political and moral order are respected and to safeguard the principles of representative democracy, of the rule of law, of social justice and respect for fundamental rights'.

—Commission memorandum April 4 1979: 'on the EC becoming signatories of the European Convention on Human Rights'.

—European Parliament Resolution on Draft Union Treaty imposing the express obligation on the Union 'to protect fundamental rights and freedoms'.

—European Parliament Resolution April 1989 enumerating fundamental rights.

[16] *Opinion 2/94*, see below.

[17] See e.g. Case 1/58 *Stork* v *High Authority* [1959] ECR 17; and Case 40/64 *Sgarlata* v *Commission* [1965] ECR 215, in which the Court refused to allow the treaty to be overridden by a plea based on fundamental rights.

[18] E.g. Case 29/69 *Stauder* v *City of Ulm* [1969] ECR 419.

European Court identified a respect for fundamental rights within the Community legal order itself. These fundamental rights take the form of **general principles of law**, and will be discussed in detail later in the chapter.

In addition to that, the European Court has named specific treaty items as fundamental rights: namely, non-discrimination on grounds of nationality in Article 12 EC and the four fundamental freedoms of goods, services, persons and capital.[19] They have also referred to equal pay (Article 141) and equal treatment as fundamental rights.[20] The new legal basis introduced by Article 13 of the EC treaty for non-discrimination legislation has already had an impact on fundamental rights legislation.[21] Some fundamental rights exist as secondary legislation rather than treaty provisions: the equal treatment directives are good examples.[22]

There is no clear, conceptual underpinning to the rights protected under EU law, probably because they have been developed in such an *ad hoc* way. The rights protected under EU law also take all forms – to use the terminology of the American jurist, Wesley Hohfeld, they exist as claim rights, imposing positive duties on others (i.e. social rights) as well as liberty rights, such as freedom of expression, powers and immunities.[23] So many things have been called 'fundamental rights' in the EU context that we seem to have an *embarras de choix* and a choice to suit any fantasy, in the guise of what might be called, in psychoanalytic terms, a floating signifier, namely a concept which can mean whatever its interpreters wish it to.[24] As has been suggested,[25] one may have to employ some sort of definitional refinement, otherwise the fishing rights claimed by the Spanish fishermen in *Factortame* will be jurisprudentially indistinct from 'cruel and unusual punishment'. It is, however, difficult to find such a refinement within the *acquis communautaire*, or more particularly, within the case law of the ECJ, a fact which surely made the case for an EU Bill of Rights all the more necessary.

---

[19] See Case 240/83 *Procureur de la République* v *ADBHU* [1985] ECR 520, 531 where the Court stated, 'It should be borne in mind that the principles of free movement of goods and freedom of competition, together with freedom of trade as a fundamental right ...' This 'elevation' is regretted by Coppell and O'Neill in 'The European Court of Justice: Taking Rights Seriously?' (1992) 29 CMLRev at 689.

[20] Case 149/78 *Defrenne II* [1978] ECR 1365 at paragraph 27.

[21] Article 13 reads as follows: 'the Council . . . may take appropriate action to combat discrimination based on sex, racial or ethnic origin, religion or belief, disability, age or sexual orientation.' So far, the following two directives have been adopted under Article 13: Council Directive 2000/78/EC establishing a general framework for equal treatment in employment and occupation; Council Directive 2000/43/EC implementing the principle of equal treatment between persons irrespective of racial or ethnic origin. The following decision has also been adopted: Council Decision 2000/750/EC establishing a Community action programme to combat discrimination (2001 to 2006). These three measures were adopted pretty swiftly, and it has been suggested that this swift progress was partly prompted by fears over the human rights situation in Austria after the election of a government in 2000 which included the far-right Freedom Party. Other treaty provisions of relevance include Article 3(2) EC on gender equality and Article 141(4) positive action.

[22] Such as the Equal Treatment Directive 76/207 and the discrimination directives mentioned above.

[23] W Hohfeld, *Fundamental Legal Conceptions* (Yale University Press, 1919).

[24] See R Barthes, *Mythologies* (Paris: Seuil, 1957) for one of the first uses of the term 'empty signifier'. See also Jacques Lacan, *Ecrits* (London: Tavistock, 1977); also C Douzinas, *The End of Human Rights* (Hart, 2000).

[25] I Ward, *A Critical Introduction to European Law* (Butterworths, 1996) at 139.

Maurice Cranston suggested that, in order to qualify as a 'fundamental right', the provision in question must be universal, of paramount importance and practical, thus disqualifying certain socio-economic rights, such as the right to holidays with pay, which satisfy none of these criteria.[26] These, he thought, were better characterised as political aspirations.[27] However, Cranston's criteria seem too narrow, excluding not only rights recognised under EC law (such as the right to free movement or the right of transsexuals to equal treatment recognised by the ECJ in the *P* v *S* case, discussed later in the chapter) but also under international law, in the two UN covenants, both of which include Cranston's hated right to holidays with pay. We may not wish to constrain the lexicon of rights in the way Cranston suggests. Koen Lenaerts, a judge of the CFI, proposed, more expansively, characterising human rights in the EU along a model of concentric circles.[28] Lenaerts sees the nucleus of human rights protection being that of the European Convention on Human Rights, expanded by a second circle formed by general principles of law articulated by the European Court under Article 220, with the third and fourth concentric circles made up of fundamental rights related to the status of the Community citizen and aspirational social rights. This gives greater flexibility. The new EU charter, with its six headings and about 50 rights, follows its own classification, and includes many rights that Cranston would reject. While not actually following Lenaerts' classification, nor that of the Charter, this chapter will focus on a wider frame of reference than the classic core of civil and political rights to be found in the European Convention of Human Rights or US Bill of Rights, taking in other things which the ECJ has named 'fundamental', while nonetheless approaching the EU classification critically.

Significantly, fundamental rights overlap substantially with citizenship, another concept which has been gradually developing to its present level of importance.[29] Some writers conceive citizenship in terms of rights, as did T H Marshall, who categorised the development of national citizenship through economic rights to political rights and then to a more complete realisation with the addition of social rights.[30] But a purely rights-based conception of citizenship is not necessarily appropriate to the twenty-first century EU: it fails, for example, to account for the more participatory, republican and duty – bearing elements that seem pertinent to Union citizenship. However, it is undeniable that the concept of citizenship does have a strong rights-based element,[31] which is considered in depth in the next

---

[26] M Cranston, *What are Human Rights?* (Bodley Head, 1973).

[27] An opinion shared by the CBI, in its response to the Convention's EU Charter of Rights, which includes social rights. The CBI suggested that these should not be in the Charter as they were only 'aspirations'. The CBI's document may be found on the Convention's archive website: http://db.consilium.eu.int/df.

[28] K Lenaerts, 'Fundamental Rights to be included in a Community Catalogue' (1991) 16 ELRev 376; also K Lenaerts, 'Fundamental Rights in the European Union' (2000) 25 ELRev 575.

[29] Discussed in Chapter 14.

[30] TH Marshall, *Citizenship and Social Class* (Cambridge University Press, 1950) at 11.

[31] See for example the pamphlet on 'The meaning of American Citizenship' published by the US Dept of Justice, which contains the following: 'When you took the oath of allegiance to the constitution of the US, you claimed for yourself God-given unalienable rights which that sacred document sets forth as the natural rights of all men.'

chapter. On the other hand, fundamental rights, to the extent that they are seen to be universal, pertaining to all humans, go beyond citizenship with its ties of allegiance to a particular regime. In this context, however, it is notable that most[32] of the wide variety of candidates for fundamental rights in the EU apply only to those who are nationals of an EU state. A 'fortress Europe' applies as much within the field of human rights as in international trade, a somewhat counter-intuitive and worrying feature, given that human rights are generally taken to be things we possess by virtue of our humanity, not our nationality.

THE EUROPEAN COURT OF JUSTICE AND HUMAN RIGHTS

Given the absence of any EU Bill of Rights until 2000, protection of fundamental rights for the first 40 years of European integration developed through the case law of the European Court of Justice (ECJ), which has undoubtedly played a very important role, and much of this chapter will focus on this. The same court which developed the doctrines of direct effect and supremacy of Community law, neither of which doctrines finds explicit basis in the Treaty, also developed a complex doctrine of protection of human rights, although some would claim that this doctrine has been developed with cynical motives. The late Judge Mancini, writing in 1989, summed up the position the ECJ had achieved in relation to fundamental rights in the following way: 'Reading an unwritten Bill of Rights into Community law is indeed the most striking contribution the Court has made to the development of a constitution for Europe.' But he continued by qualifying it in this way: 'this statement was forced on the Court by the outside, by the German and, later, the Italian constitutional courts.'[33] His qualification will be considered in the ensuing sections.

The development of the Court's jurisprudence has now spanned over 40 years and can be divided up into roughly four stages.

(1) 'The sins of youth'[34]

The first cases to raise human rights questions in the EC context came before the Court in the late 1950s. In the *Stork*[35] case, the ECJ refused to annul decisions of the High Authority of the European Coal and Steel Community (the equivalent of the Commission of the EC) on the basis of their incompatibility with provisions of West German constitutional law. In the *Sgarlata*[36] case of 1965, which concerned an application for annulment of two Commission regulations fixing the price for citrus fruits, brought by Mr Sgarlata and nine other citrus fruit growers, on the basis of

---

[32] With the exception of the right to petition the Ombudsman and the European Parliament.

[33] F Mancini, 'The Making of a Constitution for Europe' (1989) 26 CMLRev 595.

[34] The reference is taken from M Hilf, 'The Protection of Fundamental Rights' in F Jacobs (ed.), *European Law and the Individual* (North Holland, 1976).

[35] Case 1/58 *Stork v High Authority* [1959] ECR 17; see also Cases 36, 37, 38 and 40/59 *Geitling v High Authority* [1960] ECR 423.

[36] Case 40/64 *Sgarlata v Commission* [1965] ECR 215.

their incompatibility with fundamental rights under Italian constitutional law, the ECJ declared these applications inadmissible. The express provisions of the treaty could not be overridden by other principles, even if those principles were of a fundamental nature. The impact of these cases was not helped by the clumsy and unfortunate choice of wording used by the Court (described by Teitgen, a founder of the ECHR, as 'brutal'[37]) which made it seem all too obvious that EEC law was, indeed, inadequate in its protection of fundamental rights. Mancini, however, sees these early decisions as prompted by fear, by the resolve to protect the fragile freedom of action of the new EEC institutions against the member states.[38] And perhaps we should not be too harsh. In comparison with other courts with a human rights jurisdiction, the ECJ's progress was not so slow. The US Supreme Court decided very few human rights cases in its first 100 years and one of these was the infamous *Dred Scott*[39] case. Moreover, the European Court of Human Rights had only seventeen substantive decisions to show for its first eighteen years.[40]

(2) Defensive use of human rights

In any case, matters were soon to change. By the late 1960s, the German and Italian courts[41] were beginning to express concern at the possible erosion of fundamental rights entrenched in their national constitutions, if Community competence increased. It became increasingly clear that a shift in attitude was required by the ECJ in order to assure member states that fundamental rights could be adequately protected by Community law. The *Stauder*[42] case of 1969 gave the European Court its chance to show how this might come about. In order to deal with the Community butter surplus, one of the many unwanted by-products of the CAP, the Commission had authorised member states to provide subsidised butter to certain categories of social security recipients, who in return were to furnish the national trader with a coupon issued in their name. Stauder, who fell under this category, objected to the requirement to reveal his name on the basis that this violated his dignity, a fundamental right under German law. He challenged the scheme in the Stuttgart Administrative Court and the matter was referred to the ECJ, because it raised a point of Community law. The ECJ held that the provision in question could not be interpreted as requiring (although it did not prohibit) the identification of beneficiaries by name. Therefore the provision contained 'nothing capable of infringing the fundamental rights enshrined in the general principles of Community law and

---

[37] Cited in F Mancini, 'Safeguarding Human Rights – the role of the court' in Carpi and Orlandi (eds) *Judicial Protection of Human Rights* (Milano Giuffre, 1991). Teitgen was a former French Minister of Justice, who was responsible for the 1949 Teitgen report – and draft – of the ECHR.

[38] Mancini, op. cit. at 502.

[39] *Dred Scott* v *Sandford* 60 US (19 How) 393 (1857).

[40] C Gearty, 'The European Court of Human Rights and Protection of Civil Liberties – an overview' (1993) CLJ.

[41] These jurisdictions placed particular stress on observance of fundamental rights, given their recent history.

[42] Case 26/69 *Stauder* v *City of Ulm* [1969] ECR 419.

protected by the Court'.[43] As it was not necessary to identify a recipient of sub-sidised butter by name, any possible discrimination or infringement of the right to human dignity could be avoided by interpreting the measure in this way. Thus, the doctrine of fundamental rights finds its first mention in Community law. (And, somewhat ironically, an applicant who did not wish his name to be revealed, became famous in Community law, for that very reason.)

However, there were still problems. In referring the issue to Luxembourg in the *Stauder* case, the Stuttgart court had given a thinly veiled warning to the Community institutions, stating:

> ...the Community Institutions were called upon to assume, in their fields of jurisdiction, a responsibility for the protection of fundamental rights that had previously been guaranteed by the national courts of West Germany; for if the European Court of Justice would not constructively fulfil its duties, then the national courts of the Federal Republic of Germany would, in spite of the disruption of such a result, feel compelled to reserve for themselves the ultimate power of examining the constitutionality of Community acts ...according to the fundamental rights laid down in the West German constitution.[44]

This was no idle threat. Article 79 of the German Basic Law states that no amendment of the Constitution may diminish fundamental rights protection. Article 24 permits transfer of sovereignty to international organisations subject to the rules of the first chapter of the Basic Law (which guarantees fundamental rights and binds all institutions of the state to them). Therefore, the EEC could have had no lawful power to infringe fundamental rights of the German constitution. This warning, that national courts would themselves review the compatibility of EEC acts with national constitutional principles, struck at the heart of the principle of supremacy of Community law, which had been established in 1963 in the *Costa v Enel*[45] case and reaffirmed in many subsequent cases. It therefore looked as if the lack of a Community charter of fundamental rights would pose a real threat to the supremacy of Community law.

This matter was revisited the next year in the famous *Internationale Handelsgesellschaft*[46] case. This did not at first appear to be promising fundamental rights material, being another Common Agricultural Policy case. The applicant company, Internationale Handelsgesellschaft, was suing the national authorities responsible for administering Community law. The applicants were claiming the return of a (very large) deposit which had been confiscated when the company failed to export its full projected export of corn. This forfeiture was required under EEC Council Regulation 120/67 which set up a common market in cereals. The applicants claimed that the forfeiture was a violation of their basic rights under German constitutional law, namely, the principles of freedom of action and disposition, of economic liberty and proportionality. The national court referred the system's validity to the European Court of Justice.

---

[43] Ibid.
[44] Ibid.
[45] Case 6/64 *Costa v Enel* [1964] ECR 585. See chapter 7.
[46] Case 11/70 *Internationale Handelsgesellschaft* [1970] ECR 1125.

Here was a difficult question for the European Court. On the one hand, it would be disastrous for the Community legal system, as mentioned above, if national courts started to invalidate EEC provisions for their non-compliance with constitutional law. EEC law must take priority, the Court stated, holding that 'Recourse to the legal rules or concepts of national law in order to judge the validity of measures adopted by the institutions of the Community would have an adverse effect on the uniformity and efficacy of Community law. The validity of such measures can only be assessed in the light of Community law.'[47] On the other hand, the prestige of the EEC would be considerably eroded if the Community were found to be breaching national and international standards of human rights and nothing could be done about it.

The Court went on to find an ingenious, if somewhat devious, solution to this problem. It suggested that Community law itself might protect these very same fundamental rights:

> However, an examination should be made as to whether or not any analogous rights guaranteed inherent in Community law have been disregarded. In fact respect for human rights forms an integral part of the general principles of Community law protected by the Court of Justice. The protection of such rights, whilst inspired by the constitutional traditions common to member states, must be ensured within the framework of the structure and objectives of the Community. It must therefore be ascertained . . . whether the system of deposits has infringed rights of a fundamental nature, respect for which must be ensured in the Community legal system.[48]

After examining the grounds of infringement alleged, the ECJ concluded that there had been no infringement, as the restriction on the freedom to trade was not disproportionate to the interest which the deposit system sought to advance. Such a holding did nothing to halt disquiet in Germany and, when the case was resubmitted to the German constitutional court, the *Bundesverfassungsgericht*, that court gave its infamous judgment, otherwise known as *Solange I*, where it stated that, while it recognised that the Community constituted an independent legal order derived from autonomous sources of law, it, however, suspected that effective protection of fundamental rights had not been assured with sufficient certainty within the EEC, at least at that stage of the integration process, since the Community contained no formal catalogue of fundamental rights.[49] The *Bundesverfassungsgericht* therefore considered itself competent, so long as these conditions were not satisfied, to check whether Community law was compatible with fundamental rights enshrined in the German Basic Law, the *Grundgesetz*.

In describing the European Court's resolution, Joseph Weiler has written: 'the surface language of the Court is . . . the language of human rights. The deep structure is all about supremacy...'[50] Indeed, Coppell and O'Neill suggest that the

---

[47] Ibid. para 3.
[48] Ibid. para 4.
[49] The *Bundesverfassungsgericht's* first *Solange* decision is reported at [1974] 2 CMLR 540.
[50] Weiler, Cassese and Clapham (eds) *Human Rights and the European Community* (Baden-Baden: Nomos, 1991) vol II at 58.

European Court has instrumentalised rights as tools for European integration.[51] It might seem that the Court's strategy is here vulnerable to a post-modern critique of law, which asserts that forms of legality which are supposedly liberating in nature, such as civil liberties or judicial review, in fact participate in an all-determining instrumentalisation of social control, normalisation and governance. Gaete, for example, suggests that the libertarian project of human rights is trapped as 'the instruments of liberation tend to become the means of manipulation'.[52] And so human rights become a means to the legal system's self-aggrandisement and success.[53]

However, EEC law could not be entirely successful or manipulative while the prospect of a clash of national constitutional courts and the European Court of Justice remained. The ECJ's strategy was, nonetheless, reasonably successful, despite initial caution by the Italian[54] and German constitutional courts, and in subsequent case law the ECJ developed its fundamental rights jurisprudence. In the *Nold* case in 1974, it made its first reference to the European Convention on Human Rights[55] stating that 'the protection of property ownership constitutes . . . one of the guarantees recognised by Community law . . . based on the constitutional traditions of member states and acts of public international law such as the ECHR'.[56] In the *Hauer* case, Liselotte Hauer claimed that her right to property (in this case to grow a vineyard) had been infringed by regulations issued under the CAP. The ECJ, in a judgment which has since operated as a strong precedent,[57] considered the right to property in detail, giving special attention to the right under Protocol 1 of the ECHR. Other important decisions followed.[58] Therefore, by the late 1980s, the German Constitutional court seemed to think that the Community standard of protection was now adequate, when it gave its *Wunsche Handelsgesellschaft* judgment, otherwise know as *Solange II*.[59]

---

[51] Coppell and O'Neill in 'The European Court of Justice: Taking Rights Seriously?' (1992) 29 CMLRev at 689. Coppell and O'Neill claim that their conclusion is backed up by their survey of outcomes – i.e. that in very few of the cases where the Court boldly uses the rhetoric of fundamental rights does the applicant actually succeed in their assertion of that right. The vehemence of the Coppell and O'Neill claim is only matched by those who seek to defend the European Court against such accusations of bad faith, such as Weiler and Lockhart in their article '"Taking Rights Seriously" Seriously: The European Court and its Fundamental Rights jurisprudence' – part I (1995) 32 CMLRev 51, part II (1995) 32 CMLRev 579.

[52] R Gaete, 'Postmodernism and Human Rights: some insidious questions' (1991) 2 Law and Critique 149 at 150.

[53] See Foucault, *Power/Knowledge* (New York: Pantheon, 1980); Marx, *On the Jewish Question* [reprinted in Waldron (ed.) *Nonsense on Stilts* (Methuen, 1987)].

[54] *Frontini v Ministero delle Finanze* [1974] 2 CMLR 372; see also the discussion in Chapter 7 on supremacy.

[55] Although references to the ECHR had previously been made in pleadings and by Advocates General.

[56] Case 4/73 *Nold* [1974] ECR 491.

[57] However, notably, although the Court acknowledged the existence of a right to property under Community law, the applicant did not succeed in her claim: Case 44/79 *Hauer* [1979] ECR 3740.

[58] See cases discussed under section 3 below.

[59] Case 69/85 *Wunsche* [1986] ECR 947 also known in German as the *Mittlerweile* decision. See also *Bundesverfassungsgericht*'s judgments of 1993 in *Brunner v European Union Treaty* [1994] 1 CMLR 57, and now of 2000 in the *Bananas II* judgment: Order of 7 June 2000 2 BvL 1/97.

(3) Binding the member states

So far, the application of fundamental rights provisions to acts of Community insti-tutions themselves has been considered. But what about member states? For they also have a considerable role to play in the application and administration of Community law. Are member states required to observe human rights principles when they apply Community law? The answer must certainly be yes. Just as, with-in the US, the guarantees of the Federal Bill of Rights came to be incorporated and extended to acts of the state governments,[60] so the European Court of Justice, hav-ing 'discovered' fundamental rights in the national provisions of member states and international documents, and weighed community actions against them (a sort of 'upward' incorporation'), then turned and applied these rights to actions of member states, a consequent 'downward' incorporation. A fundamental issue then becomes **which** acts of member states are covered by this process?

The *Rutili* case of 1975 appeared to lay the foundations for these principles. In this case, the French Ministry of the Interior sought to restrict the movements of an Italian national, Rutili, on the basis of his political activities. In doing so, the French government had to derogate from Article 39 of the EC Treaty which deals with the free movement of workers within the EC. The grounds for doing so are set out in Article 39(3) of the treaty and must be based on 'public policy, public security or public health'. The ECJ held that the scope of the public policy derogations could not be determined unilaterally by member states but was a matter for Community law. The ECJ then went on to suggest that the limits of member state action under EC law were parallel to certain provisions of the ECHR: 'These limitations are a specific manifestation of the more general principles enshrined in Articles 8, 9, 10 and 11 of the European Convention on Human Rights ... which provide, in identi-cal terms, that no restrictions in the interests of national security or public safety shall be imposed on the rights secured by the above quoted articles other than such as are necessary for the protection of the interests in a democratic society.'[61]

Therefore, in the *Rutili* case, not only did the ECJ expressly invoke specific pro-visions in the European Convention but it applied them, not to acts of Community institutions, but to an act of a member state **derogating** from Community freedoms, thus indicating a willingness to police the boundaries of EC law. Several other cases followed[62] which established an incremental expansion of the area of member state action which would be subject to fundamental rights validation by the ECJ.

It would seem certain that member states, when they are enforcing Community policy and interpreting Community rules, as well as derogating from Community law, as in *Rutili*, must observe fundamental rights. However, the requirement may go further than that. In the *ERT*[63] case, the ECJ made it clear that member states

---

[60] Through the 14th Amendment which was added after the Civil War. Before that, the guarantees in the Bill of Rights applied only to the federal government.

[61] Case 36/75 *Rutili* [1975] ECR 1219.

[62] E.g. Case 63/83 *Kent Kirk* [1984] ECR 2689; Cases 60 & 61/84 *Cinétheque* [1985] ECR 2605; Case 12/86 *Demirel* [1987] ECR 3719; Case 5/88 *Wachauf* [1989] ECR 2609.

[63] Case 260/89 *ERT* [1991] ECR 2925.

are bound by fundamental rights, stating that: 'as soon as any such legislation enters **the field of application** of Community law this Court is sole arbiter in this matter'. Therefore, it seems that the only actions which the ECJ might decline to vet would be those falling within the member states' exclusive jurisdiction. This was the interpretation of Advocate General Van Gerven in the *Grogan* case who stated: 'Once a national rule is involved which has effects in an area covered by Community law…then the appraisal of that rule no longer falls within the exclusive jurisdiction of the national legislator.' This is a very wide interpretation indeed,[64] and of relevance in the context of Article 51 of the EU Charter of Fundamental Rights, which defines its scope, and will be discussed later in the chapter. Given the scope and width of Community law it may conceivably come into contact with just about any area of national law. An illustration of how this might come about leads us on to a fourth stage in the development of the ECJ's human rights jurisprudence.

(4) Member state nationals exercising Community rights

The *Konstantinidis*[65] case is an interesting example of the possible development of the law. Kristos Konstantinidis was a self-employed Greek masseur and aromatherapist who lived and worked in Germany. When he got married he noticed that his name had been wrongly transliterated into the marriage register and he tried to get it rectified. Unfortunately, the outcome was not what he had hoped for and his name underwent a further transliteration to become *Hrestos Konstadinindis*. The applicant, finding this spelling intensely distasteful, lodged an appeal against this transcription on the ground that it misrepresented his name. The German court took the view that the dispute raised problems of the interpretation and application of Community law.

The European Court itself gave a straightforward ruling, based solely on the right of establishment in Article 43 EC, which it referred to as one of 'the fundamental legal provisions of the Community'. Although there was nothing in the EC Treaty to prevent the transliteration of a Greek name into Latin characters in civil status registers, this transcription could not actually discriminate against foreign nationals by interfering with the unfettered exercise of the right of establishment under Article 43. Thus it held that it would be contrary to Article 43 for a Greek national to be obliged to use, in the pursuit of his occupation, a transliteration of his name whereby its pronunciation is modified and the resulting distortion exposes him to the risk of potential clients confusing him with other persons.

The real interest of this case, however, lies in the opinion of Advocate General Jacobs and in its implications for EC law and fundamental rights. According to the Advocate General, the fundamental rights issue broke down into two further questions. First, was the treatment of Mr Konstantinidis, as regards the spelling of his name, contrary to the European Convention on Human Rights or to any other

---

[64] Coppell and O'Neill criticise such a wide application as an attempt by the Court to accelerate the process of economic integration in the member states.
[65] Case C-168/91 *Konstantinidis* [1993] ECR I-1191.

human rights instrument or constitutional principle, the observance of which the Court must ensure within the sphere of Community law? Second, if that were the case, was the mere fact that Mr Konstantinidis was exercising his freedom of establishment under Article 43 EC sufficient to bring the case within the sphere of Community law for these purposes?

As regards the first question, the Advocate General found the German authorities' treatment of Mr Konstantinidis to be contrary to fundamental rights documents.[66] More difficult to determine was the second question of whether a person who exercises their right of free movement under EC law is entitled, as a matter of Community law, to object to treatment which constitutes a breach of their fundamental rights, even where the authorities' treatment is not discriminatory. Put simply, can the violation of fundamental rights, *per se*, interfere with the free movement of persons? Advocate General Jacobs considered that it could, writing, 'a Community national who goes to another member state as a worker or self-employed person…is…entitled to assume that wherever he earns his living in the European Community, he will be treated in accordance with a code of fundamental values, in particular, those laid in the European Convention on Human Rights.'

In fact, Advocate General Jacobs' opinion would extend the protection of fundamental rights under Community law quite considerably. The Court of Justice has never sought to examine the compatibility with the European Convention of national legislation lying outside the scope of Community law. But the scope of Community law is constantly expanding and the ambit of the free movement of persons provisions would take a particular leap with Advocate General Jacobs' opinion. By suggesting that these provisions might apply, even where no discrimination on grounds of nationality has occurred, the possibilities of assessing national law for its compatibility with the European Convention would be hugely increased.[67]

In the years since the *Konstantinidis* case, the ECJ seems to have rejected AG Jacobs' invitation to extend the scope of fundamental rights scrutiny,[68] finding the fact that the applicant is a migrant worker to be insufficient of itself, but requiring

---

[66] Although the European Convention on Human Rights does not contain any specific reference to the individual's right to their name, or any express provisions regarding their dignity or moral integrity, Advocate General Jacobs found this omission to be repaired by provisions in the Constitutions of many member states, which do include such explicit references. Thus he thought it possible to infer, from the constitutional traditions of member states and a broad interpretation of Article 8 of the Convention, the existence of a principle according to which the State must respect the individual's dignity, moral integrity and sense of personal identity. These rights would be violated if the State compelled someone to abandon or modify their name. Indeed, there appeared to be a particularly gross violation in Mr Konstantinidis' case, since the new transcription would also destroy the Christian character of his name.

[67] This was no revolutionary suggestion, given that the Court had held that non-discriminatory laws could be obstacles to the free movement of goods for many years, and more recently acknowledged non discriminatory laws as obstacles to the free movement of persons: see Case C-281/98 *Angonese* v *Cassa di Risparmio di Bolzano SpA* [2000] ECR I-4139.

[68] By Advocate General Gulmann in *R* v *Ministry of Fisheries, Agriculture and Food, ex parte Bostock* [1994] ECR 955.

also some element of EC policy to be at issue. It did consider fundamental rights issues to fall within the scope of EC law in the *Familiapress*[69] case, brought in the context of newspaper publishing, in which the ECJ cited the judgment of the European Court of Human Rights in the *Informationsverein Lentia*[70] case. However, in two other cases, the ECJ declined jurisdiction. In *Kremzow*,[71] a case which aroused a lot of interest, perhaps because of its facts, it readily drew a line round the outer boundaries of EC law. Kremzow, a former Austrian judge, convicted of murder, brought proceedings against Austria after being sentenced to life imprisonment contrary to Article 6 of the ECHR.[72] He argued that fundamental rights as general principles of EC law applied to his case because, as a citizen of the EU, his rights to free movement were infringed by the unlawful penalty of imprisonment. The ECJ did not follow AG Jacobs in *Konstantinidis* but instead held his claim to be outside the scope of EC law, stating that, while deprivation of liberty may impede a person's exercise of their right of free movement, a purely hypothetical prospect of exercising that right does not establish a sufficient connection with EC law to justify its application. As AG La Pergola noted, Kremzow's criminal sanction was the result of the application of a norm defining the crime of murder which had no connection with the free movement of persons. Similarly, in *Annibaldi*,[73] the ECJ held that the fact that national regulation deals with a policy area, such as agriculture, which is also regulated by the EU, does not necessarily of itself bring that area within the scope of EC law. It is only where there is a more specific link, such as where the national measure is introduced to implement EC law, or where it impinges on its effective application, that there will be jurisdiction. These cases are in line with the ECJ's *Opinion 2/94*,[74] in which it held that the EU lacked a general human rights jurisdiction, and also with the Court's more cautious approach to jurisdictional issues in the 1990s, as if it were fearful of invoking too much opposition.[75]

(5)   The continuing development of a fundamental rights jurisprudence

The ECJ has recognised a variety of rights in its jurisprudence: rights to trade and to property, and to engage in economic activity; procedural rights, such as to a fair hearing; freedom of expression and to privacy; rights of access to information;

---

[69] Case C-368/95 *Familiapress* [1997] ECR I-3689. Familiapress, an Austrian newspaper publisher, brought proceedings against Heinrich Bauer Verlag, a publisher of newspapers established in Germany, for an order that Bauer cease selling in Austria publications with prize-winning games, in breach of an Austrian law on unfair competition. The ECJ held that a prohibition such as the Austrian law might be capable of infringing Article 28 of the EC treaty on free movement of goods, as well as Bauer's fundamental rights to freedom of expression. However, it also noted that Article 10 of the ECHR, which protects freedom of expression, permits derogations from that freedom for the purpose of maintaining press diversity. Bauer did not have an unfettered right to freedom of expression.

[70] *Informationsverein Lentia* ECHR (1993) Series A No 276.

[71] Case C-299/95 *Kremzow* [1997] ECR I-2629.

[72] As found by the ECHR in *Kremzow v Austria* [1993] Series A No 268-B.

[73] Case C-309/96 *Annibaldi* [1997] ECR I-7493.

[74] Discussed later in this chapter.

[75] For a greater discussion of this matter see Chapter 5.

rights to non-discrimination on grounds of sex; some social rights.[76] In addition to the cases already cited, the ECJ has decided other recent cases on fundamental rights, raising issues of general importance, which give a flavour of its growing caseload.

In *X v Commission*[77] the ECJ gave an important decision on the right to respect for one's private life. The applicant claimed that his rights under Article 8 ECHR had been infringed because he was subjected by the Commission medical service, against his will and without his knowledge, to a dissimulated AIDS test, in the course of a job application. The ECJ overruled the CFI's judgment, in which that court held that a Community employee could not refuse to submit to this type of test. Instead, the ECJ held that a right to respect for private life, which included the right to keep one's state of health secret, required a person's refusal to be respected in its entirety. AG Van Gerven distinguished two aspects of the right to respect for private life: that of physical integrity or inviolability and the right to determine of oneself what information to divulge; both, he thought, had been infringed here. However, neither the Court, nor AG Van Gerven recognised an unfettered right of privacy. Both cited a passage from *Commission v Germany*:

> the rights (of the ECHR)...do not constitute unfettered prerogatives and may be restricted, provided that the restrictions in fact correspond to objectives of general interest pursued by the Community and that they do not constitute, with regard to the objectives pursued, a disproportionate and intolerable interference which infringes upon the very substance of the rights guaranteed.[78]

Nonetheless, this was a strong holding on privacy, and as the ECJ's handling of this right had previously appeared shaky in the *Hoechst*[79] case, it was encouraging.

The *Bosphorus*[80] case shows the ECJ grappling with the issue of the balance between fundamental rights and the public interest, in a context of worldwide importance. Bosphorus, a Turkish airline, had leased a plane from Yugoslav national airlines. This plane was impounded in Ireland as a result of Article 8 of Regulation 990/93, which was designed to implement at Community level UN sanctions imposed on the Federal Republic of Yugoslavia. Given that the aeroplane was owned, rather than controlled, by Yugoslav interests, Bosphorus argued either that sanctions under Article 8 did not apply, or that they would be contrary to their fundamental rights to peaceful enjoyment of property and their freedom to pursue a commercial activity. The ECJ disagreed, elaborating on what it had said about the right to property in *Hauer*, holding that Article 8 did apply and that the measure, although an interference with Bosphorus' property, was proportionate. The Opinion of AG Jacobs in the same case additionally made reference to the right to property in Protocol 1 of the ECHR, and Convention case law, such as *Sporrong and*

---

[76] See the following discussion.
[77] Case C-404/92 *X v Commission* [1994] ECR I-4737.
[78] Case C-62/90 *Commission v Germany* [1992] ECR I 2575 (at para 23).
[79] Discussed below.
[80] Case 84/95 *Bosphorus* [1996] ECR I 3953.

Lonroth,[81] in which the ECHR held that states may control the use of property in accordance with the general interest but that an appropriate balance must be struck. He also cited the 1994 EC case of *Germany* v *Council*,[82] concerning the organisation of the banana market, in which the ECJ held that the right to property and the freedom to pursue a trade or business were part of the general principles of EC law, but not absolute, and must be viewed in relation to their social function. Therefore, although Bosphorus' fundamental rights were at issue, there was also seen to be a strong public interest in enforcing the embargo measure of the UN Security Council. Indeed, according to AG Jacobs, it was difficult to imagine what stronger interest there might be than stopping civil war. Unavoidably, such sanctions affected property rights, including those of innocent economic operators. And so, like Ms Hauer and the banana traders, whose rights were at issue in *Germany* v *Council*, the applicants found their property rights subjected to a more general communal interest. This might seem to leave a surprising margin to the Community interests. Indeed, the *Germany* v *Council* case was subject to criticism and the ECJ blamed for what was seen by some as a superficial treatment of fundamental rights.[83]

In the case of *Connolly* v *Commission*,[84] the CFI considered the right to freedom of expression. Bernard Connolly was a middle-ranking Commission official who became notorious for publishing a book entitled *The Rotten Heart of Europe: The Dirty War for Europe's Money*,[85] in which he expressed contempt for 'Lotharingian' Christian Democrats, who aimed to build a new Charlemagnesque European state. He had not, however, received permission to publish this work, the content of which, according to the Commission, was detrimental to his participation in EMU (he worked in the unit of the Commission dealing with EMU), as well as to the image and reputation of Community institutions. He was subjected to disciplinary proceedings for violating the statutory obligations imposed on Commission officials and then dismissed. Connolly sought annulment of the decision to dismiss him, claiming, *inter alia*, that this interfered with his freedom of expression (accusing the Commission of 'intellectual terrorism' in stifling any serious minded attempt at what he called 'open minded discussion' of European monetary issues).[86] By the time his case came before the CFI, in February 1999, the Brussels executive had been put on the defensive over their alleged culture of secrecy and unaccountability.[87] Connolly alleged a breach of Article 10 ECHR, claiming his case to be a forerunner to that of Paul van Buitenen, the Dutch audit officer suspended by the Commission for attempting to highlight corruption. The currently poor reputation of the Commission did not help him. The CFI found that freedom of expression, as a fundamental principle of Community law, must certainly apply to Community officials,

---

[81] *Sporrang and Lonroth v Sweden* [1982] EHRR 35; Examples of the ECHR's growing jurisprudence under Protocol 1, which was rather ignored in its earlier years.

[82] Case C-280/93 *Germany v Council* [1994] ECR I-4973.

[83] See the discussion in Chapter 7.

[84] Cases T-34/96 and T-163/96 *Connolly v Commission* [1999] ECR IA-87, II-463.

[85] Faber and Faber, 1995.

[86] See J Palmer, 'The Belly of the Beast', (The Guardian, 10 November 1995).

[87] See Chapter 2 for a discussion of the events of the 1999 Commission mismanagement debacle.

but that his freedom of expression had not been undermined by his need to respect the dignity of his post and his obligation of loyalty. Such an approach, which places boundaries around the right to freedom of expression, is in line with the jurisprudence of the ECHR (indeed, Mr Connolly himself admitted that 'no national civil service would tolerate one of its employees publishing such a book', and he had also expressed the somewhat premature hope that 'Brussels has a tradition of allowing more individual expression')[88] but provides less protection for freedom of speech than the US, where the first Amendment has considerable weight. One of its most extreme advocates, Justice Hugo Black, stated, 'It is my belief that there **are** "absolutes" in our Bill of Rights. Indeed, the importance of freedom of speech in the US is signified by its place in the Bill of Rights. It is the **first** amendment.'[89] In contrast, it is only the 10th article of the ECHR and Article 15 of the EU Charter.

In the *Baustahlgewebe* case,[90] the ECJ considered another Convention right: the right to a fair hearing under Article 6 ECHR. Baustahlgewebe appealed to the ECJ from the CFI about, *inter alia*, the excessively long time they had to wait for the CFI to give judgment. They had brought an action in 1989 for annulment of a Commission decision which imposed a fine of 4.5 million ECU on fourteen producers of welded steel, for agreements which infringed Article 81(1) EC by price fixing and market sharing. The CFI did not give judgment until April 1995 (a duration of nearly six years), in which it partially annulled the decision and reduced the fine. Baustahlgewebe claimed that this infringed their right to a hearing within a reasonable time, as well as constituting a *Prozesshindernis* (a bar to proceeding with the case). The ECJ held that the reasonableness of such a period had to be appraised in the light of circumstances specific to each case, such as its complexity, the conduct of the applicant and the competent authorities, and its importance to the applicant. In this case the applicant's economic survival was not directly endangered, although the need for legal certainty had not been ensured, given the fine which they faced. On the other hand, the case was exceedingly complex, given that it involved fourteen manufacturers, eleven applicants, three different languages, voluminous documents and facts and law of some complexity. Notwithstanding this complexity, it found the CFI proceedings had been unreasonably protracted. However, their length had not affected their outcome and so the ECJ was only prepared to reduce the amount of the fine, by 50,000 ECU, as 'fair satisfaction'. If the applicant's complaint had been as to the length of time taken by the ECJ itself, they would have been without a remedy. Given that the EU is not party to the ECHR, they would have been unable to take their case there, although such a course of action would have been of questionable value when the European Court of Rights has been as much subject to delay as the Community courts. Delay, one of Bentham's 'three headed hydra' of the legal process, is as much a feature today as it was in the early nineteenth century.

---

[88] Quoted in A Watson, 'Unity within Europe, past, present and future' (*The Times*, 11 September 1995).

[89] Quoted in C Black, 'Mr Justice Black, The Supreme Court, and the Bill of Rights' (Harper's Magazine, February 1961) at 63.

[90] Case C-185/95P *Baustahlgewebe v Commission* [1998] ECRI-8417.

Some other cases which show the ECJ engaging in an important jurisprudence of fundamental rights will be considered in more detail in the context of European citizenship and just noted here. As well as developing rights under the ECHR, and those present within the constitutional traditions of its member states, the ECJ has explored the right to equal treatment of men and women, as it is found in Article 141 of the treaty and in directive 76/207. This case law on equal treatment is too voluminous to be dealt with in any comprehensive way here, although of course, the ECJ has clearly stated that the right to equal treatment on grounds of sex is a fundamental right. However, two cases[91] are worth highlighting, as they have a capacity to move this right in new directions. In *P v S*,[92] the ECJ held that the Equal Treatment directive could be relied on by a transsexual dismissed from their employment as the result of gender reassignment surgery, stating that 'the Directive is simply the expression, in the relevant field, of the principle of equality, which is one of the fundamental principles of Community law'. For the ECJ, discrimination arising from the sex change 'is based essentially, if not exclusively, on the sex of the person concerned'.[93] However, in *Grant*,[94] the ECJ refused to extend the equal treatment principle to discrimination suffered by gays and lesbians. This was in sharp contrast to AG Elmer who suggested an interpretation of the equal treatment provisions as free-standing. The Court, however, preferred to leave the matter to the political institutions for legislation, which has since taken place, with the addition of Article 13 by the Treaty of Amsterdam, and secondary legislation based on Article 13.[95] So the EU has moved somewhat closer to a free-standing right to equality in the treaty, of the sort to be found, for example, in the 14th Amendment of the US Constitution.[96]

Another fundamental right, which has a close link with citizenship, this time in its political and civil manifestation, concerns the right to information.[97] In the past, access to information in the EC was covered by a code of conduct and secondary legislation; now it falls under Article 255 EC, inserted by the Treaty of Amsterdam, and Regulation 1049/2001 on Access to Information.[98] This regulation, however, contains a large list of exceptions allowing the institutions to refuse access under Article 4. The regulation was criticised while in draft form, by the Ombudsman Jacob Soderman, as an inadequate approach to transparency. Soderman argued that

---

[91] The Court has also given important rulings on positive discrimination in *Kalanke* and *Marschall*, which are considered in the chapter on citizenship. Also important are the *Sirdar* and Case C-285/98 *Kreil* decisions, concerning women's rights of access to the military, which are also discussed in the chapter on citizenship.

[92] Case C-13/94 *P v S* [1996] ECR I-2143.

[93] Paras 20–1.

[94] Case C-249/96 *Grant v South West Trains* [1998] ECR I-621.

[95] Detailed in fn 21.

[96] The 14th Amendment reads *inter alia* that 'No State shall . . . deny to any person within its jurisdiction the equal protection of the laws.'

[97] This is discussed in Chapter 14 on citizenship, and in greatest detail in Chapter 3, in the section on transparency.

[98] See Chapter 3 for a detailed discussion of this regulation.

the list of exceptions was without precedent in the developed world (which seems questionable, given the familiar bureaucratic secrecy of government departments). However, this situation was given a rather comic twist, with reports of Soderman and Prodi, the head of the Commission, agreeing only to appear separately before the parliamentary committee scrutinising the draft.[99] In the event, the draft was modified somewhat, but the list of exceptions remains broad.

The Community Courts now have quite a developed body of case law concerning access to information.[100] Recently, in the *Hautala*[101] case, the ECJ refused to grant the Council's appeal from a CFI decision. Ms Hautala, an MEP, had asked the Council to send her a copy of a report on conventional arms exports, which had been prepared by a working party in connection with the CFSP. The Council had refused her request on the ground that the report contained sensitive information and disclosure could be harmful to the EU's relations with third countries. The CFI had annulled this decision and had required the Council to consider giving partial access to the report. In his Opinion in *Hautala*, AG Leger referred to the principle of access to documents as a fundamental right. He also referred expressly to the Charter of Fundamental Rights, which provides a right of access to documents. He saw this as a key way of involving citizens in the management of public affairs. Although the denial of access might sometimes be justified, in particular where national defence is concerned, in this case the Council's refusal to consider partial access conflicted with the principle of proportionality and also was at odds with the right of access as a fundamental right. This strongly worded opinion clearly underlines the importance of access to information as a fundamental right, although it remains to be seen just how the Community Courts will balance the status of the right to information as a fundamental right with the long list of permitted exceptions to disclosure.

DIFFICULT QUESTIONS

This survey of the ECJ's protection of human rights raises questions. Perhaps the most obvious is the question of whether any theoretical connection may be drawn between the human rights cases decided by the Court. They concern various types of right, some procedural, some substantive. Do they share any common features other than that they all concern human rights? In the next section the following problematic areas will be discussed, which may make possible some conclusions concerning the human rights 'philosophy' of the European courts. They are as follows:

(1) Which rights are to be protected, given the reference to the 'constitutional traditions' of the member states?

(2) What is the **status** of these 'general principles of law'?

---

[99] Reported in *EU News* March 2000 Issue 13.
[100] Again, see Chapter 3 for a discussion of this case law.
[101] Case C-353/99P *Council* v *Hautala* [2001] ECR 000, upholding judgment of the CFI.

(3) Has the ECJ privileged economic integration at the expense of human rights?

(4) What **standard** of review have the Community courts provided?

(1) Which rights should be observed and protected by the EU?

The EU Charter sets out a long list of rights which will be discussed later in the chapter. However, this is non-binding and the Court's case law still remains highly relevant. The ECJ has stated that it cannot 'uphold measures which are incompatible with fundamental rights recognition and protection by the member states.'[102] Article 6(2) of the Maastricht Treaty, as already mentioned, requires the EU to 'respect fundamental rights, as guaranteed by the ECHR . . . and as they result from the constitutional traditions common to the Member states, as general principles of law'. Does this mean that the ECJ will respect a right that is recognised in **any** of the member states, even if in only one? If so, protection of rights by the ECJ would be considerable. Some writers have indeed interpreted these references as suggesting that the most extensive protection is to be applied, a so-called 'maximalist' or absolutist requirement.[103]

However, given the great range of rights protected in member states, some of which conflict (such as a woman's right to an abortion and the unborn child's right to protection in the Irish constitution) it is difficult to see how such a maximalist standard might operate. The fundamental rights protected in the member states of the Union reflect choices made by citizens about the sorts of values they wish to see protected as well as the best means of securing them. One cannot talk about law, and most certainly not about rights, without entering the realm of value. HLA Hart tried, and some would argue failed, to do so, in *The Concept of Law*.[104] Not all will wish to see a right to abortion,[105] or a people's right to a clean environment, for example, among them. To enforce a right protected in one member state on nationals of another could be divisive and disruptive.[106] It is not clear that human rights will always be an integrationist or unifying force, even among member states which are signatories to the same human rights instruments. For example, in the *AM & S* case,[107] the ECJ derived a principle of confidentiality between lawyer and client from a comparative survey of the laws of the member states. Yet, as is evident from the comments of Advocate General Warner in this case, not all member states were happy with the conclusions of the Court as to this supposedly common principle. He reported that: 'The French Government went so far as to suggest that the present

---

[102] Case 44/79 *Hauer* [1979] ECR 3740.

[103] See e.g. Besselink, who argues for maximum protection, in Besselink, 'Entrapped by the Maximum Standards: On Fundamental Rights, Pluralism, Subsidiarity in the EU' (1998) 35 CMLRev 629.

[104] HLA Hart, *The Concept of Law* (Oxford: Clarendon, 1961).

[105] Consider the controversy over the US Supreme Court's holding that there was a constitutional right to an abortion in *Roe* v *Wade* for example.

[106] See e.g. Weiler, 'Fundamental Rights and Fundamental boundaries: on the conflict of standards and values in the protection of human rights in the European legal space' in Weiler, *The Constitution of Europe* (Cambridge, 1999) 102.

[107] Case 155/79 *AM & S Europe Ltd* v *Commission* (1982) ECR 1575.

case represented an attempt to foist on the Community what was no more than a domestic rule of English law.' However, the Advocate General concluded that despite these objections there was a general principle which could be distilled from the various states even if the 'conceptual origin' of the principle and 'the scope of its application in detail differ from Member State to Member State'.[108]

Indeed, if the ECJ were to enforce **all** the fundamental rights protected in member states it surely would be going beyond its own constitutional role and instead enforcing the member states' own constitutional law. Rather, the Court is observing a European (albeit sometimes more minimal) standard of protection inspired by the common constitutional traditions of the member states.

For some commentators, however, the problem is not that the ECJ adheres to too maximalist a standard but rather that it is too perfunctory in its scrutiny. Writing in 1991, Andrew Clapham observed that 'the Court's method so far has been to selectively distil common practices from some member States'.[109] adding that 'references to specific national legal systems are often perfunctory and haphazard'. These criticisms will be considered in further detail in ensuing sections.

(2) The status of general principles of law

The status of fundamental rights as general principles of law is important and somewhat intriguing. How do such principles operate within the EC – as binding rules, or as something vaguer, as guidelines? This is a crucial question.[110] The protection given to human rights may vary, depending on the interpretation adopted. Unfortunately, the ECJ has given no clear indications on this issue.

The OED defines a principle as: 'a fundamental . . . proposition on which others depend; a general statement or tenet forming the basis of a system of belief . . . a primary assumption forming the basis of a chain of reasoning',[111] thus suggesting a foundational status. However, in addition to having a fundamental, important status, the use of principles within legal theory and law also suggests a degree of generality or even vagueness. In *Taking Rights Seriously*,[112] Ronald Dworkin contrasts legal principles with legal rules, stipulating that, while legal rules operate in an 'all or nothing' fashion, principles do not, but instead have a dimension of weight, while not denying that they may bind courts.

Therefore, it seems that principles are more difficult to identify than rules. Dworkin suggests that they cannot be identified by way of any positivist rule of recognition, and builds a whole theory of his own, indicating the part that principles pay in adjudication.

---

[108] Ibid. 1587.

[109] A Clapham, *Human Rights and the European Community: a Critical Overview* (Baden-Baden: Nomos, 1991) 50–1.

[110] For a discussion of general principles, see T Tridimas, *General Principles of EC Law* (Oxford: OUP, 1999); J Bengoetxea, 'Principles in the European Constitutionalising Process' (2001) 12 King's College Law Journal.

[111] *The Shorter Oxford Dictionary* (1993 edn).

[112] Dworkin, *Taking Rights Seriously* (Duckworth, 1977).

How has the ECJ proceeded in identifying general principles of law? The terminology of the ECJ is instructive: it refers to the fundamental rights found in international treaties and national constitutions as an 'inspiration'.[113] Koen Lenaerts[114] compares them to the 9th Amendment of the US Constitution, which states that 'the enumeration in the Constitution of certain rights shall not be construed to deny or disparage others retained by the people'. The situation remains the same in the post-Charter EU. Although, for Manfred Dauses, this nevertheless means that general principles must be categorised as 'more than a conceptual guide, but a primary source of directly binding law' others have found their status to be more uncertain. So, as has recently been observed, 'Applying the ECHR "as general principles of Community law" (Article 6 § 2 TEU) must probably be distinguished from applying it per se; otherwise the question would arise why the substantive provisions of the ECHR had not already been integrated as such into the Treaties. That applies even more to the ECHR's Protocols, which have not yet been ratified by all the European Union's member States; Protocol No. 7, for instance...has been ratified by only eight of the fifteen member States.'[115]

For Andrew Clapham, the characterisation as 'inspirations' is a weak point, enabling the ECJ to 'selectively distil common practices from some member states',[116] which are then only treated as guidelines. Poiares Maduro agrees, stating that 'It is therefore abundantly clear that international human rights treaties and national constitutions . . . do not bind the ECJ.'[117] If so, then the ECJ's characterisation is quite distinct, offering less protection than those of rights theories, such as those of Dworkin or Rawls,[118] in which rights are seen as having lexical priority over community goals. Dworkin presents his famous image of the right as a trump card. A status as 'guidelines' is a long way from these obligatory categorical imperatives, whereby rights are things that must be respected and it certainly fails to capture the strength and urgency of rights. The same is true of the non-binding, 'inspirational' Charter.

But some such principles must bind the court: under the Vienna Convention on the Law of Treaties, any treaty is void if it conflicts with peremptory norms of international law (*jus cogens*).[119] Not everything which the ECJ categorises as a general principle would however qualify as a *jus cogens*, which is of the most fundamental sort, such as the prohibition of torture, rather than say the principle of proportionality, which the ECJ has also categorised as a general principle of law.

On the other hand, general principles do seem to be what the ECJ has identified as sufficiently important, part of the common legal and political heritage and morality.

---

113 For example, in *Internationale Handelsgesellschaft* [1970] ECR 1125 at 1134.
114 Lenaerts, 'Fundamental Rights be included in a Community Catalogue' (1991) 16 ELRev 376.
115 Per Fischbach and Krüger, Council of Europe observers, 'Comments on document Convent 13 CHARTE 4178/00 cb 2 JUR EN 16.3.2000'.
116 Clapham op. cit. at fn 109.
117 M Poiares Maduro, 'Striking the Elusive Balance Between Economic Freedom and Social Rights in the EU' in Alston (ed.) *The EU and Human Rights* (OUP, 1999) 453.
118 Dworkin op. cit.; Rawls, *A Theory of Justice* (Harvard, 1971).
119 Articles 53 and 54 Vienna Convention.

This is still admittedly very vague, as vague as Dworkin's instructions to his ideal judge Hercules: 'Hercules' theory of adjudication...identifies a particular conception of community morality as decisive of legal issues; that conception holds that community morality is the political morality presupposed by the laws and institutions of the community. He must, of course, rely on his own judgement as to what the principles of that morality are...'[120] This leaves much scope for the subjective preferences of judges, always a problem in the context of fundamental rights and the subject of much debate in the US, where the power of judicial review of the Supreme Court is enormous. The proclamation of the EU Charter of Fundamental Rights in December 2000 has certainly not solved this problem. Its non-binding status raises the question of how the rights therein function – as guidelines, or aspirations? Most likely in exactly the same way as general principles.

(3) Economic integration or rights?

One specific problem with the ECJ as a key guarantor of fundamental rights in the EU, is that this Court has seen economic integration as one of its key objectives. A Human Rights Supreme Court, such as the European Court of Human Rights, on the other hand, has, as its main concern, the protection of human rights. What happens when the objective of economic integration is in conflict with fundamental rights? The *Grogan*[121] case provides an example of the sort of conflict which can arise.

In 1989, the Society for the Protection of the Unborn Child brought a case against student unions in Ireland, seeking an injunction to prevent students from distributing publications containing information about abortion clinics in the UK. They saw this as being contrary to the 1983 Irish Constitutional amendment which states that: 'The State acknowledges the right to life of the unborn and with due regard to the equal right to life of the mother, guarantees in its laws to respect and, as far as practical by its laws, defend and vindicate that right.'[122]

The student organisations, on the other hand, defended their actions as falling under the freedom to provide services protected by Article 49 of the EC Treaty. So, there seemed to be a conflict between the economic right of the freedom to provide services and the right to life of the unborn child protected in the Irish constitution. Would the ECJ, to which the case had been referred by way of a preliminary reference, recognise and protect the Irish right, given that Ireland was the only member state to give constitutional status to this right? Cases like *AM&S* tend to suggest that a right protected under only one constitution may still be protected under EC law. But in *Grogan* this 'maximalist' approach was not followed. In its judgment, the ECJ held that abortion could qualify as a service under Article 50 of the treaty, therefore the manner under which this facility might be available became justiciable under EC law. Article 49 prohibits any restriction by a member state on the freedom

---

[120] Dworkin, *Taking Rights Seriously* at 126.
[121] Case C-159/90 *SPUC v Grogan* [1991] ECR I-4685.
[122] Article 33 Irish Constitution.

to provide services throughout the EC (subject to member state derogations under Articles 46 and 55). However, the ECJ did not get as far as looking at the grounds for derogation under Article 46 as it decided that the link between the British abortion clinics and the student information was 'too tenuous' for the Irish injunction to be regarded as a restriction within the meaning of Article 49. Thus the ECJ escaped having to deal with any of the vexed moral issues involved. But what would have happened if there had been a formal relation between a British abortion clinic and the activities in Ireland? The obvious response for the Irish government would have been to claim derogation under Articles 46 and 55 of the EC Treaty. However, since *Rutili* and *ERT* such derogations must be justified in terms of their compatibility with the ECJ's interpretation of the ECHR and the status of the right to life of the unborn is far from certain under the ECHR. In the *Dublin Well Woman* case[123] (which ran in tandem with *Grogan* on a very similar point, namely, as to whether the constitutional ban on information about abortion was contrary to Article 10 of the ECHR, which provides for freedom of expression, rather than the EC freedom to provide services)[124] the European Court of Human Rights held that the ban on information was contrary to Article 10 of the ECHR, but did not decide the extremely controversial issue of whether the unborn is protected under Article 2 of the Convention, which protects the right to life (or indeed whether there is a right to an abortion under Article 8 of the Convention which concerns the right to respect for one's private life).

Some commentators have seen *Grogan*, and other cases, as indicating the danger that member state constitutions can be subordinated to economic interests under EC law[125] (which latter have been alluded to by, for example, Advocate General Van Gerven as 'fundamental rights').[126] This is perceived to be a worrying development. Indeed, it has even been suggested that economic rights, such as the right of free movement of services, are at the kernel of rights protection in the EU. Norbert Reich suggests that 'The economic rights of market citizens are certainly the nucleus of any rights granted by the European Community or Union...'[127] This characterisation is very different to that of Lenaerts quoted earlier.[128] Is it accurate?

That economic interests might be so prominent is not surprising, for two reasons. First, for a long time, the fundamental impulse of the EEC was primarily economic in nature, and second, companies, with their economic interests in mind, have been the main litigants before the ECJ, and the European Court's jurisprudence reflects this.[129]

---

123 *Open Door Counselling & Dublin Well Woman v Ireland* [1992] E Ct HR Series A No. 246.

124 See the article by Conor Gearty on the flurry of litigation in Ireland, following the Irish constitutional amendment: C Gearty, 'The Politics of Abortion' (1992) 55 MLR.

125 E.g. Coppel and O'Neill, 'The European Court of Justice: Taking Rights Seriously?' (1993) 29 CMLRev 689.

126 In his Opinion in the *Grogan* case.

127 N Reich, 'A European Constitution for Citizens' (1997) 3 ELJ 131.

128 The significance of market rights in EC law is discussed in detail in the chapter on citizenship.

129 E.g. Case 11/70 *Internationale Handelsgesellschaft* [1970] ECR 1125 (right to property, economic liberty); Case 4/73 *Nold* [1974] ECR 491 (right to ownership); Case 44/79 *Hauer* [1979] ECR 3727 (right to property); Case 5/88 *Wachauf* [1989] ECR 2609 (right to compensation), to name but a few.

One of the founding influences on the EEC was that of ordo-liberalism, with its basis in free market transactions and economic efficiency. However, the ECJ has not always upheld claims based on a fundamental right to property (it did not do so in *Hauer*, or *Bosphorus*). But there is no doubt that the economic freedoms, particularly the free movement of goods, have been highly developed by the ECJ, requiring the elimination of member state restrictions on free movement including those which are not discriminatory in nature but also those which simply restrict trade, domestic or imported.[130] Until recently, free movement of persons under the treaty has not been given such broad scope.[131] The most highly developed aspect of EU citizenship is market citizenship[132] and the right to economic activity: political and social rights have been far less developed. Although the EC has had some sort of social policy from the outset, and the right not to be discriminated against on grounds of sex has been highly developed by the ECJ, aside from that, it is rare for the ECJ to affirm fundamental social rights as general principles of EC law. The Community courts sometimes seem quite uncertain about the status of social rights: in *Comité Centrale*[133] the CFI was less sure of its handling of the rights of workers to keep their jobs, and of their representatives to be consulted, than in the case of its usual more confident handling of property rights. However, this has not always been the case and it remains to be seen what sort of interpretation the Community Courts will give to the new discrimination directives. The *Comité des Sages* were appointed by the Commission to look into civic and social rights in 1995. In their report they argued that if the EU was to become 'an original political entity, it must have a clear statement of the citizenship it is offering to its members. Inclusion of civil and social rights in the treaty would help to nurture that citizenship and prevent the EU being perceived as a bureaucracy assembled by technocratic elites far removed from daily concerns.'[134]

A stress on free market rights and interests can sit uneasily with fundamental rights protection: in most constitutions and international rights documents greater priority is given to civil and political rights. They make no appearance in the US Bill of Rights, and little more in the ECHR, where the right to property in Protocol 1 has only quite recently come to the awareness of the rights-bearing public. Some writers suggest that economic rights do not need a superior level of protection: Alexander Meiklejohn, for example, argued that distinguishing the two types of right was of great importance and that a constitutional regime that linked the two was 'in constant danger of giving to man's possessions the same status, the same dignity, we give to man himself'.[135] Coppell and O'Neill comment: 'It would seem, then, that there is

---

[130] See for example, Case 8/74 *Procureur du Roi v Dassonville* [1974] ECR 837; Case C-76/90 *Säger v Dennemeyer* [1991] ECR I-4221.

[131] But see now Case C-281/98 *Angonese v Cassa di Risparmio di Bolzano SpA* [2000] ECR I-4139.

[132] For a greater discussion of this concept see Chapter 14.

[133] Case T-96/92 *Comité Centrale d'Entreprise de la Société Générale des Grands Sources v Commission* [1995] ECR II-1727.

[134] Report of the Comité des Sages, *For a Europe of Civic and Social Rights*, chaired by Maria Lourdes Pintasilgo, Brussels (1996).

[135] Meiklejohn, *Free Speech and its relation to self-government* (New York: Harper, 1948).

no distinction and hence no hierarchical relationship being posited by the European Court between the basic human rights outlined, for example, in the European Convention on Human Rights and the free market rights arising out of the treaties of the European Community.'[136] If economic rights are indeed fundamental, then the Cranston test for fundamental rights must surely be rejected, as economic rights are surely not universal and arguably not of paramount importance.

However, we may locate this privileging of economic rights in a sound historico-philosophical tradition. For Locke, property rights were the prototypical natural rights which became translated into a civil right under the law.[137] This Lockean exegesis is sometimes seen as an explanation of the prevalence and paradigmatic status of property rights in Anglo-American jurisprudence from Blackstone on. Indeed, Blackstone effulged over property rights, 'There is nothing which so generally strikes the imagination and engages the affectations of mankind . . . as the right of property.'[138] Mary-Anne Glendon, who deplores this privileging of property rights as leading to what she has derided as the atomistic 'lone rights bearer' of US law, suggests that in continental European political theory and practice, where Rousseau had greater influence than Locke, a different discourse on rights developed.[139] In the *Contrat Social* Rousseau suggested that property rights were always subordinate to the overriding claims of the community.[140] We see such an approach in the jurisprudence of the ECHR under the first Protocol, and more particularly in cases like *Hauer* and *Bosphorus*.

As already remarked, a formative influence on the EU single market was an ordoliberal economic theory of the market, but one in which market freedoms are seen as intrinsic to the notion of human dignity, as well as upholding theory of contract and private property rights.[141] Thus, rather than uplifting the economic rights to the same status as a right to human dignity, it might be said that, under this vision, human dignity is achieved by the functioning of a free and equal market society. Ordoliberalism is closely related to the neoliberalism of Hayek,[142] which claims that the protection of a free and equal society ensures prevention of the atrocities of Nazi Germany and the like. Along with the traditional politico-economic liberalism of Locke, these versions of liberalism hold that economic rights are secured in return for our surrender of our natural state, in the belief (or perhaps 'fantasy') that society

---

[136] Coppell and O'Neill op. cit. at 669. See also EJ Mestmacker, 'On the Legitimacy of European Law' (1994) 58 RabelsZ 615, and E-U Petersmann, 'Proposals for a new Constitution of the European Union: Building Blocks for a Constitutional Theory and Constitutional Law of the EU' (1995) 32 CMLRev 1123.

[137] Locke, *Second Treatise in Two Treatises on Government*, Laslett (ed.) (Cambridge: CUP, 1963). See also Nozick, *Anarchy, State and Utopia* (Oxford: Basil Blackwell, 1974).

[138] Blackstone, *Commentaries on the Laws of England* (Oxford, 1768) Book III at 4.

[139] M-A Glendon, *Rights Talk* (Macmillan Free Press, 1991) at 16.

[140] Rousseau, *The Social Contract* (Oxford: OUP, 1994) 178–81.

[141] See Petersmann, 'National Constitutions, Foreign trade policy and European Community law'(1992) 5 European Journal of International Law 1; see also D Chalmers, 'The Single Market: from prima donna to journeyman' in Shaw and More (eds) *New Legal Dynamics of the European Union* (Oxford: 1996) who suggests that the European Court is now less influenced by ordoliberal theory than in its early days.

[142] Hayek, *The Road to Serfdom* (London: ARK, 1976).

can be unified and rationally organised, a promise which may remain undelivered. It is certainly questionable whether such a basis is sufficient for a twenty-first century EU which has moved beyond a common market. The EU must avoid the danger of what Terry Eagleton has termed 'commercial humanism', by which the citizen is defined not by political virtue but by rights to and in things.[143] This is a ready pitfall if there is too great a focus on market rights and market citizenship.

(4) Evaluation of the ECJ's review

There are three principal areas by which the ECJ's activities in human rights may be evaluated. First, qualitatively – in terms of how substantial the Court's judgments are in this area. Second, by way of outcomes – how many applicants are successful in their rights claims? Third, a procedural issue – the question of access to the Court in these types of claim.

(a) The character of judgment

Some discussion of this aspect has already taken place, in discussion of the way in which the court identifies fundamental rights, and of the attention it pays to precedents from, e.g., the ECHR or national courts.

At this stage, one is again prompted to ask the question: is there any underlying coherence to the Luxembourg court's human rights judgments, evidence of some theory which unifies their approach to the great varieties of rights they consider? But a survey of the court's jurisprudence reveals a shortness, sometimes even a lack of maturity, in its analysis that one would perhaps not find in courts more experienced in dealing with human rights, such as the ECHR, or US Supreme Court. In the context of the ECHR, which itself contains a disparate array of rights, Conor Gearty has suggested that this court has managed to develop a coherent jurisprudence, writing, '"Due Process" is the core unifying concept of the Convention and its case law; it is the underlying process which renders intelligible a body of decisions that would otherwise seem fragmentary and occasionally inconsistent with each other.'[144] Similarly, one can extract some sort of judicial philosophy in the human rights cases of the US Supreme Court, albeit one which changes over time and is not shared by all of its members at any one time. So for example, one can identify economic liberty in the late nineteenth/early twentieth century,[145] or civil rights in the 1950s and 1960s Warren court era. It is more difficult to identify such movements in Luxembourg. If one can identify any general theme, it does seem to be economic integration. The fundamental freedoms of EC law have been highly developed to this end. Likewise, the concept of direct effect, introduced by the ECJ

---

[143] T Eagleton, in *Oxford Amnesty lectures: On Human Rights*, S Shute and S Hurley (eds) (New York: Basic Books, 1993).

[144] C Gearty, 'The European Court of Human Rights and Protection of Civil Liberties – an overview' (1993) CLJ 125.

[145] See e.g. *Lochner* v *New York*, 198 US 45 (1905); *Coppage* v *Kansas*, 236 US 1 (1915).

partly, in its own terms, to uphold 'individual rights'. Supremacy of Community law was at least partly the rationale for the court's introduction of a fundamental rights jurisprudence in the first place. But these developments have been in the context of general economic integration and do not always sit comfortably with the individual language of rights. Thus individual claims to property are not always upheld against the general communal interest, and the court has not always given great attention to analysis of individual rights. Admittedly, strong recognition of a Community interest seems to reduce the risk of rights being used unreasonably to constrain the public interest, to be used against the democratic process,[146] as in the US, where for example, the first amendment has been used to strike down legislation outlawing hate speech, as in *RAV v St Paul*.[147] But on closer inspection this argument is hardly a strong one. The ECJ has been accused of being anti-democratic, not because it upholds fundamental rights against the public interest, but because it imposes its view of Community interest over that of the member states, (which are arguably more democratic than the EU) thus imposing its notion of one communal interest over another.

Furthermore, the Court's analysis sometimes seems a bit peremptory. De Witte notes that the *Hauer* case is often cited as a good example of the ECJ's fundamental rights scrutiny but that in fact, when analysing the rights to property, the Court of Justice looked at only three of the member states' laws, even then in no great detail.[148] The discussions in *P v S* and *Grant* on equality or in *Kalaake* and *Marschall* on affirmative action seem thin in comparison to the consideration given in the Supreme Court's 14th Amendment jurisprudence.[149] The discussion in *X v Commission* on respect for one's private life is far less detailed than ECHR precedents on this issue such as *Dudgeon*.[150] The *Connolly* case seems a mere epigone next to great first amendment precedents such as *New York Times v Sullivan* or *Texas v Johnson*,[151] which engage in detailed discussion of the place of free speech in our society.

Admittedly this difference is partly due to the ECJ's organisation and rules of procedure. The requirement of unanimous judgments tends to produce terse opinions. If we look instead to Advocate Generals' opinions – such as those of AG Jacobs in *Konstantinidis* or AG Van Gerven in *X v Commission* – we find a deeper analysis. But what, however, is also the case is that the CFI and the ECJ might take more care to develop persuasive arguments when they reject arguments based on rights. The earlier *Banana war* cases, such as *Germany v Council*, show a great amount of deference to the Community legislature. In these cases, in the sections dealing with

---

[146] For a critique of the undemocratic nature or a rights-based review, see J Waldron, 'A Rights-Based Critique of Constitutional Rights' (1993) 13 OJLS 18.

[147] *RAV v City of St Paul* 112 S Ct 2538 (1992).

[148] B De Witte, 'The Past and Future Role of the European Court of Justice in the Protection of Rights' in Alston, *The EU and Human Rights* (OUP, 1999) 859.

[149] For an example of US Supreme court jurisprudence an affirmative action see *Adarand Constructors v Federrico Pena* (1995) 112 S Ct 2097.

[150] *Dudgeon v United Kingdom* (1983) 5 EHRR 573 ECHR.

[151] *New York Times v Sullivan* 376 US 254 (1964); *Texas v Johnson* 491 US 397 (1989).

fundamental rights claims, the language of rights hardly shines through the discussion of international trade, and reads too much like Teitgen's 'brutal' sins of youth, decided 40 years earlier.

(b) Outcomes

Several commentators have noted that not so many applicants have been successful in their fundamental rights claims in the Community courts. In many of the cases in which the ECJ has adopted the language of fundamental rights Community law has nonetheless prevailed against claims as to their violation. Coppell and O'Neill, already mentioned, suggest this follows from an instrumental manipulation of human rights, citing the *Wachauf*[152] case as an example of fundamental rights being treated as principles of interpretation, rather than universal and overarching principles of validity.[153] However, their claims have been stringently contested by the Court itself, and by Weiler and Lockhart, who cite a number of cases in which rights have been successfully invoked: for example, rights to a fair hearing or defence in *Orkem*,[154] and the right to equal treatment. Weiler and Lockhart are not themselves totally uncritical of the Court however, adding their own (mild) critique of cases in which they see fundamental rights as having been compromised by the ECJ. They cite, *inter alia*, *Van Duyn* (in which a Dutch scientologist was denied entry into the UK on grounds of her scientology, although this was not a prohibited activity in the UK), *Henn and Darby*, in which Dutch pornography was banned from entry into the UK although similar materials were available in some areas of the UK, and the *Diatta* and *Demirel* cases (concerning the residence rights of third country nationals in the EU), as examples of cases in which the ECJ was too deferential to the political and constitutional sensibilities of its member states.[155]

Coppell and O'Neill are not the only writers to point to the low success rate of applicants. Foster (albeit writing in 1987)[156] found few cases in which the ECJ had held that a provision of the ECHR or a national constitution had actually proved a successful ground for upholding a claim, citing the *Kent Kirk* case,[157] on the non-retroactivity of laws, as one of the few. By the late 1980s Foster could find little advance in the success rate for pleading fundamental rights in the twenty years since the ECHR was first raised as an issue before the ECJ. Out of the 45 cases in which the ECHR had been raised over those twenty years, in only sixteen had it been referred to in the Court's judgment and in only two of these had it been of any assist-

---

[152] Case 5/88 *Wachauf* [1989] ECR 2609.
[153] Coppell and O'Neill op. cit.
[154] Case 374/87 *Orkem v Commission* [1989] ECR 3283.
[155] Case 41/74 *Van Duyn v Home Office* [1974] ECR 1337; Case 81/87 *R v Henn and Darby* [1979] ECR 3795; Case 267/83 *Diatta* [1985] ECR 567; Case 12/86 *Demirel* [1987] ECR 3719. It is not only the ECJ, but also the ECHR which may be subjected to this criticism. *Muller v Switzerland* and *Otto Preminger v Austria* are good examples of cases in which that court seems to have been over-deferential to Community standards.
[156] N Foster, 'The European Court of Justice and the European Convention for the Protection of Human Rights' (1987) 8 HRLJ 245.
[157] Case 63/83 *R v Kent Kirk* [1984] ECR 2689.

ance to the party (*Kirk* and *Rutili*). He therefore concluded that fundamental rights had been of little concrete assistance to parties.

Writing over a decade later, de Witte makes a similar complaint,[158] arguing that the cases where the ECJ finds an actual breach of fundamental rights to have been committed by the EC are very rare indeed, and that, consequently, the standard of protection of rights in the ECJ is lower than that of the ECHR and national constitutional courts. *Hoechst*[159] and the *Banana* cases[160] are examples of the failure of the ECJ to protect rights – in both cases the right at issue was considered to be a fundamental right under German constitutional law. In *Hoechst* the right under consideration was that of the inviolability of the home, held by the Court not to be protected in EC law, although it was under German law (a good example of the ECJ not applying a maximalist standard). In the *Banana* cases, German commentators have suggested that the German courts would have handled fundamental rights differently (in this case the rights to property and the freedom to pursue a trade).[161] However, the ECJ does seem to have been more sensitive to rights in its more recent judgments in the *Banana* cases,[162] giving, for example, closer scrutiny to the Council regulation amending the original banana regulation and finding some of its provisions in breach of a general principle of non-discrimination.

(c) Access to justice in the Community courts

As discussed in the chapter on judicial review, standing under Article 230 is very restrictive. Applicants who want to challenge EC law in Luxembourg on the grounds that it infringes fundamental rights must be directly and individually concerned by the measure. This is very difficult for private litigants to establish, given the stringency of the *Plaumann* test.

The ECJ has suggested that individuals and companies which have no standing in the ECJ might use their national courts, which could then make preliminary rulings under Article 234. In this way, it has asserted that a complete system of remedies does exist under the treaties, designed to permit the ECJ to review the legality of measures.[163] But recourse to national courts is not always available. In such a case there might be a conflict between the right to a judge under Article 6 of the ECHR and the system of the treaties. There may be no domestic legislation which implements the Community act in question and the applicant may be left with the tough

---

[158] B De Witte, 'The Past and Future Role of the European Court of Justice in the Protection of Rights' in Alston, *The EU and Human Rights* (OUP, 1999) 859.
[159] Case 46/87 *Hoechst v Commission* [1989] ECR 2859.
[160] See Chapter 7 for a discussion of these cases.
[161] E.g. U Everling, 'Will Europe Slip on Bananas?' (1996) 33 CMLRev 401; T Stein, 'Bananen-Split? Entzweien sich BverfG und EuGH uber den Bananenstreit?' (1998) EuZW 261.
[162] E.g. Case C-364/95 *T Port* [1998] ECR I-1023 and Case C-122/95 *Germany v Council* [1998] ECR I-973.
[163] See Case 294/83 *Les Verts* [1986] ECR 1339.

choice of breaking the law if they wish to challenge the EC act, an unattractive prospect, and a situation in which justice cannot always be done.[164]

The ECJ itself mentioned the possibility of a relaxation of its standing rules at the IGC in 1996. This is in many ways desirable: if they were relaxed to a test whereby the applicant be 'adversely affected' they would resemble the core liberal standing rules in the US and UK.[165] Standing under Article 230, however, remained unaltered by the Treaties of Amsterdam and Nice,[166] and is unlikely to be much altered in the near future: a fear of floodgates being prompted by existing delays in the courts.

Alternatively, it has been suggested that a special individual human rights complaint procedure might be created based on existing remedies in member states, such as the German *Verfassungsbeschwerde* (also mentioned by the Court in its preparatory report for the 1996 IGC) or the Spanish *Amparo*.[167] This would exist only for alleged breaches of fundamental rights and not for cases of other types of judicial review. Such a procedure would reduce the possibility that justice is not done in individual cases. The fact that the ECJ itself is suggesting such changes indicates that all is not well regarding access to justice and that the member states would do well to take these suggestions into account in future.

HUMAN RIGHTS AND EXTERNAL RELATIONS

Much of this chapter has been taken up with analysing the work of the ECJ, but other institutions have played their part in the human rights field, particularly in the context of external relations. Until recently, the external relations of the EC were concerned mainly with trade, rather than with general foreign policy, which became a matter of serious EU concern only with the introduction of the Common Foreign and Security Policy by the Maastricht Treaty. However, human rights issues can play a significant role in overseas trade and, since 1983, the EC has been adopting reports on human rights in the world and Community policy on human rights. So, for example, foreign trade agreements may be made conditional on the other party's observance of human rights: if they fail to do so, the treaty may be terminated, a practice increasingly used since the early 1990s. Aspirant members of the elite EU club may also find their membership hopes dashed if they are revealed to have an unsatisfactory record on human rights – a fact which can be quite galling, as the practices of the EU's current members may not always be as pristine in the human rights arena as is desirable. A noticeable feature of the EU's human rights policy in the external arena is that it does not always practise what it preaches to others. Another feature is that it does not actually possess a coherent policy. As an Amnesty report stressed, 'The whole sphere of the Union's external policy is riddled with

---

[164] See the commentary on this point in Convention paper for the Draft Charter of Fundamental rights CHARTE 4111/00 20 January 2000 at 6.

[165] See the discussion of standing in Chapter 10.

[166] With the exception of the expanded *locus standi* of the European Parliament under Article 230.

[167] See De Witte op. cit. at 893 *et seq.*

competing competences, on the one hand among the member states and the Union, and on the other among the pillars of the Union. In such circumstances it is not surprising that the objectives of human rights policy are not being fully served.'[168]

The following sections outline the most important human rights mechanisms currently operating in the field of external relations.

Human rights as a condition of entry to the EU

This is a very basic example of the EU setting human rights standards for other countries. The Treaty of Amsterdam added a new[169] Article 49 TEU, requiring candidate countries for EU membership to respect the principles of Article 6(1) TEU, namely 'the principles of liberty, democracy, respect of human rights and fundamental freedoms, and the rule of law'. EU institutions must be satisfied that this is the case: there must be unanimity in the Council of Ministers, an absolute majority in the Parliament, and the opinion of the Commission is also important in the context of the accession of new member states. These principles are taken seriously, as can be seen in the *Agenda 2000*[170] document, prepared by the Commission, which gives some indication of how the criteria can be met by prospective applicants. So, for example, the Agenda specifically stated that Slovakia did not satisfy the criteria, on account of its lack of proper democracy. However, although Article 49 TEU for the first time brings respect for human rights of candidate countries within the treaty framework, such criteria have unofficially played a role for a longer time through the *Copenhagen criteria*, laid down by the European Council in 1993 as political criteria for membership. According to these criteria, countries must have achieved 'stability of institutions guaranteeing democracy, the rule of law, human rights and respect for and protection of minorities'.[171] Notably, this emphasis on protection of minorities has not been included in Article 6(1) TEU,[172] a factor which may increase in significance on the future accession of East European states.

The principles in Article 6(1) resemble those in Article 3 of the Statute of the Council of Europe, which lay down criteria for membership of that institution.[173] However, the admission to the Council of Europe of countries such as Albania, Croatia and Russia might raise doubts as to the seriousness of the Council of Europe

---

[168] Amnesty International memorandum: Proposal for a strengthened protection of human rights by the EU in the context of the IGC 11996. RAC 04/96. Nor has consistency been a feature of the EU's CFSP as a whole: see S Douglas-Scott, 'The Common Foreign and Security Policy of the EU – reinforcing the European Identity' in Bergeron and Fitzpatrick (eds) *Europe's Other* (Ashgate, 1998).

[169] Prior to this, the main treaty criterion for entry was that the country concerned be a 'European' state.

[170] *Agenda 2000 – for a stronger and wider Union.*

[171] Bull EC 6–1993 pt I.13.

[172] Article 6(1) of course applies to present states of the EU, some of which, such as France, do not recognise minorities (Reservation of France to Article 27 International Covenant on Civil and Political Rights). See also Nowak, 'Human Rights Conditionality in the EU' in Alston (ed.) *Human Rights in the EU* (OUP, 1999).

[173] Article 3 reads as follows: 'Any European state can become a member of the Council of Europe provided it accepts the principle of the rule of law and guarantees human rights and fundamental freedoms to everyone under its jurisdiction.'

in applying its own criteria.[174] In the context of EU membership, the situation becomes somewhat ironic, with existing members showing a poorer record, for example, of ratification of international human rights instruments, and their protocols, than some candidate countries.[175] And, of course, the EU is not itself a member of the ECHR. We may cite the words of Samuel Johnson's Prince Rasselas to the venerable philosopher: 'Have you then forgot the precepts . . . which you so powerfully enforced?'[176] As Weiler and Alston comment, 'EU Leadership would be best achieved by example.'[177]

The human rights clauses

Since the early 1990s, human rights clauses have been included in certain international agreements entered into by the EU with third countries, such as bilateral trade and cooperation agreements, some association agreements, Mediterranean agreements and Lomé agreements. These reflect the changing nature of the world and the emergence of fragile new democracies. These clauses allow for the suspension of the agreement if the other partner breaches human rights, and indeed they came about as a result of difficulties faced under general international law in suspending agreements. The principle of *pacta sunt servanda* was thought to preclude termination of a treaty agreement on the grounds of another country's unsatisfactory human rights record. For example, the EU had found itself unable to halt payments, on grounds of Amin's notorious abuse of human rights, of about 7m ECU to Idi Amin's Uganda in the 1970s under Lomé I.

Human rights clauses were not included in EC international agreements until Lomé IV, but, even then, no suspension clause was included. However, in the 1990s 'essential element' clauses began to be used in agreements with new democracies in Eastern Europe, which unequivocally spelled out the conditions for suspension and termination of the agreements. These were strengthened by non-compliance clauses: the so-called 'Baltic' and 'Bulgarian' clauses.[178] In 1995 the EC adopted a decision[179] setting out the basic elements of these clauses to ensure consistency, which now serves as a model for new treaties.

---

[174] Nowak op. cit. at 692 cites the former Deputy Secretary-General of the Council of Europe, Peter Leuprecht, outspoken in his critique of the admission practice of the Council of Europe, who resigned because he did not wish to continue to serve in an organisation which had become 'feeble and flabby' in its role as the standard bearer of democracy, rule of law and human rights in Europe (*Frankfurter Rundschau*, 3 July 1997).

[175] E.g., not all EU states have ratified the main UN human rights instruments: Belgium and Ireland have not ratified the Convention Against Torture. Many have not ratified various protocols of the ECHR, e.g. Protocol 4 has not been ratified by Spain or the UK. Many have not ratified the European Convention on Regional or Minority Languages (ratified by the UK 1 July 2001).

[176] Samuel Johnson, *Rasselas*, (ed.) B. Brown (New York: 1964).

[177] Weiler and Alston, 'An "Ever Closer Union" in Need of a Human Rights Policy: The European Union and Human Rights' in Alston op. cit. 3.

[178] For example, the Baltic clause reads as follows: 'The parties reserve the right to suspend this Agreement in whole or in part with immediate effect if a serious breach of its essential provisions occurs' (Article 21(3) treaty with Baltic states).

[179] Bull. EU 5-1995 pt 1, 2.

There has been some doubt over the legal basis for these human rights clauses in the treaty. In *Portugal* v *Council*[180] the ECJ rejected Portugal's argument that the cooperation agreement between the EC and India should have been based on Article 308, which requires unanimity in the Council, and instead upheld the legality of the human rights clause of the agreement under Article 181 EC, on the basis of Article 177(2) EC which provides that: 'Community policy in this area shall contribute to the general objective of developing and consolidating democracy and the rule of law, and to that of respecting human rights and fundamental freedoms.'[181]

The EU's increasing tendency to use these clauses may be illustrated by the fact that, by late 1995, the 70 ACP states, twenty OSCE states, fifteen Latin American countries, two Mediterranean states, six Asiatic states and South Africa had agreed to such human rights clauses. However, the popularity of these clauses is in tension with their actual implementation.[182] So Riedel and Will note, by mid 1999, 'not a single formal suspension of a treaty…has been based solely on human rights violations, even though there was ample occasion for it'.[183] Thus, the purpose of these clauses is to establish dialogue and communication, rather than to be used as a blunt instrument for terminating agreements (and termination may have an unfortunate impact on traders in third countries who are not responsible for that country's human rights record). Riedel and Will go as far as to say that, 'One might…even argue that the human rights clause has missed its point, if it actually has to be applied by way of treaty suspension.'[184]

Trade preferences

The EC may also be willing to grant unilateral trade preferences to trading partners conditional on respect for, e.g., fundamental labour standards. These may be withdrawn if the third country is found to breach these, by, for example, allowing the practice of forced labour which is in breach of the Geneva and ILO Conventions. In this way, in March 1997, the Council of Ministers withdrew access to tariff preferences to Burma because of its forced labour. However, the EC does not always withdraw such preferences. It may instead offer 'special incentive arrangements' to countries satisfying standards set in ILO Conventions.[185] The General System of Preferences (GSP) was the first instrument to contain such an incentive clause. Such preferences are unusual in the field of international trade law which seems to permit trade restrictions prompted by human rights concerns only to a very limited extent.[186]

---

[180] Case C-268/94 *Portugal* v *Council* [1996] ECR I-6177.
[181] For more commentary on this, see E Riedel and M Will, 'Human Rights Clauses in External Agreements of the EC' in Alston (ed.) op. cit. 723 at 732.
[182] A fact noted by Riedel and Will, op. cit. at 743.
[183] Ibid.
[184] Ibid 751.
[185] Such as freedom of association and the right to collective bargaining.
[186] See the discussion on this point by B Brandtner and A Rosas, 'Trade Preferences and Human Rights' in Alston op. cit.

But it may be questionable whether EU practice on trade preferences always operates to the benefits of human rights. As Brandtner and Rosas note,[187] 'limiting trade may have unfavourable implications for the interests of traders (who may also be stakeholders in a human rights discourse) or for the situation of the affected population (and its economic and social rights)'.[188]

Human rights in the context of the EU's common foreign and security policy (CFSP)

Of course, trade is not the only dimension of external relations in which human rights issues can arise. They are also likely to play their part in general foreign policy. Like the Blair government in the UK, the EU aspires to have an 'ethical' foreign policy. Article 11(1) TEU sets a basic obligation on the EU 'to define and implement a common foreign and security policy', one of whose specific objectives is 'to develop and consolidate democracy and the rule of law and respect for human rights and fundamental freedoms'.

So far, the EU's CFSP has not been noticeably successful.[189] More particularly, so far, it has not produced a satisfactory EU human rights foreign policy. Part of the problem has been a lack of consistency in foreign policy on human rights, and part, a difference of opinion over human rights foreign policy among its member states. The EU's position, or lack of it, on China, is an example of this. When the Council of Ministers formalised its position regarding human rights in China, for the purpose of a resolution, it was in fact to announce that the EU would not be acting, and nor would its member states be, in China. This was seen by some as 'putting markets before morality',[190] and also involved a 'levelling down' of positions which might have been individually taken by the more radical member states of the EU.

Part of the problem of inconsistency within the CFSP relates to its rotating presidency, every six months. According to one recent commentator, 'when they do act, the six month rotation of the Union presidency makes it almost impossible to follow a consistent line, because each country has its own priorities'.[191] On the other hand, there is now a permanent head of the CFSP, currently Javier Solana, so there is room for some continuity.

THE WAY FORWARD

Worries such as those outlined above concerning protection of human rights within the EC have meant that accession of the EC to the ECHR or the creation of the EC's own Bill of Rights – what de Witte has referred to as the 'two Loch Ness Monsters

---

[187] Ibid.

[188] Ibid at 721.

[189] See Douglas-Scott, 'The CFSP: reinforcing the European Identity?' in Bergeron and Fitzpatrick op. cit.

[190] Amnesty, 'The EU is putting markets before morality,' cited in Clapham, 'Human Rights in the Common Foreign Policy' in Alston op. cit. at 647, fn 62.

[191] I Mather and R Fox, 'Adrift in a vale of Tears' (*The European* 19–25 Jan 1998) at 14.

of the EU' – have always been on the agenda, as a means of giving more adequate protection of human rights. The EU now has its own Charter, which will be discussed shortly, but what of access to the ECHR?

Accession to the ECHR?

Traditionally, accession to the ECHR was seen as less controversial than creation of the EC's own Charter, as all member states of the EC are already contracting parties to the ECHR. From time to time, the issue of EC accession to the ECHR has been explicitly on the political agenda.

There would be many advantages in EC accession to the ECHR. A formal linking of the EC and ECHR could be seen as underlining Community concern with human rights, especially for aspiring member states emerging from totalitarian regimes, given that the ECHR is seen as part of European cultural and political heritage. It would also minimise the danger of conflicting rulings emanating from these courts (i.e. the Community Courts in Luxembourg and Court of Human Rights in Strasbourg) given that they could now rule on virtually identical issues. The problem of conflicting rulings has already arisen in the context of the right to respect for private life under Article 8 ECHR. In the *Hoechst* case, which concerned a Commission investigation into a company's anti-competitive behaviour, the ECJ was asked to apply Article 8 to the company's business premises. It refused to do so, holding that Article 8 applies only to private dwellings, stating that, 'the protective scope of that article is concerned with the development of man's personal freedom and not however be extended to business premises'.[192] But in the *Niemietz*[193] case, the ECHR held that to interpret 'private' and 'home' as including certain business premises would be in keeping with the object and purpose of Article 8, which is to protect individuals against arbitrary interference by public authorities. Similar conflicts also arose in the context of Article 6 in the *Orkem* and *Funke* cases.[194]

EU accession to the ECHR would also alleviate the situation in which individuals may find themselves when faced by possible breaches of the ECHR by EU institutions, but no remedy. At present, unless Community law has been implemented by some member state act, there is no possible action in Strasbourg (in which case it would be against that member state). This was established in the *CM & Co* case, in which a company had been fined by the Commission for breach of Article 81(1). The ECJ rejected the company's complaint that Article 6 had been infringed. The applicants' application in Strasbourg was held inadmissible as the EU is not a party to the Convention.[195] This seemed to leave a gap in judicial enforcement. However, attempts to fill gaps can create other problems, as the *Matthews*[196] case illustrates.

---

[192] Case 46/87 *Hoechst* [1989] ECR 2859.
[193] *Niemietz v Germany* (1993) 16 EHRR 97 ECHR; see also *Chappell v United Kingdom* (1990) 12 EHRR 1 ECHR.
[194] Case 374/87 *Orkem v Commission* [1989] ECR 3283; *Jean-Gustave Funke v France* [1993] 1 CMLR 897 ECHR. Indeed in *Orkem*, AG Darmon stressed that the ECJ is not bound by the ECHR.
[195] Application *CM & Co v Germany* 13258/87 13 February 1990.
[196] *Matthews v UK* [1998] 28 EHRR 361.

Matthews, a resident of Gibraltar, had applied to be registered as a voter in the elections to the European Parliament. She was informed that Gibraltar was not part of any electoral constituency for the European Parliament under the 1976 Community Act.[197] Matthews asserted before the European Court of Human Rights that the UK had breached her rights under Article 3 of Protocol 1 of the ECHR, which guarantees the right to free elections under secret ballot. Gibraltar is a dependent territory but not part of the UK as such: executive power is vested in the Governor as the Queen's representative. It was accepted that Article 3 of Protocol 1 applied to Gibraltar and that EU legislation was capable of affecting Gibraltar, under Article 229(4) EC. There were two main questions. First, could the UK be responsible for the lack of European Parliament elections in Gibraltar, given that the 1976 Community act had treaty status? The European Court of Human Rights held that it could. The problem with this holding is that member states may now be held individually responsible for EU joint actions. Second, did Article 3 Protocol 1 apply to the European Parliament? Again, the European Court of Human Rights held that it did. It found the Parliament to be 'the principal form of democratic political accountability in the Community system'.[198] It has been suggested that this case marks the end of the horizontal relationship between the Community Courts and the Strasbourg Court, which now seems to be moving toward 'a de facto vertical dimension for the Court of Human Rights'.[199] In *Matthews*, the European Court of Human Rights demonstrated that it felt able to scrutinise primary Community law, contrary to previous holdings. It is true that the applicant would otherwise perhaps have been left without a remedy, although it seems that the Community Courts could probably have decided the case by means of a preliminary reference. This really makes the case for EC accession to the ECHR all the more important. If the Strasbourg Court is going to scrutinise EC law, its decisions would have more legitimacy if the EC were a member of the ECHR.

However, there are also major problems with EC accession to the ECHR. The Council of Europe and its institutions are not designed with supranational entities in mind. Who would represent the Community in the Strasbourg court, for example? Would non-member states of the EU have a right to bring proceedings against the EU in the ECHR? The requirement for exhaustion of domestic remedies under the Convention could also lead to extremely long litigation if EC law were at issue and preliminary rulings had already been made to Luxembourg.

With these concerns in mind, the Council of the EU requested the opinion of the ECJ (under Article 300(6) of the EC Treaty) as to whether the accession of the EC to the ECHR would be compatible with the EC treaty. According to the Council, no decision on the principle of opening negotiations could be taken until the court had considered whether accession was compatible with the EC treaty.

---

[197] 1976 Community Act concerning the election of representatives of the European Parliament by direct universal suffrage. This is annexed to Council Decision [1976] OJ L278/1 but has treaty status.
[198] *Matthews* para 52.
[199] I Canor, 'Primus inter pares. Who is the ultimate guardian of fundamental rights in Europe?'(2000) 25 ELRev 3.

Several member states argued, at the hearing in November 1995, that accession would be incompatible with the Treaty. The French government, for example, pointed to the danger of proceedings involving EC law being submitted to Convention organs consisting of nationals of Council of Europe states which were not members of the Community. Other states pointed out that accession to the Convention would put in question the exclusive jurisdiction of the ECJ, under Articles 220 and 292 of the EC Treaty.

The ECJ held that, as Community law now stands, the Community has no competence to accede to the Convention as there was no adequate legal basis in the treaty for accession, rejecting the argument that Article 308 might serve as a base. Therefore, accession could only be brought about by way of treaty amendment.[200] The Court's reasoning has not been found satisfactory by all. Weiler and Alston contrast the Court's finding, without demurrer, that the EC could accept the dispute resolution of the WTO.[201] However, perhaps the ECJ was responding to fears of some member states over the growing expansion of EC competences. After all, this was not so long after the German Constitutional Court's *Maastricht* judgment.

So the two institutions continue on their separate ways.[202] Toth has suggested the dramatic solution of the withdrawal of EU states from the ECHR and its incorporation into EU law by protocol.[203] In this way, the EU could gradually replace the ECHR as the guardian of human rights in Europe. This seems a very unsatisfactory proposal. First, it would drastically increase the workload of the Community courts by introducing all sorts of human rights cases which are usually not litigated there. Delay is already enough of a problem in the Community courts. Second, it would seem to be an abandonment by western Europe of its important democratic role in the post-communist European legal order. It is important that judges from western Europe sit alongside those judges from countries which have just emerged into democracy, and share their experience of the cultural, philosophical and moral phenomenon that is human rights law. This case law has grown up over 50 years and needs to be handled by those who know its jurisprudence, as well as by newcomers. It is also the case that the ECJ and CFI are not so experienced at handling human rights claims, as has already been suggested in a preceding section. A less radical solution was suggested by Koen Lenaerts who suggested that it was desirable to build a procedural bridge between the Community Courts and the Court of Human Rights in Strasbourg.[204] But this also raises the problem of very slow procedures.

Given the difficulties of accession, it is not surprising that the EU has more recently turned its mind to the creation of its own Bill of Rights.

---

[200] *Opinion 2/94* [1996] ECR I-1759.

[201] Weiler and Alston, 'An "Ever Closer Union" in Need of a Human Rights Policy: The European Union and Human Rights' in Alston op. cit. 3.

[202] Although the issue of accession is not completely off the agenda: the European Parliament called on the 2000 IGC to take steps to ensure that the EU accedes to the ECHR (report on European Parliament's proposals for the IGC – motion for a resolution A5-0086/2000). This has not been taken up yet.

[203] A Toth, 'The European Union and Human Rights: The Way Forward' (1997) 34 CMLRev 491.

[204] K Lenaerts, 'Fundamental Rights to be included in a Community Catalogue' (1991) 16 ELRev 376.

THE EU CHARTER OF RIGHTS

On 7 December 2000, the EU Charter of Fundamental Rights was proclaimed by the respective presidents of the EU institutions. It was not a high-profile occasion, overshadowed by the wrangling over the forthcoming Treaty of Nice. The Charter's apparent lack of importance seemed to be underlined by the fact that the Institutional presidents were not even given the time to complete their speeches.[205]

The Charter was proclaimed by the EU institutions, rather than by the member states, but this should not undermine the fact that this Charter was a member state initiative, first presented by the German Presidency in the first part of 1999, its operational structure detailed in the Presidency conclusions of the Cologne and Tampere European Councils of June and December 1999 and finally agreed by the European Council in Nice 2000. Although it was proclaimed in Nice, it is not yet legally enforceable, and, if it is to have any future legal effect, this too will be a decision for the member states.

The President of the European Commission, Romano Prodi, introducing the Charter in the welcome page of the Commission's Charter website,[206] stated that the objective of the Charter is 'to make more visible and explicit to EU citizens the fundamental rights they already enjoy at European level'. Thus it brings together, in a concise text, rights scattered throughout many different sources. This echoes the Presidency Conclusions of the Cologne European Council of June 1999, which, in paragraph 44, stated that fundamental rights applicable at Union level should be consolidated in a Charter and 'thereby made more evident'.

Some would dispute that this is necessary. Joseph Weiler has suggested that 'the citizens of Europe appear to "suffer" from a surfeit, rather than a deficit, of judicial protection of their fundamental rights'[207] and that 'The real problem of the Community is the absence of a human rights policy with everything this entails: a Commission, a Directorate-General, a budget and a horizontal action plan from making those rights already granted by the treaties and judicially protected...effective.'[208] In this, both the Bar Council of England and Wales and the Law Society agreed, in the submissions which they made to the Convention.[209]

However, although the EU may lack a human rights policy,[210] surely this does not mean that it may not also have a Charter. There is a great deal to be said for a Charter of Rights as a 'road map' to human rights protection in the EU and the

---

[205] Editorial (2001) 38 CMLR at 1.

[206] At http://europa.eu.int/comm/justice_home/unit/charte/en/welcome.html.

[207] J Weiler, 'Editorial: Does the European Union Truly Need a Charter of Rights?' (2000) 6 ELJ at 95.

[208] Ibid. at 96.

[209] Submission by the General Council of the Bar of England and Wales, Brussels, 2 May 2000 CHARTE 4234/00 CONTRIB. 108; a contribution submitted by the Law Society of England and Wales, Brussels, 22 June 2000 (26.06) CHARTE 4380/00 CONTRIB.

[210] Although there is now a Commissioner with responsibility for human rights, and also a new Human Rights unit responsible for human rights and democracy in the DG for External relations. See also the references made by Commissioner Chris Patten at the *Human Rights Discussion Forum* in recognition that the Commission lacks a coherent strategy regarding human rights. (report available on http://europa.eu.int/comm/dg1a/human_rights/intro).

several pages already spent in this chapter merely introducing in a very summary form, human rights protection in the EU up to the introduction of the Charter, surely illustrate this need.

Therefore, previous incoherence regarding human rights would, it is argued, be sufficient to justify the EU introducing its own Charter. There are also other reasons why a Charter might be thought necessary, and these may be dealt with briefly. First, notwithstanding Joseph Weiler's remarks regarding 'human rights saturation' in the EU, there are, in fact, currently, areas in which human rights protection is not satisfactory. For example, the near absence of judicial control over the third pillar matters (PJCC) and little control over Title IV EC regarding asylum and immigration.[211] There is also the fact of continuing opaque decision-making in the EU, notwithstanding continuing initiatives such as the proposed White Paper on Governance.[212] The Charter is likely to bring about improvements in both of these areas. Second, the ECHR, drafted over 50 years ago, although a 'dynamic'[213] instrument, is unsuitable for dealing with certain contemporary developments. In this respect, the introduction into the Charter, for example, of provisions concerning protection of personal data (Article 8) or particular rights regarding the integrity of the person in the fields of medicine and biology (Article 2) are to be welcomed.

There is also another way in which the Charter might be innovation, rather than mere confirmation. A reason given by the Commission[214] supporting the need for a Charter was that 'the European Union has entered a new and more resolutely political stage of integration'. The European Parliament, in its draft Resolution on the drawing up of the Charter in January 2000,[215] described the Charter as providing the basis of an EU constitution. Such a reason might strike fear into the hearts of Eurosceptics, especially those who fear the German urge for a truly 'constitutional' IGC in 2004. But it cannot be ignored. Although the ECJ has on some occasions[216] described the treaties as a constitution of the EU, they do not look really very constitutional in nature. With a Charter of Rights incorporated, they might begin to appear more so, especially if this were done in the context of a redrafting of the treaties at an IGC in 2004.

THE CONVENTION

This was the chosen name of the body that drafted the Charter. The name is significant. 'Convention' was the term used by those delegates who gathered in Philadelphia to draft the American Constitution. It was also used by gatherings

---

[211] See Articles 68 EC and 35 TEU regarding ability of ECJ to give preliminary rulings on these matters.

[212] Information about this is available at: http://europa.en.int/comm/governance/index.

[213] See F Jacobs and R White, *The European Convention on Human Rights* (Oxford: Clarendon, 1996) who state (at 31): '...the interpretation of the Convention must be 'dynamic' in the sense that it must be interpreted in the light of developments in social and political attitudes.'

[214] At http://europa.eu.int/comm/justice_home/unit/charte/en/FAQ.html.

[215] B5-0110/1999 OJ C54 25.02.2000 at 93.

[216] E.g. in Case 294/83 *Parti Ecologiste 'Les Verts' v European Parliament* [1986] ECR 1339.

during the French Revolution. The less evocative IGC is the body/structure which is used to bring about significant changes in EU law, and which has altogether a different sort of resonance, that of international law, in which sovereign states negotiate through their representatives. The term 'Convention' makes the EU Charter sound like more of a constitutional initiative.[217] Just how significant was the structure and organisation of the body which drafted the EU Charter?

There is no doubt that in some respects it was new and radical. The time limit was very short: only nine months in which to produce a Charter. The Convention had 62 members, drawn from four areas: member state governments (15), the Commission (1), the European Parliament (16) and national parliaments (30). There were also two representatives from the Court of Justice and Council of Europe (one from the Court of Human Rights) who had observer status.[218] It first convened in December 1999 and met thereafter every week.

Notably, it operated in an atmosphere of transparency, according to the principle of openness: both its hearings and documents submitted for hearings were public,[219] and the latter available on its website. Such openness was encouraging, and certainly not the case in the context of the IGC,[220] nor was it the case in the drafting of the ECHR, which proceeded by way of a committee on administrative questions which reported to the Committee of Ministers. On the other hand, the US Bill of Rights[221] was engendered in public. The press were admitted to the US House of Representatives, in which it was debated, from its first session. However, they did not have the advantage of those who follow our contemporary Charter's proceedings, having to proceed in dim light, with quill pens and poor acoustics, rather than the relative ease of web site.

The Convention's methods were unorthodox. The Praesidium (namely, the President, the Commission representative and the three Vice Presidents representing the Council, European Parliament and national parliaments) would put forward a proposal which would be extensively debated in the Convention itself, with the aim of reaching consensus without a formal vote. It succeeded in producing a final text in nine months. In both its transparency and working methods it set a fine example to the 2000 ongoing IGC.

Furthermore, the Convention provided an institutional (if we are to count national governments, which were well-represented) response to the need for a Charter. However, even if national and the European Parliaments were well-represented, civil society had no place on the Convention itself. Neither NGOs nor human rights experts had a place on it. This did not, however, mean that civil society had no

---

[217] Even if it may also bring confusion in sounding as if it refers to a human rights instrument, such as the ECHR, rather than a drafting body.

[218] The Convention's detailed membership is to be found on the European Parliament's Charter website: http://europarl.en.int/charter/composition_en.htm.

[219] Available at the Convention website, http://db.consilium.eu.int/df, which contains a large number of documents, both the Convention's working papers, and observations of various groups.

[220] Or certainly not until recently. Secrecy was one of the charges made against the 1996 IGC which preceded the Treaty of Amsterdam.

[221] Unlike the Philadelphia Convention, which drafted the US Constitution of 1787, which proceeded without publicity, reports of which were not even published until considerably later.

voice. For example, 70 associations representing various interest (churches, trade unions, asylum, gays and others) took part in a hearing on 27 April 2000, and then most of these produced a written submission. But there was no requirement for the Convention actually to heed their views, although it did apparently do so in at least some cases, for example that of the European trade unions.[222] On the other hand, there was no parliamentary selection process (in the UK at least) for the governmental and parliamentary representatives on the Convention.[223] The Charter was not debated in the UK Parliament and the average person knew very little, if anything, of it. One commentator[224] has remarked on the irony of Lord Goldsmith, selected by the government, telling us what our rights are. Some[225] saw the nine-month time span as far too short both for adequate preparation and consultation. However, it was a much longer time than was taken for the drafting of the US Constitution in Philadelphia, only from June–September 1787, although half as long as the time taken for the drafting of the European Convention on Human Rights (which, however, was volleyed back and forward through debate in the Council of Europe Parliamentary Assembly, as well as its Committee of Ministers).

THE LEGAL EFFECT OF THE CHARTER

The Charter is not currently legally binding, although it may become so. According to Declaration 23 on the Future of the Union attached to the Treaty of Nice:

> 4. Following a report to be drawn up for the European Council in Göteborg in June 2001, the European Council, at its meeting in Laeken/Brussels in December 2001, will agree on a declaration containing appropriate initiatives for the continuation of this process.
> 5. The process should address, inter alia, the following questions:
> — how to establish and monitor a more precise delimitation of powers between the European Union and the Member States, reflecting the principle of subsidiarity;
> — the status of the Charter of Fundamental Rights of the European Union, proclaimed in Nice, in accordance with the conclusions of the European Council in Cologne;

There has been a clear division of opinion between those who wish to see the Charter binding and those who do not. Among the former we may cite the Commission[226] which has stated its belief that the Charter 'is destined to be

---

[222] See the convention archive website, detailed at fn 219, for details.

[223] The UK's representatives were Lord Goldsmith (for the Government), Lord Bowness (for the House of Lords) and Wyn Griffiths (for the House of Commons). Andrew Duff MEP commented that the representatives of national parliaments on the Convention were somewhat of a 'curiosity': unlike the EP representatives (whose Constitutional Affairs committee had prepared them for it) they had no mandate, simply putting forward their own views. See HL select committee on EU affairs 67 24 May 2000, 'The EU Charter of Fundamental Rights'.

[224] Professor Conor Gearty, at the Conference on the Charter at King's College London, October 2000, also referring to 'some sort of Platonic guardianship' at work.

[225] For example, the British Institute of Human Rights, cited in HL select committee on EU affairs 67 24 May 2000, 'The EU Charter of Fundamental Rights'.

[226] Commission communication on 'The legal nature of the Charter', Brussels 11 October 2000 COM (2000) 644 Final.

incorporated sooner or later into the treaties', and among the latter, the UK government – Tony Blair, for example, stating in November 2000, 'The Charter is simply a statement of policy and the UK is not the only member state to oppose something of a binding legal nature.' (Surely there is something somewhat ironic about this pronouncement: support being given by the UK government for the Charter only if it had no effect.)

However, the Charter was drafted from the outset 'as if' incorporated into the treaties, drafted in a formal way, as a document suitable for incorporation into the treaties, even although the Convention did not know what the final outcome would be: they left the choice to the European Council.

In any case, regardless of its legal status, the Charter has already begun to have a legal impact. For example, in *BECTU v Secretary of State for Trade and Industry*, AG Tizzano spoke of the Charter as a 'substantive point of reference' and in *P Z v European Parliament*, AG Jacobs stated of the Charter, 'whilst itself not legally binding, [it] proclaims a generally recognized principle . . . '[227] In the *Hautala* case, AG Leger referred to the right to information to be found in the Charter as evidence for its status as a fundamental right.[228] Therefore, although these Advocates General recognised that it was not legally binding, they stated that this did not mean that it could not have legal consequences. They saw it at the very least as enumerating in a systematic way those rights which are part of the Community *acquis*.

This is all very well. It indicates that the Charter will have, for the next couple of years at least, a fairly high status of soft law. Its effect will not be negligible. However, as a public statement, the message presented is not optimal. The Charter will subsist, in some sort of legal twilight, albeit as a reference point for the citizen, a clearer statement than previously existed, but with its status as a proclamation revealing a lack of confidence on the part of the EU and its member states about citizens' rights and the relationship between the individual and authorities in the European legal space. There are already enough such Solemn Declarations on human rights by EU institutions. On a symbolic level this says much. It carries forward the ambiguities and ambivalence which have characterised the very *sui generis* process of European constitutionalism over the past fifteen years or so. If we wish to know why the European public still makes so little of its status as a European citizenry, we need look no further than the status of the Charter proclaimed in December 2000.

THE CONTENT OF THE CHARTER

There are plenty of rights here. The Charter has, for example, at least twice as many rights as the Declaration of Fundamental Rights adopted by the European

---

[227] Case C-173/99 *BECTU* [2001] ECR I-4881; Case C-270/99 *P Z v European Parliament* [2001] ECR 000.
[228] Case C-353/99P *Council v Hautala* [2001] ECR 000.

Parliament in 1989,[229] and about three times as many as the ECHR (without its Protocols). The 50 rights in the Charter are set out in six Chapters, with the headings Dignity, Freedoms, Equality, Solidarity, Citizens' rights and Justice: names that are 'meaningful and easy to remember'.[230] Each of the Charter's 50 rights are taken from a 'precursor' text, such as the ECHR, the European Social Charter, the Community Charter of Social Rights of Workers, common constitutional traditions, rulings of the ECJ and Court of Human Rights, as well as international conventions of the Council of Europe, UN and ILO. Some of the rights are specifically introduced to deal with contemporary problems such as protection of personal data, given the proliferation of information about persons in the more barrier-free Europe,[231] or new innovations in bioethics.

However, the Charter is innovative in containing, in the same instrument, both economic and social rights along with the more traditional civil and political rights, which has never been done before in an international human rights instrument. In this way the Charter presents in sharpest relief the **indivisibility** of human rights.[232]

At a first glance, the Charter might seem to present a series of rights founded on an agreeable view of society and of the worth of human beings. For too long it has been possible to charge EU law with being over preoccupied with commercial interests and with rights of the 'market citizens', as has already been discussed in this chapter. Therefore, it is encouraging to see that economic and social rights have been included in the Charter, even against the wishes of industry and employers' groups.[233] It also counters the views of those who believe that economic and social rights are of a singular nature and difficult to incorporate into human rights documents because of the positive action which they require of governments.[234] Such rights address the concerns of everyday people and the inclusion of rights recognising the fundamental status of workers' rights in the Community Charter is important. The rights of solidarity set out in Chapter IV of the Charter have an impressive breadth and scope.

The rights of the Charter might seem to provide an example of what John Rawls has called an 'overlapping consensus.'[235] In modern societies, where there is no shared, comprehensive account of the good, or morality, Rawls defined political liberalism as a public culture formed by a shared fund of implicitly recognised ideas

---

[229] EP Resolution adopting the Declaration of Fundamental Rights and Freedoms Doc A2–3/89 OJ C 120/51. See also the Draft Constitution of the European Union adopted by the European Parliament in 1994 which contained a section on human rights largely based on its earlier 1989 Declaration – A3–0064/94 OJ C 61/166.

[230] Editorial, (2001) CMLR.

[231] E.g. the Schengen Information System or Europol.

[232] 'Commission Communication in the Nature of the Charter – the legal nature of the Charter', Brussels 11.10.2000 COM (2000) 644 Final.

[233] E.g. CBI submission to the Convention on the Charter – 12 April 2000, CHARTE 4226/00 CONTRIB 101.

[234] See e.g. the views of Schermers in giving evidence to the House of Lords select committee, noted in their report no 67 2000; also submissions of the CBI CHARTE 4226/00 CONTRIB 101.

[235] J Rawls, *Political Liberalism* (Columbia, 1993) 55.

and principles.[236] There does seem to be some sort of shared, normative consensus in the EU. Principles such as citizenship, human rights (Article 6 TEU refers to the 'common constitutional traditions of the member states'), respect for democracy and the rule of law, suggest some sort of existing, public, consensus in the EU which goes beyond the desirability of economic efficiency and free markets. The Charter seems to be a further such example, taking what is perceived as best from the common European heritage of human rights, suitable for what in MacCormick's terms is the 'mixed commonwealth' of the EU.[237]

SPECIFIC PROBLEMS

However, there are significant problems which indicate that the Charter might promise more than it can return. The first of these is the often opaque language in which its provisions are drafted, although opaque language is nothing new in EU law. Article 29 states that 'Everyone has a right of access to a free placement service.' In the Explanatory note for the Praesidium,[238] this provision is stated to be based on Article 1(3) of the European Social Charter and point 13 of the Community Charter of the Fundamental Social Rights of Workers. It relates to a practice apparently used in Scandinavia but hardly transparent to Anglo-Saxons and of sweeping generality in any case. Another opaquely drafted provision is Article 36, concerning 'Access to services of general economic interest' which states that: 'The Union recognises and respects access to services of general economic interest as provided for in national laws and practices, in accordance with the Treaty establishing the European Community, in order to promote the social and territorial cohesion of the Union.' Once again, the explanatory notes of the Praesidium are not illuminating, merely stating: 'This Article fully respects Article 16 of the Treaty establishing the European Community and does not create any new right. It merely sets out the principle of respect by the Union for the access to services of general economic interest as provided for by national provisions, when those provisions are compatible with Community legislation.' Likewise Article 38: 'Union policies shall ensure a high level of protection.' Again, vague in the extreme and not drafted in terms of rights at all.

A second problem pertaining to the provisions on rights of solidarity concerns the way in which some of them are highly qualified. Article 27, for example, provides for a 'Workers' right to information and consultation within the undertaking' but this is only to be 'in the cases and under the conditions provided for by Community law and national laws and practices'. Similarly for Articles 28, 34, 35 and 36. A gen-

---

[236] Rawls op. cit. at 8.

[237] See N MacCormick, 'Sovereignty, Democracy and Subsidiarity' in *Questioning Sovereignty* (Oxford: OUP, 1999).

[238] CHARTE 4473/00 Text of the Explanations relating to the complete text of the Charter as set out in CHARTE 4487/00 and CONVENT 50, of 11 October 2000.

eral limitations clause set out in Article 52[239] applies to all of the rights in the Charter. Once again, the status of something as a 'fundamental' right in EU law is compromised by a myriad of possible limitations on it.

SCOPE

Article 51 raises difficult questions. It reads as follows: 'The provisions of this Charter are addressed to the institutions and bodies of the Union with due regard for the principle of subsidiarity and to the Member States only when they are implementing Union law...'

But what exactly is covered by member states in the act of implementing EU law? As Laws J commented in *First City Trading*,[240] 'This is a deep question. It concerns the depth of the Community's bite.'[241] In the *ERT*[242] case, the ECJ stated that 'as soon as any such legislation enters **the field of application** of Community law this Court is sole arbiter in this matter'. Therefore, is it the case that the only actions which the ECJ might decline to vet would be those falling within the member states' exclusive jurisdiction? This had seemed to be the interpretation of Advocate General Van Gerven in the *Grogan* case who stated: 'Once a national rule is involved which has effects in an area covered by Community law...then the appraisal of that rule no longer falls within the exclusive jurisdiction of the national legislator.' This is a very wide interpretation indeed. Given the scope and width of Community law it may conceivably come into contact with just about any area of national law.

There are also some other questions regarding scope. Beyond the issue of member state liability there is that of **which** EU and member state bodies are covered by the Charter. In the context of member states there is the question of how to define public authorities. It is suggested that the existing case law of the ECJ in the context of horizontal/vertical direct effect might be applied in this context.[243] Related issues might apply in the EU context. Will the Charter apply not only to formal EU institutions but to entities established within the framework of the EU context, such as Europol? Surely it must do so?

Secondly, should individuals be bound by the Charter? It is not usual for international human rights documents to bind individuals, although the issue of

---

[239] Article 52 reads as follows:
Any limitation on the exercise of the rights and freedoms recognised by this Charter must be provided for by law and respect the essence of those rights and freedoms. Subject to the principle of proportionality, limitations may be made only if they are necessary and genuinely meet objectives of general interest recognised by the Union or the need to protect the rights and freedoms of others.

[240] *First City Trading* [1997] 1 CMLR 250.

[241] At para 24.

[242] Case 260/89 *ERT* [1991] ECR 2925.

[243] E.g. Case C-188/89 *Foster* v *British Gas* [1990] ECR I 3313. The test was set out by the ECJ para 20 of this judgment, in which it stated that a public body was '...a body, whatever its legal form, which has been made responsible, pursuant to a measure adopted by the State, for providing a public service under the control of the State and has for that purpose special powers beyond those which result from the normal rules applicable in relations between individuals, is included in any event...'

drittwirkung is complex. The appropriate course here might be that followed in the UK's Human Rights Act, namely to impose obligations on public authorities and to leave it up to the courts as themselves public authorities to decide whether and how to give horizontal effect.[244] Also, the South African Constitution of 1996 and its concept of *mittelbaredrittwirkung* might be cited here, namely that human rights have an indirect impact on the development of all jurisprudence by means of a constitutional requirement that 'when developing the common law...every court must promote the spirit, purport and objectives of the Bill of Rights'.[245]

CONCLUSIONS

The last issues border on the arcane. There will be time enough to deal with them if and when the Charter becomes binding. On balance it seems beneficial that the EU is now to have its own Charter of Rights, both for reasons of clarity and transparency. It simply is not right that protection of rights in the EU is managed in such an incoherent way. Citizens ought to be able to know what their rights are. But a Charter of Rights is also important on a symbolic level: an EU Charter could have as much significance as the US Bill of Rights or the European Convention, both beacons of individual protection. It might mark the EU's coming of age as a polity. However, we should not, as already remarked, become too obsessed with rights and charters of rights. We could do worse than remember the references made at the time of the drafting of the US Bill of Rights to the 'ship of state' metaphor', drawn from Jonathan Swift's *Tale of a Tub* of 1704. In this story Swift describes how sailors, encountering a whale which threatened to damage their ship, flung it an empty tub by way of amusement to divert it. In the US context, this was used to refer to the fact that Madison had proposed rights amendments rather than those designed to change the structure or essence of the new government: in this way, it was said, Leviathan was diverted and the ship of state sailed away intact. Likewise in the EU. We should beware of being diverted by the prospect of a Charter of Rights from the need for real democracy in the EU. Fundamental rights in the EU must not be allowed to become the phenomena of 'smoke and mirrors' derided by Karl Marx.[246]

---

[244] See the discussion of this concept in Chapter 8.

[245] Ref. made by the General Council of the Bar (in CHARTE 4234/00) to a plea, made by Sidney Kentridge QC in 'Lessons from South Africa' in Markesinis (ed.) *The Impact of the Human Rights Bill on English Law* (OUP, 1999).

[246] Marx, 'On the Jewish Question' (reprinted in Waldron (ed.) *Nonsense on Stilts*, Methuen, 1987).

14

IN SEARCH OF UNION CITIZENSHIP

The constitutional scholar, Alexander Bickel, once characterised American citizenship as 'at best, a simple idea for a simple government'.[1] The same could not be written of European Union citizenship. In spite of a growing wealth of material, both of a practical and scholarly nature,[2] the concept remains complex, elusive and fragmented. At a practical level, the components of Union citizenship lie scattered across the *acquis communautaire*. Some of these are clustered in the semi-constitutional provisions of Articles 17–22 of the EC Treaty; other legal manifestations of citizenship are peppered across EC law in its non-discrimination, free movement and social policy provisions, with no great logic or coherence; and still more are to be derived from the case law of the European Court, whose *Martinez Sala*[3] decision raised optimistic hopes about the future of European citizenship. Thus, in so far as it has been realised at all, European citizenship is far from a 'simple idea', but rather a phenomenon to be perceived by process of induction from a myriad of empirical sources.

Nor does there seem to be a clear conceptual model of citizenship to provide a paradigm for the future development of the Union citizen. At the conceptual level, the components of, and candidates for, citizenship are as contested and uncertain as in the legal field. A large variety of (often mutually incompatible) conceptions of citizenship offer themselves, each holding up something of relevance to the contemporary EU: market citizenship; active or republican citizenship; social citizenship; global citizenship, each subject to its own internal as well as external critique, each

---

[1] A Bickel, *The Morality of Consent* (Yale University Press, 1975) 54.
[2] E.g. C Closa, 'The Concept of Citizenship in the Treaty on European Union' (1992) 29 CMLRev 1; H-J d'Oliveira, 'European Citizenship: Its meaning, Its Potential' in R Dehousse (ed.) *Europe After Maastricht: An Ever Closer Union?* (Law Books in Europe, 1994); E Meehan, *Citizenship and the European Community* (Sage, 1993); D O'Keeffe, 'Union Citizenship' in D O'Keeffe and P Twomey (eds), *Legal Issues of the Maastricht Treaty* (Chancery Press, 1993); S O'Leary, *The Evolving Concept of European Citizenship* (Kluwer, 1996); Preuss, 'Problems of a European Citizenship' (1995) ELJ 267; J Shaw, 'The Interpretation of European Union Citizenship' (1998) 61 MLR 293; J Weiler, 'To be a European Citizen: Eros and Civilisation' in *The Constitution of Europe* (Cambridge University Press, 1999).
[3] Case C-85/96 *Martinez Sala v Freistaat Bayern* [1998] ECR I-2691; the case is discussed later in this chapter.

bearing some sort of vital relation to human rights, therefore raising the question of the relationship between citizenship and human rights.[4]

Another twist to the tortuous problem of European citizenship is offered by the difficulty of grounding citizenship in a transnational community. Citizenship is usually defined in terms of an individual's relation to the state or nation. Can there be such a thing as post- or trans-national citizenship and, if so, what sort of identity might it give rise to? Thus, citizenship is problematic on two different dimensions or planes, which also interact: the horizontal, involving disagreement of an analytical sort about the nature of citizenship, and the vertical plane, which raises the problem of membership of a supranational polity, certainly not the 'simple government' of Bickle's definition.

At present, in this tangle of complexity, Union citizenship seems to operate at a symbolic level, as a contemporary preoccupation, not yet fully realised, looking to the future, but drawing on past traditions of political philosophy and theory, as well as law. Citizenship, it seems, just might offer remedies for the present dissatisfaction, unease, and even alienation which individuals feel for the EU, if only we knew how to actualise it.

POST-NATIONAL MEMBERSHIP

Is citizenship possible at supranational level? This seems to be the most fundamental question in the context of European citizenship and will be examined first. Much recent debate concerns questions of post-national membership and identity. This contemporary preoccupation with issues of citizenship, identity, and, more specifically, European identity, is unsurprising. As Habermas[5] has written, the feeling that pervaded the mid-1980s, that we were entering the era of post-history, vanished some time ago. History reasserted itself, shattering certainties, if any existed. Unsettling events, such as the break-up of the Soviet Union, or, most recently and dramatically, the terror attacks of 11 September 2001 and beyond, disturb perceptions of a settled world order as well as affecting tangible physical borders, eroding any psychological meanings these had to offer. Identity becomes a focus.

Concurrently, the projects of the EU for 'an ever closer union' seemed to have reached one sort of limit by the 1990s, in the sense that one well-pursued strategy of integration, the Monnet method of neo-functionalism, no longer seems adequate.[6] As well as the need for instrumental policy-making to further economic integration, prosperity, and peace, there is a preoccupation with the question of the EU's own identity as a transnational polity. However, there remains a gap between the fact of legal, institutional and economic integration, and any meaningful identification with this fact by individual Europeans.

---

[4] This issue is discussed below.
[5] J Habermas, 'Citizenship and National Identity' (1992) 12 Praxis International 1.
[6] B Laffan, 'The Politics of Identity and Political Order in Europe' (1996) 34 JCMS 81.

How can the power of the economic and part-political community that is the EU be channelled into the creation of the sense of identity and belonging necessary for citizenship? An **affective** dimension to integration is required. Karl Deutsch suggested that integration was synonymous with a 'sense of community', of 'we feelings' and 'trust'.[7] For some writers, this type of integration is not possible in the EU. From this viewpoint, the perceived lack of European *demos*, a people sharing a collective identity and loyalty forged by language, history and ethnicity, shows the futility of seeking a European identity.[8] This view owes much to the Romantic view of the nation as a seamless web, an organic unit, developed by eighteenth and nineteenth-century writers such as Herder and Fichte.[9] If European identity depends on being part of a *demos* or an *ethnos*, a community with a shared cultural heritage, then prospects for post-national community and, more particularly, an EU identity and meaningful citizenship, are not encouraging. However, there are several responses to such a pessimistic approach. First, the *ethnos* or *demos* definition of community tends to undermine itself. The nations which are held up as being founded on shared culture were often themselves artificial, constructed communities in the nineteenth century. Gellner, for example, saw the formation of nation states in Europe as a necessary accessory to the processes of industrialism and the needs of nineteenth-century capitalism, writing, '[n]ationalism is not the awakening of nations to self-consciousness, it invents nations where they do not exist'.[10]

Second, most contemporary writers prefer to understand *demos* in non-organic civil terms, on the basis of shared values, rather than a shared *ethnos*.[11] But what may these shared values be, which are capable of giving rise to a common sense of identity and community? Earlier attempts by the EU to create such values and to inculcate an identity from the 'top down' seem almost laughable. The founders of the EEC attempted to foster a distinctive European identity to replace former warring identities and, as British, French, Italians and Germans had done in their deliberate nation-building myths of the nineteenth century, set out to create new myths and symbols to replace the old. The Adonnino report in 1984 outlined a series of measures needed to strengthen and promote a 'citizen's Europe'.[12] This report stressed the necessity of 'strengthening the Community's image and identity in order to enhance the sense of belonging and identity with the Community'. This was to be achieved by the creation of new symbols of 'Europeanness', i.e. a European anthem,

---

[7] K Deutsch, *Nationalism and Social Communication* (Wiley, 1953).

[8] Kirchhof, 'Europäische Einigung ünd der Verfassungsstaat der Bundesrepublik Deutschland', in Isensee (ed.) *Europa als politische Idee and als rechtliche Form* (Berlin, 1993).

[9] For an account of German Romanticism see I Berlin, *The Roots of Romanticism* (Chatto and Windus, 1999).

[10] E Gellner, *Nations and Nationalism* (Blackwell, 1983); see also Hobsbawm, *Nations and Nationalism since 1780* (2nd edn, Canto, 1992) and Anderson, *Imagined Communities* (Verso, 1992), who agree on the constructed nature of nation and community although do not necessarily share Gellner's views on the reasons for this construction.

[11] See e.g. J Weiler, 'Fin de siécle Europe' in Dehousse (ed.) *Europe After Maastricht* (Beck, 1994); Habermas, see fn. 5.

[12] Adonnino, *Report of the ad hoc Committee on a People's Europe to the European Council*, Supp. 7/85-Bull EC; see also the Tindemans report of 1975, Chapter 7 of which is entitled 'Towards a Europe of Citizens', Bull EC(8) 1975 II, for another early attempt.

day (9 May, the day on which Schuman gave the speech which led to the Coal and Steel treaty, hardly a date well-known to the citizens of Europe), driving licence, town-twinning, youth exchanges, as well as the flag adopted from the Council of Europe: somewhat hesitant first steps towards the construction of a European identity.[13] But the Adonnino committee's symbols of a European identity may have been less effective at fostering effective support for Europe than in giving the impression of a European elite trying to legitimate its own ideology. Any causal link between top-down manipulation and attitude changing is far from clear. The public does not yet appear to feel very 'European', as Reif's analysis of Eurobarometer surveys indicates (56 per cent said that they never felt European).[14]

On a more abstract level, in the realm of contemporary liberal political theory, there has been discussion of the sort of shared values which might be identified and utilised in the development of a European citizenship. The shared values of human rights, an increased participatory public realm, or a common sense of justice, have been singled out as obvious candidates. Thus, Habermas'[15] 'constitutional patriotism' has been much discussed, although, as this has been inadequate to provide the foundations for solidarity in Germany,[16] it is unlikely to prove adequate for the European Union. Alternatively, it has been suggested that deep diversity might somehow be accommodated around a shared sense of justice, as elaborated in John Rawls' *Theory of Justice* and *Political Liberalism*, works which set a blueprint for uniting individuals of radically differing actual circumstances around principles which are just because fair, neutral, and bargained for in circumstances free from bias. Relatedly, Joseph Weiler writes of the EU treaties as potentially a 'social contract' between the peoples of Europe rather than just between the member states.[17]

However, Rawls' earlier theory of justice as fairness has been criticised as too universalising and thus unsuitable for a culturally plural society such as the EU.[18] In such a case, it has been argued that there must be a need to accommodate special interests by way of different, rather than neutral, treatment, and special rights rather than the same equal rights for all.[19] A further problem lies in the absence of an effective public realm at EU level, a 'public space' for citizens, in which shared values could develop. The public space of the EU is splintered into national units, thus rendering the creation of a deliberative and dialogic democracy difficult at transnational level.[20]

---

[13] Other Adonnino recommendations found their way into the provisions of Articles 17–22 EC and are discussed below.

[14] Reif and Inglehart (eds) *Eurobarometer: The Dynamics of European Public Opinion* (Macmillan, 1991).

[15] J Habermas, see fn 5.

[16] Dijkink, *National Identity and Geopolitical Visions: Maps of Pride and Pain* (Routledge, 1993) 34.

[17] J Weiler, 'To be a European Citizen: Eros and Civilisation' in Weiler, *The Constitution of Europe* (Cambridge University Press, 1999) 346.

[18] Rawls has of course reworked his earlier theory of justice specifically to account for the problems caused by a multicultural community in *Political Liberalism* (Columbia University Press, 1993). This reworking is specifically discussed in Chapter 15.

[19] W Kymlicka, *Multicultural Citizenship* (OUP, 1995); Young, 'Polity and Group Difference' in R Beiner (ed.) *Theorising Citizenship* (New York University Press, 1995).

[20] This issue is discussed further below.

The fragmented nature of the public space in the EU relates to the multiple *demos*, identities, and thus citizenries in the EU, a feature which has been put to productive use. A number of writers have suggested the possibility of an identity, a citizenship of 'concentric circles', an attachment of different levels of intensity,[21] a phenomenon which would seem to sit well with the fragmented nature of postmodern identities generally. Thus, it has been said, one might be Scottish, British, and European, no one of these excluding the other. In this way, European citizenship need not take on an exclusive nature, a possibility which has in any case been seen as dangerously culturally imperialistic by writers such as Delanty.[22] Such a vision of 'multiple citizenries' also concurs with contemporary theories of sovereignty, such as those of MacCormick, who writes of overlapping sovereignties, rather than the exclusive sovereignty of either the national parliament or the EU.[23] In this way we are unlikely to see our identity as stemming from one definitive cultural or geographical source, just as it becomes less easy to derive the authority of law from one fundamental source or *Grundnorm*.

Therefore, an albeit sketchy consideration of the issues raised by a transnational polity seems to suggest that membership or citizenship of such a polity is a possibility, providing these following factors are borne in mind. First, there must be some shared values to create a sense of belonging, but the recognition of such values, while entailing the respect of all individuals as equals, must also be willing to accommodate special needs and interests, rather than imposing in a universalising way. Second, this citizenship will be one of a series of multiple identities which individuals possess. The question which must now be addressed is whether contemporary accounts of citizenship, either as they are already actualised within the EU, or within citizenship theory on which the EU can build, can satisfy these requirements.

CITIZENSHIP

As Peter Schuck[24] has suggested, citizenship talk proceeds through different tropes. Sometimes it functions as a powerful aspirational ideal, expressing our deepest commitments to a communal life. As such, it requires equality and full participation in the life of society. Alternatively, citizenship functions as a positive concept which describes the citizen's legal-political status and relations between the individual and the polity.

---

[21] E.g. Weiler, 'The Selling of Europe: the Discourse of European Citizenship in the IGC 1996' (Harvard Jean Monnet Working Paper, 1996); Breton, 'Identification in Transnational Political Communities' in Knop *et al.* (eds) *Rethinking Federalism: Citizens, Markets and Governments in a Changing World* (University of British Columbia Press, 1995). Similarly Anthony Smith writes of a 'European family of cultures' in Anderson and Gowan (eds) *A Vision of Europe* (Verso, 1997).

[22] G Delanty, *Inventing Europe: Idea, Identity, Reality* (Macmillan, 1995).

[23] E.g. N MacCormick, 'Beyond the Sovereign State' (1993) 56 MLR 1; *id*, 'The Maastricht-Urteil: Sovereignty Now' [1995] ELJ 1; see also J Tully, *Strange Multiplicity* (Cambridge University Press, 1995).

[24] P Schuck, 'The Re-evaluation of American Citizenship'; EUI Working Paper RSC No. 96/26.

On neither of these levels is the concept of citizenship well developed within the EU. Therefore, the European Commission, in its second report on citizenship,[25] highlighted three '*desiderata*' for the development of European citizenship: the increasing participation of the individual in European affairs, strengthening the protection of individual rights and promoting the idea of Europe.

The present legal 'resources'[26] of citizenship within EU law seem to be inadequate as a basis for the development of the EC's *desiderata*. The EU citizen only gained formal recognition with the Maastricht Treaty and the explicit enumeration of certain rights in Articles 17–22. These provisions are well known, namely, a personal right to free movement and residence subject to the limitations and conditions laid down in the treaty and secondary law; electoral rights in the European Parliament and municipal elections in the place of residence; protection by diplomatic and consular authorities of any member state in a third country where the citizen's own member state is not represented; access to non-judicial means of redress, through access to the Ombudsman and a right to petition the European Parliament. They are not free-standing, but confer the status of Union citizenship on those who are already nationals of the member states of the EU. They are not a coherent bundle of rights, but a collection of provisions, for the most part already existent in some aspect of EC law: a mixture of free movement rights and political rights, some of which require migration and some which do not. Perhaps the most enigmatic of these provisions is Article 18, which continues to perplex with regard to its status.[27] The European Court has made little contribution to the development of these principles until recently.[28] Article 17(2) also refers to the fact that Union citizens are subject to 'duties' imposed by the Treaties. Duties are traditionally correlated to rights of citizenship in the context of the nation state, where they may take the form of an obligation to pay taxes, to do military service, defend the realm, and so on. EU law however imposes few duties on individuals, and it is difficult to fathom which duties of citizenship it might introduce. Therefore it would seem that Articles 17–22 are unlikely of themselves to provide a foundation for a meaningful concept of European citizenship.

---

[25] *Second Report of the European Commission on Citizenship of the European Union*, COM(97)230 (Office for Publications of the European Union, 1997) at 3–4.

[26] A term cited by J Shaw, in 'The Interpretation of European Union Citizenship' (1998) 61 MLR 293, borrowed as she acknowledges from A Wiener, *Citizenship Practice: Building Institutions of a Non-State* (Westview, 1991).

[27] Article 18 was most recently amended by the treaty of Nice which replaced its existing second paragraph and added a third. The new second paragraph removes the requirement for unanimity in the Council when legislating measures under this provision. The new third paragraph removes certain matters: 'provisions on passports, identity cards, residence permits or any other such document or to provisions of social security or social protection' from its ambit.

[28] Those cases in which some issue of citizenship has arisen are Case C-193/94 *Sofia Skanavi* [1996] ECR I-929; Case 214/94 *Boukhalfa v Germany* [1996] ECR I-2253; Cases 64/95 and C-5/95 *Stober and Pereira* [1997 1 ECR I-511; Cases C-64/96 and C-65/96 *Uecker and Jacquet* [1997] ECR I-3171; Cases C-85/96 *Martinez Sala* [1998] ECR I-2691 and Case C-274/96 *Bickel and Franz* [1998] ECR I-7637; Case C-378/97 *Wijsenbeek* [1999] ECR I 6207; and Case C-184/99 *Grzelczyk* [2001] ECR I-6/93. These cases are discussed below.

However, most commentators look beyond the explicit grounds of Article 18 to other sources of citizenship. These include the prohibition on discrimination on grounds of nationality, which forms a component of EC policies such as free movement, agriculture, social policy, and so on, as well as existing as a free-standing provision in Article 12. Furthermore, since Amsterdam, and the introduction of Article 13, there has been a legal basis for the EU to legislate on discrimination generally. This overarching prohibition on discrimination was curiously not consolidated into the citizenship provisions, although it expresses the fundamental importance of the equality principle, which must surely be a key feature of any account of European citizenship. Also perceived as part of an enlarged concept of citizenship are the provisions on free movement of persons and services, which involve market, consumer, and social elements, as well as the provisions of the newish Title IV of the EC Treaty. The broader spectrum of citizenship must also encompass democratic rights, including rights of access and transparency, such as those in Article 255 EC.

Since Maastricht, EU law has been full of the rhetoric of citizenship, partly in an attempt to ensure a greater sense of belonging and participation of the individual. But what we presently have is a very uncentred notion of citizenship – the relevant provisions in EU law lack transparency as they are spread throughout the treaties, secondary legislation and case law – like a scattering of jigsaw pieces which at first glance do not seem capable of fitting together into any articulated notion of citizenship.

This wider range of provisions will be examined in the light of distinct conceptions of citizenship. In the myriad of definitions of citizenship, three in particular stand out and will be examined in detail: first, a private or passive conception, which focuses on individual rights and the ability to state preferences; second, on the other hand, the notion of active citizenship, a republican conception with its roots in Aristotle;[29] third, a more recent conception of social citizenship, which is currently seen by many as an essential element of European citizenship, although this may be the most difficult of the three to realise.[30] All three of these conceptions already have some recognition within the broader spectrum of citizenship in EU law outlined above. Their suitability for a Union citizenship of the twenty-first century will also be examined in the light of the requirements set down in the last section, namely: the realisation that recognition of an equal membership of a culturally diverse community requires more than formal equality as well as the potential for multiple identities and citizenship in the EU. In order to satisfy the conditions of post-national membership it will be argued that the EU must shift from too great a reliance on the first, market conception of citizenship, already strongly realised in the body of EU law, to greater actualisation of participatory and social citizenship.

---

[29] Aristotle, *The Politics* (ed. S. Everson, Cambridge University Press, 1988).
[30] This identifying of three different types of citizenship has a certain resonance with TH Marshall's definition of citizenship, which took it to be the realisation of three types of rights: civil, political, and social. Marshall is discussed later in the chapter.

THE MARKET CITIZEN

This private notion of citizenship has been incipient in EC law from the outset. This model is generally perceived as being passive in nature, stressing not a capacity for engagement in public life, but rather human nature as a bundle of passions and interests satisfied in market relations and private sociability – it implies a privatised consumer society – and thus requires a neutrality of institutional arrangements in order to protect competing notions of private freedom. The liberty of the market society is thus a passive liberty, comprising the right to enjoy and accumulate property, and the classic civil liberties of freedom of expression and from arbitrary arrest, rather than the freedom of the civic paradigm which involves the freedom to participate in the creation and ordering of civic society. This market conception of the individual's role in society was derided by Marx in his earlier writings,[31] who criticised the bourgeois version of economic man, urging socialist embrace of the Aristotelian ideal which would allow man to realise his own true nature.

The market citizen of the EEC was identified (probably not for the first time) by the German lawyer, Ipsen,[32] in 1972, as encompassing the role of the individual as *homo economicus*, the individual who acts as participant or beneficiary in the common market. Indeed, this is the only concept of citizenship which has had any meaningful realisation in EU law to date. Unfortunately, it has tended to operate as an exclusionary blueprint, inadequate for the future development of the EU.

What identifiable rights does the market citizen actually have in EU law? These have a broader base than just Article 18 and may be isolated as: the so-called fundamental freedoms in EC law, in particular freedom of movement throughout the Union under Article 18 and certain consumer rights,[33] as the market citizen consumes as well as trades. The market citizen also benefits from a cluster of fundamental rights or general principles developed by the European Court in its case law: for example, Ms Hauer's right to property or Nold's right to trade,[34] evidencing a well-forged link between citizenship and fundamental rights.

Market citizenship has been beneficial for the business community, which has taken advantage of its rights as market citizen, encouraged by the European Court's invention of the direct effect of Community law, which enabled it to litigate in its own courts against recalcitrant member states which it perceived to be infringing its rights to trade across borders. The language of individual rights and their 'effective protection' in the national courts became a tool for the furthering of European integration and the completion of the internal market.

---

[31] Marx, 'On the Jewish Question', in McLellan (ed.), *Karl Marx: Selected Writings* (OUP, 1977).

[32] Ipsen, *Europäisches Gemeinschaftsrecht* (Mohr, 1972). See also M Everson, 'The Legacy of the Market Citizen' in J Shaw and G More (eds), *New Legal Dynamics of the European Union* (Clarendon Press, 1995) for a very comprehensive account.

[33] E.g. concerning product liability, as realised through the Product Liability Directive, or unfair contract terms, realised through the Unfair Contract Terms Directive.

[34] Case 44/79 *Hauer v Rheinland-Pfalz* [1979] ECR 3727; Case 4/73 *Nold v Commission* [1974] ECR 491.

It has not been so beneficial for others. The somewhat self-satisfied enthusiasm which attaches to this conception of market citizen tends to overlook the heavily instrumentalist nature of the rights and the conception of subjecthood underlying them.[35] The citizen must be involved in the internal market and thus the unemployed, or those not recognised as formally economically active, are excluded. Despite the grand rhetoric of Union citizenship, the individual right to freedom of movement has been circumscribed to date. The status of Article 18 is perplexing: the provision states that this right is subject to the limitations and exceptions in the existing *aquis*[36] which suggests that this is not a freestanding right but one dependent on the exercise of economic activity. The market citizen has the right to move freely[37] from one member state of the Union to another, in order to work or follow a profession (even if the work is part time as established in *Levin* and *Kempff*,[38] but true to his, and sometimes her, status as *homo economicus*, the work must be of a truly economic nature: *Bettray*)[39] or to provide or receive services (even if those services turn out to be in fact obtaining an abortion, as characterised by the ECJ in *Grogan*).[40] Even the expansive conception of citizenship delineated by Advocate General Jacobs in the *Konstantinidis*[41] case, which would allow an individual in the words of the Advocate General to state loftily, '*civis Europeus sum*', must still involve migration within the framework of the EC Treaty, and thus, for the most part, relies on the notion of market citizenship. Unless financially self-sufficient, in which case the citizen is able to move freely, providing he or she does not become a burden on the host state under Directive 90/364, the citizen must be engaged in economic activity.[42]

The Court of Justice, in its post-Maastricht case law, has done little to alleviate this state of affairs. Although Advocate General Leger, in *Boukhalfa*,[43] stated that 'every citizen of the Union must, whatever his nationality, enjoy exactly the same rights and be subject to the same obligations', those Union citizens who are economically inactive have not enjoyed free movement and residence rights unless they have come within the residence directives. In cases where the prospect of citizenship

---

[35] As Everson writes,' [b]eing instrumentalised, the market citizen had no choice but to become instrumentalist', see fn 32, at 88.

[36] This point is discussed further below.

[37] Although may still be subjected to border checks and frontier controls in the absence of harmonised measures governing the crossing of external frontiers, as the *Wijsenbeek* case illustrated: Case C-378/97 *Wijsenbeek* [1999] ECR I 6207.

[38] Case 53/81 *Levin v Staatssecretaris van Justitie* [1982] ECR 1035; Case 139/85 *Kempff v Staatssecretaris van Justitie* [1986] ECR 1471.

[39] Case 344/87 *Bettray v Staatssecretaris van Justitie* [1989] ECR 1621.

[40] Case C-159/90 *SPUC v Grogan* [1991] ECR I-4685.

[41] Case C-16891 *Konstantinidis v Stadt Altensteig* [1993] ECR I-1191.

[42] Directive 93/96 concerning students exercising the right to vocational training [1993] OJ L317; Directive 90/365 concerning employed and self-employed people who have ceased to work [1990] OJ L180/28; and Directive 90/364 concerning persons who do not enjoy a right of residence under Community law [1990] OJ L180/26. Under these directives member states are required to grant the right of residence provided those concerned have adequate resources so as not to become a burden on member state social assistance schemes, and are covered by sickness insurance.

[43] See fn 28 at 2271.

has arisen, such as *Sofia Skanavi* and *Stober and Pereira*,[44] the ECJ preferred to rely on specific treaty provisions such as Article 43, rather than relying on the citizenship provisions in Article 18. Nor have the national courts been encouraging in their interpretations. In *ex parte Vitale*[45] the Court of Appeal (without making a reference to the ECJ) rejected the argument that Article 18 creates a directly effective free-standing right of residence on the basis that the 1990 residence directives would otherwise be redundant. A chance for the ECJ to consider the nature of Article 18 was also lost when the reference to Luxembourg from the Divisional Court in *ex parte Adams*[46] was withdrawn (for the best of reasons) when the exclusion order applied to Gerry Adams was lifted at the start of the peace process. Thus, in the absence of a finding that Article 18 was free-standing, a complex combination of treaty provisions and secondary legislation has governed citizens' rights of entry and residence. The member states' implementation of the residence directives has also been unsatisfactory, leading to enforcement action by the Commission.[47] Unsurprisingly perhaps, then, the Commission in its second report on citizenship[48] suggested that Article 18 should be revised at the IGC so as to provide a single, comprehensive legal instrument dealing with the European citizen's free movement and residence rights.[49]

The Treaty of Amsterdam did not bring about a revision of Article 18. Although the draft treaty referred to 'an area of Freedom, Security and Justice', and it might have been hoped that this would mark a shift away from the market orientation of EC law, such hopes have not been rewarded. In 1999, the Commission once again highlighted the inadequacy of member state attitudes to rights of free movement and residence, this time in its report to the Council and Parliament on the implementation of the residence directives.[50] This report notes the unsatisfactory implementation of these directives, as well as the great uncertainty experienced by citizens regarding the practical application of the directives. To remedy this, the Commission identifies four objectives for enhancing the effectiveness of the right of residence, namely: stepping up efforts to inform citizens; ensuring compliance with existing Community law; making Community legislation on the free movement of persons clearer, with particular emphasis on the concept of European citizenship; and beginning discussion on substantive changes to existing legislation. The identification of such goals is to

---

[44] See fn 28.

[45] *R v Secretary of State for the Home Department, ex parte Vitale and Do Amaral, The Times*, 25 January 1996, 34.

[46] Case C-229/94 *R v Secretary of State for the Home Department, ex parte Adams* [1994] OJ C275/18. See S Douglas-Scott and J Kimbell, 'The Adams Exclusion Order Case: New Enforceable Rights in the Post-Maastricht European Union?' [1994] PL 516.

[47] See e.g. Case C-96/95 *Commission v Germany* [1997] ECR I-1653; Case C-344/95 *Commission v Belgium* [1997] ECR I-1035.

[48] See fn 25, at 17.

[49] Notably, in May 2001 the Commission proposed a draft Council and Parliament directive on the rights of citizens and family members to move and reside freely within the territory of the member states. The aim of this draft proposal is to streamline and simplify existing arrangements for freedom of movement and to bring all current measures within one single instrument: COM (2001) 257 Final.

[50] Report from the Commission to the Parliament and the Council on the Implementation of Directives 90/364, 90/365 and 93/96.

be welcomed, but the Commission's objectives are undoubtedly ambitious, and it may take a considerable time to fulfil them.

However, some commentators saw the *Martinez Sala*[51] case as augmenting the rights of citizens under Article 18. Martinez Sala, a Spanish national resident in Germany since 1968, although not working for the whole period, claimed to be entitled to a child-raising allowance, as a German national would have been. She challenged the authorities' refusal on the basis of her rights as a Community worker under Article 39 and her Union citizenship. The ECJ rejected her claim under Article 39, holding that she was not a worker at the relevant period. However, the court did find her entitled to the grant on the basis of her status as a Union citizen, which required her to be treated equally with German nationals. What the ECJ in *Martinez Sala* did not, however, establish was that she had actually had residence rights under Article 18. Such a finding the Court held to be unnecessary, as it found that the German authorities had in any case given her leave to reside. Given that she was a lawful resident she could make use of her citizenship rights under Article 18, which entitled her to equal treatment. The *Martinez Sala* case therefore is not authority for the recognition of a general, directly effective right of residence of Union citizens under Article 18, nor does it clarify the relationship between Article 18 and the conditions imposed on its exercise by secondary legislation. However, *Martinez Sala* does seem to mark an important advance in the availability of welfare rights to Union citizens, in particular to those who are not economically active, and thus does something to mitigate the instrumental nature of market citizenship.[52]

Exclusionary citizenship

As well as being for the most part instrumental in the development of the internal market, Union citizenship has a tendency to be exclusive and exclusionary. If the individual does not have the nationality of a member state of the Union, he or she does not benefit from Union citizenship;[53] therefore nine million people who live and work in Europe are denied its status.[54] O'Keeffe has complained that the internal market provisions merely serve to entrench a national state ethic of 'discrimination, racism, xenophobia...and incitement to hatred and racial violence'.[55] Additionally, while the language of Union citizenship is gender neutral, that neutrality perpetuates the invisibility of women. So the right of free movement, critical to the concept of European citizenship and the single market, has been constructed in gendered ways which contrasts the independent (male) citizen (or 'worker') and

---

[51] See fn 28.
[52] This point is discussed further below.
[53] Although non-EU nationals do have the right to petition the European Parliament (Article 194) and to apply to the Ombudsman (Article 195), rights discussed in the next section.
[54] See A Geddes, 'Immigrant and Ethnic Minorities and the EU's "Democratic Deficit"' (1995) 33 JCMS 197–217; and Ward, 'Law and the Other Europeans' (1997) 35 JCMS 96.
[55] D O'Keeffe, 'The Free Movement of Persons and the Single Market' [1992] ELRev 3 at 19.

his dependants, including the spouse.[56] For Iris Marion Young the discourse that links civic public with fraternity is not merely metaphorical: '[f]ounded by men, the modern state and its public realm of citizenship paraded as universal values and norms which were derived specifically from masculine experience...respectful competition and bargaining among independent agents; discourses framed in unemotional tones of compassionate reason'.[57]

As is well known, for many individuals, rights under EU law have been derivative only, for example the rights of family members are essentially parasitic on the family relationship with the worker. If a migrant worker husband loses his right of residence, the family's derivative rights have been lost, increasing the vulnerability of the spouse.[58] In the well-known *Diatta*[59] case, the ECJ held that a third-country-national spouse did not lose her right of residence in an EC state on separation from her EC husband, implying that she might, however, do so on divorce. The situation was well summed up by Weiler who, commenting on the *Diatta* case, wrote '[f]or the Court to say that at the moment of her divorce she does not only lose her derivative rights under Community law (which is acceptable), but also protection of fundamental rights, is to strip her of humaneness. It is to acknowledge that under Community law she is mere instrumentality.'[60]

It might have been hoped that Title IV of the EC Treaty, created by the Treaty of Amsterdam, would improve this situation. This title deals with visa, asylum, immigration, and other policies related to the free movement of persons, thus bringing together matters previously dealt with separately, and confusingly, under Justice and Home Affairs, Schengen, or secondary legislation. Here was a chance to put the rights of Union citizens and third-country nationals on a more coherent basis. Such coherence is unlikely to come about yet as Title IV is a prime example of Europe '*à la carte*', as it does not apply to Ireland, the UK or Denmark.[61] It also operates essentially on an intergovernmental basis as unanimity is required for the first five years of its operation (Article 67) and, as only courts of final resort are permitted to make preliminary references (Article 68), is likely to give rise to conflicting national

---

[56] See C Ackers, 'Women, Citizenship and European Community Law: The Gender Implications of the Free Movement Provisions' (1994) 4 Journal of Social Welfare and Family Law 391. See also below.

[57] I-M Young, 'Polity and Group Difference' in R Beiner (ed.), *Theorising Citizenship* (State University of New York Press, 1995). See below for a greater discussion on discrimination based on sex in the EU and discrimination generally.

[58] The High Level Panel on free movement of persons recommended the introduction of a right of residence for divorced third-country nationals: see *Report of the High Level Panel presented to the European Commission* on 18 March 1997 at 57. The spouse, of course, is even more vulnerable if a 'mere' cohabitee: see e.g. Case 59/86 *Netherlands v Reed* [1986] ECR 1283. The High Level Panel also recommended amending Regulation 1612/68 [1968] OJ L257/2, to take account of social change.

[59] Case 267/83 *Diatta v Land Berlin* [1986] ECR 567; see also Case 12/86 *Demirel v Stadt Swabisch Gmund* [1987] ECR 3719, where the applicant, a Turkish worker in Germany, was unable to rely on the right to respect for family life under Article 8 ECHR because his case fell outside the scope of EC law, there being no EC law permitting family reunification. See also Case C-277/94 *Taflan-Met* [1996] ECR I-4085.

[60] Weiler, 'Thou Shalt Not Oppress a Stranger: On the Judicial Protection of the Human Rights of Non-EC Nationals – a Critique' (1992) European Journal of International Law 65–91 at 90.

[61] See the Protocol on the position of the UK and Ireland and the Protocol on the position of Denmark.

jurisprudence. Thus it seems likely to perpetuate the present fragmentary and exclusive situation.

Economic rights

Market citizenship is simply inadequate for today's EU. This is partly because it reflects and reinforces the continuing prioritisation of economic rights in the EU. Norbert Reich has suggested that, '[t]he economic rights of market citizens are certainly the nucleus of any rights granted by the European Community or Union...the European Constitution might thus be said to resemble a Russian doll which at its core contains a basic (economic) structure'.[62] That the economic rights of the market citizen should be so prominent is not surprising as, being set up as an economic community, for a long time the fundamental EEC constitution was primarily economic in nature. The fact that a large part of the European Court's specific jurisprudence on fundamental rights concerned rights to property reflects this.[63] But this sits uneasily with fundamental rights protection: in most constitutions and international rights documents greater priority is given to civil and political rights, which are themselves core rights of citizenship.[64] Some writers suggest that economic rights should not enjoy a superior level of protection: Alexander Meiklejohn, for example, argued that distinguishing the two types of right was of great importance and that a constitutional regime that linked the two was 'in constant danger of giving to man's possessions the same status, the same dignity, we give to man himself'.[65] However, a privileging of economic rights has traditional historical origins. Locke's theory of political obligation rests on security of property rights.[66] For, according to Locke, in an original hypothetical 'state of nature', individuals had property in their own person and in their labour and when they 'mixed' their labour with something by removing it from its natural state they thereby made it their own property 'at least when there is enough and as good left in common for others'.[67] Individual property rights therefore preceded government and the preservation of property was, according to this view, 'the great and chief end for which men come together in commonwealths'.[68] Therefore, for Locke, property rights were the prototypical natural rights which became translated into a civil right under

---

[62] N Reich, 'A European Constitution for Citizens' [1997] I ELJ at 131.

[63] E.g. Case 11/70 *Internationale Handelsgesellschaft* [1970] ECR 1125 (right to property, economic liberty); Case 4/73 *Nold* [1974] ECR 491 (right to ownership); Case 44/79 *Hauer* [1979] ECR 3727 (right to property); Case 5/88 *Wachauf* [1989] ECR 2609 (right to compensation) to name but a few.

[64] Coppell and O'Neill comment: '[i]t would seem, then that there is no distinction and hence no hierarchical relationship being posited by the European Court between the basic human rights outlined, for example, in the European Convention on Human Rights and the free market rights arising out of the treaties of the European Community': Coppell and O'Neill, 'The European Court of Justice: Taking Rights Seriously' (1992) 29 CMLRev 689.

[65] A Meiklejohn, *Free Speech and its Relation to Self-Government* (Harper, 1948).

[66] Locke, *Second Treatise* in *Two Treatises on Government* (ed. Laslett, CUP, 1963). See also Nozick, *Anarchy, State and Utopia* (Basil Blackwell, 1974).

[67] Locke, see fn 66, at 395.

[68] Ibid.

the law: Locke's justification of property rights as a way of legitimating the power of the rising classes in seventeenth-century England is sometimes seen as an explanation of the prevalence and paradigmatic status of property rights in Anglo-American jurisprudence from Blackstone on.[69] Although it is unlikely that the drafters of the EEC Treaty had Locke in mind, it has been suggested that the basis of the EU single market was that of an ordoliberal economic theory of the market in which market freedoms are seen as intrinsic to the notion of human dignity, as well as upholding theory of contract and private property rights.[70] Under ordoliberalism, which is closely related to the neoliberalism of Hayek,[71] the protection of a free and equal society ensures prevention of the atrocities of Nazi Germany and the like. Economic rights are secured in return for our surrender of our natural state, in the belief (or, perhaps, 'fantasy') that society can be unified and rationally organised.

However, this version of citizenship, being essentially premised on self-interest, cannot create strong allegiance, nor a sense of belonging, given that, in the context of the EU, it excludes so many from its ambit. The instrumental nature of market citizenship rights has undermined the ability of the EU to create a culture in which rights are meaningful to all. In *L'Autre Cap*,[72] Derrrida points to the instrumental nature of the EU, to the dominance of capital, of technology, in a Europe which has forgotten its history and needs to resurrect *capitale* (cultural heritage) over capital. The need for a European cultural heritage has also been stressed by other writers. Ignatieff, for example, notes the necessity of the contribution of intellectuals to the unity of Europe: '[s]ince 1945 European intellectuals have been arguing that European integration should not be left to the politicians: it is a unity to be constructed in the mind and heart, and in the works of culture. And what is the result? We now have European debate dominated entirely by bankers, economists and politicians.'[73]

Market citizenship specifically fails the test of citizenship in a post-national community identified earlier: an inclusive multicultural citizenship that respects all interests, as well as recognising multiple identities. In the *Contrat Social*, Rousseau suggested that property rights should always be subordinate to the overriding claims of the community[74] but the conception of market citizenship provides no dimension of community. It also fails to provide any identifiable public space other than the

---

[69] Indeed, Blackstone effulged over property rights, '[t]here is nothing which so generally strikes the imagination and engages the affectations of mankind . . . as the right of property' Blackstone, *Commentaries on the Laws of England* (University of Chicago Press, 1979) book 3 at 4.

[70] See Petersmann, 'National Constitutions, Foreign Trade Policy and European Community Law' (1992) 5 European Journal of International Law; see also D Chalmers, 'The Single Market: From Prima Donna to Journeyman', in Shaw and More (eds), *New Legal Dynamics of the European Union* (Clarendon Press, 1996), who suggests that the ECJ is now less influenced by ordoliberal theory than in its early days.

[71] F Hayek, *The Road to Serfdom* (ARK, 1976).

[72] Published in English by Derrida as *The Other Heading – Reflections on Today's Europe* (Indiana University Press, 1992).

[73] M Ignatieff, *Where are They Now?* (Prospect, October 1997).

[74] Rousseau, *The Social Contract* (ed. M. Cranston, Penguin Books, 1968) 178–81.

market place, fragmented by individual interests and biases. What is needed are further dimensions of citizenship which will do this.

THE 'GOOD' CITIZEN

This conception of citizenship lays stress on active and virtuous participation in public life: that of the 'good' citizen. Charles Taylor has suggested that this mode of citizenship defines 'participation in self-rule as the essence of freedom...an essential component of citizen capacity'.[75] On this understanding (sometimes referred to as 'republican' citizenship), which has its origins in ancient Greek thought, primarily that of Aristotle, although also close ties with contemporary communitarian reasoning, citizenship involves membership in a specific political community, defining a particular identity over and above that of family, clan, tribal or religious affiliations. In this way, the concerns of citizenship become aspirations for an autonomous political community, rather than of atomised individuals.

This might seem to be a more promising matrix for citizenship in today's EU, but, at present, there seems little scope for the fulfilment of such a conception. Indeed, the most notable aspects of the political realm of the EU have been its infamous democratic deficit, and the lack of available channels for citizens to play their part in EU public life. An unelected Commission responsible for the initiation of legislation (also suffering from the stinging criticism of the independent experts' report highlighting the Commission's 'lack of responsibility and accountability in the face of fraud and mismanagement'[76]) and a weak European Parliament with, until recently, few or no powers to initiate or veto legislation, could hardly inspire the citizen.[77]

Attempts have of course been made to change this. Article 19 EC formalised a package of political rights: the right to vote in municipal or European Parliamentary elections in another member state, to petition the Parliament or the Ombudsman. But these rights do not go very far and certainly do not introduce the necessary structures for active citizenship and have not even been properly implemented by some member states.[78] As d'Oliveira has noted, 'the political dimension of EU citizenship is underdeveloped. The instruments for participation in the public life of the Union are lacking as is public life itself, is virtually non-existent.'[79] For example, the present provisions of the Treaty on voting, as implemented by Directive 94/80 EC, only grant voting rights without mentioning other important rights, such as freedom of association and expression, which are preconditions for meaningful exercise of

---

[75] C Taylor, 'The Liberal Communitarian Debate' in Rosenblum (ed.) *Liberalism and the Moral Life* (Harvard University Press, 1989) at 178.

[76] Committee of Independent Experts, *First Report on Allegations Regarding Fraud, Mismanagement and Nepotism in the EC*, presented to the European Parliament, 15 March 1999.

[77] Although the Committee of the Regions and Ecosoc do something to enhance the democratic representation of popular interests.

[78] See e.g. Case C-323/97 *Commission v Belgium* [1998] ECR I-4281.

[79] H-J D'Oliveira, 'European Citizenship: Its Meaning, Its Potential' in Dehousse (ed.), *Europe after Maastricht: An Ever Close Union?* (Law Books in Europe, 1994).

voting rights.[80] Even in the context of the only direct political link which individuals have to an EU institution, the European Parliament, the national political agenda continues to dominate elections, with citizens voting on the basis of national party political concerns, rather than a European political agenda. Since 1979, voter participation in European Parliament elections has actually declined from 63 per cent to 59.5 per cent in 1994.[81] The grant of non-national voter rights under Article 19 does not seem to have made citizens feel closer to the EU, with a very low participation rate (an average of 11.81 per cent turn-out of non-national Union citizens, with as little as 1.55 per cent in Greece).[82]

In the absence of an EU legislature which can command effective support, attention has focused on the transparency of the EU decision-making process and rights of access to information. A lack of information about EU activities, along with the fact that the main legislative body, the Council of Ministers, operates largely in secret, has made it difficult for an active engagement with citizenship. The present consolidated treaties, which have renumbered provisions so they lose the familiarity they once had (even if only for a few lawyers, or European specialists) is a paradigm example of lack of transparency, albeit one carried out in the name of transparency. The process of comitology, whereby EC law is implemented, or even created, by unaccountable member state appointees, who oversee the Commission's work, also excludes the citizen in an almost Kafkaesque scenario. The EU often seems to operate by depriving its citizens of information they need to make intelligent choices and to assess the benefits and burdens of proposed legislative policies. Frustration is often misdiagnosed as apathy or indifference to public affairs.

In spite of recent initiatives taken at EU level aimed at encouraging transparency in the EU lawmaking process[83] secrecy has very often prevailed. Advocate General Tesauro's claim in *Netherlands* v *Council* that 'the right to information, including information in the hands of public authorities . . . [is] a fundamental right of the individual'[84] has not always seemed to have been fulfilled by the outcome of cases.[85] In *Netherlands* v *Council* the Court rejected the challenge brought by the Netherlands

---

[80] A point which was recognized by the Commission in its 1997 report on citizenship of the Union.

[81] Eurobarometer surveys, no 41 July 1994. Participation of UK voters in the June 1999 European Parliamentary elections was at an all-time low, with some constituencies reporting as little as a 2 per cent turnout.

[82] Commission second report on citizenship, fn 25 above.

[83] E.g. Declaration 17 to the Final Act of the Treaty on European Union which declares the right of access to information; Commission Communication on 'Public Access to Institutions' OJ 1993 C156/5; Commission and Council Inter-Institutional Agreement which enumerates principles governing public access to documents in their possession (OJ 1993 L340/41); Council Code of Conduct on access to minutes, Bull. EU 10/ 1995. Also Decision 93/731 on public access to Council documents, OJ 1993 L340; Commission Decision 94/90 ECSC/EC/Euratom on public access to Commission documents. For a general survey of freedom of information in the EU see Birkinshaw, 'Freedom of Information and Open Government: The European Community/Union Dimension' [1997] Government and Information Quarterly 1; O'Neill, 'The Right of Access to Community-Held Documentation as a General Principle of EC Law' (1998) 4 European Public Law 403.

[84] Case C-58/94 *Netherlands* v *Council* [1996] 2 CMLR 996 at 1002, para. 6.

[85] See Chapter 3 for a more detailed discussion of the Courts' case law on transparency.

government to the legal basis of the Council Decision[86] concerning public access[87] to Council documents, on the basis that the application was directed against the Community code of conduct, an expression of purely voluntary coordination not intended to have legal effects. In the *Carvel* case[88] the journalist, John Carvel, was refused Council documents on the basis of confidentiality. The Court of First Instance held that, in exercising its discretion, the Council must engage in a balancing exercise, weighing the interests of citizens' access against its own interests in maintaining confidentiality. As the Court found that no such balancing exercise had been conducted, it held that access had been wrongly refused. This may seem progressive; however, the Court would not go as far as to uphold the Dutch government's argument that the fundamental right of access to information should not be merely a matter of the Council's internal rules of procedure. In this context, Armstrong has commented, 'the essentially inter-institutional nature of EU governance has not changed, leaving the Union citizen as a rather ambiguous identity within the Union's political and legal systems... At no point does John Carvel as a Union citizen ever become constructed in the Court's mind.'[89]

Nevertheless, since then, the CFI does seem to have been more willing to annul institutions' refusal to give access to documents.[90] However, in spite of the introduction of a plethora of legal instruments on access to information, the Community Courts' case law often seems to be reasoned on the basis of a requirement to give reasons, a duty which always existed in EC law rather than on the basis of a right to information. Craig and de Búrca argue that the giving reasons requirement should be mutated into a participatory right, forcing the Commission to enter into dialogue with those who put forward arguments for or against participation, which would give it a more truly deliberative, democratic nature.[91]

Further attempts have been made to strengthen a right of access to EU information. The three own initiatives of the European Ombudsman all concern transparency of information.[92] The Treaty of Amsterdam amended Article 1(1) TEU to incorporate the requirement that decisions should be taken '*as openly as possible*

---

[86] Council Decision 93/731, OJ 1993 L340/42.

[87] The Netherlands had challenged the legal basis of Article 207(3) which empowers the Council to adopt rules of procedure, as inappropriate for the purposes of giving effect to a fundamental right.

[88] Case T-194/94 *Carvel v Council* [1995] 3 CMLR 359.

[89] K Armstrong, 'Citizenship of the Union? Lessons from *Carvel* and the Guardian' (1996) 59 MLR 582, 586.

[90] See, for a sample of the Court's case law, Case T-10595 *WWF (UK) v Commission* (1998) ECR II-313; Case T-124/96 *Interporc v Commission* [1998] ECR II-231; Case T-83/96 *van der Wal v Commission* [1998] ECR II-545; Case T-174/95 *Svenska Journalistforbundet* [1998] ECR II-2289; Case T-14/98 *Heidi Hautala v Council* [1999] ECR II-2489; Case T-188/97 *Rothmans International v Commission* [1999] ECR II 2463; Case T-309/97 *The Bavarian Lager Co Ltd v Commission* [1999] ECR II 3217.

[91] P Craig and G de Búrca, *EU Law* (2nd edn, Oxford: OUP, 1998) 120. The creation of participatory rights might also further mutate into rights of access to justice where necessary and thus help widen the rules of individual standing before the ECJ, under Articles 230 and 232 EC, which are one of the most glaring aspects of a citizen's lack of access and thus power.

[92] See e.g. *The European Ombudsman's own initiative inquiry into public access to documents*, 20 December 1996 (616//PUBAC/IJH).

and as closely as possible to the citizen'. Amsterdam also introduced a new Article
255(1) which states: ' [a]ny citizen of the Union, and any Member States, shall have
a right of access to European Parliament, Council and Commission documents, subject to the principles and conditions to be defined in accordance with paragraphs 2
and 3'. However, as paragraph 2 limits access on grounds of 'general principles' and
'grounds of public or private interest', given the Court's interpretation of similar
provisions in secondary legislation, one may be sceptical as to the effectiveness of
the right. Article 255 was supplemented in May 2001 by the adoption of the long-
awaited Regulation 1049/2001 on *Access to Information*,[93] which it is hoped will
add body to the still rather thin citizen's right to information.

The earlier Dublin draft[94] of the Amsterdam Treaty commenced with the impressive phrase: '[t]he EU belongs to its citizens'. However, these proposals were very
modest, and, as Weiler[95] notes, 'at worst, the proposal represents another symptom
of the degradation of civic culture whereby the citizen is conceived as a consumer'.
Weiler also derides the disempowerment of the European citizen, writing, 'as the
Community has grown in size, in scope, in reach and despite a high rhetoric including the very creation of "European citizenship", there has been a distinct
disempowerment of the individual European citizen, the specific gravity of whom
continues to decline as the Union grows'.[96] Habermas has taken a similar view, sum-
marising the European public realm in this way: '[f]or the citizen, this translates into
an ever greater gap between being affected by something and participating in changing it…citizens have no effective means of debating European decisions and influencing the decision making process'.[97] Given the imperceptible effect that the
Amsterdam and Nice Treaties have had on Union citizenship, a more accurate heading for the draft Treaty might have been 'The EU ignores its citizens'. The
Commission's solution to this lack of progress has been optimism in the success of
the *Citizens First* initiative and the action plan for the internal market:[98] initiatives
which may at least remedy the lack of information about European citizenship, but
do nothing to improve the lack of an identifiable public, political space in the EU.

Therefore, active citizenship in the EU has remained hypothetical only, a pale relation of its more actualised but imperfect counterpart, the market citizen, capable of
producing only an anaemic political discourse and an anaemic Union citizen.
However, active citizenship remains an attractive ideal which, if realised, can

---

[93] This regulation is also discussed in Chapter 3.

[94] *The European Union today and tomorrow – adapting the European Union for the benefit of its peoples and preparing it for the Future*, Conf. 2500/96.

[95] Weiler, 'The European Union belongs to its Citizens: Three Immodest Proposals' (1997) 22 EL Rev
151.

[96] Ibid., at 153. Weiler's own suggestions for reversing the disempowerment are his 'three immodest proposals': a limited form of direct democracy, through a European legislative ballot; the *Lexcalibur*
initiative which proposes placing EU decision-making on the Internet to enhance accessibility and transparency; and the creation of a Constitutional Council on the French model, to adjudicate *ex ante*
challenges to EU legislation.

[97] Habermas, 'Citizenship and National Identity: Some Reflections on the Future of Europe' (1992) 12
Praxis International 1.

[98] EC Commission, *Second Report on Citizenship*, fn 25 above, 19 ff.

become more than just a status defined by rights and duties but a matter of identity-membership of a political community. But how can any coherent political identity be experienced in multicultural Europe? The problem of attaining some sort of shared, overlapping, consensual values which might contribute to, or even create, such an identity re-emerges.

Determining the public realm

One movement in political theory looks to a deliberative democracy as a solution, whereby such a civic realm can be created dialogically. Michelman, for example, defines politics as a discursive engagement which the community has as to the terms of its common life, with citizenship defined as 'the constant re-determination by the people for themselves of the terms on which they live together'.[99] Indeed Michelman insists that 'the self is constituted by or comes to itself through, such an engagement'.[100] By this account the individual is therefore a truly political creature, with no particular pre-political identity, unlike the account given under market citizenship, whereby the individual is antecedently situated to any communal attachments. But, importantly, this republican account is dependent on an institutional public space capable of structuring and sustaining the debate. In the US context, Bruce Ackerman looks to the Constitution, which 'has always provided us with the language and the process within which our political identities could be confronted, debated and defined'.[101]

Even if such an account is desirable in the US context (and that is debatable) it seems unworkable and inappropriate for the EU. First, there is no single written Constitution for Europeans with the power and aura of the US constitution, although it is true that a conception of active citizenship may be derived from provisions such as those in the Swiss Constitution or Article 33 of the German Constitution. But at a European level all that exists is a discouraging medley of treaties and legislation propagated by elites (even if the ECJ is happy to characterise the treaties as a 'constitution'), which engender no sense of belonging in the peoples of Europe.

Republican accounts of citizenship attempt to move the dialogic realm beyond that of formal constitutions, however, seeking sources of self-government in the local community, religious groups, unions, so that, as Christodoulidis notes, 'eventually, social controversy as such becomes synonymous with republican debate'.[102] In this way, Cass Sunstein has suggested, 'citizenship understood in the republican fashion, does not occur solely through official organs'.[103] Thus, Sunstein suggests that we may 'multiply the points of access to government and generate institutions

---

[99] F Michelman, 'Law's Republic' (1988) 97 Yale LJ 1493 at 1518.
[100] Ibid., at 1523.
[101] B Ackerman, 'The Storrs Lectures: Discovering the Constitution' (1984) 93 Yale LJ 1013 at 1072.
[102] E Christodoulidis, 'A New Constitutional Reality for Civil Society: Some Cautionary Remarks' in Bellamy, Bufacchi and Castiglione, (eds) *Democracy and Constitutional Culture* (Lothian Press, 1995).
[103] C Sunstein, 'Beyond the Republican Revival' (1988) 97 Yale LJ 1539 at 1573.

that will produce deliberation among the differently situated'.[104] Would this enlarged republican discursive citizenship be an attractive model for the EU? Such a theory of deliberative democracy seems to be suitably inclusive, garnering support from writers such as Martha Minow, who suggests that '[t]he introduction of additional voices may enable adversary dialogue to expand beyond a stylised either/or mode, prompting new and creative insights'.[105]

Adherents of this inclusive deliberative democracy seem to suggest that it is possible for all types of viewpoints, including the marginal, outsider voices in society to become part of a community's 'normatively consequential dialogue', to enter the public space. In this way, civil society is given a constitutional, legal reality.[106] But even this version seems unlikely to work well in the EU. Such a conversational political self-determination may succeed at national or sub-national level, but a reliance on spontaneous dialogue in unofficial contexts is less likely to work across national frontiers. Barriers of language and culture continue to make it unlikely for such conversations to grow up on an *ad hoc* basis. Rather, it is just the lumbering, formal mechanisms of the European institutions which attempt to make cross-border co-operation possible. Dialogue still has to be initiated in this way and, as such, appears rather stilted. There is no spontaneous public space or spaces at European level. Institutional support, even if it is the *Citizens First* variety, is still needed.

This must be the rather disappointing conclusion at this stage. An increased participatory realm seems vital in the construction of a desirable active citizenship for Europe. But such a forum cannot be created spontaneously. Europe's institutions must still play a prominent part in its creation. This is a troubling acknowledgement at a time when, following the Independent Experts' report, the European Commission in particular is suffering from the lowest levels of credibility. The imperative seems to be that European institutions must become more open, and Joseph Weiler's three immodest proposals, including 'Lexcalibur', the placing of all draft EU legislation on the internet, seem to be no bad start.[107]

A HUMAN RIGHTS FOUNDATION FOR CITIZENSHIP?

Some commentators have suggested that citizenship does not have to be politically and economically determined, but might be founded on a human rights determination; indeed, it is quite common for contemporary accounts to conflate these two concepts. T H Marshall's classic definition portrayed citizenship as built on the back of the establishment of civil and political, social, and economic rights through time. So, for example, Siofra O'Leary writes, 'the establishment of a connection between the Community's commitment to fundamental rights and Community citizenship could promote the protection of individual rights as one of the central objectives of

---

[104] Ibid., at 1585.
[105] M Minow, 'Justice Engendered' (1987) 101 Harvard LR 10 at 88–9.
[106] E.g. U Preuss, 'Problems of a Concept of European Citizenship' (1995) ELJ 267.
[107] See Weiler fn 95.

Community law and might help displace nationality as the single most important condition for the full enjoyment of Community citizenship'.[108]

O'Leary also suggests that human rights and citizenship could be defined to help foster a Community identity which is absent at present. These optimistic suggestions have drawbacks, which turn mainly on the sort of conception of human rights which is likely to emerge. At present, what exists in the EU is, for the most part, a liberal human rights philosophy, with a strong support for economic rights, which has much in common with the principles underlying the European Convention or US Bill of Rights, even if its legal form is somewhat incoherent, owing to the past lack of a formal catalogue of fundamental rights in EU law. Weiler notes the resonance of Community nationalism 'with Enlightenment ideas, with the privileging of the individual, with a different aspect of liberalism which has as its progeny today the liberal notions of human rights'.[109] The danger of such liberal, universalising principles is that, in their neutral, apparently equal application, they may operate to the detriment of the dispossessed, the excluded, as well as tying us to an unacceptable norm of equality, which often turns out to be anything but.[110]

One response of European writers to scepticism about this conception of human rights and its concomitant conception of personhood has been to suggest that the insertion of a human rights discourse into EU law is still beneficial. This suggestion has been made by those who hold themselves to be agnostic or sceptical about human rights generally. Grainne de Búrca suggests that the criticism that the concept of rights, with its individualising language and practices, is incompatible with a genuine participatory democracy, is the least apposite in the context of the EU.[111] For, she writes, the criticism presupposes a fully developed and functioning democratic system which is not what we have in the EU, and in this context, rather than undermining the democratic process, it is possible that the language of rights has an empowering effect in giving voice to interests which are largely excluded from the political processes. On one level, de Búrca's contention is correct. There is a need for a greater injection of certain types of rights into the body of EU law, namely participatory rights and social rights or second-generation rights, rather than the negative, liberal, first-generation rights traditionally protected under European law.

However, there is also a need for caution. Since Maastricht, human rights have been seen as a therapy for alienation and dissatisfaction within the EU. But will a greater embrace of human rights have the desired effect: will human rights bring people closer to the EU? In contexts such as the ECHR, human rights have played a vital role in post-war Europe and continue to play an important role in the context of citizenship. However, as Joseph Weiler cautions, most rights set 'walls of liberty' around the individual against public authorities. A focus on human rights may not therefore be psychologically appropriate to making Europe appear 'closer' to its

---

[108] S O'Leary, 'The Relation between Community Citizenship and Fundamental Rights' (1995) 32 CMLRev 519 at 542.

[109] Weiler, 'Does Europe need a Constitution? Demos, Telos and the Maastricht Decision' (1995) 1 ELJ 219.

[110] See below.

[111] G De Búrca, 'The Language of Rights and European Integration' in Shaw and More, see fn 32.

citizens. Human rights can also have a potentially divisive and disintegrative effect, not always in tune with the 'social solidarity' necessary for citizenship. Rights clash with each other. There may be reference in Article 6(2) of the Maastricht Treaty to the 'common constitutional traditions' of member states, but these traditions on occasion approach human rights quite differently, as the *Grogan*[112] case showed. So, in the context of the ECHR, the European Court of Human Rights continues to allow a 'margin of appreciation' to member states, with resulting different outcomes to cases, particularly in the fields of morality and culture.[113] Disputes as to the types of rights which should be enforced and recognised may reveal disputes and even deep disagreement on how the political realm is conceived, i.e. whether libertarian, socialist, and so on. In the long run, this disagreement cannot be solved by 'more rights' but rather by some political authority.[114]

In their disintegrative aspect, human rights simply re-raise the fundamental questions about the nature of the European polity, and its identity, which remained unanswered in the citizenship context. The answers must lie in a greater legitimacy of political institutions in the EU brought about by increased democracy. As Weiler writes, human rights are not the principal hallmark of citizenship although they may be part of the package. Human rights are the hallmarks of humans. The hallmark of citizenship is that it enables and habilitates representative institutions and this is where action must be taken.

SOCIAL CITIZENSHIP

For Marshall, citizenship was of course constituted by the possession of social rights, as well as civil and political rights. These were thought to be essential if individuals were to become full members of the Community. It has become fashionable to perceive social citizenship as an indispensable element of EU citizenship, a way of bonding the individual to the EU.[115] But is the fulfilment of social citizenship an appropriate aspiration for the EU?

On the one hand, social citizenship, as realised through social rights and social justice, seems to be an essential means of tempering the socially exclusionary effects of the market. The provision of social rights ensures that individuals are able to take advantage of their market freedoms and their civil and political liberties. According to John Rawls, 'below a certain level of material and social well-being, and of training and education, people simply cannot take part as citizens'.[116] Similarly,

---

[112] Case C-159/90 *SPUC* v *Grogan* [1991] ECR I-4685.

[113] See, in this regard, *Muller* v *Switzerland* [1991] 13 EHRR 578; *Otto Preminger Institute* v *Austria* (1995) 19 EHRR 34.

[114] See R Bellamy, 'The Constitution of Europe: Rights or Democracy?' in Bellamy, Bufacchi and Castiglione (eds), *Democracy and Constitutional Culture in the Union of Europe* (Lothian Foundation Press, 1995); J Waldron, 'A Rights-Based Critique of Constitutional Rights' (1993) OJLS 18.

[115] E.g. I Ward, '(Pre)conceptions in European Law' (1996) Journal of Law and Society 198; E Meehan, 'European Citizenship and Social Policies' in Vogel and Mann (eds), *The Frontiers of Citizenship* (Macmillan, 1990); J Shaw, 'Citizenship of the Union – towards Postnational Membership?' Harvard Jean-Monnet Working Paper 6/97.

[116] Rawls, *Political Liberalism* (Columbia University Press, 1993) 166.

Dahrendorf describes 'a degree of poverty that deprives those who suffer it of civic participation'.[117] Remedying this by social rights satisfies the demand of inclusiveness set earlier as a requirement of post-national citizenship, albeit in a manner designed to operate in the contexts of national welfare regimes. In this way, individuals may be liberated from the operation of market forces, and from what Esping-Andersen termed 'commodification'.[118] The recognition of social citizenship also produces a different conception of personhood, whereby the worker is perceived not as a factor of production, but rather as a human being, leaving a space for the development of the multiple identities which individuals may possess. Such a humanising conception emerged in nineteenth-century labour law, in the work of Otto Gierke and the German historical school, who attacked the view that labour was a commodity whose value was determined, not by the principles of social justice, but exchange. In contrast, Gierke described labour as 'human flesh and blood' and advocated 'the emancipation of human work as a legal conception from the nexus of property law'.[119] In this way, labour is not a commodity to be exchanged, since a person's working power is part of, and inseparable from, the person him- or herself.[120] Thus, introduction of social rights through welfare regimes aids this process of decommodification.

Therefore, it might seem that realising social rights could temper the undesirable focus on the market in the EU, ensuring that all individuals can benefit, regardless of circumstances. However, the following problems emerge in this context.

First, a definitional problem. What is meant by social citizenship? This concept suffers from as much uncertainty as citizenship generally, with candidates as varied as industrial, cultural, welfare, and even market citizenship, for social citizenship. Second, there is the problematic status of EU social policy and the question of the EU's competence in this area. Given that the EU was founded as an economic community, tensions form between economic and social policy. There is also the real fear that EU social policy may intrude into national sovereignty over welfare and finance.

Nonetheless, there seems to be more than the germ of social citizenship in EU law, which must be developed if post-national EU citizenship is to be worthwhile and meaningful. This might be the way to redress the imbalance of capital to *capitale* in the EU highlighted by Derrida, opening up the prospect of a Europe which embraces multiple identities, rather than focusing on the bankers and business community.

---

[117] R Dahrendorf, 'Citizenship and Social Class' in Bulmer and Rees (eds), *Citizenship Today: The Contemporary Relevance of T H Marshall* (UCL Press, 1996).

[118] Esping-Andersen, *The Three Worlds of Welfare Capitalism* (Polity, 1990).

[119] O Kahn-Freund, *Labour Law and Politics in the Weimar Republic* (Blackwell, 1978).

[120] See Hepple, 'Social Values in European Law' (1995), *Current Legal Problems* 53, who notes that 'various laws and codes on the contract of employment which emerged, starting with the German BGB of 1896, the Dutch Law of 1907 and the French *Code du Travail* of 1910 reflect this gradual transformation'.

A concept of social citizenship

Maurice Roche has suggested that 'social citizenship refers to rights and duties of citizenship concerned with people's welfare in the broad sense including work, education and quality of life'.[121] This definition will be adopted here, with the following qualification: that the purpose of social citizenship is (following Marshall) to enable individuals to participate fully in the life of the community. It is submitted that social rights are in fact prerequisites for the enjoyment of the principles of liberty and equality and of foundational status, rather than afterthoughts.[122] The principle of liberty underpins civil and political rights: the freedom to contract and own property and the freedoms of expression and association. Keith Ewing has argued that 'people without an income, without a home or adequate health care can hardly expect to take much interest' if they are 'completely unsure about food and shelter in the coming days'.[123] The same is true if people have to work long hours for a modest return and therefore have no time to use their legal and political freedoms. Social security is thus a precondition of legal and political liberty.

Protection of social rights also has a bearing on the principle of equality, requiring equal protection by the law, equal access, and the condemnation of irrational discrimination. Citizenship is not just a matter of the rights necessary for the exercise of political freedom, or the right to participate in the exercise of political power, but also about the 'right to share to the full in the social heritage and to live the life of a civilised being according to the standards prevailing in society'.[124]

It is recognized that this is a very loose and broad definition of social citizenship. Given the inchoate nature of social citizenship in the EU, this definition at least has the merit of not ruling anything out at an early stage of development. However, it is recognised that, if pursued strictly in the context of the EU, social citizenship may turn out to have implications for national welfare sovereignty, one of the most serious problems which the EU must face in developing a meaningful concept of citizenship.

Problems of a European social citizenship

In addition to the difficulty of defining social citizenship, specific problems arise in the context of the EU's jurisdiction in the field of social legislation. Given that the Treaty of Rome, as already discussed, was based on neo-liberal ideology, social policy played small part in the early days of the EEC, and was in any case perceived to be, for some at least, incompatible with the achievement of economic efficiency. Article 2 of the Treaty of Rome originally set out the task of promoting

---

[121] Roche, *Rethinking Citizenship: Welfare, Ideology and Change in Modern Society* (Polity Press, 1992) at 3.
[122] For an expression of this view see K Ewing, 'Social Rights and Constitutional Law' (1999) Public Law 104.
[123] Ibid; see also J Waldron, *Liberal Rights* (Cambridge University Press, 1993) at 287.
[124] TH Marshall, *Citizenship and Social Class* (Cambridge University Press, 1950) at 11.

'an accelerated raising of the standard of living' which was to be performed by establishing a common market and approximating the **economic** policies of member states. As Hepple[125] notes, the original Title II on Social Policy was a compromise between French and German policies, both grounded in economic considerations.

EC social policy was for a long time hampered by the lack of a clear legislative basis.[126] Articles 94 and 308 (formerly 100 and 235) of the EEC Treaty were used in the 1970s,[127] but, given the terms of Article 94, this meant that much social legislation had to be linked to the common market rather than fulfilling autonomous social goals. Even so, some member states were not in any case too happy with the EEC's social legislation: it was seen to intrude into sensitive areas of national sovereignty and even history, in which disputes about the allocation of public goods and benefits had been resolved only after hard-won battles. So, for example, the UK, Belgium and the Netherlands insisted on a long implementation period for the first social security directive. Other provisions on positive action, retirement and parental leave suffered from neglect and member state vetoes and had to wait for the different climate of the 1990s for implementation. A social policy dimension was conspicuously missing from the 1985 White Paper, and the new Article 100a (now 95), introduced by the Single European Act to bring about legislation based on a majority vote, expressly excluded legislation on the free movement of persons and the rights and interests of employed persons. Even the Community Social Charter of Fundamental Rights of Workers of 1989, which attempted to lay a new foundation for social rights, could do little to remedy this situation, being only a non-binding political declaration. The later social chapter, appended by protocol to the Maastricht Treaty, created no new enforceable fundamental social rights but rather simply made it easier for new measures to be adopted and gave a central role to social dialogue. Fundamental rights to association and to strike were expressly excluded. In the 1990s, a climate more favourable to the pursuance by the EU of social legislation emerged, with the incorporation of the Social Chapter into the EC Treaty and, for example, the 1996 Comité des Sages report on a 'Europe of civic and social rights' stressing the need for the involvement of groups and individuals in the development of citizens' rights, an approach which embraced the cultural as well as the welfare context.[128]

But, for the main part, as Hepple has suggested, 'the legislative and decision making [mechanisms in the EU] remain firmly rooted within a social universe created and shaped by the economics of the market and not by independent social values'.[129]

---

[125] Hepple, see fn 120, at 41.

[126] See Joined Cases 281, 283–285 and 287/87 *Germany and Others v Commission* [1987] ECR 3203, which concerned the Commission's attempted use of Article 118 in its original form as a legal basis.

[127] E.g. Article 308 was used as the basis for the Equal Treatment Directive.

[128] Report by the Comité des Sages chaired by Maria de Lourdes Pintasilgo (OOPEC, 1996).

[129] Hepple, see fn 120, at 46.

Equality and equal treatment

The principle of equal treatment is an essential dimension of social citizenship, even if it has not been expressly linked to citizenship in the EC Treaty. Within EU law, the principle of equal treatment finds no coherent protection. It finds expression in the requirement of equal pay for equal work in Article 141 and the Equal Treatment Directive, both of which concern equality of the sexes. It also applies as a general prohibition on discrimination on grounds of nationality running as a thread through EC law, expressly prohibited in Article 12 and applied by the ECJ in its case law. A more general principle of non-discrimination has been applied as a general principle of law by the Court in certain contexts, for example within agricultural or competition policy. But the principle of equality has not been applied as a free-standing principle at all in other contexts, such as race, religion, or sexual orientation, although, following the introduction of Article 13 EC, it now can be, and has been, used as a basis for introducing such legislation.[130]

Furthermore, as de Búrca observes,[131] the principle of equality has also evaded uniform interpretation by operating in differing ways. Thus, it has been applied instrumentally, so as to help achieve the eradication of obstacles to the single market. It has also functioned as a side-constraint, modifying EU measures. Additionally it has operated as an independent value and goal in its own right.

Equal treatment between the sexes at work: Differentiated citizenship?

Equality on grounds of sex is essential to citizenship. If a woman is not an equal, she is not a full member of the community. Indeed, Kant and Rousseau excluded women from the status of citizenship because they did not perceive women to be equally rational beings and thus capable of full participation in society.[132] Sometimes, the application of these equal treatment provisions in EC law has functioned so as to empower women; however, an exploration of the ECJ's case law reveals some of the dilemmas to be encountered in trying to ensure equal treatment, which may in some circumstances require **special** treatment, a factor noted in the initial discussion on post-national citizenship.

At first glance, EU equal treatment law seems to reveal two different underlying rationales. On the one hand, the aim of a common, or internal, market was and is to strengthen member state economies and bring them close together, the goal being

---

[130] See Council Directive 2000/78/EC establishing a general framework for equal treatment in employment and occupation; Council Directive 2000/43/EC implementing the principle of equal treatment between persons irrespective of racial or ethnic origin. The following decision has also been adopted: Council Decision 2000/750/EC establishing a Community action programme to combat discrimination (2001 to 2006).

[131] G De Búrca, 'The Role of Equality in European Community Law' in Dashwood and O'Leary (eds), *The Principle of Equality in Community Law* (Sweet and Maxwell, 1997).

[132] For an analysis of Rousseau's treatment of women see e.g. Schwartz, *The Sexual Politics of Jean Jacques Rousseau* (University of Chicago Press, 1984).

an economic one: the individual being seen as a factor of production, a close relative to our old friend the market citizen. On the other hand, some case law under
Article 141 reveals attempts to perceive the worker as a **human being.**[133] The
European Court refers to Article 141 as a 'fundamental right'.[134] But it must be
remembered that Article 141 was originally inserted at the demand of the French,
who, having more advanced non-discrimination laws on equal pay than the rest of
Europe at that time, were anxious to secure that they would not be at a competitive
disadvantage by the relocation of work in member states more profitable to employers, so its impetus was very much economic.

In the area of discrimination, one strategy (preferred by feminists of a certain 'liberal' sort) has sought to remedy the exclusion of women from the full status of legal
subject by insistence on sex-blind equality. Discrimination takes place if a woman in
the same or similar situation to a man is treated differently. EU law clearly sometimes takes this approach: there is no defence to a charge of direct discrimination
under Article 141. This approach seems to rely on a neutral conception of citizenship and legal subjecthood. But, it is argued, this equal treatment approach in fact
assumes a substantially **male** conception of legal subjectivity. Catherine Mackinnon
makes the point this way – that equality conceals 'the substantive way in which man
has become the measure of all things'.[135] This legal conception of subjecthood based
on formal equality has functioned as an obstacle to women's progress. Equal citizenship has not led to social justice and equality. If social citizenship is to fulfil its
potential as a vehicle to full membership in society, we must move beyond these paradigms and utilise a concept of equality that enables us to do so.

The concept of indirect discrimination attempts to redress the problematic dominance of the male norm. Indirect discrimination addresses situations in which
employment practices, while treating both sexes alike in the formal sense, have the
effect of excluding more women than men. This concept is not included in Article
141 but has been developed in the case law of the European Court, especially in
those cases dealing with part-time workers.[136] In these cases, the Court appears to
recognise that the anti-discrimination principle extends beyond requiring women to
conform to the male norm of full-time working. So, for example, in the case of *Bilka
Kaufhaus*,[137] the European Court held that the arrangement whereby part-time
employees could obtain pensions under an occupational scheme only if they had
worked full time for fifteen out of twenty years was capable of constituting discrimination, although it would be capable of objective justification if it could be

---

[133] An expression used in the context of free movement of persons by AG Trabucchi in Case 7/75
F v Belgian State [1975] ECR 679.
[134] Case 149/77 *Defrenne II* [1978] ECR 1365, para 27: 'There can be no doubt that the elimination of
discrimination based on sex forms part of those fundamental rights.'
[135] C Mackinnon, *Feminism Unmodified: Discourses in Life and Law* (Harvard University Press, 1987)
36.
[136] See most recently Case C-167/97 *Seymour-Smith and Perez* [1999] ECR I-623. It has also been
applied by the Court in the field of free movement of workers: see Case 379/87 *Groener v Minister of
Education* [1989] ECR 3967; Case 152/73 *Sotgiu v Deutsche Bundespost* [1974] ECR 153.
[137] Case 170/84 *Bilka Kaufhaus* [1986] ECR 1607.

shown to correspond to a real need on the part of the undertaking.[138] However, there are limits on the reach of indirect discrimination. First, as mentioned, the employer may argue that the practices are justified for reasons not due to the sex of the worker, such as 'a real need on the part of the undertaking'[139] (and, thus, market forces may be used to justify indirect discrimination, albeit in accordance with the principle of proportionality)[140] or a 'necessary aim of social policy'.[141]

In such cases, equal treatment cannot be seen as a fundamental right but merely as a presumption which can be trumped.[142] Second, on a practical level, this approach does not make sufficient inroads into the male norm: it does not demand resolution of the underlying structural problems which beset women in the workplace.[143]

An alternative approach seeks not to efface difference (whether between sexes, races, nations, etc.) but instead to transcend comparisons with a male norm, by acknowledging certain characteristics as unique and special, and by using legislation to protect differences between the sexes, an approach sometimes known as 'difference' feminism.[144] The conception of subjecthood, it claims, should not be based on the neutral, rational, male norm springing from the Kantian conception, but instead a conception which seeks to respect difference while treating people as equals and to recognise the radical potential of that injunction.

Are there any traces of this conception in EU law? It has been suggested that it is in the subject of pregnancy that the European Court has made the greatest strides in protecting equality by recognising special rights for specific situations. It may in this context be contrasted to some approaches of the English courts, which held that, to establish discrimination, a woman must show that she had been treated less favourably than a man would have been treated. In the early case of *Turley* v *Alders*[145] it was held that dismissal on grounds of pregnancy could not constitute discrimination under the Sex Discrimination Act 1975, there being no male comparator. But this approach is inadequate: pregnancy as a genuine difference should be treated as such without forced comparison with a male norm. In *Dekker*[146] the European Court held that the Equal Treatment Directive protected a woman denied a job on grounds of pregnancy despite being the most suitable applicant and did not attempt to formulate the claim by reference to a male comparator. Instead it held that

---

[138] See also Case 127/92 *Enderby* v *Frenchay* [1993] ECR 5535; Case 33/89 *Kowalska* [1990] ECR 2591; Case C-1/95 *Hellen Gerster* v *Freistaat Bayern* [1997] ECR I-5253; Case C-100/96 *Brigitte Kording* v *Senator für Finanzen* [1997] ECR I-5289.

[139] The requirement laid down by the ECJ in the *Bilka* case at para 36 of the judgment.

[140] The ECJ has also engaged in judicial legislation to mitigate the temporal effects of its judgments so as to reduce costs on employer and pension funds: see Case C-109/91 *Ten Oever* [1993] ECR I-4879 and Case C-262/88 *Barber* [1990] ECR I-1889.

[141] Laid down in Case 171/88 *Rinner-Kuhn* [1989] ECR 2743 at para 14 of the Court's judgment.

[142] As pointed out by Fredman in 'European Community Discrimination Law: A Critique' (1992) 21 ILJ 119 at 125.

[143] Although it is likely that Directive 97/81 on part-time work [1997] OJ L14/9, aiming at the removal of discrimination against part-timers, may do something to remedy this.

[144] See N Lacey, *Unspeakable Subjects* (Hart Publishing, 1998) at 191.

[145] *Turley* v *Alders Department Stores Ltd* [1980] ICR 66.

[146] Case C-177/88 *Dekker* [1990] ECR I-3941.

the most important reason for refusal to recruit applied exclusively to one sex: only a woman can be refused employment on grounds of pregnancy and such a refusal was direct discrimination. Thus the Court refused to allow economic considerations to override the social dimension and to affect its perceptions of a right to equality. This approach acknowledges pregnancy as unique and special, a feature of women, rather than a flaw comparable to disability in men.[147] The Preamble to the Pregnant Workers Directive, 92/85,[148] also seems to reject a conflation of pregnancy and illness by stating: 'the concept of an adequate allowance in this case of maternity leave...should in no circumstances be interpreted as suggesting an analogy between pregnancy and illness'.[149]

There are, however, conceptual difficulties in moving away from the paradigm of neutrality, towards a concept of differentiated citizenship. Iris Marion Young suggests that, in such circumstances, the situation calling for different treatment should be understood, not as lodged in the differently treated workers *per se*, but as in their interaction with the structure and norms of the workplace. In this way, the claim for special rights is perceived not as a need to compensate for an inferiority, 'but as a positive assertion of specificity in different forms of life'.[150] Just how far should law go in respecting difference? There may be a thin line between recognising difference and undesirable stereotyping. The thinness of this line is revealed at a conceptual level by the attempt of the French feminist and psychoanalyst, Luce Irigary, to redefine the category of rights. Irigary critiques the capacity and contractual-based notion of the subject as rights bearer, suggesting that redefining the right to civil identity is one of the urgent tasks of our time. However, many of the images which Irigary invokes – virginity, motherhood, peace and so on – resonate with conventional images of womanhood and may have adverse rhetorical effects from a feminist point of view. In *Je, Tu, Nous*, Irigary proposes 'a right to motherhood as a component of female identity. If the body is a legal concern, and it is, then the female body must be civilly identified a virgin and potential mother.'[151] Not necessarily a strategy to the benefit of women, and one illustrating the 'double bind'[152] in the strive for equality.

---

[147] But in other cases, the equivocal nature of equality has asserted itself. In Case C-179/88 *Hertz* [1990] ECR I-3979 the ECJ held that where pregnancy-related illness extends beyond the period of maternity leave, there must again be comparisons with a male comparator. This approach was again upheld in Case C-400/95 *Elisabeth Larsson* [1997] ECR I-2527, where the ECJ held that there was no reason to distinguish a pregnancy-related illness from any other type. But in Case C-394/96 *Brown v Rentokil* [1998] ECR I-4185, in a ruling that seemed to conflict with *Hertz* and *Larsson*, the Court held that there could be no dismissal at any time in pregnancy for absence due to a pregnancy-related illness. This approach is preferable: if pregnancy is unique to women then surely so are its consequences. See also, more recently, Case C-207/98 *Mahlburg* [2000] ECR I-549 in which the Court held that it was contrary to EC law to refuse to appoint a woman for an indefinite period on grounds of pregnancy, and Case C-109/00 *Melgar* [2001] ECR 000, in which the Court held that the dismissal of a pregnant woman constituted direct discrimination, even if her contract was for a limited period.

[148] [1992] OJ L348/1.

[149] However, the Pregnancy Directive also moves away from treating pregnancy as an issue of equal treatment by adopting as a legal basis Article 138 on the health and safety of workers.

[150] I-M Young, see fn 57, at 220.

[151] L Irigary, *Je Tu Nous* (Routledge, 1993) at 88.

[152] A term taken from Lacey, in 'Feminist Legal Theory Beyond Neutrality' (1995) 48 Current Legal Problems 10.

The problems involved in developing a concept of differentiated citizenship have been subject to consideration in decisions under the Equal Treatment Directive, which raise some issues already discussed, in particular that of 'double bind' and special rights. In the case of *Eckhard Kalanke*,[153] Mr Kalanke and Ms Glissmann were found to be equally well qualified for the promotion for which they were applying. This finding then triggered the application of a German law, the *Landgleichstellungsgesetz* on equal treatment for men and women in the public service, which provides that priority should be given to women in a tie-break situation. A reference was made to the European Court regarding the compatibility of the Bremen *Land* law with the Equal Treatment Directive, Article 2(1) of which provides: '[t]he principle of equal treatment shall mean that there shall be no discrimination whatsoever on grounds of sex either directly or indirectly or by reference to marital or family status'.

The Court, following the Advocate General, held that the Bremen positive discrimination system was not compatible with Article 2(1). Notable in the approach of the Advocate General is the assumption that the male is the norm, that substantive equality places women in the same position as men.[154] This approach was followed by the Court. It has been suggested that '*Kalanke* might be characterised as a typical liberal holding, giving absolute priority to the individual right not to be discriminated against'.[155]

The issue of positive discrimination raises crucial issues of neutrality, equality, and special rights. A 'neutral' application of equal treatment provisions, some suggest, requires treating men and women alike – there shall be no discrimination. Positive discrimination, it is alleged, breaches this principle. On the other hand a 'neutral' approach may ignore endemic structural inequality in society, which is why positive discrimination is thought necessary in the first place. Appointing a woman over an equally qualified man, or applying a quota system, it is argued, cannot be an example of discrimination, because to treat it as such would be to override equality as a societal goal. This is familiar territory in US constitutional law. In the US Supreme Court, Justice Stevens, dissenting in the *Adarand*[156] case (where the majority found a federal affirmative action scheme to be unconstitutional), held that invalidating such a programme on account of its violation of equal treatment ignored the difference between a 'no trespassing' sign and a 'welcome' mat.[157]

Such a result in the *Kalanke* case brought the European Court in line with the US precedents, which are full of the language of neutrality, of the 'color blind' constitution, and brings the EU firmly in line with the image of the neutral autonomous rights bearer. Here the European Court found a 'sex blind' Directive.

---

[153] Case C-450/93 *Eckhard Kalanke* v *Freie Hansestadt Bremen* [1995] ECR I-3051.

[154] *Kalanke*, above fn 153, para 15.

[155] See Peters, 'The Many Meanings of Equality and Discrimination – A Conceptual Analysis' (1996) 2 ELJ at 192.

[156] *Adarand Constructors Inc.* v *Federico Pena* (1995) 112 S Ct 2097.

[157] For a commentary on *Adarand* see S Douglas-Scott, 'Affirmative Action in the US Supreme Court' (1997) Public Law 43–54.

The EC Treaty has been amended to counteract the Court's judgment in *Kalanke*, notably in Article 3(2) EC, to read, '[i]n all the activities referred to in this article, the Community shall aim to eliminate inequalities and to promote equality between men and women'. Article 141(4) includes a positive action programme 'with a view to ensuring full equality in practice'. In the *Marschall* case[158] the European Court, contrary to the opinion of Advocate General Jacobs,[159] upheld a similar *Gleichstellungsgesetz* requiring priority for women in the context of 'equal suitability, competence and professional performance' but this case is not directly comparable to *Kalanke*, as the provision in question also contained a 'savings' clause by which the female candidate need not be preferred if 'reasons specific to the male candidate tilted the balance in his favour'. However, the Court seemed to recognise that formal equality of opportunity might be insufficient to ensure equality in practice, as it stated that 'the mere fact that a male candidate and a female candidate are equally qualified does not mean they have the same chances'.[160]

A more general non-discrimination right?

At present EC law does little to protect the equal rights of groups such as gays, lesbians, and ethnic minorities. Until recently, there were no specific provisions equivalent to those discussed which secure equal pay and treatment for women, although Article 13 now provides a basis for such legislation. Recent case law demonstrates how the achievement of full citizenship status by minority groups can be impeded by a lack of specific legislation, as well as by conservative interpretations of the principle of equality.

P v S and Cornwall CC[161] is the most intriguing in its implications. P had not been allowed to continue her job with Cornwall CC following a sex change operation. The argument had been put that this refusal could not be discrimination on grounds of sex as that required male/female comparisons, and here any alleged discrimination was due to the applicant's sex change. The Court did not accept this, holding the Council to be in breach of Article 2(1) of the Equal Treatment Directive stating, 'to tolerate such discrimination would be tantamount, as regards such a person, to a failure to respect the dignity and freedom to which he or she is entitled and which the court has a duty to safeguard'.[162] Advocate General Tesauro was more expansive in his opinion, stating that, while there was no explicit provision specifically and literally intended to regulate the problem, such a

---

[158] Case C-409/95 *Marschall* v *Nordrhein Westfalen* [1997] ECR I-6363.

[159] AG Jacobs found at para 47 of his Opinion the provision to infringe the Equal Treatment Directive on the basis that it went further than promoting equality of opportunity and required equality of result (a test which he held to have been set by the Court in *Kalanke*). Other cases have followed along similar lines, e.g. Case C-407/98 *Abrahamsson and Anderson* [2000] ECR I 5539; and Case C-158/97 *Badeck* [2000] ECR I 1875.

[160] *Marschall*, see fn 158, para 30.

[161] Case C-13/94 *P v S and Cornwall CC* [1996] ECR I-2143.

[162] Ibid., at para 22.

provision could be readily and clearly inferred from the principles and objectives of Community social law, observing:

> I regard as obsolete the idea that the law should take into consideration and protect, a woman who has suffered discrimination in comparison with a man, or vice versa, but denies that protection to those who are **discriminated against**, again by reason of sex, merely because they fall outside the traditional man/woman classification.[163]

What to make of this? It is a decision which one can only applaud, impressive in its rhetoric. Paragraph 17 rejects the need for any male/female comparison,[164] thus appearing to escape the pitfalls of the neutral, rights bearer standard, and also appearing to take us well beyond our traditional conceptions of personhood. Yet it was Tesauro who, in *Kalanke*, found the Bremen scheme to be in breach of the Equal Treatment Directive. Is it possible to applaud *P v S* and to dislike *Kalanke*, based as they both are on the Equal Treatment Directive and the imperative of equal treatment?

However, in *Grant v South West Trains*[165] the European Court seemed less willing to protect homosexuals than transsexuals. Ms Grant had contested South West Trains' refusal to award her female partner travel concessions which, under her contract, were granted to married members of staff and to common law partners of the opposite sex. The European Court held that this refusal did not constitute discrimination prohibited by Article 141 or Directive 75/117,[166] holding that, because SWT's regulations applied in the same way to both male and female members of staff, this could not be interpreted as constituting discrimination on grounds of sex–discrimination on grounds of sexual orientation was not 'based essentially on sex'. The Court seemed content to note that, under the Treaty of Amsterdam, the EU has been able to take measures to eliminate discrimination based on sexual orientation,[167] thus preferring to leave sexual orientation discrimination to be dealt with by the political institutions.[168] One may however have cause to be optimistic given

---

[163] AG Tesauro in *P v S*, see fn 161, at para 17 (emphasis in original).

[164] This parallels the insertion of a new general non-discrimination clause in Article 13 by the Treaty of Amsterdam.

[165] Case C-249/96 *Jacqueline Grant v South West Trains* [1998] ECR I-621.

[166] The relevant secondary legislation dealing with equal pay.

[167] See Article 13 introduced by the Amsterdam Treaty. The relevant Directives which have so far been adopted under Article 13 EC (but are not yet in force) are detailed in fn 130.

[168] For a commentary on the *Grant* case see Wintemute, 'Recognising New Kinds of Direct Sex Discrimination (1997) 60 MLR 344. Another opportunity to assess whether discrimination on the basis of sexual orientation is contrary to the Equal Treatment Directive was lost when Case C-168/97 *R v Secretary of State for Defence, ex parte Perkins* [1997] 3 CMLR 310 was withdrawn. But see Case C-273/97 *Sirdar v Army Board* [1999] ECR I-7403, in which AG La Pergola rejected the argument that defence matters fell within the exclusive competence of the State, illustrating a willingness to scrutinise discrimination in the armed services. But the ECJ ruled that the Royal Marines was a special combat unit for which sex was a determining factor; they were entitled to exclude women. See also Case C-285/98 *Kreil v Germany* [2000] ECR I 169, in which a female applicant challenged, on the basis of the Equal Treatment Directive, the German law which excluded women from joining the armed services. The ECJ held that legislation barring women outright from army jobs was contrary to the principle of equal treatment, although derogation might be possible where sex constituted a determining factor for access to some special combat units.

the speedy introduction of non-discrimination legislation under Article 13. *Grant* was followed by *D v Council*[169] in which the CFI showed itself unwilling to assimilate homosexual stable relationships to those of married persons, holding that a Community official living with a same sex partner was not entitled to a household allowance.

An alternative approach, not taken by the Court in *Grant*, would have been to broaden the way in which the legal imagination conceives of sex and gender, and to seek to shift from rigid formalities of male/female to a recognition of sex and gender as a continuum or spectrum, a recognition of the possibility of differentiated identities. In this respect it is a clear retreat from *P v S*, in which the Court, as stated by Advocate General Elmer in *Grant*, took a decisive step away from interpreting the principle of equal treatment on the basis of the traditional comparison between male and female. The application of equality as an **individual** right, and especially as a principle of consistency, may also overlook the fact that what is required is the recognition of an individual's relationship with others, the value of their group identity. The impulse to atomise individuals has to be resisted.

The dilemmas thrown up by these cases reveal some of the problems specific to the notion of equality and, more particularly, the problems to be encountered in developing an inclusive concept of social citizenship. The goal for the EU must be to find a way of promoting an equal citizenship which does not suffer from the 'dilemma of difference'[170] or the 'double bind' identified by feminists.

The broadening of non-discrimination on grounds of nationality

The operation of the equality principle has also always been problematic in cases where the application of EC law has been unclear. Where there has been no economic activity it has been unusual for Article 12 EC to operate so as to give rise to equal treatment in the field of social assistance, for example. The potential welfare burdens on member states and the dangers of 'welfare tourism' were thought to rule this out. Therefore, in the *Brown*[171] case, the ECJ held that a migrant student would not be entitled to a maintenance grant on an equal footing with national students, unless they could directly link their studies with their status as a worker.[172] In *Lebon*,[173] the child of a retired migrant worker in Belgium, who was over 21 and not dependent on her parent, nor qualified as a worker herself, was not able to claim unemployment benefit. On the other hand, in the *Cowan*[174] case, the ECJ held that

---

[169] As already detailed at fn 130.

[170] M Minow, 'Learning to Live with the Dilemma of Difference' [1985] *Law and Contemporary Problems* 157.

[171] Case 197/86 *Brown v Secretary of State for Scotland* [1988] ECR 3205.

[172] In which case they could claim the grant under Article 7 of Regulation 1612/68 [1968] 10 L257/2: see Case 39/86 *Lair v Universitat Hannover* [1988] ECR 3161.

[173] Case 316/85 *Lebon* [1987] ECR 2811.

[174] Case 186/87 *Cowan v Le Trésor Public* [1989] ECR 195.

a British tourist mugged in Paris was entitled to compensation for his injuries on an equal basis to a French national. Notably, this entitlement was reasoned on the rather tendentious basis of a right to receive services under Article 49.

Perhaps at last the equal treatment principle may have been divorced from the need for economic activity, and thus from the shackles of market citizenship. The ECJ seems to have made a move in this direction in *Martinez Sala*,[175] which has already been discussed in the context of market citizenship, and which Fries and Shaw describe as 'representing the beginning of a new phase of EU incursion into national welfare sovereignty'.[176] They suggest that, since *Martinez Sala*, we are now close to a universal non-discrimination right. The basis for this suggestion is the ECJ's finding that 'a citizen of the European Union...can rely on Article 6 [now 12] of the Treaty in all situations which fall within the scope *ratione materiae* of Community law, including the situation where that Member State delays or refuses to grant to that claimant a benefit that is provided to all persons lawfully resident'.[177] This holding seems to eradicate linkages which were previously required for the non-discrimination requirement to apply.

Given this apparent expansion of the scope of the non-discrimination principle in *Martinez Sala*, what then is the status of cases such as *Brown* or *Lebon*? The *Brown* decision seems to have been justified on the basis of a lack of EC competence in the field of education and a recognition of the problems which member states would suffer if there were a Community-wide entitlement to maintenance grants. However, this reasoning seems incompatible with *Cowan* and *Martinez Sala*, in which the ECJ would not let the exercise of a Community law right be restricted by virtue of the fact that public funds were implicated. As if at least to partly confirm this reading, the ECJ held in the *Grzelczyk*[178] case that students residing in a member state other than their own are entitled to receive a minimum subsistance allowance on the same conditions as those of the host national state. The Court did however qualify this by stating that member states may still require students to declare (in accordance with the relevant Directive) that they have sufficient resources to avoid becoming a burden on the host member state. But it also stressed that a student's position may change, so they may subsequently have recourse to assistance. The Court specifically justified its holding by reference to the provisions on citizenship and non-discrimination in the EC treaty.

Grzelczyk may seem like some sort of half-way house. However, there will be considerable opposition from member states if the widest interpretation of *Martinez Sala* is taken. On the one hand, it seems that there will not be effective enjoyment of meaningful social rights as part of Community citizenship until equality in the field of social benefits is divorced from the role played by the citizen in the process of economic integration. On the other hand, social policy is highly contentious, both

---

[175] Case C-85/96 *Martinez Sala* [1998] ECR I-2691.
[176] S Fries and J Shaw, 'Citizenship of the Union: First Steps in the ECJ?' (1998) 4 European Public Law 53.
[177] *Martinez Sala*, see fn 175, at para 61.
[178] Case C-184/99 *Grzelczyk* [2001] ECR I 6193.

at the national level, where the welfare provisions of the different states of the EU have different policy and historical foundations, and in the context of the EU, whose democratic deficit makes it a controversial forum for contested policy. If the wide interpretation of *Martinez Sala* is taken possible long-term consequences may include a re-thinking of national social policy and the scope of entitlements with a race to the lowest levels of provision.[179]

Martinez Sala could be seen as one of a series of cases in which the ECJ and its Advocates General have attempted to extend the scope of the non-discrimination principle, such as *Cowan, Konstantinidis,* and *Bickel and Franz.* In *Bickel and Franz,*[180] an Austrian and a German national were charged with criminal offences in Bolzano, a town in the Trentino-Alto Adige region of Italy, in which, due to the presence of a German-speaking minority, Italian residents had the right to use German in criminal proceedings. Bickel and Franz wanted the proceedings to be conducted in German but had been denied this by the authorities. The ECJ held that the subject matter of the case fell within the EC Treaty (on the basis of Article 49, *Cowan,* and Article 18) and that Article 12 would be breached if proceedings were not held in German. Advocate General Jacobs went even further, suggesting that, even though it was unnecessary to determine whether all criminal proceedings against a citizen fell within the scope of the treaty for the purposes of Article 12, regardless of whether the citizen had exercised his or her right to free movement, such a question should be answered affirmatively, given that citizenship of the Union was introduced partly to give expression to the EU's character 'as more than a purely economic union'.[181] This, albeit an *obiter* statement, is a wide-reaching conception of the possible expansion of Articles 18 and 12 which the Advocate General held out to the Court, for future consideration.

There still remains the problematic status of Article 18. The Court in *Martinez Sala* did not make clear the basis of the applicant's lawful residence in Germany. If she was lawfully resident, not under EC law, but on the basis of national law (since the German authorities had not requested her to leave), then it may be the case that member states will have an incentive to exclude citizens whose status under EC law is questionable (i.e. because they are not economically active or do not satisfy the provisions of the directives).[182] As O'Leary notes, the policing of migrants would be more difficult in the UK and Ireland, which do not make use of identity cards but control migrants at the point of entry.[183] The ECJ has also, recently, in the *Swaddling* decision,[184] made inroads into the UK's test of 'habitual residence', which was supposed to prevent 'welfare tourism'. However, British nationals

---

[179] See Fries and Shaw, fn 172, at 558.

[180] Case C-274/96 *Criminal Proceedings against Bickel and Franz* [1998] ECR I-7637.

[181] Ibid., paras 23 and 24.

[182] In *R v City of Westminster, ex parte Castelli* (1996) 28 Housing Law Reports 616, in the context of a homeless Italian migrant who was HIV positive, the Court of Appeal seemed to suggest that, until the UK took steps to exclude the applicant, he was not unlawfully resident in the UK and was entitled to benefit.

[183] S O'Leary, 'Putting Flesh on the Bones of European Union Citizenship' (1999) 24 EL Rev 68 at 78.

[184] Case C-90/97 *Swaddling* v *Adjudication Officer* [1999] ECR I-1075.

returning from other EC countries were as likely to fail the test of habitual residence as migrants from elsewhere. In *Swaddling*, the applicant, a UK national, had been working in France, and argued that the application of the habitual residence test to UK nationals returning from working abroad was contrary to Article 39 as it hindered free movement. The ECJ agreed, holding that the UK authorities must take into account previous periods of residence in the UK.

Therefore, if *Martinez Sala* does involve a broadening of the concept of Union citizenship (and that remains to be seen, given, for example, the disappointment of *Grant*, following on from *P v S*) it also brings the danger of a reaction from member states, such as expulsion of non-nationals of questionable status, or a possible lowering of the level of benefits under state social security and assistance schemes, if EC law is seen to be intruding into national welfare law. The demands of social citizenship will not be easy to resolve.

REALISING EUROPEAN CITIZENSHIP

European citizenship is a fragmented concept, difficult to present coherently, as well as not yet fully actualised. Its future hangs from threads which are currently woven into the fabric of EC law, some dormant, some of which may peter out. However, it cannot be built on the back of just one of these threads, but must emerge from a complex, interwoven design. A vision of citizenship which conceives of individuals only as instruments of the market will not capture the hearts and minds of Europeans. Clearly, however, the political and social aspects of citizenship are difficult to resolve in the EU and raise threats to national sovereignty. This will take time to manage.

It is important for EU law to develop and embrace a complex notion of citizenship which is capable of capturing the different identities, attachments, and aspects of their personhood which individuals adopt in a multicultural supranational community. As Lacey and Frazer write: '[o]nce we recognise the complexity of human subjectivity – the way in which we can hold multiple commitments, relationships, views, desires and roles together without collapsing under the weight of incoherence – the idea of the unitary subject becomes less attractive'.[185] These particular tensions may lead us in the EU context to a richer conception of citizenship. But we must recognise that this will bring difficulties and double binds, and even perplexity.

---

[185] E Frazer and N Lacey, *The Politics of Community* (Harvester Wheatsheaf, 1993) at 199.

15

A CONSTITUTION FOR EUROPE?

'Neither morals, nor riches, nor discipline of armies,
nor all these together will do without a constitution'

(*John Adams*)

This final chapter starts with two (briefly argued) premises. They are not particularly controversial, but lead fairly swiftly to a third point, which is the kernel of the argument. The first is that the EU already has some sort of Constitution, albeit not one in the traditional sense. The second is that the existing constitutional order in Europe is now problematic and unsatisfactory. It is in a state of flux, and best seen as a plurality of overlapping orders, as characterised by MacCormick and others.[1] This being the case, there will inevitably be problems regarding the relationship of these orders, and the question of ultimate authority, which cannot be resolved by recourse to the traditional hierarchical legal order posed by legal theory. This European polity is also unsatisfactory; even if the state is not taken as a model for constitutionalism, the EU is too undemocratic, too chaotic, too impenetrable to be meaningful to today's Europeans, to capture their hearts and minds, their imagination and their respect. New solutions have to be found for this new constitutional age. The third and major question which therefore arises is: how can we do better? What issues should a reforming European constitutionalism address? How might it resolve them? This last question involves issues of law and politics, political theory and philosophy. The conclusion on these issues will be the (perhaps unfashionable) contention that Europe needs a remodelled, clearly principled constitutional framework, built on a foundation of shared values, and that, although Europeans may engage in mutual conversations over their legal and political order, a new constitutional architecture will be as significant for the developing European polity as a flourishing discursive democracy. Whether the EU will obtain such a meaningful constitutional framework depends on future developments – including the deliberations of the convention on the future of the EU, and on what is decided at the IGC in 2004.

---

[1] As discussed in Chapter 7.

(1) THE EU ALREADY HAS A CONSTITUTION

Elements of a constitution

The notion of what is a constitution is, of course, as much contested as the concepts of justice or law. This vexed issue will not be directly addressed, but rather the very broad definition provided in *The Oxford Companion to Law* will be adopted, which defines a constitution as: 'the basic principles and laws of a nation, state, or social group that determine the powers and duties of the government and guarantee certain rights to the people'.

Such a definition might seem so broad as to be almost banal. This is not, however, fatal, as at this stage, the concept is being addressed only in what in Dworkin has described as a pre-interpretive sense,[2] rather than an in-depth analysis which would consider the point of constitutions, what they are for.

Thus, within the body of EU law we have important elements of what are to be found in a Constitution understood in this very broad sense. All of these have been discussed in previous chapters of this book and they may be summarised in the following way:

(a) The EU treaties operate constitutionally, they go well beyond what is usually to be found in treaties of international law. The EC has exclusive competence (legislative sovereignty) over a very wide range of matters, and, in a departure from intergovernmentalism, a huge amount of legislation is passed on the basis of qualified majority voting in the Council of Ministers, and takes effect immediately without need for transposition into international law. Even if the EEC did conform to the status of international organisation in its early days (which is unlikely) it has now moved well beyond that.[3]

(b) The EU has institutions which function in ways comparable to government. It has a Parliament which is directly elected and whose powers have considerably increased since the early days, most recently with the Treaty of Nice, which increased its powers of legislative co-decision with the Council of Ministers. This adds a political and democratic element not usually found in international organisations.

(c) The European Court of Justice has made its contribution. It is common in this context to read of how the European court has 'constitutionalised' the

---

[2] See R Dworkin, *Law's Empire*, (Fontana 1986) chaps 2 and 3.

[3] Evidence of this may be found in the fact that the EU treaties may not be amended according to the rules of international law. Under international law parties to a treaty may revoke it at any time, even disregarding provisions in the treaty stipulating a special procedure for amendment and withdrawal: see the Vienna Convention 1968. Although in its early days, the EEC treaty was amended in this way, more recently the ECJ has held that the treaties may only be amended according to Article 48(1), a statement which would be illegitimate if the EU existed only according to the norms of international law. See Pescatore, *L'ordre juridique dés Communauté européennes* (Liége: Presses universitaires de Liége, 1975) 62–3.

treaties.[4] Federico Mancini, a judge of the European Court, wrote in 1989 that 'If one were asked to synthetise the direction in which the case law produced in Luxembourg has moved since 1957, one would have to say that it coincides with the making of a constitution for Europe.'[5] The doctrine of supremacy of Community law, established in *Costa, Internationale Handelsgesellschaft, Simmenthal* and *Factortame*,[6] is a keystone of the doctrine of European constitutionality. Equally important is the doctrine of the direct effect of Community law, originally introduced in *Van Gend en Loos*, which provides that much of EC law is directly effective, giving individuals rights which can be enforced in their national courts.[7]

In other case law the ECJ has stressed the constitutional status of the treaties, describing them as a 'constitutional charter' in *Les Verts* and its first opinion on the draft EEA agreement, *Opinion, 1/91*.[8]

(d) The EU treaties manifest other features which may be considered constitutional. A commitment to the rule of law and fundamental rights, for example. Article 6 of the TEU states, 'The Union is founded on the principles of liberty, democracy, respect for human rights and fundamental freedoms, and the rule of law, principles which are common to the Member States.' In *Les Verts*, the ECJ stated that the EC 'is a Community based on the rule of law, inasmuch as neither its member states nor its institutions can avoid a review of the question whether the measures adopted by them are in conformity with the basic constitutional charter, the Treaty'. According to Jean-Claude Piris, 'this means the Treaty has superior legal values, in the same way as a Constitution does . . . The rule of law is perhaps the most fundamental of constitutional guarantees, because all other values depend on it, for them to be upheld at all.'[9]

Article 6(2) TEU goes on to strengthen the Union's commitment to fundamental rights, by stating 'the Union shall respect fundamental rights, as guaranteed by the European Convention . . . and as they result from the constitutional traditions common to the member States, as general principles of Community law', a provision which reinforces existing ECJ case law. The EU has also, since December 2000, possessed its own, albeit non-binding, Charter of Fundamental Rights.

(e) Finally, there is the somewhat vexed question of the division of powers between the EU and its member states. It is now difficult to fathom where

---

[4] Weiler refers to the 'constitutionalisation of the Community legal structure' naming the doctrine of supremacy as one key doctrine in the constitutionalising of the treaties. Weiler, *The Transformation of Europe'* at (1991) 100 Yale LJ 2413. See also the discussion in Chapters 5–9 of this book.

[5] Mancini, *The Making of a Constitution for Europe* (1989) 26 CMLRev 5933.

[6] Case 6/64 *Flaminio Costa v ENEL* [1964] ECR 1251; Case 11/70 *Internationale Handelsgesellschaft* [1970] ECR 1125; Case 106/77 *Simmenthal* [1978] ECR 629; Case C-213/89 *R v Secretary of State for Transport, ex parte Factortame* [1990] ECR I 2243.

[7] Case 26/62 *Van Gend en Loos* [1963] ECR 1.

[8] Case 294/83 *Parti Ecologiste 'Les Verts' v European Parliament* [1986] ECR 1339; *Opinion 1/91 (Draft Opinion on the EEA)* [1991] ECR I-6079.

[9] Jean-Claude Piris, 'Does the European Union have a Constitution? Does it need one?' (1999) 24 EL Rev 557 at 561.

any remaining core of state sovereignty might reside. The somewhat relentless process of European integration, particularly in its swifter form of the
1980s and 1990s, along with the introduction of qualified majority voting
and completion of the internal market, has removed many areas of state competence (as maintained by the 'spillover' concept of functionalist theory).[10]
Thus, for example, transfer of competence in Justice and Home affairs to
intergovernmental level, results in an encroachment of state sovereignty in
matters of national security.[11]

Many federal constitutions set out a division of competence between the federal government and its constituent units. While edging toward constitutionality,
the EC treaty is silent about the division of competence between the EC and the
member states, although of course it allocated the power to act to the EC in certain areas. The division of powers is thus unclear. The ECJ, as might be expected,
has developed a jurisprudence regarding the respective competences of the EC
and member states, through the development of the doctrines of exclusivity and
pre-emption. In some areas, such as the Common Commercial Policy, it has held
that the EC is exclusively competent.[12] Elsewhere, there is concurrent competence, and if the EC has not acted in a particular area, the member states may
take action. However, for the member states, as Lenaerts[13] writes, there is 'no
constitutionally protected nucleus of sovereignty'.

'A new legal order'

Given that this 'new legal order' of the EU demonstrates such features, it is not
surprising that even the *Bundesverfassungsgericht*, in its now famous *Maastricht
Urteil*, was forced to concede that the treaties were 'in a certain sense' the EU's
constitution.[14] However, although the EU may 'in a certain sense' possess a constitution, this is not the sense in which its member states do so. The EU fails to
conform to the traditional state paradigm for the following reasons:

(a) Although sovereign in many areas, it lacks the full sovereignty often seen as
    characteristic of the modern state. It lacks the omnicompetence of say the
    Hobbesian or Austinian sovereign. The EC and EU have no independent sover-
    eignty or '*Kompetenz-Kompetenz*'.[15] As a corollary of this, it lacks complete
    authority over all persons and things within its territory (it governs by way of

---

[10] See e.g. L N Lindberg, *The Political Dynamics of European Integration* (OUP, 1963) for an example
of a neo-functionalist approach to European integration.

[11] Since the Treaty of Amsterdam, a substantial section of the Justice and Home affairs pillar has been
transferred to Title IV of the EC treaty, and the remaining section renamed Police and Judicial
Cooperation in Criminal matters.

[12] *Opinion 1/75* [1975] ECR 1355.

[13] K Lenaerts, *Constitutionalism and the Many Faces of Federalism* (1990) 38 AJCL 205–63 at 220.

[14] Although the BverfG went on to conclude that the member states were still the '*Herren der Vertrage*'
or 'masters of the treaty'. *Brunner v The European Union Treaty* [1994] 1 CMLR 57 at para 55 (p 83).

[15] Although the ECJ sometimes gives the impression that they do: Case 314/85 *Foto-Frost (Firma)* v
Hauptzollamt Lubeck-Ost [1987] ECR 4199.

attributed powers: under Article 5 EC it may legislate only in those areas covered by the treaties). It lacks **external** sovereignty in all areas of international relations, a key feature of the state in international law. It may conclude treaties only for those matters within its field of competence. And it has no power to wage war or to make peace (although the CFSP is being developed).[16]

Furthermore, it also lacks the **indivisibility** of traditional sovereignty as there is no single, law-creating body within the EU.

(b) The EU's system of governance is incomplete. It lacks the legal means and administration, finances and coercive force of its member states and consequently relies on them to provide these in many instances. In this way the EU is not independent and self sufficient but complements the states. According to Ulrich Preuss,[17] there exists an 'osmotic' relationship between the EU and the state constitutions, which is different in nature from the well-known dualism of federal and state constitution in the context of e.g. the US or Germany. In traditional federalism, the respective roles and functions of state and federation are preordained and well worked out in 'an overarching concept of political unity' whereas, in the context of the EU, there is no preordained order, but rather an ongoing process of institutional interaction.

(c) Finally, and not least importantly, it lacks the ties and affinities with its people which characterise the nation state. It lacks an affective dimension. There are few ways in which individuals may relate to the EU. The EU lacks a coherent identity, a fact which is underlined by the TEU provision which stipulates that 'the Union shall respect national identities of the Member States' (Article 6(3)). It gains its legitimacy by validation, i.e. ratification by its member states, rather than its peoples. Contrast the preamble of the US constitution, which refers to 'We the People of the United States'. The Rome Treaty refers to 'ever closer union among the peoples of Europe'. Europe is not made up of one people, as the *Bundesverfassungsgericht* has somewhat notoriously remarked. The EU is a contract between states in the form of an international agreement and not yet one between citizens and government in the Lockean or Rawlsian sense.

Perhaps we should not get too carried away with this last point. After all, although the US Constitution may state that 'We the People of the US . . . do ordain and establish a Constitution', it was of course the states which ratified it. Additionally, the ECJ has made it clear on several occasions that the subjects of the constitutional charter which are the EC treaties are 'not only the Member States but also their nationals'.[18] The ECJ of course also gave its citizens a stake in the enforcement of EU law by way of introducing the concept of directly

---

[16] See conclusions of the Cologne European Council June 1999. See also S Douglas-Scott 'The Common Foreign and Security Policy of the EU: Reinforcing the European Identity?' in Fitzpatrick and Bergeron (eds) *Europe's Other* (Ashgate, 1998) at 126.

[17] U Preuss, 'The Constitution of a European Democracy and the Role of the Nation State', (1999) 12 Ratio Juris 417 at 420.

[18] *Opinion 1/91 (EEA)*, see above fn 8.

effective rights in *Van Gend en Loos*. Recently Joseph Weiler has described the EU treaties as potentially a 'social contract' between the peoples of Europe rather than just between the member states.[19]

In conclusion it might be said that, as a result of its novel constitutional status, the EU exhibits the following features. It is polycentric in character – power is fragmented and dispersed in the EU – what Preuss describes as a 'nebulous and hardly comprehensible network of pluralist actors'. It is also dynamic in character: while member states may be primarily concerned with the preservation of their institutional identity and stability, the EU is concerned (conversely) with its own permanent self-transformation, both regarding its policy goals and institutional set up. It has been described as a '*Wandel-Verfassung*'.[20]

(2) THE TRANSFORMATION OF EUROPE HAS NOT BEEN ENTIRELY SATISFACTORY

The problematic relationship between Community and member states

The EU experiences a problematic relationship with its member states, which still prefer to see their own legal orders as sovereign. Thus, the supremacy of EC law in the UK is attributed to section 2(4) of the ECA, and in France to Article 55 of the French Constitution. While, according to the ECJ, EC law stands at the very apex of the legal order, for many member states, their own constitutions, or concepts such as parliamentary sovereignty, occupy that position. We therefore find a clash of two constitutionalisms, with apparently no authentic method for resolving the conflict. This conflict is also not purely theoretical, as dilemmas raised by the Banana wars illustrate. Such a conflict is also liable to lead to a lack of legal certainty and a crisis of confidence in the authority of law.

It is time to return to the question raised at the end of Chapter 7. What is the nature of the legal order in the EU? In that chapter it was suggested that we would have to move beyond the sort of theorising about law and legal systems which had been engaged in for centuries, and that the idea of law as a hierarchical system had had its day. Therefore, tenacious as the doctrine of sovereignty, or the notion of the ultimate authority of law manifested by some *Grundnorm* or Rule of Recognition may be, they need to be replaced by a different way of thinking about law.[21] Older theories simply support the clash of titans of legal orders.

---

[19] Weiler 'To be a European Citizen: Eros and Civilisation' in Weiler, *The Constitution of Europe* (Cambridge, 1999) 346.

[20] An expression used by Preuss in op. cit. at fn 17.

[21] N MacCormick, *Beyond the Sovereign State*; *The Maastricht Urteil: Sovereignty Now* (1995) 1 ELJ 259; P Eleftheriadis, *Aspects of European Constitutionalism* 21 ELRev 1996 at 37; P Eleftheriadis, *Begging the Constitutional Question* (1998) 36 JCMS 255; M Kumm, *Who is the final arbiter of Constitutionality in Europe?* Harvard Jean Monnet Working Paper, 1998 http://www.jeanmonnet-program.org/papers/papers98.html, paper 10/98.

Instead, it seems feasible to look to a complex interaction of overlapping legalities as a better way of explaining the nature of contemporary Europe.

Along with this goes perhaps the recognition that doctrine itself cannot explain the authority of law in any case.[22] Rather, we must look to some substantive assessment in order to evaluate the claim made on behalf of the legal order. In this way, the *Bundesverfassungsgericht* offered a justification of the sovereignty of the German state on the basis of *demos* or *Staatsvolk* of Germany as at the pinnacle of the constitutional order. The framers of the American Constitution looked to Federalism and to the Separation of Powers to do away with the sovereign indivisibility of the body politic. The EU has not yet provided such a compelling justification.

The EU's claim to sovereignty currently rests on inadequate normative foundations

In spite of its constitutional, or neo-constitutional status, the EU suffers from a serious democratic deficit or 'perversion'.[23] Modern liberal theory requires government to be democratic in order to respect the principles of individual (and increasingly popular) autonomy and self-determination. Although it need not be the case that democracy in the EU mirrors that of its member states,[24] it must at least do a better job than present EU governance in terms of providing its citizens with opportunities to participate in its law-making; in rendering those in power in the EU accountable; and in providing reliable constraints on those in power. Given the increase in the EU's competences, and the ECJ's attachment to the doctrine of supremacy, these are no small issues. If the EU fails to provide an adequate basis for itself as a constitutional order and its claims to sovereignty, it fails to take its citizens' liberty and rights to self-determination seriously: it also fails itself, because it is unable to create a polity with an affective dimension, in which the people of Europe have respect for their (European) law.

(3) HOW CAN THE EU DO BETTER?

A constitutional convention

If the current perception is that there is in some sense a European constitution, albeit an unsatisfactory one, how then might this generation of Europeans, anxious to improve their polity, proceed? Of course some might think such an

---

[22] For Derrida, the origin of authority is 'a violence without ground', a logical aporia. J Derrida, *Force of Law: The Mystical Origins of Authority*, in Cornell (ed.) *Deconstruction and the Possibility of Justice* (New York: Routledge, 1992) at 14; see also Goodrich who describes the source of legal authority as 'hidden' and 'obscure': P Goodrich, *Reading the Law* (Oxford: Basil Blackwell, 1986) at 62. See also P Eleftheriadis, *Aspects of European Constitutionalism* 21 ELRev 1996 at 37.

[23] Weiler, 'The Case against Statehood' (1999) 4 ELJ 43 at 45.

[24] MacCormick for example suggests a 'mixed commonwealth ' as a possibility in 'Sovereignty, Democracy and Subsidiarity' in N MacCormick, *Questioning Sovereignty* (Oxford: OUP, 1999).

exercise unnecessary and might seek to justify the *status quo* on the grounds of the same old hierarchical paradigm described above. One might argue for the supremacy of Community law within a monistic legal order which included both national and European law. Its justification might be the preservation of peace and the rule of law, and economic prosperity. But such an account fails to do justice to the complex reality of millennial Europe. It accords supremacy, but fails to provide any sufficient arguments for that supremacy. What is needed is a constitutional framework which combines the advantages of European union with the protections of the modern democratic state: fundamental rights, democratic accountability and a rich sense of citizenship and so on, the sort of exceptional thought which prompted the framers of the US Constitution to 'split the atom of sovereignty'[25] and argue for and introduce divided power and federalism.

Might this not be the occasion to start afresh, with the European Convention which commenced work in the spring of 2002, a 'constitutional convention', along the lines of that held in Philadelphia in the summer of 1787? Certainly, discontent with the current state of the EU, especially after the crisis of mismanagement in the Commission in 1999,[26] might seem to indicate the need for a major reworking of the EU structure. Maybe, at the dawn of the new millennium, Europe is undergoing what is, in Ackerman's much quoted, grand phrase, a 'constitutional moment'.[27] This may turn out to be the case in retrospect, but the current lack of popular, or media interest in, or even awareness of, such an event, indicates inability to provoke a shift in the constitutional **episteme**, or consciousness, in Europe. On a more mundane level, however, it might be contended that there have already been many, many 'constitutional moments' in the history of European union, given the dynamic nature of the EU's *Wandel Verfassung*.

Almost all are agreed that Europe needs a greater affective dimension: it needs to capture the hearts and minds of Europeans, and to include them in the European polity, which has so far been dominated by bureaucratic elites. In order to do this, there must be a shift in both individual–EU relations, whereby at least some EU citizens will have an attitude of respect of the EU law and polity, but also of individual–individual, whereby Europeans will recognise other Europeans as citizens of the same polity with reciprocal rights and obligations. But any attempt to do so must grapple with the following fundamental problems. First, how to create an ethos of constitutionalism in a Europe of some 400 million citizens, operating in what might be described as conditions of **reasonable pluralism**.

---

[25] Per Kennedy J in *US Term Limits Inc v Thornton* (1995) 514 US 779 at 838 (S Ct): 'Federalism was our Nation's own discovery. The Framers split the atom of sovereignty. It was the genius of their idea that our citizens would have two political capacities, one state and one federal, each protected from incursion from the other.'

[26] See, for example, Anatole Kaletzky, writing in *The Times* on 18 March 1999 (the week of the resignation of the Commission): '. . .This week may mark a great leap forward for the "European project". . . a full scale constitutional reform is now required . . . the need for a new constitutional settlement for Europe, analogous to the Constitutional Convention that created the USA in 1789, is the one issue that unites almost all honest thinkers on Europe.'

[27] B Ackerman, *The Future of Liberal Revolution* (Yale University Press, 1992).

The framers of the American Constitution believed themselves to be dealing with self-evident, universal truths. We have become less sure of all-embracing status of our values since then. Second, how to ensure that any commonly agreed provisions which might be articulated can satisfy at least some of the diverse needs and demands of both individuals and groups to recognition? How to ensure that identities are not subsumed in some European standard, rather like the apocryphal food standards (uniform bananas, chocolate etc.) emanating from Brussels, which the popular press so lampoons? These two concerns are related, but work in tension with each other, and seem to be at the heart of the project of creating a democratic constitution in today's Europe. In the course of working at these concerns, I shall consider, and reject, two very influential contemporary accounts which stress the discursive importance of the constitutional domain, preferring instead a constitutionalism that stakes itself on getting its **content** right, in drafting a new document of explicit values that will create and nourish a new European constitutional consciousness.

Reasonable pluralism

As already has been remarked, the legal orders of Europe are pluralistic: no one is dominant from any outside perspective (if indeed we could occupy such a perspective). But this pluralism also operates within the legal orders themselves, albeit not usually as a pluralism of legal orders, but of values and peoples. This is no novel obstacle to constitution building. Joseph de Maistre, writing in the context of the French constitution of 1795 wrote, 'The Constitution. . .was made for **man**. But there is no such as man in the world. In my lifetime I have seen Frenchmen, Italians, Russians etc;. . .but as for **man**, I declare that I have never in my life met him; if he exists he is unknown to me.'[28] The *Bundesverfassungsgericht* could find no European *demos*, but it becomes ever more difficult to find a national *demos* within single European states, an *existentieller Gemeinsamkeit*.[29] National identities may not be taken for granted, or if they may, they no longer, if they ever did, sum up an individual's sense of identity and allegiance: there are Scots who are also British, Venetians who are Italians.

However, most contemporary writers prefer to understand *demos* in terms of non-organic civil terms, on the basis of shared values, or *ethos*, rather than a shared *ethnos*.[30] But what might these shared values be, which are capable of giving rise to a common sense of identity and community across Europe? Earlier attempts by the EU to create such values and to inculcate an identity from the 'top down' seem almost laughable. The Adonnino report of 1984 outlined a

---

[28] J de Maistre, *Considerations on France* (Cambridge University Press, 1974) at 97.
[29] An expression used by the *Bundesverfassungsgericht* in the *Brunner* case [1994] 1 CMLR 57 (para 57).
[30] See e.g. J Weiler, 'Fin de siècle Europe' in R Dehousse (ed.) *Europe After Maastricht* (Munich: Beck, 1994); J Habermas, 'Citizenship and National Identity' (1992) 12 Praxis International 1.

series of measures needed to strengthen and promote a 'citizen's Europe'.[31] This report stressed the necessity of 'strengthening the Community's image and identity in order to enhance the sense of belonging and identity with the Community'. This was to be achieved by the creation of new symbols of 'Europeanness': i.e. a European anthem, day, driving licence, as well as the flag adopted from the Council of Europe, somewhat hesitant steps towards the construction of a European identity.[32]

On a more abstract level, in the realm of contemporary liberal political theory, there has been discussion of the sort of shared values which might be identified and utilised in the development of a European constitution. But there exists little in the way of a readily identifiable, homogeneous set of values within one member state of the EU, let alone throughout the EU. As the European Court of Human Rights has often recognised 'there is no common European consensus on morality'.[33] Thus it has often allowed a 'margin of appreciation' or subsidiarity in human rights matters.

Individuals in contemporary liberal democratic society are undeniably committed to a range of different and often contradictory conceptions of the good.[34] This being so, the challenge is to devise an adequate response to such diversity, heterogeneity and often incompatible beliefs, practices and customs. This situation is of course by no means unique to the EU, but is exacerbated by the sheer variety of culture, history and law in the EU. John Rawls, in *Political Liberalism*, labels this dilemma which faces modern liberalism, 'reasonable pluralism', i.e. one in which diverse religious, political and moral doctrines exist, incompatible but reasonable.

The fact that such pluralism exists has not prevented the modern belief that constitutions can be drafted on the basis of, and can unite a populace around, shared, normative values; they can sum up a community's 'moral membership'. For Ronald Dworkin, the only way to ensure that people are treated with equal concern and respect is to entrench a cluster of primary, substantive requirements for the containment of popular decision-making, in a constitution.[35] These requirements will take the form of individual rights. In many societies the shared values of human rights, a more active sense of citizenship, or a common sense of justice, have been singled out as obvious candidates to accommodate deep diversity.

John Rawls has, in his later works, expounded a theory based on 'public reason'. According to Rawls, the 'burdens of judgement' (namely, causes and

---

[31] P Adonnino, 'Report of the ad hoc Committee on a People's Europe to the European Council', Supplement 7/85 Bull EC.

[32] Other Adonnino recommendations found their way into the provisions of Articles 17–22 of the EC treaty.

[33] E.g. *Handyside* v *UK* [1976] 1 EHRR 737; *Otto Preminger* v *Austria* [1995] 19 EHRR 34.

[34] See J Raz, *The Morality of Freedom* (Oxford: Clarendon, 1986) for an account of why liberal society must promote a competitive moral pluralism which gives rise to a need for toleration.

[35] E.g. R Dworkin, *Taking Rights Seriously* (London: Duckworth, 1977) and *Freedom's Law* (Oxford: OUP, 1996).

sources of disagreement) ensure that there will be reasonable disagreement.[36] In such circumstances, Rawls suggests that the citizen will accept the value of reaching agreement based on public principles of justice, thereby forming an 'overlapping consensus', in spite of lacking a shared comprehensive account of the good. Rawls therefore defines political liberalism as a 'public culture as a shared fund of implicitly recognised basic ideas and principles'.[37] And because such an overlapping consensus lacks a comprehensive foundation, it may escape charges levelled at other liberal doctrine, such as Rawls' own earlier theory of justice, or some rights-based political theories, such as those of Nozick, of being too universalising and thus unsuitable for a culturally plural society such as the EU.

Such an overlapping consensus might be identified in the context of the EU. Principles such as citizenship, human rights (Article 6 TEU refers to the 'common constitutional traditions of the member states'), respect for democracy and the rule of law, suggest some sort of existing, public, normative consensus in the EU which goes beyond the desirability of economic efficiency and free markets. Further implicit values might be made explicit. Such shared principles operate perhaps only as a bare minimum but might be, as La Torre suggests, suitable for what in MacCormick's terms is the 'mixed commonwealth' of the EU.[38]

The problems of reasonable pluralism

Might a Rawlsian political liberalism work in the context of the EU? Can we form a powerful, explicit articulation of the public values Europeans implicitly hold? Any European consensus is assuredly thin – for some, too thin to function as a basis for conflicts of value and culture which undoubtedly exist in the EU. For example, should the right to abortion be a protected constitutional right? Should gays and lesbians have the right to marry? Rawls suggests that his theory of political liberalism may resolve such conflicts by operating at a higher level of abstraction: 'The work of abstraction is a way of continuing public discussion where shared understandings of lesser generality have broken down.'[39] But it may be the case that a higher level of abstraction only renders the consensus less determinate. For example, does an overlapping consensus, operating as it does, as a form of 'public reason', affect intimate relations which at first sight appear to be private and non-political? How are we to identify the public domain within which the overlapping consensus is to operate? In *The Idea of Public Reason revisited*[40] Rawls suggests that '. . . the government would appear to have no interest in the particulars of family life, or of relations among the sexes, except in so far as that form or those relations in some way affect the orderly

---

[36] John Rawls, *Political Liberalism* (Columbia University Press, 1993) 55.

[37] Ibid. at 8.

[38] See Massimo La Torre, 'Legal Pluralism as evolutionary achievement of Community law' (1999) 12 Ratio Juris 182, and N MacCormick, 'Sovereignty, Democracy and Subsidiarity' in *Questioning Sovereignty* (OUP, 1999).

[39] *Political Liberalism* at 45–6.

[40] Rawls, *Collected Papers* (Harvard University Press, 1999) at 587.

reproduction of society over time. Thus appeals to monogamy as such, or against same sex marriages, as within the government's legitimate interests in the family, would reflect religious or comprehensive moral doctrines.'

The US Supreme Court was clearly not of Rawls' opinion in *Bowers* v *Hardwick*,[41] in which it held that there was no constitutional right to homosexual sex by which a Georgia law outlawing such conduct could be invalidated. According to the majority, constitutional recognition could not be given to such a claim because, 'to claim that a right to engage in such conduct is "deeply rooted in this nation's history and tradition" or "implicit in the concept of ordered liberty" is, at best, facetious'. Thus the Supreme Court acknowledged the Georgia State government's interest in regulating such conduct. In *Grant* v *South West Trains*,[42] the ECJ appeared to rely on similarly 'comprehensive' views, based on tradition, refusing to extend travel concessions to a lesbian couple in a stable relationship, on the basis of the equal pay and treatment directives, although stable heterosexual couples would have qualified. In finding that such discrimination was not discrimination based on sex, the ECJ stated that cohabitation by two persons of the same sex was not treated as equivalent to a stable heterosexual relationship in most member states of the EU, nor 'recognised in any particular way' in those countries or under the case law of the ECHR.

In both these cases, the courts concerned approached the issues on the basis of a state interest, rooted in history and tradition, thus differing from Rawls in what they considered to be the private domain. But distinguishing the private from the public domain is no new problem. An account based on an overlapping consensus of public reason has to deal with arguments based on a public morality of a sort raised by James Fitzjames Stephen and later by Lord Devlin.

But to protest the difficulty of the public/private division is perhaps not to do more than to join in the traditional attack on the indeterminacy of rights-based theories, and indeed of liberal theory generally.[43] But rights never operate in an absolute manner: to use a Hartian metaphor, they are normally applied within a core of settled meaning (e.g. a right to privacy covers unmarried heterosexual sex) and a penumbra of more doubtful application, in which context they are often balanced against state interests, such as national security, or even popular morality. The fact that disputes exist over the exact meaning of self-respect or privacy in a particular case does not mean that the liberal agenda must be abandoned, nor that an overlapping consensus, which can prove workable in at least some of these cases, cannot be found. A European constitution with a clearly drafted bill of rights is better than an EU with no such charter, which was the situation until December 2000. Those who disparage a constitution of substantive values as a means of resolving disputes should show how their proposals may do better. These claims will be considered immediately below.

---

[41] 478 US 186 (1986).

[42] Case C-249/96 *Grant* v *South West Trains* [1998] ECR I-621.

[43] See R Bellamy, 'The Constitution of Europe – Rights or Democracy?' in Bellamy, Bufacchi and Castiglione (eds) *Democracy and Constitutional Culture in the Union of Europe* (Lothian Foundation Press, 1995).

More problems of reasonable pluralism

Indeterminacy is not the only problem to be faced by proponents of a constitutional 'overlapping consensus.' A further critique maintains that the search for, or presupposition of, shared, implicit norms of a Rawlsian public reason, or indeed, of any common values, is misplaced.[44] Such a claim emanates from those who aspire to a politics of recognition, and insist that the aim of negotiations over cultural recognition is not to reach agreement on universal principles, but to bring the negotiators to recognise differences and similarities. For this to take place, it is necessary to shift the focus from the external conduct of participants (i.e. whether, as a matter of observation/empirical fact, citizens in Europe really do adhere to values of human rights etc.) to a shift to a concentration on the inner beliefs and motivations underlying this conduct – in other words, to take a more hermeneutic approach.

Most Western jurisprudence, especially of the Anglo-American kind, has not exhibited a great tendency to approach human action in this way. Austin is the clearest example of an undiluted external approach to law, but even Hart, introducing the 'internal point of view' into his account of a legal system as a union of primary and secondary rules, as a feature which supposedly takes account of the approach of officials and insiders of the legal system, is still really operating within the empiricist paradigm, rather than looking to inner beliefs and motivations. The internal point of view becomes yet another fact.[45] What do those writers who insist that we abandon our 'view from nowhere', our attempt at objectivity and neutrality in our search for shared principles, suggest that we do? What methodology do they propose? James Tully, in his influential book *Strange Multiplicity*, looks to Wittgenstein's *Philosophical Investigations*,[46] in which Wittgenstein compares language to an ancient city, which has grown up through long use and practice, overlapping and interacting in the endless diversity and strife of human affairs. For Wittgenstein, the grammar of words is too multiform to be represented in a comprehensive rule. Tully suggests that this metaphor also holds for the language of constitutionalism – the activity of understanding is a 'language game' – we grasp a concept, as Wittgenstein suggests, in the same way we learn to play a game like tennis, by serving, returning, rallying and so on. So, Tully further suggests that, transferred to the language of modern constitutionalism, this does not involve the comprehending of others within one's own language of redescription, but rather, proceeding by analogy, example, a working out rather analogous to the reasoning employed in individual cases at common law.[47] General concepts are not like rules, which must be followed in an all or nothing fashion.

---

[44] J Tully, *Strange Multiplicity* (Cambridge University Press, 1995) at 131.

[45] N Simmonds, *The Decline of Juridical Reason* (Manchester University Press, 1984) makes this critique at 9–11.

[46] *Strange Multiplicity* at 104.

[47] Tully also refers to the interchanges between Hale and Hobbes in this context.

Tully's approach has much in common with hermeneutic approaches, which aspire to an understanding of the other with radically different beliefs and practices. To do so, we must place these alien beliefs against analogous 'home' practices. We are then forced to notice a range of factors which often remain obscure when a model of 'neutrality' is used – most particularly, that these strange practices are in fact from the other's perspective social practices with value.[48] As expressed by Betti, such an understanding 'recognises and reconstructs a human spirit, communicating with the interpreter through the forms of its objectivization, and causing him to sense an affinity with it through their common humanity'.[49]

We are therefore required to understand the facts about other human agents accurately, to treat them as serious and important matters, and, where relevant, take these beliefs into account. Such an approach increases the self perception of individuals that their views are considered and given some weight by legal institutions, a factor necessary in order to ensure their identity with the legal system.[50] It might also help to inculcate a sense of true community, vital to take us beyond the Europe of the free market.

Translated to the constitutional context this approach requires, according to Tully, that a contemporary constitution 'should be seen as an activity, an intercultural dialogue in which culturally driven sovereign citizens of contemporary societies negotiate agreements on their ways of association over time in accordance with the conventions of mutual recognition and consent and continuity'.[51]

This, as Tully recognises, is not the traditional modern approach to constitutionalism. Hobbes and Pufendorf, as he recounts, required uniformity in a constitution, as this would they said lead to the unity, strength and power needed to compete with other European powers. On the other hand, they saw diversity as leading to disunity, weakness, dissolution and death. *The Federalist Papers* also drew the same conclusions regarding uniformity and unity.[52] Indeed, Hobbes uses entertaining architectural metaphors in order to expound his theory. If a constitution is to be anything than 'a crasie building, such as hardly lasting out their own time' then it must be constructed with 'the help of a very able Architect' continuing that, 'The skill of making and maintaining Commonwealths consisteth in certain Rules, as doth Arithmetique and Geometry; not (as Tennis-Play) on Practise only.'[53] Three hundred years later, we see the same sort

---

[48] See C Taylor, 'What is Human Agency?' in his *Human Agency and Language: Philosophical Papers I* (Cambridge University Press, 1985); E Betti, 'On a General Theory of Interpretation' (1987) 32 The American Journal of Jurisprudence 245; M Malik, 'Faith and the State of Jurisprudence' in Oliver, Tadros and Douglas-Scott (eds) *Faith in law: Essays in Legal Theory* (Hart, 2000).

[49] Betti op. cit. at 35.

[50] See article by Richard Cohen in *New York Times* of 14 January 2000, 'Europe in Search of an Identity' which cites Kreil, a litigant who had taken her case to the ECJ as saying 'I feel a little bit more European' after the decision of the ECJ (in the context of access of women to the German military) in her favour.

[51] Tully, *Strange Multiplicity* at 184.

[52] Hamilton, Madison and Jay, *The Federalist Papers*, (ed. Rossiter, New American Library, 1961) at 38.

[53] Hobbes, *Leviathan* (ed. Tuck, Cambridge University Press, 1991) at 105 and 146.

of metaphors being employed in the context of the European Union. The EU is a structure with 'three pillars' across which there must be consistency and unity, rather than the undesirable, unsystematic Europe of 'bits and pieces'.[54]

But how would these intercultural negotiations, this hermeneutic dialogue of 'mutual recognition' operate in today's EU? 'Mutual Recognition' is a concept with which Europeans are already familiar and comfortable. They have been applying it in the context of free movement for at least twenty years, dating from the ECJ's *Cassis de Dijon* decision. Professional diplomas have been subject to mutual recognition. In the context of free movement of goods, the concept has introduced Europeans to a new range of products which they otherwise might not have experienced, often because of age-old traditional practices of their own country. Germans have been able to buy beers in Germany which had not been produced according to the ancient *Reinheitsgebot* (although these laws continued to govern German law making). Italians are able to experience other types of pasta than those made traditionally in Italy with durum wheat, even if according to Gide, Italians do prefer their pasta glistening 'de deux côtes de la fourchette'.[55] But this concept of mutual recognition has operated within the context of the so-called *Cassis* 'mandatory requirements' or rule of reason: the foreign product may be denied access if it can be objectively justified on grounds of some legitimate aim, in legal doctrine sometimes called the rule of reason. The call for recognition can be rebutted, home practices do sometimes prevail, diversity is not maintained. Alternatively, sometimes a particular product may be harmonised, leaving no scope for diversity or national preference; EMU might be cited as an example of this.

So, although it appears to have resonances with concepts already employed by EU law, Tully's 'mutual recognition' might not be in complete accord with them. Furthermore, there still may be problems in applying this concept in the field of claims to self-respect based on cultural difference and recognition as in the field of human rights. One way in which claims to difference or diversity might be given recognition is in the introduction of special rights, applying not to the whole population, but only to some, who have special needs, such as European Charter for Regional or Minority Languages. But there are difficulties with moving away from the paradigm of neutrality and uniform application. Just how far should law go in comprehending and respecting difference? As discussed in the last chapter, there may be a thin line between recognising difference and undesirable stereotyping, a thinness which is revealed by Irigary's attempt to redefine the category of rights. Irigary has criticised the notion of the subject of rights bearer as it appears in traditional liberal theory, suggesting that redefining the right to civil identity is one of the urgent tasks of our time. However, many of the images Irigary invokes – virginity, motherhood, peace, and so on – resonate with

---

[54] D Curtin, 'The Constitution of the Union: a Europe of Bits and Pieces?' (1993) 30 CMLRev 17.

[55] See S Weatherill, *Law and Integration in the EU* (Oxford: Clarendon Press, 1995) who cites AG Mancini's opinion in the *Drei Glocken* case (Case 407/85 *Drei Glocken* [1988] ECR 432). Mancini referred to the diaries of André Gide in his Opinion, including the extract above.

conventional images of womanhood and may have adverse rhetorical affect from a feminist point of view.[56] Such conversational claims to 'special rights' may turn into a constitutional Tower of Babel. It is suggested that arguments such as Tully's fail to convince us that the identification and application of shared terms, such as those of public reason really is misplaced in the construction of a European constitutionalism.

Discursive democracy

However, Tully's notion of a constitution as a continued intercultural dialogue has resonances with notions of discursive democracy, which stipulate that the civic realm be created dialogically. So, for example, Michelman defines politics as a discursive engagement which the community has as to the terms of its common life, in which citizenship becomes 'the constant re-determination by the people for themselves of the terms on which they live together'.[57] Such a notion is attractive as it accords to individuals the liberty, self-determination and involvement which the EU has so far failed to grant them. Indeed, Michelman insists that 'the self is constituted by, or comes to itself through, such an engagement'.[58] This notion of a 'dialogical democracy' has been further explored by Michelman himself in recent works[59] and by Habermas, who describes as valid those laws 'to which all possibly affected persons could agree as participants on rational discourse'.[60] These authors proceed on a procedural paradigm for constitutionalism which may be contrasted to the substantive 'public reason' of John Rawls, or Dworkin's 'moral community'. Such a procedural account is attractive, because it creates a 'responsive' democracy, issuing from conditions of popular sovereignty, in which everyone can identify themselves as an 'owner', responsible for the laws, because everyone has had some part in the 'conversation' which created them.[61]

But dialogical democracy finds as many problems in constitutionalism as does a hermeneutic approach. Two such will be considered here. First, that dialogical democracy is dependent on there being an institutional public space capable of structuring and sustaining the debate (with the rider that such a public space does not yet exist in the EU). Second, that such theories of democracy must contend with the paradox of democracy: namely that the populace itself cannot determine the nature of the fundamental rules which structure public debate, and

---

[56] Irigary L, *Je, Tu, Nous* (Routledge, 1993) at 88.
[57] F Michelman, 'Law's Republic' (1988) 97 Yale LJ 1493 at 1518.
[58] Ibid. at 1523.
[59] F Michelman, *Brennan and Democracy* (Princeton University Press, 1999).
[60] J Habermas, *Between Facts and Norms* (Oxford: Blackwell, 1996) 107.
[61] See e.g. R Post, *Constitutional Domains* (Harvard University Press, 1995).

hence at this level, there is no democracy, as the people are not self governing in the creation of these fundamental laws, which have been imposed on them.[62]

The inadequate public realm

Dialogical democracy is linked to a certain notion of citizenship which stresses the active and virtuous participation in public life. But there is little scope for the fulfilment of such a conception in today's EU, given its democratic deficit and lack of available channels for citizens to play their part in the EU's public life. An unelected Commission responsible for the initiation of legislation (albeit now trying to reinstate itself after the stinging criticisms of the Independent Experts which highlighted the Commission's lack of responsibility and accountability in the face of fraud and mismanagement)[63] and a Parliament that was little more than a consultative assembly until relatively recently have hardly been inspirational to citizens. Attempts have been made, of course, to change this: Articles 17–22 of the EC treaty formalised a package of citizens' rights, including some 'political' ones, but these do not go very far. Public life in the EU overall is almost non-existent. In the absence of an EU legislature which can command affective support, attention has focussed on improving the transparency of the EU decision-making process and rights of access to information. A lack of information about EU activities, along with the fact that the main legislative body, the Council of Ministers, operates largely in secret, has made it difficult for active engagement. The present consolidated treaties, which renumber provisions so they lose the familiarity they once had (even if only for a few lawyers or EU specialists) is a paradigm example of lack of transparency, albeit one carried out in the name of transparency. The process of comitology, whereby EU law is implemented, or even created, by unaccountable member state appointees, who oversee the Commission's work, excludes the citizens in an almost Kafkaesque scenario. In spite of Article 1(1) TEU, which requires that decisions should be taken 'as openly as possible and as closely as possible to he citizen', the EU often seems to operate by depriving its citizens of information they need to make intelligent choices and to assess the burdens and benefits of proposed legislative policies. The results include a very low turn-out at European Parliament elections and frustration is often misdiagnosed as apathy or indifference to public affairs.

One may contrast these EU provisions with more concrete ones in the 1990 Round Table draft for a united German constitution. Article 35 of the 'Round Table' draft provided for a right to participation of associations and movements. Article 36 gave such associations a democratic constitutional forum, representing a sphere of public debate, to enable them to be key participants in the

---

[62] There is also a third objection, which will not be considered in this context – which is that the notion of a self created by continuous engagement in the public space is unattractive and unrealistic – and denies the ways in which we are apart from our public, communal selves. Benjamin Franklin, for example, described humans as not political creatures but 'toolmakers'.

[63] Committee of Independent Experts: *First Report on Allegations regarding Fraud, Mismanagement and Nepotism in the EC*, presented to the European Parliament 15 March 1999.

Willensbildung. The German draft constitution was not implemented any more than the European Parliament's draft European constitution of 1984, but this provision is an indication of the ways in which a more participatory European forum might be introduced if there were a will.

Determining the public realm

Some dialogical theories are dependent on an institutional public space, as a host in which to structure and sustain public debate. Michelman looks to the courts, Ackerman to the US constitution itself, which 'has always provided us with the language and process within which our political identities could be confronted, debated and defined'.[64] Cass Sunstein finds such a forum in Congress.[65]

Even if such an account is desirable in the US context (and that is debatable) it seems unworkable and inappropriate for the EU. First, there is no single written Constitution for Europeans with the power and aura of the US constitution. At a European level all that exists is a discouraging medley of treaties and legislation propagated by elites (even if the ECJ is happy to characterise the treaties as a 'constitution'), which engender no sense of belonging in the peoples of Europe.

Discursive and Republican accounts attempt to move the dialogic realm beyond that of formal constitutions and institutions. Rather they look to more informal gatherings: the local community, religious groups, unions, so that discussion in such groupings as such becomes synonymous with republican debate.[66] Thus, Sunstein[67] suggests that we may 'multiply the points of access to government and generate institutions that will produce deliberation among the differently situated'.[68] Would this enlarged republican discursive citizenship be an attractive model for the EU?

Such a theory of deliberative democracy is certainly attractive by virtue of its inclusive nature[69] and supporters of this inclusive deliberative democracy seem to suggest that it is possible for all types of viewpoints, including the marginal, outsider voices in society, to become part of a community's 'normatively consequential dialogue', to enter the public space. In this way, civil society attains a constitutional, legal reality.[70] But even this version seems unlikely to work well in the EU. Such a conversational political self-determination may succeed at national, regional or local level, but a reliance on spontaneous dialogue in unofficial contexts is less likely to work across national frontiers. The public space of the EU is fragmented into national units, thus rendering the creation of a delib-

---

[64] B Ackerman, 'The Storrs Lectures: Discovering the Constitution' (1984) 93 Yale LJ 1013 at 1072.
[65] C Sunstein, 'Beyond the Republican Revival' (1988) 97 Yale LJ 1539.
[66] E Christodoulidis, 'A New Constitutional Reality for Civil Society: some cautionary remarks' in Bellamy, Bufacchi and Castiglione (eds) *Democracy and Constitutional Culture* (Lothian Press, 1995).
[67] Sunstein, 'Beyond the Republican Revival' at 1573.
[68] Ibid. at 1585.
[69] M Minow, 'Justice Engendered' (1987) 101 Harvard LR 10 at 88–9.
[70] E.g. U Preuss, 'Problems of a Concept of European Citizenship' (1995) 1 ELJ 267.

erative and dialogical democracy difficult at transnational level. Barriers of language and culture continue to make it unlikely for such conversations to grow up on an *ad hoc* basis. Rather, it is just the lumbering, formal mechanisms of the European institutions which attempt to make cross-border cooperation possible, even if they do not do it very well. Dialogue still has to be initiated in this way, and as such, appears rather stilted. There is no spontaneous public space or spaces at European level. Institutional support is still needed. Perhaps one exception to this might be on a functional level, where in particular policy areas cross-border networks may be forming a nucleus of a transnational public space. Multiple *demoi* are arising in sectors, lobbying the Commission in areas such as competition, agriculture or environmental policy. In this way Kohler-Koch advocates a 'federal pragmatism' which focuses on efficiency rather than on democratic responsibility'.[71] The growth of multiple *demoi* may be encouraging, but their growth based on efficiency, the old justification for the EEC, is less so.

This may seem a rather disappointing or pessimistic conclusion. It does seem vital that Europe have an increased participatory realm and a European public space, or at least spaces. But it will be very difficult to create these spaces spontaneously. Europe's institutions still play a major, vital role in its continuing project. This is troubling, as European institutions still suffer from lowish levels of respect, especially the Commission after the events of 1999. However, attempts are being made to excite public interests in the future of Europe, even if it is of the *White paper on Governance*, the *Future of Europe debate* or the *European Convention First* variety. These may not be earth shattering events (as a perusal of the comments on their discussion fora often reveals) but along with the huge amount of EU material now available on the EU's websites, they play their part in increasing the European debate, as well as keeping the public better informed.

The paradox of constitutional democracy

Those advocating discursive democracy have not only to deal with the problem of the lack of an adequate public space in Europe. They must also provide some account of how a European constitution which constrained and contained the European law-making process could be compatible with the popular decision making they advocate.[72] As Michelman asks in *Brennan and Democracy*, is constitutional democracy possible if democracy is understood as concerning individual freedom and self-government? This paradox is of course very evident in the context of the US constitution, where the judiciary – the 'least dangerous branch', and most particularly the Supreme Court – engages in powerful judicial review of legislation. But it is also highly relevant in the European context, in

---

[71] B Kohler-Koch, 'A Constitution for Europe', Mannheim Working Papers 1999, http://www.mzes.uni-mannheim.de/publications/wp/wp_E.html

[72] But this is of course no less a problem for those who advocate substantive constitutional constraints, who sometimes, however, wear their counter-majoritarianism or perfectionism unashamedly on their sleeves.

which a more participatory public realm is seen as a remedy for the democratic deficit. Should the EU become more democratically accountable, the decisions of the ECJ might take on a higher profile than at present.[73]

The paradox is difficult to resolve. Michelman's suggested resolution takes the form of a 'responsive' democracy with a difference.[74] Such a democracy would allow one to identify with and to respect a legal system, even if one had personal objections as to its individual laws. Such allegiance would be based on a combination of a belief in the moral rightness of that country's fundamental laws (i.e. values such as tolerance, the rule of law) but the belief would be ultimately grounded in a faith in the democratic nature of the system's procedures. According to Michelman, such a system can be democratic even in the presence of strong judicial review if its institutions and fundamental laws are subject to constant exposure to the opinions of all interests in society. So Michelman's account allows procedure-independent standards of rightness but only if those standards are exposed to and react to popular opinion.

Such an attempted resolution appears attractive; it allows for standards of objective rightness to take their place in constitutional formulation, but also makes way for valuable critique. However, such a resolution is ultimately unsatisfactory in the EU at present. This is partly for the reasons already considered above: Europe lacks a common public forum, a space in which criticism could be voiced. There is also the important practical issue of whether judges do in fact listen to and react to public debate. Sometimes it seems as if they do. In the context of positive discrimination, the *Marschall*[75] decision of 1997 might be seen as a partial retreat from the Court's earlier *Kalanke*[76] holding, in the light of the fierce critique which surrounded the earlier case. The ECJ's somewhat subdued case law of the early 1990s in the internal market field may also be seen as a reaction to public criticism that the ECJ had been going too far too fast.[77] But sometimes there seems to be very little response. Fundamental, wide-ranging constitutional principles of EC law were created by the ECJ (i.e. direct effect and supremacy) in its early 'heroic period' with little response or reaction save from specialist lawyers.[78]

However, those who attempt the complex reconciliation of self-determination and constitutional containment must also contend with another objection based on the **status** of public opinion and critique within this formulation. Michelman denies that his suggestion would involve a complete return to 'responsive' democracy of the type proposed by Post. This is because what is important in this

---

[73] But see H Rasmussen, *On Law and Policy in the European Court* (Martinus Nijhoff, 1986), discussed in Chapter 5, for a strong critique of the ECJ.

[74] Michelman, *Brennan and Democracy* at 58–61.

[75] Case C-409/95 *Marschall* v *Land Nordrhein Westfalen* [1997] ECR I-6363.

[76] Case C-450/93 *Kalanke* v *Freie Hansestadt Bremen* [1995] ECR I-3051.

[77] See e.g., Cases 267–268/91 *Keck and Mithouard (Criminal Proceedings Against)* [1993] ECR I-6097 in this regard, as well as the discussion in Chapter 5.

[78] This may of course reflect the youth of the EEC in those early days, and the fact that it was simply not considered to be any sort of political forum.

context is not so much that legal institutions **respond** to individual input but rather the **epistemic** or truth-finding value of these contributions. According to Michelman, they help us to find the 'right answer'. Open debate and discussion which includes all possible viewpoints helps us to find the 'truth' of the matter. This, says Michelman, was Brennan's[79] view of democracy. But it is by no means a neutral view. The contention that there should be free discussion of all viewpoints, with the rider that this has an epistemic value – it helps us find the truth – is often advanced as a structural feature of liberal society. The truth-finding capacity of free expression is also often advanced as a justification for free speech.[80] But the view that all opinions should be permitted is not one that finds favour throughout Europe, throughout the liberal, democratic Europe of the European Convention. In some European countries it has for some time been a criminal offence to deny that the Holocaust took place.[81] Such legislation has been challenged by 'revisionist' historians such as David Irving, on the basis that it interferes with free speech rights such as those under Article 10 of the ECHR. But such challenges have been rejected by the Convention's institutions, not just on the basis that such speech may interfere with the rights of others (such as the right of Jews to be free from offensive speech) but that the exercise of freedom of expression in this context threatens the very exercise of democracy.[82] This approach derives from a different approach to the role of freedom of expression from that of Justice Brennan or Michelman, one that stresses that the 'free' speech of some must be curbed to permit other voices to be heard, to allow all to take their part in society. It thus might be questionable whether such an absolute free flow of criticism does have epistemic value which enables us to surmount the paradox of democracy, if it is acknowledged that free speech for all may sometimes 'skew' debate. If this is so, then it can be acknowledged that discussion and debate can sometimes be constrained by substantive moral constraints.

Constituting the *pouvoir constituant*

We now return to the issue with which section 3 started: the pluralism of the European *pouvoir constituant*. It is my conclusion that neither the hermeneutic (nor mutual recognition) approach, nor that of discursive democracy, are appropriate models for rendering the people of Europe more constitutionally involved, of instilling the 'we feelings' and trust necessary for a more effective and

---

[79] Brennan was a very influential Justice of the US Supreme Court during the path-breaking Warren era, and beyond.

[80] E.g. as is offered by Mill in *On Liberty* (Harmondsworth: Penguin, 1985).

[81] In Germany the '*Auschwitzlüge*' offence (literally 'lie of Auschwitz' offence) under Articles 130 and 194 of the Criminal Code prohibits the approval, trivialising or denial of Nazi crimes or the crimes of other violent regimes. The laws of other European countries, such as France and Austria, also create similar offences.

[82] *T v Belgium* (1983) 34 DR 158; *Kunen v Germany* (1982) 29 DR 194.

affective European constitutionalism.[83] Instead, I shall conclude by contending that clearer, substantive constitutional provisions might do this, might 'kickstart' Europe into a new era of constitutionalism. But first, a further problem, or paradox even, must be noted, also related to matters raised at the outset of section 3. As Rousseau asked, are constitutions the effects of the 'social spirit' or the causes of it? For Rousseau, in constitutional politics, effects must become their own causes, as 'the social spirit, which should be created by those institutions, would have to preside over their very foundation; and men would have to be before law what they should become by means of law'.[84] The question is this: do constitutions articulate demands of pre-existing social identities or do they in fact constitute those identities (and continue to constitute them)? We see this issue arising in the context of the US Declaration of Independence, of which Derrida has famously written, '[W]e cannot determine whether independence is stated or produced by this utterance.'[85] But, by the time of the Constitution, the American populace have become most definitely 'We the People' but, as has been endlessly remarked, we are still engaging in ever closer union of the peoples of Europe.

I would submit that constitutions have a dual function – they are both constitutive of and descriptive of a constitutional morality (if not a people) – hardly a very radical view. But the latter function is particularly important – constitutions are constitutive, they create subjects and social relations – as Durkheim stressed, the Declaration of the Rights of Man and Citizen created the kind of man and citizens and men it envisaged. But constitutions cannot perform this role if they are not transparent and meaningful to their reading public, if they do not capture the political and social imagination. And for a constitution to do this, it must be, as Ian Ward has written, seen as an 'aesthetic' entity.[86]

It is difficult to perceive the current EC 'constitutional charter', comprising the treaties, as an 'aesthetic' entity. Contrary to Tully's rejection of the Hobbesian metaphor, I would suggest that the EU **is** in need of an architect, of the restructuring of the present 'crasie building' that is the EU. Lastly, also **contra** Tully, I believe that such remodelling would also **increase** the discursive and conversational impact of a European constitutionalism, because a more transparent, well-planned, thoughtful European order is likely to take on more subjective importance to Europeans. It remains to be seen whether the present European Convention, and IGC in 2004, will be capable of this task.

---

[83] As stipulated by the neo-functionalists, Scheingold and Lindbergh, as requirements for an affective dimension; Lindberg and Scheingold, *Europe's Would be Polity: Patterns of Change in the EC* (Eaglewood Cliffs NJ: Prentice Hall, 1970).

[84] Rousseau, *Social Contract* (Hackett, 1987) Book II Chap ii, 'On the Legislator'. See also Hegel, 'The German Constitution' in *Hegel's Political Writings* trans TM Knox (Oxford: Oxford University Press, 1984). For Hegel, a constitution is a political and legal expression of the prior socially constituted identities, a view which has not been abandoned by the *Bundesverfassungsgericht*.

[85] Derrida, *Declarations d'Indépendance*, Otobiographies (Paris: Galilee, 1984) at 18.

[86] I Ward, 'The European Constitution, the Treaty of Amsterdam and the Search for Community' (1999) 27 Georgia J Int Comp L 519.

A PROPOSAL

In conclusion, both to the fairly complex reasoning of this chapter, and to this whole book, I set out the following proposal. It is of a pragmatic nature, aimed at increasing transparency, of creating a more, dare I say it, harmonious European order, but also aspires to stimulate a European constitutional order which enters the public imagination.

Ideally, the construction of a desirable European constitutional order would proceed by way of a constitutional convention of the sort held in Philadelphia in 1787. Ideally too, it would be a convention in which not only the 'usual suspects' – the European elites which participate at IGCs – would take part, but in which European citizens could participate, although the basis for selecting such participants would require a great deal of thought.[87]

Such a Convention should attempt to construct a European constitutional order around the following requirements. It would:

(1) incorporate fundamental shared moral principles, such as the principle of toleration, and would enumerate basic rights;

(2) it would provide mechanisms to make those in power accountable; and

(3) it would provide a means for the increased participation of the European citizen in the decision making process.

These three requirements are a bare minimum for the EU. Set out in such simplistic form, they function as aspirations, but aspirations which must find their way through the hazardous maze of modern liberal democracy with its problems and paradoxes which have been discussed in the previous section.

The following steps might be taken on the basis of these aspirations. They are presented on an undetailed basis as the focus of this chapter has been on the underlying level of theory, but they are well-tailored to the argument made above.

The constitutional element of EU law, at present a constitutional charter derived from provisions in the EU treaties, as well as even some secondary legislation, must be simplified. The consolidated treaty produced at Amsterdam did not do this. A basic simplified constitution for the EU would consist of institutional provisions arranged along more democratic lines, a bill of rights, the fundamental freedoms of the internal market, and a more clearly defined role for the EU in external relations and foreign and security policy.

Thus the key changes of a new simplified treaty would comprise:

(1) **A Bill of Rights.** Fundamental rights are already respected under EC law, but the position is complex, as respect for rights arose under the jurisprudence of the ECJ, on an *ad hoc* basis, rather than under a bill of enumerated rights under the treaties. Tricky questions as to the nature of rights respected under EC law arise. This would be alleviated by the incorporation of a legally

---

[87] See A Weale, 'Democratic Legitimacy and the Constitution of Europe' in Bellamy and Castiglione op. cit., for a discussion of the methods used for selecting representatives at the Philadelphia Convention.

binding Bill of Rights into the treaties. The rights incorporated should include at least those protected under the ECHR, as well as those additionally already recognised under Community law, such as the right to freedom of movement, non-discrimination and social rights, as well as the political rights of citizenship. Such a Charter was proclaimed in December 2000. However, it still remains to be decided whether, and if so how, the Charter should be integrated into the treaties. It is submitted that such integration is essential.

(2) **A coherent determination of the division of competence between the EU and its member states.** This would involve a clear statement of the Union's exclusive powers (already a contested area, as discussion over the provisions under Article 5 EC, concerning subsidiarity, has illustrated). There will inevitably still be divisions over concurrent powers of EU and member states, a state of affairs which exists under some national federal systems, and is probably inevitable.

(3) **Increasing democratic legitimacy in the EU.** Firstly, the European Parliament should be given its own right of legislative initiative. However, as the constitutional order of the EU is different to that of the traditional member state, giving more power to the European Parliament does not necessarily make the EU more democratic. Account has to be taken of the pluralistic nature of the EU legal order, and its 'osmotic' relation with its member states. In this regard, it is important to enhance democratic legitimacy at the level of national parliaments in the EU, by increasing their role. This must involve national parliaments in the possibility of controlling their ministers in EU affairs. The Amsterdam Treaty annexed a 'Protocol on the role of national parliaments in the EU' giving the national parliaments the right to be involved in any EC matter. But this protocol should be given constitutional status by being included in the treaty, rather than addended by protocol.

(4) **Simplified and transparent institutional arrangements in the Commission and Council of Ministers.** This involves: (a) greater transparency in the working arrangements of both, as well as increasing rights of access to information (a state of affairs which is coming about due to greater reliance on Article 255 of the EC treaty); (b) also these institutions are unwieldy in the light of further enlargement of the EU. They will have many members, and voting procedures are already Byzantine enough. This problem was not completely solved by the 2000 IGC.

(5) **Finally, there should be complete competence for the EU in the field of external trade.** Although the EC has exclusive competence over the Common Commercial Policy, its status in external trade generally is uncertain. In its *Opinion 1/94*, the ECJ held that the power to approve the WTO Uruguay round agreement was shared by the EC and the member states. This means that the EC cannot speak with a unified voice at the WTO. (On the other hand, it is still not yet possible for the EU to have complete competence in

foreign policy and security and defence, given the (neutral) status of some of its members and an enhanced role in foreign relations.)

This would not be a huge task for the EU, but it could have a possibly transformative effect. In this regard, those in the EU should bear in mind the words of Archibald Cox, who writing of the framers of the US Constitution, wrote, 'In retrospect we can see that much of the genius of the founding fathers, perhaps forced upon them by their very difficulties, lay in their remarkable capacity for saying enough but not too much.'[88] That is what is required at this stage of the transformation of Europe: to say enough, but not too much.

---

[88] A Cox, *The Court and the Constitution* (Houghton Mifflin, 1987) at 377.

INDEX